Almost a hundred years after the demise of the London & North Western Railway and the Shropshire Union Railways & Canal Company, their names survive painted on an end gable at Longport Wharf in the Potteries. [page 216] *Simon Middleton*

The launch at Market Drayton in 1972 of one of the present Llangollen horse-drawn trip boats. It was constructed by 'Holidays Afloat' in the building which had previously been used for making concrete products. [page 201, 232] *Tim & Lisa Machin*

The restored wharf building at Llanymynech has displays about the canal, limestone quarries and tramroads. Since 2005 volunteers have provided trips on the *George Watson Buck* on the half-mile of rewatered canal, which includes crossing the border from England into Wales. [page 275] *Author*

Is this the future of boating on the canals? Solar-powered *Solar Flair III* impressed spectators at the IWA's 2008 National Trailboat Rally at Welshpool. [page 261] *Author*

The Shropshire Union Canal

The Shropshire Union Canal

From the Mersey to the Midlands and Mid-Wales

Peter Brown

RAILWAY & CANAL HISTORICAL SOCIETY

First published 2018
by the Railway & Canal Historical Society

www.rchs.org.uk

The Railway & Canal Historical Society was founded in 1954
and incorporated in 1967.
It is a company (no.922300) limited by guarantee
and registered in England as a charity (no.256047)
Registered office: 34 Waterside Drive, Market Drayton TF9 1HU

© Peter Brown 2018

All rights reserved
No part of this publication may be reproduced, stored in a retrieval system
or transmitted in any form or by any means, electronic, mechanical or photocopying,
recording or otherwise without the prior permission of the author,
other than for personal study.

Every reasonable effort has been made to acknowledge correctly and contact
the copyright holders of material in this book. The RCHS apologises for any
unintentional errors or omissions which should be notified to the publisher.

ISBN 978 0 901461 66 7

Designed and typeset by
Malcolm Preskett
Printed and bound in Great Britain by
Short Run Press, Exeter

Contents

Editorial Notes 6
Acknowledgements 7
Introduction 8

The First Canal Age

1 Between the Severn and the Mersey 10
2 The Chester Canal 20
3 The tub-boat canals of east Shropshire 38
4 The Shrewsbury Canal 48
5 The Ellesmere Canal 56
6 The Montgomeryshire Canal 80
7 The Ellesmere & Chester Canal 94
8 The Birmingham & Liverpool Junction Canal 110
9 Creating the Shropshire Union 126
10 The Shropshire Union Railways and Canal Company 140
11 The First Canal Age 193

The Second Canal Age

12 Decline 210
13 Revival 230
14 The Second Canal Age 267

Appendices

A Mileage and locks 275
B Montgomery Canal: progress of restoration 275
C Chronology 276
D Dividends 277
E Senior officers 278
F The Egerton and Leveson-Gower families 279
G The Plas Kynaston Canal 280

Bibliography 283
Index 284

Editorial notes

Names

Parts of the canal were in Wales, but most of the canal companies' secretaries were English, which made for some idiosyncratic phonetic spelling – for example, 'Ffrwd' was always written 'Frood'. For clarity and consistency, the principal spelling on current Ordnance Survey maps is used throughout the book, regardless of the canal companies' usage.

The term 'Black Country' refers to the West Midlands conurbation north-west of Birmingham, from Smethwick to Wolverhampton (although to purists that town should not be included) and from Dudley to Walsall. 'South Staffordshire' is the term the Shropshire Union Canal Company used for the Black Country plus the Wombourne–Stourbridge–Kidderminster area (part of this area is actually in Worcestershire).

The names generally used for some features changed over the years. Again, for ease of understanding, just one name is used throughout the book.

The term 'tramroad' is generally used for narrow-gauge railways where the wagons were pulled by horses so as to distinguish them from (steam-hauled) railways and (urban passenger) tramways. (This nomenclature is not exactly in accordance with that used by specialist transport historians, but is thought to be clearer for the general reader.) The tramroad from the end of Trevor Basin is referred to as the Ruabon Brook Railway in the early years; after conversion to a standard gauge railway it is referred to as the Pontcysyllte Railway – in both cases, this is what the canal company called it. The other main exception is the Glyn Valley Tramway, because that is so well known by that name, both in its horse-drawn and steam-powered eras.

Key people

Brief biographic notes about key people have been put in box-outs. For the relationship between the Egerton (Bridgewater/Ellesmere) and the Leveson-Gower (Stafford/Sutherland) dynasties, see Appendix F.

Weights and measures

Because the canal's designers and managers used imperial or traditional measures, they have been used throughout the book.

1ft = 0.3048 metres 1 mile = 1.6093km 1lb = 0.4536 grams

Prior to the Weights & Measures Act 1824 the interpretation of hundredweight and ton (in particular) could vary; for example, some canals used a hundredweight comprising 120lb, the ton therefore having 2,400lb. The 1824 Act defined the ton and hundredweight as 112lb and 2,240lb respectively, but the traditional weights continued to be used for tolls on some types of traffic for much of the rest of the 19th century.

Money and prices

All amounts are shown in pounds, shillings and pence. (A pound comprised 20 shillings or 240 pence.)
There is no reliable meaningful method of converting 18th and 19th century money into current values – life, and people's needs, were then too different.

Updating

Updates and corrections can be found on the website of the Railway & Canal Historical Society *www.rchs.org.uk* and by following the link to 'Publications'.

Abbreviations

BCN	Birmingham Canal
BLJC	Birmingham & Liverpool Junction Canal
BTC	British Transport Commission
BTW	British Transport Waterways – the correct formal title [1953–63]
BW	British Waterways – the name commonly used for the for both the British Transport Waterways and the British Waterways Board [1953–2012]
BWB	British Waterways Board – the correct formal title [1963–2012]
CMS	Conservation Management Strategy [for the Montgomery Canal]
CPRW	Council for the Preservation of Rural Wales
CRT	Canal & River Trust [2012–]
DIWE	Docks & Inland Waterways Executive [1948–53]
ECC	Ellesmere & Chester Canal
GJR	Grand Junction Railway
GVT	Glyn Valley Tramway
GWR	Great Western Railway
IWA	Inland Waterways Association
IWAAC	Inland Waterways Amenity Advisory Council
IWRAC	Inland Waterways Redevelopment Advisory Committee
LBR	London & Birmingham Railway
LMSR	London Midland & Scottish Railway
LNWR	London & North Western Railway
MBR	Manchester & Birmingham Railway
MSC	Manchester Ship Canal
SNCA	Shrewsbury & Newport Canals Association
SNCT	Shrewsbury & Newport Canals Trust
SSSI	Site of Special Scientific Interest
SUCS	Shropshire Union Canal Society
SU	Shropshire Union Railways & Canal Company – or sometimes more loosely as the area served by the canals of that company
SURCC	Shropshire Union Railways & Canal Carrying Company
SWC	Staffordshire & Worcestershire Canal
TMC	Trent & Mersey Canal
TNA	The National Archives
UNESCO	United Nations Educational, Scientific and Cultural Organization
WRG	Waterway Recovery Group of the Inland Waterways Association

Acknowledgements

I am grateful to all those who helped me prepare this book, though I did not always adopt their suggestions.
The responsibility for any errors in the text is entirely mine.

In particular I wish to thank those who read various chapters in draft: Joseph Boughey, Alex Brown, Ray Buss, Neil Clarke, Tim Day, Richard Dean, Wendy Freer and Stephen Rowson. And those who provided information on specific matters, including Malcolm Reed, Peter Cross-Rudkin, John Milner and Cath Turpin – and my apologies to those whose names I have omitted.

Also the patient archivists at Shrewsbury, Stafford, Chester, Ruthin, the Institution of Civil Engineers and the National Archives (Kew), and especially Linda Barley and John Benson, the Archivists of the Canal & River Trust at Ellesmere Port.

But more than anyone I wish to thank my wife and 'research assistant', Quita, for all her help in the decade this book has taken to write.

Peter Brown

Ellesmere Canal stone showing the boundary of the canal company's property. *Author*

8

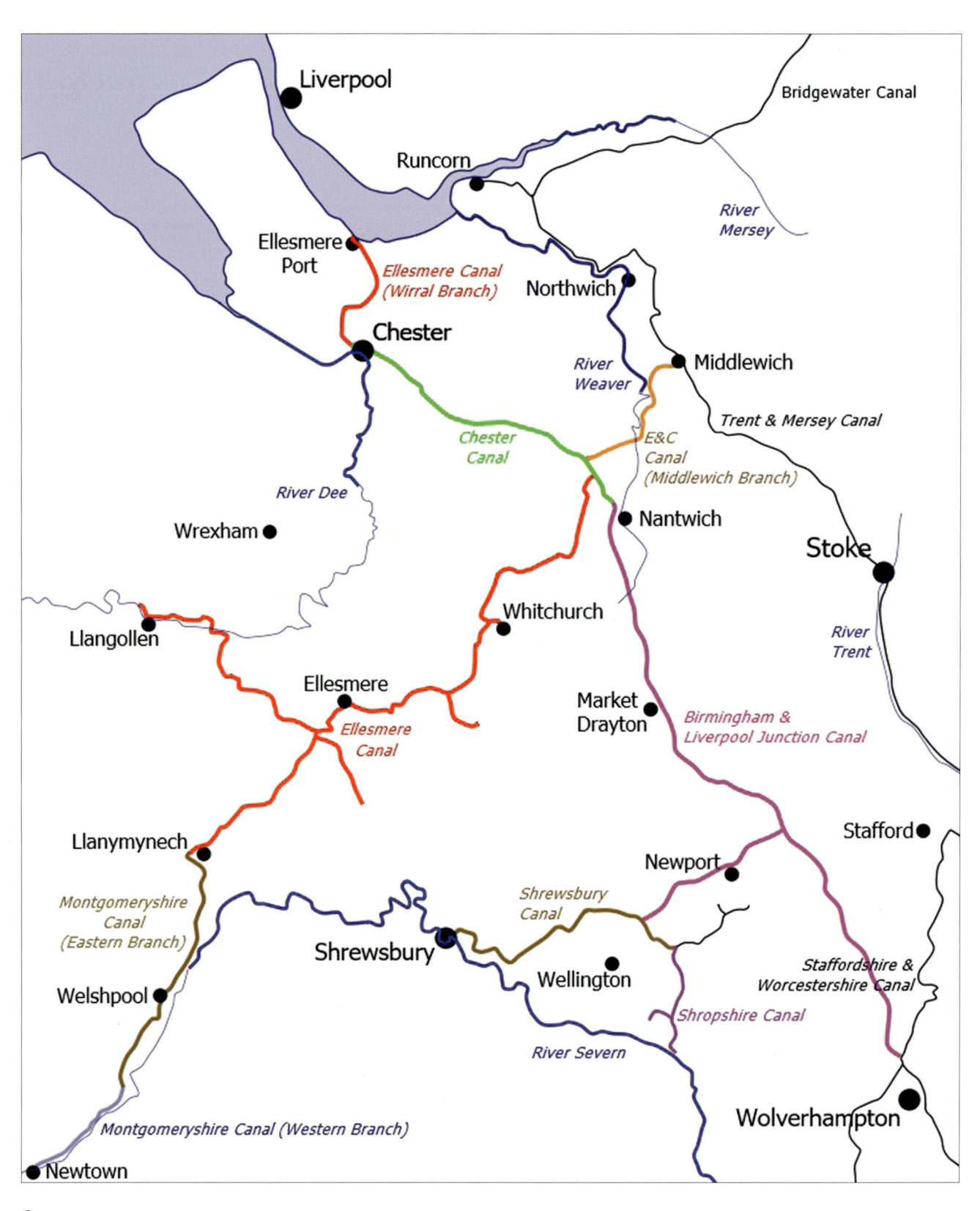

Introduction

In the middle of the eighteenth century the population in the large triangle of fertile land between Wolverhampton, the Mersey and just over the Welsh border was largely self-sufficient. Socially, the area was dominated by a few families, with a spread of landholdings and with rural mansions surrounded by parklands. Below them the gentry class provided the justices of the peace, who ran the counties as well as being the magistrates.

Most of the population lived in villages, not travelling further than the local market town. The two major towns, Chester and Shrewsbury, served a wide hinterland of north and central Wales respectively.

There were two exceptions to this relatively quiet rural isolation, both based on coal and ironstone: the east Shropshire area close to the Severn Gorge, now sometimes referred to as 'the cradle of the Industrial Revolution', and the Wrexham/Ruabon area of Denbighshire.

Over the seven decades from 1770, enterprising men promoted canals, most often to improve the prosperity of their lands or businesses – those who did it in the expectation of big profits were usually disappointed – and these local canals eventually became part of a national transport network. As this book will show, canals helped transform some places whereas some others, though canal-served, were almost unaffected. With the coming of the railways, which was relatively late in Shropshire and the Welsh border area, canals lost their importance and by the 1950s had become commercially irrelevant.

The major change in attitude in the last few decades has been that canals are recognised as a major environmental and leisure asset. National and local government no longer need convincing about their importance, particularly the economic and health benefits they can bring. Local communities too appreciate their canals, with increasing use being made of the towpaths. There are active schemes to restore much of the network which was lost in the 20th century.

Map of Shropshire Union Canal network, distinguishing the constituents, and showing the connections with other canals.

The Shropshire Union Canal

Nowadays the name Shropshire Union Canal is usually understood to mean just the canal from the north-western edge of Wolverhampton, through Market Drayton, Nantwich and Chester to the Mersey at Ellesmere Port, together with its branch to Middlewich. But for most of its life, the Shropshire Union (SU) included the long 'Welsh Branch' from Hurleston Junction, a little north of Nantwich, via Whitchurch, Ellesmere, Llanymynech and Welshpool to Newtown, together with its branch to Pontcysyllte and Llangollen; and also the branch from Norbury Junction past Newport and Wellington to Shrewsbury.

The very name 'Shropshire Union' is misleading because only about 39% of the length of the canal was in Shropshire – 29% was in Cheshire, 13% in Staffordshire and 19% in Wales.

The SU was unusual in being formed by the coming together of several earlier companies with the ostensible aim of converting many of their canals into railways and building further railways. In the event, only one railway was built – from Stafford to Shrewsbury – and the canal company was leased to the mighty London & North Western Railway (LNWR).

This book looks at the history of the constituent companies, comparing their policies and progress, follows the SU under railway control, examines the reasons for the decline and closures, then brings the story up to date with nationalisation, revival and restorations. In particular, it regards the canals as businesses and as part of local history, stressing the social and economic aspects. It is less concerned with the engineering and the boats. To keep the length manageable, it concentrates on the SU canal network itself. Ellesmere Port, Liverpool docks and the cross-Mersey trade are considered only to the extent that they relate to the canal network – they deserve a full length book to themselves. The SU's boating and carting activities in Birmingham, south Staffordshire and the Potteries are also largely omitted.

To make it easier for the reader to follow the developments, the book is organised thematically, subject by subject, rather than chronologically. However, this has the disadvantage that sometimes events appear out of their order; for example, because the chapter on the Shrewsbury Canal precedes that on the Ellesmere Canal, Thomas Telford is first encountered when appointed as Engineer to the former in 1795, with his more important appointment as General Agent of the latter in 1793 being discussed later.

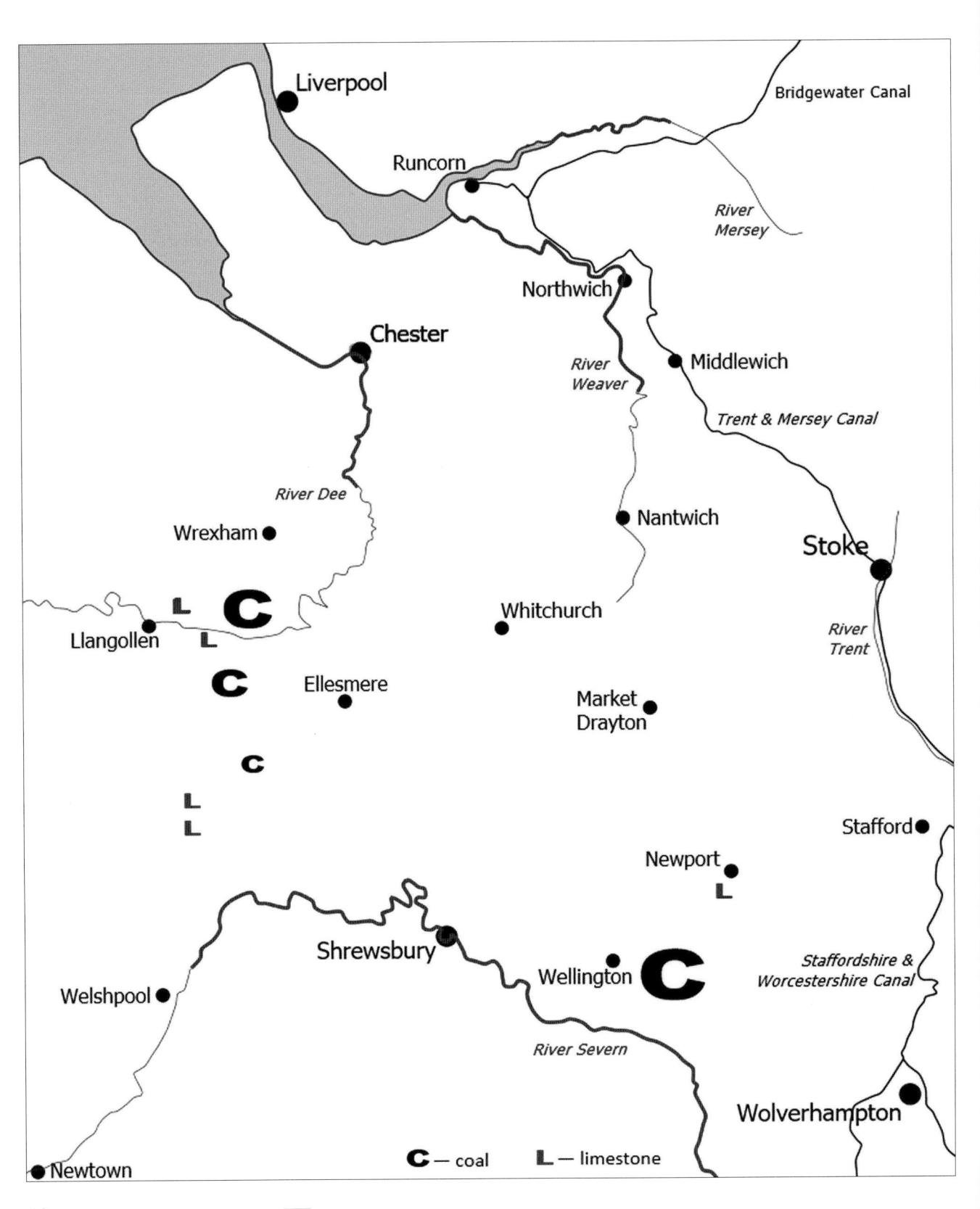

10

1
Between the Severn and the Mersey

Local history, which includes the history of canals, is closely dependent on the geology and geomorphology of the area. Together with climate, they determined the agriculture – the crops grown and the livestock kept – which in turn affected the nature of the settlements. The geology determined the opportunity for exploiting minerals such as coal, ironstone and other metal ores, building stones and slates. These, together with the availability of wood for burning or for making charcoal, and rivers or streams suitable for powering machinery, influenced the location of industries. Agriculture and industries needed towns for markets; some of these towns then developed into regional administrative centres. To benefit from the best method of communication in medieval times, the main towns were often located at strategic points on a navigable river.

Canals were built to fulfil an economic need: to move raw materials to where they could most profitably be used and to take products to, or to bring products from, more distant markets. Unlike the development of railways, there was rarely any consideration of them as a national or even regional network. Thus their construction was determined by the same factors as influenced the local agriculture, industries and settlement pattern. Their exact routes were dependent on the local geomorphology, the river valleys and the hills. Particularly in the 18th century, a general aim was to minimise the engineering necessary, though this might mean a more circuitous route. Even the materials used for their construction were dependent on the local geology: the availability of suitable stone or brick-making clay.

The lie of the land

The area with which this book in concerned is bounded to the north-west by the highlands of Wales and to the south-west

Map of Shropshire Union area, showing the principal towns, Severn, Dee, and Mersey, indicating the sections which are navigable (plus the navigable Weaver), the 'first generation' canals (Bridgewater, TMC, SWC), and the main areas of minerals.

by the river Severn. To the north is the Mersey Estuary. The eastern boundary is not strongly defined by natural features, rather it is by the 'first generation' navigable waterways canals linking Wolverhampton, Stafford, Stoke-on-Trent and Middlewich, together with the river Weaver.

Geologically, much of the area consists of Triassic sandstones and mudstones, with two principal sedimentary basins: in central Shropshire north of the Severn, and in central Cheshire. Dividing the area are several broken sandstone ridges, in Cheshire and north Shropshire aligned approximately northeast to south-west, and in the Shropshire/Staffordshire border area running roughly north to south. These sandstones are generally poor as building materials, though there are excellent outcrops at Grinshill (seven miles north of Shrewsbury) and at Cefn Mawr (near Wrexham).

The northern part of the area was significantly affected by the last Ice Age. The river Severn was diverted from its earlier northwards course to a route south into a large lake; when this drained it cut the Severn Gorge. When the ice retreated it left a glacial till of sands and gravels and, especially near Ellesmere, hollows which became the meres and mosses.

Important outcrops of limestone occur in the Welsh border area at several locations between Llangollen and Llanymynech; the other major source in the Shropshire Union area is at Lilleshall (between Newport and Telford). The Welsh border area also yielded slates and granites.

Coal measures occur in east Shropshire (now the town of Telford) and in the Wrexham/Ruabon/Chirk area, and there is a minor coalfield west of Shrewsbury.

Metal ores have been found in several places. The east Shropshire and Ruabon areas yielded ironstone. The hills west of Shrewsbury, somewhat outside the Shropshire Union area, were once one of the country's most important sources of lead; quantities were also found at certain places in the Welsh border area. Copper has been mined at Llanymynech and at Clive (eight miles north of Shrewsbury).

The suffix 'wich' is a reminder that large deposits of salt lie under the Middlewich/Northwich area and also at Nantwich.

11

The economy of the Shropshire Union area in the late 18th century

As a generalisation, up to the 18th century most farming was mainly for subsistence, with a small surplus being sold locally in order to buy the things not made by the farming community. Thus most farms were mixed, with both arable and livestock, being too far from major conurbations to benefit from specialisation. However, by the middle of the 18th century the trend was towards larger farms. Investment in farm buildings, soil enrichment, land reclamation and in improving the strains of crops and animals all meant that a much larger proportion of the output could be sold in the markets, with farms concentrating on the type of production best suited to the local circumstances. This surplus helped feed the quickly-growing urban population, though of course it needed a transport system to get the products to their destinations. In much of the Shropshire Union area, particularly the lower-lying land with its heavy soils, the land was best suited for cattle, the surplus milk giving rise to the Cheshire and Shropshire cheese industry.

At the time when the canals were being developed, much of the land in the Shropshire Union area formed part of the estates of wealthy landlords, for example, Earl Gower (later the Marquess of Stafford) in east Shropshire, the Duke of Bridgewater in north Shropshire, Earl Grosvenor in west Cheshire, the Earl of Powis in Montgomeryshire and the Williams-Wynn dynasty in south-east Denbighshire.

The next tier of gentry had large land-holdings in more local areas: these men, as justices of the peace, were the backbone of county administration. Landlords who actively wished to increase their rental income encouraged the trend towards larger farm units and often were a major source of the money needed for investment. Consolidation could be effected by agreement or by the passing of an Inclosure Act; the peak years for this were during the Revolutionary and Napoleonic wars with France when demand for agricultural products rose because imports from continental Europe were not available.

Two towns have historically dominated the Shropshire Union area. Chester on the river Dee was a Roman city, the base for one of the legions, and has retained its importance, the former abbey church becoming a cathedral in 1540. Shrewsbury was a Saxon foundation on a superb defensive site in a loop of the river Severn. In 1801, both towns had a population numbering about 15,000. As well being the administrative and commercial centres of their counties, Chester and Shrewsbury served a wide hinterland of north and central Wales respectively. Both too were politically divided; elections were sometimes rife with allegations of manipulation of the franchise and bribery.

Local needs gave rise to a pattern of market towns, mostly with a population of about 2,000 to 3,000 in 1801, which were generally about twelve to fourteen miles apart – Newport, Wellington, Market Drayton, Nantwich, Whitchurch, Ellesmere, Oswestry, Welshpool, Newtown, Wrexham and Llangollen. The anomalies were Wellington and Wrexham, which had a rapidly increasing population because of the industrialisation based on their coalfields, and Llangollen, which even at that date was showing signs of developing as a leisure and retirement centre.

Most of these towns, together with the two county towns, were beginning to have some small-scale manufacturing. For example, Newtown, Welshpool and Llangollen had textile workshops making use of Welsh wool; Market Drayton had paper mills; and Nantwich had shoe-making.

East Shropshire is sometimes regarded as the place where the Industrial Revolution started, as it was at Coalbrookdale that Abraham Darby I successfully smelted iron ore using coke rather than charcoal. However, the resultant pig iron was suitable only for cast-iron products and was rather too brittle for conversion into wrought iron. It was not until the second half of the 18th century that techniques improved sufficiently for coke-smelting to become the dominant technology. In the 1750s nine blast furnaces were built in the coalfield, transforming its economy, which was to be dominated for more than a century by large concerns which leased mines from landowners, extracted coal, iron ore, clay and limestone, smelted iron ore, converted the pig iron to wrought iron, and made iron castings and a wide range of products. In 1788 the east Shropshire area produced 38% of the Britain's output of iron. The population of the coalfield grew from about 20,000 in 1760 to 34,000 in 1801.

The second most important coalfield to be served by the Shropshire Union – or, to be more exact, which was intended to be served by one of the Shropshire Union's constituents – was Wrexham and its hinterland. John Wilkinson's ironworks at Bersham (two miles to the west of Wrexham) was in the late 18th century one of the most productive ironworks in western Europe, and the mineral resources of Ruabon parish (six miles south-west of Wrexham) were starting to be exploited.

River transport

RIVERS have been used as transport systems since time immemorial. There is some evidence that even relatively small rivers were used, with portage over land between the headwaters.

The major rivers were important transport arteries for heavy goods in medieval Britain, but they had serious defects. The route could be excessively long because of meanders in those sections with little fall in the level of the land. At other places excessive fall in the land caused rapids. Mills and fish weirs obstructed the passage of boats; mills in particular caused conflicts of interest concerning water supply. There was usually no towpath. Worst of all, in summer the river could be shallow because of drought whereas in winter and early spring the flow could be excessive, causing flooding; in both cases, boats could not travel.

On the other hand, rivers had a natural water supply and they rarely froze. The worst shallows could be deepened; locks could be created to bypass rapids and to assuage the millers; a towpath could be constructed. Most important of all, the basic channel existed – it did not have to be dug by hand.

CHAPTER 1 : BETWEEN THE SEVERN AND THE MERSEY

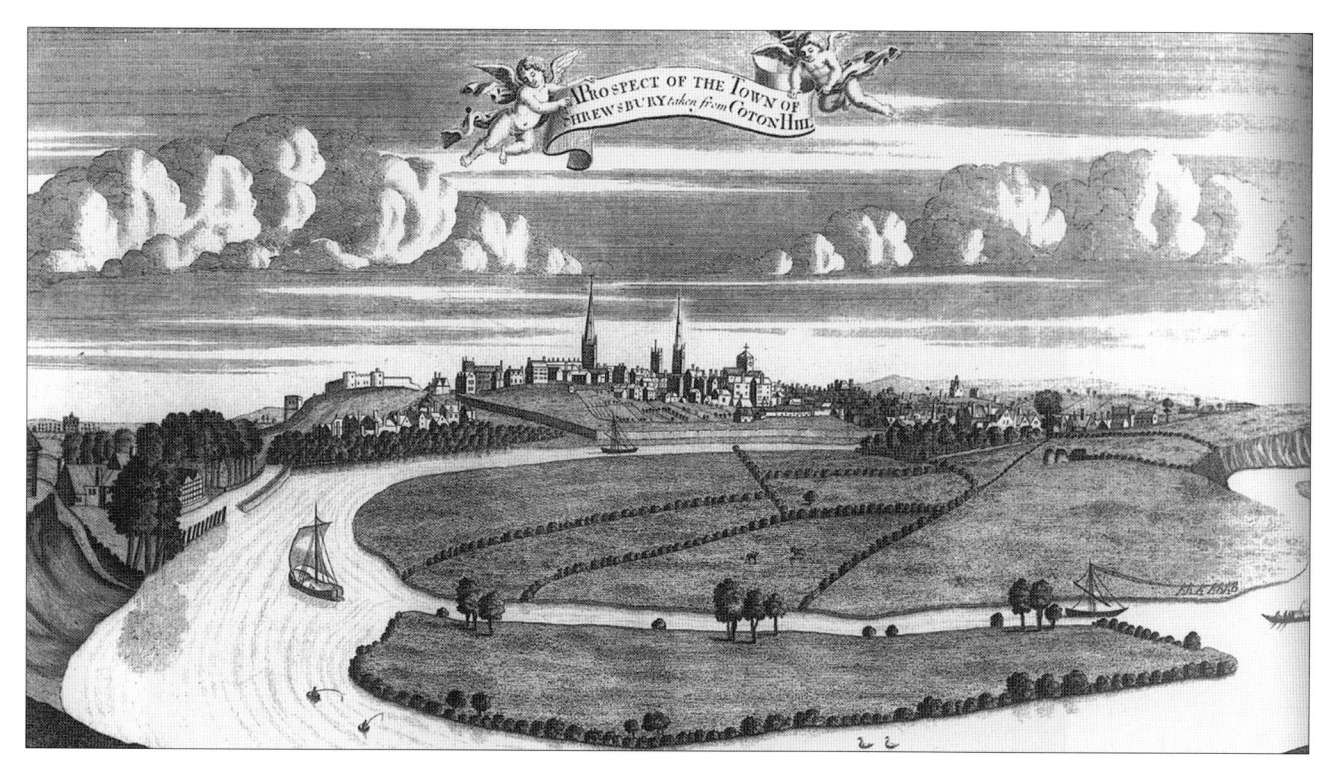

18th-century view of Shrewsbury, showing the barge gutter at Frankwell.
Shropshire Archives

River Severn

SHROPSHIRE'S principal transport route until only two hundred years ago was the river Severn. Remains of a Roman quay have been found at Wroxeter. Because the water level could vary greatly and quickly, up as far as Pool Quay, three miles short of Welshpool, the Severn was unobstructed by weirs for mills and other water-powered machinery, these industries being better sited on the more manageable feeder streams.[1]

More than forty sites of fish weirs have been identified in Shropshire, with further ones downstream in Worcestershire. Not all were in operation at the same time but the last one, at Preston Boats near Shrewsbury, survived until 1910. The fish weirs were bypassed by channels called 'barge gutters', some of which were dug through the adjacent flood plain, creating the characteristic islands or 'bylets' at each site.

In medieval and early modern times the river was navigable for 155 miles from the mouth of the Bristol Avon up to Pool Quay. It was known as a 'free river' from the absence of tolls. Boats went downstream with the current; many vessels, particularly those engaged in the coal trade, waited for a 'fresh' – a rise in river levels caused by rainfall in mid-Wales. The principal method of taking a boat upstream was by bow-hauling, up to the beginning of the 19th century by men, but usually by horses after the towpaths had been made. Sails could be used, either upstream or downstream, when the winds were in the right direction. Suitably designed larger vessels (trows) could navigate below Gloucester, usually to Bristol. Typically, boats of 60 tons could navigate to Coalport, of 40 tons to Shrewsbury and 20 tons beyond Shrewsbury. However, a reliable service could not be guaranteed because of the floods and droughts.

Thomas Telford considered that the matter had been made much worse by the embankments which had been raised in the last part of the 18th century in Montgomeryshire and west Shropshire to protect the riverside lands. He wrote:

> Formerly, when the river had risen at a moderate height, it overflowed these low lands to a great extent, which thereby operated as a side reservoir, and took off the top waters of the high floods; and these waters returning to the bed of the river by slow degrees, proved a supply for the navigation for a long time after the flood began to subside, but being now confined to a narrow channel, they rise suddenly to a greater height, and flow off with more rapidity than formerly; whereby the navigation is at one period impeded by uncontrollable floods, and, at another, left destitute of a sufficient supply for its ordinary purposes.[2]

In the 1780s proposals were made to improve the navigation by the construction of locks. Many land-owners were opposed, but the strongest hostility came from the barge owners who did not want to start paying tolls for the use of the formerly 'free river'. To support their argument they stressed how many watermen would be put out of work. When the scheme was defeated it was said that the barge owners 'shouted themselves hoarse and tossed their caps in honour of victory over attempts to improve the channel'.

The towpath from Bewdley to Coalbrookdale was not completed until 1800, and its continuation to Shrewsbury had to wait until 1809. The records of the towpath trust show that the number of boats drawn upstream to Shrewsbury by horses averaged 288 a year in the period 1815–20, increasing to 363 in 1825–30.

Joseph Plymley, writing at the very end of the 18th century, stated in his *Agriculture of Shropshire*:

> Wines and grocery goods are brought up the Severn from Bristol and Gloucester, to Shrewsbury, and so on to Montgomeryshire; and from Coalbrook-dale many vessels are laden with coal, and with the produce of their iron-works, potteries, etc. ... Flannels are exported from Shrewsbury, and grain, cheese, and lead. Soap is both imported to Shrewsbury from Bristol, by retail dealers, and soap made in Shrewsbury is exported down the Severn, and starch.[3]

At Shrewsbury the warehouses were grouped around Mardol Quay and Frankwell Quay – these dealt with such cargoes as hops, cider, spirits, grain and lead. Union Wharf, near the castle, was constructed as late as 1823–6.

A significant river-borne traffic was bar iron (cast-iron pigs) from the Severn Gorge to forges both downstream, particularly to those in the Stour Valley, and upstream to such places as Upton Forge (on the river Tern) and Bromley Forge (near the mouth of the river Perry) – even as far as Clawdd Coch, twelve miles up the river Vyrnwy, near its confluence with the river Tanat.

The trade on the Severn generally increased in the early 19th century except for the traffic to charcoal-powered forges, which were displaced by changes in technology for producing wrought iron. The Shrewsbury trade diminished immediately the Shrewsbury Canal was connected to the main canal network in 1835 (discussed in Chapters 4 & 8), and by 1850 only about two barges a week were going to Shrewsbury. The principal Severn traffic, coal and iron from the wharfs in the Severn Gorge going downstream, was progressively lost when the railways were opened through the industrial area of east Shropshire to Coalbrookdale (1854) and Coalport (1861). The opening of the Severn Valley Railway from Shrewsbury to Bewdley and Hartlebury in 1862 presaged the end for the Severn Navigation. The last recorded cargo on the Severn above Bewdley was a load of bricks from Jackfield in 1895.

River Dee

THE weir at Chester probably dates from the 11th century. It incorporated corn mills; by the 14th century there was a fulling mill; and in 1607 waterwheels were added for raising drinking water for the city. At times of very high tides, boats could pass over the weir. When the height of the weir was raised in 1916, a 'watergate' was incorporated in the structure – a single gate acting somewhat like a flash lock. Although the weir was reduced to its previous height in 1922, the watergate was retained, though it has actually been little used.

Chester had been a significant port since Roman times. For example, in medieval days it had been one of only five English ports through which wine could be imported. In particular, it was the principal port for the crossing to Ireland. However, larger sea-going vessels and the difficulties of shifting sandbanks meant that ships often had to be anchored downstream along the Wirral shore at places such as Neston, Heswell and Parkgate.

The River Dee Company was formed to provide a channel 15ft in depth at high-water spring tides up to Chester. To help finance this, the Company was authorised to reclaim land from the estuary down to Burton Point, about 7,000 acres in extent. Between 1737 and 1771, the training works were constructed, with a long straight channel of constant width to Connah's Quay on the Welsh side of the Dee, a sharp bend at Saltney and an even sharper one at Chester.

The 'new' river did not follow the natural line which was by the Wirral shore. The ebb tide no longer scoured the river so the required depth could not be achieved or maintained – even at spring tides boats drawing only 8½ft could sometimes not reach Chester. The loss of the scour in the estuary meant that sandbanks built up. To quote Vernon-Harcourt, a leading consultant on rivers and canals, writing in 1896:

> If it had been desired to destroy the navigable capabilities of the estuary of the Dee, it could hardly have been accomplished in a more effectual manner than by the works actually carried out by the River Dee Company.

He blamed the concept of combining land reclamation with the improvement of navigation, as the financial incentive was to give priority to the former.[4]

By the late 18th century, Chester was losing the battle for the Irish trade to the fast-growing port of Liverpool, and the Irish packets were sailing from Parkgate, not from Chester. Nevertheless, in the 1790s three boats provided a regular service from Chester to London, the *Chester*, the *William* and the *Conquest*. At Chester they loaded at the Old Crane, where John Whitby was broker and wharfinger; at London at Yoxall's Wharf, where Rhoda Yoxall was broker and wharfinger. The *Bristol*, the *Peter* and the *Peggy* went to Bristol. These services prove that in certain circumstances, transport by sea was a viable alternative to transport overland. Other boats traded along the north Wales coast as far as Barmouth.

The Flintshire coalfield was being developed in the second half of the 18th century, the pits being connected to the Dee by tramroads, at first with wooden rails, later with cast iron. At the wharfs the coal was transferred into boats for conveying to

Chapter 1 : Between the Severn and the Mersey

A detail from a print by T.F.Burney showing a barge being hauled upstream under the newly-built Iron Bridge. The towing line was attached to the mast. Shropshire Archives

Chester. In addition, there was one short canal off the lower Dee: Sir John Glynne's Canal, built in 1768 to carry coal from the Sandycroft Colliery near Bretton.

Above Chester Weir the Dee was navigable to Holt and, with more difficulty, as far as Bangor-is-y-coed. An Act of Parliament of 1550 had provided for the improvement of navigation up to Corwen. Andrew Yarranton surveyed the river in 1674 and suggested that if it were made navigable southwards it could be used for conveying goods to London via the Severn and the Thames. Nothing came of these proposals, of course.

In the late 18th and early 19th centuries, the small square-rigged open-decked flats or barges were hauled by men upstream – at times the tide could help as far as Farndon – and returned downstream powered by the current. Loads included gravel and stone dredged from the Dee opposite the mouth of the Alyn, sand, timber, manure, grain and other farm produce. Malt and barley came overland from Shropshire to Bangor. Boats were built at Bangor for the Bridgewater Canal and for the Mersey & Irwell Navigation. Virtually all trade had ceased by the 1830s.

In more recent years, the only commercial boats have been the pleasure boats operating from Chester. From Chester Weir to Farndon Bridge, navigation is the responsibility of Cheshire West & Chester Council, having inherited the function from Chester City Council.

River Weaver

An Act empowering a group of men to make the Weaver navigable from Frodsham to Winsford was passed in 1721 but the works, including eleven wooden locks and a towing path for the haulage of boats by men, was not completed until 1732. The navigation was not properly maintained, and in 1760 another Act was obtained, replacing the original 'undertakers' by a new body of 105 trustees. They built brick locks and increased the depth; a towpath for horses was made as far as Anderton by 1793 and later extended to Winsford.

The navigation was enhanced throughout the 19th century, locks being enlarged, the depth increased, and access to the Mersey and the docks at Weston Point improved.

An unusual feature of both the 1721 and 1760 Acts was that surplus revenue would be paid to Cheshire County Council, being used principally for road and bridge improvements. Payments started in 1771, ceased after a few years, then resumed. Unlike the Severn and the Dee, the Weaver continued to thrive until the second half of the 20th century.

Road transport

It is popularly assumed that roads in the late 18th century were atrocious, virtually impassable in winter and not much better in summer. This is a misleading over-statement, certainly as far as turnpike roads were concerned.

As a general rule, roads were a parish responsibility, being maintained by residents obliged to work on them for a certain number of days in the year, under the supervision of someone appointed as the unpaid surveyor. Whilst this system may have been just about adequate for local traffic, it was inappropriate for longer-distance traffic – and especially for the roads between the major cities and ports.

The solution was turnpike roads: toll roads administered by non-profit-making local trusts, which could borrow money in order to make improvements, repaying the loans with interest (at a maximum rate of 5%). The powers lasted for twenty-one years, but almost invariably extension Acts were obtained. Drainage ditches would be made alongside the road, and the surfaces would be improved through the use of gravel, small stones or (in industrial areas) slag. More ambitiously, roads could be straightened and gradients eased by making cuttings and embankments – ideally the maximum gradient would be 1 in 20, which was the steepest that a trotting horse could still pull a carriage, but in hilly country the gradient could be as severe as 1 in 8.

The first turnpike Act was passed in 1663 for part of the Great North Road, but it was not until the period from 1696 to 1714 that many more Acts were passed. Shropshire's first turnpike Act was in 1725, for the road from Shrewsbury to Ivetsey Bank on Watling Street and from Oakengates to Shifnal. West Cheshire's first Acts were for Stone to Nantwich in 1728 and Nantwich to Chester in 1743.

The main period for creating turnpikes was the twenty-five years from 1750. Almost all of the turnpikes in the Shropshire Union area date from this period. Although the routes of some existing turnpikes were extended after 1775, new trusts tended to be created only in the developing industrial areas. The one rare exception was the road from Whitchurch to Tarporley (now part of the A49), which was turnpiked as late as 1829.

The success of turnpikes depended largely on the activity and consciousness of the local trustees, and on the quality of the paid surveyor they appointed. Other important factors were the availability of suitable road-building materials and the nature of the traffic, very heavy loads being prone to damage the road surface. And busier roads were usually better than quieter roads, if only because more income was available for improvement and maintenance.

The quality of the turnpike roads was improved progressively until the parallel railways opened, removing most of the long and medium distance traffic, and therefore considerably reducing the income. During the later 19th century, mainly between 1860 and 1880, the trusts were dissolved and the roads taken over by the county administration.

Three authors, all writing about the year 1800, commented on the roads in their areas. G.A. Cooke, writing about north Wales, was an enthusiastic supporter of turnpikes:

> The general turnpike act was a happy one for agriculture, commerce, and every species of internal improvement.[5]

Joseph Plymley said about Shropshire's roads:

> The turnpike roads of this county are, in general, tolerably good, where they have not an over proportion of heavy carriage; but as that is likely to be taken off in a great degree by the introduction of canals, it is to be hoped that roads, ere long, will be greatly improved.[6]

He particularly praised the state of repair of the roads in the Oswestry area. On the other hand, he was highly critical of roads maintained by the parishes:

> The private ones, particularly in the clay part of the county, are almost impassable to any but the inhabitants.[7]

Henry Holland was cautious in his opinion about Cheshire's roads:

> Though the roads in Cheshire are far from being good, they are greatly better than they were twenty years ago; and may certainly be considered at present as in a state of progressive improvement.[8]

He blamed the general flatness of the county, the clayey surface, the amount of rain, and in particular the shortage of hard material for the road surface.

The most dramatic improvement in the early 19th century was in the road from London to Ireland via Birmingham, Shrewsbury and Llangollen and on through north Wales to Holyhead. West of Shrewsbury the previous turnpikes were taken over by a government agency, then realigned and rebuilt under the direction of Thomas Telford between 1815 and 1829. He also advised on the roads east of Shrewsbury, but there the administration was left with the original trusts.

The effect of successive improvements to turnpikes is demonstrated by the reduction in the time taken by the Shrewsbury to London coaches. The journey time was progressively reduced from four days in 1753 to two days in 1764 and to between 22 and 30 hours (non-stop) in 1788; by the early 1830s, the *Wonder* and the *Nimrod*, both large coaches, were getting to London in about 15 hours.

The timings of the stage coach from Chester to Birmingham via Nantwich, Market Drayton, Newport and Brewood, which operated from 1834 until 1837 (when the competing railway opened) provides evidence of the quality of less strategic turnpikes. This coach took 9¼ hours for the 90 mile journey; after allowing a total of an hour for the breaks at Nantwich (southbound), Audlem (northbound) and Brewood (both directions), the average speed was almost 11mph – and this does not include any allowance for the time taken to change the team of horses elsewhere.

More relevant to the development of canals was the use of the road system for non-passenger traffic. By the later 18th century the carrier trade was well-developed, and could be divided into three categories: London, regional and local. The carriers to London tended to be quite large well-organised concerns, the best-known being Pickford's, which started its business in Manchester. Regional carriers tended to restrict themselves to journeys which could be accomplished in a day, that is, twenty to thirty miles; they would probably have only one wagon and team of horses, starting from an inn close to their base one day, staying overnight at an inn at their destination, and returning the following day. Local carriers would make just one or two journeys a week to the nearest market town, there and back in the same day; this was not likely to be their only business. The trade continued throughout the year, though journeys took longer in winter and charges were higher.

For example, the following carriers' services were operating from Chester in about 1795:

– To London by fly wagon in six days, travelling overnight: three journeys a week operated by Wakeman & Co., each using a different route (Wakeman later went into carrying by canal);

– To other destinations in England: Warrington & Manchester (3 times a week); Middlewich (3); Whitchurch (3); and Shrewsbury (1);

– To destinations in Wales: Wrexham (3); Denbigh (2); Bala (2); Corwen (1); St Asaph & Abergele (1); Holywell (4); Mold (4); Ruthin (1); Mostyn (1); Pwllheli (1); plus occasional journeys to Conway, Llanrwst, Bettws-y-Coed, Bangor & Beaumaris and Welshpool.

– In addition, there would have been several carriers coming in from the local villages on Wednesdays and Saturdays, the market days.[9]

Early canals

CONTRARY to the impression sometimes given, Britain did not pioneer canals. The Romans built canals for irrigation, flood control and transport, including the Fossdyke, between Lincoln and the river Trent. The Grand Canal in China, completed by 1327 but largely built many centuries earlier, was over 1,000 miles long; it was between 10ft and 30ft deep and often 100ft broad. In AD984 the Chinese built the first pound lock – a lock with gates at both ends, thus minimising water usage. In Europe the first canal to cross a summit, the Stecknitz Canal (in northern Germany), was built at the end of the 14th century. The pound lock with mitre gates was drawn by but not necessarily invented by Leonardo da Vinci and used on canals in the Milan area in about 1500.[10] The Canal de Briare, linking the Loire with the Seine, was started in 1604 and completed in 1642; the Canal du Midi, between the Mediterranean Sea and the river Garonne (which flows into the Atlantic) was started in 1665 and opened in 1681. These early European canals were financed by governments. In the mid 1600s, an extensive system of transport canals (trekvaarten) was constructed in the Netherlands; these were financed by the cities they served.

In Britain, various rivers were improved for navigation by the building of locks and artificial cuts. The earliest pound locks with vertically rising (guillotine) gates were built on the Exeter Canal in 1564–6, and the first pound locks with mitre gates on the river Lea in 1576. River improvements in the 18th century tended to have a greater proportion of artificial cuts; for example, well over half of the length of the Kennet Navigation between Newbury and Reading (1715–23) was not on the line of the river.

The first British canal to be constructed over a summit was the Newry Canal in northern Ireland, which was completed in 1742 by Thomas Steers, the Liverpool Docks engineer. Steer's pupil and successor, Henry Berry, was the engineer for the Sankey Brook Navigation, which, despite its name, was the first canal in England independent of a river; this received its Act in 1755, and opened in stages from 1759 to 1772, when it reached St Helens. Its most significant innovation was that it was privately financed by issuing shares to the general public – indeed, this concept is often regarded as the principal British contribution to the history of canals worldwide.

Liverpool-financed surveys in 1755 and 1757 showed that connecting the Weaver and the Trent was practicable, and another survey in 1758 proposed making the Trent navigable as far as Stoke. That same year Earl Gower of Trentham and Lord Anson of Shugborough, together with others, engaged James Brindley to make a survey for a canal independent of the river from the Potteries down to Wilden Ferry, on the Trent near Derby. The 43-year-old Brindley had no experience of building canals, but he was highly regarded as an innovative millwright, a job which entailed the manipulation of water supplies; he had installed pumps for Earl Gower and had built a steam-driven engine for another leading advocate of the project, colliery owner Thomas Broad. Britain had at that time no experience of canal-building on such a scale, much finance would have to be raised, and public opinion was sceptical. Pamphlets were published; the rival schemes debated.

In 1760 Brindley resurveyed the line at the sole expense of Lord Gower but the time was not yet ripe for an application to Parliament. An Act of Parliament was necessary in order to have powers to purchase land even when the owner was unwilling to sell; it was also needed to create a limited liability company, one where the shareholders would not be individually liable to pay the debts if the company failed.

The Bridgewater Canal

EARL Gower was the brother-in-law and guardian of Francis Egerton, who in 1748 became the third Duke of Bridgewater. (For further information about the relationship between the Duke of Bridgewater and Earl Gower, see Appendix F.) Worsley, one of the twelve estates inherited by the Duke, was some seven miles north-west of Manchester and had large reserves of coal. In 1759 he obtained an Act for a canal from the mines to Salford. The detailed plans were devised by John Gilbert, the manager of the Worsley estate and the younger brother of Thomas Gilbert, Principal Agent for both Earl Gower and the Duke of Bridgewater. Later that year a more ambitious scheme was developed: to cross the river Irwell and take the canal to close to the centre of Manchester, with the potential of extending it towards Liverpool. At this stage James Brindley was brought into the team. A second Act was obtained, and the canal to Manchester built, including the crossing of the Irwell at Barton on a three-arched aqueduct, the centre arch being 63ft wide and 38ft high. Completed in 1761, the canal was a success in every way: spectacular engineering, profitable for the Duke, and reducing the price of coal in Manchester substantially.

The Act for the extension of the Bridgewater Canal westwards to the deeper waters of the Mersey was obtained in 1762, but little was done on the ground for another couple of years.

The Grand Trunk and Staffordshire & Worcestershire Canals

THE success of the Bridgewater Canal had a major influence on public opinion. Pamphlets and meetings to advocate a canal link between the Mersey and the Trent resumed, Josiah Wedgwood emerging as a driving force, working closely with James Brindley. Earl Gower had excellent contacts with the government and in Parliament. The promoters realised the importance of the cooperation of the Duke of Bridgewater, with the result that the northern connection would be with the Bridgewater Canal not, as would have been more natural (and cheaper), with the Weaver. The project was renamed the 'Grand Trunk Canal', which was both accurate and good marketing, but is now generally referred to as the 'Trent & Mersey Canal'.

The key meeting to launch the project was held on 30 December 1765 at the inn at Wolseley Bridge, north of Rugeley – a meeting which has been described as 'the birth of the First Canal Age'. Earl Gower set out the potential benefits; Brindley gave the details of the scheme. It was unanimously agreed that application should be made to Parliament, also that the promotion of a line to the Severn should be left to separate promoters.

One decision was to have a long-lasting effect on canal development in England: that the locks should be built to accommodate boats 7ft wide and 72ft long. Up until then, the dimensions of navigations and canals had been determined by the size of boats using the estuarial waters, typically with a width in the order of 14ft, but the implications of making Harecastle Tunnel, over 1½ mile long, at that time by far the longest tunnel in the world, meant that the width was considerably restricted.

The impression is sometimes given that Brindley had the concept of a 'Grand Cross' of canals joining the ports of Liverpool, Hull, Bristol and London, and almost single-handed led the canal movement towards this goal. In reality, the impetus to build canals came from local communities, principally the manufacturers and merchants, together with those major landowners who saw the potential of improving the productivity and hence the rents of their estates. Brindley, a tireless advocate of canals and a prodigiously hard worker, remained the most sought-after engineer for such projects.

The first of these other projects was the Staffordshire & Worcestershire Canal, from a junction with the Trent & Mersey at Great Haywood, skirting Stafford and Wolverhampton, and continuing via Kidderminster to the river Severn, at a location which came to be named Stourport. This was promoted principally by a group of Wolverhampton businessmen led by James Perry. It obtained its Act on the same day as the Trent & Mersey Canal: 14 May 1766.

Other local proposals

BACK in April 1762 James Brindley recorded in his notebook that he had 'set out for Chaster and Sropshire survey or a raconnitoring', in four days visiting Whitchurch, Wem, Shrewsbury, Ellesmere, Bangor-on-Dee, Wrexham and Chirk. A few pages later in his notebook is a sketch map of a route between Chester and Lee Brockhurst passing Whitchurch and Wem. It is not known who commissioned him – possibly he was looking at alternative routes between the Mersey and the Severn – and no record survives of what he told a meeting of Chester City Council later that year.

One of the opponents to routeing the canal from the Trent to the Mersey via the Potteries was Sir Richard Whitworth of Batchacre Hall, four miles north of Newport, who described himself as 'an ingenious gent'. In early 1766 he issued a pamphlet advocating a line through Stafford and Nantwich, via the gap used much later by the Grand Junction Railway (now the West Coast Main Line). This would have avoided the need for the long tunnel at Harecastle. From Nantwich his canal would have gone to Winsford, there joining the river Weaver. There would have been a branch from near Ecclleshall, passing through the grounds of Batchacre Hall, linking with the

Chapter 1: Between the Severn and the Mersey

river Severn close to Attingham Hall. By having a much lower summit level it would probably have been cheaper and quicker to construct, but it had the severe disadvantages of serving neither the Potteries nor the West Midlands industrial area and of entering the Severn too high for efficient navigation.

Two years after the Trent & Mersey and Staffordshire & Worcestershire Canals received their Acts, Whitworth issued a further pamphlet urging the citizens of Chester to opt for a route by Farndon, Whitchurch and Hinstock, joining his original Stafford–Severn route at Batchacre. This advice was not heeded. Undeterred, Whitworth enlarged an ornamental pool on his Batchacre Estate to become a substantial reservoir, with another at a slightly higher level, and constructed at least half a mile of the line of the canal.

No other serious proposals emerged for canals in the next couple of decades within what was to become the area of the Shropshire Union apart from the Chester Canal (discussed in the next chapter) and the private Donnington Wood Canal (Chapter 3). However, one canal project just outside the area would eventually have a significant effect on the Shropshire Union: the Birmingham Canal.[11] Its 1768 Act authorised a line from Birmingham to the Staffordshire & Worcestershire Canal at Aldersley Junction, with branches to Wednesbury and Ocker Hill. Construction was completed in 1772.

Notes and references

1. The weir below Shrewsbury was built under the provisions of the Shrewsbury Corporation Act 1909, long after the river had ceased to be used for commercial navigation. The Act required rollers for the use of pleasure boats to be provided, but this was never done.
2. Thomas Telford, in Joseph Plymley, *General View of the Agriculture of Shropshire*, second edition 1813, p.287
3. Joseph Plymley, *General View of the Agriculture of Shropshire*, second edition 1813, pp.83–4
4. Leveson Francis Vernon-Harcourt, *Rivers and Canals*, Vol.1, Rivers, 1896, pp.290–3 & plate 9, fig.13
5. G.A. Cooke, *Topographical and Statistical Description of the Principality of Wales, Part 1, North Wales*, p.63
6. Joseph Plymley, *General View of the Agriculture of Shropshire*, second edition 1813, p.279
7. Joseph Plymley, *General View of the Agriculture of Shropshire*, second edition 1813, p.273
8. Henry Holland, *General View of the Agriculture of Cheshire*, 1808, p.302
9. *The Universal British Directory*, Vol.2, Part 2, 1793–8, p.724
10. Mitre gates: a pair of lock gates which meet to form an apex facing the direction of the higher water; pressure holds them tight against each other, minimising leakage.
11. The Birmingham Canal is now popularly known as the 'BCN' – Birmingham Canal Navigations. Many canal acts of that period included 'Navigation' in the title of the canal.

The Chester Canal, derived from a 1895 map of the Shropshire Union Canal with peripheral detail removed.
Canal & River Trust

2

The Chester Canal

Obtaining the Act of Parliament

By the late 1760s the leading citizens of Chester were rightly concerned about the future of their port. In 1766 the Grand Trunk Canal, later generally known as the Trent & Mersey Canal (TMC), had been approved by Parliament, and this would clearly become the natural outlet for the industrial area of the Potteries – Chester would be bypassed. Although the danger had been realised, Chester had made no attempt to seek a clause enabling a canal to be made from the city to the Grand Trunk, apparently under the impression that Parliament would permit this at a later date.

A clause in the Grand Trunk's Act permitted the Duke of Bridgewater, the 'Canal Duke', to construct the northernmost five miles of the canal from Preston Brook to Runcorn, that section then becoming part of the Bridgewater Canal. (The western end of the Bridgewater Canal was originally to be at the Hempstones, about 1½ miles upstream of Runcorn.) This had not been the only option discussed by the promoters of the Grand Trunk Canal. The most natural and cheapest northern terminus would have been to join the river Weaver, about where the Anderton Lift was built over a hundred years later. The most ambitious would have involved an aqueduct across the river Mersey near Runcorn, then a canal just north of the Mersey along to Liverpool. Yet another option considered was to have taken the canal via or near Chester to Ince, on the Mersey estuary.

Members of James Brindley's staff carried out a survey in the autumn and winter of 1768/69 on behalf of the 'gentlemen of Chester' for a canal between their town and Middlewich. Various Chester men met Brindley on a few occasions and also had discussions with the members of the committee of the Grand Trunk Canal.

A meeting was called by the Mayor of Chester, Charles Boswell, and the principal local landowner, Lord Grosvenor of Eaton Hall, on 25 November 1768 to promote a Bill for the canal. The City Corporation's support was formally given when the Assembly resolved to attach its seal to a petition to Parliament. However, there is no record of the proceedings of a Bill in Parliament, nor of the presentation of the petition. Brindley's covering letter with his account for his men's time states that he had 'not charged any thing for my self, as your Bill did not go forward, though I had a good deal of trouble – but I leave it to you and the rest of the gentlemen of your city, to allow me what you think proper'. A note on the account shows that they gave him 30 guineas for his efforts.[1]

The second attempt

After a lapse of a year, a meeting was held on 23 April 1770 to consider how to promote the Chester Canal. The newspaper advertisement referred to the 'present subscribers', but this probably meant the subscribers to the previous attempt, as at a later meeting it was resolved to reimburse expenses 'hitherto incurred'.

A survey was commissioned from Samuel Weston, who had been a junior member of Brindley's surveying team: he had been paid 2s.6d a day, whereas John Varley, who had led the team, had been paid 10s.6d a day. Although he described himself as an 'engineer', Weston had little experience. He had worked for Brindley for a couple of years as a staff-holder and leveller, and about this time he with another person undertook an earthworks contract on the Leeds & Liverpool Canal. He had made small arches but had never made nor supervised the construction of locks or bridges. Nor had he ever undertaken land valuation.

No doubt it was not a totally new survey but a refinement of the one Weston had been involved in a little more than a year earlier; the various landowners on the route were noted and supplies of water were identified. He estimated the total cost as £32,399, of which £8,250 was for the land.

The canal was to leave the Dee at Boughton Ford, about a mile above Chester weir, rise by a series of locks to Christleton, then take much the same line as the present canal as far as Tilstone. From there it would have taken a fairly direct line to the village of Wettenhall, down the south side of the valley of Ash Brook, crossing the river Weaver near Twelve Acres Farm in Wimboldsley parish. The final couple of miles into Middlewich would have been similar to the line of the later Middlewich

21

Branch. There was one major engineering work, the aqueduct taking the canal 60ft above the river Weaver. At this stage there was no proposal for a link to Nantwich.

An advertisement was placed in a local Chester paper inviting 'all noblemen, gentlemen, merchants ... desirous of carrying on the undertaking' to a meeting at the Talbot on 31 August. It also asserted that if carried out the canal would 'not only turn out to the advantage of the subscribers but also be of greatest utility in preserving and promoting the trade of the City, Middlewich, Nantwich, Tarporley and adjacent parts and of great advantage to land owners'.

The share capital was to be £40,000 in £100 shares, and more than this sum had been promised by the end of this first formal meeting of the subscribers.

At a meeting a week later a committee of thirteen was elected; all seem to have been men of Chester. Widdens & Potts were appointed solicitors, though they resigned three months later, possibly because of a potential conflict of interest with their role as legal advisers to the River Dee Commission, an appointment which they held until 1870.

At an early meeting Weston was instructed to survey two other routes in the Chester area which would bring the canal into the Dee a mile below the weir, as a result of which the committee selected the route below the city walls via Northgate. The engineering would be more difficult, including a deep cutting and 120 yards of tunnelling, and more expensive land would need to be bought, but the operational advantages would be considerable as the entrance to the canal would then be adjacent to Crane Wharf, the city's principal wharf for sea-going vessels. The canal wharf for trade between Chester and the hinterland would be in the most convenient location too.

The committee must have had some misgivings about the experience of their engineer, as they asked John Longbotham, the engineer of the Leeds & Liverpool Canal, to look over the course and tell them whether any improvements could be made. He must have been too busy, because they then repeated the request to Hugh Oldham of Manchester, a land surveyor who had also worked for Brindley – again, he must have been busy, because the supporting engineering evidence to Parliament in February 1771 was given by Thomas Yeoman, a well-respected engineer much experienced in river navigations. However, Yeoman admitted that he had not actually seen the ground where the canal was to be made, nor was he acquainted with the prices of labour and materials in that part of the country. His positive contribution was to say that he thought that Weston had taken great pains and understood the subject.

Petitions in favour of the Bill were obtained from the Potteries, Middlewich, Nantwich, other parts of Cheshire, and north Wales. Supporting evidence was given to Parliament by John Chamberlaine and James Folliott, both Chester merchants, and John Latham, Surveyor of the Port of Chester. A petition against came from Northwich. But much more important was the negative attitude of the Trent & Mersey Canal and its influential backer, the Duke of Bridgewater.

This had been recognised as a major issue from the beginning. In October 1770 two committee members had met with representatives of the TMC, the latter being concerned that a canal from Middlewich to Chester would reduce their income in the Middlewich to Preston Brook section, which the Chester members could hardly deny. Widdens & Potts were asked to contact everyone sympathetic to the Chester Canal whom they thought was likely to be an investor in the TMC, exhorting them to attend the next General Meeting of the TMC and vote in favour of agreeing to a junction. A letter was written to the Duke of Bridgewater 'to recommend the intended scheme for his favourable opinion and approbation, and to solicit his concurrence and assistance'; this was sent via the Duke's Lancashire Steward, John Gilbert, whose brother, Thomas Gilbert, was then Chairman of the TMC. (Thomas Gilbert was General Agent for six of the Duke's estates, as well as being Earl Gower's General Agent. As MP for Newcastle-under-Lyme he had chaired the House of Commons Committee which had examined the TMC's Bill in 1766.) The Duke would of course also lose income on his canal between Preston Brook and Runcorn if the Chester Canal were built, so it is hardly surprising that he gave no assistance. Worse, although the Bill passed the Commons, it was defeated in the Lords in May 1771, probably mainly through the influence of the Duke of Bridgewater and the other major landed investors in the TMC, such as his brother-in-law, Earl Gower of Trentham Hall.

Third time 'lucky'

JUST eleven days after the Bill had been defeated, it was decided to open a new subscription to apply again to Parliament in the autumn. The summer was spent gathering support, leading to a General Meeting on 13 September at which a committee was elected.

At this meeting it was also decided to apply for a branch from Tilstone Heath to Nantwich, and Samuel Weston was asked to carry out the necessary surveys. His revised route was similar to that previously agreed between the river Dee and Tilstone but then it continued south-east for a further 2½ miles to Wardle before making a right angle turn and going north-east to rejoin the earlier route near Wettenhall. The Nantwich branch from Wardle went south-east to a terminus three-quarters of a mile short of the centre of Nantwich – in other words, the canal from Tilstone to Nantwich was to be as it now is. This amendment to the Middlewich line minimised the total length of canal which was to be built; more importantly it reduced the height of the summit level by at least 25ft.

A more positive effort was made to get support from Chester's hinterland, but one wishes one knew what lay behind one tantalising minute:

> That an answer be wrote to Mr Yoxall of Nantwich to desire that he would thank the inhabitants for their intentions but that the committee cannot think of acquiescing to their terms.

Chapter 2 : The Chester Canal

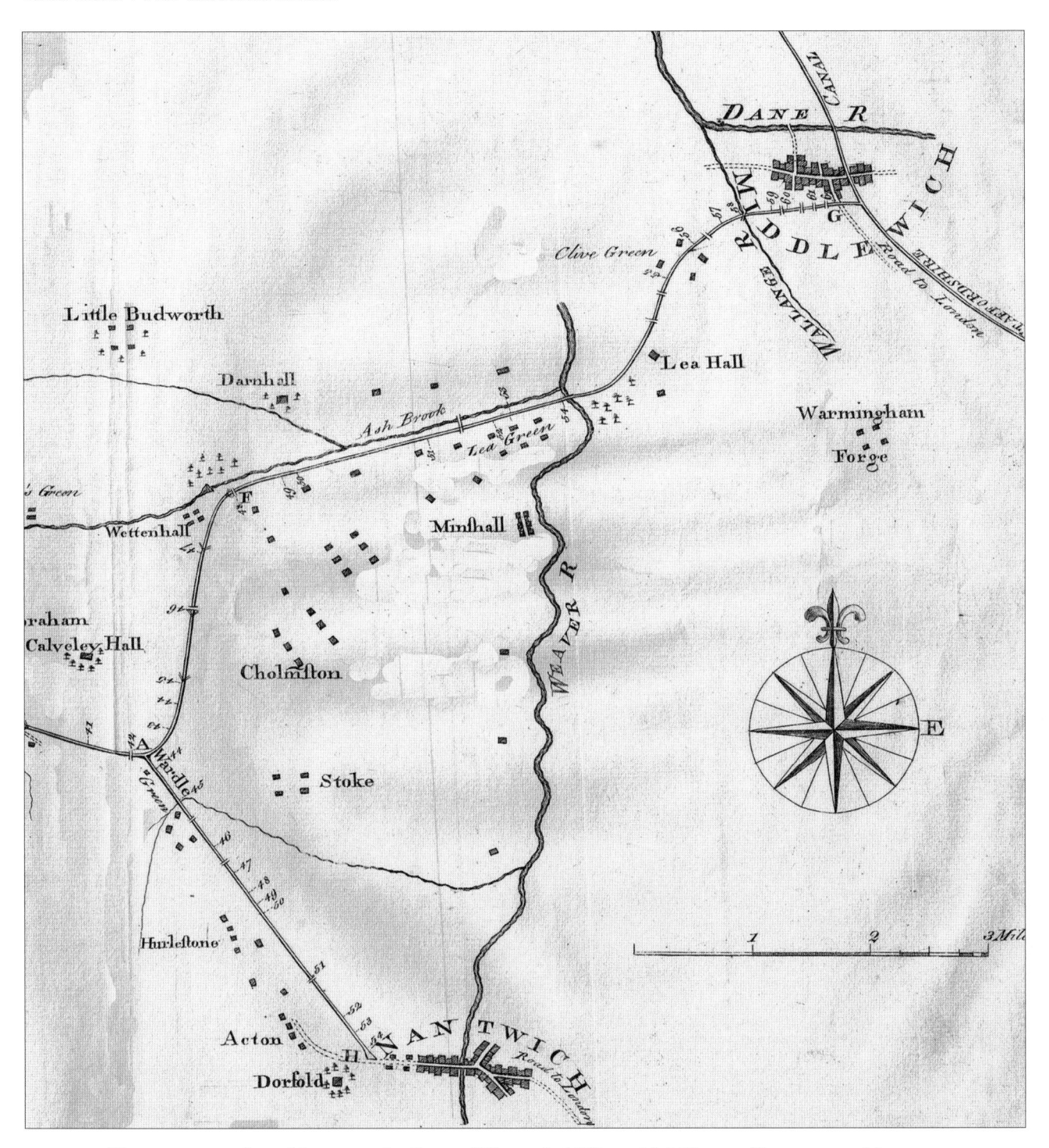

The eastern section of the survey by Samuel Weston in 1771 to which Thomas Yeoman gave his name. Unlike the Middlewich Branch built in the late 1820s, the Chester Canal would have crossed the river Weaver north of Church Minshull. The map, which shows the intended positions of locks, is not accurate, being somewhat diagrammatic, and the implied levels are clearly wrong. Nevertheless, this formed the basis of the application to Parliament. *Richard Dean*

Perhaps they wanted their involvement in the management to be formally included in the Bill.

A letter in *Adam's Weekly Courant*, the local newspaper, a few days later outlined how the prosperity of nations developed from hunting via pasturage and agriculture to manufacturing and trade before citing a number of reasons why the canal should be made: increasing commerce adds to prosperity, the price of carriage of goods is reduced, existing manufactures are promoted and new ones established, ports prosper because of the increasing sea trade, mineral resources can be exploited, fewer horses need be kept, the water of the canal would help farmers in times of drought, and lower food prices would benefit the poor.[2]

The principal outstanding problem was of course the issue of joining the TMC at Middlewich. When the Bill was about to come before Parliament, the three committee members who were in London to give evidence were authorised to have negotiations with the TMC and the Duke of Bridgewater. They met the latter, who said he would not oppose the Bill if there were a clause prohibiting the Chester Canal from crossing Booth Lane (the main north–south road), thus preventing it from entering the TMC. On being informed of this, the Chester committee agreed the terms and sent the Duke their 'most humble thanks ... for this great act of kindness and condescension'. Nevertheless they still hoped that he would induce the proprietors of the TMC to allow the junction, and a week later they asked whether he would be willing to ask the TMC proprietors whether they would be willing to agree to a junction if payment were made.

In the event, the clause in the Act was even more restrictive than the Duke's suggestion: the Chester Canal would not be allowed to build within 100 yards of the TMC. Charles Dupin, a Frenchman writing some fifty years later, commented that this clause:

> though it is uncommon of its kind, it shews, that even among nations where the legislator is the most enlightened, he may be surprised into granting restrictions, contrary to the general spirit of his acts, and injurious to the public good.[3]

It destroyed any chance that the Chester Canal would succeed on its main aim of attracting through trade from and to the Potteries. The double transhipment would add significant costs, make dispatch arrangements more complex, and increase the chance of the goods being damaged. Apparently not appreciating the significance of their defeat, the committee was delighted when the Bill received the Royal Assent on 1 April 1772.

Samuel Butler was a flour dealer in Chester. He appears not to have taken an active part in the management of the Canal Company.

Grosvenor Museum, Chester

The construction period (1772–1779)
Management

NOWADAYS we expect any organisation to have a chairman, someone who leads the management team and acts as the public face of the organisation, but this was not always the case in the 18th century. The Chester Canal had a group of individuals who worked long and hard on the project, meeting virtually every week, sometimes twice a week, for many years, but no one of them was the chairman, neither in name nor spirit. The members of this group were all leading citizens of Chester: John Chamberlaine and James Folliott were merchants, Thomas Griffies dealt in timber, Alex Denton was a physician, Hugh Speed was Deputy Registrar of the Diocese of Chester, and Walter Thomas, Thomas Moulson, John Rogers and Peter Panton were all at some point described as 'gentlemen'.

They were unpaid except for travelling and subsistence when on canal business – in fact, as committee members had to own five shares and all but one were probably dead before the shares brought even a meagre return, their involvement cost them dearly in money as well as in time and worry. The one exception was John Chamberlaine, who in April 1774 was paid 100 guineas 'for the whole of his extraordinary trouble had in this undertaking to this day'. Sometimes the committee members supplied materials but this does not seem to have been used as a way of making excess profits; for example, one minute authorised hay and oats to be bought from Dr Denton at a market price, but a minute at the next meeting instructed to buy Mr Miller's hay as it would suit better.

Although those who regularly attended committee meetings were all from the city of Chester, the Annual and Special General Meetings were sometimes chaired by one of two major shareholders from its hinterland: Revd Sir Thomas Broughton of Doddington Hall, about five miles south-east of Nantwich; and John Crewe of Crewe Hall, who was an MP for Cheshire. (The other MP for Cheshire was Samuel Egerton, who was destined to play a significant role in the history of the Chester Canal.)

Canal companies' committees generally got much more involved in the details of management than would now seem normal, but the Chester Canal Company took this micromanagement to extremes.

Judging by the turnover of the staff in the key jobs, they were unable to attract able people with suitable experience – partly this would have been because canal construction and operation was something new, but poor pay and an excess of interference were surely major factors.

For the Clerk to the company the committee wanted someone 'who is not of the law, to keep the books and accounts'; the qualifications expected were 'book-keeping, measuring timber, surveying of lands, and a competent knowledge of mechanisms'. Philip Norbury was appointed on £60 a year, plus the use of a house which would contain the committee room. The following year his annual salary was increased to £70. However, in October 1773 he was dismissed because of a cash deficiency, and replaced by John Moon on a salary of £100 a year. Shortly afterwards Moon was given an assistant clerk, Charles Hill, initially on £20 a year, rising to £30 a year 'according to his behaviour'.

In later years it was the common practice for canal companies to engage a consulting engineer who chose the route, designed the main engineering works, gave general advice and conducted a periodic survey. However, the Chester Canal was one of the earliest canals to be promoted, and expert talent was scarce and expensive. The committee therefore appointed and closely supervised a full-time Engineer. Samuel Weston was formally appointed in May 1772, on a salary of £150 a year, with John Lawton as his assistant on £100 a year, and with Weston's son as his clerk on £20 a year. Lawton died in January 1774 and does not seem to have been replaced.

The following are examples of the instructions given to the Engineers:

– Ordered that Mr Weston make a report at every General or Committee Meeting what is intended or necessary to be done on the course of the canal each succeeding week and that he follows the directions given at such weekly meeting and do not vary from the same without first giving notice thereof at a subsequent meeting.

– Ordered that Mr Weston do begin to stake and set out the canal under the directions and orders of Messrs Thomas, Chamberlaine and Rogers.

– Ordered that Mr Morris do at all times take his instructions from the Committee for the breadth of all bridges to be built on the canal before he fix the same determinable.

Contrary to general canal practice, initially most of the earth-works were done by labour employed directly by the company. The committee gave specific instructions about the number of men to be employed; for example, in February 1773 they stated the maximum number of men to be employed as cutters were '40 men between Golden Nook and the Brockholes, 60 ditto between the Trooper's and Waverton Quarry ... 20 in getting up rock and rubbish at Chester'.

Later the practice seems to have been to work mainly through gang-masters, though still specifying the maximum number of men in each gang. Contractors tended to be used only for items for which craftsmen were needed, such as brickwork and masonry; these contracts were each small in value.

The division of duties between the Clerk and the Engineer was not clear-cut. For example, Philip Norbury was instructed to 'agree with Ellis Makings and Henry Rigby carpenters to make a good sufficient rail road in John Griffith's garden, upon as low terms as he can, not to exceed 2s.6d per rood for laying the said rail road'. Presumably this was for transporting material to or from the construction site, aspects which one would expect the Engineer to deal with.

Another example occurred when Richard Graham, one of the overlookers of works, refused to obey an order from the Clerk concerning the repair of a dam, saying that he took orders only from the Engineer – the committee said it 'do very much disapprove of this behaviour' and told him that he had to obey all orders given to him by the Clerk too.

In February 1774 Samuel Weston was dismissed, the immediate cause being the collapse of part of the aqueduct over the river Gowy. However, this seems to have been the culmination of a series of problems about the quality of his supervision. The previous month it had been minuted:

> If the Engineer certifies the bill and the work has not been duly performed, the said charge or charges shall be deducted out of the Engineer's salary, and besides this the Company shall think him guilty of a high offence.

Perhaps too he had not been spending enough time on site; he was also together with a partner carrying out a four-mile-long earthworks contract on the Leeds & Liverpool Canal.

The company wrote to Thomas Morris, who was then in Ireland, inviting him to take over as Engineer. Morris had worked for Brindley on various canals and he was probably in charge of the Bridgewater Canal works from Altrincham to Runcorn until their near completion at the end of 1772. He had had a minor involvement with the Chester Canal previously, as back in 1770 he had advised Weston when the latter was seeking a suitable water supply. He accepted, though he was unable to start until later in the year. Morris was given a four-year contract at an annual salary of £150 but this was increased to £200 after two years.

Despite having a more experienced engineer – or perhaps a sign of lack of confidence in him – the company engaged three better-known engineers to survey the canal and give their opinions: Thomas Yeoman, who had given evidence on behalf of the Chester Canal promoters in their second attempt to obtain an Act; John Golbourne, a Chester man who was Engineer to the River Dee Company and who was then engaged on making the Clyde navigable up to Glasgow; and Robert Whitworth, formerly one of Brindley's team of engineers and at that time Surveyor to the Navigation Committee of the Corporation of London. In 1771 Yeoman had chaired the first meeting of the Society of Civil Engineers; Golbourne and Whitworth were also founder members of the Society. They all reported in 1776, though the actual payments were so small that they could not have spent more than one or two days each in the area.

In the same year, Josiah Clowes was asked to assist Morris

viewing the line between Wardle Green and Middlewich. Early the following year Moon was instructed to ask Clowes to survey that line, prepare an estimate and give evidence to Parliament. The committee was told that he had agreed and that the estimate would be ready the following week; two days later they were told that he had turned down the request. The committee then instructed Moon, along with Morris, to prepare the estimate.

In June 1777 Morris told the committee that he wished to leave when his contract ended the following May, but in August they dismissed him, paying £75 in compensation for the early termination. Relationships had obviously soured. For most of 1777 Morris had not been being paid his full salary because of the financial crisis. The involvement of other engineers and the lack of clarity of his and Moon's respective responsibilities cannot have helped. The committee passed a resolution which hints at the recognition of the problem:

> Whenever a future Engineer is employed ... he shall have the sole direction of any works he shall undertake and be answerable to the committee for any failure.

John Moon, the Clerk, then temporarily undertook the additional role of engineer. A 'properly qualified' engineer was advertised for, without success. That autumn, John Golbourne was invited to be engineer, but he refused. Then in April 1778 Josiah Clowes was appointed 'General Surveyor or Overlooker of the Works' at an annual salary of £200, with the conditions that he lived in the neighbourhood of the works and did not absent himself without the committee's permission in writing. The first was not a problem as his home was at Middlewich. He must have known that he was unlikely to fulfil the second condition as he had other business interests, principally his business as a carrier on the Trent & Mersey Canal; he was also assisting Thomas Dadford senior in building locks on the Stroudwater Canal in Gloucestershire.

Just 14 weeks later the committee resolved:

> The Company's Concerns ... suffer greatly on account of Mr Clowes Absenting himself from their Works. ... If he shall continue to absent himself, this Committee will be under the disagreeable necessity of directing his Wages to be stopped in proportion to the time he shall be absent.

It can have been of no surprise to anyone when he was dismissed at the end of November. Once again John Moon took on extra duties, for fifteen months assisted by William Cawley, who was employed on a temporary contract.

No engineer was appointed. For the rest of the independent life of the Chester Canal, one of the committee members acted in effect as engineer. Initially this was Joseph Turner, an architect.

Occasionally the committee had to deal with unusual issues. In 1779, for example, Edward Turley, an apprentice employed by Edward Bird, who was constructing boats for the company, was impressed into the navy. Legal action was taken as apprentices were exempt from impressment (as were 'gentlemen'); one hopes this was successful.

Gauge

ONE of the first decisions made after the Act was obtained was to decide that the locks should be made 15ft wide. At first sight this seems logical, as it was normal for the gauge of a canal linked to the sea to be determined by the size of coastal boats in that area – for example, the 'narrow' TMC was built broad from the river Trent as far as Burton-on-Trent, to accommodate the boats which traded up to Nottingham. In the case of the Chester Canal it is less obvious, as the main trade was always intended to be boats plying to and from the Potteries and the West Midlands, and these would be only 7ft wide, the TMC and Staffordshire & Worcestershire Canal being narrow.

The gauge was one of those fundamental decisions which should be made before costs were estimated, before the share capital required was determined and before the Act was applied for, as it had a significant impact on the cost of the engineering works and land purchases. A broad canal cost about 40% more than a narrow canal.

It also affected the water supply needed, as a broad lock passes twice as much water as a narrow one. It might be thought that this was not material, as the broad boats had about double the capacity of narrow boats. However, this assumes that all boats were fully loaded. For many types of traffic, it was not possible to load even a narrow boat to its full 20 or 25 ton capacity, not unless departure of the boat was delayed until a full load could be obtained to its ultimate destination. As the boats coming from the Potteries would be narrow, if they then went singly through the locks, half the water would inevitably be wasted. Indeed, in many drier summers the committee later found it necessary to require narrow boats to wait until they could be paired up.

A boat going from Middlewich to Chester would traverse a summit, so would use a lockful of water ascending to the summit, then another lockful descending the other side. It is doubtful whether an adequate supply of water had been identified to permit this, the original plans not even including a reservoir to enable some winter water to be stored until the summer.

Furthermore, in the specific case of the Chester Canal, the 'staircase' of five locks at Chester (where the lower gate of one lock is the top gate of the next) would pass more water per boat than conventional pound locks – five times as much if boats go each way alternately, or three times as much if they arrive randomly in each direction. A sea-going boat bringing (say) coal from the Flintshire coalfield, going up the staircase and unloading at one of the canalside industries which developed at the eastern edge of Chester, then returning empty for another load, inevitably used several lockfuls of water but paid little in tolls, which were charged proportionately to the mileage travelled.

The entrance lock from the Dee

To make matters worse, the Act stated that the entrance lock from the Dee was to be no wider than that needed to take boats 7ft broad without the consent in writing of the River Dee

Company. The latter refused to agree to a wider lock, claiming it would be 'injurious to their Company', despite the fact that one would have thought they would do everything they could to encourage trade on the river. It said that it would agree to a greater width if all boats passing to or from the Dee paid a special tonnage, so it seems that its attitude was really just opportunism. It may be significant that the River Dee Company was an organisation based in London, not in Chester.

The Act stated that the canal company could give a year's notice of exercising their rights once boats could navigate through the 'rock' at Northgate; this was first done on 27 December 1774, so they served the formal notice – and this asked for an entrance 27ft wide into a basin which should have 'a pair of good and substantial gates ... in order to retain the water ... so that vessels may at all times safely lie afloat therein'. In other words, it was to be a 'wet dock'.

It was not until June 1775 that Thomas Yeoman, who had been engaged by the River Dee Company, designed the entrance, for which the Chester Canal Company was to reimburse the cost. His instructions were to make the entrance 7ft wide, but the canal company refused to pay for anything which was not in accord with its wishes, which in turn prompted the river company to initiate legal action. In August two members of the canal company's committee were deputed to go to London to negotiate but it was not until the following April that a settlement was agreed whereby the River Dee Company would be paid one half penny per ton on coals and all other articles (except stones, gravel, limestone, flint stone, potters clay and slate) which passed from the canal into the basin or vice versa.

Thomas Morris, by then the canal company's engineer, was instructed to prepare plans for the basin and the entrance 27ft wide, but in June 1776, less than a month later, the committee decided that a 15ft entrance would be 'more advantageous'.

An Act to confirm the changes was passed in March 1778.

Progress

THE Mayor of Chester cut the first sod on 4 May 1772, but as there was no report of the event in *Adam's Weekly Courant*, it is not known where this took place.

The City Corporation had concerns about the City Wall and Northgate Gaol, for which they were responsible. When the Northgate route was first suggested, the Corporation had sought the advice of John Golborne, who thought that there was no probability of either the City Wall or the Northgate being damaged if the canal was kept four yards distant. With this reassurance, the Assembly had formally backed the project.

Making the cutting through which the canal was to run necessitated the demolition of a part of the gaol and the removal of the link between the gaol and the Chapel of St John. Five canal committee members met the Sheriffs of the City to settle how prisoners were to be prevented from escaping whilst the works were being carried out in the grounds of the gaol. John Chamberlaine gave a bond as security for the costs arising from any escapes, the committee subsequently indemnifying him. The Corporation wanted the canal arched over; the canal company refused to do this but said it would reconsider once the works had been completed. In the end, a bridge was made from the garden of Northgate Gaol to the chapel.

Navvies were usually mentioned in the newspapers only when there was a riot or a death, but in February 1776 the *Chester Chronicle* reported that a number of canal workmen,

> being out of employ from the severity of the weather, drew a waggon loaded with coals, 38 hundredweight, from Madeley in Staffordshire to this city, above thirty miles distance, and after collecting money on the road and round the city for two successive days, they unyoked at Mr Speed's, in the Abbey Square, one of the proprietors of the canal, and presented the coals to him.[4]

The entrance from the Dee into the canal was opened on 13 November 1776, and the following month it was reported that a canal barge of about 60 tons burden, had for the first time on 10 December descended the 'five-fold lock lately completed' in order to bring coal back.

Curiously, it was not until June 1778 that the sill of the lowest lock of the staircase was fixed as 2½ft above low water mark, implying that the lock had to be adapted.

The Act of June 1777 confirmed John Moon's and Thomas Morris's revised lines both to Middlewich and to Nantwich, the former on a similar route to that built half a century later. Immediately after Morris had left in the August, Moon was instructed to survey and make accurate estimates of the canal from Bunbury Lock to Nantwich and from Wardle Green to Middlewich, the wording implying that reaching Nantwich was now the top priority. The estimates were considered at two General Meetings chaired by Sir Thomas Broughton. It was decided that the canal from Wardle Green to Middlewich should be built for boats 7ft wide, saving £20,000 and enabling the whole canal to be completed within a total cost of £87,000, a figure that was later revised upwards to £106,000.

In April 1778 advertisements were placed for 'properly qualified persons' to submit tenders. Lot 1 was to complete the canal from the top of Beeston Brook Lock to Nantwich, part of the works having already been done by direct labour. This was the first time the Chester Canal had invited tenders for significant portions of work. The tender for Lot 1 was awarded at a price of £3,764.13s to an experienced contractor, James Pinkerton, who on this occasion was in partnership with William Jessop. The latter is better known as a the country's leading canal engineer of his generation – and this was his only venture as a contractor.

Lot 2, for the whole of the canal from Wardle Green to Middlewich, including the aqueduct over the Weaver, did not then go ahead.

The abandonment of the old summit proposal east of Tilstone with its feeder from Eaton meant new sources of water would be needed. The first, known as the Horsley Bath Drain, was constructed by direct labour. Even before the dismissal of Josiah Clowes, it was John Moon who was instructed to survey possible additional sources. One he identified was on Bunbury Heath, and he produced a plan for a reservoir with two embankments, one 22ft high, the other 10ft high, which would hold a total of 1,384 locks of water. He was instructed to make a more modest plan with an embankment 16ft high with provision to increase it to 22ft if that later proved necessary, which Pinkerton agreed to build. (This reservoir was out of use by the time that the Tarporley to Whitchurch turnpike was created in 1829. This road, now the A49, crosses it at map reference SJ558565.) Later, additional streams in the summit level were tapped.

Pinkerton & Jessop took on additional works: they rebuilt the bridge at Barbridge which had been faultily constructed by direct labour and also made the basin at Nantwich. However, not everything went smoothly. In April 1779 James Pinkerton was said to be 'highly blameable' because there had been slips in the cutting at Wardle Green which meant that the company had not been able to impound the recent rains. The committee insisted that he returned and completed the works immediately, threatening to do the works by direct labour and charge the contractor. They could not have known (or did not care) that the soil in that area was very soapy, especially when wet, and most unsuitable for making stable embankments or cuttings – as Thomas Telford was to discover fifty years later.

Operation (1775–1779)

CANAL companies often provided wharves and warehousing, either managed directly or leased to others, but the Chester Canal Company went one stage further and proposed to trade, despite there being no provisions to do so in its Act.

The opening of the canal to Beeston in 1775 enabled trading to start. A passage boat had been ordered, 40ft long, 12ft beam, 'finished in the best & most convenient manner possible'. Its original summer timetable was to leave Beeston at 6am on Wednesdays and Saturdays, returning at 5pm; on Sundays it would leave Chester at 8am and return at 6pm. On Tuesdays it would leave Chester at 7am, but no return journey was mentioned in the minutes. The fare was to set at 6d single and 9d return, with passengers in the Grand Cabin paying double these amounts. On Mondays and Thursdays it was available for hire for one guinea a day. Later a second boat, 45ft long, to be fitted up 'in a genteel manner' for passengers, was ordered.

The company also ordered several barges and flats, the latter presumably for trading in the Dee and round to the Mersey.

When the canal was opened to Beeston, wharves were made there and at Crow's Nest (the nearest location to Tattenhall). Coal was to be sold for 6d per hundredweight, so when after a few years they realised that a loss was being made when small quantities were sold, the price where less than a ton was bought was raised to at least 7d per hundredweight.

The principal wharf in Chester was established by Cow Lane Bridge. Designed by Joseph Turner and John Moon, it included a crane and a weighing machine. Here too was the canal's office and maintenance depot.

Full opening to Nantwich in November 1779 brought about a period of activity in which every effort was made to encourage trade. Joseph Turner drew up the plans for a moderate size warehouse, house and stable at Nantwich and a limekiln was erected there too. Wharfingers were appointed at Nantwich, Beeston and Cow Lane. A boat to convey passengers and merchants' goods was to leave Chester for Nantwich at 7am on Tuesdays and return leaving Nantwich at 7am on Fridays.

It was still hoped that traffic could be attracted from the Trent & Mersey Canal, though it would have to travel some nine miles overland between Wheelock and Nantwich. Joseph Turner was asked to survey that road in order that notice might be given to the overseers of the townships to repair the road 'as the law requires'. (This road, now the A534, was not turnpiked until 1816.) Land was bought and a warehouse erected at Wheelock, and a contract was made with Joseph Holland of Sandbach to carry goods from Wheelock to Nantwich. Two boats were hired from Josiah Clowes, and the policy established that the charge for conveying goods from Birmingham and the Potteries to Chester for exporting would be the same as charged by the Trent & Mersey Canal for conveyance to Liverpool. Advertisements in the press gave a long list of traffics and their prices. The service proved unsuccessful and was discontinued in August 1780.

Turner arranged with Joseph Bostock to carry goods from Nantwich to Audlem, Market Drayton and Newport at set prices.

Nantwich, as its name implies, was a town where salt was found. The industry had peaked in the mid-16th century but there was still some production in the second half of the 18th century. In an attempt to create a profitable trade, a set of boring rods was bought. Joseph Turner went to Northwich to see the rock pits and brine springs there, and, on returning to Nantwich, employed two teams of borers. He selected sites in which to bore and offered a premium of ten guineas to the team of borers who first found rock salt. Nine months later the project was abandoned.

A committee member was asked to write to correspondents in Caernarvonshire to encourage limestone and paving stones

---

Joseph Turner (c.1729–1807)

JOSEPH TURNER was a Chester architect and contractor, his works there including the Bridgegate, the Watergate and the Bridge of Sighs and the rebuilding of the Inner Pentice. In north-east Wales his works included the Flintshire County gaol, the bridge over the river Elwy at St Asaph, the lighthouse at Point of Ayr, and what is now Ruthin Library, as well as several churches. A member of the committee of the Chester Canal, from 1778 until 1795 he acted as its engineer, in effect. He was an advocate of the eastern route of the Ellesmere Canal.

Chapter 2 : The Chester Canal

Cow Lane Wharf, c.1840, by an unknown artist. Chester Cathedral looks rather different because it was substantially altered (more than a 'restoration') between 1868 and 1874. Grosvenor Museum, Chester

to be brought to Chester. John Moon was authorised to buy these as cheaply as possible and bring them up to Cow Lane Wharf.

Finance (to 1779)

The Act had authorised the issuing of 420 £100 shares and the borrowing of up to a further £20,000. At that time, potential shareholders did not have to pay a deposit, they merely had to make a promise to pay. (The law was later changed.) By ten months after the passing of the Act, calls of £20 per share had been made but almost £2,000 – over a fifth of the money due – was still unpaid. On several occasions committee members either lent the company money or gave a legally-enforceable post-dated promise to the person owed money.

And as time went on, collecting the money from the shareholders became more and more difficult. Financial penalties for late payment were proposed but were ineffective. The Clerk was instructed to visit subscribers to ask for the money, and if the subscriber did not pay by the third visit he was to be told that his shares would be advertised and sold in accordance with the Act.

The fourteenth call on shareholders in March 1775 brought the total of the calls up to the full amount of £100 a share. By that time only eight miles of the canal were completed, from Chester to Crow's Nest. Opening of the next section to Beeston Lock was imminent, and works were under way to Bunbury and also on the flight of locks down to the river Dee. Thus about half the intended canal works from the Dee to Middlewich had been done – and the remaining half included the main engineering feature, the aqueduct over the Weaver. One would have thought that it was obvious that the total cost would be at least double what had already been spent, implying a further £40,000 was needed, plus say £10,000 for the Nantwich Branch. Yet the likely total cost never seems to have been discussed.

Finance was debated at the Annual General Meeting in April 1775, where the general feeling was that further calls totalling £25 should be made, but this was not a formal decision as the meeting was inquorate. At the reconvened meeting this proposal was agreed, but with the condition that 90% of subscribers agreed. Unsurprisingly, such a high proportion proved impossible to achieve, so an alternative proposition was then approved: that subscribers should be asked to lend £25 per £100 share, with interest of 5% being paid. Loans would also be sought from others.

Samuel Egerton, the wealthy owner of Tatton Hall, was the Duke of Bridgewater's second cousin and an MP for Cheshire; he was also the largest single investor in the Trent & Mersey Canal. Asked to lend the £10,000 he declined but made an offer that was in effect as valuable: he would act as guarantor for loans to the company. In a letter he stated

> It gives me great pleasure to be of service ... and that it may turn out to be to the benefit of the County as well as to the proprietors is my earnest wish.

The alternatives, according to a counsel's opinion, were to have additional calls on the existing shareholders, to issue new shares, or to borrow, but it would be necessary for the holders of at least 200 shares to be present at the meeting at which the decision was to be made. This was just achieved at a Special General Meeting in the October, when it was agreed to have five further calls of £5 each on the existing shares, and also to borrow £10,000. This time there was no condition concerning the assent of shareholders not represented at the meeting. One call was made immediately, but in January 1776 the Treasurer reported that a lot of subscribers were refusing to pay extra calls unless compelled to do so by law. The previous decision was then reversed: the full £20,000 would be borrowed, with Samuel Egerton providing the security. By July 1776 about half the money needed had been obtained, including a £4,000 loan from Richard Reynolds of Ketley. There were practical problems getting the bonds counter-signed. On one occasion, John Moon went to Tatton Park to see Mr Egerton, but discovered that only that morning he had left for London. Moon therefore went on to London, using the opportunity whilst there to try to get money from the London shareholders.

Mr Snow, the company's solicitor after the resignation of Widdens & Potts, offered to lend £9,000 at 5% interest, but this was declined because the committee thought the money could be borrowed at a lower rate of interest, though they had previously paid 5%. (One hopes this was not money held by Snow in trust for his clients.)

The shortage of money interfered with progress. In December 1776 all the staff except Moon and Morris were temporarily suspended, the men working on the canal beyond Beeston Brook were dismissed, and only those finishing the canal to Beeston Brook or which were 'absolutely necessary ... to preserve the canal from misfortune or waste' were retained.

A note of desperation can be detected in the letter sent to shareholders summonsing yet another Special General Meeting in January 1777:

> The Committee, finding it impossible to carry on the works much longer without the further aid of Parliament, and being desirous of having the opinions and concurrence of all the proprietors about the mode of application for the completion of the canal ... your attendance is absolutely necessary. ... Not a day is to be lost.

It was agreed to ask Parliament to authorise the borrowing of a further £10,000 in addition to the £20,000 previously authorised and also the raising of a further £60 per share. The extra £60 per £100 share would be a voluntary contribution; interest at 5% would be paid only to subscribers who made this voluntary contribution, but it would be payable on the full £160. Only once there was sufficient profit to cover this would other subscribers start to receive dividends.

The Act was passed in June 1777. Prior to this, in the April, it was resolved to start the six month period during which the subscriptions were to be made, though the terms were not to become binding until £10,000 had been subscribed. By June, £6,000 had been subscribed, and after six months the total was still far short of the target.

It was clear that if more money was to be raised, some form of compulsion would be required to make the more reluctant shareholders part with further cash. It was decided to apply for an Act with a compulsive clause to raise an extra £80 per original £100 share and also to be able to borrow £10,000 in addition to the £20,000 in the 1772 Act. This received the Royal Assent on 27 March 1778, and calls totalling £50 were made over the next two years.

That autumn action started to be taken against subscribers whose calls were in arrears. Shareholders in arrears were warned and sent a copy of the relevant section of the Act; then the forfeited shares were auctioned, though in practice most of the shares were bought for a nominal sum (usually one shilling) by a nominee then held in trust for the company. The first auctions were held in November 1778 and January 1779 in which just over a quarter of the 420 original shares were sold, including twenty owned by 'the Companies of Chester'. Auctions continued throughout the rest of the independent life of the company, though these merely showed that the shares were thought to be worthless.

When counsel's opinion had been taken three years earlier, he had recommended that it would be more effective to take action for non-payment of the sum owing, rather than forfeiture. His recommended method would have forced the payment of the debt, whereas forfeiture gave the subscriber the option of assessing whether paying would be throwing good money after bad.

At the Annual General Meeting on 2 April 1779 a unanimous decision was made which was fundamental to the future of the Chester Canal: once the canal from Chester to Nantwich was completed, no action was to be taken about continuing to Middlewich for the time being. Another decision was that subsequent calls were to be used towards discharging the bond debts currently secured by Samuel Egerton in such a way as future General Meetings might decide. A later meeting modified the latter decision: future calls were to be used first to pay off the various contractual debts, and secondly for the bond debts.

The most important contractual debts related to the land purchase in the summit level. This was to be the major cause of the water feeders being disrupted, as discussed later in this chapter.

Extensions

FINANCIAL problems had not prevented the company from looking at possible extensions. Presumably to access the coalfield, in 1772 a survey was carried out of the land from the south side of the river Dee to Gresford and on to 'Cae Gidog Bridge', the latter probably meaning Sydallt, where the river Cegidog joined the river Alyn. Then just before he was dismissed Samuel Weston was paid for his expenses in carrying out survey work in Shropshire; unfortunately there is no hint about whether the contemplated extension was to Whitchurch, Market Drayton or even as far as the river Severn.

The canal company retained the expectation that it would be able to join the Trent & Mersey Canal, the construction of which had concentrated on the southern end and the Harecastle Tunnel. It was not navigable from Preston Brook to Middlewich until some time in 1775 and was not fully open until 1777. Samuel Egerton was reported in March 1774 as promising 'to use his utmost influence with the Duke of Bridgewater to obtain a junction as soon as we approach each other, and that he has no doubt of succeeding'.

John Chamberlaine and John Rogers went to a committee meeting of the Trent & Mersey Canal (commonly then known as the 'Staffordshire Canal') in February 1775 and to its General Meeting the following month, having been given authority to make an appropriate offer concerning the junction (subject to final approval by the company). Their report back was optimistic:

> The Staffordshire Canal proprietors were pleased to give them a very favourable reception and promised to take their printed paper of remarks and calculation into consideration and if it appear to them after such consideration that the junction will not be injurious to that concern they should not have any objection to give their consent thereto.

But it was not to be: once again the request was refused.

Trading whilst insolvent (1779–1790)

THROUGHOUT the next period of the history of the Chester Canal, finance, management, maintenance and operation were intimately interconnected. The income was not enough to meet the day-to-day expenses, so maintenance suffered, making it even more difficult to achieve adequate income. Trade tended to be transferred to the hands of agents, whose interests did not necessarily coincide with those of the company. And there was no way that the debts on the capital account could be repaid.

To make matters worse, Samuel Egerton, who had been an active supporter of the Chester Canal, died on 10 February 1780, his estate passing to his sister Hester who died only five months later. Next in succession was her son, William Tatton of Wythenshawe, who then took the surname Egerton. For a long while Samuel's estate remained in the hands of trustees, their agent being James Tomkinson of Dorfold Hall (close to Nantwich Wharf), a lawyer whose central concern was to maximise the financial benefits to his clients and in the process became wealthy himself. The story of the next fifteen years was to be one of continual tension between the canal company and the guarantor of its bonds totalling £20,000 and of the interest which had to be paid on them, usually at 5%. Tomkinson had little or no concern for the other creditors of the company: the people it had not yet paid for the land it had taken, its contractors and suppliers.

In April 1780 the General Meeting resolved to sell all land that was not essential for the real use of the canal – where the canal divided land holdings the company had often had to buy parcels of land it had not really wanted – and also to sell all the boats except for the Beeston market boat and the two passage boats. Similar resolutions to sell surplus land were passed several times in the next fifteen years, which shows that they were not acted upon conscientiously. Nor were the boats sold at this time: the flats *Bootle*, *Peploe*, *Speed* and *Egerton* were laid up in the basin below the Phoenix Tower, and their rigging stored at Cow Lane. The *Speed* and the *Bootle* were later leased out but the latter sank near Rhuddlan, and the *Egerton* and *Peploe* were hastily re-rigged to go and raise it.

The intention had been to pay the proceeds to William Egerton but in fact the money was used for paying the ongoing expenses of the company. The minutes sorrowfully stated:

> The Company are daily harassed with demands and actions commenced against them and for the payment of which the Company have no other funds ... by reason thereof many of the workmen and other creditors of the Company are liable to be defrauded and injured.

James Tomkinson tried to get the wharfingers to pay him any money they received but the company was adamant that he had no power to do this. What the company desired was for Egerton to take full possession of the navigation and its assets, providing he would undertake to pay the outstanding contractual debts, many of which the individual committee members had underwritten. However, Tomkinson was too canny to agree, as this would make Egerton responsible for either continuing the operation of the canal, presumably at a loss, or incurring the odium of closing it – it was much more advantageous to keep the pressure on whilst avoiding all responsibility for the outcome.

In July 1780 the salary of the Clerk, John Moon, was reduced from £100 to £80, and that of his assistant, Charles Hill, from £40 to £30. As a further economy measure, two carpenters were to act as masters of the passage boats. Two years later, Hill was given three months notice, and Moon told he could continue as Clerk but could leave at his own discretion. He resigned shortly afterwards, and Hill was kept on as Clerk at an annual salary of £42 plus £10.10s towards the rent of a house and 'extra for fire and candles at the discretion of the committee'.

Over the years there were several changes in arrangements concerned with management of the wharves and maintenance of the canal and of its feeders, usually in an attempt to reduce costs. For example, in March 1780 the wharfinger at Nantwich was also made responsible for day-to-day oversight of the canal from there to Bunbury; the Beeston wharfinger was to look after the canal from Bunbury to Crow's Nest and also the feeder from the reservoir; and the Chester wharfinger was responsible for the rest of the canal. Employment on the canal was precarious, and when money was particularly tight, wages were withheld, the Clerk being instructed to pay those men he judged 'most needy'.

The landowners who were owed money began to take direct action. John Fenna of Brown Hills drew the paddle to drain Bunbury Reservoir, aiming to deprive the summit level of water and thus force the company to pay him. Thomas Wicksteed of Wardle Hall, through whose land passed the Horsley Bath Drain, a main feeder for the summit level, also took direct action by diverting the water back to its original course. The company had little choice but to ask John Spurstow, the Treasurer, to make rental payments and to promise to reimburse him by the sale of the *Peploe* and *Bootle* flats – money which Tomkinson had expected to be paid. Actually neither boat was sold at that time, so neither Tomkinson nor Spurstow was paid. A few months later, Spurstow was declared bankrupt, with the problems of the Chester Canal no doubt being a contributory cause, but after four years he was back on the committee.

The Dean & Chapter of Chester, being owed three & a half years' rent, distrained on timber, crops and everything else on their piece of land, although these actually belonged to Thomas Griffies and another under-tenant, as well as distraining on the passage boat moored there. The committee thought this was unjust (one of the four members present being Griffies) and that the sale of the passage boat would mean the loss of a principal means of earning profits. In the event the boat was not sold, and Griffies personally gave security to pay the rent himself if the company did not. Egerton was told, but as usual did not respond.

Charles Bate had sold to the company the land on which the wharf at Nantwich had been constructed, but the purchase price of £240 had never been paid. He put a chain across the canal, demanding to be paid a fee for all timber and other items loaded or unloaded there, and it was agreed that he could take possession of the wharf.

Samuel Hulse, a neighbour of Bate, who was owed £150 for land and had refused to accept £7.10s a year in lieu, followed Bate's example by placing a chain across the canal, preventing boats from getting to the wharf. The committee was unwilling to take any action without William Egerton's approval, having just received a writ from James Tomkinson on behalf of Egerton. They clearly could not pay the money owing to Egerton, nor could they afford to defend the action, which meant the case would be lost by default. They therefore agreed to write to William Egerton personally asking him to stop proceedings. In this they must have been successful, as no further action is recorded. On the other hand, the dispute with Hulse dragged on for several months before agreement was made for £20 to be paid immediately and £10 a year thereafter.

There was a succession of other writs and distraints, some affecting the earning capability of the company. For example, the crane at Chester wharf was sold on behalf of a creditor.

Tomkinson's and Egerton's unwillingness to get more closely involved in the affairs of the company sometimes worked against their own interests. Two parcels of land had been sold in 1779 for a total of £166, but although the two purchasers took occupation of the lands they refused to pay the principal (or even rent or interest) because, they said, they would not have good title unless it was legally evidenced that the lands were not subject to Egerton's mortgage. This remained outstanding for twelve years.

Throughout this time there were several engineering problems, evidence of a lack of day-to-day maintenance. Beeston Brook Lock, which was at that time a staircase pair, failed in the summer of 1780 and was repaired. Then in April 1782 a culvert under the Chester–Nantwich turnpike at Barbridge collapsed, the water then undermining the foundations of the tollhouse, causing a 3in. gap to appear in the brickwork of the gable end; when it rained, over sixty yards length of the road was flooded. A serious incident happened in October 1782 when a boat was coming through the staircase of five locks at Chester: one of the bottom gates gave way when the lock was almost full. Joseph Turner was requested to effect the repairs, the cost being borne out of the next tonnage money that could be spared. In June 1783 part of Tilston Mill Lock collapsed, blocking the canal; Turner again was asked to deal with the repairs at an estimated cost of £80, which was to be financed by the sale of the *Peploe*. It was a year before the works were completed.

In a short-sighted attempt to save money, three banksmen were discharged at the end of September 1783. The company's porter was to go up the canal as far as Golden Nook each week and attempt to stop any leaks he found.

By 1787 the timber bridge by the entrance lock from the Dee was in a ruinous and dangerous state. It was desirable that it should be replaced by a masonry bridge, but of course the company had no money to do this. Voluntary contributions were sought from the people of Chester, as the bridge would be 'of great public utility', but little money could have been forthcoming as an agreement was made for the River Dee Company to build the bridge and be reimbursed by the canal company when money was available.

In November 1787 disaster struck: the walls of the staircase lock at Beeston Brook gave way because the sand in which this lock was built had been washed out. A report in 1794 shows the extent of the damage:

> the hollow posts betwixt the locks being torn to pieces by the sinking of the foundations ... the breast of the lock

given way, part of the side walls of both locks sunk, the counter arch of the upper lock shook to pieces and part carried away, the apron or floor of the lower lock burst and part of the planks torn off.

As repairs could not be afforded, for the next ten years the canal was operated in two sections, with the inconvenience and expense of transhipment at Beeston Brook.

In January 1790 part of the south-west wing wall at Barbridge Aqueduct fell down and caused the bank to slip there, then the following month somebody breached the canal at Christleton by cutting the bank. Repairs to these and certain bridges were to be financed by demolishing a shed at Cow Lane and selling the materials, and by selling various items of scrap, including 8 tons of cast iron, 432lb of wrought iron, three mill-stones, a cheese-press screw and an old passage boat – the last-named valued at only £1.1s. However, it was more than three years before all the work was completed.

Joseph Bostock, the company's wharfinger at Beeston Brook, caused the committee much grief, though he must have had merits too, as they continued to employ him. A carrier and trader at Nantwich, only a few months after being appointed there was a dispute about what was his money and what was the company's. He was later reprimanded for dealing in slates brought along the canal, whereas the agreement was that he dealt only in coals. A box belonging to Mr Taylor of Liverpool went missing; Bostock was held to be liable. In 1783 he was dismissed for being 'very inattentive to the interests of the company' but within ten days he had been reinstated and later he was engaged to carry out several major maintenance projects.

It had been agreed that Bostock could fit out the flat *Bootle* explicitly for bringing coal from Flintshire to Beeston Brook, but it was seized by the Customs House Officers at Liverpool for non-payment of duty on cannel coal loaded there. The committee tried to get the backing of the Cheshire MPs in petitioning for its release, but in vain as the boat was sold. As Bostock had breached the agreement, the committee told him to pay them the value of the boat, assessed at £68.13s.6d; he initially refused, but having been threatened with legal action, agreed to pay £50, which the committee accepted. Unsurprisingly, they dismissed him as wharfinger at Beeston Brook. Reluctant to employ another wharfinger there, they decided to advertise the wharf to the best price – and the highest tender was for £18 from Joseph Bostock, the person who knew best the opportunities there. This bid was accepted, despite their misgivings, but a few months later they were threatening legal action if he did not settle his account promptly.

Meanwhile, the company continued to operate its passage boat and tried to encourage other users. As the inland coal trade was not faring well, tonnage rates were reduced. Special rates were given to manure and to gravel, the latter only if there was adequate water. A new source of income was water used by steam engines in canalside premises.

In 1787 the committee was told that the company's mare was of little use as it would not pull the passage boat; it was sold and a more useful one bought.

A damning assessment of the canal was published in Holland's *General View of the Agriculture of Cheshire* (1808): it had been 'productive of no advantage to the internal intercourse of the country' and 'a most burdensome concern to the proprietors'.[5]

Improved prospects (1791–1795)

The coming of the Ellesmere Canal

IN April 1791 there was a rare piece of good news: John Duncombe showed the committee the plans for a proposed canal from Shrewsbury to the Mersey via Chirk, Ruabon and Chester, later to be known as the western route of the Ellesmere Canal. This caused them to write again to James Tomkinson:

> From the constant repairs and outgoings on the canal and some failure in the business the last winter ... we are fearful that we shall not be able to keep it on, which we wish for the present to do, as a proposal has been made to join us by the proprietors of the canal from Shrewsbury to Liverpool, which is likely to be so beneficial to this canal as to enable us either to make something of it for Mr Egerton or he may dispose of it then to some advantage.

They repeated their offer to give the canal up to anyone that Mr Egerton should nominate but felt that his interests would best be served by waiting until the other canal joined rather than to have a total loss. Although they emphasised that they would like to receive his opinion as soon as possible, no reply was received.

The following year an alternative proposal for a canal between Shrewsbury to Chester which stayed to the east of the Dee was discussed by the committee. For clarity this is referred to here as the 'eastern route' of the Ellesmere Canal. As it would join the Chester Canal near Crow's Nest it was clearly the better of the two schemes from the company's point of view: boats from it would travel along some seven miles of their canal; also it would bring in an extra water supply. Joseph Turner was one of its promotors.

The events leading to the passing of the Ellesmere Canal's Act are discussed in Chapter 5; here it is only necessary to note that the 1793 Act authorised the western route, with the eastern route to be constructed if all landowners agreed. The implication was that specific proposals for the eastern route were to be in a subsequent Act, but it was learnt in the summer of 1794 that the Ellesmere Canal did not intend to deposit such a Bill during that autumn. They therefore sought the support of William Egerton and John Crewe, the latter having 20 Chester Canal shares and being one of the two MPs for Cheshire, but without success. Every shareholder was written to, urging them to lobby MPs known to them and, if they were shareholders in the Ellesmere Canal, to put pressure on that company. They were also told that if they failed to get the connection, the whole Chester Canal could be 'totally abandoned'.

The original proposal had been for the Wirral Branch of the

Ellesmere Canal to be totally separate from the Chester Canal but that was soon changed to it sharing the entrance basin from the Dee, then rising by two new locks to its Wirral level. This was amended to the arrangement we see today: the bottom two locks of the staircase of five were to be closed and the Chester Canal to have a right-angle bend to join the Wirral Branch of the Ellesmere Canal, two new locks being constructed between that and the entrance basin. As well as being better operationally, assuming most boats from the Chester Canal would continue to Ellesmere Port rather than descend to the Dee, it would give a water supply to the Wirral level and reduce the consumption at the staircase. The cost of the changes would be borne by the Ellesmere Canal Company. The basin was transferred in 1796, though ownership of the soil remained with the River Dee Company, and the liability for the duty of ½d a ton continued.

Joseph Turner was asked to work with the Ellesmere Canal Company and negotiate with the Dean & Chapter, who owned the land at the new junction. The minutes describe him as 'their engineer', but in reality he was the committee member who acted as engineering adviser, and sometimes the contractor, in the absence of any consulting engineer or any relevant expertise on the staff.

Financial reconstruction

THE immediate issue was how to finance the rebuilding of Beeston Brook Lock. Turner offered to do the work for £139 exclusive of the cost of piling, as until the ruined lock had been taken down, it would not be possible to ascertain what was needed. He would give a loan at 5% interest on whatever sum the company was short. Samuel Weston, who was soon to build the Wirral Line, was also asked to give an estimate but, as that was higher, Turner's offer was accepted. However, he never actually fulfilled his promise, and the canal remained in two sections.

At the unusually well-attended General Meeting in August 1794 it was agreed to make a further £2 call on shareholders, the first call since 1780. Unsurprisingly, a large number of these calls remained unpaid, despite a threat to forfeit these shares. By June 1795 almost 60% of the shares had been forfeited. Further calls of £2 were made in 1795, 1796, 1797, 1800 and 1803.

James Tomkinson, the agent for the executors of Samuel Egerton, had died in March 1794, and it is probably no coincidence that later the same year a realistic agreement was made with William Egerton: he would accept £8,000 in settlement of the full debt secured by the mortgage, which was £20,000 principal plus £13,408 accumulated interest (to November 1794). The company would pay for the expenses of obtaining an Act of Parliament, estimated at £1,000, the cost of which would be added to the mortgage.

The second biggest creditor was the River Dee Company, and an offer was made to settle their outstanding debt for £1,000. Money was still owed for land purchases, particularly to the south of Bunbury, of course.

But how was the money to pay Egerton and the others to be raised? A letter was sent to all shareholders, pointing out that the canal's income had been £1,000 a year, with the prospect now of it being much more. If a substantial portion of the £8,000 was not forthcoming from the shareholders, the property would pass out of their hands and the benefit go to others. It concluded emotively:

> Let the blessings of peace return, and with them will return to this land the spirit of industry, enterprise and commerce. Can the waters of Cheshire alone be useless and its agriculture unfurnished with the means of improvement?

The letter proved ineffectual, only £3,300 being promised. Joseph Turner and the committee then put forward a further suggestion: to raise £9,000 to buy Egerton's mortgage and meet the cost of Act by issuing 180 shares of £50. These would be offered first to existing shareholders. The mortgage of the canal company's assets would continue, but now the mortgagee would be the owners of these new shares. This succeeded: the money was raised.

William Egerton was given a memorandum of security signed by nine subscribers, and was paid his £8,000 in October 1795. By this date the debt with its accumulated interest had reached a total of £35,176.19s.7½d. Samuel Egerton's nephew paid dearly for Samuel's well-intended guarantee.

Revival (1795–1804)

THE Commercial Canal was an ambitious proposal made in 1795 for a broad canal from Nantwich through Newcastle-under-Lyme, Burslem, the Cheadle coalfield, Uttoxeter and Burton-on-Trent to join the Ashby Canal. It was surveyed by two of the leading canal engineers, Robert Whitworth and William Jessop. Not only would it have linked the Chester Canal with the main national network, it would also have provided Chester with coal from the Newcastle area. Negotiations were held with its promoters and, in exchange for a guaranteed minimum annual toll income of £1,500 from this source, lower through tonnage rates were agreed. In December 1796 it was reported that no application had been made to Parliament because the Trent & Mersey Company had made an agreement to widen their canal south of Harecastle Tunnel. This would not have helped the manufacturers of earthenware who were trading to Liverpool, so it was proposed to apply to make a broad canal from the Potteries to Nantwich. None of these schemes went ahead. The idea for a Newcastle–Nantwich canal was revived in 1805, followed by a proposal for a tramroad – both were stillborn.

A significant change in the personalities associated with the Chester Canal occurred in 1795 when John Fletcher was elected to the committee, taking over Joseph Turner's role as the committee member who looked after day-to-day engineering matters. Like Turner, he contracted for some of the works himself. The Ellesmere Canal's minutes referred to him on one occasion as 'the Engineer of the Chester Canal Company', a title which has been repeated in various books, but this was a misunderstanding of his position.

Chapter 2: The Chester Canal

In 1796 Thomas Morris, who was Docks Engineer at Liverpool (and probably the son of the Thomas Morris who had been the Chester Canal's second engineer), was invited to prepare a plan and specification for the repair of Beeston Brook Lock. It was also agreed to widen and deepen the canal to its original intended dimensions between there and Nantwich, and to replace the seven swivel bridges on the summit level with brick bridges, but it seems that these aspects were not then done. John Fletcher contracted to repair Beeston Brook Lock and maintain it for seven years. This was completed in the spring of 1797, so, ten years after the breach, the canal was whole again.

The link to the Wirral Branch of the Ellesmere Canal was opened in the summer of 1797, giving a shorter and much more convenient link to Liverpool. These developments prompted improvements at the wharfs: the weighing machines at Chester and Beeston Brook were repaired and a new warehouse built at Nantwich. Freight charges were lowered, on the expectation that the increase in quantity would more than compensate for the reduction. A special rate was made for flour going forward to Ellesmere Port and Manchester. On the other hand, it was at long last recognised that little trade would come transported by road from the Trent & Mersey Canal, so the wharf and warehouse at Wheelock were sold.

Not everything went well. The interior of the passage boat was burnt in a fire at Nantwich wharf. Worse, in a separate incident, a large quantity of sugar loaf being transported for Messrs Bowman & Keay of Nantwich was damaged. The spoilt cargo was sold for £73.4s.7½d. The minutes do not state how much compensation had to be paid, but it must have been considerable.

In August 1797 John Fletcher made a proposal to rent the canal for two years, paying £300 in the first year and £400 in the second, but no decision was made. However, a year later the General Meeting resolved:

> That the tolls, yards, wharfs, boats, cranes, weighing machines and all other advantages arising from this concern, be advertised to be let by public auction ... for five years certain, commencing 2nd February 1799, subject to conditions.

Fletcher's bid of an annual rent of £220 – rather less than his original proposal – was accepted. The company continued to be responsible for the maintenance, and it was Fletcher who was usually employed to carry out approved works. He was not given an entirely free hand: on surveys he was usually accompanied by Joseph Turner or Thomas Atherton, another committee member.

After a year Fletcher reported that he had been prevented from navigating the canal for 49 days during the year, so this period was added, rent-free, to the end of his contract. His expenses for maintenance and minor works during the year came to just over £200 more than his rent. The works included creating a dock 16ft wide at Cow Lane Wharf, together with a swivel bridge over the entrance.

The conversion of the staircase of five locks into a staircase of three locks necessitated some adjustment of the structure and gates because the water level in the Wirral Branch did not coincide with that of the third lock down when empty. As can be seen, seven extra brick courses and a stone capping were added. *Author*

John Fletcher (1756–1835)

JOHN FLETCHER was born in Halton near Runcorn, the son of an agricultural labourer. Although not educated beyond village school level, by 1782 he was a schoolmaster in Chester. In 1783 he purchased the ailing New General Printing Office, the publisher of the *Chester Chronicle*, and for the first couple of decades he acted as its editor. He was highly critical of the self-perpetuating nature of the Corporation, which led him to be jailed in 1785 for six months after being been found guilty of libelling the town's Recorder. However, much later in his life he became accepted in town politics, and was Mayor of Chester in 1825/26 and 1832/33. As well as printing and publishing, he was involved in many entrepreneurial activities, including being a timber merchant and also an agent for medical supplies and patent medicines.

He joined the committee of the Chester Canal in 1795 and thereafter acted as its engineering adviser, sometime contractor, and for several years its lessee. He constructed much of the Ellesmere Canal from 1795 onwards, ususally in partnership with others. Other engineering works for which he was the contractor included Chester's racecourse and the turnpike roads from Wrexham to Llangollen and from Llangollen over the Oernant Pass towards Ruthin.

Telford described him as 'an able mathematician and mechanic'.

In 1800/1 Fletcher claimed that the canal was unnavigable for 51 days, and in 1801/2 for 150 days. Maintenance costs had been heavy, with several lock gates needing replacement. The number of days for which the canal was closed in subsequent years was not stated explicitly, but, one way or another, the contract was extended until February 1806.

Towards the merger (1804–1813)

ALTHOUGH the route for the link with the Whitchurch Branch of the Ellesmere Canal was agreed in 1797, it was not completed until eight years later. The junction at Hurleston was made on the summit level of the Chester Canal, so boats going from it to Ellesmere Port had to travel along 17 miles of the older canal.

The first six boats off the Ellesmere Canal arrived in Chester on 30 December 1805 – all were laden with timber, five from Shade Oak, near the end of the Weston Branch, the sixth from Montgomeryshire.[6]

Discussions, 1804–5

IN 1804, discussions about a merger were held with the Ellesmere Canal. This would be a natural development, as the Chester Canal lay between the Ellesmere's main line and its Wirral Line. These crystallised into a formal proposal from the Ellesmere Canal Company:

– That the two canals be united as a joint concern;
– The Ellesmere proprietors would have 4,000 shares of nominal value £100;
– The proprietors and mortgagees of the Chester Canal would be entitled to a further 1,000 shares (the proposal did not suggest how these shares were to be divided between the 'old' proprietors and the 'new' mortgagees); and
– The proprietors of the Ellesmere Canal would at their own expense put the Chester Canal into complete repair, erect all necessary warehouses etc, and pay all the Chester Canal's debts to a maximum of £5,000.

The Chester Canal made a counter-offer whereby the mortgagees of the Chester Canal would have a mortgage of £45,000 on both canals, at 5% redeemable in ten years, and the 'old' proprietors would have 300 shares. It is difficult to see the justification for such a high figure for the mortgage. The minute states 'it appearing to this meeting that the principal and interest due on mortgage of the Chester Canal will in a short time amount to £45,000', but the 'new' mortgage of £9,000 in 1795 plus compound interest at 5% would accumulate to a little under £15,000 by 1805. Surely they cannot have taken the Egerton mortgage as their base figure?

Realising that this was unlikely to be acceptable, an alternative counter-offer was made: that the 'old' proprietors and 'new' mortgagees of the Chester Canal be entitled to 1,200 shares. As Ellesmere Canal shares had recently been sold for £55 each, this valued the Chester Canal at £66,000. The Ellesmere Canal rejected both counter-offers.

Continuing operations

THE Chester Canal engaged Thomas Morris, by then the Resident Engineer of the East India Docks in London, to survey the line. His report listed 83 items costing a total of £2,555 (including 10% for supervision etc), the most expensive being widening and deepening the canal in the cuttings of the summit level, and building a warehouse at Nantwich Basin. It was resolved to do the necessary work and to ask the mortgagees to increase their loans by a further 10%, with interest of 5% a year to be paid. Other money would be borrowed from the bank. A tenth of the amount of the 'new' mortgage, together with interest, was repaid in December 1810; a further tenth was repaid a year later.

In 1805 John Fletcher made a bold suggestion: to replace the staircase of three locks at Chester with one 32ft deep lock with guillotine gates, whilst saving water consumption through the use of eight side ponds stacked above each other. He considered that no more than 3ft lockage would be used for descending boats, or 6ft for ascending boats. Thomas Morris was again asked to advise, and he said that the concept was sound but would be impracticable to execute because the slightest settlement in the structure or blockage to culverts or paddles would make it inoperable. He was also critical of the time which it would take to operate the lock in the way intended. William Jessop considered that it was worth spending money to get rid of the prodigious waste of water at these locks. He felt that Fletcher's idea was feasible but that fewer basins, perhaps four, would make it simpler and quicker to operate; however it would be difficult to make everything strong and watertight. The committee decided to leave the staircase unaltered.

The committee must have been concerned about the practical effect of the loss of control occasioned by letting the revenues and operation of the canal, as they took back direct control from Fletcher in 1806 without ever apparently debating the issue. They could of course have expected a big increase in income from boats coming off the Ellesmere Canal.

Thomas Broster was appointed Clerk at a salary of £40 a year but he lasted in the company's employ for only a year, being dismissed because he was negligent in keeping the accounts and did not pay money into the bank promptly. He was replaced by Charles Tomlinson, who lasted just over a year before being dismissed because it was considered that he was 'not sufficiently qualified to keep the books and accounts and also carry on the other business of the company'. Tomlinson's successor was William Cross, his salary being a more realistic £80 a year.

The minutes of the meeting in September 1808 contained two items which may be connected: a report stated that losses had been incurred by persons ordering work without proper authority, and John Fletcher was given notice to quit the wharf, timber yard and warehouse at Cow Lane, Chester. Had he been acting high-handedly as if he still had control of the undertaking? However, just two months later his lease of the wharf was confirmed. In 1809 he became Chairman of the committee but he was replaced the following year. Then in 1811 there was dispute about Fletcher's back accounts which took over a year to sort out, and he was again given notice to quit Cow Lane Wharf. Despite these differences, Fletcher took a leading role in negotiating the eventual merger with the Ellesmere Canal Company.

Another row concerning a wharf at Chester was prompted when Samuel Lythgoe erected a wall alongside the canal near the end of Queen Street (adjacent to Cow Lane Wharf) and put up a crane. The committee ordered these to be taken down, the implication being that they were blocking the towpath. Lythgoe responded by writing a long letter which was published in the *Chester Courant* (the rival to Fletcher's paper), accusing the canal company of having acted in a way which was 'monstrously unjust, cruel and illegal'. His version of events was that a few years earlier he had purchased a plot of land in front of the canal and had erected a warehouse and a crane in order to carry out the business of a wharfinger and timber merchant. After the works had been completed the canal company demanded rent for the land, which he refused to pay. Twice in the last two years his property had been attacked in the middle of the night and destroyed. Most recently the attack happened in the middle of the day, when 30 or 40 men with hatchets, hammers and spades destroyed his crane and demolished his wharf. The letter continued:

> In this situation, at present, stands the dispute between an humble individual, with a wife and family of nine children, having no other means of providing for them, and a powerful body of men, whose influence and property alone, and not their right, render them formidable.

Lythgoe considered that the dispute should have been settled by a legal action, and hinted that the real reason for closing down his business was to remove a rival timber merchant.[8] However, whatever the merits of the case, might triumphed.

Resumed discussions, 1812–3

IN 1812 the Ellesmere Canal Company put forward new terms for a merger:

> That taking into account the respective values of the gross and net income of the Chester and Ellesmere Canal companies and likewise of what appears to be the respective present values of the capital of each canal, this Committee cannot think itself justified in offering more than 500 shares to the Chester Canal Company.

The Chester Canal Company's committee recommended acceptance and proposed the following apportionment of the shares:

– Every holder of one share of £50 in the mortgage to have two & a half shares in the combined Ellesmere & Chester Company; and

– Every holder of one 'old' share of £100 (nominal) to have one quarter of a Ellesmere & Chester share.

If £9,000 had been raised by mortgage as intended, there would have been 180 such £50 shares; thus 450 Ellesmere & Chester shares would go to the mortgagees, leaving 50 for the 'old' shareholders. This implies there were still 200 unforfeited 'old' shares out of the 420 originally issued. The minutes indicate that there were somewhat fewer than 200 'old' shares, so perhaps slightly more than £9,000 was raised by the issue of the £50 mortgage shares.

Taking into account the extra loan in 1805 and the repayments in 1810 and 1811, and allowing for compound interest at 5%, an original loan of £50 would have accumulated to about £105 in 1813. This would imply a value of about £42 for each Ellesmere & Chester share.

The mortgagees gained the most from the financial aspects of the merger, but that was reasonable because they rescued the company from foreclosure. Each 'old' share was valued at about £10 in this package, which seems fair.

The General Meeting which was called specifically to consider the merger resolved unanimously to accept the terms 'as it appears advantageous to both Companies, will actually cement interests which are already virtually united, will remove many difficulties in the management, and give facilities which separately neither possess'. However, no doubt everyone wished that they had accepted the more generous terms offered in 1804.

An Act of Parliament was needed to effect the merger. The companies were formally united on 1 July 1813.

Notes and references

Most of the information for this chapter is derived from the minutes of the Chester Canal Company (The National Archives: RAIL 816). The principal source for the history up to the passing of the Act is 'Chester Canal Projects' by Edwin Shearing, published in the *Journal of the Railway & Canal Historical Society*, November 1984 (pp.98–103) and March 1985 (pp.146–153).

The Chester Canal is the only one of the constituent canals of the Shropshire Union which has been the subject of a full-length book: *The Old Chester Canal*, edited by Gordon Emery (2005).

With the exception of the statutory General Meeting held on the first Friday in April, there seems no significant difference between what is described in the minutes as 'General Meeting', 'Committee Meeting' and 'Meeting of Proprietors and Committee'. They are therefore all referred to as 'Meeting'.

1. Cheshire Archives, ZTAV2/55
2. *Chester Courant*, 17 September & 1 October 1771
3. C. Dupin, *The Commercial Power of Great Britain*, Vol.1 (translated from the French, 1825), p.257
4. *Chester Chronicle*, 5 February 1776
5. Henry Holland, *General View of the Agriculture of Cheshire*, 1808, p.312
6. *Chester Courant*, 31 December 1805
7. The capital of the Ellesmere Canal comprised 4,000 shares of nominal value £100, though £133 had actually been paid for each share. The nominal value was merely a paper figure – the actual value was of course what someone was willing to pay for a share.
8. *Chester Courant*, 16 April 1811

The tub-boat system of east Shropshire, before the construction of the Shrewsbury Canal.

3

The tub-boat canals of east Shropshire

TOWARDS the end of the 18th century the east Shropshire area, now the modern town of Telford, was one of the most important industrial areas in Britain. Here were the essential raw materials for making iron – ironstone and coal, with good deposits of limestone not far away – and people with the talent and finance to exploit them.

A major problem was transport, both to bring the raw materials together and to take the finished products away to the customers. The area seemed unsuitable for canals, being hilly and without a reliable source of water for the locks. William Reynolds found the solution by designing the country's first successful canal inclined plane. This carried rectangular tub-boats, which led to the development of a small network of tub-boat canals.

These canals were all closely related in traffic, technology and personalities. Some stayed independent, a section of the Wombridge Canal was bought by the Shrewsbury Canal, and the Shropshire Canal was leased to the Shropshire Union for a few years before being sold to the London & North Western Railway.

Donnington Wood Canal

EARL Gower was a major landowner in east Shropshire, his estates including the coal and ironstone deposits at Donnington Wood, Priorslee, Wombridge and Snedshill as well as the limestone at Lilleshall.

In the 18th century the coal pits in the Wrockwardine Wood and Donnington Wood area were small and shallow. As was then the normal practice, the landowners did not get directly involved in mining, instead they let the rights to chartermasters. Most of the coal was sold to other entrepreneurs, with some being sold in the domestic market.

Lilleshall limestone was of two types: white and, in a lower stratum, grey. Neither were particularly suitable for building but

Tub-boats were about 6ft 2in. wide and 20ft long, typically carrying 5 tons, and could have been constructed in wood or iron. They were pulled in short trains and, being rectangular, they did not need to be turned at their destination. *John Howat*

A rather fanciful view of a boat passing Lilleshall Abbey on the Donnington Wood Canal as depicted by Samuel Ireland. The painting was first published in Thomas Harral's *Picturesque views of the Severn*, Vol.1 in 1823/4, but it must date from some time in the period from 1790 to 1797. *Shropshire Archives*

the white limestone was ideal as a flux in the manufacture of iron – one contemporary geologist thought it the best in the country for that purpose. The grey limestone would produce a cement which would harden under water, which was much in demand for dock-building. Limestone, burnt in kilns then spread on the land, was used in agriculture to reduce the acidity of soil and increase crop yields.

In 1764 Earl Gower went into partnership with Thomas Gilbert, his Agent, and Thomas's brother John, a mining expert. Half the profits of the partnership were to go to Lord Gower, the other half to be shared between the Gilberts.

The need for transport was soon identified as important, so a canal 5½ miles long was made between Wrockwardine Wood and Pave Lane, two miles south of Newport on the turnpike road to Wolverhampton. Only one section of the route was not on Gower's estate, and this section was leased from the land-owner, Mr Cotes of Woodcote, for a period of 500 years. Because neither compulsory purchase powers nor limited liability were needed the canal was built without an Act of Parliament. A minor consequence of this was that the canal had no formal name: at various times it was called Earl Gower's Canal, the Marquess of Stafford's Canal, the Pave Lane Canal, and the name used in this book, the Donnington Wood Canal.

Work was started in 1765 and finished three years later. At the Wrockwardine Wood end, the canal continued underground to the coal faces, just as John Gilbert had done at Worsley. Four limekilns were erected at Pave Lane.

About 1768 a branch was built from Hugh's Bridge to the limestone quarries and mines at Lilleshall; with five shallow locks, this had a complex of arms leading to the various workings. Coal was also taken to Lilleshall, where there were several limekilns. An extension to the new Pitchcroft limestone mine was made in 1797.

The branch canal was 42ft 8in. below the main line at Hugh's Bridge. The original arrangement was that the boats entered a tunnel which continued to just short of under the towpath of the main line. Here there were two shafts where the loads, mainly limestone, were lifted in pallets by crane and swung into the waiting boat on the main line. This was similar to an arrange-

Chapter 3 : The tub-boat canals of east Shropshire

The main drive of Lilleshall Hall, now one of the UK's National Sports Centres, uses a short length of the bed of the former Donnington Wood Canal, including this bridge. Author

ment at Castlefield, Manchester, on the Bridgewater Canal, engineered by James Brindley and John Gilbert.

Following the success of the inclined planes at Ketley and on the Shropshire Canal (described below), an inclined plane was constructed at Hugh's Bridge in 1797.

It is not known at whose initiative a plan was drawn in 1792 by George Young, a surveyor from Worcester, for a canal from the end of the Donnington Wood Canal to the Staffordshire & Worcestershire Canal, showing four alternative locations for junctions near Penkridge. Nothing came of this.[1]

A stock list of 1798 shows a total of 109 boats on the canal: 70 eight-tonners, 20 five-tonners and 19 'large boats' which implicitly could each carry about 15 tons. This indicates how busy the canal was.

Following the deaths of John Gilbert in 1795 and brother Thomas in 1798, their shares were in the hands of executors. Earl Gower (by then the Marquess of Stafford) wished to cease his involvement and seek new partners. As a first step, Lord Granville Leveson-Gower, the Marquess's younger son, acquired the Gilberts' shares. A new partnership, known as the Lilleshall Company, was formed in 1802; Lord Granville had a half interest, with various local industrialists holding the other half interest between them. The new partnership got much more involved in industrial production such as ironworks and potteries. By 1815 the partnership had three blast furnaces at Wrockwardine Wood and two at Donnington Wood.

The canal was included in the properties leased by the Marquess of Stafford and his successors to the Lilleshall Company. The latter charged tolls to anyone else using the canal and presumably did whatever maintenance was necessary.

A short branch canal was built to the Lilleshall Company's Lodge Furnaces when these came into operation in 1825 and remained in use until the furnaces were blown out in 1888.

The peak period of limestone extraction at Lilleshall was from 1800 to 1840. By the latter date the main workings were running out and there were concerns about future reserves. By the 1850s, most of the limestone production was from the Pitchcroft mine. Other shafts were sunk, but water ingress became a significant problem. With the flooding of the Pitchcroft mine in 1860 that arm became disused and was dammed at its junction. The closure of the last limestone mine in 1883 brought about the abandonment of the Lilleshall branch and the incline. The limestone quarries and mines were never rail-connected, neither to the Shropshire Union Railway which ran past the Pitchcroft site from 1848, nor to the Lilleshall Company's own extensive private rail network – almost all of the hundreds of thousands of tons of limestone extracted would have gone out by the canal.

The Pave Lane end of the canal was officially closed on Christmas Day 1882.

The western end of the canal, about as far as the modern Donnington Wood Way, stayed in water until shortly after the Second World War although the link to the Shrewsbury Canal closed in 1921. The collieries served by the canal had closed by the end of the 1920s.

The Wombridge Canal

William Reynolds is generally considered to have been the ablest of all the east Shropshire ironmasters. In 1786–7 he discovered valuable deposits of coal and ironstone near the surface of the ground at Wombridge and put into practice an idea he conceived some years before of open-cast mining, uncovering the strata of ironstone and coal which lay near the surface, so as to extract all the minerals.

During the spring and summer of 1787 he designed, engineered and built at his own expense a private canal at Wombridge

41

on the land of St John Charlton of Apley, the main purpose being to take coal and ironstone to the blast furnaces at Donnington Wood in which he was a partner. He also wanted to expand into chemical production of sulphuric acid, soap, dye, alkali and glass, creating a fully integrated chemical process using tub-boats to transport by-products along a chain of works. Reynolds invested £1,640 in the construction of the canal, 1¾ miles long with no locks, from just south of the Wombridge Church to close to the Donnington Wood Canal at Wrockwardine Wood.

The formal agreement for the connection with the Donnington Wood Canal was not signed until 1794, two years after the link had been made with the Shropshire Canal.

William Reynolds sold to the Shrewsbury Canal the section from the top of the Trench Incline to the junction with the Donnington Wood Canal, 1 mile 188yds in length, for £840, reserving the right that his internal traffic could travel toll-free.

Most of the remaining part of the Wombridge Canal went out of use when the Wombridge Iron Works was built across its line in 1818, leaving just a short section in water from the top of the Trench Incline to the ironworks.

The Ketley Canal

THE Ketley Canal was a private canal two miles long constructed by William Reynolds in 1787-8 to convey coal from Snedshill to his ironworks at Ketley. The most interesting feature was the country's first successful inclined plane on a canal, near the Ketley end. With a fall of 75ft and horizontal length 210ft, it was by far the steepest of any of the six inclined planes eventually built in east Shropshire.

The tub-boats used on this canal were 3ft 10in. deep, carrying 8 tons.

William Reynolds died in 1803, the ironworks and canal passing to his half-brother Joseph. After that the ironworks began to be run down; in 1816, when there was a downturn in the iron-

Coalbrookdale token depicting the Ketley inclined plane.
Jim Ruston

founding industry following the end of the war with France, it was put up for sale. The purchasers demolished the old furnaces and erected two new ones but they did not retain the inclined plane, developing instead an effective tramroad system.

Use of the upper part of the canal diminished through the first half of the 19th century. It is unlikely that there were any boat movements on it after the closure of the adjacent part of the Shropshire Canal in 1859.

The Shropshire Canal

IN 1788, 24 blast furnaces in Shropshire made 24,900 tons of iron, about 38% of the national total. To the north of the river Severn, the principal ironworks and their management were:

– Coalbrookdale and Horsehay: After the death of Abraham Darby II in 1763 the Coalbrookdale Company was dominated by his wealthy son-in-law, Richard Reynolds. The works were managed by Abraham Darby III.

– Ketley and Madeley Wood ('Bedlam'): Ketley was started by Richard Reynolds but developed by his eldest son, William Reynolds; by 1806 it was the second largest in Shropshire and the fifth largest in England. The Madeley Wood ironworks was a smaller concern, close to the river Severn.

– Donnington Wood: The furnaces were built in 1785 by William Reynolds and Joseph Rathbone, and were sold to John Bishton and his partners in 1796.

– Snedshill and Hollinswood: These were developed by John Wilkinson, whose principal works were at Bersham near

> **William Reynolds (1758–1803)**
>
> WILLIAM REYNOLDS was an innovative ironmaster, industrial entrepreneur and engineer. Richard Reynolds (1735–1816), his father, who had married Hannah, daughter of Abraham Darby II, managed the Coalbrookdale ironworks during the minority of Abraham Darby III. William studied chemistry with Dr Joseph Black in Edinburgh. In 1781 he became a partner in the Coalbrookdale Company, managing the Ketley Ironworks, which he retained when the partnership was wound up in 1796. Other industrial activities included glass and pottery production and the tar tunnel at Coalport.
>
> He built the Wombridge and Ketley Canals, surveyed, promoted and was closely involved in the management of both the Shropshire and Shrewsbury Canals. He provided the iron for the aqueduct at Longdon-on-Tern and was probably principally responsible for its design.

Wrexham, at Bradley in the Black Country, and at New Willey, near Broseley on the southern side of the river Severn. Snedshill was taken over by John Bishton and his partners in 1793 when the lease expired, and the Hollinswood furnace ceased operation. Wilkinson later constructed a furnace at Hadley.

- Old Park: These works at Malinslee were controlled by the Botfield family. They were started in 1788; by 1806 they were the largest in Shropshire and the second largest in England.

- Lightmoor: In 1787 these ironworks were taken over and developed by Francis Homfray and John Addenbrooke. The Homfray family had been long established in the Broseley coal trade, and in 1784 had established the Penydarren Ironworks at Merthyr Tydfil.

The various works were generally on leased land. The landowners took rent payments and royalties but were not normally directly involved in the mines or ironworks.

A transport system was needed to bring in the raw materials, principally coal, ironstone and limestone, and to take out the finished products, both pig iron and castings. As making a canal across the industrial area from Wrockwardine Wood to what was to become Coalport, serving most of the main ironworks on the way, was too big a project to be undertaken by one person, an Act of Parliament was needed to create the company and to acquire the necessary compulsory purchase powers. However, the finance, and hence the control, was initially firmly local. Thus the Shropshire Canal project was launched at a meeting in January 1788, with a capital of £50,000.

The landowners who committed themselves to £100 shares included Isaac Hawkins Browne (30 shares), the Marquess of Stafford (20), the Earl of Shrewsbury (10), Lord Berwick (10), Elizabeth Clayton (10) and Sir William Jerningham (5). In addition, Thomas Gilbert held 10 shares.

The Darby, Reynolds and Rathbone family between them held 155 shares. Abraham Darby III was not himself an investor but his brother Samuel had 5 shares and his brother-in-law Joseph Rathbone had 60. Richard Reynolds also had 60 shares; his son William had 10 and his daughter Hannah (who was married to William Rathbone) had 20.

The other major shareholder, with 55 shares, was John Wilkinson. His partner at some of his ventures (and his wife's sister's husband), Edward Blakeway, had 10 shares – he was to become a founder of the Shropshire porcelain industry and a partner at the Coalport Pottery. William Ferriday, another ironmaster who had previously been a partner of Wilkinson at New Willey, had 10 shares.

Significantly, the Botfields and Homfrays were not shareholders, which influenced problems later faced by the company.

The Shropshire Canal never employed an outside engineer. William Reynolds advised on the route. The necessary survey was done by George Young of Worcester who a few years earlier had surveyed the river Severn from Worcester to Coalbrookdale. William Jessop gave evidence to Parliament in support of the Shropshire Canal's route and the estimated cost.

Originally the canal was to start at Hollinswood, but John Wilkinson persuaded the other promoters to extend it to Snedshill and on to Wrockwardine Wood, where it would join the Donnington Wood Canal and the Wombridge Canal. Initially the Marquess of Stafford and John Gilbert were opposed to this, but they were eventually convinced that it would actually benefit their enterprises.

In addition to the inclined planes at The Hay and Windmill Farm, this extension required a third at Wrockwardine Wood – and this would be the only one where the main traffic would be against the gradient. There were also to be three short tunnels on the 7¾ mile long main line. The Brierly Hill Branch (also known as the Lightmoor or Coalbrookdale Branch), 2½ miles long, was originally intended to continue via another inclined plane to Coalbrookdale.

The boats for which the canal was designed were to be only 3ft deep, carrying five tons instead of eight. This change may have resulted from the experience of operating the inclined plane on the Ketley Canal, or perhaps it was a response to the expectation that some of the loading would be ascending inclines.

The Act was obtained in June 1788. David Davies, a Madeley solicitor, was appointed Clerk; he continued in this role until 1820.

Construction

JOHN Lowdon was appointed surveyor to make and supervise the contracts; he also controlled the men employed as direct labour. A house was built for him at Snedshill. His terms of engagement made it clear that the committee, which usually in practice meant William Reynolds or Cornelius Reynolds, were in day-to-day control. (The latter was John Wilkinson's Agent in the east Shropshire area; he was not related to Richard and William Reynolds, as far as is known.) Lowdon lasted only fifteen months in the job, though he did carry out some work under contract later. His successor, Joshua Heatley, lasted just twelve months. Michael Middleton, the next person appointed, was dismissed after seventeen months, probably because the works by then were substantially finished. Judging from the amount of repairs which had to be made in the early years, these surveyors were generally ineffective.

Work started with the extension of the Ketley Canal, a lock being built because the level of the Shropshire Canal was to be one foot higher than that of the slightly older canal. This was not a mistake in 'setting out' but was an explicit decision of the Shropshire Canal Committee. It proceeded in stages southwards to Southall Bank, then the Brierly Hill Branch was constructed. Next came the section between the junction with the Ketley Canal and the junction with the Donnington Wood Canal, and finally the main line between Southall Bank and what was then called Broad Meadows but was to become Coalport. The contractors for the various sections were John Pixton, Thomas Ford and James Houghton.

William Reynolds was obviously not totally satisfied with the recently completed inclined plane on the Ketley Canal because he was present at the committee meeting where it was decided to offer a reward of fifty guineas to the person who put forward 'the best means of raising and lowering heavy weights from one navigation to another' – wording vague enough to embrace lifts, cranes or innovative designs of locks, as well as inclined planes.

Several people submitted plans and models. Having consulted John Wilkinson and James Watt, it was decided to award the prize to Henry Williams and the company's then surveyor, John Lowdon. It is not clear whether they had made a joint submission or whether their proposals were separate but similar. Their proposal was for an inclined plane which differed from that at Ketley in one important respect: the arrangements for getting the boat out of the top canal onto the incline. At Ketley there was a lock at the top; when the water was drained out, the boat settled onto the carriage. The guillotine gate at the end of the lock could then be raised for the boat on its carriage to descend. The water was put back to the upper canal using a small steam pump. In the winning design the boat was put on the carriage whilst it was in the upper canal, then the pair were drawn over a lip and onto the incline. Thus no water was lost, but it did mean that some power was needed, even where descending loads predominated. This design was adopted for the three inclines on the Shropshire Canal, as well as for the later inclines at Trench (Shrewsbury Canal) and Hugh's Bridge (Donnington Wood Canal).

As well as the principal prize, the committee thought that other models also merited some award: they made nine awards ranging from 1 guinea to 15 guineas, totalling 50 guineas, including one of 4 guineas to Henry Williams 'in consideration of the great trouble and expense in making his machines'.

Inclines were constructed at Windmill Farm and The Hay, supervised by Henry Williams and Cornelius Reynolds. In the short term – about two years – horse-powered winches were used before the steam engines were installed. The rails used were heavy-duty versions of plateway rails, 8in. wide, 2in. thick, with a 3in. flange. William Reynolds constructed the incline at Wrockwardine Wood and supervised the installation of the steam engines at the other two inclines.

A different solution was adopted at the top of Coalbrookdale. It was agreed that the Coalbrookdale Company would sink shafts from the terminus of the branch canal and drive in a tunnel to meet these shafts, and would take all the receipts from tonnages. In 1794 the tunnel and shafts system was replaced by a tramroad incline.

Despite the use of inclined planes, water supply problems continued to trouble the company. Randlay Reservoir was created by making a dam 20ft high, later further raised, and a steam engine was purchased to raise the water into the reservoir. A further reservoir at Horsehay was added in 1796.

As was permitted by the Act, the partnership of the Marquess of Stafford and the Gilbert brothers constructed the 58yd long connection between the bottom of the Wrockwardine Wood incline and the Donnington Wood Canal. In 1798 the partnership paid 20 guineas for the right to use it without charge in perpetuity.

At what was to become Coalport the canal did not actually link with the river, tub-boats not being suitable for use on the Severn, so arrangements had to be made for transhipping the coal, pig iron and other traffic. Before wharfs could be created the bank had to be piled and stabilised, the cost being shared between the canal company and Richard Reynolds, the lessee of the land.

The first income from tonnages was in the summer of 1791, and the canal was completed in 1793.

If the £50,000 share capital did not prove adequate, the Act permitted an extra £10,000 to be raised from the shareholders or borrowed. In the event, only £1,300 was borrowed, and that only for a short period, so the canal must have been built virtually within budget – a rare occurrence for any canal company, and especially commendable as this canal incorporated new and almost untried technology. Perhaps this slightly overstates the achievement: the canal down Coalbrook Dale, authorised by the Act was not built, and (far more importantly in the long run) it seems that much of the land over which it ran was leased, not bought. In doing so it had followed the practice of the tramroads of the area.

Management

IN 1794 Henry Williams was appointed Agent (or Superintendent) – in effect, General Manager – having been advising on several issues, not just the inclined planes, since 1791. He was paid £200 a year, which was reduced to £180 a year in 1798, but had to meet the costs of employing clerks and assistants. He lived rent-free at Snedshill.

Once the canal was opened for traffic, the committee became much less involved in its working. From 1803 onwards it usually met only twice a year; sometimes the only business was to declare the dividend.

Tonnage disputes and their consequences

THE Act fixed the maximum tonnage at *2d* per ton per mile, and an equal rate had to be applied for the whole length of the canal. However, at the General Assembly meeting in 1792 it was decided that charges of *3d* per ton should be made at the

---

Henry Williams (1753–1842)

HENRY WILLIAMS had been constructing engines for the Coalbrookdale Company at Ketley since 1779 and designed the inclined planes on the Shropshire Canal. He became Agent of the Shropshire Canal in 1794 and Agent & General Superintendent of the Shrewsbury Canal in 1797, retaining these posts until retiring in 1839. He became a partner in the Ketley ironworks in 1818. Amongst his other activities was rebuilding the stretch of the Holyhead Road through Oakengates.

Chapter 3: The tub-boat canals of east Shropshire

Wrockwardine Wood and Windmill Farm inclines and 1½d per ton at The Hay – the minute explicitly stated that this payment was 'over and above the tonnage due by the Act', so the members should have been aware that it was not legally enforceable. The following year the charge at The Hay was also made 3d per ton.

Unsurprisingly, various coal companies objected to the charges. John Bishton of the Snedshill Company attended the 1794 General Assembly, representing several mining companies, where it was decided to halve the tonnage to 1½d and to remove it altogether when the dividend reached 8%, provided the mining companies agreed within a month. If they did not agree, the threat was that the engines would be removed. In the event, the mining companies agreed, albeit reluctantly.

Having seen a financial statement of the costs of operating the inclined planes, the 1795 General Assembly decided to increase the tonnage on the inclines to 2d. By the time of the 1796 General Assembly, still no reply had been received from the three main concerns: the Marquess of Stafford & Company, the Snedshill Company, and the Old Hill Company. A financial statement showed that losses were still being made on the inclines, so the tonnage was increased to 3d, the figure at which it had originally been set. The resolution added that if anyone refused to pay that amount, the steam engines would be removed and horse-powered winches used instead; nevertheless, they said that they were still willing to get agreement by arbitration.

The dispute dragged on for several more months until a Special Assembly in May 1797 called specifically to discuss the issue instructed the engines to be removed if users did not agree to pay a reduced amount of 2d per ton. As this threat was never implemented, those companies which continued to use the canal presumably agreed to pay the tonnage demanded.

Meanwhile, John Bishton initiated retaliatory action by assembling agreements for wayleaves for what became known as the Sutton Wharf Railroad, an 8 mile long tramroad from Snedshill to Sutton Wharf, a little downstream of Coalport. Apart from the incline from Sutton Wharf up to Sutton Common this was open by the end of 1797; the incline was completed by the end of 1802.[2] The tramroad was reputed to have cost only £5,000 to build, a tenth of the cost of the canal.

The tramroad was also used extensively by the Lilleshall Company, the successors to the Marquess of Stafford & Company. In 1807 the Lilleshall Company bought the Snedshill works, John Bishton having died the previous year.

In 1812 Thomas Bishton, also representing the Lilleshall Company, negotiated an agreement whereby £500 compensation would be paid by the Shropshire Canal Company twelve months after the tramroad was taken up. Henry Williams was authorised to enter into an agreement with the Lilleshall Company to convey their coal, iron and other articles to the Severn 'upon such terms as he shall judge expedient'. The implication is that a favourable rate would be granted – this would have been good commercial practice as it would remove a rival and attract the extra trade, but was dubious in law, as all users were meant to pay the same rates. The tramroad must have ceased operation in 1814, the £500 being paid in 1815. This relatively low price implies that the tramroad had not been particularly successful, or possibly that some of the landowners (some of whom were also shareholders in the Shropshire Canal) were seeking significant increases in their lease terms.

Back in 1794, at the request of William Reynolds, the tonnage on limestone was reduced to 1d a ton. This time other customers subsequently benefited from what had been Reynolds's special pleading. The tonnage on sand was similarly reduced in 1802. Both reverted to the statutory maximum of 2d in 1814. The previous year the method of calculating a ton had been changed from 120lb per cwt to 112lb per cwt.

The effects of mining

The Act stated that the company would not be entitled to coal or other minerals found in making the canal, nor to coal under the canal. It was silent about who would be liable for the injurious effects of extracting coal from under the canal, an omission which was to cause long-running arguments with some of the proprietors and lessees of mines.

In 1794 the Lightmoor Company was sent a bill for £24.10s, the cost of rectifying damage caused by their mining, but they refused to pay. The following year it was reported that the Marquess of Stafford & Co. had mined under the Wrockwardine Wood incline, damaging it and nearby buildings. Having obtained counsel's advice which said there was a legal right to recover the costs, it was agreed that mining companies should be charged for the damages they caused.

Some agreed to pay – on a number of occasions the Snedshill and Ketley Companies repaired the tunnel, bridges and towpath when their mines caused subsidence and damage – but the Lightmoor Company continued to refuse. By 1812 the cost of the damage was said to be averaging £5 a month, so having sent several solicitor's letters without effect, the canal company obtained a counsel's opinion prior to taking legal action through the courts. However, this opinion must have been unfavourable, as no further action was taken.

Perhaps the other mining companies took note of this, as the effects of subsidence were to be the single biggest problem during the rest of the life of the Shropshire Canal.

Operation

A transport development in the late 1790s was the introduction into the east Shropshire coalfield of railways with the flanges on the rails instead of on the wheels – terminology varied, this system being referred to as tramroads, plateways or (locally) 'jenny' or 'jinny' rails. There was no standard gauge, at least six different gauges being used in the coalfield. In 1800 the Coalbrookdale Company was given permission to put this style of tramroad on the towpath between Horsehay Wharf and the end of the Brierly Hill Branch, mainly for conveying coal. The towpath would still be usable for the haulage of boats. A compensation toll of one penny per ton for everything transported along the tramroad was to be paid, the distance being about a mile. Other people could use the tramroad on payment to the Coalbrookdale Company of 2*d* a ton.

This tramroad between Coalbrookdale and Horsehay replaced an edge-rail line which had been built in the 1750s, but it was short-lived, being succeeded in 1811 by a tramroad linking Coalbrookdale with Horsehay and Dawley Castle through the Lightmoor valley (thus replacing the incline by a longer but more gradual ascent), parts of which remained in use until 1932. This new line used about a quarter of a mile of the towpath, from Castle Furnace Bridge at Dawley to the bridge carrying the lane from Little Dawley to the Moors. The agreed tonnage was 1*d* per ton per mile, but a few years later the charge was consolidated as £10 a year, and later still this was reduced to £2 a year. After a few years the canal company forgot to collect the money due, and in 1838 a bill for £87 was raised for the back rents.

In 1800 the ropes at Windmill Farm incline and The Hay incline were replaced by chains, but the following year a chain broke on The Hay incline and four of Botfield's boats were damaged.

Major works were carried out at Coalport in conjunction with William Anstice, the landowner, in 1810. Because of the congestion caused by mining companies leaving full tub-boats at the terminus of the canal, a basin to hold sixty boats was created. Removal of a gravel spit in the river was contemplated, but it was considered that it was the responsibility of the Severn towpath company.

Under new management

UNTIL 1825 the committee had been dominated by local industrialists, then this suddenly largely changed. A Special Assembly elected a new committee of eleven members, with only Thomas Rose continuing from the previous committee. The previous other ten members had disqualified themselves by selling their shares – these included Richard Darby (son of Abraham Darby III), Barnard Dickinson (the manager of the Coalbrookdale Company and son-in-law of Abraham Darby III), both of whom from the mid 1830s were to resume being shareholders and committee members, and were often to chair the meetings.

Joseph Sutton, the Shrewsbury physician who regularly chaired meetings of the Shrewsbury Canal, chaired that Special Assembly meeting, and most of the meetings in the following six years. The new committee included one member connected with the Coalbrookdale Company: Joseph Reynolds, grandson of Abraham Darby II and half-brother of William Reynolds. Another member was Robert Waring Darwin of Shrewsbury, father of Charles Darwin, and a substantial investor in the Trent & Mersey Canal. Most of the committee had little if any connection with the coalfield area.

At the time of the 1825 Special Assembly the biggest single shareholding, 85 shares, was owned by Edward Loyd, a partner in a Manchester firm of bankers. It was surely not coincidental that this was exactly the total number of shares that had been owned by the ten 'disqualified' previous committee members.

The reason for this virtually complete change in control is a matter for speculation. The most likely reason is that it was done to release money which the sellers needed for other purposes. The Coalbrookdale Company was certainly then at a low ebb.

It was definitely not the case that the sellers had 'insider information' about trouble ahead for the canal company. But nor does it appear to be the case that the buyers could see some potential they thought they could unlock – the policies stayed essentially the same for in excess of a decade, the annual dividend continued to be £7.10*s* or £8, as it had been since 1818, and the day-to-day management remained unchanged.

Henry Williams was Agent until he retired in 1839, aged 86. He was succeeded by John Hewitt, who had been appointed Tonnage Clerk of the Shrewsbury Canal two years earlier. His salary was initially set at £70 a year, much less than Henry Williams had received.

William Nock, a Wellington solicitor who had become Clerk when David Davies retired in 1821, continued in the post until 1852.

The Brierly Hill Branch, by then long disused, was sold to Lord Craven, lord of the manor of Little Dawley, in 1841. That was also the year in which the issue of the ground rents payable became significant. Robert A. Slaney of Hatton Grange, lord of the manor of Dawley, wanted to increase the rent on the land occupied by the canal and its reservoirs. Other landowners – the Earl of Shrewsbury, the executors of Richard Mountford, William Amphlett, George Deakin and Samuel Whittingham – initiated similar action. Counsel confirmed that the rents were not permanently fixed, so compromise settlements had to be made.

James Foster was a West Midlands ironmaster whose main works was at Stourbridge but who also had interests in several concerns in east Shropshire including blast furnaces at Wombridge and mines on the Madeley Court estate. In 1841 he complained that the engine at Windmill Farm was not sufficiently powerful, preventing him from sending his coal and iron to Wombridge. A sub-committee was instructed to look into the matter and see to the erection of a more powerful engine if the members 'think it necessary or expedient'. The outcome is not recorded, but some action must have been taken as a couple of years later he wrote saying there was 'an absolute and indispensable necessity' to halve the tonnage on his minerals and bricks being transported between Madeley and Wombridge. This was refused, the canal company explaining that it could not favour any one customer. The predictable outcome was that the other ironmasters applied for reductions in tonnage, but these too were refused. Foster solved his problem by erecting three furnaces at Madeley Court and selling those at Wombridge.

Throughout the life of the Shropshire Canal, except for a short period for certain cargoes, the maximum tolls allowed by the Act were charged, plus an extra-statutory 3*d* per ton on the inclines. This enabled a dividend of from £6.10*s* to £8 on the nominal £100 shares to be paid consistently every year between 1816 and 1845, followed by four years when the dividend exceeded £8, peaking at £9.10*s*.

Lease and sale

In 1845 three sets of railway promoters offered to buy the Shropshire Canal. The Shrewsbury & Birmingham Railway's deposited plans showed a branch leaving the main line at Hollinswood, just east of Oakengates Tunnel. For much of its route it would have used the bed of the canal, then entered Coalbrookdale on a relatively easy gradient, terminating near the turnpike road down the Vale (close to where Green Park Halt was opened by the GWR in 1934). This branch was authorised in the 1846 Act but was never built.

However, the Shropshire Canal's General Assembly in October 1845 selected the Shropshire Union Railways & Canal Company as the preferred purchaser. Two of the committee had already met two Shropshire Union (SU) representatives and provisionally agreed terms of £125 a share, to be paid within six months of the passing of the SU Bill for constructing a line through the canal's district. This was confirmed by a Special Assembly three weeks later.

After this hasty action, matters went worryingly quiet. The SU's Act for the railway between Stafford, Wellington and Shrewsbury was passed in August 1846. The branch through the industrial area served by the canal was to have been included in the Bill for the Shrewsbury to Worcester line, but this had been withdrawn. Eventually in April 1847 the SU's Secretary wrote confirming that the Joint Committee of the SU and the London & North Western Railway (LNWR) had nevertheless agreed to buy the Shropshire Canal. A Bill was prepared for the 1848 session of Parliament but later withdrawn; instead the SU made an offer to lease the canal for 21 years or until an Act could be obtained. This was accepted. Actually there were two leases which came into effect on 1 November 1849: the tolls and dues for £3,125 a year, and the land and property for a nominal £1 a year. A clause in the lease required the canal at the termination of the lease to be in as good a state of repair as it had been at the start.

The company continued in existence to receive the lease payments and to pay the dividends. A committee was meant to be appointed to check that the SU maintained the canal according to the agreement, but it never seems to have met. In fact, the SU had increasing problems in trying to keep the canal open, as is discussed in chapter 10.

Several years went by – the Bill was not submitted to Parliament until 1857. It passed in July that year, with the canal being sold to the LNWR itself, not to the SU. The purchase price of £125 per share was paid in February 1858, and a final distribution was made to the shareholders.

This price, which had been agreed back in 1845, would have been based on past earnings and dividends, rather than on future expectations. By the late 1840s, east Shropshire was declining as an industrial area. The Shrewsbury & Birmingham Railway's branch from Madeley Junction to Ironbridge was authorised in 1847, though it was not to opened as far as Lightmoor until 1854, and this would inevitably have taken some of the trade. The canal was suffering from subsidence and the plant at the inclines was elderly. Prospects were not good – shareholders were indeed fortunate to receive £125 per share.

Notes and references

The principal source for the Shropshire Canal was the company minutes (The National Archives: RAIL869/1). The best books for background information about this area are Barrie Trinder's *The Industrial Revolution in Shropshire* (2000) and *The Victoria History of Shropshire, Volume XI: Telford* (1985).

1. Plan, 1792: Staffordshire Record Office, D3186/8/1/30/57
2. Paul Luter, *The Short History of the Sutton Wharf Tramway (1796–1814)*, privately published, 2004, p.4.

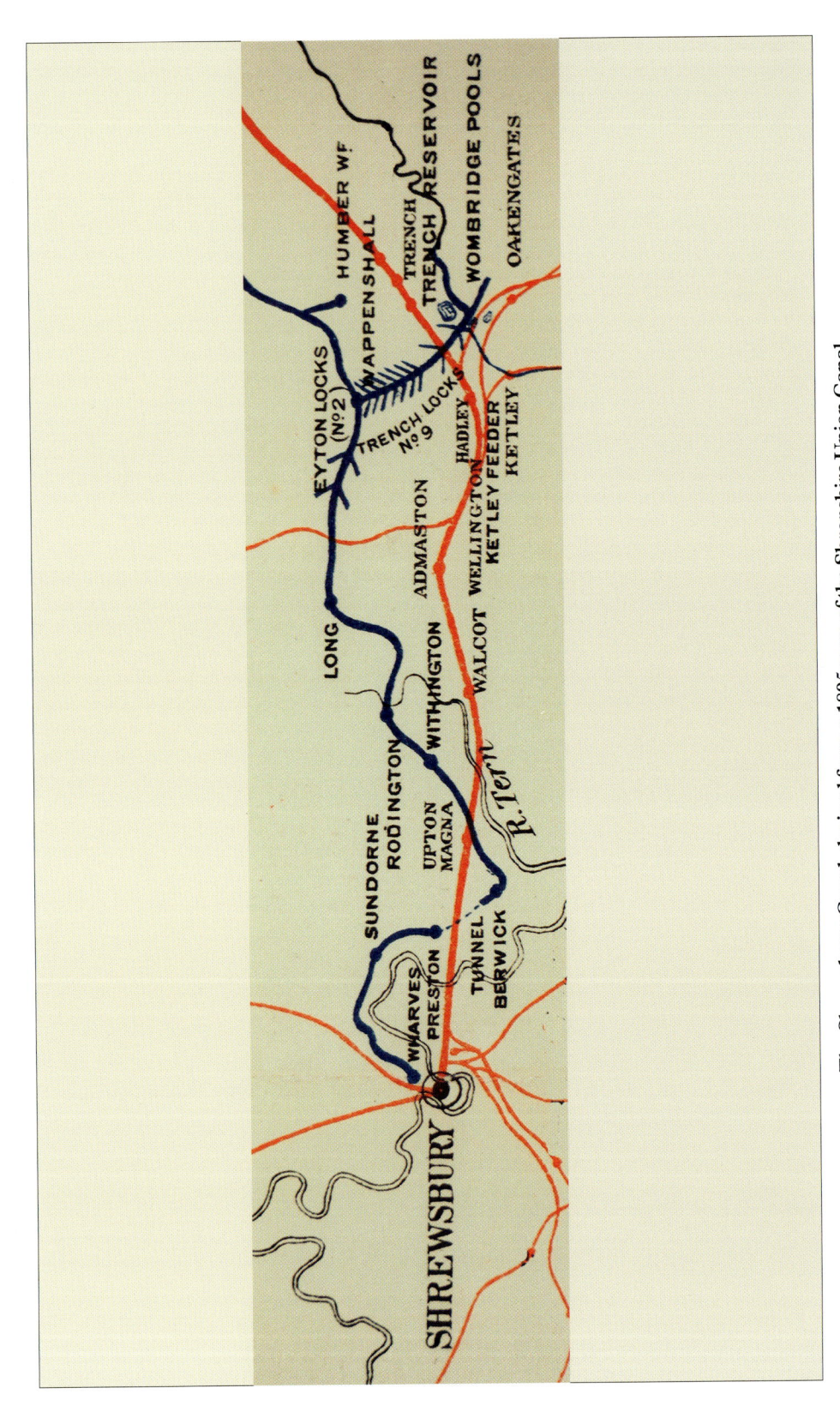

The Shrewsbury Canal, derived from a 1895 map of the Shropshire Union Canal with peripheral detail removed.
Canal & River Trust

4

The Shrewsbury Canal

Promotion

In the late 18th century merchandise was conveyed on the river Severn up to Shrewsbury but it rarely seems to have used to bring coal, although this was an important river cargo downstream from the Ironbridge area. Some of Shrewsbury's coal came by road from the small coalfield to the south-west of the town; the rest came by road from the Ketley area. It was said that the turnpike road from Wellington had become almost impassable because of the damage done by the constant succession of heavy coal carriages, despite large annual maintenance expenditure.[1]

The reasons why the Shrewsbury Canal was promoted were therefore simple: to provide Shrewsbury with cheaper coal, with the expectation that much more would be sold, and also to transport lime and manure for land improvement.

The usual method for promoting a canal would be the holding of a public meeting, a resolution to appoint an engineer or surveyor, the issuing of a prospectus, and then an application to Parliament. The *Shrewsbury Chronicle* makes no mention of the early stages: the first item about the canal is in the issue of 7 September 1792, when notice was given for application to Parliament for a canal 'from the north end of the canal known as the Shropshire Canal ... to the town of Shrewsbury'. It therefore seems likely that the leading local townsmen and gentry, industrialists, businessmen and bankers got together informally to work up the scheme.

This was to be a tub-boat canal, with its eastern terminus at Wrockwardine Wood, where the Shropshire Canal met the Donnington Wood Canal. The new company would buy 1 mile 188yds of the Wombridge Canal. An inclined plane 669ft long would lower the boats 75ft to the main section of the Shrewsbury Canal at Trench.

Almost all of the £50,000 share capital needed was raised locally, with only £800 of the initial subscription being held by people whose local connection has not been identified. The Marquess of Stafford, the Gilbert brothers and the Marquess's agent at Trentham had a total of 70 £100 shares; the Reynolds family, father Richard, sons William and Joseph and son-in-law William Rathbone, had 61. John Bishton and John Wilkinson, who both owned coal mines and ironworks, each had 20, as did Samuel Charlton, who owned much land in the Wellington/Ketley area. Other major landowners with 20 shares were Thomas Eyton, John Corbet and William Tayleur. Only one other person held 20 shares: Stephen Leeke of Chester, a relative of Egerton Leeke who was to become the Shrewsbury Canal's Clerk, and a partner of Charles Potts, the Ellesmere Canal's Clerk. A great number of the medium sized holdings, 5 or 10 shares, were held by gentry and clergy in the Shrewsbury area, whereas the owners of the smallest holdings, 1 to 3 shares, tended to be rather wider spread around central Shropshire.

Five of the eleven initial committee members including

Thomas Eyton (1753–1816)

THOMAS EYTON inherited the Eyton estate, which comprised land at Eyton on the Weald Moors, Wellington, Wrockwardine and Kynnersley, on the death of his father in 1776. He became High Sheriff of Shropshire in 1779 and later Deputy Lord Lieutenant, and in 1791 was Mayor of Shrewsbury. He married Mary, daughter of John Rocke, and they lived in Wellington.

He set up banks in both Wellington and Shrewsbury, and in 1787 was appointed Receiver General of the Crown in Shropshire, with the duty of forwarding to the Exchequer taxation collected in the county, such as land tax.

He invested £1,300 in the Shropshire Canal, £2,000 in the Shrewsbury Canal and £2,000 in the Ellesmere Canal. All three companies banked with the Shrewsbury bank of Eyton, Reynolds and Bishop. He was active in the management of the first two-named of the canals until 1797, his involvement diminishing thereafter.

He committed suicide on 22 January 1816, after which it was discovered that he had been embezzling funds in his role as Receiver General.

William Reynolds were involved with coal mining; five were Shrewsbury gentry or clergy; and one, Thomas Eyton, the chairman, was a landowner and banker. During the independent life of the canal company the industrialists became less active in its management – by 1845 only two industrialists were on the committee.

The survey for the Act was done by George Young of Worcester but it seems likely that the engineering decisions, which included recommending an inclined plane, were made by William Reynolds, as he had for the Shropshire Canal, and that Young merely did the physical survey and mapping.

Construction

AFTER the passing of the Act on 3 June 1793, the committee's first choice for engineer was William Jessop but he was far too busy elsewhere. Their second choice was Thomas Dadford Junior – judging from what happened on the Montgomeryshire Canal, the Shrewsbury committee was fortunate that he refused the appointment. Third choice was Josiah Clowes, who by then had wide-ranging canal experience. Clowes was not actually appointed until the first day of 1794, when it was agree that he should survey the canal four times a year, more often if the company thought it necessary, and that he would be paid three guineas a day.

Even before the offer was made to Clowes, the committee had made several decisions that would normally have been made by the engineer. James Houghton, John Houghton and Thomas Ford were contracted to construct 5¾ miles of the canal from Trench, below the intended incline, to just short of the river Tern near Longdon. They were also to estimate the cost of making the inclined plane, and if this cost was acceptable to Henry Williams, designer of the inclines on the Shropshire Canal, they were to proceed to make it.

William Reynolds was asked to order from the Coalbrookdale Company an engine for the inclined plane similar to the one used at the Wrockwardine Wood incline on the Shropshire Canal and to arrange for its erection. A little later, after Clowes had been appointed, the committee resolved that the cast-iron rails for the inclined plane were to be bought from William Reynolds, the price being that paid by the Shropshire Canal Company for the rails used at the Windmill Farm inclined plane.

All this activity seems to confirm that William Reynolds, the one person on the committee with practical canal-building experience, was acting in effect as the company's engineer. This is probably why the canal is unusual in having guillotine gates instead of mitre gates at the ends of its eleven locks, all of which lay within the first contract length. They also had a further gate a quarter of the way along, so they could pass one, three or four tub-boats, making the most economical use of water. One would not expect a conservative canal engineer like Josiah Clowes to have designed these – much more likely that it was an innovative man such as Reynolds.

The Act authorised the company to purchase the section of the Wombridge Canal from Wrockwardine Wood to the head of the inclined plane from William Reynolds & Company, for which it paid £840. The banks along this section were raised and a junction made with the Donnington Wood Canal.

Edward Bishop was appointed to superintend the contractors, and some aspects, such as the building to house the engine for the incline, were constructed by directly employed labour supervised by him.

Clowes' first act on taking office was to agree to pay Houghtons £9,721.1s.2d for the section from Trench to near Longdon; this opened in 1794. Houghtons also agreed a price of £20,370 to complete the canal by 29 September 1795. This section included the earthworks for the incline, aqueducts at Longdon, Rodington and Pimley and the 970yd tunnel near Berwick Wharf, 50yds longer than originally intended. On William Reynolds' advice, the tunnel had a towpath through it, the first time this had been done in a tunnel more than 100yds long. This towpath, which was made of wood, was 3ft wide, thus reducing the width available for boats to 7ft, but as the water could flow freely below it, the boats were not unduly impeded.

However, Clowes died at the end of 1794; the accounts imply he had spent only sixteen days on the business of the Shrewsbury Canal. The news of his death may have taken some time to reach Shropshire, as it was not reported in the *Shrewsbury Chronicle* until the issue of 13 February 1795 – and the same issue reported the damage to bridges, mills and other property caused by the widespread flooding on 10–12 February.

The masonry aqueduct at Longdon was severely damaged, and at the committee meeting on 23 February Thomas Telford, who was County Surveyor and by then also General Agent of the Ellesmere Canal (see Chapter 5), was asked to inspect it and the one at Rodington. (Work had not yet started on the smaller aqueduct at Pimley.) At their meeting held five days later in the Coffee Room of County Hall Telford was formally appointed to survey the works in the place of the late Josiah Clowes and instructed to make plans for 'alterations and

Josiah Clowes (1735–1794)

JOSIAH CLOWES came from a family of North Staffordshire coal mine owners. His first involvement with canals was in connection with the Trent & Mersey Canal's Harecastle Tunnel. Later he became involved in canal-related trading, based at Middlewich, his home for the rest of his life. In 1778 he took over as 'General Surveyor and Overseer of the Works' of the Chester Canal but he was soon discharged for not spending enough time on the job. In 1783 he became resident engineer of the Thames & Severn Canal, which included Sapperton Tunnel, then the world's longest; later he completed Dudley Tunnel and became consultant to various canals in the West Midlands. Clowes advised the Shrewsbury Canal and engineered Berwick Tunnel. He began building a masonry aqueduct at London-on-Tern but died shortly before the works were destroyed by the great flood of 1795.

Chapter 4 : The Shrewsbury Canal

Longdon Aqueduct in about 1950, still in water.
Railway & Canal Historical Society

additions' to the aqueduct at Longdon. Just a fortnight later the committee resolved:

> That an iron aqueduct be erected at Longdon (agreeable to a plan to be approved by Mr Telford) by Messrs William Reynolds & Company, that such aqueduct to be erected at an expense not exceeding the sum of £2,000. Messrs William Reynolds & Co agreeing to compleat the said aqueduct on or before the 14th day of September next and to uphold the same for the space of five years.

In the chapter on canals which he wrote for Joseph Plymley's *Agriculture of Shropshire*, Telford said that it was Thomas Eyton, who chaired the General Assemblies of the canal company, who first suggested making the aqueduct in cast iron. This is surprising as Eyton was a landowner and banker, and there were several ironmasters on the committee. Telford continued that once the principle had been agreed, he and William Reynolds had several consultations, formed and considered various plans before determining upon the structure as built.[2] As this was written within three years of the event for a book which would be read by most of those present, it must be correct, though it probably flattered Eyton's contribution.

Telford is usually given the credit for Longdon and it is certainly true that by agreeing the design he bore the ultimate responsibility. On the other hand, Reynolds had visited the pioneering iron aqueduct, Pont-y-Cafnau, at Merthyr Tydfil the previous year, making a sketch of it. He carried out stress tests of suitable cast-iron sections in March. What most convinces me that William Reynolds did most of the design work is the appearance of the aqueduct: with the exception of the side plates shaped like voussoirs, it does not look like a structure designed by a person who had trained as a stonemason and architect. One can contrast it with Buildwas Bridge, also cast iron, undoubtedly designed by Telford, and exactly contemporary – and which shows an architect's eye for aesthetics.

The castings for the aqueduct were done at Ketley then taken by road to the partly-completed canal, along which they were brought to the aqueduct site. The aqueduct was completed by March 1796, six months later than promised but still remarkably quickly in the circumstances.

The canal fully opened in 1797, the last parts being the completion of the tunnel and the laying out of the wharfs at Shrewsbury. Telford's consultancy was ended, and he was paid £210 'for his trouble and expenses in attending to the concerns of the Company'. Henry Williams, who had a similar role on the Shropshire Canal, was appointed Agent and General Superintendent at a salary of £200 a year.

Operation

DURING the next thirty years, with the canal isolated from effective competition, there were few events of note. Indeed, in many years no committee meetings were held, just the annual General Assembly.

As with many canals, water supplies were a continuing problem. A reservoir had been constructed at Wombridge by Houghton and Ford in 1794; in 1797 this was supplemented by a second reservoir at Wombridge. (It is not clear which of these, somewhat reduced in size, is now known as 'Middle Pool'.) These proved inadequate, so a site just over 20 acres in extent was bought in 1803 and Trench Pool constructed – this survives, and is still the responsibility of the Canal & River Trust despite not now serving a canal. In addition, an agreement was made to take waste water from the Donnington Wood Company which drained its ironstone and coal mines by means of an underground level.

Shortly after the canal opened an ice-boat was purchased, and some time later a formal policy was made for icy conditions: the canal was to be kept open until the cost of ice-breaking in the week exceeded the expected tonnage income for the week. However, in 1821 it was resolved that in future the canal company would not incur any expense in ice-breaking, the committee hoping that the traders would provide a sufficient supply of coals before the frost set in.

A second boat was bought in 1805 – this one for use by the committee and the Agent.

The towpath through the tunnel was removed in 1819. No reason is given in the minutes, but as it was made of wood it had probably rotted during its 22 years of use.

In 1819, William Lawrence was appointed Clerk at a fee of 40 guineas a year following the resignation of Egerton Leeke, who had held that office since the canal company was formed. Seven years later Lawrence resigned and was replaced by Henry Morris Junior.

A significant new trade started in 1820, conveying coal to Shrewsbury Gas Works, which had been built canalside. From 1828 to 1841 there was a coal mine close to the canal three-quarters of a mile south of Uffington. The mine failed, the

Locks with guillotine gates.

The older style lock *(left)* had a counter-balance weight suspended over the forebay of the lock behind the gate and the two wheels on the top of the superstructure were parallel with the lock. The later style *(right)* had an iron counter-balance weight in a well beside the gate and the wheels were at right angles to the lock.

Left: **Shucks Lock, c.1935.** *Shrewsbury & Newport Canals Trust*
Right: **Eyton Upper Lock, c.1954.** *Railway & Canal Historical Society*

lessee going bankrupt, but the brick and tile works on the site continued for the rest of the century.

Connection to the national canal network

THE Shrewsbury Canal was not destined to be isolated from the main canal network permanently. As will be discussed in Chapter 8, the Birmingham & Liverpool Junction Canal (BLJC) was originally intended to have a branch to join the end of the Donnington Wood Canal at Pave Lane but in 1826 its committee reconsidered the matter and opted instead for a branch from Norbury Junction through Newport to meet the Shrewsbury Canal at Wappenshall.

The Shrewsbury Canal's committee endorsed this idea, and set about considering implications for its own canal. The BLJC was a conventional narrow canal, taking boats up to 7ft wide and 72ft long, whereas the Shrewsbury Canal was designed for tub-boats, 6ft 4in. wide and 20ft long. For boats off the national network (referred to in the minutes as 'long boats') to reach Shrewsbury it would be necessary to widen the two guillotine-gated locks at Eyton and to ensure the width of all bridges at water level was adequate. Longdon Aqueduct had been built with a trough 9ft wide to allow water to pass freely by the sides of loaded boats but was only 3ft deep; the maximum draught of boats was therefore 2ft 9in. compared with the 3ft 4in. maximum on the BLJC (itself somewhat shallow by national standards). This constraint meant that fully-loaded narrow boats could get no further than Wappenshall Junction. Now that the towpath had been removed, Berwick Tunnel was wide enough.

Henry Williams estimated that the cost of altering the locks and bridges would not exceed £1,000, and the extra income which would be received would give an ample return. The works were started in 1831, at least eight bridges needing alterations, and were completed by 1833. Williams was instructed to borrow a narrow boat loaded with 20 tons to check that the clearances were adequate but he probably never did this because of the difficulty of getting one there.

Delays building the connecting canal meant that narrow boats from the national network did not reach Shrewsbury until 2 March 1835. A committee of inspection later that year found that although the width at water level was sufficient, the passage of boats through bridges at Withington, Longdon and Long Lane would be eased if the width of the towpath were reduced.

Chapter 4 : The Shrewsbury Canal

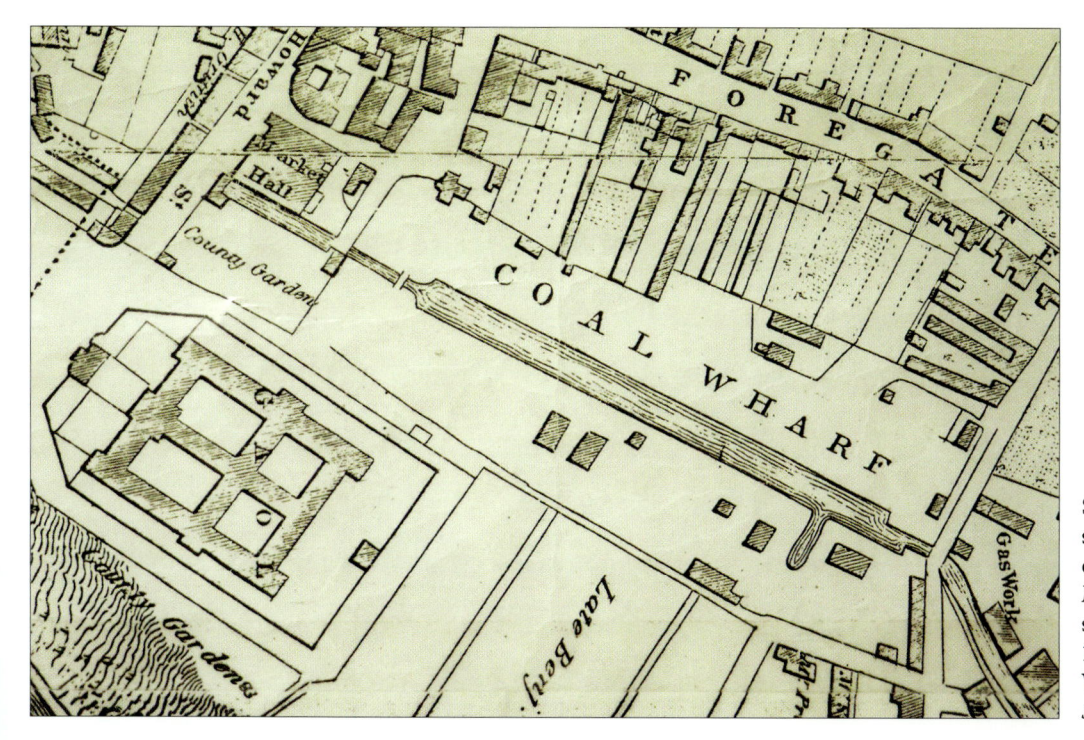

Shrewsbury Basin soon after the construction of the Market Hall, as shown in John Wood's 1838 map. West is at the top.
Shropshire Archives

William Hazledine, who a few years earlier had taken a 21-year lease of part of the wharf at Shrewsbury and erected a range of warehouses, made a side cut there to enable 70ft-long boats to turn. (Tub-boats, which were rectangular, could work in either direction without turning, of course.)

Some, perhaps all, of Hazledine's facilities were assigned to William Griffiths in 1836. That year Griffiths' market hall, later known as the Buttermarket, opened as a rival to the Corporation's market. He now extended the canal basin to alongside the market, and built a footbridge over the extension. Griffiths was at the time the Governor of Shrewsbury Gaol, but was later dismissed because of his outside activities.[3]

Staff changes

In October 1837 Henry Williams, by then aged 84, resigned as Agent & General Superintendent after working for the company for over forty years. It was decided to split his job, John Hewitt of Ketley being appointed as Tonnage Clerk at £70 a year, and John Beech of Pontcysyllte being appointed Engineer & General Superintendent of the Canal and Works, to be paid £80 in his first year, £90 in his second and £100 in his third.

Beech was only 21 years old and had been Tonnage Clerk at Pontcysyllte on the Ellesmere & Chester Canal, so was not an obvious choice for an engineering role. As well as being responsible for the state of repair of the canal and the sufficiency of water supply, he was responsible for supervising the workmen and controlling the materials used. He also had to check the weight of laden boats and the tonnage declared when he suspected under-payment of tolls.

Perhaps because of his inexperience – or perhaps because the committee members thought that Henry Williams had been too dominant in his job – it was made very clear that Beech would be allowed little independence. The committee was to meet monthly in future, Beech was to attend and submit a statement of works to be done and materials to be used, and then to do 'no works but such are of immediate necessity' without the committee's approval.

However, Beech must have been found particularly satisfactory, as his annual pay was increased to £180 in 1842.

Engineering developments

The last major issue on which Williams had advised was the widening of the canal from Wappenshall Junction up to Trench, which included nine locks. Obviously it was desirable to avoid the inconvenience and cost of transhipment but it was felt that only the part of the iron trade which entered below the incline would benefit, whereas most of the trade actually entered above the incline. In 1836 it was therefore decided not to go ahead.

Two years later this was also to be Beech's first major issue. He reported that widening a lock would cost just under £200. One of the leading ironmasters, James Foster, who had the ironworks at Wombridge, put forward a case showing that there would be a reasonable return if the locks were widened; Beech investigated, and thought that the extra water usage would mean the construction of an additional reservoir. This was enough to deter the committee.

The extra traffic brought some operational issues. William Hazledine, who operated tub-boats carrying coal to Shrewsbury, complained that boats blocked the canal at Wappenshall Junction and 'that the passage through the tunnel is obstructed by the long boats lying therein', though why any boat should stop there is not obvious. This led to the following unworkable resolution concerning the tunnel:

> That no boat shall be permitted on any pretence to be therein but shall proceed straight through provided always that where two boats shall have entered the tunnel at the same time the party which shall have first passed the centre of the tunnel shall proceed and the other party shall return so as to allow the other to pass where both are laden but where one train is unladen such train shall turn back.

John Beech suggested improvements to the guillotine gates of the locks which were adopted when repairs to gates became necessary. Over the years all but three gates were altered. Of the two which do survive, Hadley Park Lock (alongside the Silkin Way) has the original design and Turnip Lock (the next one south) is as rebuilt.

Beech recommended changes to the incline, replacing the timber sleepers by stone and, more fundamentally, using edge rails instead of plateway rails – in other words, the flanges were to be on the wheels of the trolley in normal railway style instead of on the rails. The committee authorised an experiment, but the changes were not effected until 1848. The ropes used on the incline were lasting less than two years, so the purchase of two wire ropes, each 300 yards long and ¾in. diameter, from Newall & Co. of Dundee was approved.

The engine of the inclined plane also needed to be replaced. Quotations were obtained from five companies and that of the Coalbrookdale Company was accepted. The high pressure steam engine on the Cornish plan, capable of providing up to 25 horsepower, cost £400; setting it up and repairing the machinery and the incline cost a further £576. A further replacement was a new iron carriage for the incline, purchased from the Coalbrookdale Company for £90.

Trade and tonnage

THE Act specified a maximum tonnage of 2*d* a mile on everything conveyed but in 1797 the General Assembly decided the rate for coal, the principal item carried, should be 1½*d* a mile. As an experiment it was decided that the tonnage on coal should be reduced to one penny a mile from April to September 1798, representatives of the three principal firms – William Reynolds on behalf of the Ketley and Hadley Companies, John Bishton on behalf of the Snedshill Company and Thomas Morris on behalf of the Marquess of Stafford & Company – having undertaken to pass on the reduction to the customer and in addition reduce the cost by 4*d* per ton on top coals and 1*d* per ton on others. This may have been a public relations gesture, or possibly it was a way of increasing summer sales. A third possibility is that it was partly retaliation against the road hauliers who were still carrying coal to Shrewsbury. This is hinted at when Egerton Leeke, the Clerk, reported that he had taken legal action against people who were using more horses in their teams on the Watling Street turnpike road than was permitted by the general Highways & Turnpike Act. Whatever the reason, the rate for coals reverted to the maximum amount of 2*d* a mile after just two summers.

In the winter of 1799 *Eddowe's Salopian Journal* complained that 'the hopes of being benefited by water conveyance have been so far from being realised that the town pays two to three shillings per ton more than it did before'.[4]

A curious decision was 'That Mr William Reynolds be permitted to carry all goods, wares and merchandises (except coals, bricks, timber, slates, tiles and cinders) on the canal for the space of twelve months from the 25th day of March next [1800] free of tonnage.' No explanation was given – could it have been in recognition of the engineering services he had rendered without charge?

Of wider benefit, especially to landowners, was the decision 'That limestone do pass on the canal from the 1st day of October to the 1st day of April free of tonnage (except the tonnage on the inclined plane) provided it be burnt within one hundred yards of the banks of the canal.' This was repeated for several years.

The tonnage rate for coal and iron continued at its statutory maximum level for a long time, which was much resented, particularly by the residents of Shrewsbury. In January 1841, when coal had become scarce in the town because the canal was iced over, it was reported in the *Shrewsbury Chronicle* that the 'extraordinary efforts' of Joseph Bleadon of Horton Wood brought 500 tons to Hazledine's wharf at his personal expense. He had employed nine horses and eighteen men and boys to bring 40 or 50 boats, which in ordinary times would have been brought by a single man and horse. (The exact figures are implausible, but that's a detail!) It was said that the canal proprietors 'refused to subscribe one shilling' towards the cost of ice-breaking, despite charging 2*d* per ton a mile.

In 1843 a petition was sent by the leading east Shropshire industrialists – William Horton on behalf of the Lilleshall Company, John Horton of Snedshill Ironworks, Beriah Botfield of Hinkshay and Stirchley, James Foster of Wombridge and Madeley Court, Abraham Darby of Coalbrookdale and Horsehay, and the Ketley Company – complaining about the high tonnage charges, particularly on coal, and claiming that if the charges were reduced much more would be carried.

The immediate reaction of the committee was to assert that even if the whole toll was taken off, sales of coal would not materially increase unless the price of coal at the pits was considerably reduced. It would not therefore reduce the tonnage charged until it became convinced that the canal company would not be worse off.

The following summer it was more conciliatory, offering to recommend a reduction in tonnage on coal of a farthing or a half-penny a ton if the coal masters would reduce the price at Shrewsbury by 2*s*.6*d* a ton. The coal masters must have agreed,

Chapter 4 : The Shrewsbury Canal

as at the General Assembly in November 1844 the tonnage on coal and coke was reduced by ½d a ton. The tonnage on iron was unchanged, however. This exchange demonstrates how the changing pattern of ownership mentioned earlier affected the policies of the canal company.

One traffic which proved unwelcome was gunpowder for the lead mines to the west of Shrewsbury. On 29 June 1839 a large quantity was landed at Tilston, Smith & Co.'s wharf at Shrewsbury. Whilst the waggon to convey it to the Bog Mine was being loaded, a nearby chimney caught fire and burning soot fell on a canvas sheet which was covering the casks containing nearly a ton of gunpowder, setting one alight. William Mason, the warehouseman, climbed onto the waggon, tore the canvas off and removed the burning cask and rolled it in some standing water; he next extinguished the fire completely by pouring a bucket of water over it. He then went back onto the waggon and turned over all the casks, checking that there was no more fire. Munslow, the waggoner, put water on the casks after they had been turned over. He then loaded the cask which had been on fire back onto the waggon and drove off.

The *Shrewsbury Chronicle*'s initial report gave the credit for rescuing the town 'from becoming a heap of ruins' to Munslow but three sworn affidavits said that it was Mason's courageous action which had prevented an explosion. A public subscription raised only £15. Munslow claimed a share, and it was a year and a half later before the Corporation decided that Mason should receive the full amount.[5]

Finance

The Act authorised the company to raise £50,000 by issuing shares of £100 each, and, if necessary, to raise a further £20,000. Calls totalling £100 had been made by January 1796, which proved insufficient. Of the options available – further calls on the original shares, a second share issue, or borrowing – it was decided to opt for further calls on the original shares. The preponderance of locally-owned shares made this the simplest solution. Thus further calls totalling £25 per share were made, the final call being made in May 1797. The canal must therefore have cost about £62,500, including land, buildings, legal, parliamentary and incidental expenses. Compared with many other 'Mania' canals, this was a relatively small over-spending.

The canal proved immediately successful, the first dividend being declared the following January. For most canals it was the General Assembly which declared the dividend, whereas initially for the Shrewsbury Canal it was the committee. For the first couple of decades the dividends were declared at irregular intervals; it was not until 1817 when the General Assembly took over the responsibility that dividends settled down to a regular pattern of being paid half-yearly – and at a rather higher rate than had previously been the norm. Between 1823 and 1835 the annual dividend was from £9 to £11 a share (equivalent to 7.2% to 8.8% on the sum originally invested). As a consequence of the extra trade brought because of the connection to the national canal network, in the period between 1836 and 1842 the dividend fluctuated between £13 and £16 (equivalent to 10.4% to 12.8%), dropping back to £10 a share (8%) thereafter.

One unusual feature in the 1793 Act was the charge authorised for traffic using the inclined plane: one penny a ton 'until the canal pays a dividend of eight per cent when this ... rate shall cease'. The dividend exceeded £10 a share (that is, exceeded 8% on the sum originally invested) in 1827, and the supplement for the inclined plane was duly withdrawn.

In January 1816 Thomas Eyton, a partner in the company's bank as well as frequent chairman of meetings of the company, committed suicide when it was about to be revealed that he had embezzled £300,000 in his role as Receiver General of Taxes for Shropshire. Trading at the bank ceased immediately as the property was seized by the government but when it was appreciated that the bank itself was solvent it resumed trading. The canal company was given a scare but did not lose any money.

Because no reserves had been built up, the money needed in 1832 and 1833 for the improvement works to make the canal suitable for narrow boats was borrowed from the company's bankers. The loan of £1,000 was repaid by the end of 1835 because income increased even more than had been forecast.

Sale of the company

In the summer of 1845 a letter was received from the Ellesmere & Chester Canal (ECC) stating that it proposed to convert its canal into a railway. The Shrewsbury Canal's committee recommended adopting the same policy; in addition to sending the ECC a copy of this resolution, it was sent to the Grand Junction, London & Birmingham and Great Western Railways and to the promoters of the Shrewsbury & Birmingham Railway, with the offer of all information and the invitation to visit to inspect the line. The ECC and the Shrewsbury & Birmingham Railway accepted the invitation,

Within a month of the original letter, the ECC made the offer of £150 per Shrewsbury Canal share, paid by conversion into the new railway stock. This offer, which subsequent events were to prove was excessively generous, was unanimously accepted by those attending the Special Assembly on 28 August 1845.

The sale was effected on the date that the Act creating the Shropshire Union was passed, 3 August 1846, and the final dividend was paid in January 1847.

Notes and references

The principal source for this chapter was the minutes of the Shrewsbury Canal (The National Archives: RAIL868).

1. Thomas Telford in Joseph Plymley, *General View of the Agriculture of Shropshire*, 1813, p.297; Barrie Trinder, *Barges and Bargemen*, 2005, pp.75–6
2. Thomas Telford in Joseph Plymley, *General View of the Agriculture of Shropshire*, 1813, p.300
3. Information from Alan Brisbourne
4. *Eddowe's Salopian Journal*, date not stated, as quoted in Charles Hadfield, *Canals of the West Midlands*, second edition 1969, p.163
5. *Shrewsbury Chronicle*, 12 July, 19 July & 2 August 1839 and 20 November 1840

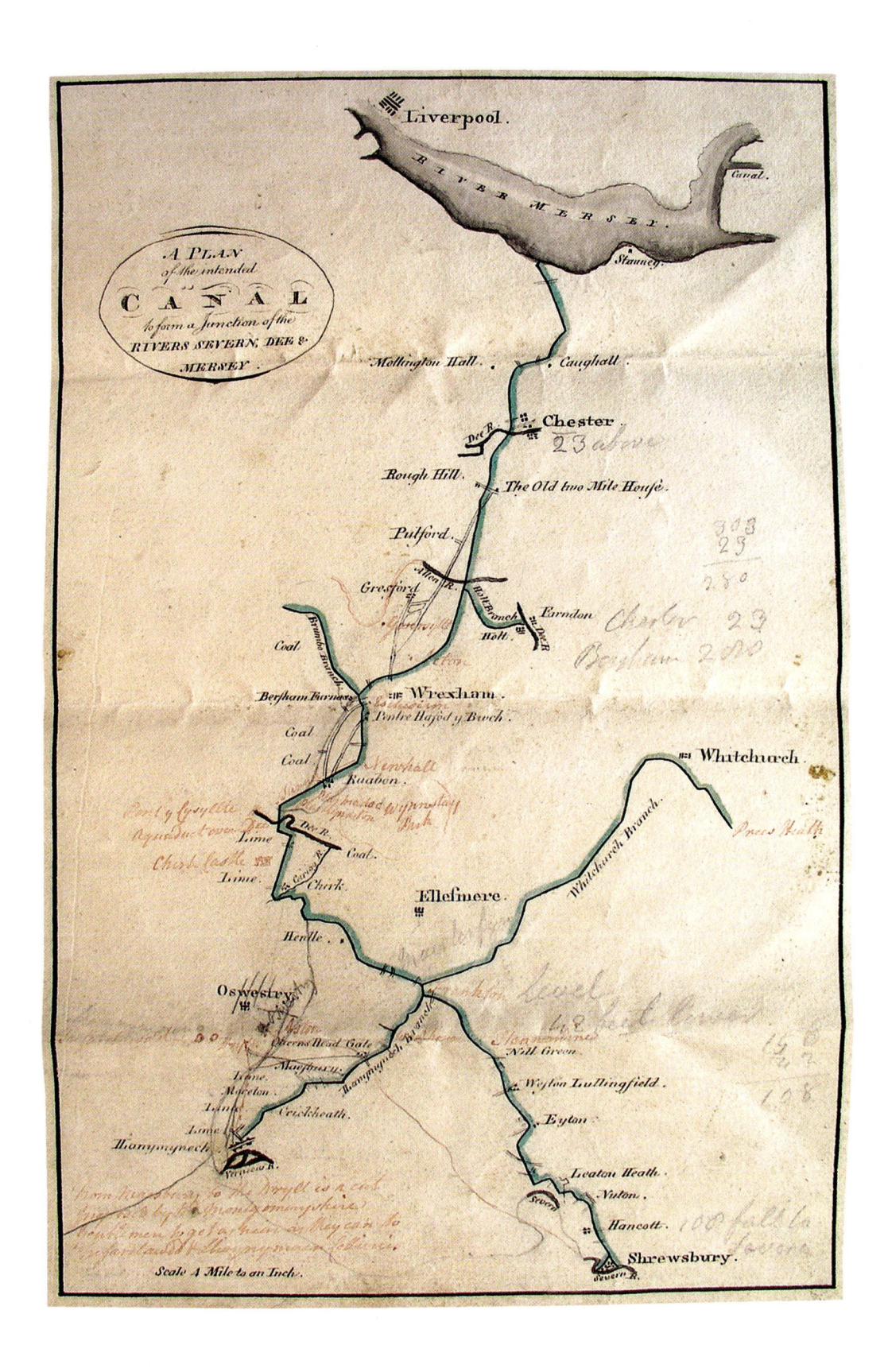

A PLAN of the intended CANAL to form a Junction of the RIVERS SEVERN, DEE & MERSEY.

Scale A Mile to an Inch.

5

The Ellesmere Canal

The origins

IN 1789 or 1790 three north-west Shropshire land-owners, John Kynaston MP, John Robert Lloyd and William Mostyn Owen MP, conceived the project which was to become the Ellesmere Canal. Kynaston's estate was at Hardwick, about a mile and a half west of Ellesmere; Lloyd's at Aston, two and a half miles south-east of Oswestry; and Owen's at Woodhouse, four and a half miles east of Oswestry. Owen also owned an estate in Montgomeryshire and, more significantly, the Plas Kynaston estate at Cefn Mawr in the parish of Ruabon, where there were coal mines and the beginnings of an iron industry, despite the inadequacy of the transport system.

They canvassed other land-owners who might be interested, notably George Herbert (2nd Earl of Powis of the second creation), his nephew Edward Clive (who later became the 1st Earl of Powis of the third creation) and Rowland Hunt of Boreatton Hall near Baschurch. Together they commissioned John Duncombe, an Oswestry surveyor, to make a preliminary survey.

The first formal meeting of the promoters was held on 28 June 1791, when Kynaston, Lloyd and Owen, together with others whose names were not recorded, met at the White Horse Inn at Overton to consider promoting a canal from the river Severn to the Mersey. Duncombe estimated the cost to be £100,000, assuming a canal 25ft wide on its surface, 16ft wide at the bottom and 5ft deep. These figures betray his inexperience: assuming the bottom width and depth as given, the surface width would be more like 36ft, with a commensurate increase in excavation and land purchase. It was decided to advertise in the local papers and make personal contacts with the principal landowners. Naturally, the Denbighshire industrialists began to take an active interest too, notably John Wilkinson of Bersham, Edward Rowland of Trevor and Richard Kirk of Ffrwd.

A further meeting was held at Ellesmere on 31 August, chaired by Rowland Hunt. The minutes of the meeting give two reasons why building the canal was desirable: it would benefit the landed and commercial interests of the country in general, and would pass through or near several extensive coal, lime and slate works. A third reason for the canal was identified at a public meeting at Shrewsbury, that of long distance communications. Shrewsbury's main transport route for goods was of course the river Severn to Worcester, Gloucester and Bristol – by then the Thames & Severn Canal had opened, giving a water route to the river Thames and hence to London. The proposed canal, it was thought, would be 'supplying the only link in the chain wanted to effect a direct communication from London to York'. More realistically, it was believed that it would benefit the town by providing a 'cheap and expeditious conveyance' to Chester, Liverpool and Manchester. It must be remembered that although France did not declare war on Great Britain until February 1793, relationships between the two countries were tense and an inland route between Bristol and Liverpool would be safer than the coastal route.

The meeting formally decided to go ahead with promoting a canal from Shrewsbury to the Mersey via Chirk and Ruabon, including a branch to Llanymynech, the site of limestone quarries. (The minute is not totally clear: it could have been that Chirk and Ruabon were to be reached by branches, though I think that less likely.) Further branches were contemplated to Wem and Whitchurch. Messrs Potts & Leeke of Chester were appointed solicitors. Duncombe was requested to make a further survey.

Incidentally, the canal seems to have been named the 'Ellesmere Canal' for no better reason than the company's meetings, subsequent to the first one, were held at Ellesmere – and that was probably because it was the most convenient place for the leading promoters to get to. It was certainly not the most important town served, nor did it indicate the geographical range of the project.

By the next meeting a fortnight later, an issue which was to vex the company for the next decade and more had emerged:

Map of Western route, published in 1793.
Canal & River Trust

The principal promoters of the Ellesmere Canal

Sir John Hill, 3rd baronet (1740–1824)

SIR JOHN HILL was the younger brother of Sir Richard Hill, 2nd baronet, of Hawkstone, and succeeded to the baronetcy on the death of his brother in 1808. He was a Whig MP for Shrewsbury 1784–96 and again 1805–06, though he was never active in Parliament. In the 1796 election he was defeated by William Hill of Attingham following an exceptionally expensive campaign.

John Hill chaired the first General Meeting of the Ellesmere Canal Company and many of its subsequent meetings (1793–1818).

His agreement to act as bondsman for Thomas Eyton, the Receiver General (for land tax) for Shropshire, cost him £5,000 when, following Eyton's suicide in 1816, it was discovered that the funds had been embezzled.

Hill lived at Prees Hall until the death of his brother, then moved to Hawkstone Hall. He was called 'the father of heroes', five of his sons, including Sir Rowland Hill (later the 1st Viscount Hill) having distinguished themselves in the Napoleonic wars; when he was presented at Court in 1815, the Regent informed him 'I am glad indeed to see the father of so many brave sons'. He was a typical country squire, still actively fox-hunting when he was 80. He died in 1824, 'easily and happily after scarcely one whole day's illness'.

Rowland Hunt (d.1811)

ROWLAND HUNT lived at Boreatton Hall, two miles south-west of Weston Lullingfields. He was a leading county magistrate, taking a special interest in prison administration. Hunt was one of the principal promoters of the Ellesmere Canal, owning ten shares and chairing various meetings (1794–1807). He gave the oration at the opening of the Pontcysyllte Aqueduct in 1805.
He was described as 'learned, judicious, and pious'.

Revd John Robert Lloyd (c.1758–1803)

REVD JOHN ROBERT LLOYD was successively rector of Whittington (1784–1801) and Selattyn (1785–1802), both near Oswestry. His residence was Aston Hall, 1 mile north-west of Queens Head. Much involved in county affairs, he was Mayor of Oswestry in 1795 and High Sheriff of Shropshire in 1787.

More a land-owner than a clergyman, he was given a Gold Medal by the Society of Arts for planting 60,000 oaks on his estate. He also kept a pack of harriers.

He was one of the people who met in 1789 to put forward the proposal which later became the Ellesmere Canal. He had ten shares in the Ellesmere Canal Company and chaired six meetings (1797–9).

William Mostyn Owen (c.1742–1795)
William Owen (1775–1845)

WILLIAM MOSTYN OWEN lived at Woodhouse (4½ miles east of Oswestry) but also owned Bryngwyn Hall (in Montgomeryshire, some 5 miles west of the Vyrnwy Aqueduct) and, of more significance for the history of the Ellesmere Canal, the Plas Kynaston estate at Cefn Mawr. He took the surname Owen when his mother inherited the Woodhouse estate following the death of her grandfather.

He was an MP for Montgomeryshire from 1774 until 1795. Although Owen was originally returned for the county on the interest of the Earl of Powis, he retained the seat from 1780 with the support of the rival interest of the Williams Wynn family, whose politics he shared. In 1789 he joined the Whig Club. He was a gambler and a big spender, mortgaging his assets when he got deeper into debt. The mortgage on Plas Kynaston reached £19,000, with multiple charges against the same property.

William Mostyn Owen was one of the people who met in 1789 to put forward the proposal which later became the Ellesmere Canal. He attended almost every meeting of the Ellesmere Canal committee until his shortly before his death, but never acted as chairman.

His son, William Owen succeeded in 1795 and had the task of sorting out his father's considerable debts. The Bryngwyn estate was sold in 1802; the Plas Kynaston estate was advertised for sale in 1813 and had been sold by 1819. He seems an honourable man; for example, he jointly stood bail for three miners who had been accused of rioting at Cefn Mawr. He occasionally attended meetings of the canal's committee from 1795. He married the sister of Thomas Crewe Dod of Edge, Cheshire, another committee member.

(Sir) John Kynaston (Powell) (1733–1822)

(SIR) JOHN KYNASTON (POWELL) of Hardwick (about a mile and a half west of Ellesmere) was the son of John Kynaston and Mary Powell; he added his mother's surname to his own in 1797. He was created a baronet in 1818. About 1800 he unsuccessfully revived a claim originally made in 1731 by his ancestor John Kynaston to the Barony of Grey de Powys.

He was returned nine times as an MP for Shropshire, sitting from 1784 to 1822, but never had to contest an election. Politically he was a Tory but he was always a back-bencher.

He chaired the meeting in 1789 which put forward the proposal which later became the Ellesmere Canal. He owned nine shares in the Ellesmere Canal Company and chaired various meetings (1796–1821).

John Kynaston was patron of Madeley Church, where Telford was employed to design the new church in about 1792.

He suffered bouts of ill-health after 1807. An obituary commended him for his integrity and urbanity.

should the main line of the canal be Duncombe's recommended line west of the river Dee, or should it be east of the Dee? The latter would be simpler, avoiding a high-level crossing of the river in the Trevor area and a further difficult crossing at Chester, but it relegated the mining and industrial area of Denbighshire to a long branch from Overton.

Back in April, even before the first formal meeting of the promoters, John Duncombe had attended a meeting of the committee of the Chester Canal and had shown the members there the draft plan, which was of course for the route west of the Dee. They noted that 'it does not appear (at present) that any opposition should be given by this Company ... and it may prove to be an advantage to this canal'. Later the Chester Canal's committee – and specifically Joseph Turner, who had not been present at the April meeting – came to realise that a route east of the Dee joining their canal outside the city would be positively advantageous to them, bringing both traffic and much-needed water.

At the meeting of the provisional committee of the Ellesmere Canal on 15 September 1791, a detailed scheme for the eastern route was put forward by Joseph Turner. This had a 'Colliery Branch' crossing the Dee on an aqueduct just below Overton Bridge, then locking up to the Ruabon coalfield and past Llangollen to Valle Crusis, serving the Oernant slate quarries, with an arm to Bersham, site of John Wilkinson's internationally renowned ironworks. As well as branches to Llanymynech and Whitchurch, a branch was suggested to serve Wem, perhaps continuing to the Whitchurch–Newport turnpike at Bletchley and to the vicinity of the Grinshill quarries. The cost of the main line was estimated at £90,648, plus £36,310 for the branch across the Dee into Denbighshire and £44,140 for the other branches, a total of £171,098.

Joseph Turner also provided an analysis of the likely trades and forecast the annual income:

		£
Coal from Ruabon area to the various towns	50,000 tons	3,750
Lime, limestone, and slack & coal to burn it	30,000 tons	2,250
Slate	10 million slates	1,250
Pig, cast and bar iron	2,000 tons	250
Freestone mainly from Grinshill	2,000 tons	167
Smelted lead and lead ore	1,000 tons	167
General merchandise to & from Shrewsbury		4,000
Produce to & from Montgomeryshire		2,250
Whitchurch Branch		500
Wem, Bletchley & Grinshill Branch		500
Salt & sundries trade on the Wirral		250
Other		121
Passage boats		1,000
		16,455

His proposals were approved unanimously. Did the Denbighshire promoters realise the disadvantage of being relegated to a branch? The minutes of the Provisional Committee do not record who was present, so perhaps their views were never put. John Duncombe, assisted by Joseph Turner and his cousin William Turner, a Whitchurch entrepreneur, were instructed to make a detailed survey and identify the landowners, preparatory to application to Parliament.

A prospectus was prepared which showed the canal and its branches to be 115 miles in length, with a summit level of 45½ miles forming a reservoir which meant that water needed for locks would be 'a mere trifle'. It was predicted that the traffic would give 'a fund of such magnitude to pay an interest of ten per cent in the first instance'; however as the forecast annual income was only 9.6% of the capital cost, no allowance seems to have been made for maintenance and other running costs.

The evidence to Parliament would require greater engineering expertise than Duncombe and the Turners. At the November 1791 meeting of the Provisional Committee it was agreed to obtain the advice of 'an engineer of approved character and experience'– their preferred choice being William Jessop, at that time generally regarded as the country's leading waterways engineer. He was asked to report not only on the line which had been approved at the previous meeting but also on the other lines which had been proposed.

Jessop made a preliminary report nine weeks later but his full report was not received until the following August, presumably because he was so busy elsewhere. He considered that the coal and lime trades were far more important than the general mercantile trade, so expressed a strong preference for the route to the west of the Dee which served the industrial area well. Furthermore, if the eastern route were adopted, coal for Chester and Shrewsbury would have to take such a circuitous journey that the cost at the towns would not be significantly reduced. Indeed, he doesn't seem to have carried out any detailed engineering assessment of the eastern route despite it being at that time the committee's preferred option. Jessop's

> ### John Duncombe (d.1810)
>
> JOHN DUNCOMBE, a surveyor from Oswestry, made the preliminary survey for the Ellesmere Canal in 1789 and was involved in subsequent surveys leading to the Ellesmere Canal Act of 1793. He worked part-time for the new company until 1796 when he was appointed Engineer. With Telford's absence in Scotland for much of the year from 1800, Duncombe bore the major share of the supervisory work on the Ellesmere Canal. In 1806 he joined Telford's team in Scotland as Superintendent of Roads.
> This move was a disaster for Duncombe, as, whether through a lack of ability or the problems of old age, Telford became increasingly critical of his output and stopped his salary in 1809, paying him instead by the completed mile. The following year he died in prison. Telford wrote to a friend: 'I am quite vexed about the old fool – his dying will not be a matter of regret but in a jail in Inverness is shocking.'

route, which was similar to that which had been surveyed by Duncombe, served the mineral and industrial areas well and had a summit level some 17 miles long, 310ft above sea level, through the upland area, assuming the aqueduct at Pontcysyllte was built at the full height. However, it had the disadvantage of a tunnel at Ruabon 4,600yds long – if built this would have been the second longest canal tunnel in Britain – and another tunnel 1,236yds long under the Chirk Castle estate. There was to be a third, shorter, tunnel between Weston Lullingfields and Shrewsbury. Jessop felt that although it was likely that his line could be improved, rather than wait a year it would be best to apply for an Act in the forthcoming Parliamentary session and to seek an amending Act in a later session. The total cost was estimated at £196,898 if a lower level crossing of the Dee at Pontcysyllte was adopted, with locks either side; £210,612 if the aqueduct was to be at full height.

The committee considered Jessop's report and correspondence from John Wilkinson, and agreed with the recommendations for the western route and for immediate application to Parliament. Two thousand £100 shares would be issued; the original subscribers had already put in £12,000 and £28,000 was reserved for landowners, leaving a further £160,000 to be sought.

Reserving shares for landowners was a common practice: it was expected that they would be more sympathetic towards the project if they were sharing in the profits. At that time landowners had a disproportionate influence in Parliament. Nevertheless, they still would have to pay the full amount for their shares.

Advertisements were placed in the local, Liverpool and London newspapers inviting potential subscribers to a meeting on 10 September at the Royal Oak Inn, Ellesmere.[1] This proved to be an embarrassing success with over £950,000 being offered by almost 1,500 investors, despite proxy applications not being permitted and a 5% deposit being required. The *Shrewsbury Chronicle* reported:

> So great was the influx of navigation speculators in this town, from the various parts of the kingdom, on Sunday evening last, that three guineas were offered for three beds by some gentlemen who came in very late, every house being filled.[2]

However, it is not obvious why this particular canal scheme was so popular. No prospectus seems to have been issued – the advertisement for the meeting merely said that Mr Jessop's report would be laid before the public – so there were no forecasts of costs and revenues.

The 'Canal Mania' was then at its height, a typical comment in a newspaper being, 'Navigation shares are so universally sought after, that a holder of that kind of property may consider himself truly fortunate'.[3] This message was reinforced by lists of canal shares then standing at a premium. Presumably many people were 'stagging' the share issue, on the assumption that they could subsequently sell the part-paid shares for a quick profit.

Of the 1,240 subscribers named in the Act, a remarkable number were from Birmingham and the towns of the east Midlands, principally Leicester, Derby and Market Harborough. Their local newspapers, to a far greater extent than those at Liverpool, Manchester and Leeds for example, reported crowded subscription meetings and spectacular prices commanded by canal stock and scrip, thus inspiring their readers to apply for shares in canals well distant from their homes. The *Derby Mercury*, for example, referred to the proposed Ellesmere Canal only once, but did so in glowing terms, calling it:

> a navigation inferior, we believe, to none other in the kingdom. The counties of Cumberland, Lancaster,

---

William Jessop (1745–1814)

WILLIAM JESSOP was the leading civil engineer of the generation after John Smeaton and before Thomas Telford. He had trained with Smeaton then became his principal assistant and, as a consequence, Secretary of the Society of Civil Engineers. During the early 1770s he worked as consultant for navigations and canals in Ireland, Yorkshire and Lincolnshire. Unsure of the direction he wanted his career to take, he invested in several businesses and in 1778, in partnership with James Pinkerton, contracted for the section of the Chester Canal from Beeston to Nantwich.

After that he concentrated on waterways engineering, including a proposal to improve the river Severn south of Coalbrookdale by building 16 locks, giving a 4ft depth of water in the driest seasons; however because of opposition from traders and landowners, it did not obtain its Act. Before his engagement by the Ellesmere Canal in 1791, he had been employed as principal engineer for many other waterways schemes, including the Trent and Soar Navigations, the Grand Canal (Ireland), and the Selby, Cromford, Grantham and Basingstoke Canals.

During the Canal Mania period of 1789 to 1796 he appeared before Parliament in connection with 27 schemes, far more than any other engineer, including such important projects as the Grand Junction and Rochdale Canals. These were all broad canals, the only narrow canal with which he was associated being the Ellesmere. He later worked with Telford on the Caledonian Canal – this was a joint appointment, but with Jessop being paid a higher daily rate, showing that he was regarded as the senior. His greatest project was the creation of the West India Docks at a cost of some £1¼ million. A cautious engineer, he had a reputation for avoiding the expense and delay of tunnels, which makes it more surprising that he initially recommended a route which included a tunnel well over two miles long at Ruabon.

The impression is that Jessop was a conscientious self-effacing individual, a contented family man with wider interests than engineering. A contemporary said that he was free of all professional rivalship and that 'his proceedings were free from all pomp and mysticism'.

Chapter 5: The Ellesmere Canal

Chester, Salop, Worcester, Gloucester, Hereford, Monmouth, and Somerset, being immediately interested in it; and, more remotely, almost every other inland navigation in England.[4]

This reveals what was the crucial misapprehension of investors, who assumed that a 'trunk' canal linking rivers would be particularly lucrative, whereas in reality local needs were far more important.

Most canal companies had provisions to favour local investors; the Ellesmere did not, perhaps another reason why it was particularly favoured by Midlands investors. This caused problems for the Ellesmere later on when it proved difficult to get some of the subscribers to pay their calls, but the subscribers were the ultimate losers as no dividend was paid until 1814.

Some confusion was caused because also on the same day in Ellesmere subscriptions were opened for a canal on the eastern route. According to the newspaper report, some people signed up for this thinking they were investing in the western scheme. A week later an advertisement signed by Joseph Turner announced a General Meeting of subscribers to the 'Eastern Canal'. This was to be held at Newport, where their solicitors were based, not at Chester or anywhere associated with its proposed line. The *Shrewsbury Chronicle* later reported:

> We have received two or three paragraphs respecting the meeting of the subscribers to the Eastern Canal at Newport, containing the resolutions of the said meeting; but as they differ widely from each other ... we would not wish to mislead our readers.[5]

The committee of the Ellesmere (western) Canal was more organised. It arranged the refund of the excess subscriptions, then set about reviewing the route of the canal. By taking the canal at a higher level at Ruabon the tunnel could be avoided, though this meant searching for a new source of water. A branch to near Whitchurch was added to the scheme, and a survey carried out for a route to connect this to the Chester Canal near Tattenhall.

During the winter of 1792–93 negotiations took place to unite the two schemes. The promoters of the western route offered to include in their Bill a branch from Welshampton to near Tattenhall, providing that the promoters of the eastern route proved to the Committee of the House of Commons that Standing Orders for the eastern route had been complied with. Eastern route subscribers would then become subscribers to the united concern. Negotiations became sticky, and on 11 January 1793 the committee unanimously resolved that although a link between the Whitchurch Branch and the Chester Canal would be advantageous, the Bill before Parliament could not be extended to accommodate it. It was another month before the eastern route's promoters formally agreed. Subscribers to the eastern route to a total of £40,000 were admitted. None of the leading promoters of the eastern route ever became directors of the Ellesmere Canal.

It was realised that uniting the schemes and adding branches would increase the cost of the project, so the share capital to be authorised was increased from £300,000 to £400,000.

Having placated the opposition, the passage through Parliament was relatively straightforward, and the Ellesmere Canal's Act was signed on 30 April 1793.

Messrs Potts & Leeke were confirmed as solicitors and Charles Potts was appointed Clerk. William Reynolds and Thomas Eyton, bankers of Shrewsbury, were appointed as joint Treasurers – as described earlier, the former was heavily involved in the tub-boat canals of East Shropshire, and both were leading promoters of the Shrewsbury Canal.

Thomas Telford: 'General Agent'

ADVERTISEMENTS were placed for a person 'qualified to superintend the works as a general overlooker, to keep accounts and pay workmen' who would work full time on the canal.

Thomas Telford, a well-connected Shrewsbury 'architect' (as he described himself) who had in 1787 become Shropshire's County Surveyor of Public Works, wrote to the canal company proposing himself as 'general agent, surveyor, engineer, architect and overlooker of the canal and clerk to the committee ... and, when appointed, to make drawings and submit them to the consideration and correction of Mr Jessop or their principal engineer'. This was a wider role than that envisaged in the advertisement – in modern terms it would be 'Chief Executive'. The committee accepted Telford's offer, except that appointing him Clerk would need the approval of the General Assembly of Proprietors.

Telford's autobiography, written almost forty years after the event, implies that, rather than applying for the post of General Agent, he was invited to take it:

> The committee of management, composed chiefly of county magistrates, having, at the quarter sessions and other public meetings, observed that the county works were conducted to their satisfaction, were pleased to propose my undertaking the conduct of this extensive and complicated work; and feeling in myself a stronger disposition for executing works of importance and magnitude than for details of house architecture, I did not hesitate to accept their offer.[6]

A letter written by Telford at the time confirms this sequence of events and gives more details:

> I was last Monday appointed sole agent, architect and engineer to the canal which is to join the Mersey, the Dee and the Severn ... You will be surprised that I have not mentioned this to you before, but the fact is that I had no idea of any such thing until an application was made to me by some leading gentlemen, though many others had made much interest for the place.[7]

The meeting which appointed Telford was chaired by John Hill, one of the two MPs for Shrewsbury. The other Shrewsbury MP, and Hill's political ally, was William Pulteney, Telford's patron – indeed, the man who had brought him to Shrewsbury.

The person most disappointed by the committee's decision to appoint Telford was William Turner, who had done many of the early surveys and had hoped to get the job of general overlooker. He wrote to William Jessop (who, contrary to normal practice, had not been consulted) explaining what had happened and asking for his opinion. Jessop's reply would better have been addressed directly to the committee than via a disgruntled candidate. He stated:

> I think as you do that no one man can properly undertake the actual direction of the whole of so extensive a concern as a man of art [in other words, engineer], and at the same time manage the accompts [accounts].
>
> I have always advised every person who had engaged in the direction of the mechanical part of a business of this kind not to divide his attention by interfering as an accomptant [accountant] because he may have full employment in the former if he makes best use of his time; and others better qualified for the latter than he probably can be may have full employment also. I am quite unacquainted with Mr Telford and his character; from the little acquaintance I have had with you I wish you might have had the direction of that part of the business which you have proposed to undertake, and I do not think that the terms you have offered to undertake it for are unreasonable. If the committee should consult me on this question, I should tell them so.[8]

This letter was considered by the committee at its meeting just before the General Assembly on 30 October 1793. Nevertheless the latter confirmed Telford's appointment as 'general agent, surveyor, engineer, architect and overlooker of the works' but declined to appoint him Clerk as well, retaining Charles Potts in that post.

Katherine Plymley, an acquaintance of Thomas Telford, wrote in her diary on 5 November 1793 that he had visited the family that day and that he 'has just received a very advantageous new appointment, the entire management of the canal that is to form a junction between the Severn, Dee and Mersey'.[9]

Telford's and Jessop's roles

OVER the years, the minutes of the Ellesmere Canal Company were not consistent about Telford's job title. He was usually described as 'General Agent' but occasionally as 'General Agent and Surveyor', 'General Surveyor and Agent', 'General Agent and Engineer', or 'Surveyor'. He was never referred to solely as 'Engineer', though this was how he was described (presumably by himself, or at least with his approval) in a schedule of the dimensions of the Pontcysyllte and Chirk Aqueducts which accompanied the official opening of the former in 1805.

William Jessop was never formally appointed consulting engineer, but it is clear that he was the person responsible for advising the company about the best course of action with regards to the most important engineering issues. The minutes referred to Jessop as 'Principal Engineer' on three occasions but he does not seem to have attended many General Assembly or General Committee meetings.[10]

The minutes contain just one hint that the Committee members were not totally satisfied with him: in July 1795 it was resolved 'that Mr Jessop be desired to report his opinion to this Committee upon his own responsibility and from such information as he may be satisfied is correct'. Were they hinting that he was too reliant on others – and, if so, whom?

The Ellesmere Canal required several Acts of Parliament. Jessop gave evidence for the initial Act of 1793 and for subsequent Acts of 1796 (two), 1801 and 1804. The 1793 Act was before Telford was appointed, of course. Jessop was assisted by Thomas Denson (John Duncombe's clerk and eventual successor) at one of the 1796 hearings, and by Telford

---

Thomas Telford (1757–1834)

THOMAS TELFORD was one of Britain's greatest civil engineers. Born in Eskdale, Dumfriesshire, he trained as a stonemason, working in Edinburgh, London and Portsmouth. He supervised various building projects but his ambition was to be an architect. At the invitation of Sir William Pulteney, who hailed from the same part of Dumfriesshire, he relocated to Shrewsbury where he restored the Castle for Pulteney, led the first excavations at Wroxeter Roman town and designed the churches of St Mary's, Bridgnorth, and St Michael's, Madeley. He was appointed County Surveyor for Shropshire, a fee-earning rather than a salaried post, the responsibilities including county bridges, of which there were just eight. He held this post for the rest of his life; by the time he died there were more than 40 county bridges.

In 1793 he was appointed 'General Agent, Surveyor, Engineer, Architect and Overlooker' of the Ellesmere Canal; after 1805 he continued as consulting engineer to the Ellesmere, later Ellesmere & Chester, Canal. Following the death of Josiah Clowes, he completed the Shrewsbury Canal. Towards the end of his career he was consulting engineer to the Birmingham & Liverpool Junction Canal.

For the next couple of decades from 1800 he worked extensively in Scotland, being responsible for making in excess of 1,000 miles of roads, 1,000 bridges and culverts, 40 harbours, 70 churches and (with William Jessop until 1813) the construction of the Caledonian Canal. Other major schemes were the Holyhead Road west of Shrewsbury including the Menai Bridge, the straightening of the main line of the Birmingham Canal, and the Göta Canal in Sweden.

From 1817 Telford was the engineering adviser to the Exchequer Bill Loan Commissioners which lent money for the construction of canals, docks, railways and other beneficial works. In 1820 he was elected to be the first President of the Institution of Civil Engineers.

Chapter 5 : The Ellesmere Canal

and Denson at the other. In 1804 Jessop was responsible for proving the engineering aspects and the estimate of cost, whilst Telford gave evidence on the need for the project and the financial position of the company – this is exactly the division of duties one would normally expect between the Principal Engineer and the General Agent.

The surviving formal progress reports made to the General Assembly meetings were presented by Jessop in July 1795 and January 1800, and by Telford in November 1801 and June 1802. In October 1803 Jessop was asked to inspect the whole canal and provide a written report but there is no mention in the minutes of the report being received.[11] Telford, as General Agent, wrote other formal reports, such as the circular to shareholders in October 1795.

The minutes sometimes distinguished between what Telford was expected to do personally and what he should leave to others. The actual making of surveys was sometimes explicitly delegated, most often to John Duncombe, but on one occasion Telford and Duncombe were asked jointly to report. John Duncombe was described as 'engineer'; he became a salaried employee in April 1795.

Telford generally let construction contracts and settled issues concerning them; on one occasion these were assigned to Jessop. Telford was in charge of the section built by direct labour between Chirk and Pontcysyllte aqueducts, 'agreeable to the directions in Mr Jessop's report'. He also let contracts for building boats, making bricks, erecting a windmill (though this was not proceeded with), constructing limekilns and for a pumping engine powered by steam. He often met and negotiated with landowners or their agents or with other canal companies and sometimes acted as a valuer, but at other times these duties were undertaken by named committee members or by outside valuers.

Occasionally Telford was specifically named in connection with purely administrative affairs: to find a convenient office and committee room at Ellesmere; to arrange the payment of interest on calls; to 'make a circuit' to collect money due from shareholders, register stock transfers and answer questions; to provide a list of shareholders who were in arrears; to place an advertisement concerning calls on shares; and to calculate interest due.

Certainly in the earlier years, much of Telford's energy was devoted to the purely management issue of resolving conflicts. In a letter he referred to the 'violent agitations ... and often clashing interests to contend with or reconcile'. Once part of the canal was open he had to spend time developing the trade; again he mentioned dealing with 'many contending and clashing interests'.[12]

Telford's autobiography, written towards the end of his long life, minimises Jessop's role. In the context of the Ellesmere Canal, the only mention of him is: 'in regard to earth work, I had the advantage of consulting Mr William Jessop, an experienced engineer, on whose advice I never failed to set a proper value'.[13] There is no hint that Jessop had wider responsibilities.

In his oration at the opening of Pontcysyllte Aqueduct, Rowland Hunt, who had been closely involved since 1791, gave a brief history of the canal project, acknowledging the contribution of the various people involved. He said:

> We will mention, as concerned in the scientific and practical construction of the works, our General Agent, Mr Telford; who, with the advice and judgement of our eminent and much respected Engineer, Mr Jessop, invented, and with unabating diligence carried the whole into execution.[14]

As a confirmation of the extent of Jessop's involvement, the accounts show that he was paid £1,103.18s for 'sundry surveys, journeys, inspections, plans, estimates, and for attending Parliament at several times'. His rate of pay was five guineas a day plus expenses, so this equates to about 180 days' work.

Thomas Telford is usually given the total credit for engineering the Ellesmere Canal – that is what is inevitably said on popular television programmes – but it is clear that this disregards the important part played by William Jessop. It is fairer to give them joint credit.

Telford's conditions of employment

Telford had offered to undertake the work for a salary of £500 a year, from which he would meet the salaries 'of his confidential foreman or inspector and clerk and other persons as shall be necessary' to be employed by him. He soon had second thoughts, and only three months later proposed that he should be paid £300 a year with the salaries of any assistants being paid by the company. This was agreed with effect from 1 January 1794.

In his letter to the committee when he made his original offer, Telford undertook 'not to engage himself in any other concern that may require his personal attendance or in any way interfere with the duties of his intended appointment ... without leave of the committee'. In a letter to a friend he wrote: 'I have reserved the right to carry on such of my architectural business as does not need my personal attendance, so that I shall retain all I wish for of that, which are the public buildings and the houses of importance'.[15] Although he was described in a Shrewsbury directory in about 1796 as 'architect', no significant commissions came his way after he was appointed General Agent of the Ellesmere Canal apart from St Michael's Church at Madeley.

However, he continued as County Surveyor, a role which carried no salary, instead being paid an appropriate fee whenever he was called upon to advise. Thomas Denson and (later) Thomas Stanton, both employees of the Ellesmere Canal Company, assisted him in this work, drawing up plans under Telford's supervision, and monitoring the contracts.

As mentioned in the last chapter, from 1795 to 1797 he advised the Shrewsbury Canal's committee about engineering aspects of the completion of its canal. Telford also continued his work in Scotland for the British Fisheries Society, mainly

Richard Kirk's mine alongside the Ffrwd Branch, as depicted in a hand-coloured aquatint painted by Edward Pugh and published in 1815 in *Cambria Depicta*, a volume of illustrations of North Wales. The drama of the scenery is greatly exaggerated, but the mine itself looks plausible. Because so much of the picture is 'artistic licence', the inclusion of the boat is not conclusive evidence that the canal was ever used – most likely it was not.

harbour works and 'town planning'. Then from 1801 he was involved in government surveys for roads, harbours and other public works in the Highlands of Scotland, culminating in his appointment in 1803 (jointly with Jessop) as engineer for the construction of the Caledonian Canal. About this time he also took permanent lodgings in London, appropriately at the Salopian Coffee House. It is clear from the summary accounts produced in November 1805 that Telford was paid his full salary of £300 every year with no diminution for his increasingly lengthy absences.

The members of the Ellesmere Canal's committee must have been aware of the use of canal company employees for Shropshire county work, as several members were also Shropshire Justices of the Peace, responsible for administering the county's services. However, there was no minute authorising this nor Telford's absences which by 1805 were probably at least two-thirds of the year, which must demonstrate the high regard in which he was held.

Construction

THE story of the construction of the Ellesmere Canal is complex, with aspirations far exceeding achievements. In brief: priority for construction was given to those sections which it was thought could produce immediate revenue. The 'Wirral Line' was the first section to be built, then a 'cross' of lines with the limestone of Llanymynech at the end of one arm. With construction costing significantly more than had been budgeted, no new contracts were let after 1797 for three years, giving a breathing space to review the whole project. This was a period of high inflation of contract prices – the Canal Mania had increased demand for craftsmen and labourers, and the supply of men had reduced because of the needs of the army and navy. Furthermore, interest rates had risen, largely in response to the government's need to finance the cost of war. The plans were amended, with sections of the original proposals being abandoned, postponed or replaced by a tramroad, the link with

Chapter 5 : The Ellesmere Canal

the summit level of the Chester Canal was made, and a new source of water obtained.

Rather than attempt an inevitably confusing and tedious chronological narrative giving the full details of every proposal, I shall deal with each part of the canal in turn and outline what happened there, then end this section with a summary of the reasons why the canal cost a third more than planned, despite less than half of its main line being completed.

The 'Wirral Line'

Although the Act authorised the 'Wirral Line' from Chester to the Mersey to terminate in the township of Netherpool within the parish of Eastham, it was decided to meet the Mersey slightly further east, in the township of Whitby. This site, on low-lying marshy ground, was virtually devoid of population, and did not have a reasonable road connection until several decades later. It soon came to be known as Ellesmere Port, the first use of that name being in the canal company's minutes on 21 December 1795.

This section of the Ellesmere Canal was the first to be tendered. It was one of the few parts where the line was (almost) undisputed, and there was the prospect of early completion with significant revenues. The contract was made with Samuel and his son John Weston for digging the 8¼ mile length – Samuel Weston had been the Chester Canal's first engineer. The locks and much of the other works were executed by John Fletcher with the Westons. The dimensions of the locks (74ft by 14ft 6in.) were slightly longer and wider than the locks on the Chester Canal but could accommodate most boats which used the Bridgewater Canal.

When the 1793 Act was obtained the assumption had been that the Ellesmere Canal would have an independent link with the river Dee. Following lengthy negotiations, the Chester Canal Company permitted the Wirral Branch to join its canal. As mentioned in Chapter 2, this connection involved closing the bottom two locks of what had been a five-lock staircase, making a right-angle bend on to the Wirral Line, and constructing two new locks to bring what now became the Dee Branch up to the level of the Wirral Line. It now seems surprising that such an important issue had not been settled when the Act was obtained.

The imminent opening of the locks of the Wirral Line caused a re-evaluation of the water supplies. The Committee instructed that a steam pump be purchased to raise water from the Mersey; several months later it endorsed John Duncombe's suggestion that one or more windmills be built; and a year later the instruction was again for a steam pump, to be bought from John Wilkinson (who also chaired that meeting). Together with its installation, it cost £1,576. It supplied one (broad) lock of water per hour but proved expensive to work.

The Wirral Branch carried some traffic as early as July 1795 when a packet-boat service started operating, and was fully opened when Whitby Locks were completed in late 1796 or early 1797. The link between the Wirral Branch and the Chester Canal was not completed until the summer or autumn of 1797. This eased the water supply problems for the Wirral Branch but exacerbated them for the Chester Canal.

In 1799 instructions were given for a survey and estimate of a four-mile extension of the Wirral Branch to Bromborough Pool where there would be consistently deeper water. Jessop advised against this extension, considering that it would not give a return to the shareholders. Similar proposals were considered on several occasions during the 19th century.

The main line: Chester to Trevor

Jessop disliked the uncertainty and delay which was inherent in tunnelling. He therefore sought an alternative to the long tunnel at Ruabon which had been approved in the original 1793 Act, and proposed a flight of locks at Cefn Mawr, raising the summit level from the previously-planned 310ft to 386ft above sea level. This would have the additional advantage of better serving the various mines and industries of the Cefn Mawr and Acrefair area as well as passing close to John Wilkinson's ironworks at Bersham; on the other hand, it would take the canal further away from Wrexham.

The length of the summit level would be reduced from seventeen miles to seven; more

Detail from Christopher Greenwood's map of Cheshire, 1819, showing the isolation of Ellesmere Port a couple of decades after it was created. *Cheshire Record Office*

significantly, it would require a source of water. It was proposed that this should come via a navigable branch a little over three miles long, from Gwersyllt on the main line of the canal to Ffrwd in the Cegidog valley. A 200-acre reservoir was to be constructed near Llanfynydd, feeding the end of the branch. Richard Kirk, a member of the Committee, undertook to pump water from his mine near Ffrwd. Immediately after the 1796 Act was passed, construction of the branch was commenced by Kirk, who was later reimbursed for his expenses, and by the contractors Fletcher & Whittle. Work was halted in 1797 after £8,922 had been spent, and it was never resumed.

After descending north-north-east from the summit level, the canal would have come close to the Dee at Saltney, just on the English side of the border. It would then have proceeded parallel to the river before crossing the tip of the point to opposite the entrance to the Chester Canal. The width of the Dee here is about 100yds and its tidal range is up to 13ft.

Negotiations were held with the River Dee Company concerning the crossing of the Dee. It is most likely that this would have been effected in a similar way to the crossing of the river Trent from the Erewash Canal to the river Soar: the crew would have gone over on a ferry, then the steerer would have returned, playing out a very long towline. After the line had been attached, the boat would have been hauled across by horse-power or a winch.

Negotiations also continued about the exact line to be taken between Trevor and Ruabon. The key person who had to be placated was Sir Watkin Williams Wynn, Lord Lieutenant of Merionethshire (from 1793) and Denbighshire (from 1796), MP for Beaumaris (from 1794) then for Denbighshire (from 1796), the richest man in north Wales and sometimes described as 'The Prince in Wales'. The optimum line of the canal went through his Wynnstay estate. At one stage the committee suggested taking the canal down to the banks of the Dee and passing to the *east* of Wynnstay Park – this would have allowed a low-level crossing of the Dee but would have added considerably to the length of the canal and would have removed much of its commercial purpose. A sensible compromise was reached, with the line of the canal passing through the western edge of the estate, partly in a cutting, well over a mile from Wynnstay Hall itself. As Sir Watkin owned much of the land in the Cefn Mawr and Ruabon area, including the valuable mineral rights, it was in his financial interest for the canal to serve the area well.

Jessop recommended a revised line for the canal from Ruabon down to Chester, and this was submitted to Parliament in the autumn of 1795. There followed protracted negotiations with landowners such as John Humberston Cawley of Gwersyllt Park and John Parry of Gresford Lodge in an attempt to reach a compromise which minimised any interference with their (and other landowners') estates but without creating an unreasonable extra cost.

By early 1797 the committee members were obviously having second thoughts about the section of the canal from Trevor via Bersham and Gresford to Chester, which required some 40 to 50 locks in the descent from Gwersyllt. In an attempt to save money they asked Henry Williams of the Shropshire and Shrewsbury Canals about the implications of replacing some of the locks with an inclined plane. Williams's report has not survived, but it would be surprising if even he, well-acquainted with inclines, would have recommended this solution to them. At that date the only inclines in Britain were used by tub-boats.

The next way investigated to save money was by the use of tramroads or rail ways – the name varied according to the type of system and the local usage. In the spring of 1798 Telford, Duncombe and Kirk went to Bugsworth in Derbyshire to view the Peak Forest Canal's tramroad which had come into use a couple of years earlier. This was a 'plate-way', that is, the flanges were on the rails, not on the wagons. Engineered by Benjamin Outram, Jessop's partner at the Butterley Ironworks, it had a gauge of 4ft 2in. and included an inclined plane 512yds long, rising 209ft. The delegation was impressed, considering that 'similar rail ways may be adopted in various parts of the Ellesmere Canal with great advantage of the Company'. The

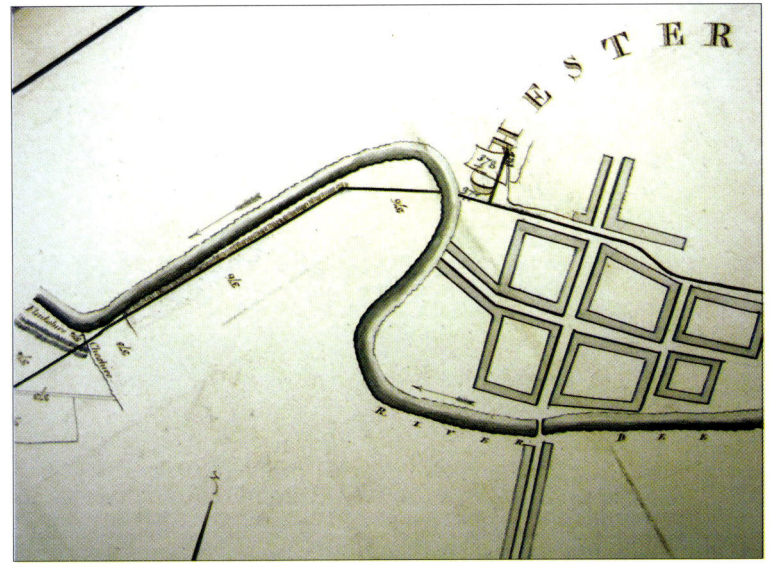

Extract from the map intended to accompany a Bill in the 1793/94 Parliamentary session which never went ahead, showing the connections to the river Dee at Chester. The original intention had been for the Wirral Branch to be totally separate from the Chester Canal. This map shows it sharing the entrance but the detail was subject to negotiations with the Chester Canal which led to what we see now. *Cheshire Record Office*

Chapter 5: The Ellesmere Canal

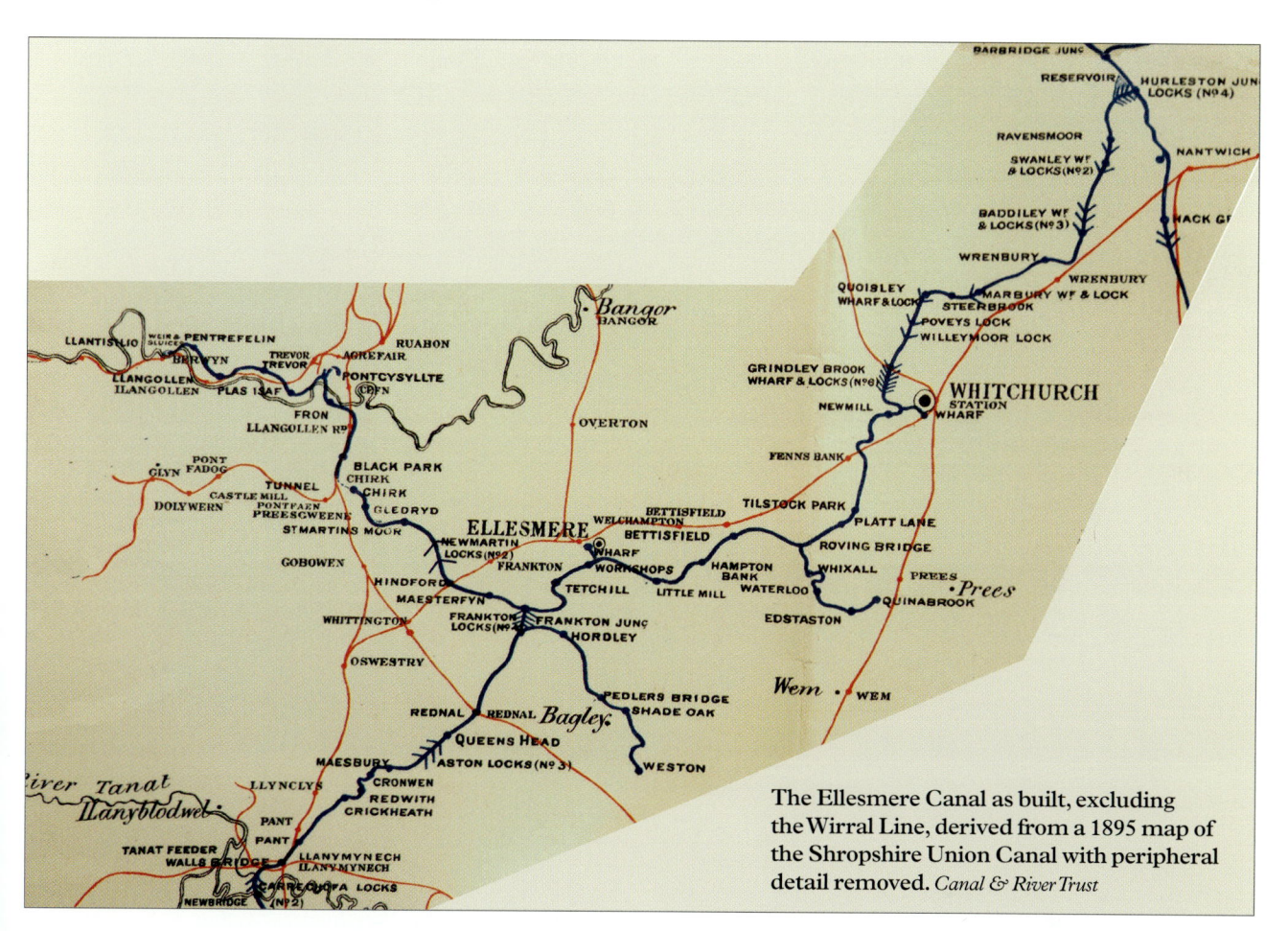

The Ellesmere Canal as built, excluding the Wirral Line, derived from a 1895 map of the Shropshire Union Canal with peripheral detail removed. *Canal & River Trust*

committee therefore instructed that the same team view the authorised route from Ruabon to Chester and advise on whether a tramroad should be built instead of a canal.

The proposal which emerged was for a tramroad from Trevor Basin to Holt on the river Dee, some 14 miles above Chester, which it was thought would both save 'a very great expense' and more effectually promote 'the convenience and advantage of the country'. Counsel's opinion was that such a tramroad was within the powers of the Company, providing landowners, tenants for life and other persons with legal rights agreed to the tramroad passing through their land. Although it was surely obvious to everybody that it was unlikely that all landowners would agree without the backing of compulsory powers, the General Assembly decided that this was the way forward.

Despite that decision, a year later land was still being purchased for the statutory line. Yet another committee of shareholders (all five being local to the area) was asked to view the country between Ruabon and Holt and between Ruabon and Rossett Green, including the Ffrwd Branch, in order to advise on what railway route would be best for the Company and the public. No action resulted from this. In his 1800 progress report Jessop stated that the opening of several collieries between Hawarden and Flint, communicating with the Dee via railways, meant that Chester was being supplied with coal much more cheaply than before. He therefore felt that a direct canal between Pontcysyllte and Chester was no longer advisable. Instead a railway was needed to connect the colliery district north-west of Ruabon with Trevor Basin, which he thought meant it could be achieved without the need to ask Parliament again. The railway was to be built with a slope of between one-eighth and half an inch per yard (that is, between 1 in 288 and 1 in 72), the intention being that a horse could pull the same number of full waggons downhill as empty waggons uphill.

This recommendation was reinforced the following year when coal owners in the Ponciau, Ruabon and Acrefair areas requested a tramroad joining their collieries with Trevor Basin. In 1802 instructions were given to draw up a specification for the tramroad and to advertise for tenders with the aim of completion within two years. A review in 1803 confirmed the tramroad as being a top priority but stated that further Parliamentary powers were necessary, so it was not until a few months after the passing of the 1804 Act that the line of the tramroad was set out. John Simpson levelled the ground, built the bridges over the various streams and supplied the stone

THE SHROPSHIRE UNION CANAL

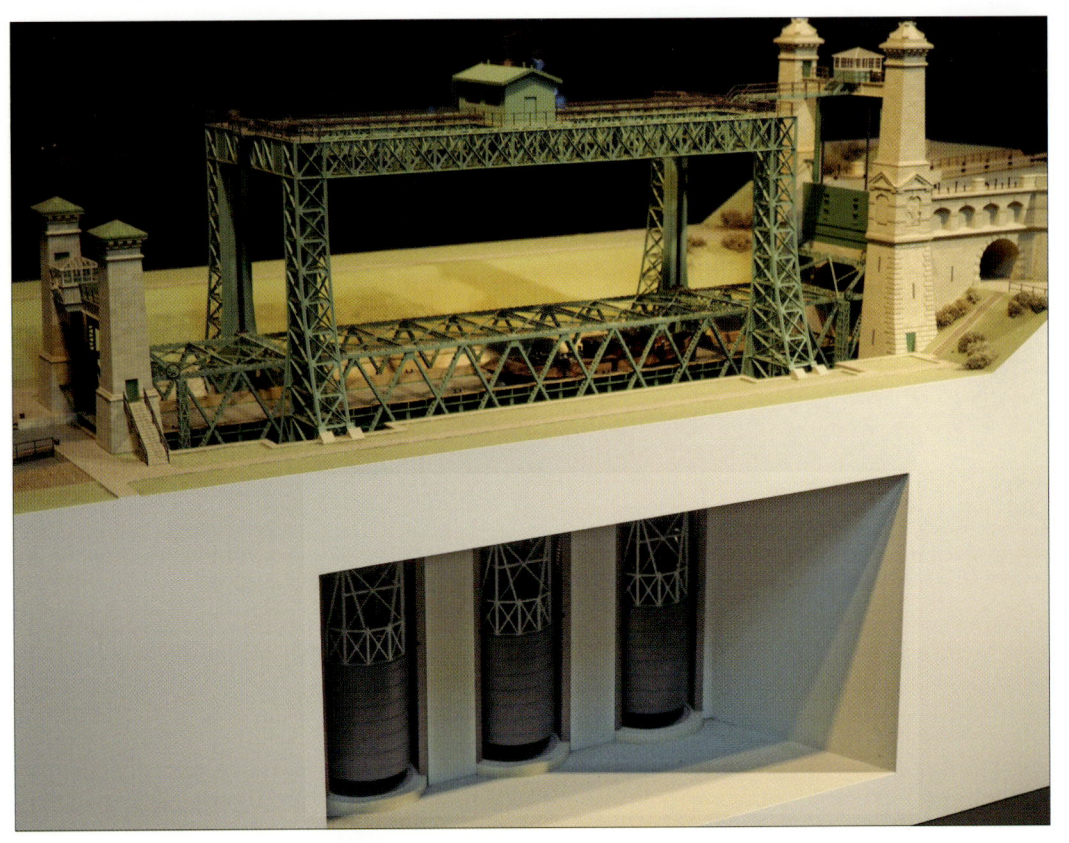

Model in the Zollverein Ruhr Museum of the original flotation lift which was built at Henrichenburg, showing the airtight tanks holding up the caisson, which is in its lowered position.
Author

sleepers; William Hazledine provided the iron rails and nails; and William Davies laid the rails. It was opened to Acrefair in 1805. By 1809 it had been extended to the place now known as Afon Eitha, the contractor being William Freeman. With a total length of about three miles, the tramroad was generally known as the 'Ruabon Brook Railway'.

The boat lift

IN the mid-1790s several inventors patented boat lifts for canals, the main attraction being the potential saving of water. One such patent was obtained by Edward Rowland, an ironmaster at Acrefair and a committee member, and Exuperius Pickering, who leased coal mines in the area. They obtained permission to build an experimental lift on the line of the Ellesmere Canal between Pontcysyllte and Chester, the company paying only if it met its satisfaction.

Technically this was a 'flotation lift': under the caisson in which the boat floated was a large air-tight tank which was always immersed in water. The size was such that the up-lift from the tank exactly counterbalanced the down-force of the weight of the assembly, making it easy to wind the assembly up and down between the canal levels, providing the framework kept the caisson exactly horizontal. At the ends of the caisson and of the canal levels were guillotine gates which could be raised to let the boat in and out.

As with most of the other experimental lifts of the time, the physics was sound but the engineering ability was inadequate. The principle has since been used successfully in three boat lifts built in Germany at Henrichenburg (opened 1899 and 1962) and Rothensee (1938). Rowland & Pickering's trial lift certainly worked but would not have been robust enough for everyday use. John Rennie, a leading canal engineer, commented in a letter to James Watt: 'It seems to me not only liable to be frequently out of order; but requires a nicety of adjustment which will be difficult to be done by the kind of men who are to use it'.[16] The experiment was estimated to have cost Rowland & Pickering a net amount of about £400, and the Ellesmere Canal Company eventually agreed to reimburse £200.

John Simpson (1755–1815)

JOHN SIMPSON, stonemason and contractor, a Scotsman from Midlothian, is best known for his works for Thomas Telford, starting with the road bridge over the river Ceiriog at Chirk (later incorporated into the Holyhead Road). Simpson built Chirk Aqueduct and completed the piers for Pontcysyllte Aqueduct. He also worked extensively for Telford in Scotland, including much of the masonry work on the Caledonian Canal.

CHAPTER 5 : THE ELLESMERE CANAL

A drawing dated 1797 by an unknown artist of Pontcysyllte Aqueduct showing the partly-completed piers. Jessop decided the dimensions of the piers partly to make it safer for the men working on them, which is a rare example of a late 18th-century engineer explicitly considering 'health and safety' issues. The piers were not built from scaffolding but built 'overhand' from inside the pier. Temporary construction decks were used at various levels. The crane looks realistic but the men are drawn far too small. *National Library of Wales*

But exactly where was it built? Various suggestions have been put forward, the most plausible being either near the Tref-y-nant Brook (a little north of Trevor Basin) or close to Home Farm on the Wynnstay Estate.[17]

The main line: Pontcysyllte Aqueduct

JESSOP'S 1792 report said that the proposed route would require an aqueduct over the Dee 970ft long and 126ft high. He added that it would be possible to reduce the cost by lowering it 24ft using three locks at each end and pumping the water back by a river-driven waterwheel. The decision was deferred at that time.

In August 1793 William Turner was asked to prepare plans and estimates for the aqueduct; his plan for a three-arched masonry aqueduct at the lower level was approved in January 1794. Telford produced plans in March 1794 which were then approved by Jessop. The contract for building the aqueduct was let to James Varley, a Chester mason, but he failed to produce the required sureties so John Simpson was made a co-partner. The cutting and dressing of the stone was begun, but construction was not commenced. Although it is generally assumed that all the stone came from the quarries at Cefn Mawr, there is some evidence that at first it came from a quarry less than half a mile north-west of the northern end of the Aqueduct – this assertion was made in a report of a field visit by geologists in the late 19th century, and the lower parts of the piers as built have a slightly different shade of stone than the upper parts.

Some time during the first half of 1795 there were second

THE SHROPSHIRE UNION CANAL

Pontcysyllte Aqueduct was the first large-scale use of cast iron as a construction material in Europe, the arches and trough being made using standardised castings. It soon became a major tourist attraction. It is debatable how much long-term influence it had on engineering practice because although cast iron is strong in compression, it is weak in tension. The largest structures continued to be built using masonry until wrought iron (and later steel) became the preferred materials.
Royal Commission for Ancient & Historic Monuments of Wales

Chapter 5 : The Ellesmere Canal

Pontcysyllte Aqueduct as depicted by Sidney Beaumont and published in *Inland Cruising* by George Westall (1908). But why is there a train crossing the 18th-century road bridge in the foreground?

William Hazledine (1763–1840)

William Hazledine was born at Shawbury in Shropshire and trained as a millwright. He established the iron foundry at Coleham in Shrewsbury which in 1796 supplied the beams and columns for Ditherington Mill, which has been described as the world's first iron-framed multistory building. He won the contract for supplying and erecting the ironwork of Pontcysyllte Aqueduct, having established a foundry nearby at Plas Kynaston. He and Telford became close friends, and he supplied the ironwork for many of the latter's major projects, including lock gates for the Caledonian Canal, Waterloo Bridge at Betws-y-Coed, Mythe Bridge near Tewkesbury, the suspension bridge at Conway, and the Menai Bridge. He had interests in limeworks at Llanymynech, mines in the East Shropshire coalfield, brickyards, timber-yards and wharfs, as well as being an active director of various Shropshire area canals.

Hazledine was an extrovert, with a positive attitude to life. Active in Whig politics, he served as Mayor of Shrewsbury in 1835–6.

thoughts about the whole concept for the aqueduct, both its height and its materials, probably occasioned by concerns about getting an adequate water supply for the locks descending both to Shrewsbury and to Llanymynech. It is not now possible to determine who initiated or led the discussions for the redesign with an iron trough, though popular opinion subsequently has had no doubt that it was Telford. However, Jessop was the Principal Engineer, and surviving correspondence shows that it was he who specified the dimensions of the piers.[18] He was also no stranger to iron, being co-owner of Butterley Ironworks in Derbyshire. But whoever had the idea, and whoever designed it, there is no doubt that it was Jessop who bore the ultimate responsibility, as it was he who made the recommendation to the committee to adopt the design.

Thus the decision for a high-level crossing of the Dee was made in August 1795 when the committee adopted Jessop's recommendation that the aqueduct should have stone piers with seven arches of 50ft span, the arches and the trough being made of iron. (The number of arches, and hence the length of the aqueduct, was later increased.) He told the committee that to lock down to a lower crossing would cause delays and loss of water. It was also agreed that the embankment leading to the aqueduct should be built by direct labour, rather than by a contractor. The material was to be boated from the cutting at Chirk – Jessop considered that this should be started at once

71

as it would take a long time, partly because only a few people could work on the embankment at any one time, also because embankments needed a long time to consolidate.

In 1797 discussions were held with John Wilkinson (of Bersham, Brymbo and elsewhere) and William Reynolds (of Ketley and Madeley Wood) to provide the ironwork, individually or jointly, for the aqueduct. The results cannot have been satisfactory, as an advertisement inviting tenders was published in various newspapers. No contract was made.

Work on the piers stopped in November 1797 in order that resources could be concentrated on Chirk Aqueduct. Having been retendered, the masonry work recommenced in 1800, the contract being awarded to John Simpson although the minute implied that he was not the lowest tenderer.

There were some thoughts about using the structure for a tramroad rather than a canal, but in November 1801 the decision for it to be a canal aqueduct was confirmed. However, the minute also instructed Telford to 'make out the necessary drawings and specifications' and to advertise for proposals from people willing to undertake it. This must refer only to the iron work, the contract then being awarded to William Hazledine with the rates paid being proportional to the weight of iron supplied: £11 a ton for castings and 8*d* a pound (that is, about £75 a ton) for wrought iron. Hazledine built a new foundry on the Plas Kynaston estate to make the castings; the wrought iron for the bolts and other fixings came from his forge at Upton Magna, five miles east of Shrewsbury.

The bottom and side plates are one-inch thick. The joints were sealed with very coarse flannel cut into pieces a little less than an inch in width and covered with white lead, the number of strips needed in each joint depending on how well the iron plates abutted. Then both sides of the joint were caulked with hemp rolled in tar and hammered into the gap.[19] It is sometimes said that the flannel was dipped in boiling sugar but there seems no written evidence for this. Also contrary to popular belief, the aqueduct does tend to leak in winter when the ironwork contracts in the cold – ashes are deposited in the trough to prevent the loss of water.

The aqueduct and embankment were completed in time for the opening of the whole canal on 26 November 1805. The report to the committee the following day gave the payments as £20,968 for stonework, £17,285 for ironwork and £246 for incidental expenses, totalling £38,499. In addition there was a little money owing at that date, hence the actual total cost of the aqueduct was about £39,000. The payments for the embankment quoted in the report totalled £8,571; again there may have been a small additional amount paid later.

The main line: Froncysyllte to Chirk Bank

At Chirk the easiest route would have required an embankment over the Ceiriog valley but at the request of Sir Richard Myddleton of Chirk Castle, the Parliamentary route involved a 1,236yd tunnel leading to a bridge further up the valley at Pontfaen. Following further negotiations, a line similar to the original proposal was adopted, with a much shorter tunnel and with an aqueduct rather than an embankment across the valley. Jessop suggested an iron aqueduct but the plan adopted was for one of masonry. In 1796 the contract for Chirk Aqueduct was awarded to John Simpson, William Hazledine and William Davies. When it was nearing completion in November 1799, a tender for iron plates and wrought-iron screws for Chirk Aqueduct was accepted from William Hazledine. The aqueduct, 68ft high and 710ft long, cost £20,899.

The most serious accident during the construction of the Ellesmere Canal occurred in May 1798 when four men were killed and one seriously injured in the building of Chirk Aqueduct. They had been rolling a stone over the scaffolding fixed between each pillar when the planks gave way and they fell more than 40ft. In contrast, only one person died during the construction of the much higher and longer Pontcysyllte Aqueduct, and this Telford later attributed to the man's carelessness.[20]

It is probable that most of Chirk Tunnel was made using a 'cut-and-cover' technique, whereby a cutting was dug then roofed over, and only part was by boring. This tunnel, 459yds long, has a towpath, one of the earliest canal tunnels to have one. This made for much quicker passages by boats, as they did not have to be 'legged' or poled through. (Of the canal tunnels in Britain still open which have a towpath, this is the second longest.) The water flows under the towpath past the boat, so its progress is not greatly impeded.

Whitehouses Tunnel, 191yds long, had a similar towpath and was constructed by 'cut-and-cover'.

The aqueduct and tunnels were finished by the end of 1801, permitting the opening of the canal as far as Froncysyllte, enabling material to be boated for the construction of the high embankment leading to Pontcysyllte Aqueduct.

The Oswestry/Llanymynech area

A principal aim of the canal company was to transport limestone from the quarries in the Llanymynech area to kilns where it could be converted into quicklime for improving land and also to supply it to the iron industry to the north of the Dee valley. As a result, the Llanymynech Branch came to be built before most of the main line was started.

When the original survey was done, it was assumed that the canal would continue to Llanymynech at the 'Queen's Head' level. The plans for the 1793 Act introduced the three Aston locks, the most likely reason for this decision being that the expectation was that the branch would join the proposed Montgomeryshire Canal in the Llanymynech area at the lower level needed to bridge the Vyrnwy. The lower route also made for easier engineering in the Pant–Llanymynech section because the canal would not then be on the side of a fairly steep slope. On the other hand, it did mean that all boats carrying limestone north would use water; under the original proposal those destined for the Shrewsbury line would not have needed to go up any locks.

Chapter 5: The Ellesmere Canal

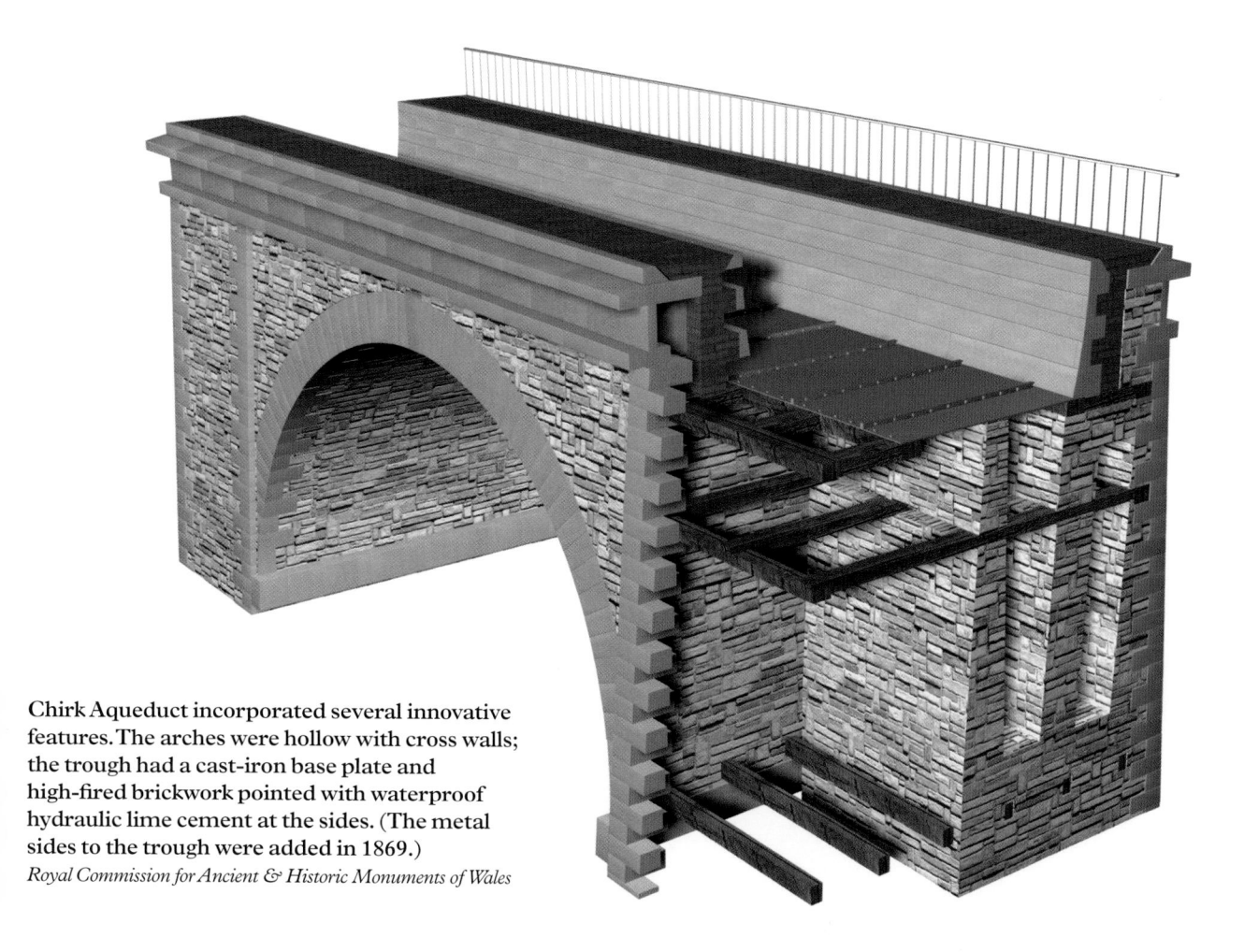

Chirk Aqueduct incorporated several innovative features. The arches were hollow with cross walls; the trough had a cast-iron base plate and high-fired brickwork pointed with waterproof hydraulic lime cement at the sides. (The metal sides to the trough were added in 1869.)
Royal Commission for Ancient & Historic Monuments of Wales

The representatives of the town of Oswestry were unhappy because the canal would be three miles away from the town, saying it would be much better served if the canal was at a higher level. Furthermore, this would also bring the line much closer to the coal mines just south of Oswestry and would make it easier to serve the Porth-y-waen quarries.

The latter were owned by the Earl of Powis, who was also a leading promoter of the Montgomeryshire Canal. It was probably at his instigation that the Montgomeryshire Canal's committee decided to continue its canal up a flight of locks to those quarries. It therefore pressed the Ellesmere Canal to adopt a higher route, its intention being that the two canals would make an end-on junction at Porth-y-Waen.

Meetings were held with representatives of Oswestry Borough and the Montgomeryshire Canal's committee, but Jessop considered that the Parliamentary line was the best. However, as a compromise, the 1793 Act included a branch to Morda Bridge, serving the nearby collieries (subject to the consent of the land-owners); it also contained a requirement for the Ellesmere Canal to put to Parliament a proposal for a higher level branch if agreement could be made with the Montgomeryshire Canal. Following such an agreement, the Ellesmere Canal's 1796 Act included a clause requiring it to apply to Parliament to make an 'Upper Oswestry Line' to link to the Montgomeryshire Canal at Porth-y-Waen. Despite pressure from the latter canal company, nothing ever happened. This topic is further discussed in the next chapter.

Meanwhile a contract had been made in March 1794 with James Houghton & Sons and Thomas Ford for the section between Maesbury Marsh and Hordley (three-quarters of a mile west of the junction below Frankton Locks, on what was to be the main line towards Shrewsbury), including the Aston Locks. That August, John Fletcher won the tender for the Llanymynech to Maesbury Marsh section.

Also that year the Revd John Robert Lloyd was granted permission to build a private canal half a mile long to Green's Gate (now Green Wicket) from the Llanymynech Branch, half a mile south-west of the Perry Aqueduct. This was actually on the line authorised in the 1793 Act but it had previously been agreed that the branch be diverted closer to Woodhouse, William Mostyn Owen's residence. In 1799 the committee agreed to reimburse Lloyd's expenses in making that canal.

The branch opened to Llanymynech in 1797; the continuation to Carreghofa opened a year later. This latter section had been surveyed in the autumn of 1793 for a proposed Bill that never went ahead. However, assuming that the land was bought by agreement without using compulsory purchase powers, no Act was necessary.

Tramroads were constructed from coal mines in the Morda area to the canal in about 1800, taking advantage of the clause in the Act permitting the owners or lessees of mines within three miles of the canal to make a tramroad to the canal.

The canal was always prone to leaking in the Llanymynech area. The problem was that when passing over limestone, the canal needed to be lined with clay puddle. The ground water level was prone to variation, and as it rose, it tended to push the clay lining upwards into the canal. When the ground water subsided, the upthrust clay could leak.

The main line: Chirk Bank to Shrewsbury

THE third section of the canal to be built, after the Wirral Line and the Llanymynech Branch, was from below Frankton Locks to Chirk Bank. The contract was let to James Houghton & Thomas Ford in 1795; it was completed in 1798.

The next three-quarters of a mile from the junction to Hordley had been included in Houghton & Ford's Maesbury Marsh contract, as already explained. The contract for the continuation to Weston Lullingfields was awarded to John Fletcher in 1796 and was completed the following year. A wharf, four lime kilns, a public house, stables, a clerk's house and a weighing machine were built by the company at Weston Lullingfields.

The original intention had been to extend this line to Shrewsbury – indeed this was the intended main line. It would have continued on the level for eight and a half miles, passing near Baschurch, Prescott, Walford and Leaton Heath to Alkmond Park, then descended 107ft (by between twelve and fifteen locks) in slightly under two miles to enter the Severn just north of Shrewsbury about where the Gateway Centre is now. The Act gave a second option for the exit to the Severn: to the east of the town near the site of the later weir, though the land levels do not seem ideal. According to some contemporary sources, the Shrewsbury Canal's Act permitted the Shrewsbury and Ellesmere Canals to join by mutual consent, though this does not actually appear in the Act. If the Ellesmere Canal had taken the line implied by the map which accompanied the 1793 Act, the two canals would have crossed each other.

A review of priorities in 1803 felt that other developments of the Ellesmere Canal system would be more immediately profitable. Diplomatically, it was then declared that 'this committee have never entertained any intention of deserting or of delaying the execution of the line from Weston Wharf to Shrewsbury'.

Nevertheless, no further work was done on the Shrewsbury line. The opening of the Shrewsbury Canal in 1797 had brought coal from the east Shropshire coalfield to the county town, and it was realised that coal from Chirk and Ruabon was unlikely to compete successfully.

The 'eastern route' and the Whitchurch and Prees Branches

As mentioned earlier, in 1793 the proponents of the 'eastern route' were promised a link between the Whitchurch Branch and the Chester Canal but it was too late to incorporate a specific proposal in that year's Act. Instead a clause approved the construction of such a link from Fenns Hall (two miles west of Whitchurch) to Tattenhall, providing all the land-owners agreed. If they refused, the authority of Parliament was to be sought within two years. Unsurprisingly, some land-owners did not agree.

The following year William Egerton, the mortgagee of the Chester Canal, was told that no application to Parliament would be made until the whole route was decided; he was also told that this did not mean that time would be lost because it would be some years before the Whitchurch Branch was completed. Another cause for delay was that Parliament had changed its rules: promoters of private acts for canals now had to submit detailed plans and books of reference showing the owners and occupiers of all land affected – and this took much longer to prepare.

The 1796 Act repealed the obligations with respect to the Fenns Hall to Tattenhall line and substituted a requirement that engineers appointed by each company should agree on the best route within five months and that the two companies should agree the line within a further three months, after which the Ellesmere Company must apply to Parliament 'within due time'. That summer John Duncombe and John Fletcher made a survey and took levels to devise the best link.

As also mentioned earlier, the opening of the Wirral Line in 1796 put a strain on the already inadequate water supplies of the Chester Canal. The two canal companies commissioned John Fletcher to survey a possible feeder from the Wrenbury Brook to the summit level of the Chester Canal. Once the Ellesmere Company decided to install a steam pump at Ellesmere Port, instructions were given for the survey to be halted, but it seems that it had already been completed. Further discussions were held concerning the feeder but the Ellesmere Company eventually withdrew, saying the proposal was too expensive, and offering instead to assist in cleansing the watercourses that already fed the Chester Canal.

A letter was sent to the Chester Canal asking for agreement for the application to Parliament to be postponed because it would be three or four years before the branch would be completed to Whitchurch and money was now scarce.

A branch by Whitchurch to Prees Heath had originally been authorised by the 1793 Act. By 1796 Jessop had recommended an improved line and also a branch on the level, passing near

Chapter 5 : The Ellesmere Canal

Wem and Prees and terminating on the Whitchurch to Newport road at Prees Heath.

The contract for the first section of the Whitchurch Branch, from Frankton Junction to Ellesmere, was made with Henry & John Mansfield and John Fletcher in early 1797 and completed by 1799. Construction was extended in sections to Tilstock Park, four miles short of Whitchurch, by 1804. The crossing of Whixall Moss was particularly tricky to make, the embankments taking a long time to consolidate. Three lime kilns were built at Hampton Bank. What became known as the Prees Branch did not reach its ultimate objective but terminated at Quina Brook, on the road from Whitchurch to Wem; this branch was not completed until 1806. The main contractor for these lines was Samuel Betton.

The 1801 Act authorised the link from near Whitchurch to Hurleston Junction, the section east from Wrenbury being based on Fletcher's earlier survey. The part from Tilstock Park to Grindley Brook was made by John & William Hughes, the rest of the line to Hurleston Junction by Messrs Fletcher and Simpson. The main engineering problem in this section was that the foundations of several of the locks were discovered to be in quicksand which required the construction of platforms, pilings and special drains. This section opened in November 1805.

The 'Water Line'

A clause in the original 1793 Act prohibited taking water from the rivers Dee or Ceiriog or from the Morlas Brook between 15 June and 15 September without the consent of Chester Waterworks.

The use of the river Dee as a source of water was mooted as early as 1795 when Sir Watkin Williams Wynn was asked for his consent to use Bala Lake (Llyn Tegid) as an occasional reservoir. A clause permitting this was included in the 1796 Act.

Abandoning the Ruabon to Chester link meant that the Pontcysyllte level was reliant on the inadequate water supplies from the Morlas Brook. The obvious solution was to seek a feed from the river Dee. Further negotiations were held with Sir Watkin concerning Bala Lake, resulting in an agreement to raise the water level of the lake by one foot. In 1804 an Act was obtained to make a navigable feeder via Llangollen. One clause caused problems much later: this required the canal company to put into the Dee above Chester the equivalent amount of water to that which they took from the Dee, topping up if necessary from streams which did not flow into the Dee.

The Water Line proved difficult to build because it was on the side of the valley, requiring a considerable amount of excavation and embanking. The uncertain nature of the work caused it to be built by direct labour rather than by a contractor. It was not completed until 1808.

Extension to Barmouth?

At the end of 1809 a proposal supported by Sir Watkin Williams Wynn came forward for a canal from the end of the 'Water Line' via Corwen, Bala and Dolgellau to Barmouth. This, according to a press report, would provide 'an inland conveyance ... for the treasures of mines of Merionethshire to Liverpool and the Metropolis'.[21] Nevertheless, if this had gone ahead, the cost would have been huge, the returns meagre.

The Whitchurch Arm

The Ellesmere Canal bypassed Whitchurch to the north. Wharves and warehouses were constructed at Grindley Brook, two miles from the centre of the town. It was considered that this distance added about 2s.6d a ton to the cost of coal, and the Whitchurch traders feared that Grindley Brook might supplant the town as the general market for the area.

The canal company's committee had decided to save money by not building the three-quarter mile long section from New Mills to Sherryman's Bridge which had been authorised in the 1796 Act. According to the minutes, this economy had been suggested by 'several gentlemen of considerable property in Whitchurch', which seems surprising, particularly in view of subsequent developments. John Knight, a Whitchurch solicitor, was a committee member and had attended this particular meeting, so would surely have contradicted this if it had been untrue.

In July 1805 a group of Whitchurch businessmen led by William Turner (who had carried out many of the company's early surveys) asked the committee for permission to build a branch canal from New Mills to Sherryman's Bridge then continue a further quarter of a mile to Castle Well. The latter terminus would be closer to the town centre and be much more convenient – from Sherryman's Bridge the road rose 38ft with a maximum gradient of 1 in 7, whereas the rise from Castle Well was only 5ft. Because of the canal company's financial difficulties, the committee readily agreed in principle, subject to them being able to take over the branch any time within ten years of its completion. However, four months' later the committee concluded they did not have the authority to delegate the powers in their Acts.

The following year an alternative proposal was made which had the same effect. The canal company was to make a contract with a consortium led by Samuel Turner (William's brother, and a Whitchurch builder) to construct a branch canal to a site known as Castle Well for the sum of £2,000, which the consortium would lend to the canal company for four years 'with lawful interest' (later agreed as 5% per annum). The company would apply to Parliament for powers for the extension from Sherryman's Bridge to Castle Well. Despite realising that they had no powers for that extension, they instructed that construction should start at Castle Well; a later meeting of the committee gave permission to start at the junction, known as New Mills, instead. The arm opened to Sherryman's Bridge on 27 June 1808. A temporary wharf was established there, but as there was no winding hole, boats had to be drawn back rudder-first to New Mills after unloading.

The canal company seems to have done nothing to obtain the Act for the extension until 1809. Knight referred to 'blunders and neglect' by Messrs Potts & Leeke, the company's solicitors, presumably concerning this delay. The pamphlet published to influence public opinion in favour of the further extension of the branch stated that no extra tolls would be charged; however, the Act clearly gave the right to charge the same tonnage rates as elsewhere.[22]

It had been thought that all the landowners affected had agreed not to oppose the Bill but two of them, William Trevor and Mr Taylor, registered their opposition and gathered signatures for a petition against it. Trevor owned the property most affected at the site of the proposed basin at Castle Well and Taylor owned the wharf land on the west bank at Sherryman's Hill (the east side being swampy and unsuitable for a wharf). Telford's plan would have given Trevor control of the land for the wharfs, so William Turner drew up an alternative plan whereby five people (including Trevor and himself) would be able to make wharfs, and it was this alternative plan which was submitted to Parliament. Knight's assessment was blunt: 'Trevor's sole object is monopoly'.[23] Knight organised a petition in favour of the Bill; and Trevor and Taylor either saw the futility of their opposition or some informal agreement was made, because they withdrew their objections. William Turner assisted Messrs Potts & Leeke in preparing the case; John Turner (who was either William's or, less likely, Samuel's son) gave evidence to Parliament; and the Act was passed.

This was not the end of the arguments with Mr Trevor and Mr Taylor. There was a difference of opinion about the amount of land to be taken for the canal, so a high-powered sub-committee, including the Earl of Bridgewater and Sir John Hill, was deputed to meet them and settle the differences. An independent surveyor was asked to make the measurements. Even that did not end the disputes. The following year, William Trevor alleged that John Kynaston Powell on behalf of the canal company had promised him that a footbridge would be erected over the Whitchurch Arm; a subcommittee investigated and, without admitting liability, offered to pay Trevor £60 in lieu.

The Whitchurch Arm opened in 1811. The various plans show a rectangular basin, but what was actually built was a narrow triangle (as at Ellesmere).

Project management

THE Ellesmere Canal took fifteen years to build, and its final form bore little resemblance to the line as approved in the 1793 Act, with less than half the intended main line being completed. There were several fundamental issues that help show why the canal was built as it was.

Crucially, there was an inability to concentrate on an agreed objective and to make firm decisions. For example, at the very first General Assembly it was decided to make surveys for two further branches, to the stone quarries of Grinshill (seven miles north of Shrewsbury) and to Mold. In trying to please everybody, the canal company finished up by not fully satisfying either investors or potential customers. The only one of the original objectives which was really achieved was to enable the farmland of north Shropshire to be improved through the use of lime – is it too cynical to observe that the most influential committee members were also major landowners in north Shropshire, whose estates came to be well served by the canal?

To make matters worse, the promise to the 'eastern' lobby that a line would be made east of the Dee, connecting directly with the Chester Canal proved an excessive price for unity when the original Act was being sought. Without that promise, the long Whitchurch branch might have been given a lower priority, enabling a greater concentration on the main line.

Also, there was no proper financial management of the project. In particular, there should have been a budget for the project which then should have been revised year by year when decisions were varied, new proposals made, land values settled or construction tenders received. The knowledge gained from what had actually happened should have been used to improve forecasts of future costs. Whose responsibility was this? Not the Treasurers, who just dealt with cash payments and receipts – they were bankers, not financial advisers. The ultimate responsibility lay with the General Committee, of course, but there was no single 'guiding hand': in the twelve years between the passing of the Act in 1793 and the effective completion in 1805, ten different people chaired the 105 committee meetings. The person who chaired most frequently, John Kynaston, nevertheless chaired fewer than a third of the meetings. In my opinion, Thomas Telford as General Agent should have drawn the Committee's attention to the inevitable crisis and made the necessary calculations to enable sensible decisions to be made.

A note written for the Directors' inspection cruise in 1900 stated that the course originally planned 'if carried out would have been in every respect much more satisfactory than that which was completed'.[24] The irony is that the canal as built was much closer to the intentions of the promoters of the 'eastern route' than it was to the line approved in the 1793 Act.

Operation

IN late 1796 or early 1797 the Wirral Line became the first section of the Ellesmere Canal to open. Two passage boats and two barges for the carriage of goods had been bought in anticipation of trade commencing.

The landowners at Whitby (soon to be known as Ellesmere Port) were asked whether they intended to construct wharves and warehouses. Fortunately for the long-term interests of the canal company, they preferred to sell their land to it. Actually, relatively little development was done here in the first three decades. Stables were provided, and wharfs with warehouses and cranes were constructed, but the normal practice was for cross-Mersey boats to travel on to Chester, where any necessary transhipment was effected. An inn was erected for the benefit of passengers travelling between Chester and Liverpool and leased out.

At Chester a public house, warehouse, offices and wet dock were built near the junction.

The first inland section opened in 1797, allowing limestone to be brought from the quarries at Llanymynech. To promote trade, the canal company financed the erection of limekilns, leasing them to people with an annual rent of 10% of the cost. The first such arrangement was at Weston Lullingfields, where the kilns were let to John Simpson.

Pontcysyllte Aqueduct was opened with much ceremony on 26 November 1805, the connection to the Chester Canal opening at the same time. By then construction of the canal was virtually complete, as it seemed to be generally recognised that the sections from Shrewsbury to Weston Lullingfields and from Trevor to Chester as originally proposed were unlikely to be built.

The company built offices at Ellesmere, including a board room first used in November 1806 and accommodation for the Resident Engineer and the General Accountant. This elegant building overlooking the junction is no longer in canal ownership. The maintenance depot, built at the same time, is the finest surviving canal depot in the country – indeed, it is a rare example of an early 19th century group of workshops, largely unchanged, still used for its original purpose. It comprised a set of buildings round a yard: a carpenter's house and workshop, a bricklayer's house and store room, a forge and a dry dock. Further dry docks were built at Trevor and Chester.

Land was leased to others for the construction of wharves and warehouses, all of which would help trade. Curiously, it was resolved that a public house at Maesbury Marsh would be advantageous and that John Jones, landlord of the King's Head, Oswestry, would be a suitable person to keep it; furthermore, there would be no objection if the local magistrates wished to make any regulations concerning Sunday opening.

Bye-laws for boatmen and boat-owners were approved by the General Assembly in 1806. These included a requirement for boatmen to drive their horses on the left side of the towpath 'as is usual on turnpike roads'. The towrope of the horse further from the water should then drop to allow a horse and boat coming the other way to pass over it – fibre ropes sank, unlike modern polypropylene ropes which float – boats therefore keeping right. All boats were to be gauged at Ellesmere; six copper index strips would be attached.

All that remained were to finish the feeder from the river Dee, which opened in 1808, and the short branch into Whitchurch. Over the next decade land and properties that were surplus to requirements were sold – the warehouses, dwelling house and other buildings at Maesbury Marsh were sold to the Trustees of the late Earl of Powis, for example.

In 1811 Thomas Telford leased a site at Ellesmere Port in order to construct graving docks and other buildings for the repair of flats and small coasting vessels. Under the agreement, after fourteen years the canal company could buy the property at valuation.

Management and staffing after 1805

The senior committee members who had guided the construction of the canal continued to be active on the committee after 1805.

The seventh Earl of Bridgewater inherited the Ellesmere estate in 1803, following the death of his uncle, the 'Canal Duke'. Despite having estates in ten counties (and an income of some £70,000 a year) he found time to chair the occasional meeting of the Ellesmere Canal Company from June 1805 onwards.

Committee meetings became less frequent after 1808. As was then always the case, members were not paid but were given a meal and drinks. A minute instructed:

> That no business relating to the Canal shall be done after dinner or be proposed unless it is of immediate importance, and in that case strangers who are not of the Committee ... be requested to withdraw.

Following the formal opening of the canal in November 1805 the management structure was reviewed and considerable annual savings made as the two Superintendents for new works were no longer required.

Thomas Telford relinquished his post as General Agent and became a consultant, his brief being to give advice not only on engineering issues but also 'to the general interests of the Company'. He was expected to report twice a year, for which he would be paid an annual fee of £100. After 1809 he appears generally to have come only once a year, usually in the winter. Some years there is no surviving evidence of him visiting. He attended few of the meetings but his reports were sometimes read to the committee, with either Denson or Stanton being instructed to take the necessary action.

John Duncombe had been formally appointed Resident Engineer back in 1795, with Thomas Denson as his assistant. Duncombe left in 1803 to join Telford's team in Scotland working on Highland road surveys. Denson replaced him, continuing in that role after 1805 with his annual salary unchanged at £150. Based at Ellesmere, he was instructed to examine the whole canal and the Ruabon Railway monthly, except for the Wirral Line, which he was to visit quarterly. He was also to visit the works at Bala Lake quarterly. Mr Fletcher – presumably John Fletcher of the Chester Canal who had been the contractor for various sections of the Ellesmere Canal – became Superintendent of the Wirral Line; as the salary was a mere £30 a year, this must have been regarded as a part-time post.

Thomas Stanton, who had been Telford's clerk since 1798, became General Accountant. He was therefore responsible for the company's finances and administration, including checking all money due was received and making quarterly reports to the committee – no doubt he had been doing that job for the previous few years during Telford's long absences. His pay was increased from £75 to £150, putting him on a par with Thomas Denson. As before, he was to be assisted by a clerk, John Stanton, Thomas's younger brother, initially paid £50 a year but increased to £80 in 1809.

Also in 1809 both Thomas Denson's and Thomas Stanton's salaries were increased by £15 to compensate them for the introduction of income tax. Following Denson's death in 1811, Stanton's took over his role too. The job was now referred to as 'General Agent', a title which had occasionally been applied to

Stanton in the period since 1805 but which had also still been used for Telford's role. Stanton's salary was first increased to £320, despite the committee's unhappiness about his work for Telford as County Surveyor; they permitted this work to continue until the following June though they minuted that 'such employment is incompatible with the due discharge of his duties'. The following summer, following Stanton's promise 'to devote the whole of his time and attention to the concerns of this company', his pay was set at £400 a year. Despite this assurance, Stanton continued to design Shropshire's bridges on behalf of Telford and to supervise their construction right up to the time of the latter's death in 1834.

The company minutes do not mention other employees, except for an incident in 1808. Ellis Davies, who superintended the weir at Bala Lake, was dismissed because he had been convicted of poaching, and Evans, who looked after the lake on behalf of Sir Watkin Williams Wynn, was appointed in his place.

The Knockin Gate

A minor but troublesome issue which was settled in 1805 was the case of a turnpike trust which asked for compensation. Turnpike trusts were non-profitmaking organisations. Improvement works were financed by borrowing at fixed interest rates. Maintenance, management costs, interest and loan repayments were then met out of the toll income. Any surpluses could be used only to undertake further works or to reduce tolls; if they made losses there was a risk they would default on their loan debt.

The particular trust which claimed compensation from the Ellesmere Canal had been established in 1772 and had a obtained a further Act in June 1792. Its main route was from Burlton (on the Shrewsbury–Ellesmere road), via Baschurch and Ruyton-XI-Towns, crossing the Shrewsbury–Oswestry road near Shotatton, then via Knockin to Llanymynech. (These are now the B4397 and B4398.) To help finance the works it had borrowed £130 from the Churchwardens of the Parish of Baschurch and £114 from the trustees of the school in Baschurch for the education of children of the poor of the village.

In June 1805 Rowland Hunt, a trustee of the turnpike as well as a member of the canal company's committee, told the latter that back in 1796 he was concerned that lime and coal traffic from Llanymynech to Shrewsbury would transfer from the road to the canal. Consequently, prior to the application to Parliament for a further Act, he said he had asked John Wilkinson, the chairman of the meeting of the committee, what consideration or indemnity should be proposed to the trustees of the Burlton–Llanymynech road. Hunt said that Wilkinson had replied (and the committee had assented), 'That the Ellesmere Canal Company would become the renters of the Toll Gate at Knockin and thus secure the interest of the concern', and that he had taken this to mean that the canal company would underwrite the sum at which the tolls were then let.

However, the 1796 minutes make no mention of this promise. The meeting referred to must have been that on 29 July, as Wilkinson had chaired only two meetings that year, and this was the only one where Hunt had been present too. There was no minute concerning applying for an Act – indeed no application was made that year as the company's 1796 Act had been approved only a few months earlier – but there was a debate concerning a contract to extend the Shrewsbury line from Weston Lullingfields. The original idea had been that it would be extended as far as the Burlton–Ruyton turnpike, but it was then thought more beneficial to continue it to the Ellesmere–Shrewsbury turnpike. (In the event, the extension was not made.)

A sub-committee appointed to investigate met Roland Hunt and Henry Bowman (the Trust's Treasurer) at Boreatton, Hunt's house near Baschurch. Hunt and Bowman explained that the tolls of Knockin Gate had been let for £115 in 1796, 1797 and 1798, but in 1803, 1804 and 1805 they had been let for only £81 – a difference of £34. It was implied that the security for the two loans was not the tolls of the Trust generally but the tolls of Knockin Gate specifically. The sub-committee members examined the accounts of the Treasurer and of the Surveyors of the Trust and found them 'correctly kept'. Hunt made an affidavit to the correctness of his statements about what had been said in 1796. The sub-committee therefore recommended that the canal company should accept responsibility for the two loans totalling £244, with interest to be paid at the rate previously agreed by the Turnpike Trust, this being recognised as full compensation to the trustees for all the financial injury done to the road by the making of the canal.

The committee received the report of the sub-committee at its meeting in July 1805 and concurred with its conclusions. The matter had to be referred to the General Assembly meeting in November 1805 before payment could be made. This was the meeting held on the day before the formal opening of the Pontcysyllte Aqueduct and which received a lengthy self-congratulatory report on the effective completion of the Ellesmere Canal, so it is questionable how much attention would have been paid to this relatively minor topic. Because it was charity money and was 'proved to be secured by this Company at a former meeting of the General Committee ... previous to the application to Parliament for the Ellesmere Canal Acts in 1796', it was agreed to pay the money 'in consequence of such promises and under the very peculiar circumstances of the case'.

The Burlton–Llanymynech Turnpike Trust was no doubt one of the poorest in Shropshire, but it does seem it was given special treatment. Rowland Hunt was a senior member of the Ellesmere Canal's committee, being one of its three most frequent chairmen. It was he who gave the oration at the formal opening of Pontcysyllte Aqueduct. Henry Bowman was also connected with the canal company, sometimes acting as its land valuer. Hunt's memory must have been at fault when he said the promise was made in connection with the 1796 Act. (He could not merely have remembered the year incorrectly, as John Wilkinson never chaired a meeting in 1795 when the application to Parliament would have been discussed.) It is much more likely that he was half-remembering the debate

Chapter 5: The Ellesmere Canal

about the extension of the canal, but of course that extension never happened. If any promise were made, one would have expected it to have been when the canal was first being discussed, as by 1796 the Weston Lullingfields line was under construction. In any event, any indemnity would have been so unusual that it should have been minuted. And why was responsibility accepted for the full amount of the loans, rather than just making up the shortfall on the tolls?

Perhaps the oddest thing is that no other turnpike trust claimed compensation for losses despite the precedent having been set, but perhaps they all recognised that the 'very peculiar circumstances' would never be applied to them.

Finances

EARLY on, there was a crucial but unminuted decision: to restrict calls on shareholders in each year to only £10 (or, in one year, £15), whereas most canal companies asked for £20 to £30. This inevitably meant that the pace of development was slow, made worse by the second half of the 1790s being a period of significant price inflation on civil engineering works, partly caused by the excessive demand for canal works and partly a result of the continuing war with France; also a succession of bad harvests had pushed up grain prices and wages.

This decision to limit annual calls was no doubt taken with the motive of protecting shareholders, many of whom were land-rich but cash-poor, but the longer the period over which the investment was spread out, the more the delay in earnings. Also from the end of 1794 to the end of 1798, interest of 5% was paid on the amount of calls paid up. Although this had the merit of encouraging shareholders to actually pay the calls, the interest had to be paid out of capital. All it really meant was that more capital had to be raised.

Parliamentary approval was obtained to raise extra money, which the company decided should mainly be done by requiring an extra £33 per share to be subscribed. A minute of 1802 read:

> It shall be stated to the proprietors in the strongest possible terms … that it will be much for the interest of this concern to have larger and more frequent calls … so that the works remaining to be executed … may be completed and the whole of the said canal brought into profit as soon as possible.

It was a pity that this hadn't been said ten years earlier. Not that it had any effect: a survey of shareholders showed that 314 owners of a total of 1,103 shares wanted to continue with £10 a year, compared with 83 owners of 332 shares who wanted more frequent calls. Most shareholders never responded. The policy therefore continued unchanged.

In 1806 the finances of the company were tidied up, £15,000 being borrowed from various shareholders, the largest amount being from the Earl of Bridgewater, plus £10,000 from the company's bankers. A further £4,000 was borrowed in 1807, specifically to extend the Ruabon Brook Railway. All these sums were repaid by 1813.

No dividends were paid during the independent life of the Ellesmere Canal Company.

Merger

THE Ellesmere Canal comprised two sections separated by seventeen miles of the Chester Canal. Trade on the latter was largely dependant on the former's Wirral Line. Merger was almost inevitable, the only issues being the terms and the date.

As described in Chapter 2, the two companies were formally united on 1 July 1813.

Notes and references

This chapter is largely based on the minutes of the Ellesmere Canal (TNA: RAIL 827). The complex story of the changing proposals for the various lines of canal is explained in detail in Richard Dean's article, 'The metamorphosis of the Ellesmere Canal' in the *Journal of the Railway & Canal Historical Society*, November 1985.

1. The Royal Oak was renamed the Bridgewater Hotel in 1806 and the Ellesmere Hotel in the 1990s.
2. *Shrewsbury Chronicle*, 14 September 1792
3. *Derby Mercury*, 12 July 1792
4. *Derby Mercury*, 6 September 1792
5. *Shrewsbury Chronicle*, 26 October 1792
6. Thomas Telford (edited John Rickman), *Life of Thomas Telford*, 1838, p.34
7. Letter from Thomas Telford to Andrew Little, 29 September 1793. Transcripts of the Little letters are in the Ironbridge Institute Library.
8. Letter from William Jessop to William Turner, 2 October 1793: Shropshire Archives, 6000/15016
9. Quoted in Anthony Burton, *Thomas Telford*, 1999, p.21
10. As the minutes do not list exactly who was present, it is not possible to create a definitive list of Jessop's attendances. However, he certainly attended on 17 January 1794, 10 August 1795 and 30 November 1803 – the last is known because he was included in the list of shareholders present.
11. The absence of any mention of this report does not mean it was never written. The minutes do not generally seem to have mentioned matters where the decision was merely 'Report noted'. Jessop gave evidence to Parliament the following spring on the issues which the committee had asked him to specifically look at when writing this report.
12. Letters to Andrew Little, 6 November 1795 & 6 March 1798
13. Thomas Telford (edited John Rickman), *Life of Thomas Telford*, 1838, p.34
14. Oration annexed to the *Report to the General Assembly of the Ellesmere Canal Proprietors*, 27 November 1805, pp.21–2: Shropshire Archives, 665/3/206
15. Letter to Andrew Little, 3 November 1793
16. Patent no.1981; letter, 19 August 1797: Birmingham City Archives, Boulton & Watt Collection
17. Richard Dean, '"The machine", a boat lift mystery solved?', *Journal of the Railway & Canal Historical Society*, December 2007, pp.750–8
18. Letter, Jessop to Telford, 26 July 1795. [Davidson papers: Gibb, Rolt, Hadfield and Burton all refer to this letter without giving its location.]
19. Letter from James Thomson to Thomas Telford, 8 May 1818, following a discussion with William Stuttle: Institution of Civil Engineers, T/EG306
20. *Chester Chronicle*, 18 May 1798; Thomas Telford, *Life*, 1838, p.45
21. *Salopian Journal*, 3 January 1810
22. *The case for the Whitchurch extension*, 12 April 1809: Shropshire Archives, 6000/15128
23. Note by John Knight: Shropshire Archives, 6000/15088
24. *Directors' Canal Excursion, Whitchurch to Llantisilio, 22 & 23 June 1900: Short history of canals*: RAIL1007/517

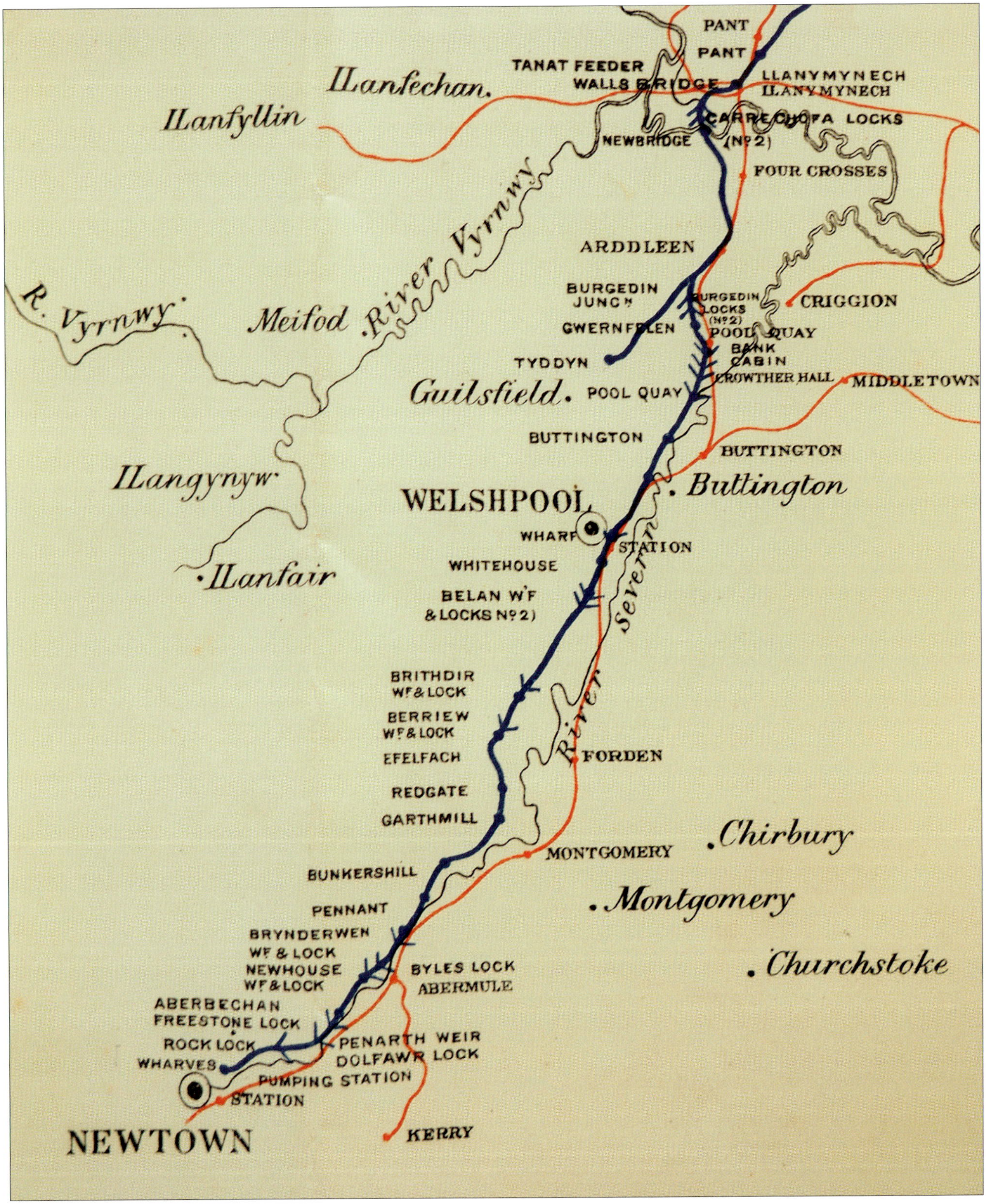
PANT
PANT
TANAT FEEDER
WALLS BRIDGE
LLANYMYNECH
LLANYMYNECH
Llanfechan.
Llanfyllin
CARREGHOFA LOCKS
NEWBRIDGE
(Nº 2)
FOUR CROSSES
River Vyrnwy
ARDDLEEN
R. Vyrnwy.
Meifod
BURGEDIN JUNCN
BURGEDIN LOCKS (Nº2)
CRIGGION
GWERNFELEN
POOL QUAY
BANK CABIN
TYDDYN
CROWTHER HALL
MIDDLETOWN
Guilsfield.
POOL QUAY
BUTTINGTON
BUTTINGTON
Llangynyw
Buttington
WELSHPOOL
WHARF
STATION
WHITEHOUSE
Llanfair
BELAN WF & LOCKS Nº2)
River Severn
BRITHDIR WF & LOCK
BERRIEW WF & LOCK
EFELFACH
FORDEN
REDGATE
GARTHMILL
Chirbury
MONTGOMERY
BUNKERSHILL
Montgomery
PENNANT
BRYNDERWEN WF & LOCK
NEWHOUSE WF & LOCK
BYLES LOCK
ABERMULE
Churchstoke
ABERBECHAN
FREESTONE LOCK
ROCK LOCK
WHARVES
PENARTH WEIR
DOLFAWR LOCK
PUMPING STATION
STATION
NEWTOWN
KERRY

6

The Montgomeryshire Canal

Promotion

On the morning of Tuesday 23 October 1792 a well-attended meeting at the Guildhall, Welshpool, approved the setting up of a committee to promote the extension of the Llanymynech Branch of the Ellesmere Canal to Berriew or beyond. At this time it was not certain whether this would be part of the Ellesmere Canal or a separate company. The meeting was chaired by William Owen, an active barrister and brother of Sir Arthur Owen of Glansevern Hall near Berriew, which he later inherited on his brother's death in 1816. The committee appointed included John Probert, Agent to successive Earls of Powis from 1769 to 1818.

'Canal Mania' was gripping the country: the committee was authorised to have discussions with groups interested in creating a canal from Berriew via Bishops Castle and Ludlow to the Leominster Canal and another down the Chirbury Vale to Shrewsbury. Surprisingly, the resolutions of this meeting make no mention of Newtown, though this was confirmed as the destination by the time that the Act was applied for.

It was usual for the Bills promoting new canals to state the canal would be 'of great public utility'. On the other hand, they were companies with shareholders, many or most of whom would like to see a large financial return on their investment – indeed, that is what their prospectuses usually promised. The Montgomeryshire Canal seems genuinely to have been an exception. It was promoted and financed principally by local people interested either in agricultural improvement or in the trade of Welshpool or Newtown. Almost 90% of the shares were bought by people who lived in Montgomeryshire or Shropshire; and just over half the shares were owned by peers or landed gentry – an unusually high proportion. Indeed, the subscription list was initially open only to 'inhabitants and landowners of the County of Montgomery'. In 1797, in a document protesting about the threat to impose a tax on canal tolls, the company wrote: 'This canal was not undertaken with a view of a large profit accruing from the tolls; for there is not even a probability that any such can arise; and therefore the subscribers ... had for their object the extension of agriculture, the reduction of horses ... the increase of horned cattle, and the preservation of the roads; with the consequent advantage to the public.'[1]

John Williams and Humphrey Jones were appointed as solicitors and David Pugh, John Pugh, James Turner and Robert Griffiths as treasurers. All had their offices at Welshpool. The choice of someone to advise on the route and engineering aspects was more problematical as the 'Canal Mania' was by then at its height. A total of 34 Acts were passed in the years 1791–3 (and a further ten were to be passed in 1794), so all the experienced engineers were fully committed. A Dadford family member was chosen: Thomas Dadford Junior, eldest son of the Thomas Dadford who was the engineer/contractor of the Glamorganshire Canal. He (Junior) was then engineer of the Monmouthshire Canal and of the Leominster Canal, so would have had little time for the Montgomeryshire Canal.

To Porth-y-Waen?

As mentioned in the last chapter, although the Ellesmere Canal's Act which had been passed in April 1793 authorised a branch to Llanymynech, that company had second (and third and fourth) thoughts about the exact route to adopt, partly because of justifiable complaints that it did not serve Oswestry adequately. In July 1793 William Jessop (for the Ellesmere Canal) and Thomas Dadford discussed the option of taking the Ellesmere Canal to Porth-y-waen, where the Earl of Powis owned limestone quarries. The following month the Ellesmere's committee resolved to apply to Parliament to build this line, though it did not in fact do so that autumn.

The route surveyed for the Montgomeryshire Canal was therefore to have an end-on junction at Porth-y-waen, no doubt much to the satisfaction of the Earl of Powis, a major investor in the Montgomeryshire Canal – and this was the line which was specified in the Montgomeryshire Canal Act, given the Royal

The Montgomeryshire Canal, derived from a 1895 map of the Shropshire Union Canal with peripheral detail removed. *Canal & River Trust*

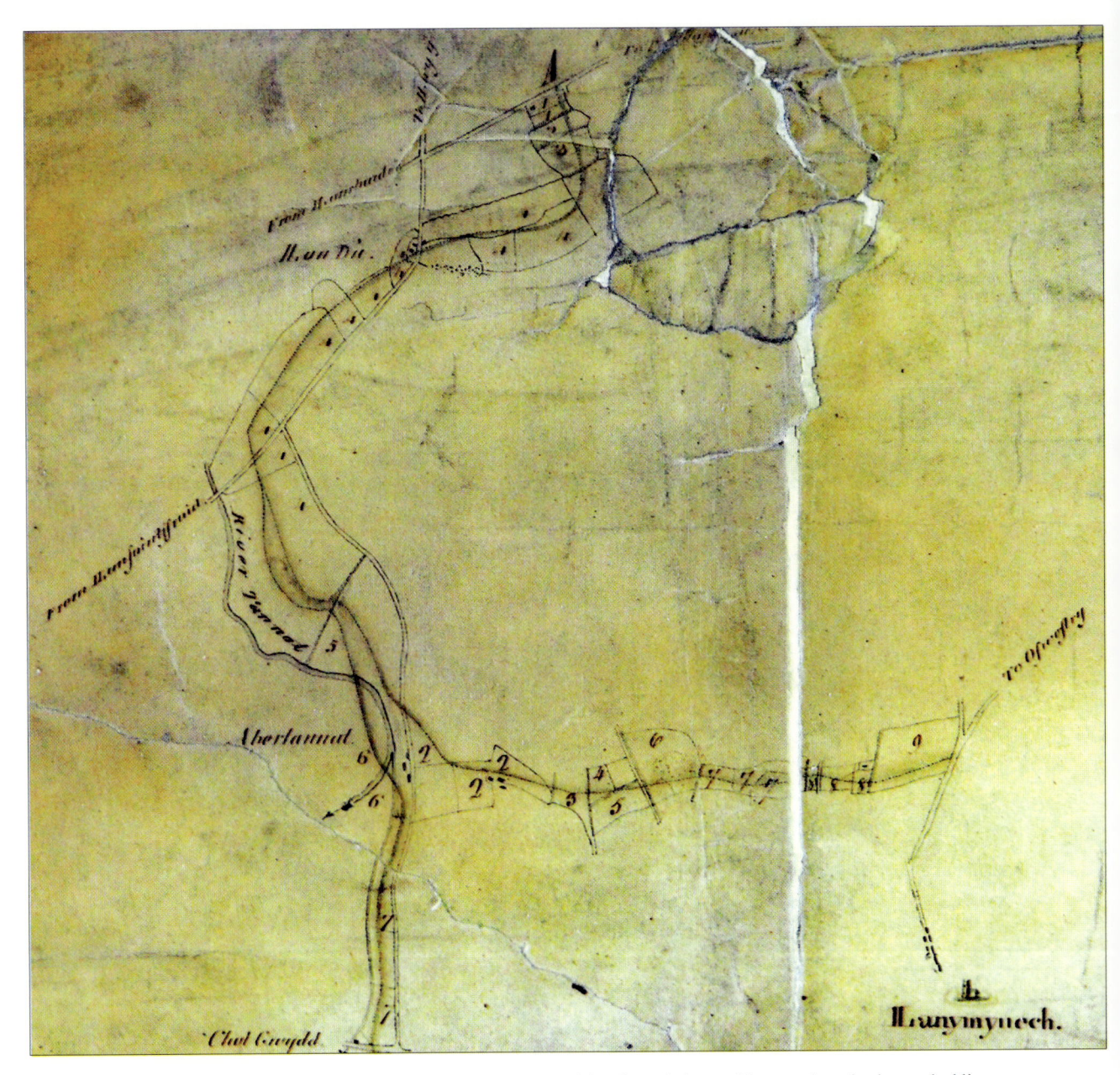

The statutory deposit map for the Montgomeryshire Canal showed it meeting the intended line of the Ellesmere Canal at Porth-y-waen, marked 'A' at the top (north) of the map. There would have been a flight of locks below the junction with a branch curving eastwards round the hill to serve the Llanymynech quarries. *Shropshire Archives*

Chapter 6: The Montgomeryshire Canal

Assent on 28 March 1794. There was also to be a short branch from about a mile south of Porth-y-waen around the south side of Llanymynech Hill to below other limestone quarries.

However in February 1794, whilst the Montgomeryshire Canal's Bill was progressing through Parliament, the Ellesmere Canal decided to proceed with the original Llanymynech scheme whilst not ruling out also building a line to Porth-y-waen. In fact the line was continued a further mile to Carreghofa, perhaps to deprive the Montgomeryshire Canal of independent access to the various limestone quarries, and the construction contract was let that August. Actually, this considerably simplified the building of the Montgomeryshire Canal, reducing its length by about two miles and eliminating the need for at least ten locks. Nevertheless, the Ellesmere Canal paid the Montgomeryshire £300 because the latter had already done some abortive work north of the crossing of the Vyrnwy.

The Montgomeryshire Canal continued to press the Ellesmere Canal to build their line to Porth-y-Waen. In the spring of 1796, the committee asked for a meeting with representatives of the Ellesmere Canal. The latter had a Bill before Parliament seeking major deviations of its approved lines; the Montgomeryshire Canal threatened to oppose this unless certain assurances were incorporated in the Bill. The Ellesmere Canal agreed to a clause stating that they would within four years put to Parliament proposals for a canal from Prees Henlle to Porth-y-wain – and that if they didn't, the Montgomeryshire Canal could make it at the expense of the Ellesmere Company.

Nothing further actually happened. The matter was mentioned in the Montgomeryshire Canal's Annual Report for 1799; a committee minute in 1801 noted that the question was asked whether their solicitor had given notice to preserve the power but there is no record of the answer. By this time both canal companies had exhausted their money, leaving their intended lines uncompleted.

The Dadford family

THE Dadford family of engineers worked mainly in the West Midlands and South Wales. Thomas Dadford (Senior) (1730–1809) had started his career as a member of James Brindley's team. He was engineer of the Trent & Mersey Canal for much of the 1780s and Surveyor of Bridges for Staffordshire from 1785 until 1792. In 1790 he starting working as engineer/contractor of the Glamorganshire Canal. His elder son Thomas Dadford (Junior) (c.1761–1801) assisted his father then became engineer to the Neath Canal (1791–2), Leominster Canal (1791–5), Monmouthshire Canal (1792–8) and the Brecknock & Abergavenny Canal (1796–1801). John Dadford (c.1769–c.1800) assisted his brother but emigrated to America in 1796. At various times between 1793 and 1798 all three were involved in the engineering of the Montgomeryshire Canal but the quality of their work was much criticised. Illness, possibly brought about by overwork, may have contributed to the Dadfords' problems.

Construction – and consequences

The engineer

HAVING obtained the Act, one of the first items of business was to formally appoint an engineer. Thomas Dadford Junior's younger brother, John, was chosen, despite being only 25 years of age. His contact was to run for four years and three months, unless the canal was not finished by the end of that time through no fault of his, in which case the contract would be extended until completion. In view of John's inexperience, the committee resolved that Thomas Junior was 'to come over and assist him with his opinion and advice as often as it should be thought necessary by the committee'.

Employing the Dadford family proved to be less than a total success. They performed well enough on their schemes in South Wales but clearly devoted insufficient time to this outlying scheme. In August 1796, because John had absented himself, Thomas Junior was asked to provide a 'proper person' to succeed him – and he proposed his 66-year-old father, Thomas Senior, which was agreed. This did not really solve the problem, as in May 1797 the committee instructed that Thomas Junior be told of their dissatisfaction, adding that he must report to the next meeting on the state of the works, and, if he did not, they would call in some other professional engineer. Thomas Senior replied that he would report to the June meeting; in the event he did not, and the committee resolved that no further payments be made to them. This prompted Thomas Junior to attend a week later.

At the request of the committee, in February 1798 William Jessop gave his opinion on the Dadfords' performance. He assured them that within the last four or five years he had not known any canal made without a considerable excess in the expenses above the estimate; that it did not appear to him that the excess in the expenses of this canal was in a greater proportion than what had commonly arisen in others; and that the canal from Carreghofa to Welshpool appeared to him to be in a good state. Subsequent events showed that this last, in particular, was a questionable conclusion. He added, 'Errors in judgement by engineers are very common and frequently unavoidable'; he therefore advised that no compensation be sought from them but he recommended termination of their contract. With much of the canal open for traffic, Jessop's recommendation was confirmed: the Dadfords were given a month's notice.

The construction contracts

IN July 1794 the main earthworks contract was let to Messrs James Green, H. Mansfield and Thomas Plevins, and the following month the contracts for the Vyrnwy Aqueduct and for the locks were let to John Simpson and William Hazledine. The latter firm also contracted for the flood-relief arches near the Vyrnwy Aqueduct, which were additional to the original plans. Other masonry work was let to John Nock.

Progress on the works was delayed. Completion had been

planned for Lady Day (25 March) 1797 but by that time the canal was finished only as far as Berriew. This wasn't quite as serious as it may have been, as the Llanymynech Branch of the Ellesmere Canal did not reach Carreghofa until mid-1798, when it was reported as navigable but not watertight. The principal reason for the delay to the works of the Montgomeryshire Canal was ascribed to the main earthworks contractors, who had 'notoriously neglected' their contract. Most of the blame was put on the misconduct of Mansfield. He, however, blamed other contractors and the lack of water for puddling. John Nock had financial problems and therefore some of his work was done by direct labour.

Costs had increased substantially. An account prepared to June 1798 showed that, compared with the original estimate of £48,000, some £68,800 had already been spent and a further £9,100 was owed, mainly for land purchase. Of the excess, £1,900 had been paid to obtain the Act, £4,300 was interest paid on the money called from shareholders, £1,000 was for wharfs, £200 for boats and £200 committee expenses – most canal estimates seemed to exclude these obvious and unexceptional costs. Works not estimated but deemed essential cost a further £5,200 (almost half of which was for the flood-relief arches), and preparations for continuing the canal beyond Garthmyl cost a further £1,600 (which implies that the construction of the canal south of Garthmyl was *not* in the original budget). The excess spending was therefore assessed as £15,500. As the paid up share capital was only £72,000, it is hardly surprising that the decision was taken to temporarily terminate the canal at Garthmyl. The Dadfords should not bear the full blame for the over-run in costs because, as noted in the last chapter, this was a period of significant price inflation.

The absence of good supervision showed itself in the poor quality of the engineering works. Belan Locks were reported as 'in a dangerous state' as early as 1799. Joseph Hill, when newly appointed in 1802, said that many of the aqueducts, locks and bridges, especially the masonry and brickwork, were 'very much out of repair, some of them dangerously'. Much of the trouble was ascribed to the locally made bricks being unable to withstand the wear. All the locks had to rebuilt from 1818 onwards, as did the small aqueducts at Brithdir and Welshpool.

The Vyrnwy Aqueduct

MOST serious, and most persistent, were the problems associated with the five-arch aqueduct over the Vyrnwy. The contractors, John Simpson and William Hazledine, each came to have a first-rate reputation – they jointly constructed the Chirk and Pontcysyllte Aqueducts, Simpson worked extensively for Telford in Scotland, and Hazledine provided the ironwork for the Menai Bridge, for example. However, their work on the Vyrnwy Aqueduct was less satisfactory, probably because of a combination of inadequate foundations and exceptionally prolonged wet weather. It was usable by February 1797 but in June was reported as being in need of repairs, part of the parapet and towpath walls having given way. Simpson and Hazledine agreed to effect the repairs and repay £500 but in August it was reported as still uncompleted.

The matter was referred to two referees with William Jessop as umpire. Thomas Telford offered to act as the contractors' nominee but the company could not find anyone to act for them; it was therefore left to Jessop to investigate and report. Jessop's award was in several parts:

– the company to pay Simpson & Hazledine £230 'towards and in full of their charges for rebuilding, repairing and securing the river aqueduct';
– Simpson & Hazledine to allow the company £24.3s in full of their penalties for not completing in due time;
– the contract bonds to be cancelled; and
– the arbitrator's charges of £59.2s to be borne £45 by the company and £14.2s by contractors.

In both this report and the one a year later on the Dadfords' performance, Jessop seems to have been excessively tolerant of the failures. Perhaps he was only too aware that a structure could fail even though the engineer thought he had done his job conscientiously – as had happened to him in 1792 when his aqueduct over the river Amber on the Cromford Canal developed a crack which threatened to bring it down.

Unfortunately, the repairs in 1797 did not cure the defects in the Vyrnwy Aqueduct. In 1799 one arch gave way because some of the stones had cracked through. Fourteen iron ties were put in: four over the arch which had given way, two over each of the three adjoining arches, and one over each pier.

The repairs carried out in 1823 by George Buck were even more substantial. He found that every arch was fractured, and concluded that this must have happened soon after its erection, blaming poor design and poor materials. The iron tie-bolts put in in 1799 had been put in much too high above the arches and were nearly all broken. He removed the clay lining and the longitudinal inside walls, which had contributed towards the failure by giving greater strength to one part of the arch than the rest. He then inserted wrought-iron tie-bolts lower down, this time in oak casing so that they could later be removed and examined. The clay puddle was replaced and new brickwork erected.

Major repairs were carried out in 1892, much of the ironwork being replaced and the upstream buttresses being made more substantial. Further repairs were done in the 1980s, and in 2009 it was considered that works estimated to cost £1.6 million needed to be done to make the structure fully secure. At the time of writing (2018) this has not been done.

Water supply

THE Montgomeryshire Canal is unusual in being a 'sump' canal, that is, it is lowest in the middle, thus requiring a water supply at both ends.

At Carreghofa the water came from two sources: the Llanymynech Branch of the Ellesmere Canal and the river Tanat. In theory the former should have been adequate for all the needs,

Chapter 6 : The Montgomeryshire Canal

The Vyrnwy Aqueduct, showing the evidence of the repairs.
Railway & Canal Historical Society

providing more boats went north from the Llanymynech limestone wharfs than came south onto the Montgomeryshire Canal, but in practice because this pound of the Llanymynech Branch leaked there was often a shortage of water to work Carreghofa Locks. The supply from the Tanat was from an extension from the leat of Carreghofa Mill. It originally came in below Carreghofa locks, presumably as the Montgomeryshire Canal did not want it to be wasted in the lowest pound of the Llanymynech Branch. The result was never wholly satisfactory, and in 1819 it was reported that boats entering from the Ellesmere & Chester Canal (as it had become) could not be loaded to more than 16 tons. This prompted the proposal to improve the supply from the Tanat by building a new weir and bringing the feeder to the top of the locks. George Buck calculated that because they could then load their boats fully, traders to Newtown would save 7¾d a ton for boats laden with coal or 3½d a ton if they carried limestone. Parliamentary approval was needed for the new feeder. The draft Bill proposed that it should navigable but land-owners objected so the clause was dropped. Having obtained the Act in June 1821 the work was done promptly. It cost £4,110, just over double Buck's original estimate, mainly because the weir was constructed in freestone instead of timber.

The southern section of the canal was to have been fed from the Severn at Newtown but this was no longer an option once Garthmyl became the terminus. A few streams came down the steeply sloping hillsides into the canal (where they still cause problems through creating gravel spits) but the volume of water from them was nowhere near adequate. A feeder was cut from the river Rhiew; to avoid a dispute, the mill at Berriew was leased. Sir Watkin Williams Wynn agreed to his large pool, Llynmawr, being used as a reservoir to mitigate summer droughts and to the canal company raising the dam by about 3ft. This still did not solve the problem. In the summer of 1800 despite all the water in Llynmawr reservoir being taken, even empty boats could not pass. The summer of 1801 was almost as bad. Whilst Llynmawr reservoir was being used a rule was in force that locks had to be worked alternately up and down, even though this caused inconvenience to the traders.

The only satisfactory solution was to provide a feeder

from the Severn. A watercourse from Newhouse Pool (a mile north-east of Aberbechan) was agreed in 1805 and finished the following year.

Operation

THE canal opened from Carreghofa to Welshpool early in February 1797, with four boats bringing in coal for the poor. Later that month it was navigable to Berriew and by August the main line was open to Garthmyl. By the following year the Guilsfield Branch was also open for traffic. Lock-houses were built at Carreghofa and Burgedin; others were added later. An office and a warehouse were built at Welshpool in 1801; two further warehouses were built at Welshpool in 1807.

Staff

RICHARD CROSS was appointed Engineer & Agent in 1798 on a salary of £80 a year but died in 1802.

Nobody responded to the first advertisement for his replacement, but following the second, William Crossley was offered the job on an annual salary of £136.10s. He declined, instead taking up the post of resident engineer of the Rochdale Canal.

The job was readvertised and this time Joseph Hill was appointed on an annual salary of £140 subject to satisfactory references. Although he had been dismissed from his previous employment as engineer of the Southampton & Salisbury Canal either no references were asked for or they must have been satisfactory. Indeed, his performance for the Montgomeryshire Canal was such that in 1806 he was paid a bonus of £50 'as a compliment'. He was absent for much of 1815 through illness, and retired in 1819, dying later that year. After he had retired it was discovered that he had been overpaid £23.12s.3d.

Following the creation in 1815 of a separate organisation for the section south of Garthmyl known as the 'Western Branch' (as discussed later in this chapter) the duties of the Clerk & Engineer were restricted to the part north of Garthmyl, the 'Eastern Branch'.

Hill's successor was George Buck, the most able engineer the company ever possessed. His annual salary was £150, increased to £250 the following year, plus an allowance for

:::
George Buck (1789–1854)

GEORGE BUCK was born near Norwich, the son of Quakers. He trained under Ralph Walker, a leading docks, river and water supply engineer. In 1819 he was appointed engineer of the Eastern Branch of the Montgomeryshire Canal, and in 1832 he was also made engineer for the Western Branch. He left the following year to become one of Robert Stephenson's senior assistants on the London–Birmingham railway. In 1837 he became Engineer-in-Chief of the Manchester & Birmingham Railway, his best-known achievements being the Dane and Stockport Viaducts. Ill-health forced his retirement in the mid-1840s.
:::

a horse. He was also given a gratuity of £100 'for his able services' in 1824. He resigned in 1833.

James Sword took over the following year but left in 1839 as a result of dissatisfaction with his accounting.

It was then decided that there was no need for anyone with special engineering experience, though the person they actually appointed, Edward Johnes, appears to have been (or became) a competent engineer. With the job title of Clerk, he had an annual salary of £150.

Details of staffing as at 1844 are given in a report by a sub-committee charged with reviewing the expenditure. The regular establishment of the company consisted of the Clerk, one wharfinger at Carreghofa, nine lockkeepers (of whom three were also wharfingers), one foreman of the works, one carpenter, one mason, one mason's assistant, one blacksmith, and six labourers. It was recommended that the mason's assistant be discharged and that temporary assistance be engaged when required.

Robert Baugh, the wharfinger at Carreghofa who was also the principal toll-collector, was shared with the Ellesmere & Chester Canal. The sub-committee was critical of his undertaking work in addition to that of the two canal companies. In 1815 he must have upset the committee by the manner in which he asked for a raise in pay because they resolved: 'That Mr Robert Baugh be wrote to desiring him to apply to the Committee in a more respectful manner for an advance of salary and to state the ground of such application without dictating to them what they ought to do'. The pay increase was then refused, but in 1819 his daily rate was increased from 2s.1d to 2s.6d – £39 a year for a six-day week.

The proposed Guilsfield diversion

THE lowest pound of the main line was the 1¼ miles from the bottom of the two Burgedin Locks to Bank Lock, the lowest of the four locks leading up to Pool Quay. In this pound the valley of the Guilsfield Brook was crossed on the Gwernfelû embankment almost ¾ mile long. A lock-free branch 2¼ miles long went up the valley of the Guilsfield Brook to Tyddyn Basin, some ⅞ mile short of Guilsfield village. This had been built to a lower standard than the main line, the minimum width at water level being 24ft, compared with 28ft on the main line.

Someone, most likely Joseph Hill, made the suggestion of altering the main line to one which followed the contour at the level of the Guilsfield Branch, leaving that branch near its far end, crossing to the other side of the valley, then rejoining the former line between the second and third locks of the Pool Quay flight. This would eliminate the need for repairing the two Burgedin Locks and also Bank and Cabin Locks of the Pool Quay flight. In October 1815 the committee decided to ask Josias Jessop (son of William Jessop, who had died one year earlier) to examine the suggestion and Hill's calculations of the costs. However, Hill went off work with a serious illness, and judging from the lack of a report back, no action was taken.

After George Buck was appointed the proposal for diversion

Chapter 6 : The Montgomeryshire Canal

Carreghofa, the principal location for gauging boats
entering the Montgomeryshire Canal, photographed after restoration in 1987.
Railway & Canal Historical Society: Shearing Collection

was resurrected, Buck's detailed report being considered by the committee in July 1820. The new line to be cut would be just over 2½ miles long; the cost, including the widening and deepening of the Guilsfield Branch, was estimated as 'not more than £6,726.15s.6d'. Buck considered that the alternative of reconstructing the four locks would cost at least £7,000, assuming they were done in the same substantial manner as those locks south of Welshpool which had been recently repaired: Rectory Lock had cost £1,877 and Brithdir Lock £1,986. There would also be on-going savings: three lock-keepers at an annual cost of £80 and maintenance of the four locks estimated at £70 a year. There would no longer be a risk of failure of the Gwernfelû embankment from an accident or from floods or other natural causes. When locks were rebuilt, stoppages and consequential loss of income were inevitable, whereas this new line could be constructed without interfering with the traffic on the canal. Once it was opened, the land across the valley could be sold and the material from the locks and bridges taken up and cleaned for use elsewhere. A practical advantage claimed for the new line was that the sump pound would then be ten miles long (a slight exaggeration), which would not necessarily save greatly on water supplies but would make them less prone to losses through leaking gates. The committee accepted that the canal's income would be increased by at least £1,000 a year because they would be able to charge traders for the three extra miles they would have to travel. This assumed that the rates of tonnage being applied continued, and that trade did not diminish. The justice of this action, and whether it would be accepted by the traders, does not seem to have been considered.

A special General Assembly meeting in November 1820 approved an application to Parliament to authorise this deviation, the Bill also to include the changes to the Tanat Feeder. This Act was passed in June 1821, including a clause that the same rates of tonnage would apply as in the original 1794 Act. The first clause in the Act gave the reasons why the measure was advantageous to the public, including 'avoiding the delay in passing several locks'. This was disingenuous: about half an hour would have been saved by the elimination of four locks, but the extra length would have taken about an hour – a net additional half an hour's journey time.

George Buck estimated that the Guilsfield deviation would cost the traders an extra 4½d a ton on coal and 2¼d on limestone but because the improved Tanat feeder would allow the boats to be fully laden the traders would be better off. Overall, Buck argued, the quantity of goods carried would not be reduced.

In September 1821 he reported on the priorities for action, recommending that the Tanat feeder should be done first, which would necessitate borrowing £1,400. As things turned out, the feeder cost far more than the original estimate and unplanned repairs to the Vyrnwy Aqueduct also had to be paid for. Rebuilding Belan and Carreghofa Locks was then given a higher priority than the Guilsfield deviation. Buck had not forgotten about the Guilsfield deviation as there is an oblique reference to it in his notes in August 1826, but in reality the idea had been abandoned. Cabin and Bank Locks were repaired in 1827 and the two Burgedin Locks in 1828–9.

Incidents at Carreghofa

The boats entering the Montgomeryshire Canal were gauged at Carreghofa Locks, which was the entrance to the canal. On 19 December 1826, Edward Perkins was on duty there, letting through a boat operated by John Humphreys of Berriew. An 18-year-old youth, John Bagley was accompanying the boat's steerer. Whilst Perkins was busy, Bagley threw a brick which hit Perkins on the head, injuring him so severely that he died a week later.

George Buck sent two men to arrest Bagley, fearing he might try to escape. (This was a couple of decades before there was a county police force.) The coroner's inquest found Bagley guilty of manslaughter, and he was sent to Ruthin Gaol to await the Assizes.

Edward Perkins' eldest son Thomas was the keeper of the lower lock at Carreghofa. He seemed conscientious and attentive, helped with the gauging of the boats and could write well, so, although only 20 years old, was appointed in his father's place.

Seventeen years later Thomas Perkins was accused of fraud through false gauging. The exact nature of the suspected fraud is not made clear in the company's records, but it seems that it was thought that Perkins short-measured loads of limestone, with the implication that he was getting a bribe from Robert Rogers, the carrier of the loads, the canal company's certification of the weight being used to pay the sellers of the limestone, one of whom was Mr D. Jones of Llanymynech. Jones must have suspected he was being short-paid and told Robert Baugh, the wharfinger at Carreghofa, of his suspicions. Baugh seems to have asked Jones to gauge boats at Llanymynech, and he would try to check them at Carreghofa, without letting Perkins realise this was being done.

All boats had three copper strips on each side of the boat; one in the middle and one about 12ft from each end. These had numbered marks showing how deep the boat was in the water, calibrated by successively adding quarter ton (600lb) cast-iron weights. In case the boat was not laden evenly, it was necessary to note the reading on all six strips. Each extra ton would put the boat about one inch deeper in the water.

A sub-committee of three members of the Montgomeryshire Canal's committee investigated the accusation, interviewing several witnesses at Llanymynech. Jones told them that he had gauged several boats at Llanymynech and found the tonnage greater than that assessed by Perkins. He had checked the strips on one side personally, and he employed a man to check those on the opposite side. However, the sub-committee found that all but one of these boats were carrying loads sold by Jones, and they felt it could be said that he had an interest in ascribing higher weights. They therefore concentrated on the remaining boat, where the tonnage returned by Perkins was said to be deficient by 1½ tons. The total load was not stated, but was probably about 20 tons.

Baugh said that he had gauged the boats a short distance from the locks at Carreghofa. He recorded the gauging numbers on both sides of the boats, though he admitted that the boat being specifically investigated by the sub-committee was not stationary at the time – one wonders exactly where he did this, as he would have had to cross the canal. Another dealer in stone stated that he would not sell stone to Rogers as he thought he did not get paid for the same tonnage as when a similar-looking load was sold to other people. The wharfinger's tonnage book showed that the tonnage of stone carried in Rogers' boats had in almost every case been reported greater since the accusation of fraud than before it.

The sub-committee felt the evidence was not good enough to lead to a conviction in the courts, but they were satisfied that it was strong enough to require the dismissal of Perkins.

To Newtown – the Western Branch

In 1797 Thomas Dadsford Junior was instructed to mark out the line of the canal from Garthmyl to Newtown and approval was given to making 1,200,000 bricks, but the following year, recognising that the funds had been exhausted, it was agreed that no further work was to be done 'until an alteration in the times and circumstances shall take place which we flatter ourselves is not too distant'.

It was a further fifteen years before extension was seriously considered again. In 1813 Joseph Hill was asked to do a survey and make an estimate of the cost. At the Extraordinary General Assembly called specifically to discuss the matter, continuation to Newtown was agreed by a narrow margin: 92 votes (shares) to 86. For such an important decision it is surprising that only a tenth of shareholders attended; including proxies, fewer than a quarter of the shares were represented. Josias Jessop was engaged to review Hill's work. His route differed somewhat from Hill's at the Newtown end, and he considered that it would be necessary to raise a further £40,000 to complete the canal. The General Assembly in July 1814 accepted Jessop's tabled report and decided to apply to Parliament for the necessary powers, but it also agreed to send Jessop's report to all shareholders. At the subsequent meeting a committee was appointed to consider the Bill, but that committee recommended not to proceed with the extension.

Opinion amongst the major shareholders was divided: the Welshpool interests such as the Earl of Powis and his Agent, John Probert, were against extension, whilst the Newtown interests such as William Pugh and John Herbert were in favour, as was Sir Arthur Owen of Glansevern (near Berriew).

A compromise was worked out, and an Extraordinary General Meeting held in February 1815 at which it was decided to go ahead. The resultant Act, passed in June that year, specified that the existing canal from Carreghofa to Garthmyl should be called the Eastern Branch and the extension to Newtown the Western Branch. (More natural would have been to call them the Northern and Southern Branches, respectively, in my opinion.) To protect the existing shareholders, a separate account would be kept of the costs, revenues, profits and dividends of the Western Branch until it achieved a 5% dividend, when the two parts would be consolidated. In other respects, the intention was that the whole would be considered to be one concern, with the same officers to be appointed to both. But, as will be seen later, it didn't work out like that.

Construction

CONSTRUCTION of the 7¼-mile extension proceeded slowly. Newtown was reached in early 1819, the terminus being on the opposite side of the river to the medieval core of the town. The Western Branch was formally opened on 1 March 1819, the *Shropshire Journal* reporting:

> A procession of 50 boats, laden with coal and lime, together with the workmen, amounting to several hundreds, passed along the new work, after which the men were treated with a substantial dinner and plenty of cwrw da [good beer]. A grand procession was also formed by a large body of land-owners, tradesmen, and other respectable individuals peculiarly interested in the success of this great undertaking, who assembled in parties to dine at the Bear's Head and other Inns, in Newtown, where it is almost unnecessary to say due regard was had both to the honour of St David and to the reiteration of those sentiments and hopes which the business of the day was so particularly calculated to excite.[2]

However, the canal was not usable to any extent for two more years because the water supply was inadequate. The original plan had been to take a feeder on the level from further up the river Severn but this proved impracticable because of the objection from owners of flannel mills who relied on waterwheels powered by the river. The canal company therefore constructed a weir downstream of all the mills and installed a pump powered by a 22ft-diameter undershot waterwheel. This was supplemented in times of low flow by a 8hp steam engine which raised water some 13ft from below the weir.

Jessop's 1816 estimate for the works, excluding land and damages, was £25,737.[3] Different sources quote different 'actual' costs for building the canal. The most reliable was probably the one given in a cumulative summary of receipts and payments given to the General Assembly in 1833, showing the works as costing £34,800, land & damages £5,100, and solicitors & engineers £3,200 – a total of £43,100 – however, this is somewhat less than figures quoted elsewhere. As well as the weir and pump at Newtown, the cost of puddling and lining throughout the canal had not been included in Jessop's estimate.[4]

The *North Wales Chronicle* enthusiastically reported in 1828 that it was proposed to extend the canal beyond Newtown to Llanidloes, but this was probably nothing more than somebody's wishful thinking.[5]

In 1834 Bryan Donkin and William Cubitt, two Vice-Presidents of the Institution of Civil Engineers, were asked to inspect the canal. They reported that the line had been well laid out and the works well executed. They concluded: 'We have not ... seen anything that was either unnecessary or useless, and ... we do not think that the sum named to us of £53,000 is either an extravagant or improvident expenditure'.[6]

Management and staffing

THE two Branches were managed separately. Unfortunately the minutes of the Western Branch have not survived, but it seems that for much of the time the two committees had no member in common. Apart from two years (1832–3) when George Buck was Clerk & Engineer of both Branches, each appointed different officers despite duplication in engineering expertise, store-keeping, administration and billing the traders. Even worse, there appeared to be animosity between the two Branches; indeed, the Eastern Branch generally had a smoother relationship with the Ellesmere & Chester Canal than it did with the Western Branch. As an example, in 1818 the Annual Report for the Eastern Branch stated: 'Of the Western Branch of this Canal, the committee can say nothing official, having never received any report of its proceedings until this morning.'

From 1819 until 1832 John Williams was Clerk & Engineer; from 1834 for the rest of the independent life of the Western Branch it was Thomas Newnham.

Financial problems

EVEN if the canal had been built within its estimated cost, it would still have been in financial trouble. Only 235 of the 400 new shares were sold and several of these were never fully paid. In 1818 a sum of £6,000 was borrowed from the Exchequer Bill Loan Commissioners. This organisation had been set up the previous year to provide loans to enable public works to be completed, the principal aim being 'affording employment for the labouring classes of the community'. Loans were to be repaid over twenty years with an interest rate of (generally) 5%; as this was the market rate or more, indeed it was the maximum that could then be charged under usury laws, this source of borrowing was a last resort. The loan to the Western Branch of the Montgomeryshire Canal was one of the first granted. Remarkably, from application to approval took only one week, the Commissioners' engineering advisor being Thomas Telford.[7]

William Pugh of Brynllwarch saved the canal from bankruptcy by lending the money which enabled the Western Branch to be completed and the principal creditors to be paid. Shortly after the Western Branch opened the shareholders showed their appreciation by giving Pugh three silver tureens and other items worth 100 guineas – an inscription referred to his 'foresight and activity' in promoting the canal and his 'indefatigable exertions during the progress of the works' but did not mention his loan.[8]

As at 29 September 1833 it was calculated that Pugh was owed the unsecured sum of £38,015.19s.2d, including accumulated interest. An Act of Parliament was obtained that year to secure that sum as a mortgage debt with rights to take over the assets in the (likely) event of non-payment. A compromise had to be made in order to get opposition to the Bill to be withdrawn: the financing of the debt was to be £25,000 by way of mortgage and £13,000 in shares. The mortgage, in £500 units, was soon sold on, though it is not known whether these units were sold at a substantial discount.[9]

On 8 November 1833 Pugh took formal possession of the Western Branch, erecting gates upon the approaches to the basin at Newtown.

Trade

MUCH is known about the amounts of the various traffics carried on the Eastern Branch of the Montgomeryshire Canal because the Annual Reports from 1807 to 1844 contained a detailed analysis. Less is known about traffic on the Western Branch.

The tonnage carried varied according to the state of the economy, canal closures for maintenance and the transport alternatives available. To give some examples: higher grain prices meant a greater incentive for land improvement and hence more limestone; whereas a great increase in the demand for iron for new railway schemes nationally caused an increase in the price of coal which led to a decrease in the tonnage of both coal and limestone carried by the canal. The Montgomeryshire Canal was also affected by what happened on the Ellesmere Canal; for example in 1808 the latter had a five-week closure in August and September, then in the following January a breach on it interfered with trade for a further five weeks.

Limestone and coal for lime kilns

THE Montgomeryshire Canal's predominant trade was limestone brought from Llanymynech and Porth-y-waen for burning in order to improve the productivity of land. The other important use of lime was in the manufacture of mortar for the building industry. The transport of limestone and its associated coal accounted for more than two-thirds of the tonnage conveyed on the canal in most years.

The Eastern and Western Branches differed in their distribution of lime kilns. On the Eastern Branch almost every settlement had kilns, though there was only one small group within Welshpool itself. Of the 58 kilns, the biggest group were at Belan (eight kilns) and Garthmyl (twelve kilns) – the latter being the original head of navigation of course, with its kilns then serving the valley up to Newtown as well as across the river to the Leighton and Montgomery areas. Some Garthmyl kilns were out of production by the 1850s, possibly earlier. Some lime from the kilns on the Eastern Branch was used for bringing upland fields into effective production, particularly in times of high grain prices. However, probably more was used by long-established and productive lowland farms such as the Earl of Powis's home farm of Coed-y-dinas.[10]

On the Western Branch, 22 of the 34 kilns were near the terminus at Newtown. Being well outside and down-wind of the main urban area, they would probably not have been particularly environmentally offensive. Although more modern than most of the kilns on the Eastern Branch, they did not differ substantially in their capacity, though the surviving two (on top of which a bungalow has been erected) have a noticeably wider arch. The Newtown kilns would have served the Severn valley up to Llanidloes and Caersws as well as the surrounding

---

William Pugh (1783–1842)

WILLIAM PUGH of Brynllwarch, four miles east of Newtown, was born in 1783, educated at Rugby School and Cambridge University, and studied law in order to be better qualified as a country gentleman and magistrate. Wealthy both by inheritance and marriage, he did much for the people of Newtown and the surrounding area. He invested over £17,000 in creating turnpike roads, was a leading promoter of Inclosure Acts and land improvement, promoted Newtown's gas works and the building of the Public Rooms, and was instrumental in getting the flannel market moved from Welshpool to Newtown. A silver epergne purchased by public subscription was presented 'by the inhabitants of Newtown as a token of their esteem and gratitude for the very great and successful exertions made by him to promote the prosperity and the trade' of Newtown.

Politically a Liberal, he strongly advocated political reform and was instrumental in calming the riotous mob in 1831. Although well-loved in Newtown (especially by the working class), his actions and ideas were not so well viewed by the leading people of Welshpool and much of the country gentry, including some who were on the Committee of the Eastern Branch of the Montgomeryshire Canal. He lent the money to enable the Western Branch to be completed but spent too much on the canal and his other ventures; worse, he had made the mistake of borrowing to help finance them. His creditors were pressing and, although he determined to sell property in order to be able to repay his debts, in June 1835 he moved to Caen in Normandy where he lived until his death.

Chapter 6 : The Montgomeryshire Canal

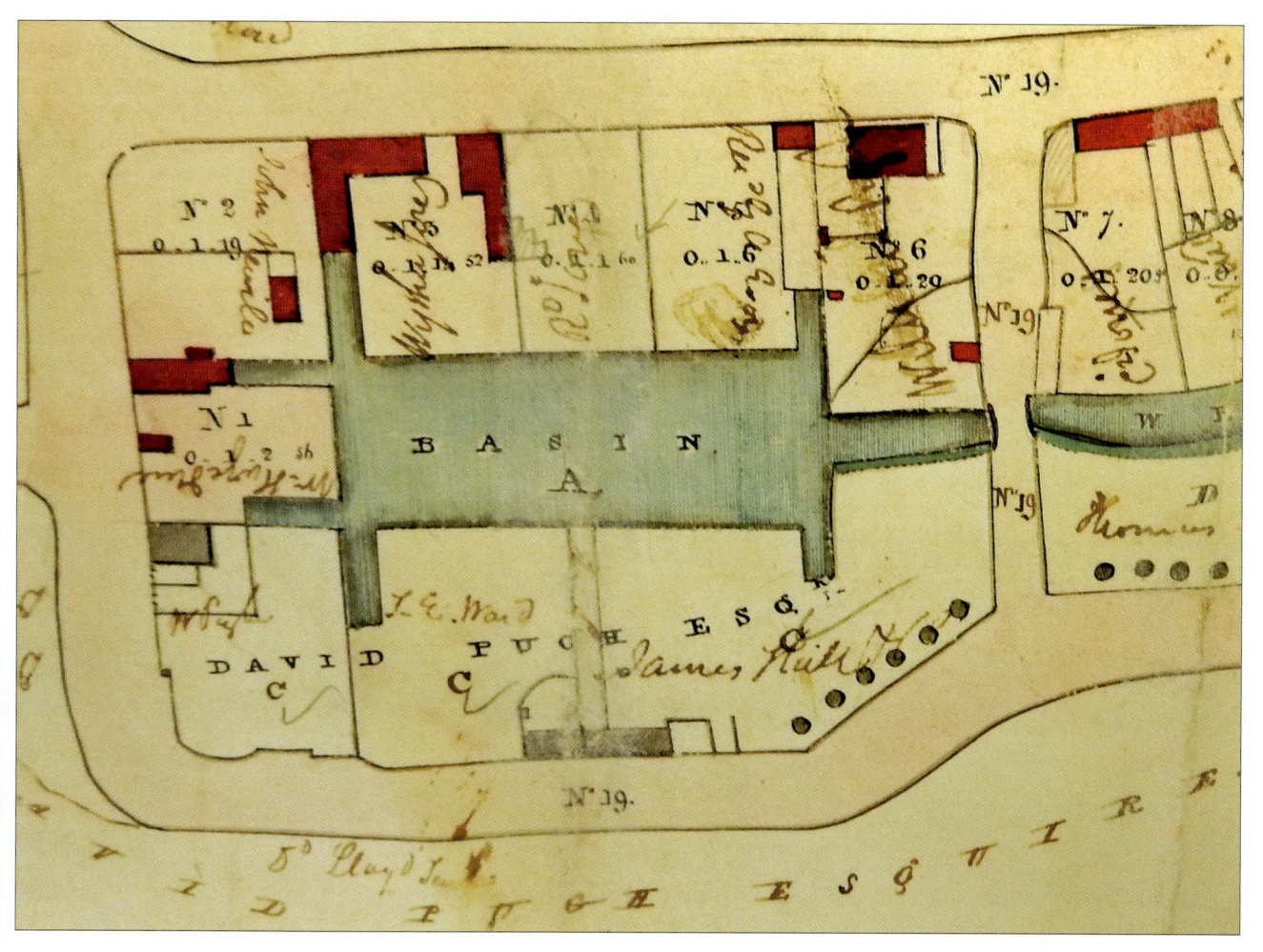

Newtown Basin, from a map prepared in August 1833 for William Pugh's taking over of the Western Branch. The hand-written notes refer to the occupiers of the various wharves.
Canal & River Trust

upland area. The production of building mortar was also probably more important at Newtown than elsewhere on the canal.

Liming the fields was a seasonal activity, taking place between the harrowing of early summer and that of the autumn, that is, between May and October. Given suitable cover, quick lime could be stored ready for sale, but production was markedly seasonal too.

For the first couple of decades from the opening of the canal to Garthmyl in 1797, the ratio of the weights of limestone to coal was approximately 4:1, later it was closer to 3:1 – this was most likely to have been attributable to the fact that many lime-kiln operators also acted as coal-merchants. At first the coal would have come mainly from the Oswestry coalfield; after 1805 Chirk and Ruabon coal became more plentiful. Thomas Edward Ward, who developed the Chirk coalfield, had twelve kilns at Newtown.

At first the canal company itself built the kilns, leasing them to entrepreneurs. For example Messrs Edwards, Simpson & Hazledine leased those at Belan and Garthmyl for a rent of 10% of the building cost; Gould & Co. leased others at Garthmyl on the same terms. The rent seems low, but probably the reasoning was that the company would make most of its money on the tonnage to be charged on the transport of the raw materials. Later kilns were built by private entrepreneurs.

The amounts of limestone conveyed on the Eastern Branch fluctuated from year to year, but after 1807 (the earliest year for which data is available) was generally between 35,000 and 55,000 tons, peaking in 1827 and 1840. In the first half of the 1830s the average quantity of limestone conveyed on the Western Branch was 26,200 tons, fractionally over half that conveyed on the Eastern Branch. (Of course, all this limestone would have travelled the whole length of the Eastern Branch as well.)

In the earlier days of the canal there was some conveyance of quicklime, which was an unstable and unpopular cargo as it reacted with water; after the mid 1820s the amount of this cargo became negligible.

Other bulk trades

THE other major trade was 'fire coals', that is, coal for domestic and industrial use. Before 1805 the amount was not up to expectations as the traders were still tending to use carriage by land; once the Chirk and Pontcysyllte Aqueducts were open, land carriage virtually ceased. The canal tonnage increased steadily until 1824, then stayed remarkably constant at about 20,000 tons a year on the Eastern Branch – about 20% of the total tonnage carried. The Western Branch carried just over half the amount of fire coal which was carried on the Eastern.

Other bulk cargoes included timber, building stone, slates, bark and coke, in order of diminishing significance. In total this group typically accounted for between 7% and 11% of the total tonnage carried. The trade in slates reduced as time went on; that in building stone increased until about 1830 then tended to diminish. Stone was the one mineral produced near the Montgomeryshire Canal, a tramroad being built from Stondard Quarry down to a wharf by the Lledan Brook in Welshpool in 1819. Slates and coke were inward traffic. Timber and bark were the only significant outward traffics, particularly welcome to the boat-owners as providing a return cargo.

Commercial goods

COMMERCIAL goods – that is, parcels traffic and other one-offs – increased steadily from an average of 1,000 tons a year in the last years of the first decade of the century to 6,000 tons in the early 1840s. This was helped by the opening of the Middlewich Branch in 1833 which gave a direct route to Manchester. Following the opening of the Birmingham & Liverpool Junction Canal in 1835 which considerably shortened the route to Birmingham, general traffic improved further. Pickford's introduced a fly-boat (fast) service to London, the first boat arriving at Newtown on 25 June and leaving on the evening of the following day. By working all day and night, it was expected to reach London on the morning of 1 July – 270 miles in under six days.[11] This may have been purely publicity as it is much more likely that the service would have been integrated with others, with transhipment at, for example, Barbridge and Birmingham. The London boat was noted as carrying an average load of three tons each way at Newtown in 1836.

In general, the pattern of trade on the Western Branch was similar to that on the Eastern. The anomalous cargo was general commercial goods, where well over 80% of the traffic was conveyed through the Eastern Branch on to the Western.

Competition

THE river Severn was navigable up to Pool Quay for boats of a maximum of 20 tons burden, though floods interfered with traffic in winter, as did water shortages in summer. By 1800 the main trades were all downstream: timber from Pool Quay, lime and lead from Llanymynech and slates from Clawdd Coch on the Vyrnwy. Traditionally the transport links from the upper Severn valley were to Shrewsbury and Bristol; the Montgomeryshire Canal however did divert some formerly Bristol traffic to Liverpool, continuing a tendency that had been in progress in mid-Wales since Tudor times.

There was only one mention in the Annual Reports of the river Severn as a rival, when it was said that contracts had been made by traders for timber and bark to go by that route and that this was especially serious as this was one of the few opportunities for back carriage on the canal. There are no references to any loads being transhipped from the canal to the river at Pool Quay, though it is possible that some timber was so handled as there is a record of the landing place at Pool Quay being covered with oak as late as the 1830s.

On the other hand, roads did give effective competition in some circumstances. When the bridge over the Vyrnwy near Llanymynech opened in the 1820s, some limestone traffic moved to the improved turnpike route.

Because Shrewsbury could not be reached from Welshpool by canal until 1835, and then only by an excessively circuitous route, a large proportion of the town's commercial goods came by road and the town's principal product, flannel, was dispatched by road. In 1828 three carriers provided a total of four journeys a week between Welshpool and Shrewsbury, and in 1835 six carriers provided a total of eight journeys.

As at Welshpool, Newtown carriers dealt with goods going to and from Shrewsbury. They also distributed items brought by canal, with scheduled services to Llanidloes, Aberystwyth, Machynlleth and Brecon. The Western Branch gave £100 and the Eastern Branch £150 towards the cost of a new road from Dolfor over the summit to Llanbadarn Fynydd in the valley of the Ithon (a section of which is now the A483 from Newtown to Llandrindod Wells), regarding this as a feeder to their canal.

The Eastern Branch repeatedly reduced its tonnage rates. When these decisions were made, there was the hope but not the certainty that an increase in the amount carried would more than compensate for the reduction in the charges. And sometimes this succeeded; in 1829, for example, it was reported that the quantity of grocery goods carried along the canal had nearly doubled since the reduction in tonnage in 1825. In 1844 the tonnage rate for gravel was reduced to the exceptionally low rate of one farthing per ton per mile; the committee recommended this 'in order that the public may be supplied with an article in which this country is deficient'.

The Western Branch was similarly sensitive to demand, though its precarious financial position meant it was unable to take any risks. In 1837 it felt forced to apply to Parliament for an increase in its statutory tonnage rates, which created much opposition in Newtown.

Finances

The share capital authorised in 1794 totalled £72,000, in £100 shares. When this had been spent the company evidently decided not to borrow the further £20,000 permitted by the Act but instead to cease construction.

Explicitly to emphasise the local benefits, the Act included a restriction on dividends whereby if clear profits exceeded 10%, the Grand Jury of Montgomeryshire was to direct the company to reduce its charges. However, with the exception of limestone, the maximum permitted tolls were higher than those on the Ellesmere Canal. Unusually, the maximum charges permitted by the 1794 Act were not uniform for the whole of the canal: they could be higher south of Garthmyl. For example, the maximum tonnage per mile for coal was 1½d on the Ellesmere Canal, 2¼d between Carreghofa and Garthmyl, and 3d south of Garthmyl; for general merchandise the maxima were 3d, 4d and 6d respectively.

The interests of the local community – or of the local people who had made loans to the turnpike trust – were safeguarded in a clause which required compensation to be paid for the diminution of tolls at the gates at Llanymynech Bridge, Pool Church, Buttington, Ceynabt, and Llanllwchaiaren. There is no record of this clause being invoked.

The Montgomeryshire Canal paid dividends in 1805 and 1806, then resumed payment in 1808, the rate peaking at 5½% in 1813 and 1814. Nothing was paid in 1819 and 1820, years when much was being spent on repairs. Thereafter the dividend for the Eastern Branch increased steadily from 2½% to 5%.

The 1815 Act enabled £40,000 to be raised in new shares for the Western Branch. No dividend was ever paid on them.

Sale to the Shropshire Union

The Eastern Branch continued to operate uneventfully until January 1845 when the report of a proposal for a railway from Shrewsbury to Welshpool and Newtown was received. A meeting was held with the Ellesmere & Chester Canal to discuss its proposals for conversion into a railway, following which William Cubitt was engaged to carry out such a survey for the Montgomeryshire Canal. Before he could report, the Ellesmere & Chester Canal offered £110 per Eastern Branch share, with the option of taking shares in the new company. A sub-committee recommended acceptance – this was hardly surprising as not only was it a generous offer, but one member of the sub-committee was the Earl of Powis, who was also Chairman of the Ellesmere & Chester Canal Company. It was also recorded that 'cordial cooperation' was established between the two Branches.

Thus the Eastern Branch was sold on 1 January 1847 to the newly-formed Shropshire Union Railways & Canal Company for £78,890, comprising £73,830 in cash and just 46 shares.

Edward Johnes, the Clerk & Engineer, was given an honorarium of 100 guineas 'for the able manner in which he has discharged the joint offices of Clerk and Engineer'. (He carried on in the employment of the Shropshire Union until 1863, after 1851 as Joint Engineer.) Robert Baugh, who had been wharfinger and toll-taker at Carreghofa for more than forty-five years, was presented with plate to the value of five guineas.

The Western Branch, controlled by its mortgagees, stayed independent for a somewhat longer. It was sold on 5 February 1850 for £33,096, initially by way of a loan at 5%.

Notes and references

Most of the formal records of the Eastern Branch of the Montgomeryshire Canal are in The National Archives in the series RAIL852. However, apart from some items relating to 1833–6 in TNA file RAIL852/10, few records have survived of the Western Branch.

1. *Case of the Montgomeryshire Canal Co. ... in respect of the proposed tax on inland navigation*: Archives of the Institution of Civil Engineers (ICE), PUCLPW
2. *Shropshire Journal*, 3 March 1819
3. Letter from George Buck to William Owen, 18 September 1832: National Library of Wales (NLW), Glansevern(6)/12498. Charles Hadfield, *The Canals of the West Midlands*, 1969, p.193 gives a figure of £28,268.
4. General Assembly of the Western Branch, 8 November 1833: TNA, RAIL852/10. An Abstract of Accounts accompanying the following year's Annual Report gives a figure of £53,000 for the initial expenses (excluding engineers & solicitors): NLW, Powysland/1965/35. Evidence of John Williams to the House of Commons, 24 March 1834: ICE, PUCLPW
5. *North Wales Chronicle*, 18 September 1828
6. Report by Bryan Donkin & William Cubitt, 1 May 1834: ICE, PUCLPW
7. Grahame Boyes, 'The Exchequer Bill Loan Commissioners as a source of railway and canal finance', *Journal of the Railway & Canal Historical Society*, November 1987, pp.86–88; TNA: PWLB2/2
8. Richard Williams, *Montgomeryshire Worthies*, 1894, pp.267–8
9. General Assembly of the Western Branch, 4 December 1833: ICE, PUCLPW; Mortgages: TNA, RAIL852/17
10. Stephen Hughes, *The Archaeology of the Montgomeryshire Canal*, 1988, pp.56–8, 112–3
11. *Montgomeryshire Journal*, 29 June 1835

7

The Ellesmere & Chester Canal

Merger

UNLIKE railway companies from the 1840s onwards, canal companies rarely merged, but in the case of the Ellesmere and Chester Companies it was a natural development. The Chester Canal linked the two sections of the Ellesmere Canal, now that thoughts of a direct route between Trevor and Chester had been abandoned; traffic on it was largely dependant on that coming down the Ellesmere Canal from north Shropshire and Wales. The Ellesmere Canal also provided the Chester Canal with a reliable water supply, something it had never previously had.

> **Edward Herbert, 2nd Earl of Powis (1785–1848)**
>
> EDWARD HERBERT was born Edward Clive. His father (1754–1839), the eldest son of 'Clive of India', had served as Governor of Madras from 1798 to 1803 and in 1804 was created Earl of Powis (of the third creation), a revival of the title which had become extinct on the death in 1801 of his wife's brother, George Herbert, 2nd Earl of Powis (of the second creation).
>
> Edward Clive became Viscount Clive when his father was made Earl of Powis. In 1807 he took the surname Herbert in accordance with his uncle's will. On the death of his father in 1839 he became the 2nd Earl of Powis. He was Lord Lieutenant of Montgomeryshire (1830–48). The family seats were at Powis Castle (Welshpool), Walcot Hall (Lydbury North) and Oakley Park (Acton Scott, near Church Stretton).
>
> He was Tory MP for Ludlow from 1806 until 1839 when he became a member of the House of Lords. A personal friend of Lord Palmerston, he had a reputation as a formidable parliamentary tactician but a poor debater. He was a clear-headed and cautious man of business.
>
> Lord Clive regularly chaired meetings of the Ellesmere & Chester, the Eastern Branch of the Montgomeryshire and the Birmingham & Liverpool Junction Canals. He became the first chairman of the Shropshire Union Railways & Canal Company. No mere figurehead, he took an active part in the various canals' affairs.

The Act of 1813 which authorised the merger stated that the name of the new company was to be 'The United Company of Proprietors of the Ellesmere and Chester Canals' – 'Canals' being in the plural. The next relevant Act, that of 1827, retitled it with 'Canal' in the singular, hence in this book I follow the practice of calling it the 'Ellesmere & Chester Canal' (ECC).

The merger was effected on 1 July 1813, and in effect, though not in law, the Ellesmere Canal Company took over the Chester. The first regular chairman at the General Assemblies was the Earl of Bridgewater, who had chaired many of the Ellesmere's meetings since 1804. In his absence John (later Sir John) Kynaston Powell or Sir John Hill, both former senior members of the Ellesmere Company, was chairman. All the senior staff came from the Ellesmere Company, as did Charles Potts, the Clerk, and Eyton & Co., the Treasurers.

The meetings of the General Assembly and of the General Committee continued to be held at Ellesmere, despite Chester being a much more important town and the location of the Clerk's offices. The remit of the Chester Sub-Committee, which had dealt with issues concerning the Ellesmere Canal's Wirral Line, was expanded to include the former Chester Canal up to Nantwich.

It was decided that the common seal should be a likeness of the Third Duke of Bridgewater (the 'Canal Duke' who had initiated and financed the Bridgewater Canal), the elder brother of the Earl of Bridgewater's grandfather, although he had never had any connection with either of the two constituent canals, not even as a shareholder.

In 1827 a further Act was obtained, repealing and replacing all the previous Acts, so simplifying the administration.

Management

THE management of the company throughout its independent existence (1813–46) was remarkable for its continuity.

The Earl of Bridgewater died in 1823. After that most General Assemblies and many of the committee meetings were chaired by Viscount Clive.

Thomas Telford continued as consultant until his death in

1834. On his advice, in 1833 William Cubitt was appointed as Consulting Engineer, bring various of Telford's proposals into fruition and then actively helping in the creation of the Shropshire Union.

Thomas Stanton had originally been employed by Telford in 1798 to manage the accounts, becoming General Agent of the Ellesmere Canal Company in 1811. He retired in 1845 aged 63 because of ill health and was granted a pension of half pay but died just four months later. On the morning of his funeral all the shops in Ellesmere closed as a mark of respect.

George Stanton, Thomas Stanton's younger son, was appointed Assistant General Agent in 1833 when the Middlewich Branch was about to be completed and the opening of the Birmingham & Liverpool Junction Canal was thought to be imminent – both events which would considerably increase the trade of the canal. He was to superintend the works of the canal generally, and given special responsibility for making arrangements for the new trade. He had previously been employed supervising the construction works on the Birmingham & Liverpool Junction Canal. Thomas Telford gave 'the most satisfactory assurances of his fitness for the appointment and of the general respectability of his character'. He doesn't seem to have mentioned that he was also George's godfather.

Charles Potts had been appointed Clerk to the promoters of the Ellesmere Canal back in 1791. Following his death in 1818 his son Henry Potts became Clerk; in 1845 he too was succeeded by his son, Charles William Potts, who had already been carrying out the complex Parliamentary work of the company for a couple of years.

Thomas Eyton, with various partners, was Treasurer of the Ellesmere Canal Company from the start. As mentioned in chapter 4, he committed suicide in 1816, after which it was discovered that he had been embezzling funds in his role as Receiver General for Shropshire. This caused his bank to suspend business, but it recovered and the new partnership continued as the company's Treasurer.

Review of management, 1822

IN 1822 two of the shareholders, Exuperius Pickering junior and Joseph Lee, carried out a thorough investigation into the state of the canal and the way it was managed. Most aspects met with their approval, though they felt the banking terms were excessively generous. Staffing levels were right, but some saving could be made on the pay rates for labourers and overseers. They agreed with the policy of doing most works by direct labour rather than contractors because they did not think that the work could be specified tightly enough. They were particularly complimentary about the way that major maintenance work such as lock gate replacement was planned, with as much as possible being made in advance and brought to the site so that the period of closure (and hence the loss of income) was minimised.

Review of management, 1836

IN 1836 a small committee chaired by Thomas Bather reported on the staffing of the company. At that time there were 99 employees, the senior salaried staff being:

Name	Post	Basic salary	Other
Thomas Stanton	General Agent	£400	£240
George Stanton	Assistant General Agent	£200	£124
George Edgecumbe	Clerk to the General Agent	£120	£7
Thomas Crimes	Superintendent, Ellesmere Port to Nantwich	£120	nil
William Jones	Superintendent, Llangollen and Llanymynech Branches and Ruabon Brook Railway	£80	£97
John Tilston	Principal Tonnage Clerk	£80	£56
Francis Lock	Works Assistant	£78	not stated

The report criticised the facts that several people had other employments which took much of their time, and that allowances could exceed the salary. The committee laid down two basic principles: everybody employed should work solely for the company, and no allowances beyond the salary should be paid for services on the line of the canal.

It described Thomas Stanton in glowing terms – 'No company can possess an agent who more ably or zealously performs his duties' – and did not refer to any outside business although until only a couple of years earlier he had worked extensively deputising for Thomas Telford in the latter's role of County Surveyor for Shropshire. However, it did criticise the fact that he no longer lived in the rent-free accommodation provided for him at Ellesmere and that he was paid 18 shillings a day if he attended anywhere other than Ellesmere. When he saw the report he threatened to resign; a compromise was reached whereby his salary was increased to £500, ostensibly in recognition of the carrying business which was being set up, but he

William Cubitt (1785–1861)

NORFOLK-BORN William Cubitt had wide-ranging engineering experience, having as a young man invented the patent sails which became the standard method of allowing windmills to work automatically regardless of the wind speed. More notoriously, he also invented the prison treadwheel, though it was originally intended as a way of occupying prisoners whilst providing a useful power source, rather than as a punishment. After a period first as a consultant to an ironworks and then as a gas-works manager at Ipswich, he moved into civil engineering. His canal works prior to his appointment by the BLJC included the Norwich & Lowestoft Navigation and straightening the northern section of the Oxford Canal. Later he became the engineer for the South Eastern Railway and the Great Northern Railway, and was President of the Institution of Civil Engineers (1849–51). He was knighted for supervising the building of the Crystal Palace for the Great Exhibition.

would only be paid expenses when working away from the line of the canal. He retained his apartments at the Ellesmere office, though there was no requirement for him to live there. In 1841 his salary was increased to £800 a year.

George Stanton's expenses added 62% to his salary, but there seemed no criticism about his attendance. He decided to resign, saying he wished to concentrate on his engineering profession, though in fact he appears to have become a gentleman of leisure.

George Edgecumbe's extra charges were minimal but, the report stated, 'He is very little employed and has various and extensive business of his own'. The committee thought he would probably resign, but in fact he did well out of the review, being appointed Resident Engineer at a salary of £300 plus accommodation at Ellesmere. He had to provide his own horse – but more importantly, he had to work full time for the company. One wonders why George Stanton was not appointed Resident Engineer instead.

Thomas Crimes was referred to as 'an old servant of the company', having been appointed back in 1806 as wharfinger at Chester, but for the last few years he had been unable to undertake any work because of a paralytic affliction. He was retired and granted a pension of £31.4s a year. In 1845 Crimes took the post of Clerk of the Grand Junction Canal but had to resign after only four months because of ill-health.

Francis Lock was promoted into the vacant position of Superintendent at a salary of £100 a year.

William Jones, whose additions and expenses exceeded his salary, also worked for William Provis, managing the latter's fluxing stone business at Trevor Rocks. To make matters worse, his accounts were confused, mixing up income from the fluxing stone and canal businesses. This was a particularly responsible job, his section of canal including the two great aqueducts, two tunnels, the deep cuttings and high embankments, and the water supply to the whole canal, 'the key of the navigation'.

> ### William Provis (1792–1870)
> WILLIAM PROVIS worked extensively for Thomas Telford in Scotland and Wales, initially preparing surveys and engineering drawings, later as a resident engineer. He was closely involved in Telford's Holyhead Road, including the designing of the Menai Bridge. Provis drafted the designs for the dock works at Ellesmere Port and also did some of the design work for the Birmingham & Liverpool Junction Canal. His first work as contractor was the Middlewich branch of the Ellesmere & Chester Canal; shortly afterwards he was appointed contractor for sections of the Birmingham & Liverpool Junction Canal. Further contract work included the improvements at Ellesmere Port (1839–43). He later resumed his career as an engineer, had various enterprises in the Cheshire and Border area, and was a major canal shareholder. William Provis married Thomas Stanton's eldest daughter in 1825. Following Telford's death in 1834, he bought Telford's London house.

Thomas Stanton thought highly of Jones, stating that he had been in the situation for thirty years and was 'an exceedingly trustworthy and suitable person'. He was duly appointed at a salary of £100 including expenses.

John Tilston had other businesses as a carrier and a timber merchant. In the latter capacity he had supplied much timber to the Ellesmere yard. Although there was no criticism of the prices charged, he was dismissed because of the incompatibility of his outside employment. The company stressed that this was done with regret and that they had no concerns about his fidelity or efficiency. He was replaced by his former deputy, Richard Beddow, the salary staying at £80.

Bather's committee's report expressed no concerns about the lower-paid employees, considering that their number did not seem excessive and their wages were in line with rates elsewhere.

The annual pay for the twenty-five tonnage clerks, most of whom were also lock-keepers, varied from £52 down to £31.4s; the five who were solely designated as lock-keepers received £26. The twenty-eight labourers received either £31.4s or £26; there were also nine overseers, all but two of them on labourer rates, which seems hardly fair in view of their extra responsibility. The élite of the manual workers were the craftsmen based at the Ellesmere depot – two carpenters (on £46.16s and £44.4s) and a blacksmith (£46.16s) – but highest paid of all was the carpenter who concentrated on Ellesmere Port and the canal as far as Bunbury, who received £54.12s.

Constables

AN innovation in 1841 was the appointment of constables with powers of arrest. Permission for such private police forces had been given in the County Police Act 1840. The constables needed to be individually approved by the Justices of the Peace.

Religious affairs

AN ethical question had to be addressed in 1839 when a deputation of clergymen requested that the canal be closed on the Sabbath. The company deflected the issue by saying that it was 'deserving of the most earnest consideration' and that they would be willing to discuss it with other public companies. Until then, they couldn't give a more definite answer. One can sense their discomfort: four of the thirteen committee members present that day were clergymen. At a later meeting (with no clergymen present) it was minuted:

> However desirable such a measure may be, this Company has not any authority to stop such traffic, the canal being a common highway for the use of all Her Majesty's subjects on payment of the tolls.

This seems a dubious if convenient interpretation of the law. Canals were not 'common highways', and the Acts included provisions which enabled bye-laws to be made concerning (for example) the hours permitted for navigation.

A couple of years later a Special General Assembly meeting refused a request for the annual payment of £50 towards the stipend of the minister of the church which was being built at Ellesmere Port. In 1843 it was agreed that the company should pay six shillings per share towards the cost of the church, with the proviso that individual shareholders could contract out.

Consolidation (1813–1825)

THE period from 1813 until 1825 was essentially one of consolidation, with the Ellesmere & Chester Canal staying isolated from the main canal network of the country.

In 1816 the possibility of a tramroad between Edstaston wharf and Shrewsbury was mooted, it being suggested that the price of land carriage would fall by more than three-quarters. In 1818 Thomas Telford made a survey and estimate for completing the canal from Weston Lullingfields to Shrewsbury, but it was felt that the income would be barely equal to the expense of maintenance and management, with little or nothing over to pay for the interest on the investment. Six years later approval was given in principle to William Hazledine constructing a railway from Weston to Shrewsbury using the canal company's powers, but he decided not to go ahead.

Exuperius Pickering senior was given permission to make the 'Water Line' navigable for half a mile beyond Pentre-felin to a place where he built the 'Chain Bridge', a suspension bridge across the river Dee. Here he made a wharf to which coal could be boated then taken on up the valley to Corwen and other settlements. Nearby he built lime kilns. The Chain Bridge opened in 1817.

Arthur Davies and Richard Jebb had carried out many of the surveys for the Ellesmere Canal, and it was perhaps during one of these that they discovered good seams of coal at Chirk Bank. Together with two others they sunk a shaft in what is now called Chirk Meadow, between the turnpike road bridge and the aqueduct.

As early as 1808 there were concerns about the effect of Chirk Bank Colliery on the structure of the canal. Thomas Denson and William Stuttle, Hazledine's foreman, had been asked to make a plan of the colliery's workings and to ascertain whether any injury to the aqueduct or other works was likely to happen. Then on 28 December 1816 the embankment at Chirk Bank failed and the canal water cascaded down into the Ceriog Valley, filling the mine with water and debris, destroying the machinery and drowning all the horses in the works. Luckily this happened on the only night of the year in which there were no workmen in the mine, they having collected their Christmas bounties. The mine owners claimed that the fault lay with the inattention of the staff of the canal company who had failed to regulate the level of the canal following a long period of rain which had raised the level of the river Dee. The canal company's first reaction was that they were not liable – indeed, compensation was owed to them as they considered that the bank had been weakened by the mining. The matter was referred to two arbitrators with a referee; two and a half years later the matter was settled, the canal company accepting the arbitration decision had gone against them for an amount of £88. However, by then the mine owner had gone bankrupt, and his assignees accepted an offer of £70. At the meeting at which this decision was made, it was also agreed to buy one pipe (126 galls) of the best port wine and one hogshead (52½ galls) of the best sherry. One hopes this was not in celebration of saving £12.

In 1822 or shortly afterwards, the line of the Llanymynech Branch was altered north of Heath House Bridge, Redwith, in order to take it further from Woodhouse, the residence since 1795 of William Mostyn Owen's son, William. This diversion, about a mile in length, meant that the canal reverted to its originally planned line, so incorporating what had been the Revd John Robert Lloyd's private canal. The diversion was paid for by William Owen, a long-standing director of the canal who chaired the meeting at which this decision was taken.

The locks of the former Chester Canal were particularly in need of repair, unsurprisingly as they were of course some twenty years older than those of the former Ellesmere Canal. In particular, the wooden gates were decayed, much of the stonework had crumbled and many needed by-weirs. The necessary repairs were effected by the mid-1820s. The worst problem concerned the two Beeston Locks, which had been built in quicksand; there had been a breach in 1818, and in 1824 these were reported as being 'in a very precarious and unsafe state'. Telford recommended a new line with two new locks, the lower one to be made with cast-iron plates instead of stone or brick sides. This was completed in 1828.

At Telford's recommendation, cast iron had already been used for various replacement lock gates and for Mollington Bridge, where the Chester–Parkgate road crossed the canal at a particularly low level. Ellesmere Port needed an extensive programme of works over the years. In particular the tide lock and the walls of the tidal basin were repaired in the first eight years of the new company's existence, and the north pier had to be rebuilt. Most of the bridges on the Wirral Line required some attention. No major works were required on the Ellesmere Canal west of Hurleston Junction except for the replacement of most of the timber bridges. The towing paths through Chirk and Whitehouses Tunnels were originally constructed of timber; these were rebuilt with stone piers and brick arches.

During the winter of 1820/21 floodwater on the river Dee caused the Horseshoe Weir to partially collapse. George Buck, the Montgomeryshire Canal's engineer, considered the root cause to have been poor construction rather than poor foundations. When it was rebuilt, the weir was capped with cast iron.

Connections (1825–1843)

To Cefn Mawr

A private canal, five-eighths of a mile long, was built from the end of Trevor Basin into the industrial area below the village of Cefn Mawr. Later known as the Plas Kynaston Canal, it was constructed in two stages, by Exuperius Pickering junior in about 1825 and by Thomas Ward in about 1830. The history of this canal is discussed in Appendix G.

The Shropshire Union Canal

Wardle Lock at Middlewich was so named because from the point of view of its owner, the Trent & Mersey Canal, the destination of the branch canal was the hamlet of Wardle, ten miles away. Because the lock cottage was built by the TMC, its style is unlike the others on the Middlewich Branch, as was the style of the paddle gear. *Canal & River Trust*

To Wolverhampton

AFTER the end of the Napoleonic War, the British economy suffered a period of depression, but by 1824 the financial market was easing and investment in transport infrastructure was again being contemplated. One project which would have had serious implications for the Ellesmere & Chester Canal was that for a railway from Birmingham to the Mersey via Nantwich and Chester. In response several leading shareholders of the Birmingham Canal contacted the ECC at the end of 1824 to propose a junction canal linking the two systems, thus giving the Birmingham Canal a shorter and much easier access to Liverpool than its existing route via the Harecastle Tunnel. The ECC reacted enthusiastically, as it would end the isolation of its canal by linking it with the Midlands and also to London by an inland route. This proposal became the Birmingham & Liverpool Junction Canal (BLJC), the subject of the next chapter.

To Middlewich: negotiations [1]

THIS activity prompted the ECC to resurrect the idea of a link with the Trent & Mersey Canal (TMC). In late 1824 it approached the TMC and the Bridgewater Trustees with the proposal for a branch from Wardle Green, a little north of Nantwich, to Middlewich. Permission from both canals was needed, as a clause in the Chester Canal Act 1777 forbade the carrying of a Middlewich branch within a hundred yards of the Trent & Mersey without both their agreements. The ECC was hoping to persuade the others that circumstances had changed, and that a link would be a benefit, not a threat. It promised extra traffic from north Shropshire, west Cheshire and north Wales to Manchester, including grain, other agricultural products, slates and minerals.

Robert Haldane Bradshaw, the conservative Superintendent of the Bridgewater Canal, could see no potential advantage from such a link 'even with the aid of Mr Telford's views and explanations', adding 'he talks of an expenditure of £150,000 in improvement and conveniences ... as if it were nothing'. However, James Loch, the Marquess of Stafford's Principal Agent and also one of the Bridgewater Trustees, eventually persuaded him that more would be gained than lost, arguing that one could not oppose both the new railway and the new canal. The Bridgewater Canal thus formally became 'favourably disposed' to the proposal and Bradshaw signed the deed under seal which was necessary to waive the right of veto.

Fifty years earlier the TMC had refused to agree to the link because it was justifiably concerned that some northbound cargoes going to Ireland would transfer to the Chester Canal, so the TMC would lose tolls between Middlewich and Preston Brook (where it joined the Bridgewater Canal). Now it must have appreciated that if the BLJC was approved by Parliament, loss of much of the Birmingham and Black Country trade to Liverpool was inevitable. There remained the concern about some of the trade between the Potteries and Liverpool, but probably a greater worry was that the Birmingham–Manchester trade would go via the BLJC and the Middlewich Branch of the ECC, thus the TMC would lose the tolls for the section between Great Haywood Junction and Middlewich.

In July 1825 the TMC committee resolved that although it might have given favourable consideration to a branch from the ECC to Middlewich, the suggestion of a canal from Autherley to Nantwich would be 'highly injurious'. It therefore declined to give an answer to the ECC until Parliament had decided whether to approve the BLJC. This decision, which does not

Chapter 7 : The Ellesmere & Chester Canal

seem to have been communicated to Lord Clive, chairman of the committees of both the ECC and the BLJC, until several months later, prompted him to decide to postpone the application to Parliament for the Middlewich Branch for a year.

The TMC's resolution alarmed Loch. Lord Stafford and his sons owned large estates in east Shropshire which were to be served by a branch off the BLJC. He was concerned that terms might be agreed which penalised traffic coming off the BLJC whilst permitting traffic which started on the ECC's Welsh Branch to pass freely onto the TMC. Although Loch was well aware that Lord Clive's personal interests were primarily in the trade coming off the ECC, he was confident that Clive would not wish to be party to a deal which especially favoured himself; nevertheless, pressure could come from other promoters, particularly those in Birmingham whose primary object was a canal to Liverpool.

The BLJC's Act received the Royal Assent in June 1826, and that autumn the ECC submitted its Bill for the Middlewich branch. The TMC's committee confirmed its intention to oppose the Bill, saying that it might have been given favourable consideration if it had not been for the passing of the Act for the canal between Autherley and Nantwich.

Inconclusive meetings were held between the parties. Bradshaw thought that 3d a ton would be ample compensation to the TMC. In the end it was left to James Caldwell (Chairman of the TMC) and Lord Clive to come to a compromise. They agreed that the final one hundred yards at Middlewich, which included one lock – now known as Wardle Lock – should be built by the TMC, and that special tolls should be paid, the maximum being:

– 9d for every ton of coal, coke, culm, limestone and rock-salt;
– 9½d for every ton of free-stone, timber, slate, iron-stone, lead ore, iron and lead; and
– 10½d for every ton of other goods.

Loch thought that Lord Clive had achieved a reasonable deal, and in a letter to Lord Stafford he particularly praised 'the manly manner in which he resisted any boon in favour of his peculiar district to the disadvantage of the Staffordshire trade'.

The tolls for timber, bricks and tiles were reduced in 1842, but these were traffics coming off the Welsh Branch, hence the TMC could only benefit from encouraging them.

Construction of the Middlewich Branch

For a 'late' canal, the Middlewich Branch has unusually deep locks: Cholmondeston, Minshull and Stanthorne are all between 11ft and 11ft 3in. deep, and Wardle Lock is 9ft 9in. deep. This compares with an average of 6ft 3in. on the near-contemporary BLJC, also engineered by Telford. The reason lies in the ECC's Act which specified the dimensions of the locks as :

not less than 77ft long, 8ft 4in. wide at the top, 7ft 1in. wide at the level of the bottom sill, 16ft 3in. in height from the bottom sill to the top of each lock, and so that the rise of each ... lock shall not be less than 10ft 4in.

The TMC's Act required Wardle Lock to be 'a lock similar to and of the same capacity as the lock ... immediately below the intended point of junction'. It went on to specify the length and width, which were identical to those given in the ECC's Act, but did not mention the fall. The objective was to ensure that boats coming off the ECC's branch, most of which would have been going on to Manchester or Runcorn, brought with them enough water to fill the TMC's locks.

The three Middlewich locks on the TMC immediately below the junction have an average fall of 10ft 10in. each, which is slightly more than the fall specified in the ECC's Act for its locks on the Middlewich Branch.[2] However, difference in water levels of the existing canals at Barbridge and Middlewich is 43ft; when the 9ft 9in. drop of the Wardle Lock is subtracted, the drop at each of the ECC's three locks on the branch must inevitably average more than 11ft.

According to the Act, the estimated cost of the branch was £68,838, which included the cost of the land as well as the engineering works. Two tenders for constructing the branch were received, one from William Hazledine, the other from William Provis, and they were referred to Thomas Telford. Telford's usual contracting method was to negotiate a price with someone whom he knew could do the job well – he did not favour competitive tendering. In this instance Telford knew both men well, but Hazledine had no experience of canal contracting during the past twenty-five years, his principal business interests being iron-founding and coal mining, and Provis had no actual experience of being a contractor. The latter had been Telford's assistant since 1808, making surveys and drawings, evolving the detailed designs and supervising contractors. He had surveyed much of the proposed BLJC and the associated extensive dock works at Ellesmere Port. (He was also the husband of Thomas Stanton's eldest daughter, Harriet.) Perhaps Provis felt the financial rewards of being the contractor would be better than being a salaried assistant to Telford – in any event, his tender of £56,900 was accepted.

Alexander Easton, who had worked for Telford since 1805, was appointed Resident Engineer with effect from the start of 1828, his salary being £200 per annum, despite fifteen months earlier having accepted a similar job for the BLJC on £700 a year with the explicit condition that he worked only on that project. Lord Clive must have been aware of the position, being Chairman of both companies.

When the exact route was being set out, Telford 'encountered an unaccommodating disposition in some of the landowners'. He made agreements with four of them to vary the line, resulting in shortening the length by 900 yards but increasing the cost by an amount originally estimated at £540 because of the extra cuttings and embankments required. The outcome was worse because, according to his autobiography:

The marly soil, of which the surface of that rich county largely consists, when used for embankment, slips and bulges in great masses, and rapidly dissolves when exposed

Barbridge Junction photographed in 1957, with the transhipment warehouse designed by Telford which was built in 1831–2 and demolished in 1959. The boats are *Ferret* and *Grantham*.
Railway & Canal Historical Society, Shearing Collection

to the atmosphere ... These evils were experienced to an enormous and unprecedented extent; and I am bound to say that ... when the height required amounts to 50, 60 or 70 feet, no estimate can safely be made, and the enterprise ought not to be hazarded.[3]

This was written with hindsight – at the time he told the committee that instead of the usual ratio of between 1½ and 2 horizontal to 1 vertical, it was proving necessary to have between 5 and 8 horizontal to 1 vertical. The most difficult section was the crossing of the Weaver Valley, where the embankment reached a height of 60ft. Cuttings too slipped; one report stated that they could be expected to do so in wet weather until they arrived at the least possible slope the soil will stand at. These problems added to the cost, and the excess seems to have been paid to the contractor.

The intention had been to make the bricks for bridges and locks from the clay found along the line of the canal. Bricks thus made proved unsuitable for facing and other outside work, so it was decided that Newcastle blue bricks should be used instead.

The branch opened for traffic on 1 September 1833, some fourteen months beyond the statutory limit for completing the works. Easton's employment was then terminated. It has not proved possible to ascertain the actual cost but it was clearly well in excess of the original estimate.

Reservoirs

BECAUSE the deep locks of the Middlewich Branch would use significantly more water than would be brought down by a boat travelling on either of the two canals feeding it, in 1829 it was decided to construct a reservoir by Hurleston Junction. Work did not commence until 1835 but towards the end of that year the contractor, Thomas Baylis, abandoned it, both Baylis and the canal company claiming the other to be at fault. Work continued slowly using craftsmen and labourers employed by the company, but the project was not completed until 1840. By an oversight, two acres had been taken for the reservoir in excess of the area agreed with the owner. Legal action was threatened, and the canal company had to settle for the best terms it could.

Chapter 7 : The Ellesmere & Chester Canal

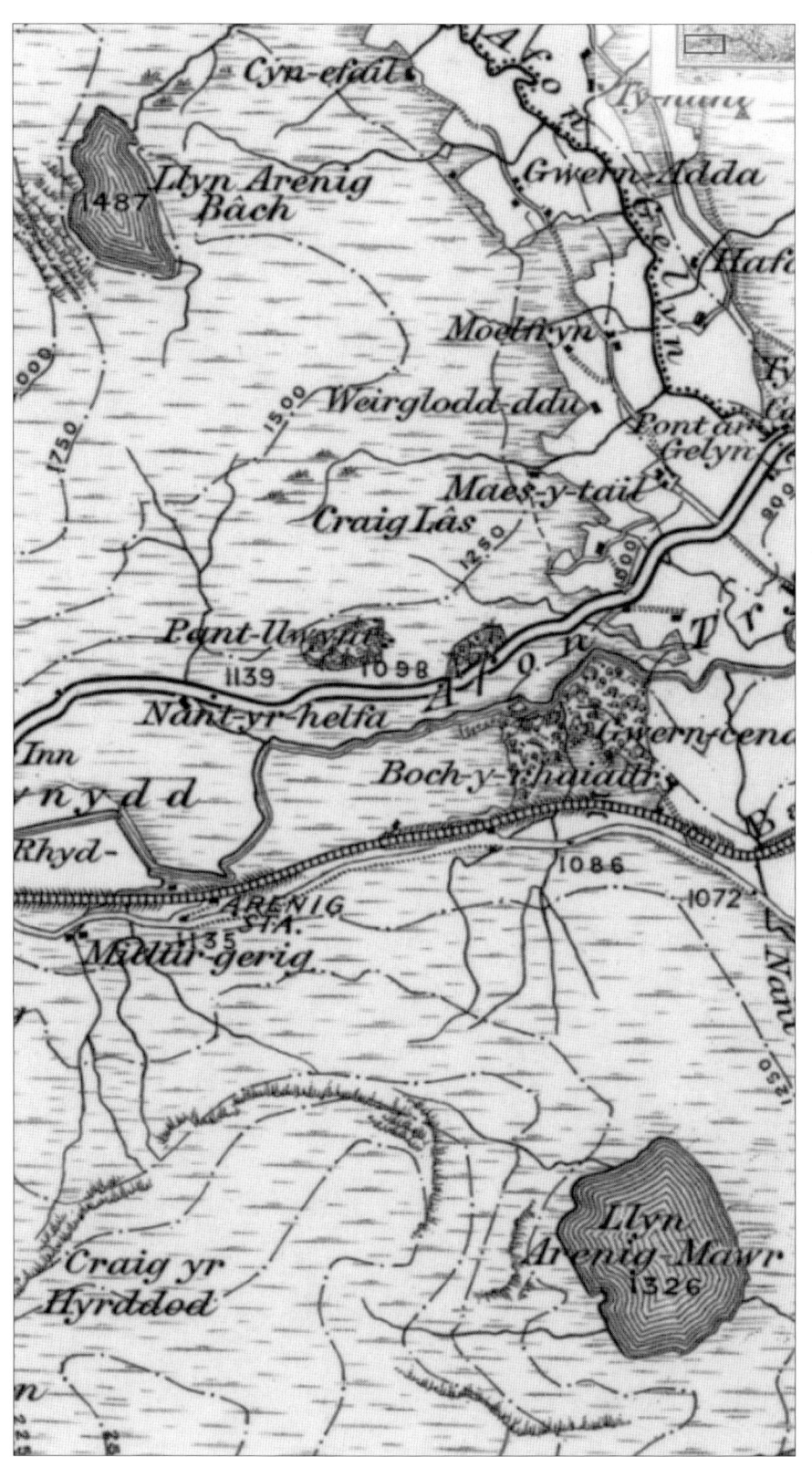

1898 Ordnance Survey 1:63,360 map (rescaled), with the two reservoirs shown as Llyn Arenig Mawr and Llyn Arenig Bach. (Current Ordnance Survey maps write the names with 'Fawr' and 'Fach'. To the Shropshire Union they were usually called the 'Large Arenig Lake and 'Small Arenig Lake'.) These lie either side of what is now the A4212, some six to eight miles north-west of Bala. The dams were a similar height, holding back a maximum depth of 16ft 4in. and 15ft 8in. respectively, but the capacities were quite different, equivalent to 12,300 locks and 4,400 locks respectively. Their water fed into the river Dee below the dam of Bala Lake.

Back in 1826 Telford had been asked to survey the lakes and streams of north Wales to find additional water supplies. The 1827 Act refers to alterations relating to Bala Lake but does not mention additional reservoirs – the fact that this is the penultimate clause of a long Act implies that it was a last-minute addition. It was not until 1832 that Telford reported that he had made the survey requested but no details are given in the minutes. A passing mention in 1836 to routine inspection of the 'Arenig Lakes' shows that the two reservoirs must have been made by then.

To Winsford [4]

In October 1830 the ECC was approached by the Trustees of the river Weaver, who were interested in creating a route to the Middlewich Branch and hence via the TMC to the Potteries.

Plans were drawn up for two options: a canal or a tramroad. Both would have taken the same line, from just south of Winsford Bridge on the Weaver (Winsford Flash not then existing) to half a mile south-west of Stanthorne Lock on the Middlewich Branch. The canal would have had seven locks at its western end and an eighth lock part-way along its course; the tramroad would have had an incline raising the line by some 67ft in about 180ft horizontally, then a slight gradient up to a basin on the canal branch.

One problem was water supply. Even the tramroad proposal would involve a loss of water when a boat went up or down Stanthorne Lock. The suggested solution was to pump water from the Weaver up to the canal using a 30hp engine located immediately to the south of Bridge 22, near Lea Hall, where the Weaver is closest to the canal.

The Weaver Trustees wanted the ECC to abandon its policy (discussed later) of charging 2s per ton on merchandise passing less than twelve miles on its canal, as most of the traffic would be passing only 2½ miles. However, their minutes make no mention of the large toll imposed by the TMC at Wardle Lock, a severe penalty for any potential traffic to or from the Potteries.

Thomas Stanton met the Clerk to the Trustees, and Thomas Telford was consulted. (Six years later, two years after his death, the Trustees paid his fee.) The canal company met in January 1831 and expressed themselves satisfied with the principle but were concerned about some of the details. The extra water provided would have to be enough for the lockage down to the Weaver, including waste by leakage, as well as the water demanded by the TMC.

Nothing further was minuted about the proposals, either by the Weaver Navigation or by the ECC. Presumably it was recognised that the tramroad proposal would be too expensive to operate because it required two transhipments, and the canal proposal would be killed by the TMC's attitude.

Other connections

Despite the evident success of the Liverpool & Manchester Railway and the recent opening of the Grand Junction Railway between Lancashire and Birmingham, William Provis obviously had faith in the future of canals when in 1838 he surveyed a direct canal between the Middlewich Branch and Altrincham. Sixteen miles long, with a mile and a quarter of tunnelling at Knutsford and a flight of six locks at Altrincham, this would have reduced the distance between Middlewich and Manchester by 18 miles. It would also have avoided the Middlewich toll by bridging the TMC. Named the Manchester & Birmingham Junction Canal, which clearly expressed its purpose, a prospectus was issued seeking a capital of half a million pounds. The provisional committee included three people associated with the ECC or the BLJC: William Hazledine, John Stanton and George Holyoake (of Wolverhampton). It also included George Fereday Smith (general manager of the Bridgewater Trust), John Horton, a partner in the Lilleshall Company and Thomas Ward (of Chirk and Plas Kynaston). Unsurprisingly, it proved impossible to raise the capital.[5]

Associated with that scheme, plans were drawn up for a four mile long direct link between just below Minshull Lock and Nantwich, with the alternative of a link between just below Cholmondeston Lock and Hurleston Junction. These seem pointless improvements: in the latter case, for example, the distance saved would only have been three-quarters of a mile, and the existing line would presumably have been kept open for traffic from the Potteries to Ellesmere Port.[6]

Ellesmere Port

Improved transhipment facilities

As was clear from its name, the main purpose of the Birmingham & Liverpool Junction Canal was to improve transport links between Birmingham and the Black Country and Liverpool, by then the country's principal west coast port. As a consequence, much more trade would pass through Ellesmere Port, requiring it to be transhipped between canal boats and vessels suitable for crossing the Mersey. It was therefore evident that the infrastructure there would need to be improved, and in 1829 Thomas Telford was instructed to design warehouses and covered transhipment facilities.

Most of the land needed was bought from the Marquess of Westminster's estate. In addition, the graving dock, slipway and buildings owned by Telford were also acquired, in accordance with the agreement made in 1811. The valuation was done by Jesse Hartley, the Liverpool Docks engineer.

The first phase of the redevelopment scheme, which included what were generally considered the finest canal warehouses ever built in Britain, was finished in 1833. When William Cubitt visited it that year he described it as 'of the highest order, both of engineering skill of the design and of practical talent of the execution'. No further major works were undertaken at Ellesmere Port for several years, mainly because the company had other priorities for expenditure.

Later developments

The 1836 Committee of Investigation identified an opportunity

Chapter 7: The Ellesmere & Chester Canal

The formal opening of Ellesmere Port docks in 1843 culminated in an 'entertainment' for 480 people in the main warehouse, as depicted in the Illustrated London News.
Canal & River Trust

for increasing trade. If, as Telford had proposed several years earlier, a sea lock was constructed sufficiently large to receive coasters and Irish traders, the company would be less constrained by shortage of room at its quays on the Liverpool side of the estuary; one transhipment would also be eliminated for loads going on to or coming from the Midlands. Trades which could be attracted included Irish cattle and agricultural produce and Caernarvonshire slate; if it were made a bonded port, even foreign goods might be brought in.

The total estimated cost of a new sea lock and of the creation of a bonded warehouse was £25,000. The site of the new dock had suitable brick clay, so the manufacture of bricks was commenced immediately, in anticipation of starting building the sea lock the following spring. Stanton was instructed to prepare working plans, drawings and specifications, and to invite tenders. In fact his wording must have been unclear, as some tenderers submitted schedules of rates – that is, prices for each unit of work, the actual payments being calculated after measuring the work done – others a total price. The committee instructed that the matter be referred to William Cubitt who submitted a detailed report which led to all the tenders being rejected.

The works were then divided into three:

- narrow locks parallel to the existing broad locks, together with the associated canal wharfs, weighing dock, patent slip, workshops and offices;
- clearing and repairing the entrance basin; and
- the ship lock and floating dock, allowing boats of up to 200 tons burthen to enter the lower basin.

Cubitt was to prepare plans and specifications for each part, and invite tenders for the first two parts from contractors he thought competent – in other words, a select tender list rather than open tendering. William Provis was awarded the contract, which was priced using a schedule of rates.

Next, Cubitt was asked to survey the strand of the Mersey in front of the Ellesmere Port premises and prepare a plan for enclosing it and building a sea wall. He actually produced two plans, costing £20,000 and £15,000; the committee accepted the latter, Provis having undertaken to do it for that price.

The works were commenced in 1839 and completed in 1843.

In 1839 the ECC decided to buy land near Brunswick Dock, Liverpool. Cubitt was asked to prepare plans for a dock and wharf. The following year 12,000 square feet of land was bought in Herculaneum Dock for £2 per square foot, and a timber dock was made to Cubitt's plan.

Ellesmere Port is situated at about the widest point of the Mersey estuary, and the scour here was not great. In 1841 Cubitt strongly recommended diverting the channel of the Beeston and Ince Brooks, which flowed into the Mersey at Stanlow through land belonging to the Marquess of Westminster, in order to increase the scouring power at the entrance to the harbour. It was agreed to go ahead immediately at a cost of about £7,000.

103

Traffic: the early years

During the 1810s and 1820s the trade on the canal grew steadily. The main traffic flows were:

- Lime from Llanymynech, Porth-y-waen and Froncysyllte to various limekilns alongside the canal, mainly for agricultural purposes;
- Coal from collieries at Chirk and the Ruabon area to the lime kilns and the various towns and wharfs as far as Beeston and Carreghofa (there continuing on the Montgomeryshire Canal to Welshpool and Newtown);
- Pig iron and iron products from Trevor to Ellesmere Port;
- A return traffic of Cumbrian iron ore from Ellesmere Port to Trevor for mixing with the local ores;
- Iron products from Edstaston on the Prees Branch to Ellesmere Port, the goods having come by road from the ironworks of east Shropshire;
- Slates from Pentre-felin (originating at the Oernant quarries) and Chirk (from quarries up the Ceiriog valley) to Chester and Ellesmere Port;
- Grain and malt from Maesbury Marsh and Ellesmere to Chester;
- Short distance traffic of fluxing limestone from Trevor Rocks and Froncysyllte to Trevor; and
- General goods from Liverpool to Chester, with some going up to Nantwich, Whitchurch, Ellesmere, Oswestry and the other towns served by the Ellesmere & Chester and Montgomeryshire Canals.

The tonnage charges were complex, and were tinkered with most years in an effort to maximise income, promote new traffics or (sometimes) for public benefit. The canal company was well aware of potential competition from alternative sources of the goods and from road transport. For example, because coal from the Flintshire coalfield was competitive with that from Chirk and Ruabon in the Cheshire market, it was decided that Denbighshire coal would be charged only as far as Grindley Brook, beyond which it would travel free. Road transport competition was particularly significant because of the circuitous route of the canal. For example, the distance from Trevor to Chester was 20 miles by road but 57 miles by canal; the extreme example was Ponciau, which was 17 miles by road from Chester but 3 miles on the Ruabon Brook Railway plus 57 miles by canal. Therefore in order to retain the trade, tonnage charges had to be well below the maxima permitted in the Acts.

Some reductions were dependent on the trader also reducing his prices. For example, in 1816 the tonnage on limestone and coal was reduced on the condition that:

> the lime burners at Hampton Bank and Bettisfield reduce the price of their lime two pence per bushell or from $15\frac{1}{2}d$ to $13\frac{1}{2}d$ – that the lime burners at Whitchurch and Grindley Brook reduce the price of the lime at their kilns

$2d$ per bushell or from $16\frac{1}{2}d$ to $14\frac{1}{2}d$ – and that the lime burners at Weston reduce the price of lime at their works $1\frac{1}{2}d$ per bushell or from $14\frac{1}{2}d$ to $13d$.[7]

This wasn't pure altruism: a lower charge to the end user would usually mean that demand increased, hence more limestone and coal would be carried.

Occasionally it was the boat firm carrying the goods which had to make the commitment. For example, in 1820 it was resolved:

> that the tonnage of wheat and flour boated from Ellesmere to Chester be reduced to two shillings per ton for the whole distance ... on the express condition that the traders ... do not charge more than $7s.6d$ for the whole freight from Ellesmere to Chester.[8]

Carriage south of Chester was entirely in the hands of private companies, particularly John & Richard Goolden, who offered regular boats to and from Nantwich, Whitchurch, Llangollen and the other towns on the ECC and Montgomeryshire Canal. Some businesses carried their own materials or products in their own boats but as they were not offering a service to the general public they do not appear in directories. For example, it is probable that the Pickerings had boats conveying limestone and coal, but no explicit evidence is known to prove this.

'Avarice and injustice'

With effect from 1 August 1827 the ECC revised its tolls, as permitted by the Act obtained that year; in particular, a new condition was to impose a surcharge of two shillings per ton on most commodities passing less than twelve miles if they went through a lock. This action was defended on the grounds that boats going from the Dee tideway up the five locks to a wharf on the main Chester level paid tonnage for only one mile yet used a large amount of water. However, the reality was that all boats entering the canal at Ellesmere Port and going only as far as Chester would have to pay this surcharge as they were travelling only nine miles – thus goods previously charged $2s.3d$ a ton would now be charged $4s.3d$ a ton.

At a protest meeting chaired by the Mayor of Chester it was declared that the new charges were 'unjust, injudicious and arbitrary', so an investigatory committee was set up to arrange a cheaper mode of transit between Chester and the Mersey. In September it reported that two-thirds of the traffic on which the higher toll would have been charged had been removed from the canal during August, and that it was hoped that a steam-boat service would soon be provided.[9]

A further public meeting was held in January 1828. The chairman of the investigatory committee asserted that 'a greater injury had never been inflicted on Chester than the cutting of the canal', his reasoning being that the river – a much cheaper method of conveyance – had then been neglected. John Fletcher, a major canal shareholder and owner of the *Cheshire Chronicle*, made the surprising claim that the local canal committee was

Chapter 7: The Ellesmere & Chester Canal

unaware of the clause permitting the higher tolls and that the Agent [Stanton] had assumed powers to which he was not entitled. This was disingenuous: Fletcher had been present at the meeting of the General Assembly which had made the decisions concerning tolls. A few days later Stanton wrote a letter to the newspapers blaming Parliament for allowing the extra charges and elaborating the reason for the crisis: factories had been erected by the canal and the boats serving them were exhausting the water, 'paralysing the navigation for 100 miles in extent'. He added that, to meet the objections halfway, the canal company had 'consented to abate half of their additional charge'. The *Chester Courant* was unconvinced, an editorial stating: 'The Company have lost the *golden eggs*, and have only the *dead goose* left, as the reward of their avarice and injustice'.[10]

The General Assembly in July 1828 modified the rules concerning the general surcharge and introduced surcharges on specific loads boating to and from the Dee – essentially, these related to the materials for and products from the canal-side factories and mills in Chester. A press report in February 1829 stated that because of the loss of traffic to river and coastal boats, the canal company had been forced to give way, adding 'and even on some heavy articles to reduce the charge below the previous rate'. The minutes do not confirm this, but sometimes minutes do not accord with what actually happened.[11]

Cross-Mersey traffic

THE canal company retained an active interest in the cross-Mersey boat services between Chester, Ellesmere Port and Liverpool, though its policy was not consistent.

The Canal Tavern at Chester and the packet boats, time-tabled boats for passengers and parcels, were owned by the canal company and let to private contractors, generally for periods of three years. In 1815, for example, they were let to Thomas Crimes for £1,000 a year – yet another example of the company's staff also having private interests in the canal.

In 1816 it was decided to acquire a steam boat for the ferry link between Ellesmere Port and Liverpool, in order to counter the competition from other ferry services which had one. If a suitable boat could not be purchased, one was to be hired until one could be built. One must have been obtained, for only the following year it was let to Thomas Crimes for £150 a year; and in 1819 it was sold.

Traffic: after 1830

Cross-Mersey traffic

THE new energy shown by the canal company which resulted in the improvements at Ellesmere Port and the links to Middlewich and Wolverhampton showed itself in another way: an appraisal of whether it should seek powers to become a carrier throughout its network. In 1829 Thomas Stanton was asked to report on whether it was desirable and practicable, the financial implications and the timing. His report was passed to a sub-committee with power to act. Although the relevant minutes have not survived it seems that the sub-committee did not think it worthwhile to become carriers on the canal, but that powers should be sought to operate boats across the Mersey. The latter were obtained in 1830.

The first proposal was to acquire the businesses and vessels of Messrs Fairhurst, Tilston & Co. and Shanklin, Manley & Co. at valuation. This was amended in 1832 to making a contract with them jointly to provide all the transport across the Mersey at agreed rates on payment of £2,000 a year to the canal company for the use of the wharfs, warehouses and clerks' houses at Ellesmere Port. The five-year contract was to commence when the BLJC opened, which was then expected to be the following year, though it did not actually open until March 1835.

Many traders complained about 'delays, vexations and unfair dealing' by the lessees. In 1836 complainants were invited to make representations to a Committee of Investigation chaired by Thomas Bather. The committee totally exonerated Fairhurst, Tilston & Co. (implicitly also Shanklin, Manley & Co.), concluding that 'no establishment of such magnitude and complexity was ever managed with less reasonable ground of complaint', and ascribing the discontent to the fact that Fairhursts were also carriers on their own account. It recommended that the canal company should take over the carrying business between Liverpool, Ellesmere Port and Chester. Fairhursts were willing, providing they were properly compensated.

The recommendations were accepted. The payment was agreed at £25,000, made up as follows:

	£
26 flats at £500 each	13,000
1 lighter	200
2 cranes, warehouse & office at the Old Quay, Liverpool	2,000
4 cranes at the Parade Wharf, Liverpool	750
weights & scales, office fixtures, trucks, chains etc at Liverpool	300
shed at Chester	400
3 cranes & 4 hoists at Chester	570
4 waggons, 3 timber carriages, 3 carts & 15 horses at Chester	900
weights & scales etc at Chester	200
goodwill including the loss of profits	6,680
total	25,000

It is not clear how this amount was divided between Fairhurst & Co. and Shanklin & Co. The former owners of the two firms became the senior managers of the carrying concern of the canal company: Thomas Balmer, formerly of Shanklin & Co., was appointed Principal Agent, based at Liverpool and in charge of the whole carrying business, being paid £400 a year; Edward Tilston of Fairhurst & Co. was appointed Principal Agent at Chester, on £300 a year; Richard Shanklin was to be Principal Agent at Ellesmere Port, paid £250 a year.

At about this time, John Tilston, the Principal Tonnage Clerk, was dismissed because of conflicts of interest with his carrying business. I have not been able to prove whether he had a connection with Fairhurst & Co. or whether he was a partner in

Tilston, Smith & Co., an inland canal carrier which seems to have been established around this date.

It was agreed to build six floats, simple decked boats without rigging, for carrying timber across the Mersey. Estimated to cost only £250 each, about a third of the cost of flats, these would be built in the company's workshop.

The idea was that the floats, and occasionally flats, were to be towed by a steam-powered vessel. Rather than purchase one, an offer from the Steam Tug Company to tow up to three boats for £3 a trip, with additional boats at £1 each, was accepted. Just a couple of months later the Steam Tug Company increased their charge to £4 per trip for up to four boats, with additional boats at 10s each. The canal company responded by deciding to have their own steam tug built, the hull by Malory of Chester and the pair of 25hp engines by Thompson of Liverpool.

In 1843, transhipment of goods to or from south of Chester was transferred from Chester to Ellesmere Port, so as to reduce wear and tear on the river craft.

Later in 1843 it was reported that the Bridgewater Trustees had greatly reduced freight rates across the Mersey, and that the ECC had been forced to do likewise. It was agreed to let to the Trustees the whole of the cross-Mersey trade except for that continuing up to Chester, the agreement being terminable by either party on giving 24 months' notice. The two steam tugs and the various flats and floats would be hired to the Trustees, together with the wharfs and warehouses. William Cubitt was to set the rent.

There was a suspicion that the permanent staff of the Trust may have encouraged this contract as a way of diverting cross-Mersey trade from Ellesmere Port to their port of Runcorn, though the agreement specified that the freight charge between Liverpool and Ellesmere Port had to be 4d a ton less than that from Liverpool to Runcorn.

Inland trades

BATHER'S Committee of Investigation also reported on the inland trade of the ECC in 1836. This identified the following main traffics:

– coal from Chirk and Ruabon to Newtown, Welshpool, Whitchurch and to a lesser extend beyond, where it came in competition with Flintshire coal;
– agricultural limestone from Froncysyllte to Whitchurch, Nantwich, Market Drayton and numerous canalside kilns;
– agricultural limestone from Llanymynech to Welshpool and Newtown;
– fluxing limestone from Trevor, and, to a lesser extent, Llanymynech, to the Black Country and the east Shropshire industrial area – much of this was taken as far as Nantwich, unloaded, then used as back-carriage for boats which had taken iron products from the Black Country and east Shropshire to Ellesmere Port;
– iron products from the Black County, east Shropshire and Ruabon to Ellesmere Port for Liverpool;
– slate from Oernant (Horseshoe Pass) and Nantyr (in the Ceiriog valley) to Manchester;
– agricultural products from various places to urban markets;
– general trade from London, Birmingham, Liverpool and Manchester to towns and villages on or near the canal.

Some traffics meant that the movement of laden boats was predominantly in one direction, the boat having to return empty. For example, in 1845 27,600 tons were conveyed from Shropshire, Cheshire and Wales to Manchester, whereas only 3,500 tons returned.[12]

The fly-boat firms, who provided a timetabled service carrying smaller quantities of goods at premium prices, requested reduced tonnage rates in 1839. Their boats were lighter loaded than those dealing with bulk goods, and competition from other modes of transport was stronger. However, the ECC declined on the grounds that their Acts prevented it. The legal issue was that the same charge had to be made to any carrier conveying a particular weight of a particular item between the same two places – preference could not be given to special types of service.

Snapshots of the traffic on the canals in the early 1840s appear in evidence used to support applications to Parliament to approve railways. For example, evidence for the Shrewsbury, Oswestry & Chester Junction Railway provided information about traffic from and to the Llangollen/Oswestry area in 1844: 85,000 tons of limestone went to ironworks near Wellington; 80,000 tons of coal from Black Park and Cefn Mawr; 15,000 tons of iron ore were imported for mixing with Welsh ore; 4,000 tons of slates and flagstones came from Llangollen and from Llangynog (at the head of the Tanat valley); 10,000 tons of timber, mostly for pit props; 3,000 tons of burnt lime; 1,000 tons of Cefn Mawr stone; and 9,500 tons of general goods.

Passengers

IMPROVEMENTS in the Birkenhead–Chester turnpike, particularly the opening of the four-mile-long New Chester Road at Bromborough in 1834, enhanced the speed and comfort of coach travel between the towns and led to the termination of the timetabled boat service from Chester to Ellesmere Port.[13]

Inland canal boats occasionally carried passengers by informal arrangements sanctioned by the carrying company, sometimes when the person was moving with a large amount of luggage.

One unusual instance occurred in April 1840, when about eighty people, mainly from the borders of Montgomeryshire, hired a boat to carry them from Newbridge (just south of the Vyrnwy Aqueduct) to Ellesmere Port, from where they crossed to Liverpool to embark for the United States. Amongst them was the Revd J. Williams, Independent Minister of Llansilin. On their journey they sang temperance hymns.[14]

In February 1844 colliers in Lancashire went on strike. Strikebreakers were recruited from the east Shropshire coalfield and travelled by canal boat from Wappenshall (near Wellington, on the branch off the Birmingham & Liverpool Junction Canal)

Chapter 7 : The Ellesmere & Chester Canal

via Nantwich and Middlewich to Runcorn. According to the press report they were 'well provisioned and full of spirit that they were going to constant work'. A second boat-load followed a few weeks later.[15]

A further example, also from 1844, was the transport of boat-loads of Irishmen for harvest work in the Midlands. The canal company charged 18*d* for the journey of between 18 and 20 hours from Chester to Wolverhampton.[16]

Canal carrier?

UNTIL 1844 the incorporation of a joint stock company – a company with shares, rather than a partnership – required royal charter or an Act of Parliament. (Limited liability companies, such as almost all canal companies, needed an Act until 1855.) In 1838 the Anderton Carrying Company sought to become a joint stock company – the ECC formally opposed this on the grounds that 'the establishment of such a company tends to a monopoly in the carrying trade dangerous to the interests of all canals'.

The canal company was unconcerned about the evils of monopoly when it proposed to be the potential monopolist. As mentioned earlier, in 1829 Thomas Stanton had written a report examining the case for becoming a carrier which is worth quoting at length:

> By an inspection of the map it will be seen that although this canal passes through 100 miles of country, which for fertility and richness of agricultural produce is perhaps exceeded by none in the Kingdom, yet with the exception of the trade betwixt the City of Chester and Liverpool, its commercial carriage is far from important. The towns on its banks are of small population and many of them (as Oswestry, Ellesmere and Whitchurch, for instance) possess comparatively short roads to market by land.
>
> The consequence is that when several carriers embark in the trade, warehouses and establishments are unnecessarily multiplied, and boats are running up and down with less than half ladings at a wasteful expense of labour and of the water of the canal while rates of freight are exacted from the public which in the hands of one respectable company would be sufficiently remunerating, but divided into numbers and exhausted in the manner described become wholly inadequate to ensure a regular and efficient discharge of the business.
>
> And the mischief does not end here. In consequence of the scantiness of the loading, the boats sail with no regularity and are frequently waiting for days together to obtain goods, whereas if the trade were in one hand and boats dispatched daily with regularity to all parts of the canal, it would frequently happen that goods would be delivered even at Welshpool before they now leave Ellesmere Port.
>
> From want of this regularity the commercial trade of the canal has suffered much. The short distances by land operating both by their speed and punctuality.[17]

The issue came to the fore again in 1841, no doubt prompted by the knowledge of how railway services were changing the pattern of carrying. The company introduced a Bill to become a carrier on its canals; this was passed the following year.

Stanton then proposed to charge the full rate of tonnage (the tolls) authorised by the original Acts, and to enforce a clause requiring boats to carry full loads – and if they didn't, to charge as if there were full loads. This was the way, he said, 'to secure the whole of the trade to the Company's vessels'. Clearly the company would have to charge very low freight rates for their actual carriage of the goods; the accounts would show the carrying concern was making a large loss which would be more than balanced by a huge increase in the income from tonnage. This action would certainly have been unethical, but whether it would have been illegal is debatable, as it would have satisfied the requirement that all carriers were charged the same tonnage.

Nevertheless, such radical action was not taken. Instead the company accepted the offer of Tilston, Smith & Co. 'our oldest and most extensive carriers' for a five year contract to carry on behalf of the company. The charge to the customers would be unchanged as long as tonnage rates were unchanged; if the company altered the tonnage rates, Tilston Smith would make a corresponding change in the charge to the customer. As well as paying the tonnage to the company, Tilston Smith would also pay £3,000 a year.

It must be remembered that carrying implied far more than merely the provision of boats and crews – or even of wharfs and warehouses. The business required continuous effort and complex organisation. Potential customers needed to be canvassed; existing customers had to be serviced and satisfied; cartage needed to be arranged, possibly at both ends of the journey; boats had to be loaded so that the goods were readily accessible at their destination; waybills needed to be sent showing exactly what was needed where; and customers needed to be billed and the money collected.

The ECC being a carrier was regarded by the other carriers as unfair competition. For example, the Neptune Conveyance Company, which had several boats based at Shrewsbury and trading to Liverpool and Manchester, placed an advertisement in the *Shrewsbury Chronicle*, accusing the ECC of attempting to create a monopoly and reassuring its customers that it intended to continue to serve them 'with dispatch and promptitude'. A fortnight later it announced that it had made arrangements for all goods to be sent to London, Liverpool and Manchester by transferring them from its boats to the Grand Junction Railway at Wolverhampton, thus speeding delivery. This project obviously failed, because a month later its advertisement extolled its boating service to Manchester and Liverpool, the latter via Runcorn. But less than two years later it was out of business and its wharf, warehouses, vaults, office and stable were being advertised to be let.[18]

Review of tolls, 1842

At the meeting which made the decision to become a carrier, the tonnage rates were reviewed and simplified. The many special rates which had been introduced over the years were abolished. Although the general trend was an increase, some tonnage rates per mile were reduced. The following are a few examples:

- limestone for making lime: formerly 1*d* as far as Grindley Brook, then tonnage free down to Hurleston; to be ½*d*;
- coal for burning limestone: formerly ½*d* as far as Grindley Brook, then tonnage free down to Hurleston; to be ½*d*;
- bricks and slates: formerly 1*d*; to be ½*d*;
- iron ore: formerly ½*d*; to be 1*d*;
- pig iron and iron products: unchanged at 1*d*;
- English (and presumably Welsh) timber: formerly 1*d*; to be 1½*d*;
- fire coal: unchanged at 1½*d*; and
- goods for which there is no specific rate: to be the maximum authorised by Parliament (which was usually 3*d*).

New minimum charges were introduced for goods boated less than twelve miles if they pass through a lock:

- slates, iron ore: 6*d* per ton;
- lime, limestone, coal: 2*d* per ton for every lock passed through; and
- other goods: 2 shillings per ton.

Trading in fluxing limestone

THE Trent & Mersey Canal Company's Act of 1776, which authorised the building of the Caldon Canal, included provision for the canal company to work the Caldon Low limestone quarries if the volume of production did not meet its requirements. Some time about 1830 the TMC took over the quarrying. The report of the ECC's 1836 Committee of Investigation stated that the TMC then supplied the ironmasters of South Staffordshire with fluxing stone at a very low price in order to retain the return trade in iron products to Liverpool.

When the BLJC opened, the ECC wanted to attract this trade, and it had good sources of fluxing stone at Trevor and Llanymynech in particular. William Provis became the tenant of the Trevor quarries, spent £2,000 opening up the quarries and installing the machinery, and Thomas Stanton agreed to the fluxing stone travelling toll free from Trevor to Nantwich, where it was deposited upon the quay for onward sale. Stanton's calculation of the cost per ton at Nantwich was as table A (right).

The 1836 Committee of Inquiry claimed to have found that Trevor stone delivered to the South Staffordshire ironmaster was still slightly more expensive than Caldon Low stone – and as Provis was having to sell the stone at Nantwich for 3*s*.3*d* per ton, he was personally actually making a loss. However, the committee thought that the company was benefiting because in the previous six months, 14,246 tons of iron had been boated from Nantwich to Ellesmere Port. During the same period 6,872 tons of fluxing stone had been deposited at Nantwich. The Committee of Inquiry considered that most or all of this was 'back carriage' – in other words, that the boats would otherwise have travelled empty. This was true as regards the BLJC, but that wasn't relevant to the ECC. It would not have been back carriage from Trevor to Nantwich as the balance of other traffic from west to east exceeded that from east to west. A second flaw in the logic, recognised but then dismissed in the report, was that some of the fluxing stone would have been going to the east Shropshire ironworks, the iron products of which would inevitably use the BLJC and ECC as there was no real competition for this traffic.

William Provis had one of the largest shareholdings in the ECC – 40 shares in 1836 – and was present at both the General Assemblies when the issue was discussed. He was also, as has been seen, the contractor responsible for most of the major works done by the ECC since 1827, as well as being Thomas Stanton's son-in-law. In my opinion he was being given special treatment, though the Committee of Inquiry denied this.

The 1841 Bill included a clause for the company to work quarries for fluxing limestone, similar to the powers enjoyed by the TMC, but this was struck out during its passage through Parliament.

In 1842 it was decided that the ECC should enter into the carrying trade for fluxing stone from Trevor and Llanymynech, charging 1*s*.8*d* per ton carriage – the same figure as used in Stanton's calculation six years earlier – and nothing for tonnage. The boats of the current carriers would be bought at valuation.

Finance

THE shareholders' patience was eventually rewarded when the payment of dividends commenced in 1814. With the exception of two years in which there was a large amount of capital expenditure, dividends of between £2 and £4 a share continued to be paid during the remaining independent life of the Ellesmere & Chester Canal.

All the capital projects – the Middlewich Branch, Hurleston Reservoir, the extensive works at Ellesmere Port and the move into carrying – were financed from retained profits or by borrowing. The maximum amount that could be borrowed was increased by £120,000.

Detailed accounts survive only for the year ended 30 June

Table A	*s*	*d*
Quarrying and loading into boats		9
Royalties		4
Repair & maintenance, administration, interest		4¼
Haulage – 45 miles @ 6*d* a mile with a load of 15 tons	1	3
Boat – 45 miles @ 2*d* a mile		5
Interest, provision for bad debts		2
	3	7¼

Chapter 7: The Ellesmere & Chester Canal

1845.[19] The following figures exclude the costs and receipts associated with the application to Parliament for the creation of the Shropshire Union:

	£	£
Receipts		
Tonnage and rents	40,100	
Duke of Bridgewater's Trustees: Ellesmere Port	10,246	
Sundry receipt	131	50,477
Payments		
Maintenance etc of canal & tramroad	6,358	
Boat account	3,171	
Salaries and wages	1,579	
Rents	1,580	
Rates and taxes	673	
Other expenses	2,471	15,832
Operating profit		34,645
Interest on loans		15,037
Net profit		19,608

The dividend paid (including taxation) was £14,259. Unlike modern accounts, there was no provision for depreciation of the assets.

Merger

THE events leading to the merger with the BLJC and the subsequent creation of the Shropshire Union are discussed in Chapter 9.

Notes and references

The company minutes are held by The National Archives in the series RAIL826.

1. The information about the negotiations is mainly derived from the correspondence between James Loch and Bradshaw, Eyre Lee and Lord Gower held by the Staffordshire Archives: D593/K/3/12–13 and D593/K/5/1–2
2. The fourth lock on the TMC's main line at Middlewich, 'Big Lock', was at that time a narrow lock, not being rebuilt for boats with a 14ft beam until 1891.
3. Thomas Telford, *Life of Thomas Telford*, 1838, p.91
4. Deposited plans: Cheshire Record Office, QPD 100; Weaver Navigation Trustees minutes, September & October 1830 and Account Books, March 1836: Cheshire Record Office, LNW4/9; ECC Committee, 4 January 1831
5. Richard Dean, 'Manchester & Birmingham Junction Canal', *NarrowBoat*, Winter 2007/08, pp.10–11
6. Deposited plan: Cheshire Record Office, QPD p.148
7. A bushel was a measure of volume, usually eight gallons, but this could vary locally – a Shropshire bushel of wheat was 9½ to 10 gallons, for example.
8. 'Freight' at that time usually meant the charge for carriage of the goods excluding the tonnage.
9. *Chester Chronicle*, 10 August 1827; *Chester Courant*, 18 September 1827
10. *Chester Chronicle*, 4 January 1828; *Chester Courant*, 22 January & 5 February 1828
11. ECC General Assembly, 24 July 1828; *Chester Courant*, 10 February 1829
12. S. Salt, *Facts and figures, principally relating to railways and commerce*, 1848, p.105, quoted in Peter Maw, *Transport and the Industrial City*, 2013, p.127
13. This new road was Thomas Brassey's first significant civil engineering contract. Brassey later built many of the railways in the Shropshire Union area.
14. *North Wales Chronicle*, 14 April 1840
15. *Eddowes Salopian Journal*, 28 February 1844; *Shrewsbury Chronicle*, 22 March 1844.
16. *Chester Chronicle*, 2 August 1844, quoted in Terry Kavanagh, *The Old Chester Canal*, p.131
17. Report of 1829, quoted in ECC Committee, 25 August 1842
18. *Shrewsbury Chronicle*, 30 September, 14 October & 28 November 1842 and 4 September 1844
19. SURCC accounts: TNA, RAIL1110/413

The Birmingham & Liverpool Junction Canal, derived from a 1895 map of the Shropshire Union Canal with peripheral detail removed. *Canal & River Trust*

8

The Birmingham & Liverpool Junction Canal

Promotion of the canal

As was mentioned in the last chapter, trade was flourishing in 1824 and credit was relatively cheap. This led to there being what has been described as a 'Railway Fever', promotion of various railway lines with horse-drawn trains, usually with the option of adopting steam locomotive traction. Some of these lines were long-distance, one being the Birmingham, Manchester & Liverpool Rail Road Company. At a meeting at Wolverhampton on 26 April the following resolution was passed unanimously:

> That a Rail Road from the town of Birmingham through the whole of the Staffordshire collieries and ironworks, and from then through the neighbourhoods of the Shropshire ironworks and Staffordshire potteries to the river Mersey with branches to the towns of Manchester and Liverpool would be of the greatest advantage to the above mentioned places and districts and productive of essential benefit to the nation at large.[1]

A committee was formed and ambitions were limited to Birmingham to the Mersey at Birkenhead (for Liverpool), the intention being to go to Parliament in 1825. A survey by Paul Padley and George Hamilton recommended a route passing near Market Drayton, Nantwich and Chester. It was always envisaged that trains would be hauled by steam locomotives.

Later in the year a second railway scheme linking Birmingham with the Mersey was being discussed. This would have crossed the Mersey between Widnes and Warrington and continued to Liverpool, with a branch to the Potteries.[2]

The previous year (1824) the committee of the Birmingham Canal (BCN) had resolved to ask Thomas Telford to recommend improvements. He reported back that September, and as well as recommending major improvements to the canal between Birmingham and Wolverhampton, which subsequently became the 'New Main Line', he recommended a new direct outlet to the Mersey. This canal, 39 miles long from Autherley, near the bottom of the twenty-one locks at Wolverhampton, to the Ellesmere & Chester Canal (ECC) at Nantwich was estimated to cost £300,000.

The BCN's committee backed this proposal, which was appropriately named the Birmingham & Liverpool Junction Canal (BLJC), and wrote to the ECC inviting its members to take up 500 shares of £100 in the enterprise. The ECC shareholders and managers responded enthusiastically. All 500 shares were taken up immediately, those having 20 shares including Lord Clive, Rowland Hunt, Thomas Stanton and Thomas Telford.

A war of words followed. An editorial in the *Chester Chronicle*, owned by John Fletcher, a major shareholder in the ECC who had taken 10 shares in the BLJC, said that 'the traversing of public roads – of gentlemen's parks – and even of the streets of towns, by odious high-pressure locomotive machinery ... must be in the highest degree annoying, and in many instances dangerous'. Other writers asserted that elderly gentlemen would not be able to cross the railroads without the certainty of being run over; there were already adequate communications by water and good roads; iron and coal prices would rise enormously because of the extra demand; and 'cattle would not graze within half a mile of the steam rail-roads'. And of course there would be the effect on canal dividends – with the usual comments about the implications for 'widows and orphans' who were reliant on their investments.[3]

An editorial in the rival newspaper, the *Chester Courant*, considered that rail-roads united safety, smoothness and speed of transit, so would render every article cheaper, increase consumption, improve the revenue and multiply the resources of the kingdom. It accepted that rail-roads would injure the proprietors of canals, just as the canals had injured the stage waggons – but it would do so by benefiting the public.[4]

With the benefit of hindsight it is obvious to us that railways were the better long-term prospect. At the time this was by no means clear. Steam locomotives were then slow, inefficient, unreliable and unable to cope with more than a gentle gradient. It was not until the Rainhill Trials of October 1829 that the steam locomotive was publicly vindicated.

Opposition from canal companies

THE proposed new canal together with a Middlewich Branch of the ECC would also give an easier route between the West Midlands and Manchester than that provided by the Trent & Mersey Canal (TMC) and Staffordshire & Worcestershire Canal (SWC). How the opposition of the TMC led to the imposition of a toll at Middlewich was discussed in the last chapter. Something similar happened with the SWC at Autherley Junction.

At that time the concept of unlimited competition had not yet been accepted – instead there was a feeling that Parliament should protect those who had invested in projects which it had previously approved. Following negotiations, it was agreed that the Bill should include a clause stating that the SWC would be paid a maximum of two shillings per ton on traffic passing to or from the BLJC at Autherley Junction.

Several years later, in 1836, seemingly at the initiative of various Birmingham Canal shareholders and Black Country industrialists, the Tettenhall & Autherley Canal & Aqueduct Company was formed with the aim of avoiding the junction toll. A Bill was presented to Parliament. The BLJC tried to seek an amicable settlement with the SWC, and when the latter agreed to reduce the junction toll to 4*d* per ton, the Bill was withdrawn.

The Stafford interest

THE Marquess of Stafford had a dilemma. Not only was he a major local landowner, under the will of the third Duke of Bridgewater (the 'Canal Duke') he had a life interest in the profits of the Bridgewater Canal but no say in its management, which was in the sole control of Robert Haldane Bradshaw, the dominant and intensely conservative Superintendent of the Bridgewater Trust. Another quirk of the Bridgewater will was that on the death of Lord Stafford, the interest in the profits would pass to his second son, Francis, not to his eldest son, Lord Gower. Lord Stafford also had ten shares in the TMC.

In October 1824 Thomas Eyre Lee, a Birmingham solicitor and a leading member of the BCN's committee, wrote to Lord Stafford's Principal Agent, James Loch, saying that he had heard a rumour that Lord Stafford was wavering as to whether he should or should not oppose their scheme for a new canal, to which Loch replied noncommittally. Loch told Lord Stafford that his Staffordshire estates would receive only small benefits from the railway proposal, and if he assented the Jury which assessed compensation would suppose he had waived all claims beyond the bare value of the land taken. This advice was accepted, and Lord Stafford continued to be neutral.

At the same time there was a vituperative argument proceeding about the proposal for a railway between Liverpool and Manchester, it being claimed that the Bridgewater Canal's monopoly compelled the public to pay £100,000 more a year than they ought to pay. A rumour spread that Lord Stafford was supporting the railway because if the Bridgewater Trust continued to prosper, his second son would have a bigger income than his first; in December 1824 Loch issued a public denial of this.

Loch was not someone who would be persuaded by the extravagant language of enthusiasm and hostility: he needed facts before he would advise. In January 1825 he investigated the capacity of steam locomotives then in use at Killingworth and Hetton Collieries and appreciated their potential. Also he had a genuine belief in the benefits of competition – and he realised that the canal/railway dispute could appear to be a conflict between the established monopolistic landowners who wanted to preserve their privileges and a new group of entrepreneurs who desired to provide cheaper transport for all. Thus his instincts were to support the railway proposals though they might seem to be against the interests of his employer.

He thought that in the long run general opposition to railways was unsustainable but that co-existence was possible, since trade multiplied if transport was improved. Furthermore, canals needed to invest in order to put themselves in a more competitive position. Nevertheless, despite Loch's doubts, from February to May 1825 the Stafford family's parliamentary strength was used to oppose and eventually help defeat both the Liverpool & Manchester Railway and Birmingham & Liverpool Rail Road Bills.

Immediately following the defeat of the Bills, Loch arranged for the newspapers to carry the story that the Bridgewater Trustees had agreed to improvements to their canal, including an additional set of locks at Runcorn, enlargement of Duke's Dock at Liverpool and additional warehousing at Manchester. He did this anonymously, forcing the hand of Bradshaw. Lord Stafford contributed £58,000 towards the cost of the works.

James Loch (1780–1855)

THE son of an impecunious Scottish landowner who was obliged shortly afterwards to sell the family estate at Drylaw, Loch was educated at the University of Edinburgh and then practised at the Bar, specialising in conveyancing and estate management. He was Principal Agent of the Marquess of Stafford (later 1st Duke of Sutherland) from 1812, supervising the Sutherland clearances and the development of new settlements 1815–20. He was also Auditor to Lord Francis Egerton (later 8th Earl of Bridgewater), the Bridgewater Trustees (Superintendent of the Bridgewater Trust from 1837), and to the trust estates of the Earl of Dudley and of Viscount Keith. He was extremely hard-working and a master of detail.

Whig MP for St Germans (1827–30) then for Wick (1830–52), his principles were liberalism, compromise and conciliation (though it was said that he was 'not superlatively endowed with tact and diplomacy'), competition, avoidance of monopoly, and strict cost control.

Although he had advised against the investment made by the Marquess of Stafford in the Birmingham & Liverpool Junction Canal he was much involved in its management and its transformation into the Shropshire Union system.

Chapter 8: The Birmingham & Liverpool Junction Canal

At about the same time Lord Stafford and his relations took 160 of the 4,000 shares in the BLJC. Certain conditions were imposed: the canal would have a connecting arm into Shropshire to benefit the Stafford family estates, and the ECC would proceed with the branch to Middlewich. James Loch and his relations took 40 shares, considering it 'a very good speculation'. Indeed, all the shares were taken up without a prospectus being issued, almost all the investors living locally, or being shareholders in the two canals it linked, or being involved in businesses of the West Midlands.

Then in late December Lord Stafford surprised the business community by investing £100,000 in the Liverpool & Manchester Railway, almost a fifth of the total share capital, acting on Loch's advice and after extensive discussions with William Huskisson, their mutual friend and a strong supporter of the railway. Eyre Lee was concerned when he read in the newspapers about the decision; like most people, he could not understand how Lord Stafford could support both canals and railways.

The Liverpool & Manchester Railway's Act was passed on 9 May 1826, the Birmingham & Liverpool Junction Canal's Act nineteen days later. Although having the biggest shareholding, the Stafford interest took no active part in the latter's management until its crisis years.

Construction

THOMAS Telford was formally appointed Engineer, Alexander Easton Resident Engineer, Thomas Eyre Lee Clerk and Sir John Wrottesley MP Treasurer. Easton, who was appointed on the generous salary of £700 a year, had first worked for Telford in 1805, and from 1807 to 1823 was the Resident Engineer of the Western District of the Caledonian Canal. Lee was a Birmingham solicitor who had been on the committee of the Birmingham Canal since 1791. Wrottesley was a Wolverhampton banker and a leading shareholder in the Staffordshire & Worcestershire Canal. Francis Holyoake, another Wolverhampton banker, replace Wrottesley in 1834.

The main line of the canal

TELFORD'S line was particularly well laid out. It started in the basin of the Trent, crossed a watershed into the basin of the Severn, then crossed another into the basin of the Weaver; nevertheless it descended all the way, so there were no intermediate summit levels requiring their own sources of water. It was fairly straight with deep cuttings and high embankments – in essence what was to become typical railway engineering.

In other ways it was old-fashioned: it was intended for narrowboats, not the boats 14ft wide which could reach Nantwich, and it was even relatively shallow, at 3ft 4in. compared with the 3ft 8in. of the canals on the route from Birmingham to London. The exposed embankments were to prove troublesome to horse-hauled boats: when unladen and therefore having a shallow draught and high freeboard, cross-winds made them difficult to steer.

The original plans had the same number of locks (29) as were actually constructed, but one would have been by Turnover Bridge (Bridge 26) near Church Eaton, rather than at Wheaton Aston.

Telford estimated that the engineering works for the main line would cost £388,451 – almost all of the share capital of £400,000. He forecast that the whole of the works would be finished by May 1831.

Negotiations were held with landowners. Telford's original idea had been to continue the canal from the end of the Nantwich Basin of the Chester Canal but in order to avoid opposition it was agreed that the canal should bypass Dorfold Hall and its park, necessitating the construction of a long embankment north of Nantwich. Rather easier to accommodate was the request for the towpath to be on the east side through the Adderley Estate.

The canal divided Thomas Twemlow's Peatswood Estate, just south of Market Drayton, part of the line being on a high embankment, 500 yards long. The canal took 16½ acres; a further 9 acres had spoil put on it. An unusual outcome was the closure of a small private canal made in the early 1790s from a marl pit to various fields. Part of its line can still be discerned in the field beside the second and third locks down the Tyrley Flight, most easily in late evening sunshine.

Most problematical were Lord Anson's requirements concerning his estates in the Norbury area, which resulted in an expensive and troublesome earthwork: Shelmore Embankment. John Freeth, Clerk to the Birmingham Canal, writing shortly after the opening of the BLJC in 1835, stated that Lord Anson had been concerned that the line originally proposed by Telford would interfere with some of his game covers and preserves. The original proposal would actually have passed almost a quarter of a mile to the east of Shelmore Wood but would have severed it from most of the farmland of the estate. Lord Anson was keen on game shooting which took place on the open fields, the wood acting as a 'holding' area for the birds. Perhaps at least as important as the shooting were the implications for farming and estate management, where he would have wanted to avoid land being severed if possible. Indeed, the canal came to be routed on the boundary of his land or just to the west of the boundary. Anson was not himself actually against the canal project, owning twenty £100 shares in it.

A branch to Pave Lane?

THE proposal in the original Bill was that there should be a branch leaving the main line near Church Eaton and following the contour for 7½ miles with just one lock to join the Donnington Wood Canal at Pave Lane. If that tub-boat canal was to be used by narrow boats it would need modernising – both widening and deepening, with some rebuilding of bridges – but the Lilleshall Company's coal mines and ironworks of the eastern end of the industrial area would then have direct transport access to the rest of the country. It would of course have been excessively expensive to rebuild the inclines at Trench and Wrockwardine Wood to make them suitable for narrow boats. Thus to get cargoes to or from Shrewsbury or Coalport, transhipment would have been necessary.

Most of the Donnington Wood Canal was owned by Lord Stafford but formed part of the long-term lease to the Lilleshall Company, in which Lord Stafford's much younger brother, Granville Leveson-Gower, held half the shares. (He was created Earl Granville in 1833.) There was some uncertainty about whether the lease of the canal merely gave the Lilleshall Company the right to use it without charge or whether they were entitled to demand tolls from third parties as at that time they were doing. Presumably as they were carrying out any necessary maintenance this was a reasonable working arrangement, even if not formally sanctioned.

One would have expected a major industrial enterprise to welcome significant improvements in its transport system, but in fact the Lilleshall Company opposed the proposal for a branch canal from the BLJC to Pave Lane. The reason given by John Horton, its managing partner, was that they thought it would injure their sales by letting in iron and coal from South Staffordshire.

The legal position of the Donnington Wood Canal was further complicated because the part nearest Pave Lane, a length of about three-quarters of a mile, was leased from John Cotes. (His house, Woodcote, was about a mile south-east of Pave Lane, and about a quarter of a mile from the line of the intended new branch.) Loch wanted the Donnington Wood Canal to become a public canal under an Act of Parliament rather than remaining private. In particular he was concerned that Cotes would demand excessive terms if he was allowed to retain ownership of a short but crucial section.

Cotes, who was well connected politically, persuaded the Shropshire MPs to oppose the BLJC Bill, which led Loch to recommend that the Pave Lane Branch be dropped from the Bill in order that the main line be unopposed. This was agreed, and the Act passed easily.

The Newport Branch

LOCH'S second reason for suggesting that the Pave Lane proposal be dropped was that he thought a line of canal could be devised which would go near Newport then pass through the estates on the Weald Moors of Lord Gower, Lord Stafford's eldest son, joining the Shrewsbury Canal near Wappenshall.

> ### John Wilson (c.1772–1831)
>
> JOHN WILSON was born at Dalston in Cumbria. He assisted John Simpson on the masonry of Pontcysyllte Aqueduct and worked for Thomas Telford extensively after that, including contracts at the western end of the Caledonian Canal, constructing roads in the Scottish highlands and being the masonry contractor for the Menai Bridge. He contracted for two sections of the Birmingham & Liverpool Junction Canal, completed by his sons after his death. (He was not the John Wilson who went with Telford to Sweden and stayed on to superintend the building of part of the Göta Canal.)

This would give a much better route to Shrewsbury and would find more favour in the county. Loch's preferred line was for the branch to pass south of Newport though this might need a tunnel under Aston Hill. However he recognised that a better line might go north of Newport and nearer to Edgmond but this would not benefit Lord Gower's estate as much.

William Provis surveyed the land on behalf of Thomas Telford. Unsurprisingly they recommended the easiest route to construct, a branch 10½ miles long with 23 locks, passing the northern edge of Newport. Telford estimated that the engineering works of the branch would cost £58,687 and the total cost would be £72,412. This was accepted at the General Assembly in July 1826, the first after the passing of the company's first Act of Parliament. The Newport Branch was approved in a second Act the following year.

At that first General Assembly Telford also recommended a 2¾ mile long link to the Lilleshall Company's limestone works at Aston. For this, he thought, a tramroad costing an estimated £6,799 would be preferable to a canal costing three times as much.

That autumn Loch considered various side branches, his expressed aim being to have 'an easy and cheap method of supplying lime and road materials to the further parts of Lord Gower's estate and an open and uninterrupted access to the market'.

His main suggestion was a branch canal to Aston. The possibility of a tramroad is not mentioned in the correspondence, perhaps because it would have involved transhipment. John Horton on behalf of the Lilleshall Company was opposed to such a branch canal. He also claimed it would not be in Lord Gower's interest either, because the coal for the lime works at Lilleshall could then be obtained easily from sources other than Lord Gower's mines at Donnington Wood.

An alternative was then explored whereby there would be a branch canal from just west of the crossing of the Kynnersley Drive to close to the turnpike road from Donnington to Trench. Limekilns would be built there, and a railway would provide a connection with the Donnington Wood Canal.

Nothing came of this at the time, though the Humber Arm which was built in 1844 was in effect a truncated version of it. Curiously, construction of this branch is not mentioned in the company minutes, implying that it was a private canal built by the Sutherland Estate, through the lands of which it ran. A tramroad was constructed from Lubstree Wharf, at the end of the Humber Arm, to the Lilleshall Company's Lodge Furnaces.

Loch's other suggestion in the autumn of 1826 was for a short branch to The Wall, on the Kynnersley to Tibberton road, thus serving the northernmost part of Lord Gower's estate. Nothing further was done about this.

Contracts

IN December 1826 John Wilson's tender for the 21 mile long section between Nantwich and High Offley was accepted in the sum of £189,100. This section included 27 of the 28 locks on the main line. Wilson had worked extensively for Telford in Scotland and had built the towers of Telford's Menai Bridge. In 1828 he bought Grove House at Market Drayton, a large house the grounds of which bordered the line of the canal – this is now the Sixth Form Centre of the Grove School.

It wasn't until June 1829 that the contract for the next section, £114,678 for the six miles from High Offley to Church Eaton (High Onn), was made. The delay had been caused by the extended negotiations with Thomas Burne, owner of the Loynton Estate, and Lord Anson. There is also a hint that financial issues contributed to the lack of haste. Telford chose William Provis to be contractor for this section, in addition to the work he was doing on the Middlewich Branch of the ECC.

By this time, Wilson's contract was proceeding well. The canal had been completed from Nantwich to just beyond Market Drayton, including the 50ft high embankment over the river Tern and Cole Brook; Tyrley Locks were started and Woodseaves Cutting nearing completion. There was a hint of trouble ahead when Telford reported in July 1829 that alternating strata of marl, clay and rock had been found in the cutting. In several places it had been found necessary to cut out the marl and support the rock by means of dry stone walls; in other places where the rock was not so firm it had been decided to slope the sides 6in. horizontal to 1ft vertical. Nevertheless he assured the shareholders that there was no doubt that the whole of the canal works would be completed 'by the stipulated time', by implication, May 1831.

At the end of 1829 Provis's tender of £77,716 for the Newport Branch was accepted. This section included twenty-three locks, the aqueduct over the river Meese and the crossing of the Weald Moors. The tender was almost a third higher than Telford's original estimate for the branch's engineering works.

The final contract for completing the main line from Church Eaton to Autherley Junction, 10½ miles, was let to John Wilson the following summer for £93,000. Wilson died in January 1831 and his sons, John and William, took over his contracts.

A few problems were encountered in 1830 and 1831. Nantwich Embankment slipped repeatedly, necessitating the widening of its base. Woodseaves Cutting was still causing trouble. As far as possible, Telford used the principle of 'cut and fill' – for example, the material cut from the cutting at Betton Wood was used for the embankment at Market Drayton – but not all the material from Woodseaves was required elsewhere so the excess was deposited alongside the top of the cutting, increasing the maximum depth to 90ft.

In January 1832 Telford was able to report that he had travelled by boat along the complete length of the Wilsons' contract from Nantwich to High Offley. However, this section could not be opened for commercial traffic because the principal water supply for the canal was to come from much further south.

The greatest problem lay in Provis's contract where Shelmore Embankment was not consolidating. However, the committee was not told about this until the following year.

The skew bridge at Forton on the Newport Branch. Beautiful architecture, but was it the best value way to make a road crossing here? *Author*

Crisis and completion

As early as November 1831 James Loch was losing confidence in Telford, commenting to Lord Clive that 'Telford is not the man he was, and that he trusts exceedingly in those in whom he has confidence, which in some instances I think has been abused'. Nor was he happy about the control of costs, telling Eyre Lee 'you must really impress on Telford that we have need of every sixpence of our money'.

It is indisputable that Telford was more concerned about exemplary engineering and architecture than about value for money. For example, a survey of the 27 highway bridges between Market Drayton and Pendeford (just outside the northern boundary of Wolverhampton) showed that all but three were skew, ten by 18 degrees or more, so necessitating the courses under the arch to be angled too. In many instances a small diversion of the road or track would have enabled the bridge to have been at right angles to the canal, hence simpler and cheaper to build. In some cases, where two bridges were close together (such as Newcastle Road and Betton Road in Market Drayton), a short section of new road would have removed the necessity for one of the bridges. We now admire the quality of Telford's stonework, but this beauty came at a cost the company could not afford.

At the beginning of 1833 Thomas Telford, by then 75 years old, was unwell and therefore unable to make his regular survey. Alexander Easton reported instead. He felt that the canal could be carried over the defective portion of Shelmore Embankment on a temporary wooden trough, which would cost about £5,000, but the committee preferred to delay a few months. The Newport Branch was progressing well, so the committee planned to open it together with the main line from Norbury Junction to Nantwich, in order that Shrewsbury and the east Shropshire coal and iron works could trade with Liverpool and Manchester. This implied using the water supply from Knighton Reservoir which, as is discussed later, was not practicable.

Loch considered that what was happening at Shelmore 'alarming'. He had little confidence in Provis, and wished that the Wilsons had been given that contract. He was particularly concerned that Telford had not suggested any remedial action and urged that another engineer be brought in. On Telford's advice, Loch invited William Cubitt to act as consulting engineer in Telford's absence.

When Cubitt inspected Shelmore Embankment he found that clay and other unsuitable material had been used, a situation made worse because the embankment was along a hillside, with the result that the material was not being deposited on level ground. He recommended that Easton be given a written instruction not to allow another load of clay or soil to be put upon the embankment, and this was done. One of the people who had accompanied him on his inspection wrote, 'It is very clear that no attention whatever has been paid to the selection of the stuff up to the present moment, the cause of the mischief we now experience'.[5]

Cubitt reported to the committee in March that Shelmore Embankment was the most important issue but it was capable of being made good. Rather than waste money removing the soft material, he recommended putting hard and heavy material on the top which would sink down through the soft, pushing it to the side. He had identified suitable good sand locally.

Woodseaves Cutting was still troublesome, the problem being caused by the marly substratum on which masses of rock rested. Frost caused the former to crumble, leaving the rock liable to fall. He had looked at the option of underpinning the rock with masonry, but felt it would be better in the long run to make the slopes at the side in the ratio of 1ft horizontal to 1ft vertical – the stone removed should prove useful for construction works. However, he was generally satisfied with the rest of the line; in particular thought that the large embankments at Market Drayton and Shebdon had kept their forms well.

In July 1833 Cubitt reported that the plan for Shelmore Embankment appeared to be successful, the work being at its full height from both ends to within 400 yards of the middle. He thought it would be at its full height and ready for puddling the channel within three months. Woodseaves Cutting was nearly completed and the rocky slope rendered 'perfectly safe and secure'. Cubitt and Telford concurred that the canal would be able to be opened by the following January.

Three months later the tone of Cubitt's report was more cautious. With regard to Shelmore he wrote:

> This important work is proceeding as well as it can possibly do under the circumstances in which it was undertaken to complete; it certainly takes more earth to make good than even I had anticipated but there is nothing to alarm or even call for a change in the mode of proceeding. ... All I can advise ... is to keep steadily and perseveringly on without the least slackness.

Nevertheless he expected to see the embankment at it full height by the end of November. The work at Woodseaves was still not quite complete. There was trouble at a new location: slips on the Newport Moors, but this he felt was the contractor's (Provis's) responsibility to put right.

Three months later Cubitt was still cheerful about the prospects, despite delays which he attributed to the wet and stormy weather. The only sign of slipping or settlement on Shelmore Embankment was at the place where the two ends met. There was still a bit of a problem with Newport and Edgmond Moors. He expected the canal to open for trade by the first day of May.

On the last day of March 1834 Cubitt reported satisfactory progress on Shelmore Embankment, though it could not have progressed as fast as he had expected three months earlier. Telford also attended this meeting and commented that the difficult works have been unusually numerous and of great magnitude. This was the last time that Telford visited the canal, though a couple of sub-committee meetings were held at his London house during the summer. He died on 2 September that year.

In June, Cubitt reported that there had been a slight slip on Shelmore Embankment, about 150yds in length, but it had only affected the puddle at the side of the channel and not the bottom of the channel. This did not particularly concern him: the embankment was getting on well but slowly. However, two slips had occurred in cuttings at places that had previously showed no signs of giving way. Up to 10,000 cubic yards had to be removed from Grub Street Cutting (north of Norbury) – Provis was trying to deal with this, and also remove spoil which he had put at the top of the cutting, but of course most of his men were at work on Shelmore Embankment. The other slip, much smaller in extent, was in the cutting just north of Avenue Bridge, Chillington.

In the following month 2ft of water were put on the embankment. Cubitt said it was perfectly watertight and showed no sign of failure, forecasting that the canal should be open for trade within six weeks. Perhaps to make people feel better about the

Landslip in Woodseaves Cutting in 2012. As can be seen, Cubitt's repeated advice to lessen the slope of the side of the cutting was never followed. Author

hoped that it could be raised to 4½ft, also that the slips in Grub Street Cutting would soon be cleared.

The canal from Autherley Junction to Gnosall, including Belvide Reservoir, opened on 22 January 1835; the remainder, including the Newport Branch and, crucially, Shelmore Embankment opened six weeks later, on 2 March. But even after the opening, problems continued. In May fifty men and three horses were still employed dealing with the movement on the eastern slope at the southern end of the embankment, and a decreasing number were employed there for several more months. To protect embankments from erosion by wash from passing boats, flagstones were placed at the sides of the cut at water level and rushes planted. The works on the moors on the Newport Branch continued to slowly subside, as they had done for the previous couple of years, and walls at two locks there had moved, though not by enough to stop trade.

Cubitt's final report of the year, in November, stated that Shelmore Embankment was standing well and that the trouble at Newport Moors had been overcome but there had been a minor slip on Shebdon Embankment at a place where one had occurred five years earlier.

Aftermath

IN the summer of 1841, William Cubitt returned to do a full survey of the canal. He was generally pleased with the condition of the works, stating

> The great evils which caused so much expense, loss of time and annoyance at the first making and opening of the canal, viz Shelmore Embankment, Grub Street Cutting and the Newport Moors are now all come to a settled state – and the former, Shelmore, is now amongst the best and safest portions of the canal.

The main outstanding problem was Woodseaves Cutting

> which from motives of economy most probably [was] cut too much upright in the sides, the consequence of which is a continual crumbling down in the winter stopping up the towing paths, filling the canal, and from the falling of large masses of rock endangering those who pass along the canal.

He thought that the slopes should be made less steep and that land should be purchased or rented to take the spoil which would be removed. As there were insufficient funds to do the whole job immediately, the work would have to be spread over several years. However, a preventative programme was never effected, and emergency repairs have been needed every few years following new falls.

Cubitt was critical of one feature in Telford's original design: the upper gates of the locks on the main line (but not on the Newport Branch) were pairs of mitre gates rather than single. These were more expensive to maintain, so he instructed Easton to replace them with single upper gates when the original gates required renewal.

delays, he added that the long dry summer had caused some canals to close and others to restrict traffic, and that if this canal had opened in May as intended, it would have had to close later for lack of water.

In his October report Cubitt said that the delays must seem 'interminable both in time and expense'. He found it 'exceedingly mortifying' that he could be so uncertain about when the canal would open. Shelmore Embankment was now slipping at its southern end, though those parts which had previously been the worst were standing well. As a precaution he had arranged for railways to be laid down on both sides of the canal on the embankment, with branches at both ends leading to stores of good earth. Heavy rain had caused a slip in Grub Street Cutting, filling up the canal for 60yds; this was being removed. In several of the other cuttings, sand and soil had been washed off the slopes and blocked the towpath.

In December 1834 Cubitt reported that progress was slow but there had been no further slips. He hoped that the canal could be opened in January. Then at the end of January he said that the embankment had 4ft of water over it, and soon he

The recess for the off-side mitre gate and the curve for the heel post can still be seen at most of the locks. This example is in the Tyrley flight. *Author*

Telford's valve house at Belvide Reservoir, with curved stonework, matching curved wooden door and cast-iron dome, contains just one large tap. Nearby is Cubitt's utilitarian valve house which also has a fireplace so can act as a refuge for the workmen. This is a striking example of how Telford's work, though beautiful, could be very poor value for money. *Author*

Chapter 8 : The Birmingham & Liverpool Junction Canal

Water supply

Reservoirs

The original plans included three relatively small reservoirs on the summit level: one at Tyrley, south of Market Drayton; one near Knighton; and Belvide Reservoir, sited alongside Watling Street. Because the main line of the canal descended from Autherley Junction to Nantwich, with most of the boats coming off or going to the Birmingham Canal – and possibly also because it may have been thought that the compensation toll being paid to the Staffordshire & Worcestershire Canal was also a payment for the water – it seems to have been assumed that water supply was not a major problem. This proved to be a serious oversight.

The reservoir at Tyrley was never built. The 52 acre reservoir at Knighton was completed by Provis by early 1833. Unfortunately, it was found that although the dam was satisfactory, the reservoir did not hold the water. It had not been lined or puddled, in the hope that the subsoil was impervious. However, even after the eastern end was puddled, the reservoir still leaked so was not used.

Meanwhile, Belvide Reservoir was completed by the Wilsons in mid-1833 with an 8ft head and a surface area of about 50 acres. In order to prevent damage by wave action, Cubitt recommended paving the surface of the slope with best Staffordshire blue brick laid endways in mortar, terminating in a curved parapet at the top, at a cost between £2,000 and £2,500. He was emphatic that any expedient would be bad, just 'money thrown away'.

After having monitored the reservoir for half a year, Cubitt recommended raising the dam by 3ft. It was later agreed that it should be raised a further foot, to 12ft; this more than doubled its capacity. The reservoir seemed totally watertight, but loss by evaporation was higher than forecast.

After the canal had opened, the reservoir requirements were reviewed. Knighton having been declared a failure, enough land was bought to increase the area of Belvide Reservoir to 200 acres, with a 25ft head. The work was completed by the addition of a stone coping in 1842.

Autherley Junction

The 1826 Act included a clause stating that the SWC would be paid a maximum of two shillings per ton on traffic passing Autherley Junction, part of the reason explicitly being to compensate for loss of water. An agreement reached in 1831 and modified in 1834 reduced this to one shilling per ton, with manure at six pence per ton, and with lime and limestone at four pence per ton. Then, as discussed earlier, in 1836 the threat of the BLJC making a direct connection with the BCN, induced the SWC to reduce the toll for all goods to four pence per ton.

The Act required the junction lock to have pairs of gates facing both ways, so that it could operate regardless of which water level was higher implying that the level of the two canals was about the same. In fact the SWC was at a slightly higher level. It has not proved possible to find out why this discrepancy occurred. One possibility was that the SWC had raised the summit level in order to increase the amount of water available to cope with dry summers, the deeper summit level acting like a reservoir. In 1831 it was agreed that one pair of gates would suffice, providing there were grooves to enable stop planks to be put in. The lock was built in 1833. A sluice adjacent was to have a meter designed by Cubitt so that the amount of extra water passing could be measured, but it seems that the meter, actually designed by the SWC's engineer, John Urpeth Rastrick, was not installed until 1838.

The amount of water taken off the summit level of the BLJC by the passage of a boat depended on the fall of the lock at Wheaton Aston. Rastrick and Cubitt met to discuss its capacity, reaching a compromise of 4,550 cubic feet. The committee of the SWC resolved that 'the difference in quantity of water to pass a loaded boat and an empty boat should also be taken into consideration'; it subsequently admitted it was in error, both laden and empty boats using the same amount of water when passing through a lock.

There were also problems getting the top gate of Autherley Junction Lock to stay closed if the difference in water level dropped to 2in. The state of repair of this gate was a matter about which the SWC complained on several occasions.

Continuing problems

To open the canal, it had to be filled with water. In 1830 a sub-committee was appointed to negotiate with the SWC and the Wyrley & Essington Canal but there is no record of the outcome.

With the opening thought to be imminent, further discussions were held in 1834. The estimated requirement was about 5,000 locks, one lock being taken as 4,000 cubic feet. The SWC refused to supply any water, though it later claimed that the BLJC could not have opened if the SWC had not provided 'a very large body of water' out of its summit level. The preferred source was the Wyrley & Essington Canal, from which it could be passed down 'along a natural valley in the neighbourhood of Wolverhampton without going into the Birmingham land at all' – presumably this means the Smestow Brook, from which a temporary cut could allow the water to enter the Staffordshire & Worcestershire Canal. The only reason I can think of for why it was desirable to avoid passing the water through the BCN, the BLJC's ally, was that as it would feed into the summit level of that canal, the water could flow south rather than the intended north. The Wyrley & Essington was willing to provide up to 4,000 locks at a cost of five shillings per lock; temporary works would be about £500.

Once the canal was open, water supplies were a continuing problem. The SWC was not passing a lock of water for every boat coming off the BCN. The SWC claimed that they had given all they could spare and it was pointless making their canal dry – this wasn't totally convincing as the boats coming off the BCN were bringing about 3,700 cubic feet of water each. At the heart of the dispute was a difference in interpretation of the Act. The BLJC thought the passage of water was an absolute requirement, whereas the SWC's interpretation was that this only applied if there was surplus water. It is surprising that the issue never came before the Courts.

The BLJC bought water from the Wyrley & Essington in the summers of 1835 and 1836.

The summer of 1840 was particularly dry, and the canal continued to operate only because Thomas Giffard of Chillington Hall allowed the company to drain his lake, for which he was compensated. This action had to be repeated in 1844.

In 1841 Cubitt calculated that by not passing in full the equivalent amount of water for every boat coming off the BCN, cumulatively they were 21,350 locks short. Without this water he thought it would be impossible to work the canal. He therefore proposed what had been investigated several years earlier in the context of tolls: a link from the BCN about a mile long, crossing the SWC on an iron trough, and locking down into the BLJC. This would stop the SWC getting the BCN's water and save customers three-quarters of the tonnage they were then paying at Autherley Junction.

The following February Cubitt reported that he had negotiated a reasonable compromise with the SWC, the main points being:

– the compensation toll would be permanently kept at 4d a ton;
– the two canals would be brought to the same level at Autherley Junction (though there is no hint about how this would have been achieved);
– the stop lock would be left open except in cases of accident or repairs;
– the stop lock would be altered so that the two gates opened opposite ways, in case one of the canals needed to lower the water level for repairs;
– Wheaton Aston Lock would be reduced in capacity to a maximum of 4,550 cubic feet;
– two cottages would be erected at Wheaton Aston for inspectors employed by the SWC; and
– the BLJC was permitted to erect a feeder from Belvide Reservoir to below Wheaton Aston Lock.

The Act to confirm the agreement was obtained that summer. Cottages were built the following year. However, it seems doubtful whether the canals were ever brought to the same level and Autherley Junction Lock left open. In 1844 the SWC complained about the state of repair of the lock gates there, and the following year it replaced the gates, recharging the BLJC for the cost. The proposed feeder from the reservoir to below Wheaton Aston Lock was never made because the cost would have been several thousand pounds.

Operation

Management

WILLIAM Hazledine, a committee member, reported in 1832 on various management issues. He recommended the appointment of an Agent to take charge of the canal and that his house, including a canal office and committee room, should be situated where it would be best for inspections and also for the convenience of proprietors attending the meetings. Here too should be a dry dock for weighing boats. His report made no mention of a maintenance depot. He thought the optimum location was Market Drayton, on land to the south of Newcastle Road Bridge (now the playing fields of Grove School). Telford advised against Hazledine's proposal, stating that renting would save £1,500. The committee took Telford's advice. The company offices were at Newport until 1843, when they moved to Audlem.

The senior staff were appointed in 1834 in anticipation of the canal's opening. The Collector of the Rates, Tolls and Dues was to be Robert Samuel Skey, who came from a family of canal carriers. He continued to serve the company and its successor until the early 1860s.

Cubitt was retained as consulting engineer. Alexander Easton was appointed Resident Engineer at a salary of £500 a year despite Loch commenting, 'He is far from active, does not impress one with the notion that he looks very sharply after the works committed to his superintendence or makes our interest his zealous and constant object'. He retired in 1851.

Opening

THE canal fully opened on 2 March 1835 but there were no formal celebrations. The *Shrewsbury Chronicle* reported:

> This important line of canal was opened to the public, pursuant to notice, on Monday morning last. For some days previous boats had passed from the Staffordshire Coal and Lime Works for a short distance along the canal near Autherley, but on this day boats proceeded from Wolverhampton to Ellesmere Port, from Wolverhampton to Shrewsbury, from Manchester to Shrewsbury, and from the Shropshire Collieries to Market Drayton.

Tolls were set at low levels to attract trade: lime and limestone was charged ½d per ton per mile, with 1d on goods and other commodities.

The BLJC issued a promotional leaflet showing the savings through using the new canal:

– Birmingham to Liverpool was 19⅞ miles shorter, with 30 fewer locks; and
– Birmingham to Manchester was 5¼ miles shorter, again with 30 fewer locks.

The leaflet also showed the tonnage tolls and the charges for wharfage and warehousing at the company's three wharves – Norbury, Audlem and Newport – and gave a ready-reckoner of distances between all the wharves, company or private, on the canal including the Newport Branch.[6] For local trade on the main line, within three years of opening there were fourteen private wharfs, four of which had warehouses.

Although the formal opening date of most of the canal was

Chapter 8 : The Birmingham & Liverpool Junction Canal

Monday 2 March, the records for Wappenshall Wharf show that on Saturday 28 February steerer Joseph Blaydon with Crowley, Hicklin, Batty & Co.'s boat number 80 arrived from Wolverhampton with 6¼ tons of goods. Either the wharf book has the wrong date, which seems unlikely in the context – there are six arrivals shown for the Monday – or the boat traversed the canal before it was officially open. This is presumably the same fly-boat of Crowley & Co. as was reported as arriving at Shrewsbury on the evening of the Monday with a cargo from London.

On the Tuesday eight or ten 'deeply laden' boats arrived in Chester by the new route, together with an inspection boat carrying several people involved in the making of the BLJC and representatives of carriers.[7]

Crowley & Co. advertised in the *Cheshire Chronicle* fly-boat services from Ellesmere Port and Chester to Wolverhampton and Birmingham with connections to London, Bristol, Oxford, Derby (and thence by road to Sheffield), Hull and numerous other places. Lock-up boats were available for the safe conveyance of wines and spirits. Other firms' advertisements quickly followed, Robins Mills & Co. for example offering to deliver goods from Chester to London in five days and to Manchester on the day following their delivery to their Chester warehouse.

The organisation of the traffic

With the canal becoming part of the national network of canals, there were two types of traffic: the quick or 'fly' trade, and the slow or heavy trade.

The fly trade was conducted only by firms of carriers, of which there were several, each with their own wharfs and warehouses. The boats could average 3mph or, with very light loads 3½mph, working day and night, with crews of four men. The horses worked stages of varying length, according to the arrangements of the individual carrier – not fewer than three nor more than five between Ellesmere Port and Birmingham, for example. The average loading was no more than ten tons.

Two distinct types of organisations worked almost all of the slow trade. The 'iron carriers' confined themselves entirely to the carriage of iron and other heavy articles which they collected and distributed direct from the works. Some manufacturing and trading businesses, principally ironmasters and timber, slate and corn merchants, operated their own boats. Slow boats tended to be heavily laden and have a maximum average speed of 2mph. They had a crew of two men (or sometimes the crew was the boatman's family), working during the day and tying up at night, and using just one horse.

Much of the trade on the canal was long distance: from Birmingham and the Black Country to or from Ellesmere Port for Liverpool. For example, Shipton & Co. of Wolverhampton, which had previously transported iron products for export through the Harecastle Tunnel to Preston Brook, transferred immediately to the BLJC route to Chester, though they reverted to Preston Brook in 1849 when they were appointed commission agents for the Bridgewater Trustees.

The trade of a typical wharf

Wappenshall Wharf served Wellington, 2½ miles away, and much of the east Shropshire coalfield area. It was operated by the Sutherland Estate, which fortuitously has meant that the detailed records of the wharf for its first 15 years have survived. What they show is typical of canal trade in rural areas before railway competition.

The most striking thing about the goods received there is the variety. The following list shows all the entries in the wharf books in April 1849 which mentioned specific goods – plenty of other entries merely stated 'box', 'truss', 'parcel' etc, or were indecipherable:

– bacon, codfish, herrings, oysters, cheese, flour, rice, biscuits, nuts, potatoes, pease, beans, fruit, figs, prunes, oranges, currants, raisins, tea, coffee, syrup, treacle, salt, spice, pepper, mustard, vinegar, lard, snuff;

– soda water, ale, porter, cider, wine, spirits, rum, whisky;

– drapery, bedding, sheets, feathers, flocks, yarn, thread, hats;

– brushes, brooms, carpet brooms, stails [handles], soap, starch, soda, naphtha, turpentine, candles, wicks, blacking, plates, tin plates, congreves [friction matches], paper, stationery, ink;

– furniture, chairs, sofa (for Revd Bird at Preston), bedsteads, pictures;

– paint, nails, wire, hoops, screws, bracket castings, rods, tubes, slates, glass, cement;

– deals [floorboards], pine boards, mahogany boards, pine logs, birch logs, scantlings, glue, varnish;

– shovels, riddles, files, lathes, grates, ash pans, fire irons;

– furnace bars (for Lilleshall Iron Co.), pumps;

– iron bars, sheet iron, steel, tin, zinc, lead, coils of lead pipe;

– plough, hoe, plough-shares, harrow, scythes, whips;

– wheat, oats, oilcake, seed, rye grass, bran, meal, hops, linseed, twigs, soda ash, potash, manure, guano;

– oil, tallow, bark rosin, grease, ropes, empty casks, leather, sacks; and

– an organ pipe.

The weights of the individual items varied considerably, some being as low as a few pounds. Few exceeded a ton. By weight, out-going goods were only about an eighth of those coming in.

By both weight and total charges the most important traffics at Wappenshall were bulk items: ironstone and limestone coming in and iron products and coal going out. The amounts varied significantly from year to year, influenced by fluctuations in the economy.

The Horsehay Iron Works, for example, had previously sent its products for export down the Severn to Bristol. With the opening of the Newport Branch, they were sent by tramroad to

The architecturally most pleasing of the Shropshire Union's company houses are those designed by Telford for the Birmingham & Liverpool Junction Canal, the design being similar to those he built for the Holyhead Road. The cottage at Tyrley near Market Drayton is the only one which survives in virtually its original condition – all the others have either been demolished or extensively remodelled. *Author*

Dawley Castle Wharf on the Shropshire Canal where they were loaded onto tub-boats, down the inclines at Wrockwardine Wood and Trench, then transhipped at Wappenshall. After a while it was decided that it was cheaper and more convenient to send them by road the six miles to Wappenshall, two or three journeys a day being made, depending on whether there was any back-carriage. Like some of the other ironworks, the company had its own boats.

Tolls

By March 1836 the BLJC had had a year's experience of operation. The implications of the SWC's junction toll was being felt: the income of the BLJC in that first year was about £8,200, but the SWC had taken about £2,000 in junction tolls. Although the route from Wolverhampton to Manchester via Nantwich was shorter and had far fewer locks than the route via Harecastle Tunnel, the tolls at Autherley Junction and Wardle Lock acted as a financial deterrent. To make matters worse, the SWC reduced its tonnage rate from 1½d to 1d a mile with effect from Christmas 1834. In order to encourage trade to use its canal, the BLJC reduced its tonnage rates on iron ore, ironstone, grain, malt, flour, timber, slates, building stone and potatoes to ½d per ton per mile.

In 1844 tonnage rates were raised, to ¾d per ton per mile for bricks, clay, ironstone, lime, limestone, ores and scrap iron and to 1d per ton per mile for all other goods. These were still very low rates compared with other canals.

Competition

Canal competition continued, of course. In 1838 the SWC identified that taking a ton load to Liverpool via the BLJC was 1s.2d cheaper than via its own route. The SWC therefore agreed with the Trent & Mersey and Bridgewater Canals to reduce charges by this amount, with the three companies sharing the discount.

But by 1838 there was an even more important competitor: the railway. The Grand Junction Railway opened from Lancashire to Birmingham for passengers on 4 July 1837 – William Cubitt travelled on it as far as Stafford later that month, on his way from Manchester to Aberystwyth – and for goods in January 1838, with its continuation, the London & Birmingham Railway, fully opening on 24 June 1838. Instead of goods taking five days to come from London, it was possible for it to be effected in eleven hours. Another advantage of the railway became clear in the winter of 1840/41 when it was reported that for the previous week the residents of Chester had been enjoying skating on the canal whereas 'the railway trains, with a slight exception, have been very regular'.[8]

The seriousness of the potential competition had been anticipated by some. Loch, writing to Lord Clive in 1834, stated:

> They are making the [rail] roads much stronger and the engines much more powerful in order to carry heavy goods, and there will be competition between it, the Grand Trunk, and ourselves, which will enrich none of us.

He added:

> I am not fidgety I assure you but I feel a very deep responsibility as to many friends, and I have very serious doubts, whether we shall be able to pay the Commissioners and keep our promise of paying those who have paid up their last instalment 5%.[9]

The Committee was heartened in early 1838 by the shortening of the BCN main line by some four miles by the new Bloomfield to Deepfield cut though Coseley Tunnel. Despite the by then evident advantages of railways, canal proposals continued to be made: from Birmingham to Braunston, from Middlewich to Manchester, and (one which was built) the Walsall Junction Canal.

In 1841, six years after the opening of the BLJC, Robert Skey wrote a report analysing the traffic, its costings and the competition. It pointed out that the railway companies owned their 'road', were the sole suppliers of motive power, were the monopoly carriers, and could divert much of their costs to passenger services; in contrast, the BLJC provided only the 'road'.

The railway companies had lowered their freight rates between Birmingham and Liverpool from 30*s* and 40*s* per ton (for the principal two categories) to 15*s* and 20*s*; even in some instances to 12*s*.6*d*. Skey concluded:

> Unless, therefore, we can save in the expense of transit, it is clear that ... we shall leave the quick trade in the possession, and the slow trade at the mercy, of the Railway Company, who, to gain or retain it, have only to content themselves with carrier's profit.[10]

He estimated that the canal tolls represented only between a sixth and a quarter of the total cost to the customer, hence it could not successfully act alone in reducing charges to meet the competition. To be effective, it needed to control all the costs, so should become a carrier.

This recommendation was accepted, and the following year the BLJC obtained Parliamentary approval to act as common carriers in the conveyance of passengers and goods, both on its own canal and on canals and rivers communicating with it, directly or via other canals. These powers included conveyance by carts, waggons etc, so a full collection and delivery service could be provided. The wording was identical to that in the Ellesmere & Chester Canal's Act, which was obtained at the same time.

Following representations from carriers, in 1842 Skey held discussions with the ECC and Birmingham Canal and agreed a drawback (rebate) of ½*d* a ton on general merchandise between Birmingham or the Black Country and Liverpool or Manchester. It was thought the concession would reduce the income of the canals by £2,000 a year.

Experimental steam tugs

SKEY'S 1841 report cited experiments on the Forth & Clyde and Union Canals in Scotland which showed that close-towing a second boat added only about a quarter to the force needed to tow one, and that a train of several boats was practicable. He thought that this could be suitable for the BLJC because of its direct course, long pounds and concentrated lockage. Skey and Easton carried out some trials and concluded that a train of about six boats drawn by two or (preferably) three horses would be ideal. The route would be divided into stages of about ten miles, with horses working once each way in the twenty-four hours. Extra horses would be stationed at the flights.

This suggestion was never put into practice, but it led to the idea of towing using steam tugs. The 1842 Act specifically permitted the use of 'steam, or other power, and machinery, for hauling, tracking and towing boats and vessels'. Further experiments gave results which appeared satisfactory, and it was estimated that the cost of moving trains of boats by steam power would be less than by using horses.

Seven iron-hulled tugs were ordered from Tayleur & Co.'s Vulcan Foundry at Newton le Willows, a leading firm of builders of ships and railway locomotives, whose founder, coincidentally, came from Market Drayton. This was in addition to the one used in the experiment.

Various building works were also needed:

– Autherley Junction: a wharf eight boats long, a coal store, and a stable for 12 horses to haul boats to Wolverhampton.
– Norbury: 'a spacious basin and wharf wall, a graving dock with a good workshop over it for the immediate purpose of fitting the steam engines and machinery into the tug boats. Stable for 6 horses to work the trade on the Newport branch.'
– Market Drayton (probably meaning Tyrley): rented stable.
– Adderley: rented stable.
– Audlem (below the locks): a basin, wharf wall, and coal store, and a rented stable.
– Hack Green: a stable for two horses.

This list reveals one of the main problems with using tugs: it was still necessary to have horses to haul the boats through the flights of locks.

The tugs hauled trains of between eight and twelve boats, the boats each carrying up to 20 tons of goods. On one occasion the train comprised sixteen boats, with 340 tons of goods. At the end of 1843 a train of boats was being dispatched daily from Autherley and from Ellesmere Port. Skey commented:

> By this means a large trade which otherwise would have been removed from the canal has been preserved and new trades which the Company could never on the old system have been brought upon it. Contracts and agreements with canal and other companies which cannot fail greatly to promote the interests of the Company have, under the sanction of the Select Committee, been concluded and others are in progress.

Easton too was pleased:

> Under all the disadvantages which naturally attend the

commencement of a perfectly novel system of trade, the steam engines and tug boats whether as regards speed or load or consumption of fuel answer fully as well as they were intended or expected to perform ... I have perfect confidence in the correctness of the plans that have been adopted.

By the following spring, seven of the eight tugs were in daily use, hauling 80 boats. After a year's experience of operation, it was clear that the experiment was not really a success. The directors' report in June 1845 to the first General Assembly after the BLJC had merged with the ECC stated:

> The system of working boats in trains though used with great advantage on the main line of the canal between Autherley and Ellesmere Port is not equally available on the Welsh and Shropshire lines and where available is not cheaper than locomotive power now is upon railways with good gradients.

The 25 miles between Autherley and Tyrley has only one lock; whereas the next 33 miles to Tower Wharf, Chester, has forty-one. Assembling suitable trains must have been administratively difficult and caused significant delays to many boats. Bridge holes do not have a great deal of room to spare; if they are on bends or if there is a side-wind (especially with unladen boats), there would have been a major problem keeping boats from hitting the sides. In January 1846 the decision was made to gradually withdraw from towing on the Main Line. At least one of the tugs continued to tow lighters on the lock-free broad Wirral Line for a few more years.

Finance

Construction

THE 1826 Act authorised the raising of £400,000 by 4,000 £100 shares, and in addition £100,000 could be borrowed by mortgaging the toll income. As already noted, Telford told the first General Assembly meeting that he estimated that the engineering works for the main line would cost £388,451. To this must be added the cost of land, Parliamentary expenses, professional fees and other day-to-day costs. There was therefore no margin for contingencies.

The 1827 Act authorised a much longer and more heavily-locked branch than that envisaged in the original Act. Despite its additional cost, no increase was made to the canal company's capital. By the next year it was known that a costly diversion would be needed near Norbury, though the exact route was not yet settled. Again, no request was made to increase the number of shares or the borrowing powers.

Following the award of the contract for the Newport Branch, a special General Meeting approved borrowing £100,000. Some of the shareholders made loans totalling £18,600.

By the summer of 1830, concern was mounting about the increasing costs. It was reported that the land would cost £40,000 more than originally estimated, and that the alteration of the line to satisfy landowners would add £38,000. No mention was made of the extra cost of the Newport Branch. It was resolved to apply to Parliament for borrowing powers for a further £80,000.

The Act having passed, application was made to the Exchequer Bill Loan Commission for £160,000. This was approved – the Commissioners' engineering adviser was Thomas Telford – and

Stretton Aqueduct, where the canal crosses the A5 (Watling Street), has this plaque bearing Telford's name and acknowledging his membership of the Royal Societies of London and Edinburgh. When the plaque is examined closely, it is just possible to discern that originally there was another row of lettering which said 'William Hazledine, Contractor'. Hazledine provided the ironwork. The unanswered question is when was it removed and why. Was it back in 1832 or 1833 on the instructions of Telford who didn't want to share the credit, or of the Wilsons who were the main contractors for this section? Or did it happen much later? *Author*

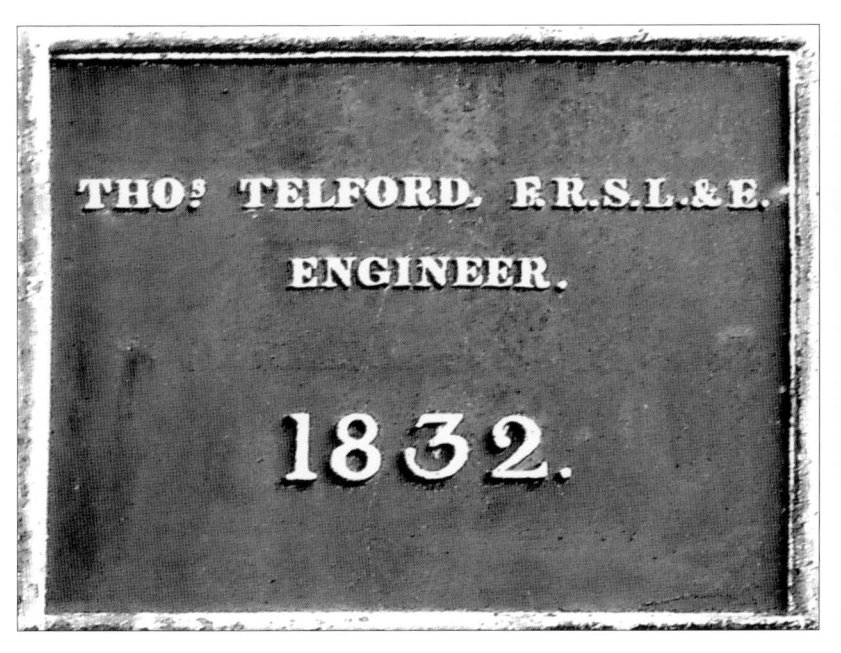

the sum drawn down over the next year. The Commissioners had to be consulted if any major expenditure was planned. For example, when Belvide Reservoir was to be increased in size, the Commissioners approved the £20,000 estimate.

By early 1834, money, or the lack of it, was becoming critical. The final call on the shares had been made two years earlier, but over £15,000 was still unpaid on shares. It was agreed to ask Parliament to authorise further calls and loans totalling £150,000; in the meantime several members of the Committee and other proprietors consented to advance the necessary sums. In the event, further calls totalling £15 were made on the existing shares, the cost of one fully-paid share becoming £115. Loans from shareholders brought in just over £61,000. There seems to have been remarkably little resistance to the demands for extra money – presumably the view was taken that a partially completed canal had no value at all, whereas a completed canal at least had some.

By the end of 1839, the amount owed to the Exchequer Bill Loan Commission totalled £252,151, interest having accumulated at 5% a year. Payments to the Commissioners started the following year. Also at the end of 1839, £29,000 was still owed for land purchases and £26,000 was due to the contractors.

From the various accounts, it can be inferred that the capital cost of the BLJC was in the order of £762,000 (excluding rolled-up interest), made up as follows:

	£
works	597,000
land and compensation	125,000
Parliamentary expenses	9,000
engineering, surveying and salaries	20,000
law and land agents charges	7,000
other expenses	4,000
	762,000

Thus the cost was more than 50% above the original estimate used for the 1826 application to Parliament, despite this being a period of stable prices.[11]

Operation

Detailed accounts survive for the year ended 31 March 1843:[12]

	£	£
Receipts		
tonnage		22,101
Payments		
repairs	6,718	
water	126	
salaries and wages	2,449	
rates and taxes	857	
other expenses	1,404	
contractors, engineering etc	3,501	
tugs	776	15,831
Operating profit		6,270
Interest on loans (excluding EBLC)		3,452
Cash surplus		2,818

The final figure was not the true profit. No payment was made that year to the Exchequer Bill Loan Commission whereas about £8,500 was due in interest, also an attempt should have been made to start repaying the sum borrowed. And, unlike modern accounts, there was no provision for depreciation of the assets.

Another real worry for the canal's management was the trend in income – this had fallen by more than 20% from the previous year's tonnage income of £27,763. Was this a temporary 'blip' caused by a downturn in the national economy, or was it a permanent trend, the result of railway competition, they wondered?

Notes and references

The principal sources for this chapter are the minutes of the BLJC and SWC (The National Archives, RAIL808 and RAIL871) and James Loch's correspondence in the files of the Sutherland Archives (Staffordshire Record Office, D593/1/K/3 and D593/1/K/5).

1. Quoted in Miles Macnair, *William James*, 2007, p.85
2. The map in Staffordshire Record Office (StRO), D3186/8/1/30/119 presumably refers to this scheme, as it seems to predate the Liverpool & Manchester Railway.
3. *Chester Chronicle*, 18 February 1825; *Chester Courant*, 23 November & 28 December 1824
4. *Chester Courant*, 23 November 1824
5. Letter from Lewis to Loch, 28 February 1833: StRO, D593/K/1/5/29
6. Table of distances and tolls, 1835: StRO, D3186/2/3/2
7. *Chester Chronicle*, 6 March 1835
8. *Chester Chronicle*, 17 July 1840 and 15 January 1841
9. Letter from Loch to Lord Clive, 23 December 1834
10. Robert Skey, *Report on the present state of competition*, 1841, pp.3–5 [Author's collection]
11. Created from Reports to the General Assembly 16 July 1835 & 2 October 1839
12. SURCC accounts, TNA, RAIL1110/413

9

Creating the Shropshire Union

In order to understand the hasty transformation in the mid-1840s of the separate canals of the north-west Midlands and the Welsh borders into a single organisation controlled by a railway company, it is necessary first to examine the transport developments in the region and the complex inter-company politics, then to consider the options available to canal companies.

The coming of the railways

The world's first inter-city railway, from Liverpool to Manchester, was opened in September 1830. Although its promoters' principal interest was to speed and cheapen the transport of goods between the two towns, it was its success in moving passengers – virtually creating a new market – which made the greatest impression on the investing public.

The merchants of Liverpool then looked to improve their communications with the Midlands, proposing a line between Birkenhead and Birmingham. This was to take a route somewhat to the east of the main line of the Ellesmere & Chester and Birmingham & Liverpool Junction Canals, reaching a summit at Whitmore, using the gap in the hills a few miles west of Newcastle-under-Lyme. There was also to be a branch to Chester. The railway was presented in two Bills, the Liverpool members dealing with the northern section as far as Chapel Chorlton (about half way between Crewe and Stafford) and the Birmingham members dealing with the southern section. The latter was rejected by Parliament; the former was progressing well until Parliament dissolved following the defeat of the 1831 Reform Bill.

The railway promoters were confident of success if they tried again, but first they reconsidered the route. Clearly, Liverpool would be better served if the trains ran to the city itself, rather than to Birkenhead on the other side of the Mersey. The proposal which emerged was the Grand Junction Railway (GJR) which was to run from Warrington to Birmingham. At Warrington it made an end-on junction with the independent Warrington & Newton Railway, itself a branch off the Liverpool & Manchester Railway; at its southern end it skirted Wolverhampton to the east then approached Birmingham from the south-east. The Bill was given the Royal Assent on 6 May 1833. On the same day the London & Birmingham Railway (LBR) was also authorised, its Birmingham station being adjacent to that of the GJR. Having bought the Warrington & Newton Railway in 1835, the GJR opened for passengers in July 1837 (and for goods six months later); the LBR opened in June 1838.

Threats to the 'Shropshire Union' area

The first incursion into the area of the canals which are the subject of this book was the line from Crewe to Chester. This was authorised in 1837 but shortly before it was opened in October 1840 it was absorbed by the GJR.

An independent line was promoted from Chester to Birkenhead in 1837 and opened in October 1840, the same month as the Crewe–Chester line. The relationship between it and the GJR was frosty; if the latter thought it was going to be able to buy it cheaply, it was mistaken.

The North Wales Mineral Railway from Chester to Wrexham was authorised in 1844 and in the following year powers were obtained for an extension to Ruabon, thus threatening to take the trade which was fed onto the canal from the Ruabon Brook Railway. The line was opened in November 1846, by which time an Act had been obtained for a continuation to Shrewsbury, the name having been changed to the Shrewsbury & Chester Railway.

Various proposals particularly affected east Shropshire and Shrewsbury. In 1836 a survey was made for a line from the GJR near Wolverhampton to Shrewsbury, then by a choice of two routes to a suggested harbour at Port Dynlleyn, on the north-west side of the Lleyn peninsula – the Irish traffic was the primary attraction, rather than serving Shropshire. Then in 1839 the GJR brought forward a proposal for a branch from its main line near Wolverhampton to Shrewsbury, but this was soon withdrawn.

In 1843 the GJR told local promoters of a line from Shrewsbury to the West Midlands conurbation that the company could not then help, but the following year it commissioned Joseph

Locke to make surveys, following which it floated a separate company to construct a line from Stafford to Shrewsbury.

Other regional developments

IN 1839 a prospectus was published for the Chester & Holyhead Railway which would create a route to Ireland along the north Wales coast and across Anglesey. Although independent, it was initially supported by both the GJR and the LBR. However, the GJR became increasing concerned about the cost of the scheme, the exact route, the details of the financing package, and the likely effect on its own revenues – it would lose the Irish mail contract, for example – so when in February 1844 the Chester & Holyhead announced its intention to buy the Chester & Birkenhead for £500,000, the GJR resolved to take no part in the undertaking. The LBR then committed £1 million capital to the Chester & Holyhead in exchange for half the seats on the board; its Act was obtained in July that year.

Meanwhile, the merchants of Manchester were seeking a line to London and the Midlands more direct than that via Warrington and the GJR. Authorised in 1837, the main line of the Manchester & Birmingham Railway (MBR) was to be from Manchester to Stafford via the Potteries, together with a branch from Alderley Edge to Crewe. Following an offer from the GJR of favourable rates, the line to Crewe was built first, opening in May 1842. The intended main line was built only as far as Macclesfield. Nevertheless, many of its directors retained the desire for a line south independent of the GJR.

In 1838 plans were deposited for the Manchester & Birmingham Extension Railway from Stone to the LBR at Rugby. Naturally, this was fiercely opposed by all the other railways affected, particularly the GJR but also the LBR, and after an unprecedented 61 days in the committee stage in Parliament, the Bill failed for lack of time. Then, in a reversal of tactics, the GJR brought forward its own proposals for a 'Trent Valley' line between Stafford and Rugby, following much the same route. It appears that the GJR invited the LBR to join them in making the line, but the latter refused on the grounds that such a line was unnecessary; following this, the GJR withdrew the scheme.

Open war between the GJR and LBR

THE GJR and the LBR were such natural partners that it now seems almost inconceivable that relations between them ever became so bad that alternative alliances were sought. Nevertheless, between the spring of 1844 and October 1845 both companies actively sought other partners to enable them to fulfil their ambitions.

A fundamental problem for the GJR was its total reliance on the LBR for access to London; by contrast, the GJR was only one of several feeders onto the LBR line, albeit the most important. For its part, the LBR wanted to reach Manchester and to develop a line to Ireland. As well as these territorial issues, there were serious differences between the two companies' freight policies which hindered the development of through traffic, and continuing disputes about station facilities at Birmingham, connecting services and through bookings. Both were ambitious companies, keen to maximise their influence and income, and led by strong personalities.

The GJR discovered from a newspaper advertisement on 13 May 1844 that the LBR was offering to guarantee the local promoters for a line from Shrewsbury to Birmingham. This was regarded as a hostile act, so the GJR appointed a committee with full powers to take any action necessary to protect their company's interests, including seeking a new outlet to London.

To try to settle the various territorial disputes, the Chairmen of the LBR and GJR made an agreement on 3 July 1844 which stipulated broadly the territory which each company would consider to be its own preserve, with the promise that neither would interfere with the other within those limits. Birmingham was defined as the boundary between their territories, though the LBR Board would not confirm this as far as the proposed Shrewsbury & Birmingham Railway was concerned – presumably because of its passage through the industrial Black Country to Wolverhampton rather than because of its continuation to Shrewsbury – and the GJR subsequently agreed that the two companies could subscribe equally. The agreement also permitted the LBR to invest in the Chester & Holyhead Railway, the GJR promising not to initiate price competition for the Irish traffic, and for the Trent Valley Railway to be taken forward as a joint project. However, this truce was not to last, as the LBR directors undermined the compromises which their GJR colleagues were prepared to accept.

In the autumn of 1844 the MBR proposed a railway from its Macclesfield Branch to Tamworth via the Churnet Valley. In response, the LBR did not openly offer support but said that it could accommodate the traffic. The GJR was of course opposed to the Churnet Valley scheme as it would then lose all the traffic between Manchester and London.

What the GJR did not know until 12 February 1845 was that the MBR had offered to sell itself to the LBR on attractive terms. During secret negotiations the LBR had agreed to purchase the MBR, to lease the Trent Valley Railway and to absorb the Churnet Valley Railway within five years of its completion.

The GJR responded by supporting the Oxford & Rugby and Oxford, Worcester & Wolverhampton Railways which had been promoted largely by Black Country industrialists anxious to break the monopoly held by the LBR. At Oxford these would join the Great Western Railway (GWR). To make a shorter route to London, the GJR assisted the promotion of the GWR-backed Birmingham & Oxford Junction Railway; when its prospectus was issued in April 1845, John Moss, the GJR's Chairman, and three of his colleagues were listed in the provisional committee.

It is not known for sure whether the GJR's flirtation with the GWR was a serious proposal or a clever ploy to put pressure on the LBR. However, what is certain is that Parliament's approval of the Oxford schemes in the summer of 1845 tended to favour the GJR's strategy at the expense of the LBR. The GJR also put pressure on the MBR by serving notice that the existing favourable terms for exchanging traffic at Crewe would be replaced by strict mileage rates.

The London & North Western Railway

THE shareholders of the various companies now began to influence events. At the half-yearly meetings of proprietors, dissatisfied shareholders in the LBR and GJR, many of whom held shares in both concerns, expressed strong feelings that the disputes should cease and the companies instead should work together.

Negotiations started on 24 September 1845, an agreement was reached on 17 October and approved by both Boards on 22 October. *The Times* reported that the two companies 'have settled their differences and are henceforward to operate cordially together'. Special meetings of the LBR and GJR companies on 7 November 1845 confirmed terms for their amalgamation, George Carr Glyn, Chairman of the LBR expressing his regrets for the 'foolish squabbling'. The LBR meeting also approved a revised agreement with the MBR. With these agreements in place, the earlier disputes were quickly forgotten. Joint meetings of the GJR and LBR boards were held from December onwards and consolidated accounts prepared. Having been approved by Parliament, the formal merger was effected on 16 July 1846, the company taking the name London & North Western Railway (LNWR).

The LNWR was the largest and most powerful railway in the country, with almost 400 miles of railway already in operation, a share capital of over £17m, and an income which exceeded a quarter of the total railway income in Britain.

The canal companies' options

WHEN faced with the threat of railway competition there were a number of tactics available to canal companies.

Opposition in Parliament

MOST obviously and simplest, they could oppose the proposals in Parliament on the ground that the railway was unnecessary because the canal already provided an adequate transport system, a tactic useful if the conveyance of goods was the main object but almost irrelevant with regard to the conveyance of passengers.

A traditional argument was that Parliament had sanctioned the canal, thus encouraging people to invest, and that therefore Parliament had a moral duty to protect that investment. Examples of such protection were the tolls which Parliament had permitted to be charged at Autherley Junction and Middlewich as recently as 1826 and 1827 respectively.

However, the mood in Parliament was changing, especially after the widening of the franchise in 1832 to include more of the mercantile middle class. When in February 1836 some of the existing railway companies, notably the GJR, petitioned Parliament in favour of some patent right of protection against competing proposals, the concept was rejected. Monopolies were no longer being seen as desirable to encourage investment but as bad because they tended to keep prices high and excessively rewarded the monopolist.

Some canal companies were paying high nominal dividends – in 1831 the Oxford Canal paid a dividend of 32% and the Trent & Mersey Canal 75%, for example – so it was easy for railway promoters to claim the canals were profiteering at the public's expense.

In May 1831 Telford wrote to the ECC and BLJC concerning the proposed railway from Birkenhead to Birmingham, following which it was agreed to oppose it in Parliament. This they were well placed to do: their Chairman, Lord Clive, was an MP, as were a few of their committee members, and some substantial investors in the canals were members of the House of Lords. Two years later the GJR's Bill was opposed by the canal companies, without success. On the other hand, in 1836 resistance to the GJR's proposals for a branch to Shrewsbury was successful.

After 1840 canal companies' policies were not so much as to object to the principle of railway bills as to try to ensure that the property and rights of the canal company were protected.

Physical improvements

Physical improvements could take the form of straightening the course (as happened between Birmingham and Wolverhampton), duplicating locks (for example, the Trent & Mersey Canal's descent from Harecastle Tunnel to the Cheshire Plain), enhanced terminal facilities or trying to speed transit. There were also serious proposals for some new canals. However, any investment needed to be financed, and if the canal company did not have accumulated reserves it would have to seek new funds – and if potential investors or lenders were unwilling, little could be done.

The BLJC had itself been promoted in response to threatened competition from a horse-powered tramroad and took a direct route; the Newport and Middlewich branches were also relatively new canals. The main line of the ECC was some forty to sixty years old but there was little opportunity for improvement, other than at Ellesmere Port where, as has been described, a major investment was being made in the wharfs and warehousing and where, in the early 1840s, the locks were duplicated.

The ECC and the BLJC had consistently supported a new canal between Birmingham and London. This idea, avoiding the descent into the valley of the Avon at Warwick, can be traced back to the London & Birmingham Junction Canal suggested by Telford in 1827; a shorter variant, the Central Union Canal, was planned by Cubitt in 1832; then in 1836 a prospectus was issued for a London & Birmingham Canal which included a seventy mile long summit level and ten miles of tunnelling, surveyed by James Green, the engineer of several canals in the West Country. Various compromise proposals were made, culminating in a meeting in Cubitt's London office in March 1838, attended by representatives of the ECC.[1] Thereafter the idea was shelved, but the Grand Junction Canal was stimulated to duplicate many of its locks, improve its water supply and introduce back-pumping.

Of more direct benefit to the ECC and BLJC would have been the Manchester & Birmingham Junction Canal from Middlewich to Altrincham, which was discussed in Chapter 7.

Improving the service to customers

ANOTHER tactic – a demonstration of the benefits of competition, one could argue – was to improve the service offered and to make it simpler and easier for customers to send goods by canal.

Whereas railway companies could generally offer customers rates covering the total cost of transport including, when required, collection and delivery, on the canals the customers dealt with the carriers who in turn dealt with the canal companies. By becoming carriers themselves, the canal companies could offer customers inclusive rates. A few canals had specific powers to do this, some others had established nominally independent carrying companies. Belatedly recognising this anomaly, the Canal Carriers Act 1845 permitted any canal company to become a carrier providing it charged all customers the same amount for the equivalent service.

Where, as often was the case, traffic needed to pass over more than one canal, more could be attracted if they would work together to offer through rates. Inter-canal co-operation was improved to a small extent during the 1830s and early 1840s, though neither the old-established Trent & Mersey nor Staffordshire & Worcestershire companies appear to have taken part.

It was not until 1842, five years after the opening of the Grand Junction Railway, that the BLJC, ECC and Birmingham Canal Company worked together to introduce a special reduction (known as a 'drawback') of one half-penny a ton per mile for general merchandise between Staffordshire and Liverpool and Manchester.

The most interesting attempt to improve the service to customers was though the use of steam-powered tugs on the main line, an experiment which wasn't to be repeated on a narrow canal for a further forty years, but it was recognised that tugs would not be economic on the Welsh line. Less dramatically, the attempt to take over the carrying trade was motivated by the idea of improving the service as well as enhancing the profitability of the company by the more efficient utilisation of boats.

Compromise

ANOTHER possibility was to compromise with the proposed railway and come to some agreement about traffics and rates. The railway company might welcome this because it would make the passage through Parliament easier by removing a major objector and it would also guarantee that there would not be a potentially injurious rates war, but people expecting to experience the benefits of competition would be vocal in their opposition.

As discussed in the last chapter, in 1825 the Marquess of Stafford had made major investments in both the BLJC and the Liverpool & Manchester Railway. He, through the energetic agency of James Loch, remained the main bridge between the railway and canal factions for the rest of the decade, part of the aim being to protect the £30 million invested in canals.

By October 1829 John Moss, then the Deputy Chairman of the Liverpool & Manchester Railway Company, had been persuaded that co-operation was the way forward. He was also concerned about the number of railway proposals being floated, even before the Liverpool & Manchester had opened and the lessons from it learnt. Consequently the Liverpool & Manchester Railway Company promised that it would not apply to Parliament for an extension to Birmingham until the 1830/31 session.[2]

Loch tried to make effective use of the respite. Lord Clive, chairman of both the ECC and BLJC, believed that the operating costs of railways and canals were about equal but the construction cost of railways was almost twice that of canals, making the eclipse of canals unlikely. Eyre Lee thought the railways would be unable to carry heavy goods as their rails and locomotives were not strong enough. Even after the Rainhill trials, Telford was sceptical about the potential ability of steam locomotives, thinking that improved canals would compete successfully. (He was also an advocate of self-propelled road vehicles on improved roads, and in the very long term he was proved right.) The canal men did not want to negotiate, the offer was never formally discussed at a General Meeting, and the opportunity passed. Loch admitted that 'it would have been at all times a matter of difficulty, without doing the same with all the canals connecting with it, and over which he had no control'. Nor were the canal proprietors attracted by an offer of shares in a Birmingham to Lancashire railway being reserved for them.[3]

Conversion

THE option of conversion into a railway was much discussed in the late 1820s. In 1829 John Moss suggested converting the partly completed BLJC into a railway, together with a similar conversion of the Bridgewater Canal. But generally it was not until the mid-1840s, by when it was evident that in the long run the railways would not be beaten, that firm proposals were made. However, nationally only about a hundred miles of canal were ever actually converted.

Sale or lease

THE final option for the canal company was to sell or lease itself to a railway company. The latter might be willing to pay a premium in order to remove opposition in Parliament and potential competition when the railway was in operation. Sometimes the railway company could make use of part of the route of the canal, building alongside it. Occasionally the canal could access places the railway could not – either outside its 'territory', as in the case of the North Staffordshire Railway's purchase of the Trent & Mersey Canal, or locally, as in Birmingham and the Black Country where the established industries were generally canalside.

First steps towards the Shropshire Union

Canal management

LOCH had little confidence in the management of the canals with which he had contact. In 1829 he wrote to his assistant, William Lewis, who represented the Stafford interest at the General Meetings of the BLJC in its early years, saying that in general canal proprietors and managers were

> a set of antiquated persons who will sit quietly still until their concerns are swept away from under them. Their resolution seems to be most carefully to avoid looking at the precipice on which they stand, to take all they can in the meantime, and they will hold up their hands and exclaim who could have thought it.[4]

He may have been thinking particularly of Bradshaw, the Superintendent of the Bridgewater Trust, but his comments probably also applied to the ECC and the other canals which some fifteen years later would merge to form the Shropshire Union.

The evidence from the canal companies' minutes supports Loch's opinion. For example, the lengthy report in 1836 of the committee appointed to examine the operation of the ECC makes no mention of potential competition from the GJR, due to open the following year. Surely they should have expected tonnage rates between Wolverhampton and Liverpool to be squeezed, at least.

Amalgamation

THE first stage towards the creation of the Shropshire Union was the proposal to amalgamate the ECC and the BLJC. The majority of the trade on the latter was in boats to or from Ellesmere Port – indeed, the construction of this canal had been the main reason for the great works done at Ellesmere Port in the 1830s. The committees of both companies were chaired by the Earl of Powis, there were other directors in common, and many people were shareholders in both companies.

However, their financial positions were quite different, the ECC having paid dividends of £3.15s or £4 annually on its shares for many years, whereas the BLJC was heavily indebted with no imminent prospect of paying its shareholders anything. Indeed, according to evidence given to the Board of Trade in 1845, the over-riding reason for the merger was the BLJC's inability to pay the interest on the money it owed the Exchequer Bill Loan Commission. The ECC feared that the Commissioners would foreclose and then auction the BLJC, resulting in it 'falling into hostile hands' – in other words a railway company. The ECC would lose the trade coming from the industrial areas of the West Midlands and east Shropshire, consequently its expensive investment in improved facilities at Ellesmere Port would become virtually worthless.

The terms of merger were intended to preserve the usual dividend paid to the ECC's shareholders whilst giving some hope of an eventual benefit to the BLJC's shareholders. Three classes of shares were to be created:

- Class 1: Preference shares, being the 3,575¾ shares of the ECC. The first call on profits would be to pay an annual dividend of £4 on these shares.
- Class 2: These would be the share bonds totalling £94,255 created when the BLJC's promoters voluntarily contributed an extra £25 per share, over and above the original £100 subscription. Once the Class 1 shareholders had been paid £4 a share, the equivalent amount could be paid to the holders of Class 2 shares.
- Class 3: The rest of the BLJC share capital.

Any remaining surplus would be distributed in proportion to all the paid-up share capitals.

The arrangements as approved by Parliament differed in that once the payments had been made to the holders of Class 1 and 2 shares, surpluses were to be divided into two equal halves, one half for the ECC shareholders, the other half for the BLJC shareholders. In the event this change proved irrelevant – there was never a surplus to be divided.

Both companies approved the merger at their General Assembly meetings in August 1844. The Act confirming it was passed on 8 May 1845, the name of the combined company being that of its dominant constituent: the Ellesmere & Chester Canal. It was agreed that few management changes should be made for the time being, with Thomas Stanton continuing as General Agent of the former ECC network and Robert Skey in the equivalent position for the ex-BLJC lines. Then in September 1845 Stanton retired because of ill health and Skey was formally appointed 'General Agent or Manager of the United Canals'.

The looming crisis

THE Crewe–Chester railway opened in October 1840, crossing the canal three times. The shallow tunnel between Christleton Lock and Greenfield Lock on the edge of Chester partially collapsed whilst it was being built, interrupting canal traffic for several hours. The railway company agreed to make and maintain a collateral canal in case any similar accident happened again. This was duly done, and the course of it can still be seen on the south side of the canal.

In the autumn of 1844 over 800 railway schemes were put before Parliament. Inevitably this worried canal companies: they foresaw that traffic would be lost, endangering dividends. And if the canal company were relatively heavily indebted, there was a danger that income would not be sufficient to pay the interest, with rather more far-reaching consequences.

That year James Loch made what proved to be an accurate assessment of the future of canals: 'long canals, if not too circuitous, having no local trade, will cease or become railways' but short ones 'such as the Bridgewater, with a very large local trade, will continue to flourish'. He anticipated that though trade might increase, income would probably fall.[5]

The committee of the new combined company expressed the realistic (if verbose) view that railways were a 'system of public conveyance which modern science and experience have shown to be better suited to the present wants and wishes of the country'.[6]

In 1846 Robert Skey gave evidence to Parliament comparing the costs of conveying by canal and by railway. He was explicit: it was cheaper to send goods by rail. For example, for 'undamageable iron' conveyed between Wolverhampton and Liverpool, the canal's charge would be between 9s.6d and 11s.6d whilst the railway's charge would be nearly 8s – the exact amounts would depend upon delivery and freight charges. He would not go so far as to say that the Grand Junction Railway was charging less than its true cost, but felt that it was clear that having their line 'in full work for passengers, they can afford to work it for goods at a rate they could not otherwise'.[7]

Conversion into a railway

Rumours

BACK in 1838 rumours had circulated that Francis Richard Price of Bryn-y-Pys near Overton-on-Dee, who owned a large property on the Wirral bank of the Mersey, was offering to buy the BLJC for £800,000 in order to convert it into a railway, to be linked to the Chester & Birkenhead Railway, then under construction. George Stephenson told George Loch (James Loch's son) that he had been consulted and, having inspected the line, considered it could be made into a railway 'at a comparatively trifling cost'; indeed he considered that some day such a conversion was inevitable. Although one of the scheme's advocates attended the Annual Meeting in early February and was told that, if they wished it to be considered, they should make a definite proposal, nothing more seems to have been heard about it.[8]

At this time James Loch was sceptical, both about whether there was such an offer – he thought it was Stephenson's idea, without any authority to justify it – and about the practicalities. He said that he remained 'incredulous as to the railway carrying goods as cheaply as the canal' and could not see how a railway could cope with traffics with different speeds, especially on a long line.[9] (It must be remembered that effective signalling systems for railways had yet to be perfected.)

Proposals

AMBITIOUS ideas about the conversion of most of their canals into railways and the promotion of additional lines may have been in the minds of several directors for some while, but by early 1845 it was being discussed seriously.

The newly-enlarged ECC recognised that it had one advantage compared with most other canal companies: its main line was constructed in a similar way to a railway, being relatively direct rather than following the contours, with high embankments and deep cuttings. William Provis, who had been the contractor for the Middlewich Branch and much of the BLJC – and who incidentally was a major shareholder in the company, owning 100 shares by August 1844 – thought that the canal could be converted into a railway for little more than half the cost at which railways could usually be built. Relatively little land would have to be bought; passage through Parliament should also be eased because no additional severance of estates would be needed. The wharf facilities and warehouses could be re-used for railway purposes. A less obvious reason for opting for conversion of the main line was that there were still worries about water supplies, as discussed in the last chapter. Provis undertook the necessary surveys, both for conversion of the 'Main Line' from Wolverhampton to Chester and of the 'Welsh Branch' from Nantwich to Newtown.

The first public mention of the proposal seems to have been when the committee appointed to recommend the arrangements for uniting and 'forwarding the general interests of the two companies' reported to the General Assembly on 12 June 1845.

The report stated that one railway Bill crossing the canal was likely to be approved soon by Parliament and that railways were being contemplated throughout the area served by the canal network. Reasoning that if these were to be built, the canal's traffic would be reduced and the proprietors' dividends endangered, the report recommended:

> No time should be lost in ascertaining the best method of converting your canals into railways and of putting the Company in a position to obtain in the ensuing session of Parliament powers to effect such conversion and to connect the lines thus to be formed with the general railway system of the country. ... In coming to this conclusion the steps they propose are not those of wild speculation, the characteristic of the present day, but are those of defence and are intended to preserve a valuable property.

This policy was adopted. A special sub-committee was set up, its terms of reference envisaging the possibility of creating extra railways and acting together with other parties. Under the chairmanship of the Second Earl of Powis (as Lord Clive had become on the death of his father in 1839), this sub-committee met in London thirteen times in the next two months.

Support for conversion of the Main Line

In late May 1845 the Earl of Powis had written to George Carr Glyn, Chairman of the LBR, informing him that the ECC intended to convert its canal into a railway. This was discussed at the LBR's Board meeting on 13 June, which resolved to 'cooperate cordially' because this would form the shortest connection with the Chester & Holyhead Railway – the implicit message being that conversion of the canal would create a line which bypassed the GJR.

One would have expected that the Birmingham Canal Company would be resolutely opposed to the conversion of the ECC main line. After all, they had initiated the promotion of the BLJC only twenty years earlier and it was now an important outlet for their trade. On being told that a section of canal would be retained at Autherley together with transhipment facilities, the members of the Birmingham Canal's delegation declared at

The Shropshire Union Canal

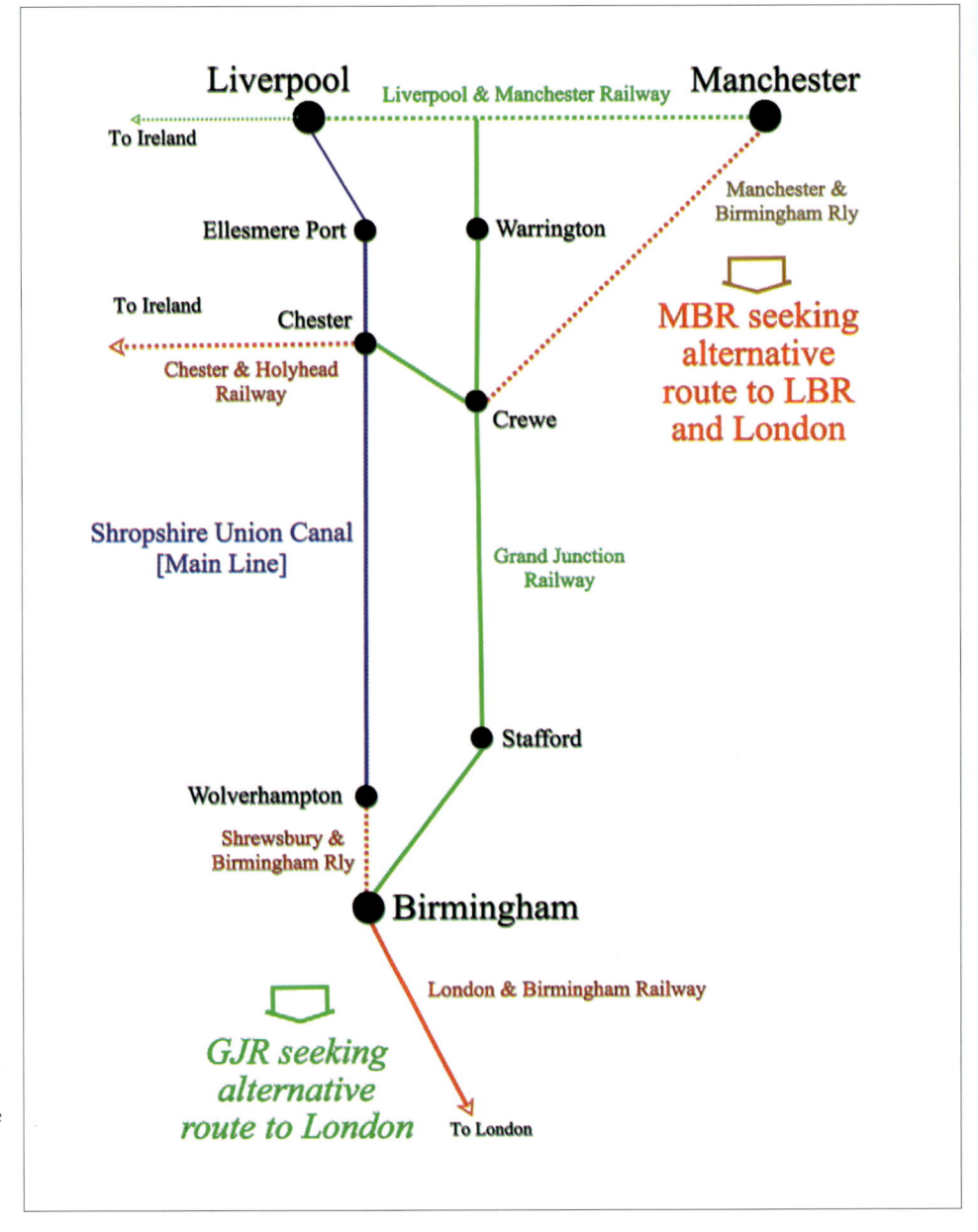

Simplified diagram showing the London & Birmingham Railway and its allies (red) and the Grand Junction Railway and its allies (green), and how the LBR could achieve an independent route north by acquiring and converting the Shropshire Union (blue).

a meeting on 4 July 1845 that they were personally satisfied but would need to seek the consent of their Board and would need to discuss it with the LBR.

The explanation for the Birmingham Canal's attitude can be traced back to the recent failure of the Bill for the proposed railway between Birmingham and Wolverhampton, mentioned earlier. On 22 May 1845 the Birmingham Canal made a provisional agreement with the LBR to jointly build a line between the two towns, much of it alongside the 'new main line' of the canal. They would each provide a quarter of the capital.

A further quarter of the capital would come from the (renamed) Shrewsbury & Birmingham Railway, if it agreed, which would build the continuation line from Wolverhampton to Shrewsbury. The other quarter would be raised from the investing public. This agreement was ratified by the LBR Board on 13 June, at the same meeting as the conversion of the ECC's main line was supported.[10]

An agreement dated 19 August meant that the LBR would provide the Birmingham Canal with a guaranteed dividend in exchange for a large measure of control.[11] For the LBR the agreement not only gave it a direct route to Wolverhampton, it also meant indirect access via transhipment to all the industries which had been built canalside during the previous seventy years.

No evidence has been found about whether the ECC's committee members were aware of the progress of discussions between the LBR and the Birmingham Canal in the period May to August 1845 – they had no committee members in common but it seems unlikely that such matters could remain secret.

In July 1845 the Chester & Birkenhead Railway also declared itself in favour of conversion of the ECC, provided the proposed railway was not extended to Ellesmere Port. The GJR had always been concerned that the Chester & Birkenhead would abstract some of its Liverpool trade but had expected that the company would inevitably be taken over, just as the Crewe & Chester Railway had been in 1840. However, the Chester & Birkenhead proved obstinate; although geographically isolated, it could see that the conversion of the ECC would give it an outlet to the south independent of the GJR.[12]

Thus the LBR, its allies and protégés were principally interested in the main line of the canal, from Wolverhampton to Chester.

Conversion of the Welsh Branch

The proposal for the conversion of the 64-mile-long branch to Newtown was partly prompted by the projection of an independent railway running parallel with the course of the canal, the Manchester & Birmingham Continuation & Welsh Junction Railway. Negotiations led to that railway giving up its Crewe to Newtown section in exchange for reciprocal working arrangements, concentrating instead on the Newtown to Aberystwyth section. Another company was further contemplating constructing a line from Newtown to Milford Haven, the idea being to give Manchester access to an alternative deep-water port to Liverpool. Both these schemes would have been hopelessly uneconomic, of course. The former reached the Committee stage in Parliament in 1846 before being withdrawn and the company dissolved, and the latter disappeared without trace.

The canal company over-reacted to the proposals, as it is unlikely that the railway companies could ever have raised the necessary capital even for a Crewe to Newtown line. Perhaps the canal directors were influenced by the 'Manchester lobby', or perhaps they were seeking an excuse for a comprehensive scheme of canal conversion.

At a meeting in July 1845 of the Eastern Branch of the Montgomeryshire Canal, the Revd John Luxmoore, its Chairman, said that his company's shares were worth £110 each and that a £5 dividend had been paid for several years. The ECC's committee recommended that these figures be accepted, with the shareholders being given the option of cash or stock in the new company.

Options concerning Shrewsbury

The committee of the Shrewsbury Canal Company had no hesitation in agreeing to the principle of converting its canal into a railway and in entering into negotiations with any other company that might help achieve this. It instructed that a copy of its resolution was to be sent to several railway companies: the GJR, LBR, Great Western Railway (which, at that time, had no presence in the West Midlands) and the projected 'Shrewsbury, Wolverhampton, Dudley & Birmingham Railway Company'. The last-named seems to be a confusion of two railway proposals: the Shrewsbury & Birmingham Railway referred to earlier (supported by the LBR) and the Shrewsbury, Wolverhampton & South Staffordshire Railway (supported by the GJR). In the event, both schemes failed in the 1845 session.

A deputation from the ECC was sent to meet the Shrewsbury Canal Company with the brief to endeavour to arrange with them for the joint construction of a line between Stafford and Shrewsbury. They reported back that the Shrewsbury company was willing to sell at £150 a share.

Having done most of the survey work for the conversion of the ECC's canals, William Provis was asked to survey a line from Stafford to Shrewsbury. Traffic estimates were also being prepared.

Negotiations intensify

On 19 July 1845 a meeting was held at Robert Stephenson's office of representatives of various railway schemes. Stephenson was the LBR's consulting engineer, so presumably only those with a friendly relationship with the LBR were invited. This was followed up by a meeting on 23 July between Stephenson and the Chairmen of the ECC and LBR, the Earl of Powis and George Carr Glyn respectively, at which Stephenson said that he recommended an amalgamation of all the interests: co-operation would avoid duplication and, in particular, avoid 'all the evils of parliamentary conflict'. All parties welcomed the idea. George Loch, who was a member of the ECC Committee and Deputy Superintendent of the Bridgewater Trust, assisted the Earl of Powis in the further negotiations and worked out a financing scheme.

Further meetings were held with the various railway companies, then Robert Stephenson and William Cubitt wrote a joint report which, with a few modifications, became the basis of the agreed scheme.

The companies concerned were:
– Ellesmere & Chester Canal
– Shrewsbury Canal
– Montgomeryshire Canal (Eastern)
– Montgomeryshire Canal (Western)
– Shrewsbury & Birmingham Railway
– Shrewsbury & Trent Valley Union Railway
– Worcester & Crewe Railway

The Shrewsbury & Trent Valley Union Railway was planned to be from Stafford to Shrewsbury. It was another project heavily influenced by Manchester businessmen but also with implicit LBR backing. Certain of its directors came to be very influential in the early days of the Shropshire Union.

Stephenson and Cubitt envisaged that a coordinated set of railway projects would be put forward:
- from the proposed Birmingham, Wolverhampton & Stour Valley Railway at Wolverhampton to Chester, largely on the line of the canal, linking with the Chester & Holyhead and Chester & Birkenhead Railways;
- from the Manchester & Birmingham Railway at Crewe to Nantwich, then via Wrenbury, Whitchurch, Ellesmere, Oswestry and Welshpool to Newtown, partly on the line of the canal;
- from Whitchurch through Wem to Shrewsbury;
- from near Ellesmere to Chirk and Ruabon;
- from the proposed Birmingham, Wolverhampton & Stour Valley Railway to Wellington and Shrewsbury; and
- from Stafford to Norbury and Wellington (two alternatives were put forward) then sharing the Wellington to Shrewsbury line.

The recommendation for a Wem–Shrewsbury line may have been influenced by a proposed Worcester & Crewe Railway. It certainly was a reason for the inclusion of a further line in the proposals agreed by the ECC's General Assembly on 18 September 1845: a line from Wellington, crossing the Severn below Coalport, then via Bridgnorth and Bewdley to Worcester and on to meet the Birmingham & Gloucester Railway, which had bypassed Worcester. The only lasting effect of this proposal was that the arms of the City of Worcester appear in those of the Shropshire Union Company.

The fifth project in the list assumed that the Shrewsbury & Birmingham's promoters would agree to join this more ambitious set of proposals, but in the event they did not.

The directors of the Chester & Holyhead and Manchester & Birmingham Railways agreed to subscribe to the new capital, and a portion was offered to the Chester & Birkenhead Railway.

'Shropshire Union'

THE name 'Shropshire Union Railway & Canal Company' was first used officially in the report to the meeting of the ECC's General Assembly on 18 September 1845.

The capital required was estimated as £5,337,417, made up as follows:

	£	£
Estimated costs of new works		3,950,000
Existing canal capital:		
shares	588,210	
loans	799,207	1,387,417
		5,337,417

This would be financed as follows:

	£	£
SU shareholders:		
existing shares	588,210	
new shares	876,766	1,464,976
Existing railway companies:		
Chester & Holyhead	300,000	
Manchester & Birmingham	200,000	
Chester & Birkenhead (offered)	150,000	
New railway companies:		
Shrewsbury & Trent Valley Union	750,000	
Worcester & Crewe	1,500,000	
Shrewsbury & Birmingham	450,000	3,350,000
Reserved for local and other interests		522,441
		5,337,417

This was rounded up to £5,400,000, to be in £20 shares.

The BLJC had borrowed £160,000 from the Exchequer Loan Bill Commission. Although some payments had been made, interest had accumulated at 5%, so by the autumn of 1845 the Commissioners were owed £286,308. This was now a liability of the combined ECC and BLJC companies, and the Commissioners were pressing for repayment. They agreed a reduction in the interest rate to 3½%, which reduced the debt to £248,746, but refused to wait for the outcome of the application to Parliament, stating that 'considering the present abundance of unemployed capital in the country and the general feeling of speculation' they felt they must take possession of the canal and advertise it for sale by public auction in January 1846. One suspects they thought that the Shropshire Union proposals were not sound, and as guardians of public money they had to be cautious. Their threat forced the ECC to take immediate action. A loan of £252,000 from the Royal Exchange Insurance was negotiated, to be repaid over three years with interest at 5%. Personal guarantees were required, but the shareholders were persuaded that the canal's assets provided adequate protection, hence the necessary signatures were forthcoming.

Eighty-four people were named as provisional directors of the Shropshire Union – not that they were expected to run the new company, their role was to impress and reassure prospective investors. And impressive the list must have seemed: five earls, four viscounts, one lord (the eldest son of an earl), three honourables and six knights; and four MPs in addition to the seven also titled.

William Cubitt, Robert Stephenson and William Provis were appointed engineers to the company. Premises for the head office were rented at 9 Great George Street, within 400 yards of the Houses of Parliament and close to Cubitt's office at 6 Great George Street.

A prospectus, prepared in September 1845 and revised a month later, showed several significant changes from the first:
- The northern end of the main line was to link to the Chester

Chapter 9 : Creating the Shropshire Union

& Crewe Railway, rather than continuing to Chester. This avoided constructing fourteen miles of railway which closely duplicated an existing railway. It also meant that the canal route from Middlewich to Chester and Ellesmere Port would remain open and available for salt and pottery traffic.

- It was made explicit that the line of the Shrewsbury Canal would remain open, and would continue to link with the Shropshire Canal (though it wasn't stated whether the Shropshire Canal was to be part of the Shropshire Union).
- Implicitly, the canal from Llangollen and Trevor to the place where it met the Crewe–Newtown railway would remain open, with interchange facilities at its eastern end.
- There would still be a branch from the Crewe–Newtown line to Wem, but its continuation to Shrewsbury was omitted.
- The railway to Worcester was to commence at Shrewsbury, the Ironbridge to Wellington section being a branch.

The revised prospectus stated that the Shropshire Union (SU) had the active cooperation of the London & Birmingham, Manchester & Birmingham, Chester & Holyhead and Trent Valley Companies, and that arrangements had been made for the consolidation of the Shrewsbury & Birmingham Railway with this company, 'which shall eventually form part of this important chain'. The links with other named existing or authorised lines were stressed, as were those with proposed lines including the North Staffordshire and, more obscurely, the Welsh Midland (which was to be from Worcester to Leominster, Brecon, Swansea and Carmarthen) and Manchester & Southampton (Cheltenham to Southampton) Railways. These last two never came into being and the Shrewsbury & Birmingham Railway never joined. The obvious omission from the list of allied existing lines was the Grand Junction Railway.

Canal conversion: the detailed proposals

THE plans for the canal conversion were drawn up by William Provis, on behalf of the two principal engineers, William Cubitt and Robert Stephenson.

The 'Main Line' railway was to be from a junction about a mile east of Bilbrook Station on the proposed Wolverhampton–Shrewsbury line to Calveley on the Crewe–Chester line. The BLJC would be closed, the section to be used by the railway being from Pendeford Bridge (Bridge 4), 1⅜ miles from Autherley Junction, to Nantwich. The canal from Nantwich to Chester and Ellesmere Port was to be retained.

Ideally on a trunk railway the minimum desirable radius of curves was one mile, though curves as sharp as half a mile radius were acceptable, which the engineers could easily achieve on the Main Line. The only significant deviation needed from the existing canal line was at Nantwich, hence the railway would have been only fractionally shorter than the canal. Indeed, for about 89% of the route, the railway would have coincided with the canal.

Conversion of the 'Welsh Branch' from Nantwich to Whitchurch, Ellesmere and Llanymynech was also proposed. Arrangements were made for the purchase of the Eastern Branch of the Montgomeryshire Canal – it was expected that the mortgagee of the Western Branch would agree too – enabling the railway to continue to Welshpool and Newtown. Thus the proposed railway ran from Crewe to Newtown, joining the line of the canal at Wrenbury Heath Bridge (Bridge 15).

These canals were typical of those built in the 1790s and early 1800s. Although they did not shun earthworks to the extent of an early 'Brindley style' canal, they tended to follow the contours, giving sharper curves and a less direct route. Thus the proposed railway would have been 12% shorter than the canals it was replacing, with less than a third of the route being actually on the line of the canals, despite accepting some curves of only a quarter of a mile radius. For more than a quarter of the route the canal would have lain outside the limit of deviation, that is, the distance (usually 100 yards) either side of the line submitted to Parliament within which the railway could be built. The longest section where the canal would have been outside the limit of deviation was across Fenns Moss; here the railway engineers chose a route unrelated to the canal's because of the ground conditions. Other significant deviations were at Quoisley, where the canal makes a loop to the north-west, between Ellesmere and Frankton Junction, where the canal picks its way through the small hills (drumlins) left by the terminal moraine, and at Llanymynech, where the railway would have gone to the south of the village so avoiding the canal's right angle bend after crossing the Vyrnwy Aqueduct. On the other hand, the railway would have re-used Ellesmere Tunnel.

The detailed statistics were:

	Main Line: Pendleford to Calveley	Welsh Branch: Swanley to Newtown
Railway exactly on the line of the canal	89%	30%
Canal within permitted limit of deviation of the railway (usually 100 yards)	99%	71%
Distance by canal	37 miles 4 furlongs	59 miles 4 furlongs
Distance by railway	37 miles 3 furlongs	52 miles 4 furlongs
Minimum radius curves	½ mile	¼ mile

Railway mergers

As discussed earlier in this chapter, in October 1845, the LBR and GJR overcame their differences and started working towards their merger. The draft agreement made at a meeting of representatives of the two companies on 17 October included a clause relating to the Shropshire Union: 'The London & Birmingham to stand perfectly neutral as respects this scheme; the Grand Junction being at liberty to oppose it or not as they may hereafter decide.' Ten days later the LBR Board approved the draft agreement with the sole exception of the Shropshire Union clause; a further meeting in Liverpool with the GJR was requested. That meeting was held the following day and, according to the note of the meeting, a proposal was 'assented to, by which certain advantages, immediate & prospective, were secured for the Shropshire Union Company, its existence as a company established, and a pecuniary guarantee offered'. A further meeting of LBR, GJR and SU representatives was held in London and a final settlement made. George Carr Glyn told the General Meeting of the LBR on 7 November that it would 'secure to them ... the whole valley of the Severn, from Worcester to Crewe'.[13]

The various reports and minutes record the decisions but not the reasoning. A reasonable inference is that the GJR representatives were unhappy about the conversion of the SU main line – it would duplicate the existing trunk railway without generating much intermediate traffic – but were persuaded by the LBR's representatives of the potential benefits of the proposals for the SU's other railway lines, bearing in mind that the SU was an established company with influential directors (unlike so many of the other railway schemes being proposed in that 'Mania' year).

If the LBR and GJR had agreed in 1843 or early 1844 to merge peacefully, would they have entered negotiations with the Shropshire Union? The original motive for negotiations – the conversion of the canal from Autherley to Calveley in order to link the LBR with the MBR and the Chester & Holyhead Railway independently (or largely independently) of the GJR's line – would not have applied.

On the other hand, it is likely that the combined company would have feared that the Shropshire Union Main Line would be taken over by a potential rival seeking a route to the Mersey. During the crucial years of 1844 and 1845 the main threat would have been seen as the Oxford, Worcester & Wolverhampton Railway (OWWR). This project had been originated by various Black Country industrialists who wanted to see the LBR's monopoly broken. In the spring of 1844 they approached the GWR asking for its assistance in promoting the OWWR. Brunel acted as its engineer, and in the late summer of that year the GWR agreed to lease it. The OWWR was approved by Parliament in August 1845. Hence during these two years it is possible that the combined LBR and GJR would have bought or leased the Shropshire Union as a defensive measure.

The impending merger of the LBR, GJR and MBR considerably altered the balance of power in the region; in particular, the LBR withdrew its active support for the proposed Shrewsbury & Birmingham Railway. The latter's directors decided to proceed alone and not join the Shropshire Union group, though this did not affect the agreement for a joint line between Wellington and Shrewsbury. It got its Act in August 1846. The line was then laid out under the direction of William Baker who had been a pupil of George Buck, later becoming a member of Robert Stephenson's team, who was also responsible for engineering the Shropshire Union's Stafford to Wellington railway. Interestingly, as early as September 1846, the Shrewsbury & Birmingham Railway's directors asked the engineer the implications of making the bridges wide enough for broad gauge, which implies they already thought that alliance with the GWR or OWWR was a possibility.

Indeed, six months later they instructed that Oakengates Tunnel be made 28ft wide instead of the normal 24ft.

To Parliament

IN April 1846, six months after the Shropshire Union had made its agreement with the LBR and the GJR, Robert Skey, its Manager, and Charles Potts, its Solicitor, gave evidence before the Select Committee on Railways and Canals Amalgamation. Skey was adamant: 'The Shropshire Union Company has no arrangement whatever with any existing railway company, nor does it propose any amalgamation with them.' He stated that the line would be competing with the Grand Junction Railway, and was then cross-examined about the promises of investments by railway companies in his company, including £200,000 from the Manchester & Birmingham. He agreed that the Manchester & Birmingham had already amalgamated with the Grand Junction, which wasn't quite accurate as it had not yet been approved by Parliament, but nevertheless repeated that he was certain that the Shropshire Union and the Grand Junction would be competing lines.[14] Did he deliberately try to mislead the Select Committee, or was he really naïve enough to believe his evidence?

The Shropshire Union proposals were put before Parliament in three Bills: Wolverhampton to Chester; Stafford to Shrewsbury; and Crewe to Newtown. It was decided not to proceed with Shrewsbury to Worcester for the time being, the reason given at the half-yearly Meeting of Proprietors being that the estimated cost was much higher than expected because of the deviations insisted on by certain land-owners.

The name was changed formally to 'Shropshire Union Railways & Canal Company' (SURCC). 'Railways' was now in the plural, but whether this was deliberate or a drafting error in the Bill is not known. The Acts vested the Shrewsbury Canal and the Eastern Branch of the Montgomeryshire Canal in the Shropshire Union; power was given to purchase the Western Branch of the Montgomeryshire Canal. The Acts also gave the power to close sections of canals replaced by railways and to discontinue the Weston, Quina Brook, Ellesmere and Whitchurch Branches. The three Acts were signed on 3 August 1846, less than three weeks after the formal creation of the London & North Western Railway.

The new Committee of Management

THE Earl of Powis was elected Chairman of the Committee of Management of the Shropshire Union Railways & Canal Company, with Joshua Westhead as Deputy Chairman. Westhead, a Manchester merchant, was Chairman of the Manchester & Birmingham Railway and a director of the Trent Valley Railway. The other members named in the prospectus were:

- George Harper   Ellesmere & Chester Canal (ex ECC)
- George Stanton   Ellesmere & Chester Canal (ex ECC)
- John Williams   Ellesmere & Chester Canal (ex ECC)
- Joseph Grout   Ellesmere & Chester Canal (ex BLJC)

Chapter 9 : Creating the Shropshire Union

The Company's official seal had the name with 'Railway' in the singular. The shield comprises five coats of arms. Clockwise from top left these represent: Shrewsbury (three leopard heads); Chester (lions and sheaves); Stafford (lion, castle and knots); and Worcester (castle and pears). The final quadrant (four lions) shows the arms borne by several Welsh princes including Owen Glendower, which was probably intended to represent North Wales. *National Railway Museum, redrawn by Cathy O'Brien*

– George Holyoake	Ellesmere & Chester Canal (ex BLJC)
– George Loch	Ellesmere & Chester Canal (ex BLJC)
– Richard Barrow	Crewe & Worcester Railway
– Thomas Groves	Crewe & Worcester Railway
– Henry Newbery	Shrewsbury & Trent Valley Union Railway
– John Meeson Parsons	Shrewsbury & Trent Valley Union Railway
– Henry Tootal	Shrewsbury & Trent Valley Union Railway
– Hon George Anson, MP	Trent Valley Railway

The Shrewsbury Canal Company nominated Barnard Dickinson and Thomas Campbell Eyton as members of the Committee of Management of the new company, but they were not appointed. Nor did any former director of either of the Montgomeryshire companies become a member of the new Committee of Management.

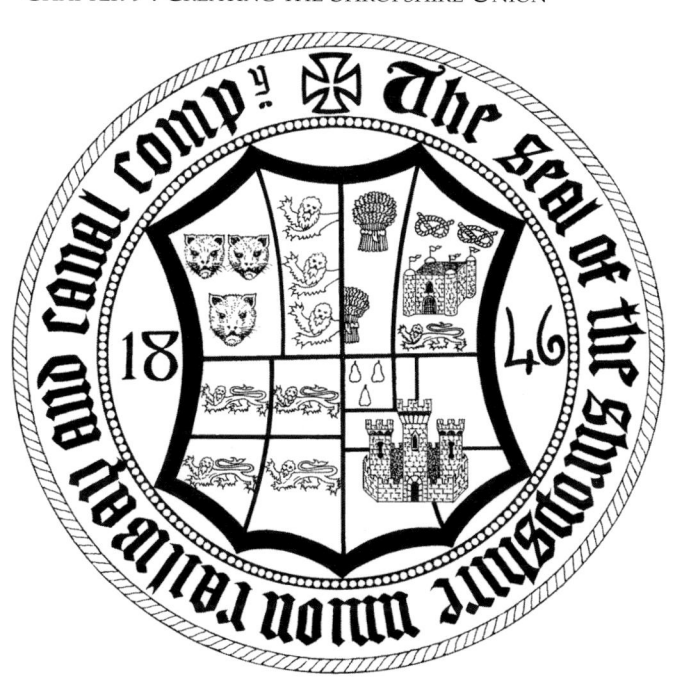

Some of the SURCC's directors were amongst the first directors of the LNWR. The Duke of Sutherland had the right to nominate directors to the board of the Liverpool & Manchester Railway; when this merged with the Grand Junction in 1845, the right to nominate one director continued, as indeed it did in the 1846 merger to create the London & North Western Railway. His nominee was George Loch. Westhead, Barrow and Anson were also initial LNWR directors; indeed, the last-named was Chairman in 1852-3. Holyoake and Tootal later became LNWR directors.

Tootal, Newbery, Parsons and Holyoake, together with the Earl of Powis, were to become the dominant directors in the early days of the Shropshire Union. Tootal and Newbery were both Manchester manufacturers; Parsons, though born at Newport (Shropshire), was a London stockbroker and for a period Chairman of the London & Brighton Railway; and Holyoake was a solicitor and banker at Wolverhampton. The Shropshire Union ceased to be a local company controlled by local people, though that was the way it had marketed itself in its prospectus.

The lease to the London & North Western Railway

Negotiations with the LNWR

IMMEDIATELY following the passing of the act, the Shropshire Union Board set up a special committee to consider the best way of carrying the newly-gained powers into effect. Two of the seven members (Westhead and Barrow) were on the Board of the LNWR, so it could have been no surprise that negotiations soon started to lease the SU to the LNWR.

On 31 August 1846 four of the committee met LNWR directors and officers; after a lengthy discussion, the SU representatives made a formal proposal. Then followed an exchange of correspondence. On 9 October the deputation again met LNWR representatives, who included Joshua Westhead (also Deputy Chairman of the SU), at the Euston Hotel, where, it was noted, the LNWR representatives were unable to agree amongst themselves, each giving their personal opinion and leaving the formal response to be decided by the LNWR Board meeting the day afterwards. However, the Board rejected the SU's proposal and another round of correspondence ensued. Robert Stephenson attended a meeting of the SU's representatives, telling them that the LNWR was prepared to give 'liberal terms', and urging the SU to come to a settlement.

The deputation attended a meeting of the LNWR Board on 17 October, when the following terms were offered to the SU:

– rental equivalent to half the rate paid on the LNWR shares;
– all profits from the SU lines above this amount to be divided

amongst the SU shareholders until the payment is 6%;
- any profits in excess of that to be divided equally between the LNWR and the SU;
- SU shareholders to be able to take part in new creations of shares by the LNWR in proportion to their capital;
- two of the three SU lines to be completed within 3½ years;
- a joint committee consisting of an equal number of SU and LNWR shareholders to be appointed;
- the decision about when the third line is be completed to be left to the joint committee; and
- a minimum capital of £12 per share to be called within 3½ years.

At a further meeting these terms were agreed, subject to a couple of amendments. The lease would start when the several lines were completed; in the meantime the SU shareholders would receive 4% on paid up capital; also the condition concerning minimum capital was removed.

These arrangements for a lease in perpetuity were approved at an Extraordinary General Meeting of the SU on 4 December 1846. The directors' report stated that they thought the shareholders would prefer a guarantee by a powerful company of a profit which was certain, to the hope of a greater profit by continuing independently.

Leasing arrangements usually specified a fixed rate of interest, but most SU shareholders would probably have thought that they had got an advantageous deal. Both the London & Birmingham and Grand Junction Railways had consistently paid their shareholders 10% during the first half of the 1840s, and the LNWR paid 10% in 1846. This had reduced to 5¼% by 1850; although it increased during the remaining life of the company, it never again reached the heights of the early 1840s.

The agreement in principle was made in time to submit a Bill to the 1847 session of Parliament. The LNWR's first draft proved objectionable to the SU directors, the most important defect being that the draft gave the LNWR extensive powers which they thought should be given to the Amalgamated Board. The Act was obtained in June 1847 but the House of Lords had inserted an amendment which placed difficulties in the way of completing the transaction, necessitating a further Act in 1854. The lease was not actually signed until 1857.

Unlike some other Acts where railway companies took over canals, there was no impartiality clause in the 1847 Act preventing discrimination against canal trade in favour of railway trade, perhaps because at that time it was assumed that the principal lines of the canal were to be converted to railways.

Financial arrangements

THE loan of £252,000 from the Royal Exchange Assurance Co. was liquidated by the payment of £100,000 in January 1847, then three equal annual instalments.

The Wilsons, the contractors who had constructed much of the BLJC in the first half of the 1830s, were eventually paid the £15,656 owing to them in July 1849.

The Shrewsbury and Montgomeryshire Canals

For each £100 nominal share Shrewsbury Canal's shareholders accepted a £150 share in the new company. This was based on dividends having been £10 per share in each of the years from 1843 to 1845. (As this was paid net of 7d in the £ income tax, the real rate was slightly higher.) This came into effect when the Act was passed on 3 August 1846.

The enlarged Ellesmere & Chester Company offered the shareholders of the Eastern Branch of the Montgomeryshire Canal two options: to accept a £110 share in the new company for each £100 nominal share, or to accept the same amount per share in cash which could be in the form of debentures paying interest at 5%. The shareholders had been receiving a dividend of £5 a year since 1839. The Montgomeryshire Canal committee made no attempt to haggle, and unsurprisingly, the great majority of shareholders accepted the cash or debenture option, with its certain interest rather than its uncertain dividends. The sale price was therefore £78,890, comprising 46 shares (owned by 11 shareholders) at £110 each and £73,830 in cash. By the time the transaction took effect in February 1847, the SURCC had been created and the decision made to lease it to the LNWR.

The Western Branch remained independent for a little longer, controlled by its mortgagees. It was purchased by the SURCC on 5 February 1850 for £33,096 in cash – again, initially financed by a loan at 5%. Its shareholders had never received a dividend; the mortgagees were repaid their loans but only about a quarter of the full interest owed.

What is clear is that the SURCC over-paid for these assets – indeed the Western Branch's only value was the land it owned. There seems to have been no realisation of the severity of the effect of the railway competition which came during the next couple of decades. The report of the Eastern Branch directors to its shareholders as recently as 1844 complacently stated:

> Your Committee cannot refrain from noticing the gratifying fact that the interests of this canal have in no way suffered from the great railway system which is extending itself throughout the Kingdom and which has operated most detrimentally upon many similar properties.
>
> Your Committee does not apprehend that the security the Company at present enjoys from this kind of competition will be disturbed; but, on the contrary, the several railways which are either in progress of formation or projected in the neighbouring counties may be regarded as tending to increase the traffic already possessed by the Company.[15]

After the lease to the LNWR

THE financial arrangements for the lease of the SURCC to LNWR were originally intended to come into effect once the planned railways had been built. With the opening of the

Chapter 9 : Creating the Shropshire Union

Shrewsbury–Stafford line and the changed circumstances concerning the other lines, the LNWR agreed that the lease could come into effect on 1 July 1849. From that date the LNWR assumed liability for the canal debt and undertook to guarantee the SURCC capital.

The calls on the 'new' £20 shares were limited to £6.10s. However, a group of shareholders took the company to court, claiming that it was unlawful for any of the money raised by the new share issue to be used for the repayment of the canal debt. The initial decision went in favour of the company, as did the decision of the Lord Chancellor on appeal.

The changed arrangements required Parliament's approval, so a Bill was prepared which also sanctioned the abandonment of some of the previously approved railway lines. Opposition came from certain shareholders and from rival railway companies but the changes were incorporated in the 1854 Act.

After 'a most protracted and difficult examination and enquiry' the LNWR's Public Accountant (in modern terminology, auditor), James Coleman, calculated the exact figures for the capital for both the canal and railway undertakings of the SURCC as at 30 June 1850. There had been no attempt to unify the structure of the share capital – it continued to reflect its origin.[16]

	£. s. d	£. s. d
Canal share capital: 8,121¾ shares:		
Ellesmere & Chester Canal:		
3,575¾ A shares of £69.15s.4d nominal	250,004.10. 5	
Ellesmere & Chester Canal:		
4,000 B shares of £37.10s nominal	150,000. 0. 0	
Shrewsbury Canal:		
500 shares of £110 nominal	75,000. 0. 0	
Montgomeryshire Canal, Eastern Branch:		
46 shares of £110 nominal	5,060. 0. 0	480,064.10. 5
Canal capital debts:		
Mortgages, bonds etc bearing interest		
at 4% or 5%	715,195.16. 6	
Owing for the purchase of land at Liverpool	14,000. 0. 0	
Railway share receipts used for repaying debt	174,263. 8.10	903,459. 5. 4
Total canal capital		1,383,523.15. 9
Railway share capital: 160,011 shares of £6.10s issued		1,040,071.10. 0
Total Shropshire Union capital		2,423,595. 5. 9

The 'A' shares correspond with the 'Class 1' shares when the ECC and BLJC merged; the 'B' shares seem to be a combination of the 'Class 2' and 'Class 3' shares. The records do not show how much of the railway share capital was subscribed by individual investors and how much came from the various railway companies.

The Shropshire Canal

THE Shropshire Canal did not form part of the original concept for the Shropshire Union but in October 1845 the SU offered to purchase it. After lengthy negotiations, in 1848 it was agreed that the purchase price should be £62,500. A Bill was introduced into Parliament to sanction this but it was withdrawn because it appeared probable that obstacles in connection with the new standing orders would prove insurmountable. An alternative working arrangement was available under the powers of the Canal Carriers Act 1845 whereby the Shropshire Canal would be leased, legislative sanction for an entire amalgamation being deferred for the time being.

The terms agreed were:

– lease for 21 years at an annual rent of £3,125;
– £6,250 to be deposited with trustees, to be returned to the SURCC when the canal was purchased but to be forfeited if the purchase were not made or if the SURCC refused to extend the lease for further periods of 21 years – the interest on the £6,250 to be paid to the SURCC;
– the lessees to keep the canal in repair.

The lease was effected on 1 November 1849.

Notes and references

The minutes and other surviving files of the Ellesmere & Chester Canal (TNA: RAIL826), Birmingham & Liverpool Junction Canal (TNA:RAIL808) and Shropshire Union Canal (TNA: RAIL623) together with those of the London & North Western Railway (TNA: RAIL384) tell part of the story of the merger and lease of the canals – the 'what' but rarely the 'why'. Hence some parts of this chapter are particularly speculative. Much of the background to the dispute between the London & Birmingham Railway and the Grand Junction Railway and their eventual merger to form the London & North Western Railway has been derived from David Hodgkins, *George Carr Glyn: railwayman and banker*, 2017, pp.175–194, and M.C. Reed, *The London & North Western Railway*, 1996, pp.31–39, 57–58. The point of view of the GWR is given in E.T. MacDermot (revised by Charles Clinker), *History of the Great Western Railway*, Vol.1, 1964, pp.180–3.

1. The irony is that, by then, William Cubitt was engineer to the South Eastern Railway, constructing the line between London and Dover.
2. Moss to Huskisson, 14 December 1829: Staffordshire Record Office (StRO), D593K
3. Eric Richards, *The Leviathan of Wealth*, 1973, pp.94, 96, 98, 100, 103
4. Loch to Lewis, 18 December 1829: StRO, D593K, quoted in Eric Richards, *The Leviathan of Wealth*, 1973, pp.90–1
5. Loch to Lord F. Egerton, 10 June 1844, quoted in F.C. Mather, *After the Canal Duke*, 1970, p.174
6. ECC General Assembly, 8 August 1844 & 26 April 1845
7. Minutes of evidence taken before the Select Committee on Railways and Canals Amalgamation, 30 April 1846, pp.680–4, 705, 709
8. Sir John Wrottesley to Loch, 23 February 1838, George Loch to James Loch, 23 February 1838: StRO, D593/K/1/3/26; Loch to Wrottesley, 3 March 1838: D593/K/1/5/34
9. Loch to Wrottesley, 26 February 1838: StRO, D593/K/1/5/34
10. Charles Hadfield, *Canals of the West Midlands*, second edition 1969, p.253; Henry Lewin, *The Railway Mania and its Aftermath*, 1936, p.177; LBR Board, 13 June 1845
11. S.R. Broadbridge, *The Birmingham Canal Navigations*, Vol.1, 1974, pp.183, 197
12. The Chester & Birkenhead Railway stayed independent until 1860, when it became a joint railway of the LNWR and GWR.
13. LMR reports, 17 & 23 October 1845: RAIL384/24; LMR Board 22 October & 6 November 1845: RAIL384/6; O.S. Nock, *North Western*, 1968, p.1; *The Times*, 8 November 1845
14. Minutes of evidence taken before the Select Committee on Railways and Canals Amalgamation, 30 April 1846, pp.650–61
15. Montgomeryshire Canal, Eastern Branch, report, 5 August 1844 : TNA, RAIL852/14
16. Report of Mr Coleman, 26 April 1851: TNA, RAIL623/46

10

The Shropshire Union Railways & Canal Company

Management

THE Shropshire Union Railways & Canal Company had its own Board and Executive Committee until the company ceased to exist at the end of 1922, but the lease arrangements meant that it did not have unfettered discretion. Its decisions were subject to rulings of the Amalgamated Board, which had equal number of representatives from the SU and the LNWR. Ultimate power lay with the LNWR, as the SU had no independent means of raising money for major investments or to cover losses. Also, of course, many of the SU directors were also directors of the LNWR.

The SU retained a fair degree of independence until 1863; after that the LNWR influence steadily grew, and from 1879 it was effectively a subsidiary of the LNWR though retaining its own day-to-day management.

Soon after the lease of the SU to the LNWR, Captain Huish, the latter's General Manager, issued sensible advice to the SU Board about running the business, in particular about maximising income, minimising expenditure and keeping good records. He stressed the importance of statistics comparing performance with that in the same period the previous year. It is noticeable how much more professionally the canal company was run after the lease – more bureaucratically certainly, but more effectively.

A minor illustration of the change in attitude was the sale of 1,449 bottles of wine which were in the company's cellars at Ellesmere. The auction in 1848 raised £232.

One feature of the SU was the remarkably long periods of service both of most of the senior Board members and of the key officers. For example, between 1848 and 1921 – over seventy years – there were only two Chairmen; between 1879 and 1911 – over thirty years – the incumbents of the two senior posts, Traffic Manager and Engineer, continued unchanged.

The Board and Executive Committee

THE first Chairman of the company, the Second Earl of Powis, died in January 1848. This was a great loss to the company, as he had been no mere titled figurehead: he had taken an active part in the various negotiations and had championed the canals in the House of Commons until 1839 and in the House of Lords thereafter. The Board minutes referred to 'his pure, steady and irreproachable conduct' and 'his indefatigable industry, commanding reputation and clear intelligence'.

His son, the Third Earl of Powis, was elected Chairman in his stead. He served as Chairman until 1891 – a total of 43 years. Like his father, he conscientiously attended most meetings. Following his decease, the minutes recorded 'the courteous and kindly spirit which always distinguished [him]'. Despite these fine words, the Executive Committee refused to contribute towards a stained-glass memorial window in Pool Quay Church.

Even longer serving was George Stanton, who served from the inception of the Board in 1846 until his retirement in 1890 and was Deputy Chairman from 1868. He was the son of Thomas Stanton, who had joined the Ellesmere Canal's staff in 1798

> **Edward Herbert, 3rd Earl of Powis (1818–1891)**
>
> EDWARD HERBERT, the great-grandson of 'Clive of India', became Viscount Clive in 1839 and, in 1848 when his father was accidentally killed by Edward's younger brother during a pheasant shoot, the 3rd Earl of Powis. He was MP for Shropshire North (1843–48), Lord Lieutenant of Montgomeryshire (1877–91) and an active participant in Shropshire and Montgomeryshire county government.
>
> A scholar and a bachelor, he was not interested in a wider public career. In his youth he had been a member of Disraeli's 'Young England' movement, a religious, paternalistic and romantic species of Social Toryism. However, when in 1875 Disraeli offered the him the Viceroyalty of India, he simply scribbled on the outside of the envelope, 'Not worth considering – Powis'.
>
> Although lacking much of his father's drive and business acumen, he served faithfully as Chairman of the Shropshire Union Company for more than four decades.

and had risen to be General Agent of the Ellesmere & Chester Canal. As mentioned in Chapter 7, George had himself been employed by the latter company from 1833 to 1836.

Henry Tootal was on the Board from the start, and was Deputy Chairman from 1851 until his resignation in 1868. A silk manufacturer in Manchester, he was involved in promoting various railway companies during the 'Mania' years, including the Manchester & Southampton. Later he became a director of the LNWR. The SU Board's minutes were particularly fulsome about his qualities:

> Mr Tootal's connection with the Board since its first formation more than twenty years ago, his assiduous attention to and knowledge of its concerns, the value of his personal experience, the prudence of his counsels, and his conciliatory manner of dealing with difficult questions and with those parties with whom the Company has had from time to time to negotiate, have been of great advantage to the Company since its first incorporation, whilst his uniform courtesy towards his colleagues has caused them to feel in addition the loss of a personal friend.[1]

The Third Earl of Powis's successor as Chairman was Ralph Brocklebank, of the Liverpool shipping family, and nephew of Richard Moon, Chairman of the LNWR. Nepotism does not seem to have been a significant factor in his appointment, as Brocklebank was highly respected in the commercial community of Liverpool. Elected to the LNWR and SU Boards in 1883, he became Deputy Chairman of the SU in 1891 and Chairman the following year. He retired in 1921, after 'long and devoted service to the interest of the Company and of its employees'.[2]

Richard Moon

THE dominant person on the Board in the last half of the 19th century was Richard Moon (from 1887, Sir Richard Moon), the forceful personality who was Chairman of the LNWR from 1861 until 1891. His earliest involvement with the SU appears to have been in 1851, when he was a LNWR nominee to the Amalgamated Board, and in 1856 he accompanied the SU Executive Committee on their two-day inspection, travelling by boat from Hurleston Junction to Welshpool – no doubt a relaxing break from his onerous railway duties.

He formally joined the SU Board in March 1865, attending most of the meetings at Euston and some of those at Shrewsbury. He had been regularly attending meetings of the Executive Committee, which then met at Chester, since April 1863. A Special Sub-Committee, comprising Moon and Tootal, was established in May 1863 to consider issues concerning traffic and rates, but soon widened its remit. This met at Euston, and took many of the decisions which had previously been the responsibility of the Executive Committee. Moon's presence on the various committees meant that the chance of an independent SU voice was much diminished.

After a couple years the key decision-making role reverted to the Executive Committee, but although Moon did not chair it,

> **(Sir) Richard Moon (1814–1899)**
>
> RICHARD MOON – Sir Richard Moon from 1887 – was the son of a Liverpool merchant. He was elected a director of the LNWR in 1847, becoming chairman in June 1861 and holding that position until he retired in February 1891. Moon was essentially conservative in his outlook, but could be innovative when he thought it in the best interests of the company. He certainly ran it very tightly. The company was employing 55,000 men in 1885, and was, at that stage, the largest joint stock company in the world.
>
> When he first became LNWR Chairman, he referred to beneficial change as coming about through 'pure and deliberate hard work and a constant watching of the concern'. Moon was incredibly hard-working and a master of detail. The depth of his involvement in the Shropshire Union – in reality only a minor part of the LNWR empire – shows much about the character of the man. George Findlay, LNWR General Manager from 1880, wrote in his book on management that his Chairman 'who keeps a watchful guard over the company's purse strings, has to be convinced that the expenditure is not only desirable but actually unavoidable'.
>
> Sir Richard Moon was described by his obituarist in *The Times* as 'the hardest of hard workers and the sternest of stern disciplinarians'. He was said to combine 'an assured confidence in the correctness of his own judgement with an autocratic spirit which hardly recognized the possibility of that judgement being criticized by others'. At the same time he was of 'a singularly retiring disposition'.
>
> He did have a human side too. When the Mersey Mission to Seamen wished to have a building at Ellesmere Port, he agreed to pay for it out of the LNWR Chairman's Fund.

there can be no doubt that he dominated it. Many detailed issues were minuted as being left to him to deal with. He attended virtually every meeting, which were normally monthly, most frequently at Chester, often at Euston, and occasionally at Birmingham, Wolverhampton, Stafford, Liverpool or Manchester.

Early in his railway career Moon considered that canals had significant advantages in the conveyance of bulk loads. However, shortly before he retired he said that he had been trying for the last forty years to make their canals pay, and could not succeed except in one case (by which he meant the Birmingham Canal), adding 'People who can make an ordinary canal yield a profit must be very clever.'[3]

General Managers, Secretaries, and Traffic Managers

WHEN the SU was created, Robert Skey continued as General Manager on a salary of £800 a year, and started attending regular meetings with LNWR officers. William Cowan was appointed under him as Secretary, on £500 a year.

In 1847 administrative offices were established in Cork Street, Wolverhampton, but two years later the offices were moved to

Chester. Then in 1850 the statutory head office in London at Great George Street was closed; Euston Station became the head office but most of the functions were transferred to Chester. This gave the opportunity to reduce staff; in particular, the employment of William Cowan was terminated on payment of a gratuity of six months' salary. The committee structure was simplified, and from then onwards many of the meetings were held at Chester instead of at London.

In 1853 the role of Secretary was separated from that of General Manager and Alfred Wragge was appointed to the new post. Skey continued as General Manager until 1863, resigning at the same meeting as Moon's Special Sub-Committee made its first report. His resignation letter hints at growing frustration and disagreement with Moon's intervention into the SU's affairs:

> Gentlemen, I have now had the honour of serving for thirty years, during the last fifteen of which I have earnestly and constantly endeavoured to draw attention to those measures which I alone considered likely to avert the crisis in its affairs that has now arrived. The opportunity for carrying out the measures I refer to has now passed by, and I feel that it may be considered that my work is done.

He was given £500 in lieu of notice, but neither the Executive Committee nor the Board minutes include any words of thanks or praise.[4]

Following Skey's retirement, the role of General Manager was added to Wragge's duties. He continued in the combined post until he left in 1872, having been offered the position of Managing Partner in an old-established firm of solicitors in London. The Board praised the 'integrity, zeal and ability which he has uniformly displayed in the performance of his duties of a difficult and laborious office'.[5]

George Jebb (1838–1927)

GEORGE JEBB was born at Baschurch in Shropshire and trained as a civil engineer under the tutelage of Alexander Mackintosh, who had been responsible for the Chester area lines of the Great Western Railway. In 1863 he went to Galicia and planned the course of the railway from Lemberg to Czernowitz (now Lviv to Chernivtsi in western Ukraine). In 1869 he was appointed Chief Engineer of the Shropshire Union Railways & Canal Company at the age of 30, holding this post for over forty years. He retired from full time work in 1919 but retained the title of Consulting Engineer. From 1875 until 1912 he was also Chief Engineer of the Birmingham Canal, which at that time had some 160 miles of waterway. Amongst his works there were the Parkhead (Dudley) and Smethwick pumping plants, which recirculated the water between the busiest levels of the canal. He was elected a member of the Council of the Institution of Civil Engineers in 1902 and was Vice President in 1912 but resigned in 1915, the year he was nominated for the office of President. It seems that he was a very private individual who avoided publicity.

The job was then split again and the post of General Manager ceased to exist. This was in line with Richard Moon's management philosophy: in 1874 he abolished the post of General Manager on the London & North Western Railway when the incumbent retired.

James Hope was appointed Secretary, but he was demoted to Assistant Secretary – and had his annual salary reduced from £350 to £250 – in 1879 when the Shropshire Union's independence effectively ceased and Stephen Reay, the LNWR's Secretary (and Richard Moon's close confidant and personal friend), was given the formal title of Secretary. From then onwards, the LNWR's Secretary was also Secretary of the SU Company, although in practice had little involvement in its affairs.

Hope continued in day-to-day charge of the Chester office, with responsibility for traffic accounts, rents and administrative matters, and he attended Executive Committee meetings as Committee Clerk. He was another long-serving officer, not wanting to retire until 1911, after more than sixty years with the canal company. The Executive Committee minuted its appreciation of his 'valuable services' and gave their 'sincere wishes for his happiness in his retirement'. Sadly, that was not to be: he died just two days before his retirement date.[6]

Following Wragge's departure in 1872, William Jones was promoted from being the company's Agent at Wolverhampton to the new post of General Traffic Manager, on a salary of £600, somewhat less than the £800 a year which Wragge had enjoyed. From 1876 Jones was also in charge of the LNWR's South Staffordshire District – the only occasion where there seemed to be a proper attempt to integrate the two businesses. However, he resigned because of ill health in 1879.

Thomas Hales then became Traffic Manager on £450 a year, based at Chester instead of Wolverhampton, having since 1876 been the Assistant at Ellesmere Port specifically responsible for the whole of the cross-Mersey business and the working of the SU's own boats. In the winter of 1893/94 he suffered from what was described as 'overstrain of the nervous system', his doctor advising him to cease all work for a time. The Company agreed to pay him his full salary whilst he had a holiday in the Mediterranean. He went to Belgium and Holland in 1906 to investigate how the canals there worked. He was Traffic Manager for over thirty years, retiring at the end of 1911. In consideration of his 'long and faithful service' he was given a retirement grant of a year's salary, by then £600.

William Whittam, who had previously been an LNWR officer, was given the title of General Manager when appointed in 1912, but his role was identical to that of Hales. He died in 1921, just 17 months before the SU's separate legal existence ceased.

Engineers

ALEXANDER EASTON, Telford's protégé who had been the Resident Engineer on the Birmingham & Liverpool Junction Canal, retired as Engineer of the Shropshire Union Company in 1851. The Executive Committee recorded its appreciation of his 'zeal, industry and fidelity'. He stayed on in the ill-defined role of

Consulting Engineer but died in 1854 when felling a tree near his home at Sutton (between Newport and Norbury).

The engineering role was then divided. Edward Johnes, who had formerly been the Manager of the Eastern Branch of the Montgomeryshire Canal, was made responsible for the majority of the canal network, on a salary of £300 a year, whilst John Beech (ex Shrewsbury Canal) was paid £200 a year to look after the works of the Shrewsbury and Shropshire Canals and the Shropshire Union Railway, also being Traffic Superintendent of the last. Neither of them had the training or experience possessed by their predecessor, and significant matters tended to be referred to the LNWR's engineers for a second opinion. For example, in 1869 William Baker, the LNWR's Engineer-in-Chief, produced reports on Knighton Reservoir, Chirk Aqueduct and potential developments at Ellesmere Port. Following Easton's death, Beech was given extra duties, and his salary increased to match that of Johnes.

In 1864 full responsibility for the Shropshire Union Railway was transferred to the LNWR, necessitating a review of duties. Beech became Engineer for the whole of the Shropshire Union's canal system, based at Ellesmere – the SU's residence there coincidentally having the name 'Beech House'. Johnes employment was terminated, a gratuity of six months' salary being paid to him.

By 1866 one can detect the Executive Committee's dissatisfaction – which probably means Richard Moon's dissatisfaction – with Beech's performance. They were critical of contract work being done without an estimate and without the order being counter-signed by the Manager, also of maintenance costs generally, and he was formally written to about them. On 14 September 1867 traffic on the former Chester Canal section of the main line was stopped because all the water from the Dee had been diverted into Hurleston Reservoir, and again he received a warning. The following year they were unhappy because he did not report to them concerns about the stability of the embankment at Lea Hall on the Middlewich Branch, which was subsiding because of brine pumping in the area, nor had he taken the action recommended by William Baker concerning Belvide Reservoir. Then in 1869, following breaches at Whixall Moss and at Soudley (south of Market Drayton), the Executive Committee decided to relieve Beech of his duties, and in lieu of notice to pay him six months salary.

His successor, George Jebb, was the SU's Engineer from 1869 until 1919 when he retired from full-time work but retained the title of Consulting Engineer. From 1875 until 1912 he was also Chief Engineer of the Birmingham Canal. Until 1887 his office was at Shrewsbury; in that year he moved to New Street, Birmingham.

Solicitors

THE longest-lasting connection with the Shropshire Union Canal and its predecessors concerned four generations of the Potts family, the Chester dynasty of solicitors. Charles Potts had been the Chester Canal's initial legal adviser in 1770, though he soon resigned. He acted for the Ellesmere Canal from the very first meeting of the promoters in 1791.

Charles was succeeded by his son Henry in 1815, and Henry by his son Charles William in 1845. The latter's son Reginald Potts formally became the SU's solicitor in 1890 though he had been advising it for many years previously; his last recorded attendance at a Board meeting was in 1894. The firm continued to work for the SU until the end of its separate existence in 1922.

The relationship may have been a long one, but the SU did not always pay its bills promptly. In December 1855, for example, it was noted that the solicitor's bills for the period from July 1850 to September 1854 totalled £2,600, of which £1,600 was still outstanding. Instead of paying the full sum due, the Executive Committee decided to pay £1,000 on account.

Relations with the London & North Western Railway

THE relationship between the Shropshire Union and the London & North Western Railway was not always harmonious. As was stated in the previous chapter, the lease terms were agreed in principle in 1846 and Parliamentary approval obtained the following year. A further Act was obtained in 1854 which gave legal approval to the actual working arrangements. However, the exact wording of the lease still needed to be agreed, and correspondence went back and forward concerning such issues as the exact amount of debt and what was to be done concerning forfeited shares. The formal lease was eventually dated 25 March 1857.

The lease left some issues in doubt. The SU Board was concerned about the implications on it of the purchase of the Shropshire Canal, which had not been considered when the original agreement in principle was made. Other matters about which the Board was concerned were claims for back dividends, dividends appropriated by the LNWR, claims for land at Chester and Liverpool, and claims for legal expenses. These were all technical points of detail, but the passage of time had allowed them to fester. The LNWR wanted informal arbitration of the points in dispute; the SU wanted formal arbitration, and this was accepted. It took a year for the two parties to agree the formal Agreement of Reference – in other words, to agree exactly what was in dispute – half a year for the arbitrators to make their judgement, and another half a year for the parties to formulate a mutually acceptable engrossment of the Agreement. This was sealed on 13 January 1860 but back-dated to the date of the lease agreement.

Even this was not the end of the matter. The LNWR had assumed responsibility for the SU's share registers and deeds, and the SU Board wanted them back. In July 1859 a compromise was reached under which these should remain the property of the SU but be in the custody of the Amalgamated Committee (that is, at the LNWR offices at Euston) with both parties having the right of access to them. However, the following summer the SU Board obtained counsel's opinion which stated that the SU's directors had the duty to be responsible for the share registers and to distribute the dividends. This time it was the LNWR which suggested formal arbitration, but the SU Board thought that as the issue was purely a point of law, a special case should be presented to the Courts for a ruling. To hasten the matter, they instructed their Solicitor to issue a formal notice requiring the books to be delivered to their Secretary. As a result of the Solicitor General's opinion, in March 1862 the SU decided to file a Bill in Chancery against the LNWR. The case dragged on, but in February 1863 Richard Moon, the Chairman of the LNWR, wrote a one-sentence rather grudging letter to the Earl of Powis, Chairman of the SU, stating, 'In order to remove any irritation which may exist at your Board, we have come to the conclusion to give up the Transfer Books – but in doing so we trust that no additional expense will be incurred in keeping the books as it costs us nothing.' Perhaps it was not a total co-incidence that, shortly after this, Moon was elected to the Board of the Shropshire Union Company.

In 1879 the SU Board voluntarily sent the books back to Euston.

The Shropshire Union Railway

IN December 1846, whilst the SURCC was still an independent company, the decision was made to construct the Stafford to Shrewsbury line first as it could be carried out quite quickly and would 'not involve the loss of any revenue derived from the canals'. (This was to be proved wrong.) The contract for the section from Stafford to Gnosall, including a spur to Norton Bridge which was never built, was let to Francis Wythes of Poole; that from Gnosall to Wellington to James Howe and Henry Jones of Liverpool. The stations, goods sheds and other buildings were the subject of separate contracts. At Shrewsbury a goods yard was built at the canal basin. The line to it descended steeply from Shrewsbury Station – the site of this curve can still be seen.

The other contracts in which the Shropshire Union was involved were all joint with other companies. The Wellington to Shrewsbury line, including Wellington Station, was joint with the Shrewsbury & Birmingham. Shrewsbury Station and the bridge over the Severn were to be paid for equally by the Shropshire Union, Shrewsbury & Birmingham, Shrewsbury & Chester and Shrewsbury & Hereford companies.

The joint line between Shrewsbury and Wellington, together with the Shropshire Union line on to Stafford, opened on 1 June 1849. Under the lease agreement the LNWR was to receive all the income and meet all the expenses of the railway though the SU had day-to-day control – an arrangement which was bound to prove unsatisfactory.

In 1846 there had been abundant finance in the money markets, a major cause of the Railway Mania which had seen 270 Bills passed authorising the construction of 4,450 miles of new railway and the raising of new capital totalling over £95 million, with borrowing powers for an additional £36 million. As calls started being made on these shares, money became tight. In October 1847, when Robert Stephenson reported to the Amalgamated Board concerning the SU's proposed Wolverhampton–Chester and the Crewe–Newtown lines, it was decided that it was not then expedient to proceed. An application was made to the Railway Commissioners for an extension of time, but in February 1849 the conversion of the canals into railways was formally abandoned. This decision had followed resolutions of the SU in September 1848 and of the LNWR in October 1848 that no new capital expenditure would be undertaken for the purpose of constructing new lines without the express sanction of the shareholders and that works in hand would be curtailed where possible.

As one of the original four partners, the SU owned a quarter share of Shrewsbury Station. With the opening of the Crewe line in 1858, the imminent opening of the Hereford line, and the approval of the lines down the Severn Valley and to Welshpool, the station needed enlargement. The SU was reluctant to meet its quarter share of the cost, arguing (with good reason) that the constitution should be reviewed to recognise the wider interests, but nevertheless it had to pay.

For the SU to have its own engineering and traffic management organisation for the railway between Stafford and Shrewsbury was wasteful, which must have been obvious to everybody except apparently the SU's Board and senior management. In the autumn of 1862 the LNWR wrote stating that with effect from 1 January 1863 it would exercise its rights to 'work and manage' the railway. The SU Board responded by saying that it would facilitate the LNWR working the railway, but emphasised that the Act reserved the *management* of both the railway and the canals to the Joint Committee (in other words, the Amalgamated Board). However, in practice from then onwards the SU had negligible input to the management of the railway.

Legally the SU railway stayed part of the Shropshire Union Railways & Canal Company, so was included in its annual accounts. However, rather than keep separate detailed accounts for the SU railway once it had effectively become part of the LNWR network, periodic assessments were made of the income. Working expenses were assumed to be the LNWR's average for all its railway operations, and a further deduction was made for depreciation. In 1881 the net annual profit was assessed as £34,000, and it was assumed that it would increase by £500 a year. Having reached £40,000 the assumed profit stayed at that figure for many years, before reverting to £34,000 in 1911.

Development of the railway network

ON issues concerning its own railway network, the LNWR tended to ignore the SU, which caused the latter to protest. For example, in September 1853, the SU Board resolved:

> That the London & North Western members of the Amalgamated Board be requested to call the attention of the directors of the London & North Western Company to the position of the Shropshire Union Company as

Chapter 10 : The Shropshire Union Railways & Canal Company

affected by the passing of the Shrewsbury & Crewe line, and the proposed renewed application to Parliament for the Shrewsbury & Newtown line.

The opening of the Shrewsbury to Crewe line in 1858 had an immediate effect on the earnings of the SU canal as it served Nantwich and Whitchurch *en route*, and it also reduced the income of the SU railway as much passenger traffic between Shrewsbury and the north had formerly gone via Stafford.

The Shrewsbury to Newtown line was a less ambitious version of an independent proposal put forward the previous year, which had continued via Llanidloes and Llangurig to Aberystwyth. However, neither that nor a scheme proposed by the Shrewsbury & Chester Railway for an extension of its Oswestry branch to Welshpool and Newtown had been passed by Parliament; instead approval had been given to the independent (and, at that stage, isolated) Llanidloes & Newtown Railway.

Sometimes the LNWR did not consult about proposals which involved the SU's own property. In 1858 the SU was sent a copy of the draft Bill which included converting the canal between Newtown and Buttington (a little north of Welshpool) into a railway; naturally the SU Board was incensed. This had been a piece of opportunism by the LNWR. The Oswestry & Newtown Railway, which was authorised in 1855, had severe financial difficulties and its contractors went bankrupt in 1858 with only the northernmost 11 of its 30 miles started. In the event the crisis passed and in 1859 the LNWR made alternative arrangements: the Shrewsbury & Welshpool Railway, authorised in 1856 and backed by the LNWR, would have running powers over the Oswestry & Newtown between Buttington and Welshpool.[7] Because the Earl of Powis was a member of the Board of the Oswestry & Newtown Railway from 1855 until 1861, one would have expected him to have been aware of what was happening, but possibly he genuinely did not know.

The SU was not consulted in advance concerning two Bills in the 1861 session of Parliament which were being supported by the LNWR: the Nantwich & Market Drayton Railway and the Oswestry, Ellesmere & Whitchurch Railway.[8] The former would run close to the SU's main line, the latter to its Welsh Branch, and both would introduce competition to towns then served only by the canal. As well as the obvious worry about the new railways injuriously affecting the canal's traffic revenue, the Board also expressed concern that the proposals would prevent the carrying out of the original intention of the conversion of most of the company's canal into railways, 'thereby seriously depreciating the value of the property'. It is interesting that more than fifteen years after conversion was suggested, it was still being contemplated. The SU realised that there was no point in opposing the proposals and that the usual protection clauses relating to the physical assets could be obtained by mutual agreement, but was 'anxious that the London & North Western Company should understand the full bearing of the schemes upon the canals'.[9]

Influence or interference?

In 1907 Sir Frederick Harrison, General Manager of the LNWR since 1893, who from 1885 had been its Chief Goods Manager, told the Royal Commission on Canals:

> I do not know of a single case where we have made use of any knowledge we may have at our disposal to divert traffic from any of the canals owned by us ... In fact we allow – to use the term not in an offensive way – the Shropshire Union Canal, who are carriers, to compete with us, and to compete with the other railway companies between South Staffordshire and the Mersey, and they also carry between North Staffordshire and the Mersey, all in competition with us.

The Commission members found this difficult to believe, but Harrison was adamant that he was correct: the SU had 'a free hand' concerning traffic.[10]

One would expect the SU and the LNWR to arrange not to work in open competition with each other, but inter-company agreements came to be much wider than that, in a way which would now be unlawful. At his first LNWR General Meeting as Chairman, Richard Moon said that the policy would be 'to work in the most friendly competition; and all we intend to go for is this, that we shall all work at equal rates and fares and under equal conditions, to which it must come in the end'.[11] This policy was actively pursued by the SU too, though, as we shall see later, the SU tended to reluctantly follow other companies' rates, rather than be the rate-fixer itself. From 1863 SU staff attended the LNWR Goods Conference.

The LNWR Board had to approve any capital expenditure by the SU. One such instance was the proposal made by the SU in August 1860 to convert the Pontcysyllte Tramroad into a locomotive railway (to be discussed in detail later in this chapter). In April 1861 a letter was received from Richard Rawlins of the Wynne Hall Colliery saying that an 8ft seam of coal had been discovered and that they would be ready in less than a month's time to forward some hundreds of tons of coal per week; this prompted the SU to stress to the LNWR the importance of an early decision. In the June the LNWR sent a committee of inspection, but the approval was not given until November the following year.

The first explicit instance of refusal to sanction capital expenditure concerned developments at Shrewsbury Wharf, which was also the site of a small SU Railway goods yard. It was proposed to buy Mr Minor's land, including his canal basin, to fill it in and make a siding to the former cheese warehouse at the end of the site. This was approved by the LNWR Board, the purchase made, and work started. However, in September 1861 Robert Skey reported that when he had met Richard Moon in Shrewsbury – this was within three months of Moon becoming Chairman of the LNWR – Moon had 'expressed a desire' for work to be halted. This was subsequently confirmed by the LNWR Board.

The one part of the Shropshire Union activities where the LNWR encouraged investment was Ellesmere Port. This particularly applied after 1889, when the Manchester Ship Canal was being constructed and a proper railway access planned from the main line railway.

Peace – and waning independence

A major reorganisation of working practices took place in 1879 'for economy and greater efficiency'. As previously mentioned, from then onwards, the Secretary of the LNWR was also Secretary of the SU. Wages and the payment of invoices were administered by the staff at Euston. Cash received at the Chester canal office was paid in via Chester station.

A report by Mr Kay, the LNWR's Chief Audit Inspector, following the integration of the accounts showed how sloppy record-keeping had been allowed to become: discrepancies were found at Ellesmere Port, Nantwich, Norbury, Trench and Shrewsbury; incorrect charges made at Birmingham, Wolverhampton and Chester; Newport and Whitchurch had allowed excessive credit periods; Market Drayton had not followed the correct accounting procedures; and the Agent at Welshpool resigned because of the cash shortage discovered. Only Manchester's and Tunstall's accounts escaped criticism.

Another round of changes took place in 1892 and 1893, with several functions being transferred to the LNWR for greater efficiency. The cartage services at Chester which the SU had provided for the LNWR were transferred, as were the similar services from the SU's wharves at Liverpool. This would have come as no surprise, as since 1889 the men and boys employed at Chester had been provided with LNWR uniforms. The SU's vans and other vehicles were to be repaired by the LNWR at Earlestown or Wolverton. Other changes involved local agents and canvassers. The keeping of canal traffic and toll accounts was brought in line with the LNWR's system for railways, made easier because the railway classification of traffic was now to be used; this meant some decentralisation, with staff being transferred to the major depots. In two instances (Liverpool and Newport) this work was undertaken by the railway station staff. The LNWR took over the cartage services in the Potteries with effect from the first day of 1896.

The year 1898 saw a simplification in the book-keeping, which also illustrated how the LNWR and its two principal associated canals were coming together. To save rendering and checking voluminous inter-company accounts, the toll to be paid by the SU to the Birmingham Canal was fixed at $6\frac{7}{10}d$ a ton, based on the average amounts for the previous three years. Similarly, for inter-company services, it was decided that the net figure (excluding Liverpool cartage) to be paid by the LNWR to the SU should be £31,000. This was increased by £5,000 when Pickford's boatage contract was transferred to the SU in 1901.

From 1880 until the demise of the SU in 1922, the meetings of the SU Board dealt with little other than formalities; the same applied to the Amalgamated Board after 1891. The day-to-day matters were dealt with by the Executive Committee. Many of these seem trivial, an extreme example (at Sir Richard Moon's last meeting) being: 'The proposed employment of a hand on alternate Sundays at 3s.6d per day to clean and feed the horses at Primrose Wharf was explained and approved.'

M.C. Reed's excellent one-volume history of the London & North Western Railway, published in 1996, which is largely concerned with managerial issues, makes just one passing mention of the LNWR's owned and leased canals. This is probably a fair reflection of the LNWR's interest in them: as long as they did not want to spend much capital money and did not cause problems for their parent company, they were left in peace, a relatively small loss being tolerated. It seems that active management, such as closing unremunerative branch canals, was considered not worth the effort.

From the 1860s until 1890, one meeting a year was usually held on an inspection boat.
In addition to their usual business, the committee members looked at the wharves, buildings and structures and made recommendations. After 1890, boat trips continued although formal committee meetings were no longer held on board. The photograph shows the SU boat *Inspector* near Colemere, c.1900. *Canal & River Trust*

CHAPTER 10 : THE SHROPSHIRE UNION RAILWAYS & CANAL COMPANY

As first built, the railway viaduct at Chirk had timber arches at each end. When these came to be replaced by masonry arches in 1858, the Great Western Railway was given permission to run a tramroad across the SU's aqueduct on the off-side. Surprisingly, seeing that the GWR was a rival, no charge was made. *Pru Stones*

Relationships with other railway companies

The 'Fighting Shrewsburys'

It was common for railway companies to be promoted locally then sold or leased to the dominant regional company on the best terms the smaller company could get. From the regional company's point of view this had the merit of enabling their network to be extended without having to raise fresh capital each time. It also meant that other people bore the speculative risk, and enabled a fair valuation to be made of the railway based on its actual construction costs and trading results. The local people got the railway they wanted, and if it was particularly successful (which rarely happened), they could sell it at a premium. Naturally they could get a better price if more than one regional company was interested.

What the local company could not wisely do was to enter into a trade war with the dominant regional company – they would almost inevitably lose. But a trade war is just what the Shrewsbury & Birmingham and Shrewsbury & Chester Railways embarked on, and their adversary was the country's (indeed the world's) most powerful railway company, the London & North Western Railway. No wonder they became known as the 'Fighting Shrewsburys'. This is not the place to discuss the details of the war, the perverse result of which was to push the Shrewsbury companies into the expanding empire of the Great Western Railway in 1854. In this book I am concerned with the impact on the Shropshire Union canal system and the incidental part it played in that war.

One of the Shropshire Union's main trades was Cumbrian iron ore conveyed from Ellesmere Port to the ironworks of the Black Country for mixing with locally-mined ore. In the autumn of 1850 the Shrewsbury Railways reduced their rates on iron ore from Saltney, on the Dee estuary, the only harbour their trains could reach without having to pass over the tracks of a company which was an ally of the LNWR.

The LNWR retaliated by persuading the board of the Birkenhead Railway to send all traffic which would normally go onto the 'Shrewsburys' by other (that is, LNWR) routes or by road. The Shropshire Union canal benefited from this as it went to or near several places which the LNWR itself did not reach, such as Ellesmere, Oswestry and Ruabon.

The forerunners of the Cambrian Railways

The first railway in mid-Wales was the Llanidloes & Newtown Railway. Authorised in 1853, its intention was to link with any of the several railways being projected to reach Newtown from Shrewsbury or Oswestry. When, for various reasons, all these proposals were withdrawn, the plan was altered so that the railway would now terminate at Newtown's canal basin. A Bill embodying this was submitted to Parliament in 1855, but that aspect was dropped on opposition for the nascent Oswestry & Newtown Railway.

Although the Llanidloes & Newtown was only twelve miles long, it was not completed until 1859. It was realised that other Newtown lines, themselves delayed, would not reach the town for another couple of years, so the concept of a branch to the canal was revived as a horse-drawn railway for goods only. This time, despite opposition from the turnpike trustees and many

147

residents of Newtown, and despite further opposition from the Oswestry & Newtown, the scheme was approved. Nothing was actually done, and in August 1860 the Shropshire Union offered to build the branch. Only a couple of months later, merger discussions between the Llanidloes & Newtown, the Oswestry & Newtown and a third local company, the Newtown & Machynlleth, started in earnest, and the canal branch was abandoned The Llanidloes & Newtown's shareholders were told that the reason was the SU's requirements for sidings and other works which were unnecessary.

In 1864 these three companies, together with the Oswestry, Ellesmere & Whitchurch Railway, merged to create the Cambrian Railways, a company which usually worked co-operatively with the LNWR. The Act gave the Earl of Powis the right to appoint a director; from 1868 until 1900 the nominee was the Hon. Robert Charles Herbert, the Third Earl's younger brother, but there seems no evidence of any special arrangements between the SU and the Cambrian Railways.

Railways in Staffordshire and Cheshire

ALTHOUGH the SU recognised that a proposed line from Uttoxeter to Stafford would benefit its railway from Stafford to Shrewsbury, it refrained from petitioning Parliament in support as it was aware that the LNWR was opposing the Bill.

One consistent aim of the SU Board was to get the toll imposed by the Trent & Mersey Canal at Wardle Lock, Middlewich, removed. (This is discussed in detail later.) The Trent & Mersey had been leased to the North Staffordshire Railway (NSR) in 1847. Two tactics were devised to put pressure on: to oppose the North Staffordshire Railway's Bills at every opportunity, and to promote a new connection between the Middlewich Branch and the Trent & Mersey. In 1852 the SU tabled a Bill for a new connection but it was later withdrawn as requested by the LNWR, who were then trying to negotiate a merger of the two railway companies. This did not come about, but a formal agreement was made in 1859 for more active co-operation. The issue of the Middlewich toll did not rank as a priority of the LNWR, despite its importance to the SU; the SU wished to oppose the NSR's Bill that year but was dissuaded by the LNWR.

When a merger between the LNWR and the Lancashire & Yorkshire Railway was discussed in 1873, the SU Board resolved that unless suitable clauses to protect its interests were obtained, the Bill should be petitioned against. Such drastic public action was never necessary as the merger did not go ahead.

The Shropshire Union canal network

APART from the developments at Ellesmere Port (the full details of which are outside the scope of this book) and the rebuilding and extension of the Ruabon Brook Railway, no major engineering works were undertaken during the life of the Shropshire Union.

Soon after the merger, repairs were put in hand to bring the Shrewsbury Canal up to the desired standard, including substituting edge rails for the cast-iron plateway rails on the Trench Incline.

The Shropshire Canal

As was stated in the last chapter, the Shropshire Canal was leased to the SU on 1 November 1849. In 1852 John Beech drew up and costed a plan for a railway through the coalfield to replace the canal, and the SU's Executive Committee resolved to refer this to Robert Stephenson or Joseph Locke.

Water supplies were an increasing concern, the problems being largely due to mining subsidence. There was a long stoppage in the winter of 1853–4. Beech investigated the possibility of providing an additional reservoir, but the best option was thought to be to accept an offer from John Horton of the Lilleshall Company to supply water from its mines through a pump at Snedshill, the cost of fixing the pump being estimated at £350.

In 1856 Beech reported that the weir at Randlay had gone down by over twelve feet and slipped laterally by about 4½ feet. In just a week about 110yd length of the embankment there had subsided by 6in. and was slipping towards the reservoir. Robert Skey, the SU's Manager, emphasised the state of the works was becoming daily worse:

> Water escaping into the pits doing there mischief for which the Company is responsible, and yet we dare not draw off the water to repair the breaches, as we have none left with which to replace it.

As an expedient, water was conveyed up the Wrockwardine Wood and Windmill Farm Inclines in tub-boats. In the five months to December 1857, for example, 5,495 boat-loads were raised, carrying a total of about 30,000 tons of water, but despite this the water level of the canal was still 8in. down. In September 1858 Skey considered that it would be impossible to keep the canal open.

Water supply was not the only problem. Following an accident at the short Snedshill Tunnel, in 1854 it was agreed that it should be opened out. On 26 September 1855 the canal broke through the roof of Oakengates Tunnel on the Shrewsbury & Birmingham Railway because a pit shaft had not been adequately capped. Joseph Locke, who had carried out the original survey had planned to take the railway 39ft below the canal but it had been built much higher. Concerns had been expressed at the time of the line's opening in November 1849 but Robert Stephenson had declared it to be 'perfectly safe'. In September 1854 the line had become part of the Great Western Railway, which accepted responsibility for the repairs.

Worse, Wrockwardine Wood Incline was falling into disrepair because of the Lilleshall Company's mining activities. Edward Jones, its Principal Mining Manager, wrote in June 1856 saying:

> I am afraid that the mining operations ... will be more injurious to you than we had at one time anticipated. The sinking may extend to the machinery and cause a depression of some feet.

And so it proved. A fissure 3in. wide opened up across the engine house and the walls supporting the drum. By 18 months later, the drum barrel and winding-out shaft had dropped so much that the top of the carriage touched when passing under.

All these troubles meant that the Shropshire Canal was likely to be lost. In November 1854 the GWR had opened its branch from Madeley Junction to Lightmoor, where there was an interchange with the Coalbrookdale Company's network of tramroads. The Wellington & Severn Junction Railway was planned to take the more difficult route from Ketley Junction (to the east of Wellington, on the GWR main line) through Horsehay and Lightmoor to Coalbrookdale. It was opened for goods and minerals as far as Horsehay in May 1857 and to Lightmoor Junction in May 1859. This became part of the GWR empire in 1861. (The extension to Coalbrookdale and across the river Severn to Buildwas was not completed until 1864.) During the 1850s the Lilleshall Company started developing its own private standard-gauge railway network, linking with the SU Railway at the Donnington exchange sidings and with the GWR main line at the Hollinswood exchange sidings.

Robert Skey repeatedly warned about the missed opportunities. For example, in September 1856 he wrote that private railway lines being projected would communicate with the GWR alone – the SU was in danger of losing 'the entire traffic of this populous and productive district'. He recommended converting the canal without delay into a railway. In his opinion the saving of the cost of working the inclined planes and the transhipment at Trench would be enough to pay at least 5% on the outlay needed 'to turn a bad canal into a good railway'.

The LNWR's directors were asked to initiate the necessary action on several occasions, with Skey's and Beech's reports being forwarded in an attempt to convince them. In November 1856 they issued the notice of intention of application to Parliament. The Act was passed in July 1857, the LNWR having agreed to meet all the costs of creating the railway. Hence it was the LNWR rather than the SU which bought the Shropshire Canal in February 1858.

As a temporary measure, permission was obtained to use the Lilleshall Company's railway from the Donnington interchange sidings for Shropshire Canal traffic, but this was conditional on the SU paying the £350 which had been promised back in 1854 for fixing the pumping engine at Snedshill. The summit level struggled on until the spring of 1859.

The construction contract for the section from the junction with the SU Railway to the summit at Priors Lee was let in August 1858, that for the continuation to Coalport in the following February. Most of the canal was closed on 1 June 1860, temporary arrangements being made for conveying the traffic. The branch line opened for goods in around September 1860 and to passengers in June 1861. In fact only the summit level of just over 2½ miles from Priors Lee to Stirchley was on the approximate line of the canal.

The canal between Tweedale Basin (below the Windmill Farm Incline) and Coalport remained open, the principal traffic being coal to the furnaces at Blists Hill. Although, strictly speaking, this was now part of the LNWR, it was administered by the SU.

Two new chains had been bought for the Hay Incline in 1859. Then in 1864 the SU suggested converting the remaining canal into a road, but this was never acted upon. The Hay Incline and the short section from there to Coalport may have been used for the last time in 1872, and certainly did not operate after 1894. It was officially abandoned in 1907. This left the pound, 1¼ miles long, between Tweedale Basin and the top of the Hay Incline. At that time the only trader using the canal was the Madeley Coal & Iron Company which conveyed coal, stone refuse, tiles and bricks between its various works. The last traffic was in about 1913 but this part of the canal was not officially abandoned until 1944.

Conversion of the Llangollen Branch?

In 1873 George Jebb submitted an estimate of the cost of converting the canal from Llangollen to Frankton and Weston Lullingfields into a narrow-gauge railway and extending it to the LNWR Shrewsbury to Crewe line at Wem. It would be interesting to know whether this was his idea, or whether he was responding to a request from a director. In any event, the Executive Committee looked at the suggestion seriously, enquiring whether they still had the powers to do this – they hadn't, the powers for railway conversion having expired and in any case never applied to this particular section of the canal system – and whether it breached any agreement with the GWR. At a subsequent meeting a simpler proposal was considered: making the interchange with the Cambrian Railways where it crossed the canal near Welsh Frankton. Moon stated that the agreement meant that the GWR would be entitled to a share of the value of the traffic passing to the Cambrian. Nothing further was done.

The Weston Branch

The branch to Weston Lullingfields, six miles long, was purely agricultural, serving no towns, and with its original purpose of linking to Shrewsbury long forgotten. Closure was considered several times but the legal advice was that Section 17 of the Regulation of Railways Act 1873 obliged the Company to keep it open. A financial appraisal using the earnings and expenditure in 1874 showed that maintenance and other costs totalling £112 exceeded the tolls of £31, but the net loss was more than offset by profit on freight (that is, on carrying) of £132.

Closure was reconsidered in 1882, prompted by gradual subsidence necessitating expenditure to raise and strengthen the embankments. As it was thought that the income was enough to cover routine maintenance, it was decided to keep it open. In 1885 George Jebb reported that the leakage from the branch was at the rate of 17 locks a day, but again the Solicitor advised that there was no power to close a canal. The first 1,300 yards of the branch, as far as Hordley Bridge, was made secure at a cost of £300, the rest of the route across the low-lying meadows being done the following year at a cost estimated at £600.

Ellesmere Port

THE full story of the development of the port and the cross-Mersey traffic deserves a book to itself, so only a bare outline will be given here.

In 1852, possession was taken back from the Bridgewater Trustees of Ellesmere Port, the SU's cross-Mersey fleet and those docks and buildings at Liverpool which were leased by the SU. The sum of £3,000 plus £150 expenses was paid in compensation.

Keeping the channel to the port open was a recurring problem, with the mud banks continually changing their position. By 1869 there were doubts that the channel could be kept open permanently even with extensive dredging, so plans and estimates were prepared for an extension of the canal by almost two miles to Poole Hall Deep, and creating a new tidal basin there. Land was purchased from the Marquess of Westminster and William Provis but the scheme was not carried out.

The docks at Ellesmere Port had no rail access until 1873 when a standard-gauge tramway was built alongside the road linking the station to the docks. All traffic along it was horse-drawn, the SU buying two horses, later increased to four, specifically for it. In 1885 the desirability of using a locomotive was discussed. A condition imposed when the land was bought from the Marquess of Westminster was that the line was to be used for a horse tramway only, but if the line was actually in the roadway (as implied by the minute) the condition did not apply. Crewe could provide a suitable locomotive for £450, but this would cost more than using horses and would provide more power than was needed, so it was decided not to go ahead.

Ellesmere Port was transformed by the Manchester Ship Canal (MSC), the 1884 revised plans of which envisaged a still-water channel along the south side of the Mersey, continuing 1¼ miles west beyond Ellesmere Port to sea locks at Eastham. It was agreed that vessels to and from Ellesmere Port would continue to have free passage to Eastham and also to Runcorn.

With the section of the MSC between Eastham and Runcorn nearing completion in 1889, the SU reviewed its commercial opportunities at Ellesmere Port and concluded that a quay 700yds long (a plan later reduced to 300yds long) with a depth of 20ft should be constructed to the west of the dock entrance. It was considered that this would be much cheaper to build if done before the water was let into the MSC. The quay wall was originally intended to be wooden, but as it proved impossible to obtain the timber, it was built in concrete instead. The necessary land was bought from the Whitby Manor Estate.

More ambitiously, Jebb was asked to make an estimate of the cost of deepening the main line of the canal. He reported that the approximate cost, including the associated works, would be £895,475, or about £13,500 a mile.

The section of the MSC which passed Ellesmere Port opened

Repairs at Berriew Aqueduct, 1889. *Canal & River Trust*

in 1891; from then onwards, the cross-Mersey boats had to pass through Eastham Lock. Although this relieved the SU of the problem of trying to keep a channel to the docks open, it brought new problems. It added half an hour to the time taken for the passage from Liverpool, the entrance to Eastham Locks was more difficult (in a two month period 19 flats sustained minor damage), and the speed of water flow in the Poole Hall rock cutting during high spring tides almost doubled, necessitating the provision of extra tugs which the MSC undertook to provide or pay for.

The horse tramway had always been considered a temporary arrangement. In 1889 the decision was made to construct a locomotive railway but land purchase took longer than expected. The railway was completed at the end of 1894.

In 1907 Jebb gave evidence to the Royal Commission on Canals. He said that in the previous 35 years about £263,000 had been spent at Ellesmere Port, including almost £80,000 on a six-storey grain warehouse, 70% of its throughput going out by canal and 30% by rail. He added that these works could not have been carried out if the LNWR had not provided the money.

Aqueducts and bridges

THE towpath over Pontcysyllte Aqueduct was replaced in wood in 1864 and again in 1879, this time using wrought-iron buckle plates. The LNWR's Engineer, William Baker reported on the 'magnificent structure', as he described it, in 1866. The only significant problems he found were that the south abutment had moved inwards and the iron ribs of the southern arch had broken in several places; these he attributed to leakage between the end of the trough and the embankment. He recommended that the trough be lengthened and the ribs repaired. The canal was closed for only eight days for the work to be done. The aqueduct was scraped and tarred in 1886.

Chirk Aqueduct needed extensive repairs in 1865 when a portion of the south arch fell and was rebuilt. More work was done in 1869, when a full metal trough, with side as well as base plates, was put in the whole length of the structure at a cost of £1,400. Following considerable leakage through the old waterway walls at each end of the trough, in 1907 new walls were put in upon a concrete invert, 50ft in length at the north end and 80ft at the south end.

Berriew Aqueduct needed extensive repairs in 1889, costing over £3,000, more than double the original estimate. At the same time, the district council agreed to meet the additional cost of enlarging the arch over the road. The canal was closed for two months. Two years earlier it was shown that the annual profit from the former Montgomeryshire Canal, taking account of maintenance and rents, was only £432, plus £1,664 profit from the carrying of traffic to and from the canal. Faced with the bill for the aqueduct, it may have seemed economically sensible to close all or part of the canal, but because traffic was still being carried the Board of Trade would almost certainly have refused an application for abandonment.

The Vyrnwy Aqueduct had given problems since it was built. In 1890 some of the associated flood arches had to be rebuilt and the following year the cutwaters of the aqueduct needed considerable repair. Other flood arches were rebuilt in 1907.

The decay of the brick arches at the ends of the Longdon Aqueduct led in 1899 to an evaluation of traffic on the western end of the former Shrewsbury Canal, but again the Solicitor advised that as there was still some traffic, an application to the Board of Trade would probably fail. Jebb considered that repairs would cost £1,500, but he was instructed to spend only such money upon it as was absolutely necessary for current purposes. Further deterioration in the winter of 1906/07 resulted in the river arch having to be supported with timber centres. It was agreed that Jebb could repair the arches at the western end and also the retaining wall on the north side.

Major repairs were needed to the aqueducts at Aberbechan (1859, following a partial collapse, and 1908), Brithdir (1867) and Pimley (1869 and 1899).

In the last quarter of the 19th century the development of traction engines and the increasing weight of vehicles put a strain on bridges, a problem which got even worse in the 20th century. The legal responsibility was not finally settled until a court case confirmed that canal companies were liable only to provide bridges strong enough for the traffic at the time they were built.

Locks

BEESTON Iron Lock, the site of which had caused so much trouble to the Chester Canal and the Ellesmere & Chester Canal, collapsed again in 1882, closing the canal for a month, during which time all possible traffic had to be sent via Calveley railway interchange sidings. The tie rods on the towpath side had failed and the floor plates, both inside and outside had given way. A new timber floor was put in and the sides strengthened and secured. George Jebb commented that the work proved very tedious and difficult because of the quicksands under the lock.

Subsidence, breaches and slippages

THE most frustrating of the maintenance problems must have been the subsidence of the Lea Hall embankment, about half a mile west of where the Middlewich Branch is crossed by the LNWR's West Coast Main Line, because the cause was in no way the fault of the SU or its engineers. In this part of south Cheshire, water was pumped into the salt strata then the resultant brine extracted. This inevitably led to subsidence for which no compensation was paid.

In 1868 the Clerk to the river Weaver Trustees wrote to the SU, alleging that the canal embankment 'was in a most unsafe condition', and if it breached it would cause inestimable damage. Beech, the SU's engineer, thought that no part of the embankment showed any weakness; nevertheless he had instructed men to strengthen it and also reduce the depth of the canal water to five or six feet. William Baker was asked to inspect it, which he did in the company of Edward Leader Williams, the Weaver Navigation's Engineer. He was dissatisfied with Beech's work, commenting that the banks were now 'very steep, almost perpendicular, and in some places sustained or kept up by the hedge'. He recommended making the slopes more secure by reducing their steepness. He was sure that there would be further settlement, as pumping of brine was continuing vigorously.

The Brine Pumping Act 1891 provided compensation to owners of property affected by subsidence but specifically excluded canals and railways. As forecast, the problem at Lea Hall persisted, and in 1900 Jebb reported that the Alkali Company was boring only 40 yards away from the canal. The embankment slipped again and had to be strengthened, but subsidence continued even after local pumping had ceased.

A serious breach occurred at Whixall Moss in 1868, when 120yds of the towpath side were carried away. This had been caused by the embankment being weakened on one side by peat extraction lowering the land level, exacerbated by the prolonged drought that summer.

The following year the canal breached at Soudley, south of Market Drayton, on the 17-mile pound between Tyrley and Wheaton Aston. If it had not been for the quick action of a banktender putting stop planks in and closing the gate designed to protect Shebdon embankment, this could have had more serious consequences – as it was only two cottages were flooded and fish were stranded in fields of corn. The cause, as so often, was a blocked culvert overloaded with water after a heavy rainstorm.

In 1903 the culvert of the Morlas Brook was overwhelmed because of exceptionally heavy rain, the water flowed over the canal and caused a 40ft breach in the bank. The canal was closed for almost a month.

Leaks on the 'Water Line' west of Pontcysyllte, with the occasional breach, were a recurring problem. The most persistent (though not dangerous) loss was through the slate rock in the Llangollen area, which Jebb cured through erecting 482 yards of walling, reducing the daily loss from the equivalent of 120 locks to just one or two.

In 1885 the main line was closed for a week because of leakage at Market Drayton caused by the embankment being honeycombed with rat holes. About 300 locks of water was lost but luckily there was no damage to downstream property.

A thunderstorm, accompanied by what was described as 'an unprecedented fall of water', on 3 June 1908 caused considerable damage near the pumping station at Newtown. The culvert under the road was unable to cope; the water overflowed, washing away some 30 yards of the road and its parapet wall, and damaged one of the company's cottages. The debris filled in the canal for a length of 70yds. Montgomeryshire County Council rebuilt the road, taking part of the company's land for the retaining wall, with a 6ft high corrugated iron fence, described as 'unclimbable', on top.

In 1912 the canal was closed at Froncysyllte for 18 days because of a slip attributed to the recent heavy rains causing water to get between the limestone cliff and the puddle of the canal. There was further leakage nearby the following year, closing the canal for 14 days.

Breaches inevitably meant that boats were delayed. Food and general goods traffic would be taken on by drays; bulk cargoes were left on board. It was usual for the boatmen to be employed to assist in mending the breach.

The cuttings of the main line, particularly those at Woodseaves (south of Market Drayton) and Cowley (near Gnosall) frequently suffered from slippages, as indeed they still do.

Weirs – and the Salmon Fisheries Acts

LEGISLATION regarding salmon dates back some 700 years to the reign of Edward I. His son, Edward II, passed a law regulating weirs, but it proved ineffective as the appointed commissioners had little power.

Following reports of diminishing numbers of salmon, a Royal Commission was appointed in 1860 to inquire into the salmon fisheries of England and Wales with a view to increasing the supply of 'a valuable article of food for the benefit of the public'. A series of Acts between 1861 and 1873 consolidated the requirements, strengthened the controls, established local Boards of Conservancy, and appointed national Inspectors of Fisheries.

The Shropshire Union was responsible for four weirs: at Newtown, where a waterwheel powered machinery to lift water from the Severn into the canal; Penarth Weir, two miles further downstream, where there was the main feeder into the southern part of the former Montgomeryshire Canal; Abertanat Weir, near the confluence of the rivers Tanat and Vyrnwy, where the water was fed into the northern part of the former Montgomeryshire Canal; and Horseshoe Falls near Llantisilio, where water was taken from the Dee into the summit level of the former Ellesmere Canal. In addition the Dee was blocked by the dam and outflow of Lake Bala, though no mention was made in the minutes of this in the context of the Salmon Fisheries Acts.

A salmon ladder was put alongside Penarth Weir in 1863 but the weir itself was damaged by floods in January 1867 and temporary repairs made. George Jebb drew up plans for a two-fall weir and fish pass. These were constructed in 1870 at a cost of £1,294, but the fish pass was almost destroyed by a flood that autumn. The following year a new fish pass was built and the weir strengthened at a total cost of £180.

The gratings at the entrances to the feeders were the main matters of dispute with the Inspectors of Fisheries. Back in

Chapter 10 : The Shropshire Union Railways & Canal Company

One of the Shropshire Union's cottages was damaged in the flood at Newtown in 1908.
Shropshire Union Canal Society, Lindop Collection

1810, following complaints from 'gentlemen who reside near the banks of the river Dee', a grating had been installed to try to prevent salmon fry from passing into the canal at Horseshoe Falls. It was replaced in 1868 with one intended to be compliant with the 1861 Act, and similar gratings were installed at the Penarth and Tanat Weirs in the following year. In 1874, some of the bars in the grating at Horseshoe Falls were removed because the accumulation of weeds was impeding the passage of water. The Dee Fisheries Board wanted their immediate restoration, but this was not done until the Board took legal action against the SU.

In 1882 the company received a letter from the solicitor of the tenant of Carreghofa Mill, demanding that the Tanat grating be removed because the restricted water flow was interfering with the working of the mill. The legal requirement for the grating was explained.

In 1885, the Severn Fisheries Board wrote to say that the grating at the Tanat Weir was 'most objectionable', then a few months later gave formal notice that 'all agreements or alleged agreements' were terminated, and that unless gratings to the following specifications were installed within 17 days, the company would be prosecuted:

– From 14 February to 31 May there was to be a grating in twelve sections each composed of flat iron bars, three inches broad, and a quarter of an inch thick, fixed horizontally as regards their length, and at a slope of 45 degrees as regards their breadth, and $7/16$ths of an inch apart.

– From 1 June to 13 February that grating may be replaced by one in twelve sections each composed of round iron bars $5/8$ths of an inch in diameter, placed vertically two inches apart.

The committee decided to oppose the proceedings but the county magistrates at Oswestry found against the SU and fined it £1 plus costs. The committee instructed its solicitor to apply to the Home Office for remission of the fine – no doubt the solicitor's letter cost more than the fine – but the Home Office refused.

The 1886 1:2,500 Ordnance Survey map shows a 'tramway' alongside the feeder from Penarth Weir to the canal but this had gone by the time of the 1902 map. Jebb had told the Shropshire Union's Executive Committee in 1881 that the rails lent by the Birmingham Canal Company for use at Penarth could not be spared at present. In the summers of 1884 and 1885 advantage was taken of the low water in the Severn to thoroughly examine and repair the weir at Penarth (and the weir at Newtown). Presumably a temporary track had been laid to assist with moving material, and the map's surveyor had mistaken this for a permanent structure.

In 1887 the Inspector of Fisheries visited Newtown following a dispute concerning the weir by the water pump: Jebb thought it was adequate as a salmon weir but the Severn Conservancy did not. The Inspector backed the Conservators. He wanted the existing weir to be reduced in height and an extra weir put in above it, forming two equal steps. He wasn't particularly concerned about its exact design or location, permitting it to be wherever was the easiest for construction. The work was done in the following summer.

153

Water supply to the Main Line

SHORTAGE of water in summer had been a recurring problem. An agreement had been made in 1856 with Mr Giffard of Chillington Hall for the SU to take up to 3ft of water from his lake, on payment of £100 a foot, and this was occasionally called upon in later years.

In 1867 William Baker recommended that the maximum water level in Belvide Reservoir be raised from 20ft to 24ft, thus increasing the capacity by almost one-half, from 13,600 locks to 20,300 locks. (The capacity of a lock was assumed to be about 27,500 gallons.) John Beech disagreed, saying that during the winter strong westerly winds threw spray over the turnpike road (Watling Street), sometimes making it nearly impassable. After further discussions, it was agreed that the head could be increased if new drains were cut to an outfall below the dam and a fence built to reduce spray.

Raising the water level caused alarm locally – the breach in July 1875 of Cwm Carn Reservoir, a feeder for the Monmouthshire Canal, which had resulted in the death of twelve people, was fresh in the memory. In February 1877 the Revd E.J. Wrottesley, vicar of Brewood, wrote to the Board of Trade on behalf of several local residents, saying that Belfields Reservoir (as he called it), 207 acres in area, was 'owing to the late heavy fall of rain, far too full, and in consequence of the apparently unsafe state of a portion of the banks, in a very dangerous condition'. He said he had written to the canal company but they had not replied. George Jebb inspected the reservoir and reported that the dams were in a perfect state of repair with 'no appearance of a slip', that they were 'of sufficient dimensions to impound with safety 24 feet of water' but that the level was only 22ft 6in. In a later letter Revd Wrottesley asserted that there was leakage of water from under the dam onto the turnpike road, but Jebb stated that this was not so, but a pipe which carried water from a land spring under the road had broken. Although these responses satisfied the Board of Trade,[12] Jebb recommended to the SU's Executive Committee that a waste weir should be constructed at the south end of the dam, with a brick channel taking overflow water to the outlet stream. It is also notable that the water level was never afterwards allowed to exceed 22ft (17,000 locks). To this day the field below the dam tends to be wet, but the Canal & River Trust's engineers are satisfied that this is not because water leaks through the dam itself but because it permeates through the underlying land.

Knighton Reservoir had never been a success. A visit by the Committee of Inspection in 1868 prompted a discussion as to its future, recommending that either its defects should be remedied or it should be disposed of. The western end of the dam head was puddled, which had not been done before, then the floor of the reservoir was puddled up to the 8ft contour. Even when filled to that level, it would hold less than 1,600 locks of water. In March 1873, a few months after the works were completed it was recorded as holding 10ft 6in. of water, but it rarely again attained that level. But in 1875 it was reported as leaking again; the new puddle was suspected to have been disturbed deliberately – a suspicion repeated following an incident five years later. It probably wasn't a coincidence that at the same meeting as the alleged danger of Belvide Reservoir was considered, the Committee decided to put in a waste weir at Knighton 'to relieve the reservoir when unnecessarily full'.

The third source of water was the Staffordshire & Worcestershire Canal (SWC) at Autherley Junction. As most of its traffic was to or from Wolverhampton, thus bringing a lockful of water into the SWC for every boat movement, the SU argued that this implied that this amount of water should be passed on. The SU thought this had been eventually agreed in 1867, but the SWC stated that this was not so but that they were 'desirous at all times to the utmost of their power to accommodate the Shropshire Union Company with respect to the supply of water' – but what this meant in practice was that they would continue to pass excess water in winter, when it wasn't needed, but less in summer when it was. The matter of the water supplies was closely connected with two other matters, the toll imposed at Autherley Junction, and the tolls imposed on traffic passing along the half mile of the SWC between Aldersley and Autherley Junctions, which are discussed later in this chapter.

Knighton Reservoir photographed from the waste weir. Although the reservoir has been out of use for many decades, it is still managed by the Canal & River Trust and subject to a safety inspection every six months. *Author*

A further potential source of water was Wolverhampton sewage works, which was built alongside the canal in the mid 1870s. Initially, outflow from the works into the canal had been refused, but in 1897 it was claimed that the water was now perfectly clear and free from taint. Wolverhampton Corporation offered to sell water to the canal after it had been filtered by a 'special process' which they were experimenting upon. The Engineer investigated, but it was decided that it was not desirable at present to make an arrangement. This decision was reversed in the 1920s, and today this is the principal source of water for the canal, though water from Belvide Reservoir is sometimes used in mid-summer and also to 'sweeten' the canal water for the sake of the fish stock.[13]

Extremes of weather

AFTER 1860 the minutes included several references to weather. Every few years the canal suffered a closure in winter because of ice. For example, in January 1867 the SU system except for Ellesmere Port to Chester was closed for 20 days, traffic required urgently being sent by rail.

The coldest temperature, minus 4°Fahrenheit (minus 20° Celsius), was recorded at several places on the SU network on 23 December 1870. Again, only the canal between Ellesmere Port and Chester was able to be kept open and much traffic was forwarded by train. Four horses were injured when trying to clear the canal; two of them had to be destroyed.

The winter of 1878/79 was particularly bad. Ice-breaking cost £803, of which £367 was hire of horses; more importantly, there were concerns about regaining the traffic lost. 1880/81 was another bad winter, the canal being closed for 24 days because of ice, followed by an 'extraordinary flood' which threatened many embankments.

In 1886 canal ice resulted in the railway line near Chester being closed for a while: ice blocked a waste weir, causing the water in the canal to overflow, which brought down a portion of the south wing wall of the tunnel.

Less frequently, water shortages interfered with traffic. For example, during the drought in the summer of 1888 as much traffic as possible was transferred to the railway. In the summer of 1896 there was so little rain that Belvide Reservoir was totally run down.

Maintenance facilities and offices

AFTER the merger, the central stores were located at Chester. The engineering depots of the constituent companies continued in use. The relative importance of the depots can be gauged from the number of maintenance boats located at each in 1884: 21 at Norbury, 11 at Chester (Cow Lane), 11 at Ellesmere and 7 at Welshpool. In addition, there were 15 at Ellesmere Port.

At Ellesmere, major alterations to the shed were made in 1879. Norbury acquired an additional storage shed in 1903. Steam-powered sawmills were used at Chester, Ellesmere and Norbury; they also each had a portable steam pump for draining locks.

In 1884 an agreement was made with Mr Davis of Whixall to extract clay for puddling from his land at a rate of 3*d* per cubic yard. Because the clay was almost exhausted, in 1911 an agreement was made with Mr Lea to extract clay from his adjacent field. (In the 1960s these clay pits were flooded and became Whixall Marina.)

In 1883 a fire broke out at the Tower Wharf offices in Chester, destroying part of the back of the building. As a gesture of thanks, £20 was distributed amongst those staff who had helped stop the fire from spreading. Other payments were made to the Chester Volunteer Fire Brigade and Chester Waterworks. Rebuilding cost £1,734, but insurance covered only £1,007.

Wharves

THROUGHOUT the period of SU management, there was a general policy of obtaining control of wharves. Those which the predecessor companies had built and then leased out were taken back; also many private wharves were leased.

The SU took over the lease of the wharf at Market Drayton in 1850. When in 1877 the freehold was auctioned, the SU bid but the price went above the amount the person bidding on their behalf was authorised to pay. The following year it was discovered that the purchaser was George Wilkinson, the SU's agent there. He then offered to sell the property to the Shropshire Union but it decided to rent for 30 years at £115 a year with power to sublet. John Hazledine became a subtenant at £60 a year for 14 years; this period was later extended to 21 years. George Wilkinson remained as the company's agent as

Welshpool wharf in 1970, with the warehouse occupied by the Montgomery-shire County Council. *John Howat*

155

Berwick wharf on the former Shrewsbury Canal. Railway & Canal Historical Society

well as its landlord. He died in 1881; in 1886 his executors offered to sell the wharf to the Shropshire Union for £3,100; it refused, but finally in 1899 the deal was done for £2,750. It was then discovered that the SU had no legal power to buy land, so a clause was added to a Bill being presented to Parliament the following year.

Edstaston Wharf, on the Prees Branch, was leased from 1860, and the lease of a warehouse at Ellesmere was taken over in 1905. Wappenshall Wharf with its warehouses had been leased from the Duke of Sutherland since about 1850; in 1911 the larger warehouse was repaired and a small hoist installed.

New wharves were made, such as Pant (1864), Edgmond (1865), Little Onn (1881), Fenns Bank (1887), Quoisley (1899), Tattenhall (1901) and Hack Green (1905).

Improvements to wharves and warehouses continued right up to the first decade of the 20th century. The biggest development at Chester was the building of a bonded warehouse, opened in 1877 and extended in 1879 and 1889. In the market towns, new or extended warehouses were built at Welshpool (1864 and 1881), Newport (1864), Llangollen (1865), Market Drayton (1870, 1887 and 1903) and Whitchurch (1877 and 1893).

Small warehouses and sheds were put up at many village wharves, including: Brynderwen (1864), Berriew (1864 and 1893), Chirk (1865), Bettisfield (1865), St Martins (1865 and 1907), Platt Lane (1865 and 1905), Garthmyl (1866), Rodington (1870 and 1906), Newbridge (1872), Belan (1872), Queen's Head (1873 and 1887, enlarged 1895, 1902 and 1905), Marbury (1875), Norbury (extension, 1877), Trevor (1884), Long Lane (1885), Brithdir (1885), Bunbury (1887), Tyddyn (1896), Tetchill (1901), Hordley (1901), Hindford (1903), Hampton Bank (1904), Cowley (1905) and Audlem (1905).

In 1869 discussions were held with Thomas Horton, General Manager of the Lilleshall Company to make the Humber Arm better suited for its traffic. The Duke of Sutherland, the owner of the wharf at the end of the Humber Arm, agreed a wharfage rate of ½d a ton. The Lilleshall Company's tramroad was converted into a standard-gauge railway in 1870. The importance of this traffic is shown by an eight year agreement made in 1880: 15 to 20 boatloads of limestone from Trevor Rocks and 5 to 7½ boatloads of haematite from Ellesmere Port was to be supplied each week. The round trip from Trevor Rocks to the Humber Arm and back took eight days, or nine and a half if the boat was laden on its return journey with coke or bricks etc.

An ulterior motive for the SU endorsing the proposal was that it was hoped that the Trench Incline, expensive to maintain and operate, could be abandoned, together with the former Wombridge Canal above the incline. This was not to come about. Coincidentally, only a couple of months after this was mooted, a boy drowned in the canal above the incline, and the inquest jury commented that the canal there was 'in a bad state'.

A few basins were constructed by the firms they served. In 1870 an agreement was made with Messrs Nettlefold & Chamberlain to pay half the estimated £1,100 cost of a basin for their proposed ironworks at Hadley, on the Trench Branch. The following year the SU's Executive Committee resolved to rebuild the locks on the Trench Branch to make them usable by standard narrow boats, presumably principally for this new trade, but the work was never carried out.

Railway/canal interchange facilities

ALTHOUGH railways came to cross the Shropshire Union canal network at several places, few interchange facilities were developed.

When the Shrewsbury & Chester Railway was constructed in 1847/48 an interchange basin was created at Rednal. The agree-

Chapter 10 : The Shropshire Union Railways & Canal Company

ment specified that it was to be used only for goods where the canal and railway were not in competition, which was largely traffic from the New British Iron Company at Acrefair. The Great Western Railway took over the line in 1854; the agreement continued but in 1862 a long-running dispute started about its interpretation. The arbitrator, John Robinson McClean MP (promoter of the South Staffordshire Railway) decided that the SU should pay the GWR half the money the latter had spent on land and works in excess of the amount the SU had spent, plus interest at 5%. The GWR had claimed £19,002; the settlement was £4,240. By 1873 all interchange traffic there had ceased. The committee decided to pull down the buildings (presumably wooden) and reuse them elsewhere, and the site was let to a manufacturer of blasting powder.

At Calveley, where the LNWR's line from Crewe to Chester came close to the canal north of Barbridge Junction, sidings were laid to a wharf in 1860. This was used not only for destinations not served by the SU's boats but also to some extent for goods going to Manchester. Principal traffics included slates from the Ceiriog Valley and Pentrefelin, timber from Montgomeryshire, bricks and pipes from Trevor, and grain from Ellesmere Port.

More problematical was a proposed railway/canal interchange at Chester. Two sites were discussed: at the station, necessitating the construction of a branch canal, or to the west side of the canal between the junction with the Dee Branch and the Cheyney Lane bridge. The former proposal would have needed a lock because of the difference in land levels, and there would have been water supply issues. The latter proposal was therefore included in a Bill submitted to Parliament by the Chester & Holyhead Railway in 1852, but it was later withdrawn.

A GWR map dated 1884 shows a travelling crane enabling interchange between the canal and a siding at Llangollen Road, just to the south of Whitehouses tunnel. No further information is known.[14]

As mentioned earlier, a proposal for the Llanidloes & Newtown Railway to have a link to the canal basin at Newtown was approved by Parliament, but the formation of the Cambrian Railways rendered the link superfluous.

In 1879 an agreement was made with the Potteries, Shrewsbury & North Wales Railway ('The Potts') for an interchange wharf where the canal crossed the railway south of Llanymynech. The wharf was built, 93 tons being transhipped in the June, but as the railway company went bankrupt the following year, the traffic was short-lived.

Tramroad wharves

The tramroads in which the Shropshire Union was actively involved, the Ruabon Brook Railway and the Glyn Valley Tramway, are discussed in detail at the end of this chapter.

The previous chapters referred to several places where private tramroads went from quarries or industrial sites to canalside wharves. ('Tramroad' is used here to describe any narrow-gauge horse-powered railway, regardless of whether it used plateway rails, where the flange was on the rails not the wheels, or edge-rails, where the flange was on the wheels. In many cases little is known about them: rarely the dates of operation, and sometimes not even the type of track or the gauge.)

Some of these early tramroads survived into the 'Shropshire Union' era:

- Welshpool, from Stondart Quarry (stone): Closed by 1854; some of the route within the town was later used by the Welshpool & Llanfair Light Railway. This used edge-rails; the gauge is not known.
- Llanymynech, from Llanymynech Rocks (limestone): Probably survived until about 1899. Certainly in later days it used edge-rails; 2ft 0in. gauge.
- Pant, from Crickheath Hill (limestone): Still operating in the 1870s. Type of track not known; 4ft gauge (or thereabouts).
- Crickheath, from Porth-y-waen (limestone): In use until 1913. Plateway; 2ft 6in. gauge.
- Gronwen, from Morda (coal): Closed about 1879. Rails an inverted 'T'; gauge 3ft 1in.
- Moreton, from Moreton Hall Colliery: No details known.
- Gledrid, from Upper Chirk Bank Colliery: No details known, indeed it may have closed before 1846. The route was later used by the Glyn Valley Tramway.
- Chirk, from Black Park Colliery: Plateway; gauge not known. Converted to standard-gauge railway about 1847.
- Froncysyllte, from Pen-y-Graig Quarries (limestone): Originally plateway, later converted to 2ft gauge edge-rail. Part of the system survived until 1956.
- Between Trevor and Llangollen, from Trevor Rocks (limestone): Four separate lines, developed over a long period; some originally plateways, later 2ft gauge edge-rails. The last line closed about 1940.
- Lubstree wharf, at the end of the Humber Arm: Tramroad from the Lilleshall Company's ironworks and coal mines. Converted into a standard gauge railway in 1870; closed 1924.

The one significant tramroad built in the Shropshire Union era was from the slate quarries near the Horseshoe Pass to the canal wharf at Pentrefelin. Constructed between 1852 and 1857, it had edge rails and a 3ft gauge. A siding from the newly-built railway between Llangollen and Corwen was made in the late 1860s, giving an alternative to canal transport. The tramway ceased operating in 1890.

A few short-lived tramroads post-dated the creation of the Shropshire Union – some are known only from their appearance on maps, further information being particularly difficult to obtain:

- Queen's Head, short line from sand-pit: No details of track or gauge known.
- St Martin's Moor, from Ifton Rhyn (coal): No details known.
- Gledrid, short line from brick kilns: No details known.
- Chirk Bank, from Quina Colliery: Opened 1871 but probably little used. No details known.

157

THE SHROPSHIRE UNION CANAL

from Penybont brick works: Operated from ... about 1881, when replaced by a standard-gauge railway. Edge-rails; gauge approximately 2ft 6in.

– Gnosall: Tramway system in the brickworks north of Cowley Tunnel and another in a brickworks south of Cowley Tunnel, both shown on the Ordnance Survey map surveyed in 1900 but not on either the 1880 or 1920 maps.

Traffic and trade

As a transport company, the SU's finances were dependent on the national economy and the health of the industrial economy in the area it served, most particularly the trade of the iron industry of the Black Country (and, to a lesser extent, the east Shropshire and the Ruabon areas) and the industries of the Potteries. The American Civil War of 1861–5 affected exports through Liverpool which, together with the increasing railway competition, prompted major cost-cutting by the SU, with many redundancies, both amongst the salaried and waged employees. Industrial output was influenced by local factors, such as strikes by miners in 1864, 1872 and 1890, by workers in the Black Country iron trade in 1865 and 1867, and by Liverpool dockers in 1890. The strikes in several industries in 1911, followed by the miner's strike in 1912, which also closed several factories, caused the most serious interference with traffic.

The iron industry

THE iron industry in the Black Country grew vigorously until the 1850s but thereafter declined. In 1870 iron and steel production totalled 589,000 tons, 9.9% of the UK total; by 1890 it was 327,000 tons, 4.1% of the total. Thereafter until the First World War it recovered slightly but nevertheless stayed below 5% of national production. A similar though not quite so extreme trend was followed in north Staffordshire. Iron and steel production in Shropshire declined rapidly over a relatively short period: from 121,000 tons in 1875 to 45,000 tons ten years later.

The reason for the changes were a combination of technical, geological and geographical. Also, West Midlands ironmasters tended to be stubbornly conservative, reluctant to innovate and invest.

During the central third of the 19th century most production was wrought iron. The Bessemer process for bulk production of mild steel was developed in the late 1850s and early 1860s but needed ores free of phosphorus to produce quality steel, hence

Pentrefelin: The line at the bottom of the photograph led to the wharf; the line crossing the lift bridge went to the slate dressing building and to the interchange with the railway.
Llangollen Museum, Gareth Benjamin Collection

large quantities of haematite ore were brought in from Cumbria and Spain. The dominance of the original Bessemer process was short-lived, as first the 'open hearth' and then the Gilchrist-Thomas process, both of which could use phosphoric pig iron, became established.

The various iron-founding industries served by the SU's boats exhausted much of their local ironstone during the 19th century. Iron ore output in the West Midlands (Staffordshire, Shropshire and Worcestershire) reduced from 3,061,000 tons in 1856 to 1,689,000 tons in 1860, then stayed reasonably steady until 1885 after which it declined sharply to 877,000 tons in 1893. Meanwhile the area still had the coal, the plant and the expertise, so a new important traffic flow developed: iron ore brought in through the Mersey ports, then conveyed to the foundries and forges – and, if these were canalside, the SU had a natural advantage. However, the exhaustion of the minerals also led to some industries being relocated: for example, the Wolverhampton Corrugated Iron Company moved to Ellesmere Port in 1904 to gain easier access to raw steel, increasingly obtained from South Wales or Belgium.

As well as ironstone and coal, the iron industry needed fluxing limestone, and the SU had a long-standing traffic in limestone from Trevor Rocks, Froncysyllte, Porth-y-waen and Llanymynech to the Black Country and to the industrial area of east Shropshire.

The fluxing-stone trade from Trevor Rocks and the Llanymynech Branch was almost abandoned in 1864. It was revived by the Llangollen Lime & Fluxingstone Company, a private company led by Henry Robertson (the owner of Brymbo Ironworks) but whose owners included Alfred Wragge (the SU's General Manager) and Charles Potts (its Solicitor). It took over the lease of the Trevor quarries and started operation in 1872, principally to supply the Lilleshall Company. As before, although most of the stone was carried direct to the customer, a stock of a few thousand tons was kept at Nantwich. The agreement between the SU, the Lilleshall Company and the quarrying company was extended for a further seven years in 1889, with 1,200 tons of stone (60 boat-loads) a month to be supplied, subject to trade fluctuations. At about the same time, the SU agreed to put in a tramroad inclined plane at Trevor Rocks at an estimated cost of £650 in exchange for stone, free of charge except the royalty payment, for surfacing towpaths. In 1893 the committee must have been shocked to hear that the quarrying company owed nearly nine months' payments, but rather less surprised the following year when it went into voluntary liquidation, still owing the SU more than £1,300. Yet another company was then formed to take over the quarries but it too soon went into liquidation. The fluxing-stone traffic had all gone by the end of the century as it had transferred to rail.

A short-lived but lucrative traffic during 1883–85 was iron pipes from the Woodside Iron Works at Dudley to the Oswestry area for Messrs Cochrane's contract for the pipeline from the Vyrnwy Reservoir to Liverpool.

Black Park wharf at Chirk in 1951, but no doubt looking much as it did a hundred years earlier.
Ian Wright / Derek Chaplin

The coal industry

COAL, the principal traffic of canals nationally, was as far as the SU was concerned essentially a local traffic: from east Shropshire to Shrewsbury and along the Newport Branch to Market Drayton and other destinations on the Main Line; from Chirk and Trevor to towns on the Welsh Branch such as Whitchurch, Welshpool and Newtown; and Flintshire coal through Chester to Nantwich. Rail competition resulted in the loss of some of the coal traffic; for example, the amount transported by canal from the Ruabon coalfield to Ellesmere and Whitchurch reduced from 8,310 tons in 1864 to 1,145 tons ten years later.

Canalside gas works at Shrewsbury, Whitchurch, Ellesmere, Welshpool (until 1862) and Brewood were major consumers of coal, the best coal for gas coming from the south Lancashire coalfield. The gas works at Newport, Market Drayton and Newtown were not canalside, and the business there was lost when the railways opened; indeed the new gas works at Welshpool was deliberately built alongside the railway.

Building materials

THE long-established building-stone traffic from the quarries at Cefn Mawr continued, probably until the 1870s.

Slates were a regular traffic from above Llangollen and from the Ceiriog Valley, some to Calveley for transhipment to northern and midland cities, with some going as far as London. George Borrow in his reminiscences *Wild Wales*, published in 1862, referred to a conversation with a boatman about this long-distance traffic:

> The boats carried slates – that he had frequently gone as far as Paddington by the canal – that he was generally three weeks on the journey – that the boatmen and their families lived in the little cabins aft – that the boatmen were all Welsh – that they could read English, but little or no Welsh – that English was a much more easy language to read than Welsh – that they passed by many towns, among others Northampton, and that he liked no place so much as Llangollen.[15]

The Ceiriog Granite Company produced stone setts for road surfacing in towns. By the last decade of the 19th century crushed stone for macadamised road-making had become an important product. In 1903 some 20,000 tons was transhipped at Chirk, which prompted the SU to agree to construct a tippler there.

Brick and tile traffic was provided by J.C. Edwards at Trevor and Penybont. On the Main Line near Bridge 32, south of Gnosall, Belshaw's had a brickworks where a steam-powered tramroad lowered bricks in small trucks to the wharf. The canalside brickyard south of Uffington on the former Shrewsbury Canal also provided a few loads.

Other traffics

THE agricultural limestone business, once so important, had virtually ceased by the mid-1860s. By then the Weston Branch had no active lime-kilns; there were none between Frankton Junction and Whitchurch; and just those at Quina Brook on the Prees Branch, which continued in operation until the start of the 20th century.

A major bulk traffic was china clay imported at Ellesmere Port and travelling along the Middlewich Branch to the Potteries. The boats returned with ceramics.

In the first half of the 19th century grain from the farms of south Cheshire and north Shropshire had been a significant traffic but as the century progressed the grain traffic in the opposite direction became much more important, the imported grain going to Chester and inland mills such as those at Wrenbury and Maesbury. Much of the grain came from Canada, but some from as far away as the Black Sea. In 1880 the agent responsible for Shropshire and the border area reported that the summer's good English harvest had 'limited the foreign grain' and so had 'considerably affected the company's traffic'.

Other long-standing traffics included timber from Montgomeryshire to the Midlands and Manchester, especially pit-props for the mines in the Black Country, and cheese, particularly from Whitchurch and Nantwich to Manchester.

The minutes alluded to other traffics but it has not been possible to ascertain how significant or long-lasting they were. Nevertheless they show the types of products conveyed by the SU in the last half of the 19th century: manure (probably 'night soil' and road sweepings) from Birmingham and Smethwick to Market Drayton and Audlem; hay from Whitchurch to the Black Country and from Oswestry to Chester, presumably for fodder; potatoes from Wem to Birmingham; flour from Chester to Manchester; bark from Welshpool to Warrington; oil cake from Liverpool to Shrewsbury; guano from Liverpool to Welshpool and Newtown; slates brought by coast from North Wales and taken to Birmingham and Shrewsbury; malt from Oswestry and Ellesmere to Liverpool and Manchester; barytes from Garthmyl to Liverpool; groceries from Liverpool to Birmingham; gypsum from Oldbury to Ellesmere Port; salt from Middlewich to South Staffordshire with a back cargo of slack; and sugar from Greenock via the Mersey to the Midlands.

Petrol was being carried from Ellesmere Port to the Potteries as early as 1870, as the SU's boat *Eagle* was reported as being destroyed by an explosion of petroleum at the north end of Harecastle Tunnel. The committee decided that it should not be carried in covered boats. Another dangerous traffic was gunpowder, four boats being altered to comply with the requirements of the Explosives Act 1875. However, in 1890 the committee decided to discontinue the carrying of gunpowder, dynamite and other cargoes enumerated in the Government's list of explosives.

To assist it to get traffic, the SU was a member of the Corn Exchanges at Birmingham, Chester, Liverpool, Nantwich, Oswestry, Whitchurch and Wolverhampton, and of other exchanges at Birmingham (two exchanges), London, Shrewsbury, Stoke and Wolverhampton. It was also a member of the News Room at Liverpool and subscribed to the *Telegraph & Shipping Gazette*.

One attempt to gain traffic would have necessitated considerable engineering work if it had gone ahead. The Weaver Hall Company's salt works was near the entrance to the Upper Flash on the river Weaver. In 1888 Jebb was instructed to consider the feasibility of putting an incline down to the river, presumably somewhere near the site of the subsidence on the Middlewich Branch which was causing so much trouble; it was also necessary for him to investigate whether the Weaver could be navigated that far up, not merely a matter of depth but also how boats would have been hauled. At the following meeting, James Hope, the SU's Assistant Secretary, said he had found amongst the company's documents a conveyance to the Chester Canal Committee dated 1773, granting the company all the rights given by the river Weaver's Act of 1733 for making the river navigable from Winsford Bridge to Nantwich. However, the Solicitor advised that as the conveyance had never been confirmed in any subsequent Act, it could no longer be put into effect.

Unsurprisingly, no further action was taken on the suggestion.

A basic problem was that many traffic flows were unbalanced. For example, on the Welsh Branch there was much more traffic eastbound than westbound, which meant there was excessive light running. Back loads were particularly welcome, such as coal to the various towns en route.

A snapshot of traffic, 1908–12

JACK Roberts, a former SU boatman, wrote his memoirs in 1969, detailing many of the trips he did and the loads carried.[16] Although most of the boats he crewed were designed for the Welsh Branch so slightly smaller, much of his time was spent on the Main Line – indeed the variety of the trips and the loads is notable, showing the flexibility of the organisation. Nevertheless, certain traffics were common, including:

– sugar, bacon, fruit, lard and butter from Ellesmere Port to wharves large and small throughout the SU network;
– wheat and maize from Ellesmere Port to various mills;
– copper bars from Ellesmere Port to the Shropshire Iron Works at Trench, with return loads of copper wire and steel wire;
– cattle feed such as macbar from Manchester to various SU wharves;
– cheese from Nantwich, Whitchurch, Ellesmere and Market Drayton to Manchester or occasionally Ellesmere Port;
– coal from various collieries in South Staffordshire and the Potteries area to wharves on the former Montgomeryshire Canal – probably house coal of a higher quality to that from Chirk;
– road-stone from Welshpool (Stondard Quarry) to various places on the Welsh Branch;
– timber from Welshpool and Ellesmere to various places on and outside the SU system;
– soda from various works in the Northwich/Middlewich area to Birmingham;
– bone ash from Ellesmere Port to Richards' bone works at Rednal; and
– chemicals in drums from Graesser's works on the Plas Kynaston Canal to Calveley interchange sidings or Ellesmere Port.

More unusual loads included:

– oakum from Shrewsbury Prison to the SU's Chester boatyard; and
– prefabricated units from the interchange sidings at Calveley to Knighton, for Cadbury's.

He was never personally involved in the limestone nor ironstone traffics.

Traffic statistics

THE Royal Commission on Canals 1906–9 was given carrying data for the years 1898 and 1905 and this is shown in Table A (left).

In addition, 587,000 tons was carried in 1898 in SU boats across the Mersey or for short distances in Birmingham and south Staffordshire, wholly outside the SU area. The equivalent figure for 1905 was not stated.

A better measure would be ton-miles, but these were not recorded. Also, it would be useful to have the Welsh Branch and the Shrewsbury Branch analysed separately from the Main Line and the Middlewich Branch.

It can be seen that over this seven year period traffic had increased by 10%. The tonnage conveyed by the SU's carrying department increased by 29%, whereas that conveyed by other carriers (regional or local), referred to as 'bye-traders' decreased by 11%.[17]

Tolls and tonnage

FOR the ultimate customer, only the total cost mattered. They were not concerned about the split between the toll – the canal company's charge to the carrier for the use of the canal – and the carrier's own charge for conveying the goods (and possibly warehousing or delivering them).

The various canal Acts specified maximum rates for tolls, which were required to be the same for the SU as a carrier as for the independent carriers. There was little consistency between the Acts of the constituent companies. Furthermore, the trading conditions of those constituent companies had led to various reductions being applied. Canal managers were aware of what

Table A	1898	1905
	000 tons	000 tons
Loaded & discharged on the SU		
Carried by SUCC	37	55
Carried by bye-traders	65	51
	102	106
Loaded but not discharged on the SU		
e.g. Ellesmere Port to the Potteries or Birmingham & the Black Country		
Carried by SUCC	87	94
Carried by bye-traders	15	13
	102	107
Discharged but not loaded on the SU		
e.g. the Potteries or Birmingham & the Black Country to Ellesmere Port		
Carried by SUCC	122	170
Carried by bye-traders	73	64
	192	234
Not loaded or discharged on the SU		
e.g. Birmingham & the Black Country to & from Manchester		
Carried by SUCC	152	151
Carried by bye-traders	0	8
	152	159

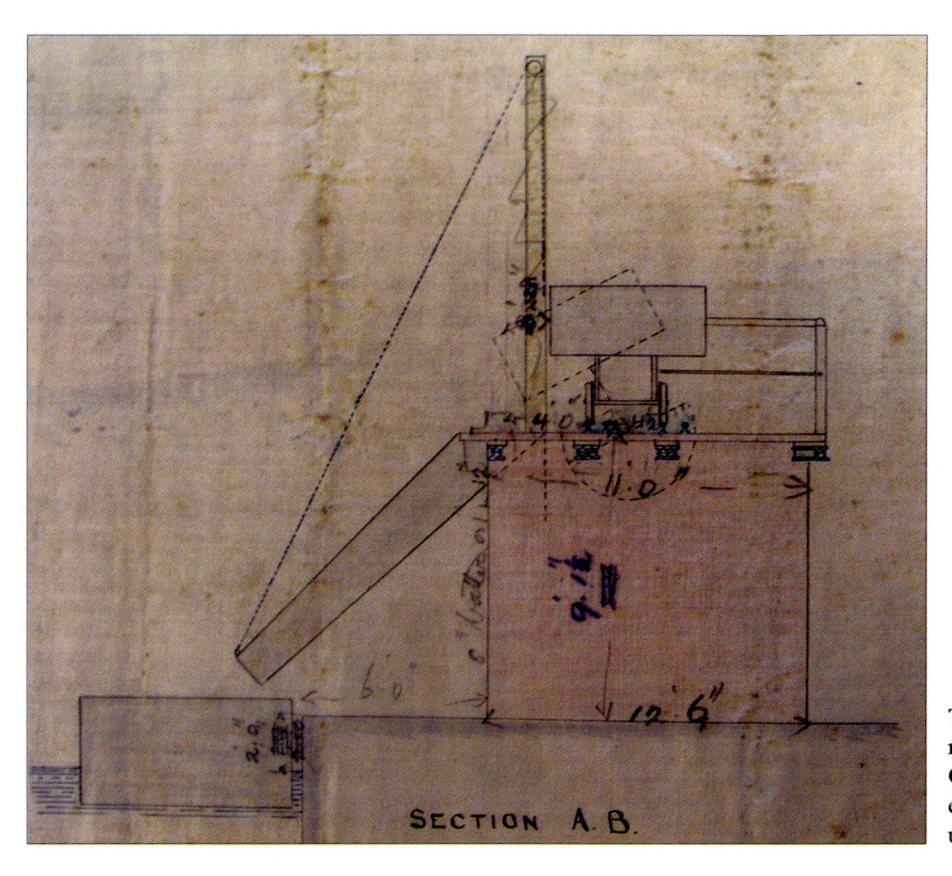

The tippler built at Chirk for the road-stone from the Ceiriog Granite Company. It cost an estimated £668, and came into use in 1905. *Shropshire Archives*

rival companies and modes of transport charged – some had shorter routes and some had better access to customers' premises – and adjusted quoted rates accordingly. Over the years a practice of high nominal tolls and numerous 'drawbacks' and other special arrangements had evolved. These made record keeping and account billing complex, and interfered with the desire to have inter-company agreement of rates. Therefore in 1854 it was decided to simplify tolls and to try to adopt the same charging principles as the LNWR.

It was easier to desire to simplify charges than actually to do so. The process always creates winners and losers: the income from winners is reduced (unless the amount they require to be conveyed is increased as a consequence), and the losers, facing a price increase, are minded to look elsewhere for their suppliers of transport. In the absence of a monopoly, the local market determines the maximum price, hence decisions such as that in 1863 that the tonnage on coal was to be halved from $1d$ to $½d$ a ton 'where found necessary'.

The Middlewich toll

As mentioned earlier, the SU Board tried to get the toll, which Trent & Mersey had imposed at Wardle Lock, Middlewich, removed by opposing Bills of TMC's parent company, the North Staffordshire Railway (NSR), at every opportunity and by proposing new connections between the two canals at Middlewich.

In 1851 a letter from Robert Smith, the canal manager of the Manchester, Sheffield & Lincolnshire Railway, which owned the Macclesfield and Peak Forest Canals (amongst others), prompted a review of what could be done to mitigate the toll. As a result, a Bill was promoted for a canal 323yds long from the east side of Rush Hall Bridge (Bridge 31) on the Middlewich Branch to a little way south of King's Lock on the TMC; there would have been a shallow lock on this link because the fall at Wardle Lock was a little greater than that at King's Lock. However, as mentioned earlier, the following May this Bill was withdrawn at the request of the LNWR.

In 1860 a petition was presented against a Bill promoted by the NSR, but without success.

Another attempt to force the issue was initiated in 1865. The SU had been under the impression that the NSR's Act of the previous year had, in effect, removed the toll but was incensed to find that not only did the Middlewich toll still apply but that the TMC charged exactly the same toll on iron products for transport on its canal from the Potteries to Middlewich as it did to Preston Brook, 17 miles further on. The SU refused to pay the toll, but the TMC then withdrew credit facilities so the SU's boats had to pay cash instead. Legal proceedings were started. A survey was carried out for a new link 2 miles 574yds long, from between Cartwright Bridge (23) and Clive Green Bridge (24) on the Middlewich Branch to just above Rumps Lock on

Chapter 10: The Shropshire Union Railways & Canal Company

the Trent & Mersey – much longer than the 1851 proposal but by skirting the built-up area would minimise opposition and possibly even be cheaper. However, nothing further was done about it pending the result of the litigation. The case was lost; an appeal then made to the Court of Exchequer Chambers – and that too was lost.

The passing of the River Weaver Act 1872, which authorised the building of the Anderton Lift, induced the SU to try again to persuade the TMC to reduce or eliminate the Middlewich toll. They pointed out that boats using the Anderton Lift would pay 1*d* a ton, whereas those passing through Wardle Lock would pay 'an oppressive and almost prohibitory toll' of 10½*d* a ton. The TMC responded by pointing out that the toll was fixed by Act of Parliament and agreed to by the Ellesmere & Chester Canal; they would not agree to any change unless it was to the mutual benefit of *both* companies.

Although the Railway & Canal Traffic Act 1888 did not explicitly abolish the Middlewich toll and similar inter-company impositions, its provisions were such as make them difficult to justify; consequently it was omitted from the schedule of rates submitted by the North Staffordshire Railway to the Board of Trade. The minute is not clear, but it seems that SU agreed to a higher rate if traffic using Wardle Lock went less than six miles on the TMC. The Canal Toll Order of 1894 confirmed that the toll had been abolished.

The Autherley toll

UNLIKE the Middlewich toll, the LNWR had no strategic objection to the SU trying to get the Autherley toll abolished. An attempt in 1864 to have it substituted by a mileage toll on the half mile of the Staffordshire & Worcestershire Canal (SWC) used by traffic to and from Wolverhampton was countered by an offer to reduce the toll of 4*d* a ton by a quarter. A survey and estimate was then prepared for a direct link to the Birmingham Canal, similar to those proposed in 1836 and 1841. Following further negotiations a compromise was reached: the toll would be reduced to 2*d* a ton, providing the SU did not obtain an Act for the direct link.

Dissatisfied, a direct link to the Birmingham Canal was considered again in 1874, Jebb estimating the cost as £24,000.

In 1888, Jebb reported that it had been arranged to pay the SWC £100 a year, on condition of their supplying a lockful of water for every boat passing either way between the Birmingham Canal and the SU. The minutes do not mention the tonnage toll, but presumably this would then be abolished. However, the Committee asked Jebb to re-survey a direct connection; he reported back an estimated cost of £22,079. The outcome was a new five-year agreement with the SWC and the Birmingham Canal, whereby the SU would pay a toll of ¾*d* a ton on all traffic between Aldersley and Autherley Junctions except lime and limestone. The SWC would supply the SU with a Wheaton Aston size lock of water for every boat which passed through Autherley Junction and, if the SU required it, an additional 50 locks a week to work the Newport Branch. It is not clear whether this superseded the agreement to pay £100 annually, but a later minute which refers to the 2*d* a ton charge on traffic passing through the lock at Autherley Junction implies that the £100 draft agreement never became operable.

The SWC's draft schedule of charges under the Railway & Canal Traffic Act 1888 continued the charge of 2*d* a ton in compensation for the water passing through the lock. This was refused by the Board of Trade, which instead allowed the SWC to charge 4s.6d where the tonnage charge for boats passing between Autherley and Aldersley Junctions would have been less. The provisional agreement about supplying water as set out in the last paragraph was also confirmed.

Nevertheless, the SWC continued to exploit its 'ransom strip'. When through rates for loads from Ellesmere Port to the Warwick canals (and vice versa) were negotiated in about 1910, the charges for 'classes A and B', that is, low value bulk loads, were:

	charge	miles	locks
Shropshire Union	1s.4d	66½	43
Staffordshire & Worcestershire	2½d	½	0
Birmingham	6½d	18	43
Warwick & Birmingham (first 4 miles)	2d	4	6
Total	2s.3d	89	92

As can be seen, the SWC took almost 10% of the income for less than 1% of the mileage, whilst incurring none of the costs of maintaining locks or supplying water.

The immediate effect of railway competition

CHESHIRE's first railway opened in 1837 and Chester, the county town, received its railway in 1840. Shropshire, despite being England's largest inland county and now regarded by many as the birthplace of the Industrial Revolution, was very late in being connected to the national network, only Cornwall being later. Shrewsbury's railway from Chester opened in 1848 and the lines from Stafford and from Wolverhampton in 1849. At both Chester and Shrewsbury the station came to be managed by a joint committee of the LNWR and GWR.

The market towns served by the Shropshire Union's canals tended to be relatively late in being connected to the national railway network (see Table B on next page).

The Shrewsbury & Welshpool Railway was opened in 1862; initially worked by the LNWR, it became a joint line of the LNWR and GWR in 1865.

Bearing in mind that the Cambrian Railways worked closely with the LNWR, there were actually few places in the canal's area which were not also readily accessible by LNWR railway freight services after 1863. It is therefore not valid to say that the LNWR's continued support for its canal was because it invaded territories which 'belonged' to other railway companies – this was true of only the Ruabon industrial area and Market Drayton.

The Birkenhead Railway, by then jointly owned by the LNWR and GWR, opened its branch through Ellesmere Port in 1863, the station there originally being called 'Whitby Locks'.

The Shropshire Union Canal

Table B		
Oswestry	1848	Shrewsbury & Chester (GWR from 1854)
Newport	1849	Shropshire Union (worked by LNWR)
Wellington	1849	Shropshire Union (worked by LNWR) and Shrewsbury & Birmingham (GWR from 1854)
Nantwich, Whitchurch, Wem	1858	LNWR
Welshpool	1860	Oswestry & Newtown (Cambrian Railways from 1864)
Newtown	1861	Oswestry & Newtown (Cambrian Railways from 1864)
Llangollen	1861	Vale of Llangollen (worked by GWR)
Ellesmere	1863	Oswestry, Ellesmere & Whitchurch (Cambrian Railways from 1864)
Market Drayton	1863	Nantwich & Market Drayton (worked by GWR)

The Wappenshall experience

WHENEVER a railway opened, the SU General Manager's monthly report mentioned that the canal's trade had reduced. In one case this can be quantified.

Wappenshall Wharf received the merchandise going to Wellington and the settlements in the east Shropshire industrial area; it was also where items were transhipped from and to the tub-boat canals. In one respect it was not a typical canal wharf serving a town: no coal was unloaded there. It was a private wharf owned by the Duke of Sutherland, and a remarkable series of trading records have survived.[18]

These show vividly the impact of the coming of the railway to Wellington. In 1847 the wharf recorded its greatest income, some 43% greater than the average of the preceding five years. This was largely attributable to the substantial amount of rails, chairs and other iron products for the construction of the railway.

The railway from Shrewsbury via Wellington to Stafford opened on 1 June 1849; that from Wellington to Wolverhampton on 12 November that year. The wharf's monthly income for the first eight months of the year averaged £48; for the last four months it averaged £25. It did not taper off – the fall was immediate. (The slight delay is because these were cash figures, and traders were allowed a period of credit before the debt was collected.) It was the smaller consignments for the local shops which virtually ceased; the bulk trades were somewhat less affected, the amount halving by the end of the following year.

The national and regional carriers soon stopped coming to Wappenshall. Crowley & Co.'s last load was in January 1850, Henshall's in August 1850 and Pickford's in October that same year, leaving the SU's own carrying subsidiary as the sole general carrier.

Comments written in 1876 by William Norris, the manager of the Coalbrookdale Company, are probably fairly typical of industrialists' opinions, especially those whose works were not canalside – in his case Wappenshall Wharf was some six miles from Horsehay Forge:

> Shipping by canal was very expensive and frequently very inconvenient, and sometimes attended with considerable losses. Boats were frozen in for weeks together during the winter, and, as horses as well as the boats belonged to the company, horse provender had to be sent from Horsehay, or money to buy it – and also money for the boatmen to provide food for himself and family, for most of the boatmen were married and had children living in the boat with them. But there were other draw-backs with this canal carrying. For instance, if you wanted to send iron to Liverpool, the company's boats could only deliver to Ellesmere Port, where they had to transfer their cargo into a Mersey flat. And if you consigned iron to South London, you could only deliver to Brentford, where you must unload into one of the Thames lighters; and if for North London or in that direction, you could go as far as the City Basin, where you had to unload for carting to the place of consignment. All these additions were expensive, some of them very heavy – especially those of London and Manchester.

He added, perhaps with exaggeration, that with the opening of the branch line railway past the works in 1857, 'iron could be rolled, loaded, and into Birkenhead before it was cold'.[19]

Competition and co-operation

THE Canal Tolls Act 1845 permitted canal companies to charge different rates per ton-mile on different parts of their line, though the various rates still had to be applied equally to all customers. Before then, specific permission had to be given in the company's private Act. This change gave flexibility to encourage specific trades and to respond to competition, and was used freely from then onwards by the SU. This was sometimes done in co-operation with other companies.

The railway companies exercised a downward pressure on rates, and the canals had to follow or lose traffic. The most drastic reductions came in 1868 when, for example, the carrying rate from Middlewich to Birmingham was reduced from 7s a ton to 4s.6d a ton.

For traffic between the West Midlands and the Mersey ports, the LNWR was the dominant railway company, but it was the Great Western Railway which tended to take the lead in reducing rates, as it had more to gain from increasing its relatively small share of the business. For example, in the 1850s the SU lost much iron ore trade to the GWR, which imported it via Saltney, until an agreement was made to equalise rates. However, the agreement was never actually signed, and was cancelled after only a couple of years. Further agreements were made later with the GWR, but in the 1860s and 1870s it was usually that company which breached the spirit of them or pressed for further reductions.

When the Oswestry & Newtown Railway partly opened in

1860, the SU's Executive Committee reacted by instructing the Manager to take all necessary steps to keep the traffic on the canal. An agreement on the rates for coal was made between the two companies in 1861 but the rate was further reduced at the insistence of the railway company early the following year. Meanwhile, the tenant of the limekilns at Belan gave notice to quit because of the railway competition, so the rent charged was lowered.

Agreements were made between the senior staff of the various companies at 'conferences'. These did not always involve only railway companies. For example, in 1863, an agreement was made between the SU and the Bridgewater Trustees – both companies being carriers as well as owning a canal – detailing equal rates between Autherley Junction and Ellesmere Port or Middlewich. As well as the tolls and carriage charges, this agreement covered such matters as cartage in Liverpool. The following year a similar agreement was made for trade between the Potteries and Liverpool; this included not only the Bridgewater Trustees but also the LNWR and NSR.

These agreements were taken seriously. When it was alleged that Mr Allerton, the company's Agent in the Potteries, had made an allowance on a consignment of goods, he and the canvasser were summoned before the committee and told that the agreement must be adhered to.

With identical prices, competition on a particular route could only be on promptness and quality of service. Some agreements didn't even allow this; for example, that made in 1882 with the Mersey Carrying Company for the cross-Mersey trade stated that 'each company shall prepare a list of its recognised customers whose trade shall be considered as non-competitive'; these lists would then be exchanged and agreed.

Competition also came from customers using alternative sources of supply. For example, the South Staffordshire iron industry could get its supplies of fluxing-stone from the Caldon quarries, rather than from the quarries on the Welsh Branch, so a watch was kept on the comparative rates. Similarly, grain bound for Birmingham could be imported via Sharpness on the Severn, rather than Ellesmere Port on the Mersey; in 1885 the SU wanted to reduce the rates in order to retain the traffic, even though income would be reduced by £1,000, but the GWR and Midland Railway would not agree.

A pooling agreement between the SU, the Anderton Company and the Mersey Weaver Company for traffic to and from the Potteries was made in 1905 and renewed in 1912.

When the Royal Commission on Canals 1906–9 was investigating the amount of true competition it made the mistake of confining its question to canal/railway competition, so the evidence given on behalf of the SU did not mention that agreement. It was told that the SU had an understanding with the GWR in respect of traffic for a few places in the Llangollen/Ruabon/Oswestry area by which the rates by canal were between 3d and 1s a ton less than the rail rate; and that there was a similar agreement between the SU and the Cambrian Railways whereby the rates by canal were from 6d to 1s per ton less than the rail rates. The evidence given by the Birmingham Canal referred to an understanding between several companies including the SU concerning all traffic between Birmingham and South Staffordshire and Ellesmere Port.

Sir Frederick Harrison, General Manager of the LNWR, explained that these were not formal agreements but 'a common understanding between competing parties that the price for a service shall be an agreed one' so that they do not underquote one another. He added, 'During the last twenty years at least the carrying interest of the country has been more sensible to the interests of the parties who invest their money in it, and they do not try to cut one another's throats if they can help it'.[20]

In the first decade of the 20th century railway companies started making major efforts to improve the efficiency of their handling of goods, particularly of bulk loads. Whereas 8-ton wagons had been the norm – this being a size originally determined by what a horse could pull when shunting in a goods yard – 15- and 20-ton wagons were being introduced, together with more effective equipment for loading and unloading. More powerful locomotives meant trains could be longer. Meanwhile the canals made little effort to increase their productivity, except at Ellesmere Port; in fairness, boat sizes could not be increased because they were determined by the dimensions of locks, and the first reliable diesel engines were not available until 1910.

Perhaps the establishment in 1906 of a lorry service for export traffic from the Potteries to Liverpool offering a door-to-door capability should have been the warning signal that the really strong competition in future was going to come not from the railways but from the motor lorry. If anyone in the SU's management recognised this threat, it was never hinted at in the minutes of its Executive Committee.

The Railway & Canal Traffic Act 1888

THE Shropshire Union's minutes do not mention any commercial disputes prompted by earlier legislation but are full of entries concerning the requirements of the 1888 Act. In accordance with the recommendations of the Canal Association (the canal companies' trade organisation) the Railway Clearing House's classification of goods was adopted, modified for canal purposes, replacing the complex and inconsistent schedules laid down by the individual Acts which had set up the companies. The Board of Trade had intended that the new regulated rates would be in place by the end of 1888 but several extensions of time were granted. The Commissioners' hearing to consider the rates proposed by the SU was started on 1 November 1893. They were told that the company's proposals would reduce its toll income by £644 and its receipts from carrying by £576.

The hearing was then adjourned as Thomas Hales, the Traffic Manager, was diagnosed by his doctor as suffering from 'overstrain of the nervous system' and instructed to cease all work for a period. The hearing was resumed on 5/6 December, when the representative of the Mansion House Association (a pressure group set up by some of the railways' and canals' freight customers, which later became the Freight Transport Association) stated that the SU's proposed charges were excessive, the company having 'ransacked all their traffic with a view of showing losses', adding that the LNWR 'had wished to prevent the canal being of any service to the trader in competition with the railways'.

The Commissioners' revised schedule was received early the following year, the rates generally being the same as those granted to the Leeds & Liverpool Canal Company. A supplementary charge for the Trench Incline had been accepted, the bonus mileage for Ellesmere Port to Chester (which had caused such a fuss when introduced in 1828) was not. It was thought that the Commissioners' rates would reduce income by about £1,300 a year. On the other hand, the new regulations had allowed the Autherley and Middlewich tolls to be challenged and eliminated.

Passenger services

Timetabled services

Two remarkable quick passenger boat services were inaugurated on 14 June 1852. These connected with trains on the Chester–Shrewsbury line, one from Rednal to Welshpool and Newtown, the other from Llangollen Road Station to Llangollen. The idea appears to have been Robert Skey's – ten years earlier he had visited Scotland and discussed the operation of passenger boats on the Forth & Clyde, Union and Paisley Canals. It was developed in cooperation with James Shipton's Wolverhampton Swift Packet Company, which had operated a similar service between Wolverhampton and Birmingham until December 1851. The advertisement announcing that service's cessation gave the reason as water shortage, but the main reason was almost certainly the imminent opening of the competing railway.

Skey was authorised to purchase three of the now surplus boats, two of which were to work to Newtown and one to Llangollen. They were specially adapted for the fast passenger services, having fine lines and light weight. The contract for the Newtown service was to run for three months, and then to be terminable by either side on two months' notice. Presumably the Llangollen service was on similar terms, though possibly it was intended to run only during the summer months, Llangollen already by then being an up-market holiday resort. Curiously, the company minutes do not mention the Llangollen service; if it were not for advertisements, one would not have known it ever had existed.[21]

Fast boats rely on a strange effect of fluid dynamics. When the speed at which a boat is towed in a confined channel is increased, there comes a point at which the water cannot go past the boat quickly enough, so piles up ahead. Towing becomes very difficult, but if the speed can be further increased, the boat then 'rides the wave' and towing becomes much easier. The speed of this wave depends on the depth of the water; for these canals the speed is about 6mph. (This technique does not work for powered boats, only for towed boats.)

The distance from Rednal to Newtown is 32 miles, with 22

One of Captain Jones's boats and its crew pose for the camera.
Llangollen Museum, Rhys Davies Collection

locks. The service also had 18 advertised stops. Train passengers leaving Chester at 10.40am or Shrewsbury at 12.35pm could catch the 1.05pm boat, timed to arrive at Newtown basin at 6.10pm. In the reverse direction the boat left Newtown at 7am and reached Rednal at 12.12pm 'in time for trains which reach Chester at 2.45pm ... and Shrewsbury at 12.50pm'. The advertisement added: 'The precise times of arrival and departure are not guaranteed, as they must depend to some extent on the arrival of the railway trains.' The fare to Newtown was 5s. first class cabin and 3s. second class cabin, and to Welshpool was 3s. and 2s. respectively.

The average speed of 6.3mph implies a speed between locks of well over 8mph, a speed which required alterations to some of the bridges. The service was organised in a similar way to stage coach operation, with galloping horses requiring to be changed frequently.

A list of the loadings each month from August 1852 to April 1853 has survived. In August and September the average monthly number each way was 125 first class and 566 second class. Loadings reduced in the winter months: the average from November to April (excluding February, when the boat was laid up for two weeks because of ice) was 33 first class and 348 second class.[22] In March 1853 it was decided that this loss-making service would cease, and notice was duly given.

The Llangollen boat made four journeys a day (except Sundays) each way, each one making a reasonable connection with trains in both directions. The fare was 9d in the first class cabin and 6d in the second class cabin; parcels under 28lb in weight were charged 6d, and those between 28lb and 56lb were charged 9d.

The short-lived (1848–1862) Llangollen Road Station was situated on the south side of Whitehouses Tunnel. The journey was timed to take just 40 minutes for the 6¼ miles, an average of 9.4mph. The public trip boats now take two hours to go from Llangollen to Froncysyllte, which is 1¼ miles short of the site of the station. Although lock-free, the route not only includes the 191 yard long tunnel, it also includes Pontcysyllte Aqueduct (336 yards) and two narrow sections totalling about half a mile where two boats cannot pass. The canal was still quite busy with boats conveying limestone from Froncysyllte and Trevor Rocks and with traffic to and from Trevor Basin.

This timing must have been found to be impractically fast, as at some point the number of return journeys were reduced to three, and the time allowed increased to a shortest of 54 and a longest of 60 minutes, giving an average speed of between 6.3 and 6.8 mph.[23]

An advertisement in June 1853 shows that while the Llangollen service continued through that summer the Newtown service had ceased.

Shipton applied to run the passenger service in the summer of 1854, presumably intending to use the canal company's swift boat. This was approved, but the charge demanded of 10s. per return trip was thought by Shipton to be excessive, so the service did not go ahead.

The next mention of such a service is in March 1856, when the proposal from another person, Mr Wilson, to run it at that toll was accepted. However, it is not certain that he went ahead. A rival omnibus service from Llangollen Road Station seems to have been more successful – that appears to have lasted until the Vale of Llangollen branch line opened from Ruabon in 1862.

Trip boats

MR Newbery of the Royal Hotel, Llangollen, started running a timetabled pleasure boat service from the Wharf to the Chain Bridge in the summer of 1881, which is thought to be the earliest such holiday usage of canals in Britain. This probably lasted only the one season.

In 1884 'Captain' Samuel Jones, a former merchant navy ship's engineer, started operating trips using two converted ship's life-boats: daily to Chain Bridge at 10.30am, 3pm and 9.15pm (fare 7d return); and on Wednesdays to Chirk and back, leaving at 11am (fare 1s.6d). By 1895 he was operating five boats, seating from 60 to 200 passengers, as well as some small craft.

A correspondent to the local newspaper in 1897 wrote, 'Along with many other signs of coming summer, one is glad to hear the cheery horn inviting passengers to join the canal boat.' Four years later, Samuel Jones was summonsed for the breach of bye-laws for causing a public nuisance, having blown his bugle after being told several times by Sergeant Wyse to desist as there had been numerous complaints. Jones didn't help his cause by replying, 'You can do what the damn you like,' and going off down the road continuing to blow the bugle. Common sense prevailed at the trial; although the magistrates dismissed the case on a legal technicality, they told Jones that he had no right to make himself a public nuisance, nor had any right to resist the police who, if he continue to offend, would take out another summons. His solicitor was sure that some arrangement could be made to allow the defendant to signal the departure of his boats in a manner that might suit all parties.[24]

Following Jones's death in 1908, the boats were bought by Isaac Roberts.

A rival service was started about 1890 by Thomas Bushby of Trevor, who was an estate agent, a corn merchant and co-proprietor of the Trevor Hall Lime Company. Under the trading name of 'The Vale of Llangollen Pleasure Boats', in 1899 he was operating a full-day trip to Chirk on Mondays and Thursdays (allowing 3¼ hours at the destination) and an afternoon trip to Pontcysyllte Aqueduct on the other weekday afternoons. He was willing to try experimental ventures. In 1893, for example, he ran 'moonlight trips' to the Aqueduct on Wednesdays, the boat *Loftus* being lit by numerous Chinese lanterns and having a string band on board; on Monday and Tuesday nights the *Great Eastern* took its passengers to Chain Bridge, with entertainment provided by a choir. Even more ambitious was his 1900 proposal for a full-day outing by boat, road and rail: canal boat to Chirk, carriage to Ellesmere for lunch at the Bridgewater Arms, an afternoon tour of the meres, then on to Ruabon for the train back to Llangollen.[25]

Pleasure boating

The canal acts generally allowed people whose lands adjoined the canal to use pleasure boats on the canal, providing they did not pass through a lock. This right was exercised by a few. For example, towards the end of the 19th century J.C. Edwards, who had made his fortune from brick and tile production, had a boathouse built close to Bryn Howel, his residence (between Trevor and Llangollen). In 1892 Colonel Lovett of Belmont (between Chirk and Oswestry) complained that he had been billed for using a boat, and the company confirmed that he had the right to do so without charge.

From mid-Victorian times, trips on the canal were popular outings for Sunday schools and similar organisations, using working boats specially cleaned for the day. Many of these were annual events, often at Whitsuntide, coinciding with the planned stoppages for maintenance which prevented longer distance carrying. They often went to the grounds of a local worthy for a picnic and organised games. A typical example was the treat provided to 400 children by the Calvinistic Methodist Sunday Schools of the Llangollen area in 1882; the boats left the town wharf between 12.30pm and 1.30pm, crossed Pontcysyllte Aqueduct then returned to Bryn Howel for tea and current bread followed by games on the lawn. They returned to the wharf by 9.30pm.[26]

Although by the 1850s the rowing of a boat for recreation was regarded as a common enough pastime on rivers and lakes, canals were private commercial transport routes and therefore not appropriate for people who just wanted to 'mess about' on water. However, the canal between Llangollen wharf and Horseshoe Falls was particularly attractive scenically; with the commercial traffic becoming much less significant and the town developing as an up-market holiday destination, this was therefore uniquely suitable for leisure use. Some visitors brought their own boats or canoes. It was not until 1882 that there is any record of rowing boats available for public hire here, though the idea had been mentioned in the local paper back in 1869.

Elsewhere there is photographic evidence that rowing boats could be hired at Welshpool from coal merchant John Jones in about 1900. However, an application in 1909 to put boats for hire at Whitchurch was refused because it was not considered safe for pleasure boats to ply with passengers on the Whitchurch Arm.

Nationally, the earliest recorded extended excursions were in the 1850s. The Thames was the most popular stretch of water – the best-known account being Jerome K. Jerome's *Three Men in a Boat*, a trip done in 1888 – but a few more adventurous people went on the canals. In 1868 three men (Harry, Will and the anonymous author who described their experiences) took a 24ft long skiff *Wanderer* and a 16ft canoe *Ranger* from Manchester to London. From Ellesmere Port they were permitted to travel on the Shropshire Union toll-free, providing they portaged their boat round locks. In fact, many lock-keepers let them through, and they had a lift through Hurleston Locks up to Wrenbury on two narrow boats, one drawn by a mule, the other by two donkeys. They also had a lift through Grindley Brook Locks. When they got to the aqueduct over the river Perry, two miles beyond Frankton Junction on the Llanymynech Branch, they took their boats out of the canal down onto the river. The following day they reached Shrewsbury, having negotiated fallen trees, cattle fences and water mills. The rest of their journey was via the river Severn, Stroudwater and Thames & Severn Canals and the river Thames.

More locally, Mr G.C. Davies of Oswestry was reported as 'paddling his own canoe' 23 miles from Maesbury to Llangollen on a Saturday in February 1869, returning on the Tuesday.

In the summer of 1894 Henry Rodolph de Salis, a director of Fellows, Morton & Clayton Ltd, holidayed in his steam-powered narrowboat *Dragonfly* for a month on the English canals. From 30 May until 4 June he was on the Shropshire Union system – covering 134 miles in just over four days. He went on to compile *Bradshaw's Canals & Navigable Rivers*, based in part on this and other trips.

1896 saw the publication of *A New Oarsman's Guide to the Rivers and Canals of Great Britain and Ireland*. This referred to the Shropshire Union system as 'a most useful one for the cruiser', supplying an easy route to the Severn at Shrewsbury, Pool Quay and Newtown, to the Dee at Llangollen or via the Ceiriog at Chirk, to the Weaver near Aston, and to the Mersey at Ellesmere Port. It described the countryside as 'nowhere unpleasing' and in parts 'very beautiful'. From the south, the expectation was that the boat will have been carted from a Wolverhampton station, 'assuming, of course, that no one travelling for pleasure will ever work through Birmingham and the Black Country'. It commented that the locks and drawbridges were in good order, and that lock-keepers would be found at all flights and most single locks, except on the Montgomeryshire section. Tolls were not cheap: 3*d* a mile for the first 25 miles and 1*d* a mile thereafter, with 5*s* for lockage. The guide advised the sights to see, such as Beeston, Chirk and Powis Castles, Chillington Hall, Lilleshall Abbey, Lady Catherine Herbert's Hospital at Preston-on-the-Weald-Moors, and churches including Norbury, High Offley, Aston, Bunbury, Whitchurch and Chirk. The reader was told that the view from Pontcysyllte Aqueduct 'though very fine, is not equal to that at Chirk', which was described as 'magnificent'.

Other sources of income

Sale of water

Water had long been used for cooling steam engines in canal-side factories, with the water being returned to the canal. Other industrial processes also needed cooling water, such as at Shrewsbury gas works and Graesser's chemical works at Cefn Mawr. Sometimes this was associated with agreements to use the canal for transport, examples from 1903 being for the Anglo-Swiss Condensed Milk Company's factory at Calveley and Brunner Mond at Middlewich.

Moreton Dock, Rhoswiel, c.1900, about where Lion Quays is now.
Canal & River Trust

Another use for water was to power machinery. Although this was generally rare on British canals, there were several instances on the Welsh Branch, both arms of which had a generous supply of water from rivers. The corn mill by Welshpool Town Lock dates from the late 1830s; the site of the water-wheel can still be seen. The bone-mill and sawmill at the Powis Estate yard were both powered by water from the canal (as well as from a nearby stream), and were there by 1840. Being a sump canal, there was inevitably water going to waste at the lowest level, hence the establishment of a corn mill at The Wern; however, this opportunity does not seem to have come into use until later in the 19th century. A farmer near Llangollen was given permission to abstract water through a 4in. pipe in order to power a small turbine. In 1895 it was agreed that the mill at Grindley Brook could be powered by a turbine using the water bypassing the staircase locks.

Agreements were occasionally made to supply water for other purposes, such as in 1848 for Chester's baths and wash-houses. The largest unreturned supply was to the London & North Western Railway at Chester. In 1874 a proposal was made for a pipe from the long pound above Christleton Lock to deliver 33,000 gallons an hour. Jebb advised that this would injure canal traffic in dry seasons; the matter was referred to Richard Moon, who authorised it. Other water supplies included those to J.C. Edwards' Penybont brick works and to the Great Western Railway at Llangollen.

The sale of water caused an argument which lasted 74 years before it was resolved. In 1870 Chester Waterworks asserted that the SU had no power to supply water for trade purposes, and asked for it to stop, and the SU responded that it would be restricted. Then in 1874 the waterworks must have heard of the proposal to supply water to the railway at Chester because they sent a letter asking for all supply to be stopped immediately, and asking for a list of the businesses supplied. The SU refused both requests. The letter from the waterworks also pointed out that the Acts required the water taken from the Dee to be returned to it, whereas of course almost all of it went into the Mersey partly via Ellesmere Port and partly via the Middlewich Branch and the Trent & Mersey and Bridgewater Canals.

In 1884 the River Dee Company asked if they could have a copy of the 1813 and 1827 Acts to complete their set; this was refused. The following year Mostyn Owen, Inspector of Fisheries for the river Dee, wrote to the *Chester Courant* alleging that the canal company was taking more water from the river than was allowed by Act of Parliament, and the fisheries were being injured in consequence. The SU committee decided to let the matter 'lie on the table'. One wonders why the newspaper was written to, rather than the company – possibly in the absence of having access to all the Acts, Owen did not really know whether his assertion was true.

However, the following year the SU made an agreement with the Dee Mills at Chester, whereby the canal company would pay £100 a year for 21 years as compensation for taking water from the river. The SU unilaterally reduced the payment by a third in 1906 following the destruction of part of the mill by fire.

The dispute was revived by the Dee Conservancy Board in 1891, which claimed that 'water is being in numerous instances and to a considerable extent abstracted from the canal for unauthorised purposes'. In response, the SU stated that it was not aware of any non-compliance, and asked whether anyone

Woodseaves Cutting, south of Market Drayton, early in the 20th century, showing the line of the canal being used for the telegraph service. Note also that the towpath is neatly surfaced with limestone chippings and slopes away from the canal to a drainage channel. This towpath through the cutting is now notoriously muddy almost all the year.
Neil Jenkins

had sustained any injury. The Conservancy Board replied that the volume of water flowing down the Dee was much reduced, which had affected navigation by diminishing the scour. It asked to see the Acts; this was again refused on the grounds that the only reason for the Board wishing to see them would be to endeavour to found a case against the company, adding, somewhat disingenuously, that 'they wish it to be understood that they do not fear a perusal of the Acts in question would disclose any breach of the company's obligations'. The company's correspondence was written by James Hope, the Assistant Secretary, not by Reginald Potts, its Solicitor – both would have been well aware that the company had exceeded its powers, but perhaps an employee could bend the truth with a clearer conscience.

Next the Dee Conservancy Board asked to inspect the gauge houses and sluices at Bala and the weir at New Marton, together with the registers kept at each place. These inspections took place eventually – in 1912 – and the Chester Corporation representatives declared themselves satisfied with the works but not with the formula for calculating the water discharged from Bala Lake.

It is possible that there was a fundamental misunderstanding concerning the matter. Jebb told the Royal Commission on Canals in 1907 that the SU more than fulfilled its Parliamentary obligations: it discharged more water into the Dee from Bala Lake than it took out at Llantisilio. However, most of the Dee's water passed through Bala Lake; what would have been more relevant was whether the amount left to go down the Dee at Horseshoe Falls was adequate.

Rents and wayleaves

LEASES, ground rents and wayleaves (granting a right of way over the company's land) provided significant income for the Shropshire Union, the properties ranging from lock-keepers' cottages to the Dee Mills at Llangollen, the Pontcysyllte Forge at Trevor and the Cambrian Mill close to Newtown Basin. In 1880, for example, the nett rental amounted to £4,410 a year.

Canalside businesses which would provide traffic for the canal were favoured. One such was Edward Richards' superphosphate artificial manure manufactory, erected in the former warehouse at the interchange basin at Rednal at the end of the 1880s, the business having previously been on the site of a canalside lead smelter at Maesbury.

By far the most important portfolio of properties, and the only one which was actively developed in the Shropshire Union era, was that at Ellesmere Port – valuable not only for rental income but also port dues and cross-Mersey traffic. Apart from the transport of grain, these properties were of little significance for canal trade.

Railways and canals provided natural direct routes for the electric telegraph network. The United Kingdom Telegraph Company contracted with the SU in 1860, part of the agreement being that the canal company's messages would be carried without charge. Wires were erected alongside the Main Line, the wayleave rent being £200 a year, and wires between Barbridge and Newtown added soon afterwards. The routes were taken over by the Post Office in 1882.

Another use proposed for the towpath was as a route for a brine pipe. In 1875 a proposal for a pipe from Nantwich to Ellesmere Port was considered, the annual rent to be £1,500 plus a royalty of 2d a ton. The solicitor advised that as the land had been bought under compulsory purchase powers for a canal, it could not be used for other purposes, so the application was turned down. A similar request in 1889 was approved, but the promoter withdrew. In 1891 there was an application for a pipe from Winsford to Ellesmere Port but on the solicitor's advice this was again refused.

Shooting and fishing

LETTING sporting rights on the canal bank could be mutually beneficial, as a duty could be imposed on the tenant to keep down rabbits, whose burrows damaged embankments.

The sale of fishing rights yielded a little income. The first such approval was granted to the Crewe Angling Society (probably associated with the LNWR's Crewe Works) in 1880. Only rod fishing was allowed, and the banks must not be damaged. Fishing was forbidden on Sundays. Fishing rights had in some places stayed with the adjacent landowner; in 1897 these rights for a twelve mile length of canal were leased from the Brownlow estate for £1 a year. Purchase of fish started in 1899, with 7,700 yearling perch being put into the canal in various places. Later purchases included roach and bream.

The independent carriers (bye-traders)

BY far the most important longer-distance carrier on the Shropshire Union's canals was the Shropshire Union itself. However, it did not have a monopoly. The Bridgewater Trustees worked between Autherley and Middlewich. James Fellows of Tipton (from 1876 Fellows, Morton & Co., and from 1889 Fellows, Morton & Clayton) also worked on the SU, occasionally as sub-contractor on SU contracts when the SU did not have enough boats.

In order to persuade Fellows, Morton & Clayton (FMC) to use the Shropshire Union Canal rather than another route to the Mersey ports, in 1893 a ten-year agreement was made, the main terms being:

– receipts from traffic carried at agreed rates (after deducting cartage) to be shared, with the SU receiving ⅜ on grain traffic and ⅓ on all other traffic for toll on their canal, services at Ellesmere Port, and freight between there and Liverpool;
– FMC to have the balance for all other canal tolls, haulage, boat hire and other services;
– SU to allow a 5% discount on their share for income over £2,000;
– FMC to be responsible for collection of accounts and for bad debts; and
– SU to provide (and charge for) facilities for stabling and feeding FMC's horses, as far as possible.

Some boats were operated by local firms, often in connection with their own businesses, but a few as general boating contractors. These tend to go unrecorded in the usual sources of history before the days of photography, so their importance can easily be underestimated. For example, in 1908 the Ceiriog Granite Company had about ten boats. At the same time, the Cheshire Farmers Association owned three small steam flats, 10ft wide, which could load 26 tons and carried corn from Ellesmere Port to Egg Bridge, Calveley and Nantwich; they also had two narrow boats which went on to Grindley Brook.

Evidence to the Royal Commission on Canals 1906–9 showed that the main cargoes carried by bye-traders were grain, coal, iron, lead, road materials, sand, bricks and manure.

The SU's managers must have had a surprise when in 1871 John Corbett, of the Salt Works, Bromsgrove, offered to pay £122.12s.6d, the amount owed for tolls by his late father, who had been a carrier on the Ellesmere & Chester Canal. This amount had been written off as a bad debt eighteen years earlier. The SU directors instructed that Mr Corbett should be thanked for his 'honourable course'.

Motive power

IT is not known for certain whether Fellows, Morton & Clayton ever used their steam-powered narrowboats on their service to Ellesmere Port. The earliest record found of a motorised boat being used on Shropshire Union waters was in 1907, when the narrowboat *Progress*, powered by a Gardner 16hp paraffin engine and owned by Edward Tailby, a Birmingham timber merchant, carried a mixed cargo including bedsteads to Ellesmere Port, returning with a cargo of timber. But until well after the First World War, the usual motive power on the Main Line continued to be the horse or, less often, the mule.

There is some evidence pointing to the generalisation that, for much of the 19th century, haulage by donkeys was at least as common, perhaps more common, than haulage by horses on the Welsh Branch. Of a sample of twelve mentions of animals in press reports concerning incidents on the canal between 1860 and 1900, nine referred to donkeys, usually explicitly pairs of donkeys. Donkeys were more docile, hardier and longer-lived than horses, and less particular about the quality of their food. They were also sure-footed and were generally unshod. However they were not as strong, and had a tendency to 'jib' – to come to a stop for no apparent reason, possibly when they thought they had done enough work for the day – and then be unresponsive to either bribery or threats.

One particularly interesting report was that in the *Llangollen Advertiser* of 29 June 1900:

LLANGOLLEN PETTY SESSIONS Samuel Rogers was charged with cruelty to two donkeys on the canal on May 18th. PC Parry gave evidence to the effect that on the date in question he saw the animals dragging a barge,

171

containing 15 tons of sand, against the stream. It was evident that the barge touched bottom, the water being muddy, and the animals had been greatly over-worked. Inspector Blake Jones said the animals were completely done up with the strain that had been put upon them. A fair load for them to tow was little more than half they had been dragging against the stream and in shallow water. Defendant had been previously cautioned for a similar offence. A fine of 7s.6d. and costs, 18s. in all, was imposed.

The following day's *Wrexham Advertiser* reported the case more briefly (and with a different figure for the costs) but gave additional information:

> Samuel Rogers, boatman, St Martins, for employing two donkeys to draw fifteen tons of sand in a barge along the canal from St Martins to Pentrefelin, Llangollen, was fined 7s.6d. and 8s.6d. costs.

The load of 15 tons does not seem unreasonable, but the canal at Pentrefelin, a mile above Llangollen on the feeder from the Dee, was (and is) certainly shallow with a significant flow of water.

The Carrying Department

ONE of the early decisions of the amalgamated company was to become a carrier throughout the Shropshire Union canal network. Notice was given to Tilston, Smith & Co. of this intention, as their lease of the carrying trade was due to expire on 1 October 1848.

As was briefly mentioned in Chapter 7, carrying was a complex organisational matter: it was not merely the provision of boats, crews, wharves and warehouses. However, there is remarkably little discussion of it in the company minutes.

The business process started with canvassing for trade, discussing transport needs with current and potential customers. This wasn't just a matter of price: speed was particularly important for perishable items or where the goods were required urgently; reliability meant that the customer's business could carry lower inventories; safety was essential for goods that were easily damaged. From the company's point of view, large loads and regular consignments were particularly desirable, as were 'back loads' – loads going in the opposite direction to most traffic, so could be transported in otherwise empty or short-loaded boats – and the creditworthiness of the customer had to be assessed. An awareness of the competitors at each place was also needed – not merely their charges but also their strengths and weaknesses and their likely reaction to price competition.

Very often, the goods would need transporting locally at one or both ends of their journey and possibly weighing and ware-housing; they would also almost certainly need loading and unloading. All these would need to be factored into the costing. But whereas the maximum canal tolls were set by law and no customer could be favoured, the carriage and 'terminal charges' were a matter for judgement and could be varied.

The network was divided into districts, each under the control of a District Goods Manager (also called the 'Carrying Agent').

He could authorise special rates, but any reduction of tolls required the approval of the General Manager. Reporting to the District Goods Managers were the Agents employed at each 'station' – the SU used the railway term for a town with a wharf at which a reasonable volume of business was done. A canvasser who worked on commission sought business at other locations.

Thus is was the Agent who was the key local presence – he represented the company in the local community, and the company's revenues depended on his enthusiasm, contacts and administrative abilities. It was normal for successful Agents to have a succession of promotions to larger stations.

The Agent collected money owed to the company. Often the recipient of the goods was liable for the transport costs: examples included most purchases from wholesalers and also 'gentleman's goods', which were items being transported for individuals rather than for firms. The Agent was also responsible for the wharfinger, whose duties included the organisation of the loading of the boats and the paperwork associated with it. Waybills were prepared showing what items had to be unloaded at the various wharves visited, including requirements for transhipping.

Traffics and boating

SIMPLIFYING, there were four types of traffic, each requiring a different type of boating.

– Fast long-distance services at predictable times, mainly for goods wanted urgently and for perishable goods, were worked by fly boats. Most fly boats had a crew of four, enabling them to work through the night. A slogan adopted by the SU was 'Collect today, deliver tomorrow'. The 'Brumagem Fly', for example, did two round trips from Ellesmere Port to Birmingham and back each week: 336 miles, 264 locks, 128 hours travelling, and 16 hours loading and off-loading cargoes. The horses were changed regularly: at Bunbury, Tyrley and Autherley in this example.

– Less urgent cargoes and long-distance bulk loads were carried in 'slow boats' (also known as 'stage boats'). Their movements were closely scheduled; for example, the timing of northbound boats was important if the load was to go on a specific ship out of Ellesmere Port or Liverpool. Slow boats had a crew of two or three, worked only during daylight, and used just one horse, mule or pair of donkeys.

– Bulk loads moving relatively short distances, mainly coal and limestone required by local industries, were carried in day boats. Because they worked close to their base, they did not have a cabin with sleeping accommodation.

– Cross-Mersey cargoes were carried in flats and floats. These also worked on the other waterways off the Mersey, including the Bridgewater Canal and the SU Main Line up to Chester. Throughout the period of SU ownership, cross-Mersey boats were generally towed by steam tugs. The flow on the Mersey was originally much slower, making it easier for barge traffic, particularly sailing flats. The Mersey bar

Chapter 10 : The Shropshire Union Railways & Canal Company

was progressively dredged to allow deeper drafted sea-going boats access to Liverpool; this increased the speed of the water in the estuary, making the use of steam tugs more necessary.

During the second half of the 19th century, the SU provided and maintained the boats. However, it supplied the horses only for fly boats. The 'steerer' (captain) of a stage boat bought and looked after his own horse, or, particularly on the Welsh Branch, mule or pair of donkeys.

The steerer was paid per trip – and had to find his own crew. Fly-boat crews were normally all male; on the stage boats the crew was often the steerer's wife and children, especially after rates fell because of railway competition.

Most of the day boats in the South Staffordshire and Birmingham area had an even more indirect organisation; the SU provided the boats, but everything else was managed by agents called 'contract steerers'.

The business of carrying

THE economics of carrying were quite different from the economics of a toll-taking canal. In the latter case most costs were largely fixed, independent of the amount of usage. For carrying, most costs were variable in the medium term, altering in proportion to the traffic.

Demand varied from year to year according to the prosperity of the various industries, from season to season, generally being highest in the spring and the autumn, and also unpredictably from day to day. One never wanted to turn away business (it might not come again) but on the other hand, it was uneconomic to keep spare crews to cover every eventuality. Provender was a major cost; a horse that was not working still incurred a cost of about half that of an active one.

Although the two aspects of the canal company's business had such different characteristics, they were not analysed separately in the half-yearly or yearly accounts. Nor did there ever seem to be any attempt to provide regular 'management accounts' to enable informed decisions to be made by the Board or the senior management.

However, a detailed analysis was calculated and published for the period from 3 August 1846 to 30 June 1850, before railway competition became really important. The following table shows the average annual earnings, costs and profit, with the profit also expressed as a percentage of earnings. (For the trades marked '#', carrying did not start until 1 July 1848, so the averages are for just two years.)

Source of trade	Earnings £	Costs £	Profit £	Profit %
Fluxingstone & iron ore	5,400	4,100	1,300	24
Liverpool & Chester (cross-Mersey)	6,200	5,200	1,000	16
Staffordshire (Black Country)	15,900	13,500	2,400	15
Birmingham #	4,900	5,100	loss 200	– 4
'North' (wharves on SU canals) #	14,400	11,200	3,200	22

Setting up the Carrying Department

SKEY was instructed to procure fifty narrow boats, so a specification was drawn up and a model made. The minutes record forty new boats being ordered, at prices ranging between £115 and £135.

Thus in March 1849 the company became the carrier throughout the whole Shropshire Union canal network. Tilston, Smith & Co. were paid £3,122 for their boats and £1,358 in respect of their wharfs and buildings at Ellesmere Port, Nantwich, Whitchurch, Edstaston, Four Crosses, Welshpool and Shrewsbury.

It was also decided to terminate the agreement with the Bridgewater Trustees concerning the cross-Mersey trade and to resume full control of the facilities at Ellesmere Port with effect from the beginning of 1853, the Trustees being paid £3,000 compensation plus £150 expenses. However, the cross-Mersey boats were initially provided by a contractor, Messrs Williams & Oulton. In 1870 their contract was ended, thirteen broad-beamed boats being taken over by the SU.

The Shropshire Union inherited the system whereby the day-to-day operation of the canal boats was managed by a haulage contractor, William Bishton. He engaged and paid the steerers and provided the horses for the fly-boats. Arrangements were made for him to use the SU's stables along the line of the canal, and he erected additional stables.

Later developments

THE company had continuing concerns about the cost of Bishton's management contract. On his part, Bishton wanted (but did not get) the security of a longer term contract. In fact in 1863 he was given less than a month's notice of the SU taking over the haulage for the 'North Trade', that is, on the branches to Shrewsbury and into Wales and on local traffic on the main line as far south as Brewood. When he later lost the Potteries trade too, Bishton concluded that his contract was so interfered with that it was working at a loss; he therefore gave notice to withdraw from the South Staffordshire and Birmingham trades. The SU took over responsibility for haulage from March 1866, and at the same time took back control of the stables at Ellesmere Port, Chester, Bunbury, Hack Green, Tyrley, Norbury and Autherley, making the repairs which had become necessary.

The SU's fleet grew by taking over the boats of other companies when they withdrew from carrying, particularly in South Staffordshire. The largest number of boats acquired this way was 85 in 1875, when the LNWR's contract with Crowley & Co. was transferred to the SU; their horses, stores and premises were also taken over. In 1901 the LNWR's contract with Messrs Pickford was taken over, with 24 boats being acquired from them.

Prompted by a report drawn up by the LNWR's Expenditure Office at Euston, in 1900 Thomas Hales, the SU's Traffic Manager prepared his own report, accompanied by full statements, showing the likely effect of the company ceasing to be a carrier and becoming a toll taker only. Its conclusions, which demonstrated that there would be no advantage to the company from such a change in policy, were accepted by the Executive Committee.

In about 1912 it was decided to stop operating fly boats to Newtown, Llangollen, Trench, Wolverhampton and Birmingham and to replace them by boats operating with smaller crews and not travelling overnight, but still timetabled and given priority. Considerable financial savings were made, but with the loss of guaranteed fast deliveries to the customers.

Cartage

IN addition to boating, the Carrying Department provided the local cartage services, both for SU traffic and for that of the LNWR in Chester (until 1892), in the Potteries (until 1895) and in some parts of South Staffordshire. The SU provided the carts, wagons and other vehicles and also the horses, which had to be bigger and stronger than the canal horses. Elsewhere, cartage services were provided by local carriers.

Haulage by horses

IN 1898 it was decided that it would be more economical for the company to provide the horses for the stage boats between Ellesmere Port and the Potteries. This proved successful, and the policy was extended to the Welsh Branch and the Main Line during the next ten years. In 1912 it was decided that as a matter of policy it was better when steerers' horses died for the company to provide them, rather than to lend money for a replacement.

Steerers could be penalised if they neglected their company horse. The extreme example was when on 28 November 1910 the grey mare 'Nellie' fell into the canal near Market Drayton and was drowned. The steerer was prosecuted, found guilty, and was fined 20s plus costs, or one month's imprisonment.

Over the years new stables were built at Bunbury (1882, for 24 horses), Autherley (1894), Trevor (1897), Church Minshull (1897, extended 1899) and Chester (1914, for 32 horses).

The stables at Church Minshull were built in order to equalise the sections the horses worked hauling the fly boats between Ellesmere Port and the Potteries. Seven horses had been needed for each boat; this change enabled the number to be reduced to five. The stables were extended when the SU started to provide the horses for the stage boats.

Some costings in the minutes in 1884 imply that horses represent about a quarter of the operational cost of fly boats. Provisioning averaged 13s.8d a week for the horses on the Main Line, by far the most important element being provender, other costs being bedding, shoeing and veterinary attendance. To this must be added the staffing, maintenance and depreciation of the stables, and the depreciation of the horse itself, which typically had cost between £30 and £35. These

The staircase locks and stables at Bunbury in about 1910. *John Howat*

CHAPTER 10 : THE SHROPSHIRE UNION RAILWAYS & CANAL COMPANY

The western part of Cow Lane wharf at Chester in the late 1880s, as depicted by George Henry Wimpenny (1857–1939). It seems to be accurate: the detail accords with the contemporary map. The building on the right was a covered wharf, an arm off the canal passing through the length of the building. The boat was *Redwing*, registered 25 at Chester in 1879, shortly after the Act requiring registration came into force, but it is not known when it was built. It was cut up in 1895. In the background is Chester Cathedral, which was extensively altered between 1868 and 1876 under the direction of George Gilbert Scott, hence its appearance is quite different from that shown in the picture on page 29.

Gallery Oldham

amounts should be compared with the sum paid to steerers, which would have been in the region of £2.10s a week, from which he would have had to pay his crew.

The number of horses owned by the SU reached a maximum of 495 in 1912.

Tugs and motor boats

DESPITE his experience of the relative failure of the 1843–46 experiment to haul boats using a steam tug, Robert Skey continued to believe that the future lay with steam haulage. In 1861 he was given permission to spend £300 to purchase an engine and equipment for a canal tug but nothing seems to have come of this.

Two years later two tugs, *Test* and *Magnet*, were hired from William Bishton for operating between Liverpool and Chester. After a couple of months trial, John Beech reported that 'no appreciable damage' was being done to the canal banks by the steam tugs, and it was therefore decided to buy them for £900. Further steam tugs were bought from the Lancaster Canal. An assessment made in 1875 claimed that towing between Ellesmere Port and Chester by tug cost 1s.8d a ton, compared with 3s a ton using horses.

The Shropshire Union Canal

The next trial of using steam propulsion on the canal was in 1876, when the 'cargo tug boat' *Wolf* was hired from the Grand Junction Canal Company – that company had just given up steam haulage following the detonation of explosives at Maida Vale. It was found that the cost of haulage between Ellesmere Port and Wolverhampton was reduced by 3*d* a ton (a later assessment was 2½*d* a ton) and the journey took four hours less, so *Wolf* was bought for £150. A second boat was put to work on the Autherley to Tyrley section of the main line, and in 1878 *Pioneer*, *Nettle* and *Havoc* were bought from the London & Staffordshire Carrying Company. With these boats a daily service from Ellesmere Port to Wolverhampton could be arranged, and it was thought that some fly boats and about 24 horses dispensed with. In September 1879 the boiler of the cargo tug *Pioneer* exploded whilst being tested at Crewe, killing two fitters; the boiler pressure on the other boats was reduced whilst their safety was being checked.

In 1885 three of the cargo tug boats working between South Staffordshire and Ellesmere Port were taken out of commission to reduce expenses, comparative costings (regrettably not recorded in the minutes) now showing that horse traction was cheaper. The hulls of these boats were retained, but Crewe had no use for the machinery. Jebb was also concerned about the effect of tugs on the canal, explaining that tugs washed the silt out of the middle of the canal and deposited it to the sides. As an experiment the screws were raised; initially it was said that this was found to considerably reduce the wash, but in 1888 Jebb repeated his concern about the effect on the banks, and it was decided that their use between Chester and Wolverhampton should cease. However, when in 1893 a large number of the company's horses were suffering from sore shoulders, two of the carrying tugs were put back into service between Autherley Junction and Tyrley.

This experience did not deter the company from trying again with steam power in 1889 when boat *Luna* was built at Crewe as the inspection packet but also usable as a tug boat. It was put to work between Ellesmere Port and Wolverhampton, and the effect on the banks was to be monitored. It is doubtful whether it was much used for inspections.

Towing between Autherley Junction and Tyrley lasted until about 1908. A typical load was fourteen commercial boats. Jack Roberts' memoirs include a record of his boat being towed by *Leader*, when the 25 miles from Autherley to Tyrley were done in five hours – and this would have included passing the unspecified number of towed boats singly through the lock at Wheaton Aston. Unsurprisingly 'there was quite a flush on each side of the boats'. Nowadays the official speed limit on this canal is 4mph but in practice the maximum is about 3mph as anything more than this causes a breaking wash. Jack's horse 'Jolly' walked alongside at his ease, Jack riding on his back for much of the way. (Because of this, the company's costs weren't actually reduced, of course.)[27]

In 1910 Messrs Gardner & Sons agreed to lend the SU a 'petroleum oil engine' – actually a diesel engine – for a six-month trial. It was put in a fly boat working between Ellesmere Port and Birmingham and, once the men had got used to it, was found to work quite satisfactorily, saving about one-sixth of the cost of working using horses. On that information, the engine was bought, but a year later, because it had frequent breakdowns and the price of oil had increased, it was decided to remove and store the engine.

A 10hp engine made by the Day Motor Co. of Putney was trialled in a canal boat in 1911, also unsuccessfully. Nevertheless, the engine was bought for use powering a centrifugal pump on the salvage barge *Lancaster*.

Mechanical towing

In 1888 the committee witnessed a trial of towing boats using a locomotive on a track on the towing path between Minshull and Cholmondeston Locks on the Middlewich Branch. The aptly-named *Tiny*, which had been brought from Crewe Works was put on a specially-laid 18-inch gauge track, three-quarters of a mile long. In the first trial, ten loaded boats were towed at about 6mph, the locomotive working steadily on the rails. A further trial was made with just four boats, these being drawn equally easily at about 7mph. The trial was deemed a success, though it was thought that stronger and heavier locomotives would be needed and that the canal banks in agricultural districts would be damaged by the wash unless they were greatly strengthened. An independent observer also noted that the test was made along a straight section of the canal, which of course favoured it. At a subsequent meeting Jebb reported on the costs of extending the trial, but it clearly was not worthwhile proceeding.

Later that year Jebb investigated and rejected cable traction, whereby a chain or cable is laid on the bed of the waterway and a tug picks it up and pulls itself along. This method had been used experimentally in tunnels; by 1888 it was fairly common on the Continent, mainly on rivers, where thirty 100-ton barges could be hauled. (The best known example in Britain was through Harecastle Tunnel, and lasted from 1914 to 1954.) Once again a major problem was the tow had to be separated to go through locks.

Boats

The basic design of narrow boats changed little through the 19th century, being built of wood, flat-bottomed, with an open hold. Across the country there were slight variations in the dimensions, depending on the exact sizes of the locks through which they were intended to work.

The typical boat on most of the Shropshire Union system carried about 21½ statutory tons (equivalent to 20 'long tons'). This was rather less than could be carried on the canal from Birmingham to London, for example, because the SU's main line was shallower: the maximum draught officially being 3ft 4in. compared with 3ft 8in. south from Birmingham. 'Fly boats' had finer lines and carried a little less. The boats used for the cheese trade were fitted with shelves enabling them to carry a full 20 ton load whilst stacking the cheeses only two high to avoid

Chapter 10 : The Shropshire Union Railways & Canal Company

The trial of mechanical towing on the Middlewich Branch. Towing by traction engine had been used in France for a couple of decades but this trial may have been the first anywhere using locomotives on rails, a system which was to be perfected on the Continent early in the 20th century.
Canal & River Trust

damaging them. They also had vents in the cratch to enable air to circulate and had cloths painted with white lead to keep out the heat of the sunshine.

The maximum load on boats working to Shrewsbury was about 15 tons because Longdon Aqueduct limited boats' draught to 2ft 6in. Britain's narrowest narrow boats were the 'Trench boats', which were only 6ft 2in. wide in order to fit the locks of the unrebuilt section of the former Shropshire Canal.

The boats without cabins used in South Staffordshire could carry about 28 tons.

The first two iron-hulled boats were bought in 1863. When in 1887 Crewe built two with steel hulls, they were made two inches narrower than the boats used on the South Staffordshire trades; this was said to be to prevent them jamming in the locks of the Welsh Branch – an indication that those locks were slightly narrower than standard. Their carrying capacity was reduced by two tons. (The Hurleston Locks nowadays have the reputation of being the narrowest on the whole canal system and are impassable by some former Grand Union boats. The company minutes show that it is not just a recent problem caused by the movement of the lock walls, as is sometimes claimed.) A further seventeen steel boats were built at Crewe the following year. These steel boats did not last particularly well, most of them being sold in 1912 and one converted into a tank for ammoniac liquor at the company's gas works at Ellesmere Port.

Tub-boats, 20ft long and 6ft 2in. wide, typically had a draught of 3ft and were capable of carrying five tons. Built of either wood or iron, they were the largest boats which could use the inclines, so loads arriving on narrow boats which needed to go up the Trench Incline would have to be transhipped at the foot of the incline or at Wappenshall. As time went on, most of the surviving tub-boats were used for canal maintenance.

Flats and floats operated between Liverpool, Ellesmere Port and Chester. Flats were up to 74ft long and 14ft 3in. wide, with cargo hatches covered with boards, and equipped with an anchor and windlass; some had gaff-rigged sails. Their draught, and hence the loading, varied depending on their main purpose. Those built for use on canals had a more rounded hull so that they could swim better in relatively confined channels. Floats were cruder in design, fully-decked for carrying deck cargoes, without rigging, and much cheaper to build.

An inspection packet was a narrow boat with a large cabin, used for the committee's annual inspection of a section of the canal. It was occasionally used for other purposes, such as in 1884, when approval was given to the Wolverhampton Chamber of Commerce borrowing it for an excursion on the canal. It was normally kept in a shed at Chester.

Other specialist boats included dredgers and ice-breakers.

The total number of boats in the fleet was shown in the

minutes from 1869 until 1919. The number grew steadily until the outbreak of the Great War, by which time it was the largest fleet in the country:

1869	1874	1879	1884	1889	1894	1899	1904	1909	1914
340	463	523	546	568	589	611	649	649	650

A full analysis showing the type of boat was recorded only for the period from 1869 to 1893:

	1869	1872	1876	1884	1893
Canal carrying					
General merchandise narrow boats	163	203	201	198	203
Coal & limestone etc narrow boats	49	80	56	55	69
South Staffordshire narrow boats	–	–	72	83	88
Tub-boats	12	12	8	8	5
Mersey flats & floats	62	106	108	116	117
Steam boats					
Canal	4	4	4	7	6
Mersey	2	3	3	3	3
Engineering & other					
Narrow boats	19	39	41	37	36
Tub-boats	9	9	9	9	21
Dredgers	1	1	3	5	5
Ice-boats	14	16	15	15	14
Packets	1	2	2	3	2
Small boats	4	5	3	7	10
Total	340	480	525	546	579

Boatyards

THE SU had four boatyards, at Chester, Wolverhampton, Pontcysyllte and Ellesmere Port. Chester was the principal yard for maintaining narrow boats, and almost all the boats that were not bought from private boat-builders or second-hand from other carriers were built there. The premises were improved over the years: in 1881 a new shed 185ft long and 43ft wide was erected, and in 1888 the shed used for the storage of the directors' inspection packet was renewed.

The boats based in South Staffordshire were maintained at Wolverhampton. There was a small maintenance yard at Pontcysyllte which also looked after rolling stock on the local railway. The cross-Mersey craft were maintained at Ellesmere Port. Boat maintenance was a major expenditure: in 1895, for example, 250 men were employed on it – 79 at Chester, 9 at Wolverhampton, 5 at Pontcysyllte (down from 10 at the start of the previous year) and 157 at Ellesmere Port, with a total annual pay-bill of about £25,000.

Boating accidents

COLLISIONS, leading to sinking of boats and damage to cargoes, were a frequent occurrence on the cross-Mersey trade. The worst period was just four weeks in 1902 when there were three incidents resulting in SU boats sinking: the flat *Thomas*, one of four in a tow, sank loaded with grain after wash from a passing steamer caused it to hit an embankment in the Manchester Ship Canal; the *Earl of Powis* with eleven flats in tow was struck by *SS Gyda* in the Ship Canal and several flats were damaged; and the SU's *George Stanton* ran into *Gamecock* in Chester Basin, Liverpool – claims were successfully made in the first two cases but only half the damages claimed was paid in the third case because *Gamecock* was occupying one of the berths reserved for the SU.

Ice-breaker being rocked, c.1910. *Railway & Canal Historical Society*

Chapter 10: The Shropshire Union Railways & Canal Company

A tub-boat carrying an Archimedes screw used for draining locks or sections of the canal. *Railway & Canal Historical Society*

Serious accidents to boats on the canals were much less common. As mentioned earlier, on 8 September 1870 the boat *Eagle* was destroyed when its cargo of petroleum exploded at Kidsgrove. On 31 October 1878 *Seal* sank near Manchester with a full load of cheese, having collided with a barge belonging to Bellhouse & Co.; the Solicitor advised that the Company had no case against the owners of the barge, but William Jones, the Traffic Manager, said he had induced them to pay £75.6s, half the loss. The most expensive incident, and one which may have caused major pollution, was when on 26 November 1910 the boat *Cyprus* ran aground at Bilston in foggy weather and sank carrying 15 tons of cyanide; an out-of-court settlement for £500 was reached.

The Shropshire Union as an employer

THE number of employees varied from year to year, of course. The only analysis given in the minutes was in 1907, when the Workmen's Compensation Act 1906 came into force:

Carrying Department	carriers, porters etc	631
	boatmen & hands (excluding wives & children under 14)	586
	flatmen	232
Engineering Department	waged staff	492
Salaried staff	earning up to £250	123
		2,064

To this must be added the salaried staff earning over £250, but these would have numbered fewer than ten. The figures above include the steerers, their adult crew and the crews of the cross-Mersey boats, which the SU appears to have accepted as employees for this purpose. The contract steerers of the South Staffordshire district made their own arrangements for their men, who numbered about 120.

Conditions of employment

PROBABLY through the railway influence, the Shropshire Union came to have quite a formal management style, employing some techniques used by large organisations today. For example, as early as 1853 a document was issued giving what we would now call 'job descriptions' for most employees – not just senior staff such as the General Manager, Secretary, Accountant and Engineer, but also wage-earners such as store-keepers, wharfingers, ticket-makers and lock-keepers – detailing to whom they reported and what their duties were. It also specified the procedures for appointments and promotions, and laid down certain employment regulations, notably:

– all employees must work only for the Company and reside where required;
– all employees must 'obey promptly the orders of his superior officers and conform in all respects to the Rules and Regulations of the Service';
– all salaried staff must provide security, normally three times the annual salary – this would usually take the form of a fidelity guarantee bond; and
– salaried staff earning under £100 a year were on two month's notice, those earning £100 or more on three month's notice.

The 1853 document also included some administrative rules, for example:

> Heads of Departments, and all employed under them, are required to use, in their communications with each other

179

The former SU boatyard at Chester. *Railway & Canal Historical Society*

in their ordinary daily business, the form of Memoranda provided for them; and their attention is particularly called to the instructions as to the use of them, on the cover of each book containing such form.

Unfortunately the accompanying 'General Chart' which detailed the forms in use has not survived.[28]

Old practices disappeared. For example, in 1854 ale ceased to be provided to labourers on canal works. More problematical were the perks of Inspectors, an issue raised by Richard Moon: first it was decided that in future they only be allowed the assistance of a man to groom their horses, but at the next meeting it was agreed that they could be allowed the assistance of one man to help get in the coal which they ordered about twice a year, they could have their horses shod at the company's expense, and they could take wood chips for lighting fires in their houses.

The men working the engineering boats had to meet all the costs of providing the 'motive power', usually a mule or donkeys, and also hire a youth to assist. These costs had to be met out of their pay, which was raised from 5*s*.6*d* to 6*s* a day in 1900.

Each steerer had a 'settling office' where he was paid for the trips he had done. However, as boats could be away from their base for long periods, advances could be obtained at other canal offices or at railway stations. It was normal also to give steerers loans for the purchase of a horse if they needed to replace one which had died. Loans were also given when boatmen were unable to work because of ice. Boatmen could travel home by LNWR train, paying a quarter fare.

In 1879 the main conditions of service other than working hours were brought in line with those on the LNWR. One benefit to employees was that they could then join the LNWR's Insurance and Provident Societies and its Pension Fund, indeed they were encouraged to do so. The minutes record that the LNWR's rule forbidding staff to have outside employments was adopted. As noted above, a similar rule had been adopted previously but had obviously fallen into disuse, as one effect this time was the dismissal of Mr Richards, the Chief Clerk at Wolverhampton, who was not only an insurance agent but also kept a pawnbroker's shop.

In 1890 the committee decided that in future men who were unable to read or write should not be taken on 'for responsible work'. The implication is that some illiterate people had previously been employed in 'responsible' jobs. This ruling did not include the skippers of boats, although they had to deal with waybills and would be assumed to know the relevant byelaws, as the wharf and toll employees did the clerical work. However, it was essential to be able to count, as boatmen were liable to be blamed for the loss of goods which may actually have been stolen by dockers or others.

The Truck Act 1896 clarified what deductions could be made from pay. In particular, no deduction could be made for bad work or injury to the employer's property unless (amongst other provisions) the deduction did not exceed the amount of the loss. The SU altered its practices so that in cases where a penalty was deemed necessary, the employee was suspended from work.

This did not apply to boatmen, where a system of fines applied, but unfortunately the minutes do not give an explanation. One

Chapter 10 : The Shropshire Union Railways & Canal Company

possibility is that they were still considered to be self-employed independent contractors; alternatively it may have been because they did not work set hours.

The advice given over the years by the company's solicitors concerning the status of the people manning the inland craft was inconsistent. When the Workmen's Compensation Act 1897 and the National Insurance Act 1911 were passed, the advice was that steerers were employees of the company but hands were employees of the steerers themselves. However, when the Workmen's Compensation Act 1906 was considered, the hands (other than wives and younger children of boatmen) were deemed to be employees.

Sunday working

The religious revival in Victorian Britain brought with it demands for Sunday observance. Motives were mixed; they included the feeling that one should not expect people to have to work on Sundays, and that if people were given the opportunity to go to church or chapel, their life and behaviour would be spiritually improved. This was a particularly difficult issue for a canal company, of course, because its role was to provide the infrastructure, with some of the carrying being done by independent firms; also, if it acted in isolation, other canals and railways would be likely to benefit. The issue was discussed by the Shropshire Union's Executive Committee on several occasions.

In 1874 it was decided that traffic by slow boats should be entirely stopped on Sundays and that fly boats should cease working during the middle of the day. When one of the directors complained that he had seen two boats carrying iron working the previous Sunday, action was taken to try to get the other carriers to follow the same rules; more effectively, the lock gates at Christleton and Northgate (Chester) were to be padlocked, which was done from 9am to 7pm. One result was that boatmen who needed to get their loads to Ellesmere Port on a Sunday had to work until midnight.

This restriction lasted well into the 20th century. For example, a notice in 1930 stated that the locks at Ellesmere Port, Chester (Northgate) and Autherley Junction were closed from 10pm on Saturdays until 6am on Mondays – except that Northgate locks were open between 11am and 1pm on Sundays, the very times one would expect them to be closed for church attendance. However, these restrictions probably were not because of thoughts of religious observance but to enable the toll-takers to work a six-day week.

The working week and holidays

THE first hint in the minutes of how many hours a week were worked was when in 1897 it was agreed that the working week for the engineering men at Norbury was to be reduced to the same as that for Ellesmere and Welshpool: 57 hours. (The minutes did not mention the Chester men.) In 1899 this was reduced to an annual average of 54 hours a week: more in summer, less in winter. (The Canal & River Trust introduced seasonal variable hours contracts in 2012, under the impression that they were a new concept.)

Boatmen did not have a fixed working week – they had to get their boat to the destination by the set time.

In 1866 engineering staff were allowed Good Friday and Christmas Day off with pay. If the latter fell on a Sunday, no extra payment was to be made – this must have been relaxed later because by 1905 it was noted that the practice was that they be allowed to have the Monday off with pay. And in 1887 all employees were given a day's holiday with pay on the Queen's Golden Jubilee, as later they were for the Diamond Jubilee (1897) and the Coronations of Edward VII (1902) and George V (1911). On the last occasion, steerers were also included, being allowed 3s.

It is not clear when general holiday entitlements were introduced. Engineering staff were granted three extra days holiday from 1890, but a similar request from the Ellesmere Port porters was refused in 1895. By 1907 the porters and waged staff of the Carrying Department were entitled to the following days leave:

– After 1 years service   3 days
– After 5 years service   4 days
– After 10 years service   5 days
– After 15 years service   6 days

These entitlements were extended to flatmen that year, and to the Engineering Department employees at Ellesmere Port the following year.

Housing

CANAL companies normally provided houses for lock-keepers, lengthsmen and wharfingers, particularly in rural areas. These employees needed to live close to their work, keeping watch over the company's assets.

A second reason for the canal company to build houses was when it needed to attract a significant number of workers to sites away from established settlements. Thus when Ellesmere Port was being developed in the 1830s by the Ellesmere & Chester Canal Company, several houses were built. More were added by the Shropshire Union when the docks were further developed.

The Ellesmere Canal also provided a house at Ellesmere for its senior manager. After the Shropshire Union Canal moved its headquarters to Chester, the house came to be occupied by John Beech. Following his dismissal, it was rented out.

As late as 1897, when the Norbury men petitioned for a reduction of half a day in their working hours on account of the distance some of them had to walk to and from their houses, the committee responded by building six cottages near the depot.

Disputes

IN 1860 'a memorial from the canal boatmen as to their wages' was received. It was referred to Mr Bishton, the boatage contractor; as there is no further mention of it, the dispute must have been settled without interference to the traffic.

Then in 1864 it was reported that steerers were refusing to take unladen boats from Ellesmere Port to Wolverhampton to pick up return loads, alleging that they had not been paid. The details are somewhat murky, but it seems that a few of Bishton's 'Staffordshire' boats were being used on the 'North Trade', that is, the service which the SU had taken back from Bishton the previous year, and that neither party was paying the men. This was soon resolved, with the SU paying the men and recharging Bishton.

Before 1871 pay and other conditions had rarely been mentioned in the minutes but from then onwards there was periodic discontent. Demands tended to be made by limited groups of workers, in the same trade at the same location, rather than by any wider organisation of the men.

In 1871 the iron porters at Ellesmere Port went on strike; this was quickly resolved. In the same year some of the South Staffordshire boatmen also went on strike, and the SU increased the rates paid. The South Staffordshire boatmen struck again in 1872, the Potteries boatmen in 1876. More serious was a seven-week strike by 202 Mersey flatmen and 84 porters at Ellesmere Port in 1890, prompted by the company's refusal to pay 6*d* an hour for overtime. A compromise was reached, involving some of the basic pay rates, some of the plussages and certain conditions of service.

Nationally, 1911 was a 'summer of discontent', from which the SU was not immune. A threatened railway strike in 1907 had been averted by the intervention of David Lloyd George, then President of the Board of Trade; while the settlement fell short of the formal recognition which the unions sought, it resulted in the establishment of a wages conciliation system. In August 1911 a national railway strike was again threatened unless (amongst other issues) the right of the unions to negotiate on their members' behalf was recognised. When the strike was actually called, Gilbert Claughton, the Chairman of the LNWR, negotiated a compromise directly with the union leaders, thus in effect recognising the unions. As usual, what affected the LNWR also affected the SU.

The strike of porters at Ellesmere Port in October 1911 was ended when increased rates of pay were agreed, but the boatmen's strike lasted longer. If their demands had been met in full, it would have cost the company £5,200; the actual settlement was estimated to cost £1,640. One element was that the Staffordshire and Humber Arm limestone trades were to be paid on 2,240lb a ton instead of 2,400lb a ton – 87 years after the imperial ton had been made standard and 33 years after it had been made compulsory. A minor concession was that the company would provide all boats with nose-tins, water-cans and boat-hooks. Early in 1912, boatyard workers' piece rate payments were increased.

In 1913 some 47 men in South Staffordshire who were members of a railway union went on strike for 16 days in sympathy with men on strike in Dublin. At about the same time, the men employed by three of the contract steerers on railway boatage work threatened a stoppage. Although these men were not directly employed by the company, it was considered undesirable to have any interference with the traffic, so the Manager requested the contract steerers to effect a friendly settlement, and the rates paid to them would be adjusted.

In 1914 it was the turn of the boat-builders at Chester and Ellesmere Port, the strike lasting

The cottage which used to be at Hurleston Junction opposite the entrance to the Welsh Branch was erected shortly after the merger of the Chester and Ellesmere Canals in 1813. The design, with its wide eaves, clearly shows Telford's influence. Photographed in 1957, it was demolished not long afterwards.

Sir John Smith, the wealthy banker and Conservative MP who had earlier encouraged the National Trust to take on the restoration of the Stratford Canal, had campaigned vigorously for its preservation. He later wrote, 'It was, in particular, the destruction of Thomas Telford's Junction House at Hurleston ... which maddened us into starting the Landmark Trust', a charity which saves historic buildings that are at risk and gives them a new and secure future.

The craft by the house is probably an early hire boat, possibly from 'Holidays Afloat' at Market Drayton.

Railway & Canal Historical Society: Shearing Collection

from 17 April until 24 August. Financially, this probably helped the company, as, because of the unsettled international situation, in July it was decided not to build some of the boats planned.

Accidents and incidents

DEATH by drowning occurred frequently – too frequently – but one gets the impression from the minutes that the main concern of the directors was that the company was not held to blame. The crewing of the cross-Mersey boats was the most dangerous occupation, a particularly black day being 19 March 1904, when Thomas Iddon, captain of the flat *Duchess*, and Peterson, a hand on the flat *Bancroft*, died in separate accidents. (Lifebelts were not carried on Mersey flats until 1903.)

Early 1890 was exceptionally unfortunate: four employees drowned in the canal in one month. And in January 1910 the wives of two steerers drowned in separate incidents in the Audlem Locks.

It is by no means certain that the inability to swim was a major factor in the number of drownings. Most accidents happened in winter. The body's rate of heat loss in water is some twenty-five times that in air at the same temperature. The gagging reflex when falling in water happens automatically, and the throat constricts, thereby the person suffocates. Also woollen clothing absorbs about one and a half times its weight of water, impeding movement. All these combine to make drowning more likely.

When 14-year-old Margaret Evans from the boat *Merlin* drowned in Christleton Lock in 1881, the inquest jury commented strongly on the bad condition of the lock. As a result, Jebb changed the paddle gear at that and similar locks so that they were worked from the land instead of from a footboard on the gate – one of the few examples where changes were made following accidents. The jury was also critical of children being employed to work locks, though by the standards of the day Margaret was virtually adult.

Many other accidents happened whilst working locks. For example, in 1908 Mrs Jones, the wife of the steerer of boat *Bee* was injured when passing through Trench Lock. Mr Jones left his windlass on the pinion of the winch whilst he went to stop his horse, but the windlass flew off and stuck Mrs Jones on the head, knocking her unconscious.

Common then, but unfamiliar now, were the accidents involving horses: several deaths and many injuries were caused by horses bolting, kicking or crushing. For example, in 1894 Thomas Bricknell, steerer of the boat *Coot*, was severely injured when he was kicked by his horse, dying later that day; this case was notable because the doctor's assistant refused to attend because that would have meant him working on a Sunday. It was not only boaters who suffered such accidents – it is often forgotten how extensive the local delivery services were which supported longer-distance canal transport.

A type of accident which still happens a couple of times a year on canal boats was asphyxiation. For example, in 1870 John Broughall was discovered dead in his bed in the forecabin of *Woodman*. The bucket which had held the fire had been knocked over and the scattered coals caused burning to the boat and to Broughall but the examining surgeon said he had not been killed by that but by carbon monoxide poisoning.

Of the loads frequently carried, round timber was the one most likely to cause accidents because it was prone to roll. The other common danger for wharf workers was a faulty crane. That at Queen's Head caused the death of 18-year-old Julia Lyth in 1901, who had been helping unload a boat. As she was the daughter of the steerer, and hence not a Shropshire Union employee, her case was not covered by the Workmen's Compensation Act 1897.

The work at Ellesmere Port could be dangerous, particularly when chemicals were being handled. For example, two men died in the autumn of 1898 after unloading basic slag, which contains large amounts of calcium phosphate, poisonous when inhaled; two other men died there that year.

Just being moored in the wrong place at the wrong time could be fatal. Henry Taylor, captain of an SU boat, was killed and Benjamin Maddocks, captain of another SU boat, was injured by flying debris when a boiler blew up at Messrs Hickman's Leabrook Ironworks at Tipton in 1856.

One curious incident recorded in the minutes occurred in the summer of 1880, when 'one of the Company's men' (which presumably implies a bank-tender, as the crew of boats were not then considered employees) was found dead on board the boat *Eyton* near Barbridge. Thomas Hales, the Traffic Manager, said that he could learn nothing which would account for the man's death. The cargo had been tampered with. Mr Hales dismissed the steerer, taking possession of the steerer's horse to cover his debt to the company.

Boating life

IN the third quarter of the 19th century, by repute boat people, especially those who had no home on land, were a world apart from normal English society. George Smith, the campaigner for occupation standards for boat cabins and for the education of boat children, wrote in 1874:

> Ninety-five per cent cannot read and write. Ninety per cent are drunkards; swearing, blasphemy, and oaths are their common conversation. Not more than two per cent are members of a Christian church; sixty per cent are unmarried, but living as husband and wife.[29]

He noted a few exceptions and was reasonably complementary about fly-boat crews, reserving his strongest criticisms for those working day boats, particularly in the iron-ore trade.

Independent evidence confirms the bad conditions, though it is difficult now to distinguish between the typical and the exceptional. One press report stated:

> The Inspector of the Nantwich Rural Sanitary Authority, Mr Davenport, in a report of some inquiries made in that

district, abundantly confirms all that Mr Smith has said as to the condition in which these people often live. He has found malignant small-pox on board a boat which was carrying the infection all through the district. In another boat a child which had died from typhus was lying unburied in the same cabin with its mother, who was ill of the same disease.[30]

Smith's campaign was successful: the Canal Boats Act was passed in 1877, though it was not truly effective until the passing of an amendment Act in 1884 which provided for the registration and annual inspection of boats, with appropriate penalties for non-compliance. The Canal Association, the trade body of the canal companies, opposed the legislation but Smith noted that several canal managers and canal companies, including the Shropshire Union, had rendered him 'valuable assistance'.

The canal boat regulations introduced in 1878 required rear cabins used as dwellings to have at least 180sq.ft of free air space and forecabins to have at least 80sq.ft, which the Company's boats were generally thought to comply with. Of the Company's total of 531 boats, 293 needed to be inspected and registered, the rest being day boats, maintenance boats and cross-Mersey flats and floats. Chester Corporation's inspector found that *Hind* had seven occupants instead of the permitted maximum of four, and the SU was warned that, as this was the third breach found, any more breaches would result in prosecution. It is a moot point whether the SU would have been held liable, as the number on the boat was the responsibility of the steerer.

The SU's minutes give an occasional glimpse of boating life. A report in 1882 stated that there were 269 boats registered as residences and 321 men in charge of boats, most of the difference being because some boats were day boats without cabins. It was estimated that 1,441 people (including dependents) relied on employment on the SU's canal boats, of whom 862 (60%) lived on board, the rest usually resident on land. Of the 862 on boats, 466 (54%) were men and boys aged 13+, 186 (22%) were women and girls aged 13+, and 210 (24%) were children aged under 13.

Education of boat children

THE SU supported the school at Ellesmere Port and appointed one of the governors. Although the company was asked on several occasions to assist other schools, these requests were almost always refused, the exceptions being a contribution to a school for boat children at Barbridge (although this possibly meant a Sunday school) and two guineas to help clear a debt of £200 in respect of Trevor National School.

School attendance between the ages of 5 and 10 became compulsory in 1880, and in 1891 became free in both state and church schools. Boaters with families who were regularly on the move found it difficult to comply, leading to criticisms by School Attendance Officers, and in a few cases prosecution. The SU directors positively encouraged education: children living on boats were issued with attendance record books and company agents were required to keep records of the number of children attending school and the reason for any absences. According to figures collected by the SU, over 90% of children attended school 'as opportunity arose'. Statistics for the SU fleet were:

Year	1884	1900
Number of boats	363	433
Adult males	574	551
Adult females	189	151
Children of school age	151	97
Number of children who could read and write	not known	32

It is not evident how it is possible that the number of boats had increased by 19% but the number of adult crew members had reduced by 8%.

Several instances were recorded of children being sent back to the boats because the school was said by the teachers to be full. Whether this was true, or whether it was an excuse not to have ill-educated and possibly bored and disruptive children temporarily in the classroom, is a matter for speculation.

Spiritual and physical welfare

IN the last quarter of the 19th century premises for religious services were provided at various places. At Cow Lane, Chester, in 1877 the SU provided an old float *Oak* for a bethel, a spire was added, and it was fitted out by the Queen Street Independent Chapel. Unfortunately it sank in late 1882; a replacement hull was provided and the bethel reopened the following autumn. It was taken out of the water and put on brick pillars in 1889. This did not prove satisfactory and a building in Victoria Place (close to Cow Lane) was given at a nominal rent instead, but in 1906 the mission room was removed to Tower Wharf.

Premises for services were also provided by the SU at Ellesmere Port and Nantwich, and a financial contribution made to the mission at Birmingham. When a building was provided at Ellesmere Port for the Mersey Mission to Seamen, most of the money (£200) came from the LNWR Chairman's Fund, as mentioned earlier. Permission was given for the erection of a mission room at the end of the Humber Arm, but it seems that it was never built.

The Boatmen's Bethel at Birmingham began a branch mission at Wolverhampton in a warehouse of the Shropshire Union Canal Company. The *Sunday School Chronicle* reported enthusiastically in its issue of 30 August 1878:

> Take last Sunday for instance, 25 boats were tied up in the canal, from these boats 33 children attended the school in the afternoon, and in the evening there were 19 adults (all boat people) and 20 to 30 children.

The Bishop of Lichfield's missionary barge was given permission to travel without charge within the diocese, that is, the Shropshire and Staffordshire part of the SU canal system, though most of its contact with SU boatmen would probably have been in Wolverhampton, the Black Country and the Potteries. The Bishop later built a mission room at Wolverhampton.

A report in 1882 by Thomas Hales gave details of the religious agencies' provision for the SU's employees:

- Ellesmere Port: Boatmen's Mission with full-time missionary/welfare worker providing Sunday services, a Sunday school and weekday bible classes; also the Boatmen's Friendly Society, providing Sunday services and welfare visits which are 'proving very successful'.
- Chester: Non-sectarian Sunday services and Sunday school provided by local volunteers in the floating bethel.
- Nantwich: Sunday services provided by the senior curate in the mission room. (Concerning this mission room, Mr Davenport, the Inspector of the Nantwich Rural Sanitary Authority, had commented that many of the parents who had been living together in an unmarried state are getting married.)
- Stoke-on-Trent: Services on Sunday evenings and Sunday school conducted by local residents in premises provided by the North Staffordshire Railway; also the Bishop of Lichfield's travelling boatmen's bethel visited periodically.
- Wolverhampton: Sunday services and Sunday school run by a chaplain.

Later, part of the warehouse at Barbridge was fitted up as a mission room for the Church Army.

At the suggestion of the Revd LaGrange Lonney, curate at Nantwich, a clothing club for boat families was established there in 1881, largely for the boaters working the fluxingstone trade. It was estimated that 30 to 40 families would benefit. The SU contributed 18*s* each year.

Hospitals were supported financially at Chester, Liverpool, Wolverhampton and Shrewsbury. More direct medical assistance was given by way of a wooden leg supplied to Morris, a member of the crew of a fly-boat, and another to Samuel Clay, who broke his leg when loading galvanised iron at Ellesmere Port and had to have it amputated.

Because of the large number of women and children on board the company's boats, in 1903 Miss Mulvany was appointed as a Lady Inspector on an annual salary of £52, with the role of visiting the cabins and exerting a 'beneficial influence', especially in seeing that children attended school. Prior to this the task had been undertaken, with considerable difficulty, by the company's Inspectors. It proved to be a job with a high turnover: Miss Mulvany resigned in 1906 and was succeeded by Miss Olive Blaney and two years later by Miss Gleave. She resigned to get married in 1910 and Miss Gough was appointed, who was succeeded by Miss Blain, then by Miss Moore in 1914. The role changed over time to one principally of nursing. Miss Gleave reported that in 1909 she visited 7,545 boats, and dealt with 282 cases of casual accidents, dressings etc, 210 cases of surgical dressings to women and boatchildren, and 128 medical cases attended to in boats.

Sick pay

In 1882 a sick pay scheme was introduced for engineering staff. Men who were off duty ill would receive full pay for the first fortnight and half pay for the following four weeks. After that, the Inspectors were to state whether the men were likely to resume duties again, and the subjects' circumstances would be specially reported to the Executive Committee for its decision. It is probable that similar rules applied to other staff (but not to boatmen).

Retirements and long service

The SU introduced pensions as early as 1852. Men with more than 50 years service would be given half their weekly wage and those with more than thirty years would get a third, but the pension was never to exceed six shillings.

Many employees worked into their 80s. In 1863, when 29 members of the Engineering Department were made redundant, this included two lock-keepers, John James (84) and Thomas Jones (82), and a bricklayer, Thomas Harper (82); Robert Baugh, the 'ticket-maker' or toll-collector at Carreghofa, had 55 years' service with the Montgomeryshire and the Shropshire Union Canal Companies, having succeeded his father in that job. Thomas Manifold, a bank tender, also had 53 years' service. Interestingly, three of the people made redundant were women: Jane Briscoe, a ticket-maker, and Mary Thomas and Mary Morris, both lock-keepers. They probably had taken over the duties on the death of their husband.

The oldest employees mentioned in the minutes were T. Richards, who retired aged 89, with 40 years service, and J. Beddow, a ticket clerk, who retired aged 88 with 55 years' service. The longest-serving employee mentioned in the minutes was S. Young of Autherley, who died in 1899 aged 79 after 65 years service; his daughter continued with the clerkage and indoor work, having performed it for her father for several years – her pay was set at £52 a year, whereas her father had been paid £81 a year. Other long-serving employees of the SU mentioned were James Hope, Secretary, who had 'over 60 years service', William King, lock-keeper at Ellesmere Port, with 63 years service, F. Challenor, steerer, latterly of the *Hussar*, with 62 years service (who was not entitled to a pension but was given a weekly gratuity), C. Talbot, lock-keeper at Newport, with 61 years service, John Roycroft, who retired as Inspector for the Norbury District after 60 years service, and J. Whitmore, foreman carpenter at Norbury, who also retired having had 60 years service. W. Barratt, steerer of the boat *Saxon*, retired in 1898 after working for Crowley & Co. (whose boats had been taken over by the SU) and then the SU for 66 years; unusually for a steerer, he was given a pension.

Thomas Ray, an Extra Porter at Chester, who died in service having been employed by the Company for 54 years, was provided with a coffin made in the Chester boatyard, at a cost of 11*s*.7*d*.

The Shropshire Union Canal

Finances

UNDER the lease agreement, the shareholders were entitled to dividends at half the rate paid to the LNWR's own shareholders. Thus the LNWR had to make good any deficiency on the SU's accounts after paying the interest on borrowings and the dividends. The SU's earnings included both those for its canals and for its railway, though once the railway became part of the LNWR network the latter was a notional rather than an actual figure. The first period for which the LNWR had to make a deficiency payment under the lease agreement was the year ended 30 June 1850.

SU canal: financial results

UNLIKE railways, canal companies did not have to make statistical and financial returns to the government. The content and assumptions of the published half-yearly and annual accounts varied over the years and it has not proved possible to create a consistent comparative statement covering the whole period of the Shropshire Union's existence.

Furthermore, company accounting was still in its infancy, and there was no such thing as accounting standards. In particular, no agreement existed about exactly what constituted 'capital expenditure' and what was 'revenue expenditure', and the accounts did not show depreciation – implicitly, it was assumed that if assets were properly maintained, they did not lose value.

One file at The National Archives shows the net income (receipts minus payments, excluding interest and dividends) of the SU canal, as used in the calculation of the deficiency charged to the London & North Western Railway for of the years 1846 to 1894.[31] This shows the following general trends:

1846–49	Net income over £50,000
1850–57	Sharp reduction to £35,000 in 1850, followed by several years about £25,000
1858–71	Reduction to £17,000 in 1858, followed by several years generally in the range £10,000 to £15,000
1872–76	Steady reduction to £1,000
1877	The first year with a trading loss (£600)
1878–89	Fluctuating results: some years showing a small profit, some a small loss
1890–94	Significant losses, averaging almost £10,000 a year

The reduction in 1850 shows the immediate effect of railway competition at Ruabon, Oswestry, Shrewsbury, Wellington and Newport; the reduction in the period 1858–63 coincided with the opening of railways serving the other market towns in the Shropshire Union's area.

The accounts prepared by James Coleman (the LNWR's auditor) for the period from 3 August 1846 to 30 June 1850 show the apportionment between the basic canal business and

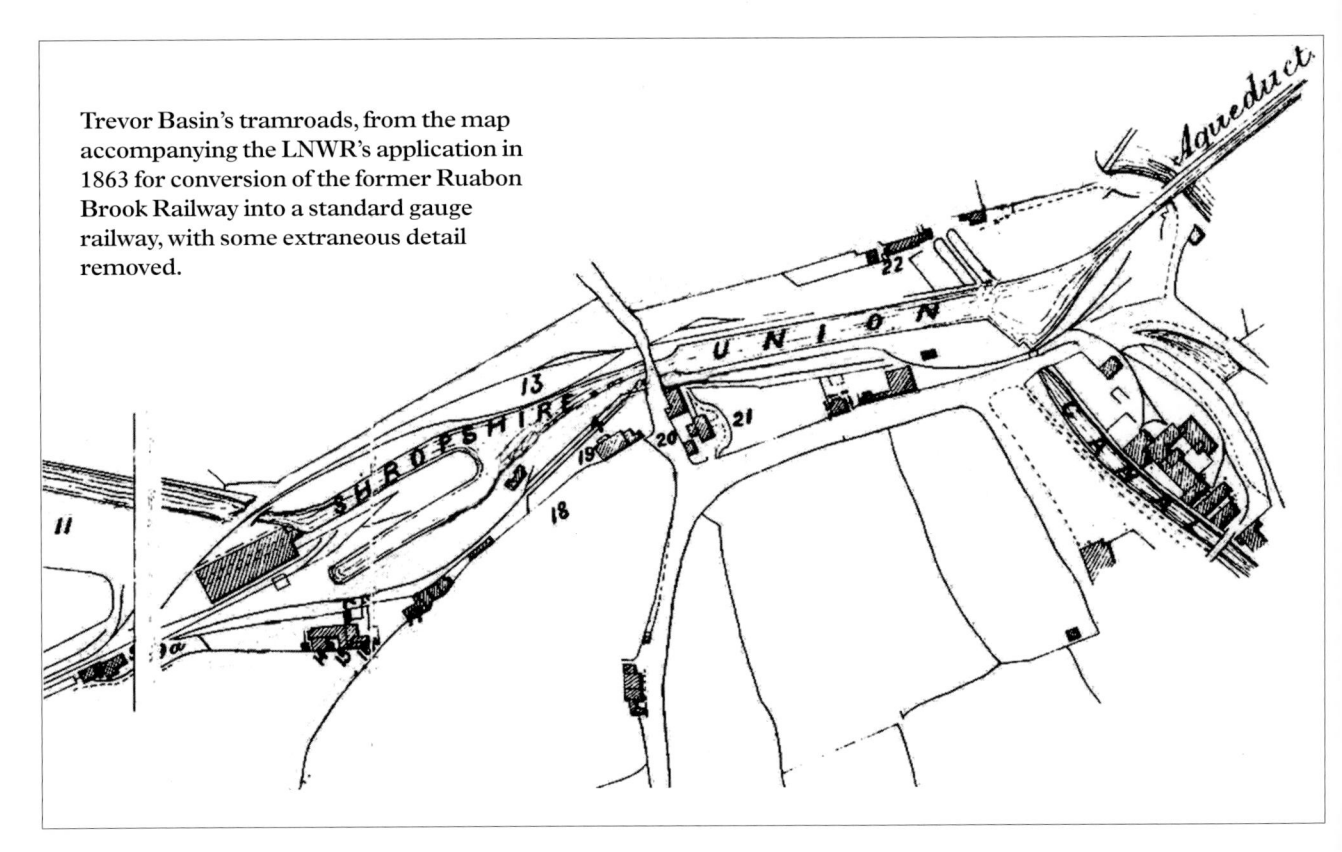

Trevor Basin's tramroads, from the map accompanying the LNWR's application in 1863 for conversion of the former Ruabon Brook Railway into a standard gauge railway, with some extraneous detail removed.

Chapter 10: The Shropshire Union Railways & Canal Company

the carrying business. The annual average figures during this period were:

	Earnings £	Costs £	Profit £
Canal: tonnage tolls etc	72,400	26,200	46,200
Carrying	46,800	39,200	7,600
	119,200	65,400	53,800
Less unallocated costs			1,200
Net profit before interest, dividends etc			52,600

Note: The costs of carrying included the tonnage tolls, the income from which is shown in the 'canal earnings' figure, as far as it related to the SU's own canals.

Although the basic canal business looks far more profitable than the carrying business during this period, it must be borne in mind that the former was created by a large capital investment whereas the latter had relatively small capital costs.

Information provided to the Royal Commission on Canals 1906–9 gives a glimpse of trends at the end of the 19th and beginning of the 20th centuries (though it is not consistent with figures derived from elsewhere):

	1888 £000	1898 £000	1905 £000
Income			
From tolls	5,400	5,500	4,300
From freight as carrier	178,900	167,700	192,300
Other	6,700	10,900	13,100
Total income	191,000	184,100	209,700
Expenditure			
Canal maintenance		25,800	33,600
Canal management		4,000	4,100
Carrier expenses		139,100	148,400
Other		14,100	16,800
Total expenditure	186,500	183,000	202,900
Net revenue	4,500	1,100	6,800

Notes: Analysis of 1888 expenditure not available.
    Income from freight as carrier includes the tolls relating to that freight.
    Excludes interest and dividends.

The Ruabon Brook Railway / Pontcysyllte Railway

The track of the tramroad to Ruabon Brook had been renewed back in the early 1830s. The rails, the length of which varied from 3ft to 5ft, were cast at William Hazledine's Plas Kynaston foundry using the original patterns – they had the initials 'EC' moulded into them, referring to the former Ellesmere Canal. This proved useful evidence in a case in 1854 when a Mr Wright was accused of dealing in stolen iron.[32]

The arrival of standard-gauge steam railways in the Wrexham and Ruabon area made the tramroad seem out-dated. The Chester–Wrexham line opened in 1846 and was extended to Shrewsbury in 1848; the Ruabon–Llangollen branch opened to freight in 1860 and to passengers the following year. Both these became part of the Great Western Railway empire, and were linked to local industries by private branches and sidings. The London & North Western Railway's only presence was through its Shropshire Union subsidiary, so it was sympathetic to proposals to extend and modernise its tramroad.

In 1857 Henry Jones offered to put 20,000 tons of coal a year on the tramroad if it was extended by about 2,000 yards to his colliery at Llwyneinion. Edward Johnes, the SU's engineer, estimated the cost to be £2,217, and Jones and his partner agreed to guarantee a return of 10% on the outlay for fourteen years. The extension was approved, but was never built.

Conversion

In March 1861 a letter was received from Richard Rawlins, manager of the Wynne Hall Colliery Company, which was at the northern terminus of the tramroad. The letter stated that an 8ft-thick seam of coal had been discovered at that colliery, and continued:

> We shall be ready in less than a month's time to forward some hundreds of tons per week from the pit. You will not be surprised therefore at our feeling anxious to know if we may look to you for railway communication, or whether we must turn our attention to what the Gt Western can do for us.

The Executive Committee of the SU was keen to accommodate the request and resolved to convert their tramway into a standard-gauge locomotive railway, but to do this they needed permission from the LNWR, which did not share the urgency. In June the Wynne Hall Colliery offered a guarantee of traffic, but as by mid August nothing had been agreed they wrote again:

> We are so awkwardly and peculiarly circumstanced in having everything ready to send off a large quantity of coal and no means of doing so but by a double loading and unloading which the low price of coal just now renders almost impossible, that we are reluctantly obliged to withdraw the guarantee we offered to you on the 8th of June last, that we may be free to endeavour to make other arrangements to accomplish the indispensable object of railway communication.

John Beech estimated the cost of conversion as £6,240, net of the value of old materials. It was another year before the LNWR's Special Affairs Committee consented to the proposal, and then the lawyers debated which undertaking should apply to Parliament, so it was not until November 1862 that the Amalgamated Board decided to go ahead, the converted line to form part of the SU. As a first stage, only the section between Wynne Hall Colliery and G.H. Whalley's Plas Madoc railway would be converted – in other words, the railway would be used to take the wagons to the GWR at Ruabon – and this was completed in April 1863.

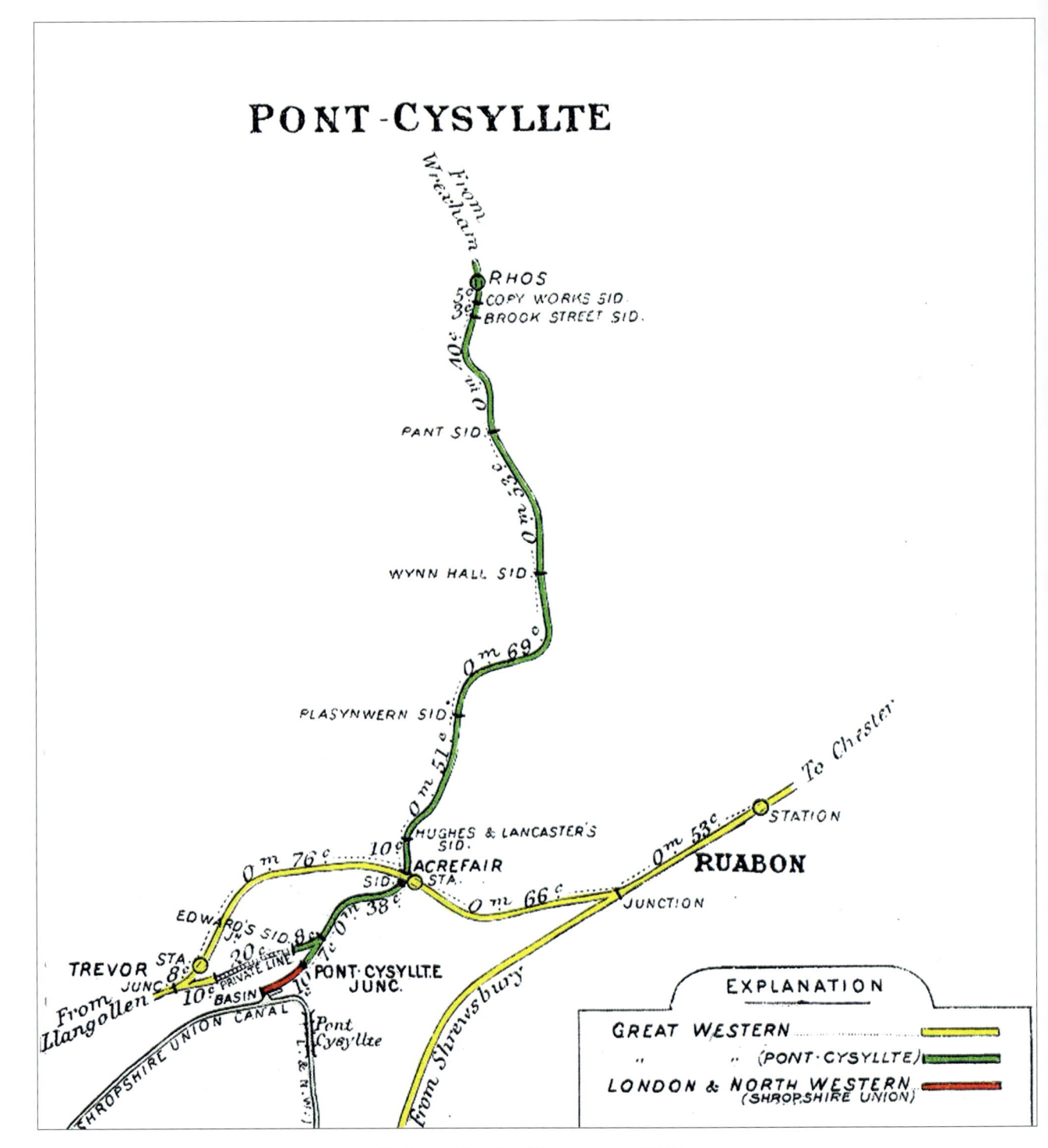

Railway Clearing House map of 1911.
The 'explanation' incorrectly shows the Pontcysyllte Railway as belonging to the LNWR.
Huw Edwards Collection

Chapter 10: The Shropshire Union Railways & Canal Company

The second stage was to be a new much shorter but steeper (1 in 31) line from Acrefair down to Trevor Basin. It was originally hoped that the land could be acquired by negotiation but this did not prove possible, so powers were added to a Bill then before Parliament. Once the Act was passed a contract was made with J. Millington & Son for the locomotive line between Plas Madoc Junction and Trevor Basin. The spoil banks belonging to the New British Iron Company and to Sir Watkin Williams Wynn's industries were used to form the embankment. The interchange arrangements at Trevor Basin were remodelled, and the railway was ready for use in April 1866.

J.C. Edwards, the brick and tile manufacturer whose main premises were at Trevor, offered to guarantee the income for a standard-gauge link between the reconstructed Pontcysyllte Railway (as it was by then known) and the GWR's Trevor station if the SU would support it. Terms were agreed for Edwards to make the link, and for SU trains to be able to work over it. This too was ready for use in April 1866.

In the autumn of 1864 the GWR proposed making a branch from Wrexham to Llwyneinion, which provoked the SU to revive its earlier proposal for an extension of the Pontcysyllte Railway to the ironworks and brickyards there. Beech estimated that a non-Parliamentary line would cost £9,700, and guarantees of traffic seemed forthcoming. The GWR's Bill was defeated, and the SU set about getting agreements to buy the necessary land and to make arrangements about the road crossings. The LNWR's approval for the expenditure was also obtained. In October 1865 a contract was made with Millingtons in the amount of £5,884 to build it. The main engineering problem was the brick viaduct over the Avon Eitha, which it was feared might be affected by mining. The approach embankment did in fact suffer subsidence, delaying the opening until the spring of 1867, half a year later than planned. Subsidence continued to be a problem; in 1869, having rejected the idea of buying the coal under the viaduct, it was decided to make it into an embankment with a culvert for the watercourse.

The extension must have been exceptionally lightly built. As early as 1872 Jebb was recommending that the track needed renewing and meanwhile that the speed limit – which was only 6mph – should be reduced.

At first the traffic on the Pontcysyllte Railway was worked by a locomotive of the New British Iron Company, but after a few months Crewe hired one to the SU. In 1870 it was decided to buy a new '4ft Shunter' locomotive from Crewe for £1,000 but instead better value was achieved by buying a small 0–4–0 tank engine named *Acton* which was surplus to the LNWR's requirements. This had been built by Sharp Brothers of Manchester in 1850 and supplied to Edward Oakley & Co., of the Coed Talon Colliery near Mold, then passed through the ownership of the Chester & Holyhead Railway and Birkenhead Railway before being taken into the LNWR stock in 1860. After *Acton* was scrapped in 1883, locomotives were hired from the LNWR for 10s a day.

The traffic on the railway never reached expectations. In 1869 Wynne Hall Colliery was drowned out and the company put into liquidation. The coal traffic from Llwyneinion was disappointing, though clay brought by J.C. Edwards from Llwyneinion to his Trevor works provided some compensation. The guarantees proved ineffective; that given by G.H. Whalley in particular being the cause of a long-running dispute. By the start of 1878 all the collieries had closed, the biggest remaining source of traffic being the Wynne Hall spelter (zinc) works.

The loss on operating the railway was estimated as £250 in 1877, but this was more than offset by the earnings on the canal from traffic coming off or going onto the railway, estimated as £413 tolls plus £164 surplus on carrying.

In June 1882 the Executive Committee travelled up the railway to Llwyneinion, discussing the actual and potential traffic. Because they found that there was little activity north of Rhosllanerchrugog (normally referred to as 'Rhos'), they decided to keep the line open only to there. Jebb was given permission to take up the rails at the further end and use them for the portion to be kept open.

In the mid 1880s, with the opening of new mines, traffic revived somewhat, and the railway showed a small operating profit. There was bad news in 1887, when the New British Iron Company, the largest of the railside industries, went into voluntary liquidation. On the other hand, in 1891 Henry Dennis enlarged his brick and tile works at The Pant near Rhos; a siding a quarter of a mile long was put in to serve it.

Sale of the Pontcysyllte Railway

In the winter of 1893/94 two rival proposals were made for serving the area between Wrexham and Rhos. The East Denbighshire Railway was locally promoted, with the expectation that it would be worked by the Wrexham, Mold & Connah's Quay Railway; a rival scheme was then put forward by the Great Western Railway. The SU initially opposed both but when the East Denbighshire Railway offered to buy the Pontcysyllte Railway for £15,000 if its Bill was successful, the SU assented and withdrew its petition.

However, that Bill failed; the GWR's progressed but later in the year was rejected by the House of Commons. Following senior level negotiations in the autumn of 1895, the GWR agreed to buy the Pontcysyllte Railway for the sum of £51,000, take on the staff employed on it, and continue to operate two trains a day to and from the canal wharf. The railway was formally handed over on 12 February 1896.

Bearing in mind that the SU had earlier been willing to sell the railway for less than a third of this amount, one must conclude that the GWR over-paid and that the SU's negotiator, Frederick Harrison, who was General Manager of the LNWR, should be congratulated.

The old tramroad

WHEN the new cut-off line between Acrefair and Trevor Basin opened, the part of the old tramroad from Acrefair to the Crane (the hairpin bend in Cefn Mawr) became redundant and the track was lifted. Complaints about nuisances were soon made. The SU was willing to sell the land to the Wrexham Highways Board, Sir Watkin Williams Wynn having agreed to give up any pre-emptive rights that he might have, but the SU's lawyers found that the company had no powers to sell it so a lease was agreed instead: £6 a year for the 800yds. The land was sold to Wrexham Rural District Council in 1915 for £131. This section of the former tramroad is now King Street.

The section of the tramroad from Trevor Basin up to the Crane continued in use, together with the extension to the Plaskynaston Colliery, which was adjacent to the GWR main line. Mapping evidence shows the extension was made some time after 1845, probably after spare rails became available from conversion of the northern part of the tramroad. There are a tantalising pair of minutes in 1869: 'Tramway – Plaskynaston Co. – This is to be done on an arrangement with the Colliery Co.', and 'Mr Smith's report ... was submitted ... as to the tramway to the Plaskynaston Colliery'. The 1870 Ordnance Survey map shows a tramway or railway (it does not distinguish between them) from Trevor Basin, past the Crane and continuing to the colliery. A minute the following year refers to 'the tramway to Cefn quarries' being completed. In 1882 it was reported that no traffic was being moved along the old tramway. The Plaskynaston Coal Company confirmed that there was no prospect of them using it, so the rails were taken up and the scrap iron sold to Crewe railway works.

Back in 1871 J.C. Edwards had been given permission 'to lay down an inner rail' on the tramroad from a clay pit near the Plas Kynaston Ironworks to his Trevor brickworks. The wording implied that the brickworks used a narrow-gauge railway within its site. By the time of the 1900 Ordnance Survey map, this line was the only surviving part of the old SU tramway.

A further 1,000 yards of the former tramway route was sold to Cefn Parish Council in 1898.

The Glyn Valley Tramway

THE river Ceiriog flows east from the Berwyn Mountains, under Chirk Aqueduct, to the Dee. Largely because it lacked a reasonable road, it remained undeveloped in the first half of the 19th century, apart from some small-scale quarrying of slate around the village of Glyn Ceiriog and some manufacturing of flannel.

In 1857 the newly-formed Cambrian Slate Company started negotiations with the Wem & Bronygarth Turnpike Trustees to provide a private horse-drawn tramway alongside the latter's proposed new road up the valley to Glyn Ceiriog, but this was opposed by Colonel Myddelton Biddulph of Chirk Castle. A standard-gauge railway, backed by the Great Western Railway, was proposed in 1865, and a counter-proposal, the Ellesmere & Glyn Valley Railway Company (EGVR) was made for a similar railway to the Cambrian Railways at Ellesmere. Thanks this time to the support of Col. Myddelton Biddulph (whose estate it avoided) and other landowners, the Act for the latter was passed in August 1866. However, the bankruptcy of Thomas Savin, a key promoter of the Cambrian Railways, and the financial crisis caused by the collapse of Overend Gurney, the largest discount house in the City of London, meant that the £120,000 needed could not be raised.

The company then put forward a much less ambitious scheme, with the capital requirement of only £25,000. The railway was to descend the Ceiriog Valley then climb steeply with a gradient of 1 in 24 from Pontfaen to interchange sidings with the Great Western Railway near to Preesgweene station and continue to the Shropshire Union Canal near Gledrid. In response to a request in 1868 to help with the construction, the SU stated that it would give 'every assistance'; at a subsequent meeting this was refined into a promise to support the scheme providing the canal interchange facilities were ready at the time the line opened and that traffic to the canal was charged the same as traffic to the GWR. The SU also said that it would 'probably' contribute £5,000 towards the share capital of the EGVR, but this was not a firm promise.

The resultant 1869 Act stated the gauge could be anything between 2ft and standard gauge, though the SU actually envisaged it would be a locomotive-operated railway of 2ft gauge.

The following year, Parliament passed the Tramways Act which relaxed certain requirements generally imposed on railways and allowed track to be laid along roads. An opportunity was seen to reduce the cost further by amending the line in the Ceiriog Valley so that for much of the way it would be adjacent to or on the road. A significant restriction was that all trains had to be horse-drawn. The EGVR's name was changed to the Glyn Valley Tramway (GVT) but its Act explicitly stated that no part of the Tramways Act shall apply. (The name is an English misunderstanding, 'glyn' being the Welsh for 'valley'.)

Before the passing of the Act the SU had stated that a condition of any subscription was that the entire balance of the money needed to make the line must be forthcoming or guaranteed. It later added a further requirement: that it would subscribe only if it worked the line.

The formal decision to invest in the GVT was made in June 1871 at a meeting at Bala of the SU's Executive Committee. The sum of £5,000 would be invested, subject to a scrutiny of the plans and specifications, with George Jebb, their engineer, having direct control over the construction of the works, and to the SU having the sole right to work the line. Alfred Wragg, the SU's Company Secretary, was nominated to be a director of the GVT.

In January 1872 the subscription was increased to £6,000, on the assurance that the rest of the money could be obtained. The shares would actually be held by nominees of the SU: the Earl of Powis (183 shares of £10 each), George Stanton (184), Richard Moon (183) and Alfred Wragge (50).

With Henry Dennis as resident engineer and Elias Griffith of Chirk as contractor, construction started in the summer of 1872. The gauge was unusual (but not unique): 2ft 4¼in.

The minutes of the SU's Executive Committee meeting on 21 April 1873 recorded that the GVT was now being worked by the SU, but as later minutes gave authority to purchase horses

Chapter 10 : The Shropshire Union Railways & Canal Company

and up to 100 wagons (to be constructed at the SU's Ellesmere Depot) and the appointment of various staff including drivers, it seems more likely that the tramway became operational in about September that year. The SU also had to lend further sums in order to provide some facilities omitted from the construction contract such as sidings, warehouses and a second track for the 925yd long incline up to the Cambrian Slate Quarry, as well as operational necessities including the wagons and several horses. The following year the SU approved the building of a house and four cottages near the south end of Chirk Aqueduct for GVT employees. A passenger service from Pontfaen (but advertised as 'Chirk') to Glyn Ceiriog started operating in April 1874.

By now, the SU realised what it had taken on. Because of the steep gradients, especially in the Pontfaen–Gledrid section, horse traction was proving much more expensive than anticipated. The use of steam power was discussed; Francis Webb, the LNWR's Chief Mechanical Engineer, considered a suitable locomotive could be built for £250.

Complaints were being made about the roadside section of the tramway: the clear width left was not always in accordance with the Act, the level of the tramway was sometimes above and sometimes below the level of the road, and where it crossed the road the rails were not flush with the road surface. The road itself was in a poor state of repair, though that was not the GVT's responsibility. Mineral trains, and even passenger carriages, were sometimes sent down by gravity.

On 19 December 1874 a gravity train carrying fare-paying passengers on a slate wagon was derailed on the sharp bend at Pontfaen, throwing its occupants and their luggage into the river Ceiriog. Three people (including one named William Shakespeare) were injured. The Board of Trade report was highly critical: gravity working was contrary to the Act, and the brakesman, who was intoxicated, failed to slow down before reaching the sharp bend over the river. The SU had to pay compensation and also to have the bend eased.

Discovery of good quality granite, suitable for setts, led to a request for the tramway to be extended for two miles further up the valley. As well as the Glyn Ceiriog Granite Company's Hendre Quarry this would serve other quarries and the Patent Gunpowder Company's factory making nitrocellulose explosives, then being newly developed. The SU encouraged the proposal, providing funding was guaranteed. It was also keen on having traffic agreements with all the companies for their entire output to be taken by the canal, so it offered rates comparable with other carriers. However, although the national canal network was extensive, it proved uncompetitive compared with the attractiveness of rail transport – and the 1870 Act had required interchange sidings with the Great Western Railway, which was crossed by the tramroad. By the end of 1876 it was clear that only about a third of the tramway traffic was being transferred to boats at Gledrid Wharf.

The granite quarry was successful; the explosive works was not. H.M. Explosives Inspectorate had found samples to be impure and potentially dangerous. In July two tons of the powder made up into cartridges for an Australian customer were dispatched on the iron sailing ship *Great Queensland*. The ship never arrived, 67 lives were lost, and an exhaustive inquiry concluded that 'in all probability, the cause was the spontaneous combustion of two tons of wood powder' for which 'the Patent Gunpowder Company are alone to blame'. The company was disgraced and ceased trading.

In 1878 Parliamentary approval was obtained for improvements to the road and to the tramway, including its extension up the valley. But the Act did not sanction the use of steam power, the use of which was essential if costs were to be contained, though the turnpike trust had consented.

Matters came to a head in September 1879 when the meeting of GVT shareholders resolved that the agreement with the SU should be ended in three months time unless the SU took steps to obtain approval for the use of steam power. Jebb reported in December that the estimated cost of making the line suitable for locomotive working would be £7,000. In February 1880 the SU directors decided that they would dispose of their interest in the GVT, but in June they took the opposite view and proposed that the SU should acquire the GVT. They may have been concerned about the loss of desperately needed traffic – or they may have fallen into the trap of considering the money they had already invested, rather than assessing the future costs and revenues. Whatever the reason for the SU's volte-face, the other GVT shareholders were determined to regain control.

The New Cambrian Slate Quarries' business was in financial trouble as its prices were uncompetitive with those for slates from Snowdonia. On the other hand, demand for setts was increasing, particularly in the towns of the North West and the Midlands. The Glyn Ceiriog Granite Company, realising that failure to secure the tramway's future could seriously damage its ambitious expansion plans, offered to take over the operation of the tramroad. The GVT Board supported this proposal, then offered to buy the plant and buildings from the SU for £1,800, leaving the canal company with its horses, harness and shares. The SU agreed to this, and ceased to run the tramway on 31 August 1881.

The Glyn Ceiriog Granite Company took over operation the following day. After much negotiation, permission for conversion to steam haulage and easing the gradient by approaching Chirk through the lands of the Chirk Castle estate were obtained, the necessary Act being passed in 1885. After immense fundraising difficulties (and major rows within the GVT Board) the converted line, now operated by the Glyn Valley Tramway itself, opened for freight in 1888 and passengers in 1891. At the western end this included the extension to the Hendre Quarry. At the eastern end the line continued beyond Chirk Station to Black Park Wharf, though the canalside granite wharf was put in later. The section from Pontfaen to the canal at Gledrid was abandoned.

In 1887 five GVT directors acting jointly on behalf of that company gave the SU a promissory note for £2,400 for the

191

purchase of the SU's shares, which had a nominal value of £6,000. Settlement was made the following March. The SU therefore had lost £3,600 on its investment, to which must be added the £5,980 net loss during the period it operated the tramway, making a total of £9,580. In fact, the amount may have been even more, as the figures reported in the minutes of the SU's Executive Committee do not take account of any loss on the horses and harness in excess of the depreciation charged.

Why should the SU, by 1871 a professionally-run organisation, have made such an error of judgement as to firstly invest in and secondly to operate a horse-drawn tramway that could not possibly cope with the projected traffic? The technology was forty years out-of-date, and it must have been obvious that this particular line was being built to below-minimum standards and including a steep adverse gradient. The Act required interchange facilities with the GWR, so the SU was unlikely to have a monopoly of the longer distance transport – and whether or not the items went by boat or main line railway, they would incur the costs and risk of damage from transhipment.

Richard Moon, Chairman of the mighty London & North Western Railway, was personally involved in all the key decisions. As mentioned earlier in this chapter, he was notoriously careful about money – on one occasion he criticised some SU officers because reports were written on only one side of the paper – and I find it incredible that he agreed to invest in the Glyn Valley Tramway, as it seems so out of character.

Shropshire Union Canal stone showing the boundary of the canal company's property. *Author*

Notes and references

The principal source for this chapter is the files of the Shropshire Union Railways & Canal Company held by The National Archives (RAIL623). For a sumptuously detailed history of the Glyn Valley Tramway, see John Milner & Beryl Williams, *Rails to Glyn Ceiriog*, Part 1, 2011.

1. Peter Braine, *The Railway Moon*, reprinted with corrections 2012, pp.39, 50, 106; SURCC & LNWR Amalgamated Board, 17 December 1868: TNA, RAIL623/36
2. SU Board, 24 February 1922: RAIL623/8
3. *The Times*, 15 August 1890, reporting the half-yearly meeting of the London & North Western Railway, 14 August 1890
4. SU Executive Committee, 26 June 1863: RAIL623/12
5. SU Board, 18 July 1872: RAIL623/7
6. SU Executive Committee, 26 April 1911: RAIL623/26
7. The Shrewsbury & Welshpool Railway was acquired by the LNWR in 1864 and became joint with the Great Western Railway in 1865, part of a group of joint lines in the Border Counties.
8. The LNWR expected the Nantwich & Market Drayton to become part of its empire, but it fell into the hands of the Great Western Railway following the promotion of the Wellington & Drayton Railway in 1862.
9. SU Parliamentary Cttee, 4 March 1861: RAIL623/7
10. Royal Commission on Canals 1906–9, Volume 3, p.280
11. Braine, op. cit., p.211
12. Board of Trade correspondence files: MT6/176/8
13. Letter from D. Green, Waterways Manager, to Edwin Shearing, 12 June 1992: author's collection
14. GWR estates map, 1884: image from Huw Edwards
15. George Borrow, *Wild Wales*, chapter VIII
16. Jack Roberts, *Shropshire Union Fly-boats*, 2015
17. Royal Commission on Canals 1906–9, Vol.4, p.104
18. Wappenshall Wharf records: Shropshire Archives, Sutherland Collection, principally 673/7/10 and 972/175
19. William Gregory Norris, *Account of Horsehay Iron Works*, 1876: Shropshire Archives, 245/140
20. Royal Commission on Canals 1906–9, Volume 3, 280; also Appendix 16, pp.52, 57
21. *Wolverhampton Chronicle*, 16 June 1852; *Salopian Journal*, 8 June 1853; *Wrexham Advertiser*, 12 August 1854
22. Stephen Hughes, *The Archaeology of the Montgomeryshire Canal*, fourth edition 1988, p.161 (The image bears the reference WM/74/107)
23. *Salopian Journal*, 8 June 1853
24. *Llangollen Advertiser*, 21 May 1897, 28 June and 2 August 1901
25. *Llangollen Advertiser*, 1 September 1893, 29 September 1899 (advertisement) and 17 August and 21 September 1900
26. *Llangollen Advertiser*, 28 July 1882
27. Jack Roberts, *Shropshire Union Fly-boat*, 2015, pp.36, 86
28. SURCC regulations & duties, November 1853: Shropshire Archives, 6147/1
29. George Smith, *Our Canal Population*, 1875 (1974 reprint), p.119
30. ibid., p.42
31. Canal earnings: TNA, RAIL623/46
32. *Wrexham Advertiser*, 24 June & 1 July 1854

11
The First Canal Age

A study of the Shropshire Union Canal and its predecessors gives the opportunity to make comparisons and draw some general conclusions about canal history.

What was the economic impact of the canals?

THE first clause of any Act to build a canal set out the advantages, typically stating that it would be 'of great public utility'. More specifically, it generally stated the canal would:

- reduce the price of coals;
- assist agriculture by the supply of lime and other manure at moderate expense; and
- encourage and assist manufactures.

The first of these claims was universally true, indeed, it was the principal reason for the construction of the Shrewsbury Canal. A letter to the *Montgomeryshire Journal* in 1835 implied that the price of coal had been reduced by a third when the canal came to Newtown. The price of coal at Market Drayton was reduced by 3d per hundredweight immediately the canal past the town opened.[1]

The second claim was often true too, though obviously the degree of benefit depended on the type of soil, the type of agriculture and the extent of previous improvements. Again using a Montgomeryshire Canal example, the Glansevern Estate archives contain a statement dated 1797 showing that the cost of lime at Garthmyl had been reduced from 18d to 13d a bushel by the opening of the canal.[2]

The third claim was more questionable. Some local industries gained improved access to fuel and raw materials, and because of lower transport costs were better able to get their products to market competitively. Thus canals promoted regional specialisation, but this also meant the destruction of some local industries because cheaper or better products could come in from elsewhere.

For example, the Ruabon area benefited by being able to sell its high quality bricks more widely. The corollary was that bricks might no longer be made close to the other settlements where they had been manufactured using poorer quality clay and expensive fuel, the only sign now of the lost industry being a depression in a field. Alternatively, bricks brought by canal might substitute for locally extracted stone. Another example was beer produced in a town brewery benefiting from economies of scale and specialist expertise might supplant that produced on the premises of the local beerhouses. Of course, these trends became even more marked when the railways arrived.

Until the 1830s, the Ellesmere, Chester and Montgomeryshire Canals were not connected to the national network which had been largely completed when the Grand Junction Canal opened from Braunston to London in 1805. Their market was thus primarily sub-regional and, via Liverpool, export. Once the Middlewich Branch and the Birmingham & Liverpool Junction Canal opened, easier access was obtained to the regional markets of the Manchester area and the West Midlands and even to London. Distribution of the area's agricultural products then became a significant part of the traffic, which also assisted the conurbations' populations to continue increasing.

The canal itself provided employment, of course. The canal companies had bank-tenders, lock-keepers and local agents. The boatmen and their crews generally had a home on shore, though as the 19th century went on a greater proportion lived on their boat. Ancillary employments included boat-building and maintenance, the provision of feed for the boat horses, and inns and beer-houses catering for the boatmen. Virtually every canalside settlement had a wharf where coal and merchandise were unloaded, and many had a warehouse or shed where goods could be temporarily stored awaiting distribution.

Siting of industries

WITHIN settlements, canals influenced the siting of industries. Obviously it was advantageous if bulky raw materials, principally coal but also, where appropriate, such inputs as cotton, timber or grain, could be brought direct to the factory or mill without the need for transhipment. It might be thought that the canal would be almost as important for distributing the manufactured products, but in practice this depended on their bulk, value, destination and urgency, much being sent by road. Even if the

The Shropshire Union Canal

Ditherington Flax Mill, later converted into a maltings – the complex includes the first, third and eighth oldest surviving cast-iron framed multi-story buildings in the world. Railway & Canal Historical Society

products of a canalside factory were sent to market by canal, this would sometimes involve road transport to the carrier's warehouse or wharf where they could be stored until there was a suitable boat.

In practice, the availability of water was a major factor in the siting of factories, particularly those with a steam engine. The low-pressure condensing engines produced in the first half of the 19th century used water for two purposes: feeding boilers and condensing steam. The latter required far greater volumes of water – something in the order of 25 times the amount used for boiler feed. This would be drawn from the waterway and the same volume returned, albeit hotter. Although high-pressure steam engines were available from the early 19th century, for several decades they tended not to be used unless there was no source of cool water.

Once established by a canal, industries and businesses tended to stay there, even after their use of the canal had ceased. For example, Orwell's coalyard traded at Victoria Wharf, Market Drayton, until 2012, many decades after it received its last load by boat.

Chester

The Chester Canal was intended to halt and reverse the city's decline as a port, particularly for traffic to Ireland. It failed to do so. Indeed, it had little immediate economic impact on the city beyond bringing in agricultural produce from the Nantwich area.

The Wirral Branch of the Ellesmere Canal provided Chester with a shorter and safer route than the Dee to and from Liverpool and the up-Mersey industries. Tower Wharf became a significant transhipment place, though it lost this role in the 1830s with the development of Ellesmere Port.

Some employment directly related to the canal. Chester became the administrative headquarters of the Shropshire Union Canal and was its principal boat-building centre, an activity which continued after the SU ceased its carrying operations.

More importantly, during the 19th century many businesses located canalside: flour mills, saw-mills, chemical works, a cotton mill and the lead works. Coal to power the steam engines was brought in from Flintshire and south Lancashire; the canal water was used for cooling purposes.

CHAPTER 11 : THE FIRST CANAL AGE

Shrewsbury

SHREWSBURY had had good water communication since medieval times, so by the end of the 18th century was well equipped with riverside warehouses and some industry, such as William Hazledine's Coleham iron works. Pigot's 1835 directory summarised the transport facilities:

> The river affords a convenient transit, for goods of every description, to Worcester, Gloucester, Bristol, and other towns; and the Shrewsbury Canal is the great medium for supplying the town with coal of an excellent quality.

The directory listed five firms boating on the Severn, and two firms offered conveyance from their Severnside warehouses to London, the first part of the journey by road, the rest by fly-boat.

As the directory entry implied, the Shrewsbury Canal supplemented the river Severn, rather than supplanting it. However, all changed that year with the opening of the Newport Branch of the Birmingham & Liverpool Junction Canal. Between 1835 and 1838 warehouses were constructed for three carrying companies: Pickford & Co., Henshall & Co. and Joseph Jobson. The Butter Market was built at the end of the terminal basin and the canal extended to it. River traffic declined rapidly before finally being killed off by the opening of the railways in 1848–9. The railway affected the canal's trade too, of course, and in about 1869 the former Butter Market was adapted as a railway warehouse.

The first of the industries which located canalside to take advantage of the cheap transport of coal was Ditherington Flax Mill. Nearer the terminal basin were the gas works (1821), two corn mills, a brickworks and an iron works.

Ellesmere Port

ELLESMERE Port is Britain's largest town that can truly be said to have been created by canals. It was founded by the Ellesmere Canal Company, developed following the opening of the Birmingham & Liverpool Junction Canal in 1835, grew during the Shropshire Union period, and thrived after the first stage of the Manchester Ship Canal opened in 1891.

The census totals for the townships of Whitby and Netherpool demonstrate these stages. Although the canal opened to the river in the winter of 1796/7, the population in 1831 still numbered fewer than 200. In the decade to 1841 it grew to 800, but the following three decades saw only a small increase to 950 in 1871. Then the growth really started, the population exceeding 10,000 in 1911. Important as the canal from Chester and the Midlands had been for the early history of the town, the numerical evidence is that the opportunity offered by the Manchester Ship Canal was actually more significant in its consolidation.

In the third quarter of the 19th century the Shropshire Union was the town's largest employer, their workers principally being dock labourers, boatmen (both on the cross-Mersey flats and the inland narrow boats) and boat repairers.

The first major industry to settle alongside the canal was Burnell & Sons, a firm specialising in galvanising founded in 1879. The Wolverhampton Corrugated Iron Company relocated from the Black Country to a site by the SU Canal in 1904, bringing in some 300 skilled workers and their families – a boost for the town but a net reduction in income for the canal company.

Three flour mills were built on land owned by the SU Canal adjacent to the lower basin or to the Manchester Ship Canal: Imperial (1905), King's (1906) and Frost's (1910), all three firms having started with mills elsewhere, at Waverton, Hanley and Chester respectively.

The Stanlow Works Estate, later renamed the Ship Canal Portland Cement Manufacturers, established a plant in the angle between the SU Canal and the Manchester Ship Canal in 1912, using the SU to supply its products to Cheshire and the West Midlands. Initially successful, it succumbed to intense price competition, production ceasing in 1932. Part of their canalside premises was sold to Colas Products who made liquid asphalt and the metal drums in which to distribute it. Although the first oil-related industry was established on the MSC's Stanlow estate as early as 1916, it was not until 1934 that refining started there. The SU Canal was used to a small extent for distribution.

East Shropshire

TODAY we call this area 'Telford', but that name dates only from 1968 when a string of industrial small towns and villages on or near the east Shropshire coalfield were grouped together with the historic borough of Wellington to form what was initially England's least successful New Town. Poor transport links were a major part of its problem, as indeed they had been in the first half of the 19th century.

The east Shropshire coalfield runs almost south–north, about ten miles long and three miles wide, from Broseley, on the southern bank of the river Severn, to Donnington in the north. The parts easily accessible to the Severn were developed first, the Severn itself being the vital transport artery for the products of the mines and iron works. As the 18th century progressed, industrial development extended northwards. In 1788 the furnaces were making nearly 25,000 tons of iron, or about 38% of the national total; by 1805–6 output had increased to nearly 55,000 tons but because iron-making had expanded rapidly elsewhere, this was down to 22% of the national production. Output peaked at nearly 200,000 tons in 1869, but by then this was less than 2% of the iron made in Britain.

The development of the coalfield and associated iron industry was assisted by tramroads and, at the end of the 18th century, by the tub-boat canals, principally the Shropshire Canal. The Shrewsbury Canal opened in 1797, with the principal aim of conveying coal in tub-boats to the county town. The mines supplying the coal were all above Trench Incline, at Wombridge and Donnington Wood. Lower coal prices at Shrewsbury resulted in increased demand. Apart from this, the economic impact on east Shropshire of the Shrewsbury Canal was limited. The

195

Pontcysyllte Forge, originally built by Exuperius Pickering Junior, photographed in 1922.
Richard Dean

ironfounders exporting through Liverpool took their products overland to Edstaston Wharf on the Prees Branch of the Ellesmere Canal after that was opened in 1805.

Two industrial premises were built alongside the Shrewsbury Canal, both above Trench Incline, close to Church Road bridge. A glassworks was built by a partnership including William Reynolds in 1792 (a few years before this section of the Wombridge Canal was sold to the Shrewsbury Canal) and in 1818 a four-storey steam-powered corn mill was erected.

It was not until 1835 that there was a link to the country's main canal network, when the Newport Branch of the Birmingham & Liverpool Junction Canal opened. (By then the Black Country, the main rival Midlands area for iron products, had had over forty years of good canal links.) This increased the area to which domestic coal was supplied – William Hazledine sent coal in tub-boats from his mines at Wombridge as far as Market Drayton, for example.

However, the canal was still not really suitable for the needs. Although the two locks between Wappenshall Junction and Shrewsbury were widened to take standard narrow boats, the nine locks between the junction and Trench were never rebuilt. Special boats 70ft long and only 6ft 2in. wide were constructed for use in this section, but of course they could not pass up or down the inclines – and the important industrial sites could only be reached by passing Trench Incline and (for many sites) Wrockwardine Wood Incline. Transhipment was done either at Trench Basin or at Wappenshall, but it added to the costs. All the major iron-making firms in the coalfield area used the new canal in several ways (except for the Madeley Wood Company, which continued to use the Severn): coal and iron products went out, and limestone from Trevor, Froncysyllte and Llanymynech came in. Some iron ore came in, initially from the Black Country, later from Cumbria and Spain via Liverpool; to some extent this was because of a shortage of local supplies but perhaps more importantly by mixing with local ores, different qualities of products could be made. Once transport patterns had settled down, only the Old Park Company continued to use tub-boats, transhipping the loads at Wappenshall; the other firms used road transport from their works to Wappenshall – not ideal, but cheaper until the arrival of the railways.

Only the Lilleshall Company had an effective solution, with the opening in 1844 of the Humber Arm and the private tramroad (later a railway) linking the basin to the company's furnaces at Old Lodge and Priorslee. Raw materials continued to be brought in throughout the rest of the 19th century.

Two ironworks were established canalside below the incline: Trench (1866) and Castle (1871). Castle Works had a basin accessed through a drawbridge, but in both cases the canal was probably more significant for its water supply than for transport opportunities. Both ironworks were also served by the Shropshire Union Railway.

Chapter 11 : The First Canal Age

Graesser's works at Cefn Mawr, c.1920.
Wrexham CBC

The Ruabon area

Before the Ellesmere Canal came, the Cefn Mawr, Acrefair and Trevor area was undeveloped except for the stone quarry, several small coal mines and Edward Rowland's iron works. The opening of the canal in 1805 provided the essential transport link to the Mersey, prompting rapid economic growth through the development of the coal and iron industries. The Ruabon Brook Railway and its later incarnation, the Pontcysyllte Railway, extended the benefits a few miles further north.

Between 1811 and 1821 the population of the parish of Ruabon, which then included Cefn Mawr and Acrefair, increased by 50% from 4,800 to 7,300; by 1831 it was 8,400; then in the decade following the opening of the Plas Kynaston Canal there was a further 35% increase to 11,300.

The principal ironworks of the area developed from that of Edward Rowland at Trevor. His son created the ironworks at nearby Acrefair, which later became the British Iron Company and subsequently the New British Iron Company. The Plas Kynaston ironworks was established by William Hazledine, initially to make castings for the Pontcysyllte Aqueduct, later supplying iron for many of Telford's bridges in Scotland and elsewhere. The foundry continued in operation until the 1930s. Both these ironworks received limestone by boat from Trevor Rocks and Froncysyllte and used the canal to send out some of their products. When the local ironstone became exhausted, the canal brought in supplies from Cumbria and Spain, enabling the industry to continue.

The Pickerings' Pontcysyllte Forge had an even closer association with the canal, being on land leased from the canal company immediately to the west of the first bridge on the 'Water Line' at Trevor. They also built a set of limekilns adjacent to the Plas Kynaston Canal, and sent coal to Llangollen and beyond from their mine at Cefn Mawr.

Cefn stone has been worked from early times and was used at Valle Crucis Abbey, Chirk Castle, Wynnstay and Erddig, for example. The opening of the canal substantially reduced the cost of transport for the construction of such buildings as St George's Hall in Liverpool.

J.C. Edward's brickworks at Trefynant, quite close to Trevor Basin, started in the 1850s, specialising in ornamental bricks and tiles. Although it had a siding from the Vale of Llangollen Railway it also used the canal to distribute its bulky product.

The chemical industry founded by Robert Graesser, which in the 20th century, when owned by Monsanto, was the major local employer, was located canalside at Cefn Mawr in 1867 principally because it would be using the waste from the area's earlier canal-related industry, though it also initially used the canal to some extent. By the 20th century the main advantage it gained from being sited by the canal was the ready supply of cooling water – this continued until the 1940s when a breach in the 'Water Line' showed that the supply could be unreliable.

Other industries which started close to the Plas Kynaston Canal included a pottery and a screw-bolt works. Neither lasted a long time, their sites becoming incorporated in Graesser's chemical works.

Several industrial concerns had sidings from the Ruabon Brook Railway. Largest was the New British Iron Company; as well as the Wynne Hall spelter works there were brickworks and collieries.

The canal company had a small yard at Trevor employing

197

a handful of men maintaining boats and tramroad wagons. During the First World War several boats were built here.

Nantwich

THE canal basin is three-quarters of a mile from the centre of the town, in the parish of Henhull and only a couple of fields away from the village of Acton. From the basin the road descends about 50ft to Welsh Bridge over the river Weaver, with the heart of the town being on the far side.

Although at the time of Henry VIII there were said to have been 400 salt houses in Nantwich, by the date of the passing of the Chester Canal Act there were only two; the last one was out of use by 1792, though it reopened from 1820 to 1856. The first cotton-spinning mill opened in 1785. The corn mill on the west bank of the river was converted to cotton spinning in 1789 and was enlarged and converted to coal-powered in 1797 – the coal being brought by the canal no doubt. In 1874 part of the mill reverted to corn milling, the rest of the site becoming an iron foundry making agricultural machinery. Nantwich's main industry in the first half of the 19th century was shoe-making, but this was a cottage or workshop industry, unmechanised until 1858, so making little or no use of the canal.

No industry was created by the canal: the basin stayed isolated. Limekilns were built there and later a warehouse was erected principally for the cheese trade.

The town's gas works was built in 1832 on the west side of the river; the coal had to be carted there from the basin, but at least it was being brought downhill.

The population of Nantwich increased by 61% between 1801 and 1851, whereas the population of most other market towns in south Cheshire and north Shropshire increased much less. However, little of this seems to be attributable to the canal. In this period Nantwich was still a sub-regional commercial and shopping centre, servicing a particularly prosperous farming area with many large estates. The liking of the great families for the town is evidenced by the number of substantial town houses built at this time. Its importance declined as Crewe increased in size.

Whitchurch

THE total population of Whitchurch and Dodington townships increased from 3,251 in 1811 to 4,413 in 1841, an increase of 36%. The increase at Dodington, where the terminus of the canal was situated, was 52%, indicating a shift in the 'centre of gravity' of the town towards the canal. These figures may be compared with an increase of only 17% at Market Drayton, where the canal did not open until 1835.

A four-storey steam-powered corn mill was constructed at the canal terminus in 1826. As at Nantwich, a warehouse was built principally for the cheese trade.

In 1828 George Trim Whitfield and John Sergeant built a canalside silk mill at Sherryman's Hill, providing working space for 200 people. It was two storeys high, but designed so that three further storeys could be added. Power was provided by a 10hp steam engine by Galloway of Manchester for four 104-bobbin doubling frames, a hard silk engine with 100 swifts, and four 100-bobbin drawing frames. It was offered for sale in 1831, and by 1851 had been converted to a warehouse by Thomas Burgess, a cheese factor and corn merchant.

The gas works was built alongside the canal at Sherryman's Bridge in 1826, a relatively early date for a works in a small town. This used the canal both to receive fuel and to dispatch the tar by-products.

Ellesmere

THE canal company itself was a significant employer at Ellesmere. Their canal offices (later known as Beech House) were built in 1805–6 as the administrative headquarters of the Ellesmere Canal Company, the committee room being in the semi-circular wing at the end of the building. There were rooms for the accounting records and for the plans, and apartments for the General Accountant and the Resident Engineer. Following the merger with the Chester Canal Company in 1813 the administrative headquarters remained at Ellesmere until 1847. Adjacent to the offices, and constructed a year later, was the Ellesmere Canal's maintenance depot, comprising workshops for the carpenters, store rooms and dry dock (principally for weighing boats). Further buildings were added later in the 19th century. Remarkably little has changed since, apart from the loss of the original crane, this continues in operation today (2018) though on a reduced scale. The manufacture of lock gates ceased in 1963. Nevertheless, as late as 1948 thirty men were employed there.

The 7th Earl of Bridgewater, John William Egerton, inherited lands at Ellesmere in 1803 and set about developing the town, laying out wharfs and erecting warehouses around the canal basin. The Bridgewater Estate's timber yard was in the square at the end of the canal arm where the Earl's agent also had offices. In addition, the Estate also had a wharf on the east side of the canal arm, between the coal wharf and the boat-building yard.

The principal trades of Ellesmere in the 1820s were described as tanning and malting, and the butter and cheese produced in that part of the county was said to be 'of the finest description'. As in most of the Shropshire market towns, tanning had virtually ceased by the middle of the 19th century and malting by the end of the century. The canal appears to have been able to do nothing to extend the life of these industries, though certainly malt was sent to Lancashire by fly-boat. Improved transport facilities may actually have hastened their demise. The canal did help the trade in dairy products, particularly after the opening of the route to Manchester, fly-boats being adapted specifically for these.

A number of businesses were located to take advantage of the canal, the most significant being William Clay's Bridgewater Foundry making iron and brass products, mainly for the agricultural industry but also the castings required by the canal company. The foundry was established in the first half of the 1850s, becoming a major employer in the town, and survived

Chapter 11 : The First Canal Age

until the First World War. After its demise its site was taken over by Great Western & Metropolitan Dairies (later United Dairies).

A gas works was built on the west side of the canal arm in 1832. John Tilston, and later Richard Tilston, were timber and building materials merchants, with wharfs on both sides of the canal basin. They were also respected boat builders, their premises being on the east side of the arm into the town, just to the north of the entrance bridge.

The civil parish of Ellesmere contained many of the surrounding villages as well as the town itself, making it difficult to use population changes as a measure of the economic impact of the canal. The indications are that, during the first three decades of the canal, the population increased significantly; thereafter the economy was steady for a couple of decades before declining for a similar period. (The coming of the railway did little to improve the town's economy.)

The canal had only a minor effect on the physical development of the town. Wharf Road was the only new road. Virtually all the new buildings in the wharf area were directly canal-related – there was minimal relocation of other industries or suppliers and no new dwellings anywhere near the wharf, apart from the houses lining one side of Wharf Road. Nor was there any new development near the canal office and depot or elsewhere along the 'main line' of the canal.

Oswestry

Although a historic borough and the town in north Shropshire with the greatest population in 1801, the canal passed Oswestry by, the nearest points being at Queen's Head and Maesbury, some three miles to the east of the town. The former became the town's principal wharf. The SU erected a warehouse in Oswestry in 1871, adding an office in 1892.

The canal thus had little impact on the town. William Cathrall's *The History of Oswestry*, published in 1855, makes no mention of the canal although it does discuss road and rail transport. Oswestry's period of rapid growth came when the railway arrived and the headquarters and engineering works of the Cambrian Railways were established there.

Welshpool

By the end of the 18th century Welshpool was the principal administrative and market town in the border area of mid-Wales, but in the 19th century tended to lose out to the faster-growing Newtown. The population of Welshpool borough increased from 2,295 in 1801 to 4,558 in 1831 but stayed virtually unchanged for the next three decades, reaching 4,844 in 1861 shortly after the arrival of the railway.

The main canalside industrial development was just outside the borough boundary to the north of the town on land owned by the Earl of Powis. The gas works opened in 1832; it lasted there until 1865, when a new gas works was opened by the railway. The 'Welshpool Company for the Manufacture of Flannel by Steam' opened its factory in 1834; it was extended in 1883 but closed in 1900.

Within the borough boundary, to the north of the town centre, a group of canalside properties included a boatyard, limekilns and a malthouse. The wharf was particularly close to the town centre. The corn mill by Welshpool Town Lock dates from the late 1830s; the site of the water-wheel can still be seen.

Stondart (or Standard) Quarry, at the western end of the town, was connected to a wharf by a tramroad from 1819 until the early 1850s.

Although the Montgomeryshire Canal had its headquarters at Welshpool it was not a major employer. A small maintenance yard was active until 1926.

Newtown

The population of Newtown plus Llanllwchaiarn (a separate parish north of the river Severn in which the canal basin was situated) grew from 4,493 in 1821 when the canal opened to 6,555 in 1831. However, to attribute this solely – or even mainly – to the canal would be fallacious. The population in 1801 had been only 1,168, so the town's most rapid period of growth pre-dated the canal's arrival. This was attributable to the water-powered weaving industry which reached its peak in the mid 1830s, located in the town and in Penygloddfa, the area immediately to the north of the road bridge. This industry made no use of the canal except for the export of some of the finished cloth, most going out by road to Shrewsbury.

Newtown's woollen industry was slow to adopt steam-powered machinery, despite the severe unemployment and social unrest caused by the growing competition from more progressive rivals such as Rochdale. The first recorded use of steam power was in 1835, but it was not particularly successful. It was not until towards the end of the 1850s that some larger steam-powered factories came to be established, including the Cambrian Mill near the end of the basin and the canalside Kymric Mill a quarter of a mile before the entrance to the basin.

A total of 22 limekilns were built near the canal at Newtown, serving not only the immediate area of the town but also the valley up to Llanidloes. Apart from lime burning, the principal canalside industry built during the independent life of the Montgomeryshire Canal was the Newtown Foundry, established by John Onions in the 1820s, which stood virtually opposite the site of the Kymric Mill. This would have brought in its ironstone, coal and limestone by canal. At the wharf there was also a malthouse by 1842 and a bakehouse by 1845.

Newtown's first gas works opened in 1827, its replacement in 1841. Neither was in the most economical location by the canal – both were on the south side of the river, necessitating coal to be unloaded from boats onto wagons and then taken three-quarters of a mile by road.

There were of course numerous wharfs at Newtown basin, some with warehouses for general goods, and others specialising in coal or timber. The price of domestic coal was said to have been reduced from 30*s* a ton before the canal opened to 21*s* a ton afterwards. The price of other commodities was reduced substantially too. This benefited not only Newtown itself, but

THE SHROPSHIRE UNION CANAL

Ellesmere Basin in the 1950s. The warehouse shows its Shropshire Union origins.
The milk depot used canal water for cooling, and the gas works originally had its coal deliveries by boat.
Ian L. Wright

also Llanidloes and the rest of the hinterland served by the extensive carriers' network.

The support services for the canal traders were also at the basin – two dry docks, boat repair facilities and stables – as well as facilities for the boatmen, in particular, two pubs. The 1841 and 1851 census returns show that almost all the houses close to the basin were occupied by people employed there.

The building of the canal had little impact on the 'shape' of Newtown, the basin area remaining a relatively isolated community. Between it and the edge of Penygloddfa was almost a quarter of a mile which had not been built over in the way one might have expected.

Llangollen

SITUATED where the Dee descended through rapids, Llangollen was ideally placed to develop its water-powered textile industry. The canal's involvement was indirect, in that it provided a water supply for the Dee Mills, which caused disputes when the canal company considered that its own needs took priority.

Even as early as 1799 the town was noted as 'a very desirable situation for those who wish to retire from the noise and bustle of large towns'.[3] In Victorian times the town became a holiday destination. This was the first place in Britain where horse-drawn pleasure trip boats started a regular service on a canal, one which continues today.

Market Drayton

THE canal came too late (1835) to have a significant effect on Market Drayton's economy. Apart from Betton Mill, built early in the 20th century as a warehouse but later converted into a corn mill, no canalside industries were created. Even the gas works (1851) was located three-quarters of a mile away. When Messrs Sandbrook & Ryley constructed a new horse-hair mill some time between 1845 and 1851, they did so by buying and rebuilding the Walkmill, on the river Tern half a mile south-west of the town centre, not by expanding their Victoria Wharf site. The two entrepreneurs who founded firms which were to become significant ironfounders and agricultural implement manufacturers both chose sites in the town centre: Gower (1842) in Stafford Street and Rodenhurst (early 1850s) in Cheshire Street.

The town hardly expanded towards the canal; indeed what few new houses were built in the mid 1800s between the town

Chapter 11 : The First Canal Age

centre and the canal were 'gentlemen's residences' rather than workers' cottages. The population of Market Drayton parish (excluding Tyrley, which was in Staffordshire) increased from 3,882 in 1831 to 4,428 in 1861; however, most of this relatively small increase was in Drayton Parva, the far side of the town centre from the canal.

Newport

THE canal also came too late to Newport to have much effect on the town, though the wharf was quite close to the town centre. No canalside industries were created. The railway opened in 1848, just 13 years after the canal, rather earlier than in most of the other Shropshire market towns.

Wellington

OF all the market towns in the Shropshire Union's area, Wellington was, with Oswestry, the least affected by its canal. It continued to receive its coal by road. All goods had to be conveyed from or to Wappenshall wharf, some two miles from the town centre, after 1835. And immediately the railway opened in 1848, general goods traffic through the wharf ceased almost entirely.

Rural areas

CANAL companies' annual reports to shareholders often emphasised with pride that they were working for the good of the local community. For example, the annual report of the Montgomeryshire Canal Company in 1811 stated that the shareholders 'are afforded the satisfaction of reflecting that, without public assistance or the intervention of strangers, [the canal] has been instrumental in bringing so many thousands of acres into cultivation; in having discharged the roads of so much heavy carriage; in the preservation of timber; and in the general improvement of so great a part of the county of Montgomery.' (The reference to the preservation of timber is probably an allusion to its substitution by coal as a fuel.) It is easy to claim one is acting for public benefit – 'spin' is nothing new – but the evidence supports the claim in this particular case.

Most villages on the line of the Montgomeryshire, Ellesmere and Chester Canals had limekilns. Initially many were constructed by the canal company itself and then leased to entrepreneurs as a way of developing traffic; later ones were developed by the entrepreneurs themselves. By the 1860s many had fallen out of use as alternative chemicals for improving land, both imported

Almost timeless – the Llangollen trip boat early 1970s. *David Wain / Ian L. Wright*

The limekilns at Pant. These were atypical is being above canal level; more commonly the limestone and coal could be fed from the canal into the kilns by gravity. *Author*

and manufactured, became available. And by the end of the century they had probably all closed, leaving just the large and relatively efficient Hoffman kiln at Llanymynech in production, which was served by a railway siding and perhaps never used the canal.

Land at the southern end of the Birmingham & Liverpool Junction Canal was improved by the spreading of urban manure from the Wolverhampton area.

Not only did the canal increase agricultural productivity, it also improved the access to markets such as Chester and Shrewsbury. From the 1830s cheese and other high value produce with a relatively long life could be taken to Manchester and the West Midlands conurbation. This encouraged specialisation; mixed farming ceased to be the norm. Several wharves were established by major landowners for use by their tenants.

Having one's farm divided by a canal could cause operational problems, splitting fields and separating fields from the farm buildings, effects partly mitigated by occupation bridges, which totalled almost half the bridges on the whole length of the canal. On the other hand, proximity to a canal increased the value of farms, as is evidenced by the many references to canals in sale advertisements in newspapers.

Various extractive industries in rural areas benefited greatly from the canal. Most significant in the Shropshire Union area were the limestone quarries at Llanymynech, Porth-y-Waen, Froncysyllte and Trevor Rocks. Slate came from the Oernant quarries to the canal above Llangollen. The Ceiriog Valley was a source of granite and slate. Coal was distributed from Chirk and Morda as well as, for a short while, from Uffington on the Shrewsbury Canal.

A number of small industries were established at rural canalside locations. For example, on the Montgomeryshire Canal there were brick and tile works at The Wern and Ardleen. The Powis Estate timber yard with its sawmill and smithy was below Belan Locks. Pool Quay had a maltings with its associated drying kiln, as did Garthmyl. A further maltings was situated $2\frac{1}{4}$ miles south of Garthmyl, at Glan-Hafren. On the Llanymynech branch of the Ellesmere Canal there was a fertiliser works at Rednal and mills at Maesbury and Queen's Head.

Elsewhere there were rural canalside mills at Grindley Brook, Wrenbury, Audlem, Calveley and Waverton. Between Calveley and Barbridge, and also near Gnosall, there were several small brick and tile works. The only village gas works in the Shropshire Union area was alongside the canal at Brewood; this operated from 1864 until 1916.

None of these industries had lasting significance. The only rural industry developed canalside which has survived into the 21st century is the food processing factory started by Cadbury's at Knighton in 1911, though it no longer has any association with its original product.

Two small rural settlements came into existence because of the canal. At Wappenshall, where the Newport branch of the Birmingham & Liverpool Junction Canal met the Shrewsbury Canal, the wharf and warehouses were built to serve the town and hinterland of Wellington; a boat repair business was established and there was a public house. At Norbury Junction, the Shropshire Union erected cottages for employees at the maintenance depot.

What effect did the canals have on society?

The canal community

It is misleading to think that there was a single canal community. Only about half of people in direct canal employment were on the boats – the others maintained the canals and the boats, worked at depots and warehouses, transported the goods to and from customers, or administered the activities. People in these latter groups would regard themselves primarily as members of their local communities.

Housing was generally provided to the canal company's employees where it was desirable for them to live close to the work and look after the company's assets – lock-keepers, lengthsmen and wharfingers – or where it was necessary to attract people to work at places not close to an existing settlement, such as the mid-19th-century 'canal town' of Ellesmere Port. Property standards and rents were generally reasonable.

Most of the boaters would have a home in a town or village, albeit possibly with long absences. Barbridge was the one village which was home to an exceptionally high proportion of boaters because it was situated at the crossroads of the local canal network, equally convenient for traffic between the Welsh Branch and Manchester as for the traffic between Ellesmere Port and the West Midlands conurbation.

There is much 20th-century evidence that long-distance canal boaters could justifiably be regarded as a 'community': children were largely brought up separately from their land-based peers; having been trained on the boats they tended to become boaters themselves; they tended to marry boaters; and they were sometimes regarded with suspicion by others. There is much less evidence available for the SU area in the 19th century. A sample of census records for the Shropshire Union area shows that most steerers and their crew members were born at places served by the SU's boats – there seemed to be little movement nationally.

Until the First World War the SU canals provided steady all-year employment. Hours were long and continued in all weather conditions, but the close discipline of factory work was absent. Wages were typical for the time rather than good, but for those who were directly employed by the SU there was the possibility of a small pension at the end of many decades of service.

Boatmen, who were in effect paid piece rates, had the opportunity of higher earning but much depended on the availability and cost of the crew, on the continuing good health of the horse or donkeys, and of course on the weather – ice meant no earnings. When freight charges came under pressure from railway competition, family boating became more prevalent. Children were then an important part of the economic unit, at the expense of their education.

The wider community

As discussed earlier, canals brought economic benefits through lower prices, particularly for fuel, and a wider choice of goods. The effects on employment were generally beneficial, though areas poor in natural resources may have suffered from the increased competition.

But canals were also a significant leisure asset. Canalside walks were popular, with local organisations sometimes providing benches. Before Chester's first swimming baths were built in 1847, in hot weather boys and young men used to swim naked in the canal, much to the annoyance of many citizens, particularly if done on a Sunday. And in many winters – for winters were generally colder in the 19th century than have been in the last fifty years – skating was popular for both sexes, again with complaining letters to the press if done on a Sunday. Fishing was a popular pastime for men; initially discouraged by the canal companies, by the end of the 19th century it was licensed and organised. As has been described, boat outings in groups started in the last quarter of the 19th century, as did pleasure boating at Llangollen. A few quieter locations had rowing boats for hire and some people tried canoeing.

However, canals were also potentially dangerous for the general public, the local papers recording several deaths every year. Particularly vulnerable were young children playing by the water and falling in. This specially applied to the age group from two to four. Older children were more aware of the dangers, incidents were fewer, and those who died were generally doing a specific activity, rather than just playing. For adult deaths the principal contributory factor (then as now) was drunkenness; in a twelve-month period in 1836/7 the *Chester Chronicle* recorded five such cases in the city, as well as two other cases where sober elderly people drowned during the hours of darkness. Sometimes drowning was deemed by the coroner's court to be suicide, occasionally attributable to depression but more often as a way out of unremitting intense pain.

Infanticide, particularly of new-born babies was not uncommon in the 19th century, and the canal was a good place to hide a body. The corpse would first sink, and when it reappeared a week or two later, it could be several hundred yards from where it was put into the water. Also the surgeon often could not tell whether the baby was still-born, died immediately after birth, or was drowned.

Crime

Transport organisations have a special problem: their owners cannot easily oversee their operations. Particularly vulnerable were boats. Back in 1841 Robert Skey wrote, 'No means have ever been found to put a stop to the pillage which has ever been the disgrace of canal conveyance'.[4] More than a hundred years later, in the early 1950s it was found that many of the boatmen in BW's Northern Fleet had been selling copper to a lock-keeper on the Middlewich Branch who acted as a middleman for professional crooks in Manchester.[5] It must not be thought that boatmen were especially criminal but of course they had more opportunities for theft than had most agricultural or factory workers.

Alcohol proved particularly tempting for personal use but almost anything was vulnerable if it could be sold. For example, in 1877 three scrap merchants of Nantwich, assisted by three boatmen, Edwin Owen, Robert Jones and Joseph Maddocks, were accused of stealing three tons of pig iron from a boat at Barbridge. A Shropshire Union employee saw them filling two carts and tipped off the police. When on their way out from Nantwich the policemen found the two carts broken down close to each other as a result of them being overloaded. The scrap merchants were apprehended; the police then went on to arrest the boatmen which they did but only 'after a free fight with the canal population of Barbridge'. The boatmen were said to have sold to the dealers for 30*s* as much of the iron as they could carry away. The scrap merchants were each sentenced to nine months' imprisonment, the boatmen to six months' imprisonment.[6]

Warehouses were another obvious target. The biggest robbery mentioned in the canal companies' minutes happened early in the First World War. In 1915 309 sacks of flour – over 7 tons – were found to have been stolen from the SU's Liverpool warehouse. The theft was thought to have taken place during the food panic at the outbreak of the war. The Liverpool police were unable to find out when or how the flour was taken, which implied it was an 'inside job'.[7]

Canal employees were not the only offenders. Warehouses were vulnerable to local thieves and boats were a target if the boaters were absent. An unusual theft occurred in 1880, when a goldfinch was stolen from the boat *Emma* at Gledrid. Louise Griffiths, the boatman's wife, said that she and her husband passed the two defendants, both colliers, on the towpath in the evening, and when they returned to the boat an hour later the bird (but not its cage) was missing, as were a pair of boots. The police found the bird in a cigar box in the accused's bedroom but not the boots. The offenders were fined 10*s* each plus costs, it being a first offence.[8]

The minutes record several instances of wharfingers and administrative staff falsifying accounts and stealing the cash which had been entrusted to them. Usually the sums were relatively small but in 1861 John Johnes, the cashier at Chester, was charged on several counts of embezzlement and forgery with a total value of about £900 (well over £50,000 in today's money). At the preliminary hearing evidence concerning only one example was given: Johnes had received £15.5*s* from M'Corquodale & Co. for waste paper but had not paid the money in. Unfortunately I have not been able to find further newspaper reports about this case. The company minutes merely mention the problems in getting restitution from the fidelity guarantee insurer.[9]

Canal Acts typically had clauses forbidding trespassing and making the master of boats responsible for any damage to adjacent properties. The Birmingham & Liverpool Junction Act, for example, had a clause forbidding guns to be carried on board, presumably because of fears about poaching.

But this didn't stop poaching. Newspapers recorded numerous cases: a couple of the more interesting examples will suffice. In 1831 a gander was stolen at Burland by three 22-year-old boatmen, Evan Evans, Charles Trow and John Jones. The farmer, Mr Nevitt, traced their footsteps to their boat, where he found them cooking the goose. They were each sentenced to four months' imprisonment with hard labour.[10]

One night in 1847, 60 pounds of hay was stolen from a canal-side farm at Berriew. Richard Lloyd's boat had been moored nearby overnight so Police Officer Hammonds inspected it at Newtown wharf and found the distinctive type of hay, Italian rye grass, concealed under the foredeck. What is particularly remarkable about this case is the quality of the detective work at this early date. Hammonds had seen footprints at the scene of the crime and instructed that they be preserved; he then took Lloyd's boots and found they made a perfect match, which convinced the court of Lloyd's guilt. Another notable feature of this case is that Lloyd was a former sergeant in the Montgomeryshire Constabulary.[11]

Canal Acts permitted canal companies to make bye-laws which, once approved by the appropriate Quarter Sessions, had the force of law. Examples of offences were wasting water, mooring in an 'improper place', and deserting the boat and cargo – in one case of the last-named in 1858, the offender was sentenced to a month in gaol.[12]

Were canals monopolies before the railways came?

Road competition – 18th and 19th centuries

ROADS in the early 19th century were better than many popular histories imply. By the late 18th century the network of turnpikes in the Shropshire Union area approximated to the present day 'A' and 'B' roads – at minimum they had drainage and had some sort of surface; often they had also been straightened and the gradients reduced by the use of cuttings and embankments.

Not only did roads improve steadily between 1750 and 1840, horses improved through better breeding, becoming stronger but also consuming less food compared with their power output. Better roads also enabled vehicles to be lighter. The combination of all these improvements meant that more could be conveyed per horse at the same speed – about two miles per hour for waggons – thus enabling charges to be lowered, or speeds could be increased. In practice, carriers' customers generally preferred lower charges to faster speeds.

Thus road competition was more significant for goods traffic than is often now realised. High value, small size goods, including the mail, almost always went by road. Merchandise, what one might call 'general goods', such as smaller-scale manufactures and stock for shops could go either by road or by canal, depending which gave the customer better value. Considerations included cost, speed, security, perishability and potential damage. Also important was whether transhipment was needed at one or both ends of the journey. Thus woollens from Newtown and Welshpool went by road to Shrewsbury, the canal route being too circuitous, hence costly and slow.

Even bulk goods, such as coal, limestone, timber and wheat, would go by road if the economics favoured that method. As was noted in Chapter 7, iron products from the Ruabon area were sometimes sent the 18 miles by road to Chester in preference to the 57 miles by canal.

Speed was more far important for passenger services, and increased as the roads improved. Hence there were few passenger services on the canals in the SU area. A passenger service on the canal from Beeston, later from Nantwich, to Chester ran fitfully in the 1770s and 1780s. In the Shropshire Union area the longest-lasting was from Chester to Ellesmere Port for Liverpool, which operated from 1795 until 1834 when the New Chester Road from Bromborough to Tranmere was completed and a new 'safety coach' service started running from Chester to the ferry terminal at Eastham. Two passenger services operated in connection with railways in the 1850s but they proved unsuccessful.

Passengers were sometimes taken on boats carrying goods, as was also done by the long distance road freight carriers, but because these arrangements were not generally advertised there are few hints of it in the usual historical sources.

Roads were of course feeders to canals as well as being rivals. This was recognised when the two branches of the Montgomeryshire Canal donated £250 between them for the construction of the summit section of the turnpike from Newtown to Llandrindod Wells.

Water-borne competition

SHIPPING, both sea and coastal, could also be regarded as a feeder to the canal, as is evidenced by the developments at Ellesmere Port. On only one occasion was it a rival, and that was when the Ellesmere & Chester Canal introduced excessive charges for traffic going from Ellesmere Port to Chester. The threat of coastal boats forced the canal company to back down.

Rivers were not significant rivals in the Shropshire Union area. The sections of the Weaver and Dee which were navigable were not served by the canal. The trade of the Severn at Shrewsbury was quite different from that of the Shrewsbury Canal. Indeed, it was the Severn which lost traffic once the canal was connected to the national network following the opening of the branch through Newport.

Canal competition was more serious. The threat of competition to the old-established canals was the reason for the imposition of the junction tolls at Autherley and Middlewich – the new 'Shropshire Union' link offered an alternative outlet for the Potteries and a better route between the West Midlands and Manchester.

Competition in transport is often thought of as alternative routes between the same source and destination. As important can be competition from alternative sources for the same goods.

To give two examples: limestone for the West Midlands iron industry could come either from the Welsh border or from Caldon Low; coal for Chester and Nantwich could come either from Chirk or Flintshire.

Thus the Shropshire Union did not enjoy an undisputed monopoly on traffic in its area – not even for bulk goods.

Did railway competition kill the canals?

RAILWAY transport had the obvious advantage of speed, though the need to aggregate traffic to train-loads meant this could not always be taken advantage of.

What is nowadays less obvious is that canals were much more affected by the weather, particularly by ice (or as it was generally called in the 19th century, 'frost'). For example, in nine of the fifteen winters from 1890/01 to 1904/05, the Shropshire Union main line was closed for at least five consecutive days, the longest periods being 40 days in 1890/91 and 38 days in 1895. In total, 172 days were lost to ice. And even when the ice was broken much traffic was diverted to the railways because of the additional cost of haulage and the potential damage to wooden boats.

Robert Skey, the Shropshire Union's Traffic Manager, in answer to a question at the General Meeting in September 1861 commented:

> It must be remembered that the stoppage of the canals during winter in former times meant a good spring trade, but now it meant the total loss of the traffic.[13]

In other words, in the first half of the 19th century ice tended to merely postpone the traffic flow, whereas after the coming of the railways the traffic was lost.

Railway competition did not generally bring financial ruin to canals, but it forced transport charges downwards. Although canals lost most of the merchandise traffic and goods where time was important, they were often able to retain bulk loads such as coal and minerals. Because factories and gas works had tended to be located alongside canals, 20 ton loads could be brought economically from ports, quarries and mines; indeed, as long as the railway was not able to put sidings into the works, canals had a positive advantage. This continued for much of the 19th century in the Birmingham and Black Country area, the vital destination for much Shropshire Union trade. However, as time went on, many old canalside industries died and new factories tended to be located alongside the railways.

The reducing income affected the carriers as much as the canal companies. Most private carriers withdrew from canal business in the 1840s, leaving the Shropshire Union's carrying subsidiary to fill the gap locally. The financial squeeze naturally reduced the income of boat crews too, resulting in more family operation of boats, some living permanently on board. However, the evidence is not available to show how general this trend was.

In the case of the Shropshire Union, railway competition never became cut-throat because rates agreements were made, not only with the London & North Western Railway but also with other railways in the area. This type of agreement would now be unlawful, of course.

The early 20th century

THE evidence given in 1907 by George Jebb to the Royal Commission on Canals highlighted one particular trend in customers' requirements:

> The traders used to buy large quantities just as the market suited them – today it is a well-known fact that the trader often orders his traffic in small consignments by telephone or telegraph as he wants it and is for ever pressing upon the railway companies the necessity for rapid deliveries.[14]

The canals were unable to satisfy these demands, at least not profitably.

An even worse threat will be discussed in the next chapter: the development of the door-to-door service provided by the motor lorry, with the charge to the customer determined by the actual costs instead of by a statutorily-prescribed formula related to the value of the items carried.

How good was canal management?

Aims and objectives

CANALS were businesses. Customers expected reliable service and they hoped for reasonable charges. The people who lent them money expected to be repaid with interest. The shareholders expected a profit – even those who had invested primarily because building a canal would help their other business interests, be that landed estates, mines or quarries, manufacturing or retailing.

In addition to wishing to be a profitable investment, the canals which became the Shropshire Union had contrasting main aims:

– Chester Canal: To develop the port of Chester.
– Ellesmere Canal: To link the Severn, Dee and Mersey; to take the industrial products of the Ruabon and Wrexham area to market; to bring coal to Shrewsbury and Chester; and to improve agricultural productivity.
– Montgomeryshire Canal: To improve agricultural productivity.
– Shrewsbury Canal: To lower the price of coal in Shrewsbury.
– Birmingham & Liverpool Junction Canal: To provide cheaper transport between Birmingham, the Black Country and east Shropshire and the port of Liverpool.

The Chester Canal was a failure until the Ellesmere Canal was linked to it – indeed it was the only failure of all the canals promoted in England in the 1760s and 1770s. The original plan was to build a canal to Middlewich to join the Trent & Mersey and abstract some of the traffic going for export or to Ireland; when this was frustrated, the canal was built to Nantwich instead. The initiative came from Chester, not from the hinterland it would be serving. The traffic just wasn't there.

The Ellesmere Canal was not a failure, but neither was it a success. Half the intended main line was never built: the line to Shrewsbury ended in a field ten miles short of its destination, and the Trevor to Chester line was not even started, the southern few miles of it being replaced by a tramroad. Bersham, which at the time of the promotion of the canal, was one of the leading ironworks of western Europe, never got its much-needed transport facility. Coal came to be supplied to Shrewsbury by the Shrewsbury Canal, and to Chester from the Flintshire coalfield. Only the agricultural development intentions of the canal were fulfilled.

Part of its problem can be attributed to there being no clarity of vision. Should it take the western or the eastern route? In the event it took neither of the routes envisaged in 1793. Most holidaymakers taking their boats up the Llangollen Canal from Hurleston Junction to Llangollen probably imagine that this was the intended route – but if this had been the route promoted in 1793, it would have been unlikely to have attracted enough investors. Similarly with the branch to Llanymynech: the canal company dithered about which route it was going to take and whether it was to serve the quarries at Porth-y-waen.

On the other hand, the Montgomeryshire Canal had a clear and limited aim, and fulfilled that purpose adequately for several decades, at least in the section as far as Garthmyl. South of Garthmyl the basic traffic aim was eventually achieved, but the capital cost was unsustainable.

The Shrewsbury Canal also had a clear and limited aim, and succeeded in fulfilling it. It received an unplanned bonus when the Newport Branch of the Birmingham & Liverpool Junction Canal was opened.

The latter's main line met railway competition within two years of opening, so never fulfilled its promise. It was old technology, a narrow canal, several decades too late.

Returns on the investment

ALL the Shropshire Union's constituent canals either cost more than had been forecast or were left unfinished. Most had to raise extra money. The following table gives an impression of the shortfall – the Shropshire Canal, although only for a short while part of the Shropshire Union, is included for completeness. Some figures are inevitably approximate.

Canal	over-spending	completion
Chester	100%	66% completed
Ellesmere	20%	46% main line; most branches
Montgomeryshire		
— as originally planned	nil	64% completed
— Western Branch	32%	completed
Shrewsbury	25%	completed
Birmingham & Liverpool Junction	52%	completed
Shropshire	3%	90% completed

The Ellesmere, and to a lesser extent the Montgomeryshire and Shrewsbury Canals, were all affected by the steep increase in prices from 1793; between that year and 1800, prices increased by about three-quarters. The other canals were built in times of reasonably stable prices. The Ellesmere's problems were exacerbated by its particularly slow development, a result of making annual calls on shareholders of only 10% of the capital required.

The engineers must nevertheless bear much of the blame for the over-spending (or under-achievement). Ironically, the best estimates were for the two canals where the scheme was designed by an industrialist rather than by an engineer: the Shrewsbury and Shropshire Canals.

The estimates of cost tended to have inadequate allowances for the cost of land, and often omitted the costs of getting the Act and paying the salaries or fees of engineers, surveyors and lawyers. Some companies paid interest on calls on shares, at least for a period, seemingly without realising that this would increase the amount of capital which had to be raised. And provisions should have been made for contingencies.

Some of the schemes were varied substantially after the initial Act was obtained, sometimes without any amendment to the capital required.

It has not proved possible to compare the actual annual income and expenditure (and hence profit) with the forecasts before the Acts were sought, if indeed quantified forecasts had been made. Unfortunately, most of the prospectuses have not survived, but quite possibly these did not say anything beyond a general reassurance that the income would be sufficient to pay a substantial dividend. Certainly some assessment was usually made: for the Ellesmere Canal William Jessop reported that he had received information from the keepers of turnpike gates, and one of the shareholders did a detailed forecast of income, albeit for the proposed Eastern Route, not the Western Route which was adopted in the Act.[15]

The Montgomeryshire, Shropshire and Shrewsbury Canals all paid dividends; the Chester and Ellesmere Canals paid dividends after their merger. In some cases the first dividend was two decades or more after the shareholders had made their initial investment. The Western Branch of the Montgomeryshire Canal never paid a dividend, but shareholders received more return than was justified when their canal was sold to the Shropshire Union. The holders of Birmingham & Liverpool Junction shares were allocated Shropshire Union shares to the extent that they had responded to appeals for additional contributions after the shares had been fully paid up.

An investment appraisal technique known as the 'Internal Rate of Return' (IRR) enables the life-long profitability of investments to be compared. The IRR is the figure which answers the question: 'Over the life of the project, what interest rate would make the value of the receipts (mainly dividends but also the proceeds of sale of the shares) exactly equal the value of payments (calls on shares)?' A negative IRR means that the investor paid out more cash than was eventually received back. (The dividends paid each year are listed in Appendix D.)

Dividend information and the IRRs for the Shropshire Union's constituent canals and the Shropshire Canal are:

Canal	Act	First dividend	Highest dividend (years)	Highest dividend (amount)	IRR
Chester	1772	1814	1842–4	1.0%	–0.4%
Ellesmere	1793	1814	1842–4	4.1%	1.6%
Montgomeryshire	1794	1805	1813–14	5.5%	2.8%
– Western Branch	1815	—	—	—	–7.4%
Shrewsbury	1793	1798	1836/39	12.8%	4.3%
Birmingham & Liverpool Junction	1826	—	—	—	–100.0%
Shropshire	1788	1793	1847	9.5	4.7%

This analysis looks at the whole life of the canal company. In practice, shares were bought and sold, so the returns to the investors would have depended on when they bought their shares and for what price. Many of the original investors may have been more concerned with the creation of an efficient local infrastructure in order to increase the profitability of their estates or business enterprises rather than the potential dividends. Those who subsequently bought the shares would probably have regarded them as a pure investment.

To assess the quality of the return on canal shares, it is necessary to consider the alternatives. The yield on government stocks varied over time, but during the period under consideration, the greatest fluctuation was in the 1790s, coinciding with the calls on the 'mania' canals' shares. 3% stock, which was at par in January 1792, was yielding 4% a year later, 4¼% at the start of 1796 and almost 5½% in January 1797, reaching 6¼% in May 1797. There was minimal risk of default on government stocks, of course. The other common investment was property, with rents generally expected to yield about 5%.

Thus the Shropshire and Shrewsbury Canals' shares were reasonable investments, providing quick returns were not wanted, but the other companies' were not. Government stocks would almost certainly have been a wiser investment – the yield was comparable, the risk minimised and they would also have been easier to sell.

Day-to-day management

DURING the 'development' period all significant decisions were made by the canal companies' committees. Once that period was over, the canal companies settled down to the somewhat easier task of maintaining their assets and trying to develop trade. The committees still were involved in day-to-day management, though as time went on meetings tended to become less frequent and fewer members attended. Committee members were local men, predominantly from the gentry class and (in the first few decades of the 19th century) included several clergymen. Few were experienced in business, banking or the management of large estates.

Where salaries were adequate to retain good staff, more tended to be delegated. However – generalising somewhat – there is some evidence that management got complacent and less cost-conscious. Few involved in canal management really faced up to the realities of railway competition, for example.

An exception was Robert Skey, General Agent of the Birmingham & Liverpool Junction Canal and later General Manager of the Shropshire Union Company, whose family background was in commercial carrying. In 1841 he wrote:

> Canals have stood still, whilst all around them has advanced; the tub that now navigates their waters is the same as first floated upon them; no attempt has been made materially to improve the boats ... no effort made to supersede or apply to more advantage the labour of man and horse, and the clumsiest contrivances, elsewhere long since discarded, are resorted to to supply the want of adequate machinery.[16]

Similar criticisms could still be made a hundred years later: the boats were essentially unchanged except for the introduction of the diesel engine in the 1920s and 1930s, and facilities for efficient loading and unloading were rare.

After the companies amalgamated to form the Shropshire Union and then were leased to the London & North Western Railway, the composition of the committee totally changed. Almost all were then businessmen, and surprisingly few had local connections to the area. The employed managers came to adopt the methods and attitudes of the parent railway company.

What was the effect of railway ownership?

THE popular opinion is that railway ownership was a disaster for the canals, with maintenance minimised, traffic being transferred to the railway and inter-canal co-operation discouraged, but the experience of the Shropshire Union does not accord with this bleak assessment.

The Shropshire Union was given considerable day-to-day independence. Any capital expenditure required permission. The only major developments happened at Ellesmere Port, where there was substantial investment in warehouses and other facilities and where the docks were connected to the railway system by a tramway from 1873 and by a locomotive railway from 1894. Nevertheless throughout the 19th century minor improvements such as the construction of new canalside warehouses were made and new boats continued to be built. There seems no evidence that the canal was allowed to deteriorate before the First World War: standards were not reduced.

The Royal Commission on Canals & Inland Navigations 1906–9 commented, 'The canal appears to be on the whole well maintained and worked.' However, the evidence to the Royal Commission concentrated on the Main Line and the Middlewich Branch; little had been said about the Welsh Branch or the Shrewsbury Branch. It also noted that the Shropshire Union was the only railway-owned canal which was also a carrier, and felt that the revenue from carrying saved the canal from being loss-making.[17]

The Royal Commission accepted the evidence given to it that traffic was not deliberately transferred from canal to rail. Competition on price was largely eliminated by agreements being made concerning rates and terminal charges, not only with the parent railway company but also with neighbouring railway and canal companies. Until 1905 at least, new traffic was actively sought and local facilities improved.

The Shropshire Union sought inter-canal co-operation, but received little or no encouragement from the two companies with which it linked directly: the Trent & Mersey and Staffordshire & Worcestershire Canals. The former was railway-owned, the latter was not.

But, as we shall see, the war changed everything.

Was what happened inevitable? : 'Counterfactual history'

WE know what happened – and there is a temptation to think that this was the inevitable outcome. This study of the Shropshire Union Canal and its predecessors shows that there were several points in the story where the outcome could have been very different, and not just for canal history.

One such tipping point was when the Marquess of Stafford decided to invest £20,000 in the Birmingham & Liverpool Junction Canal. James Loch later said the decision had been made one year too soon. Without Lord Stafford's active support that canal was unlikely to have been built, and probably not the Middlewich Branch. Some of the important Shropshire Union traffic could never have developed: no limestone from Llanymynech to the iron foundries of east Shropshire, possibly no cheese for Manchester, and of course no 'main line' loads using the Nantwich–Chester–Mersey section.

In 1839 the Grand Junction Railway surveyed a route from Shrewsbury to Wolverhampton. No action was taken, partly because of the opposition of the Duke of Sutherland who wished to protect his investment in the canals. If that investment had not been made, he would surely have been keen on improving Shropshire's transport system, as in the long run it would have increased the rents his tenants could pay. With his support, the Grand Junction would have built the branch and the Grand Junction and its successor, the LNWR, would have become the dominant railway company in Shropshire. In the longer run, at Grouping in 1923 the Cambrian Railways would have joined the LNWR in becoming part of the London, Midland & Scottish Railway rather than the Great Western Railway.

Earlier connection to the national railway network may possibly have halted the decline in the coal and iron industries of east Shropshire. This is questionable, as geology and developments in industrial technology were also relevant, as was a diminution of the enterprising spirit from the great days of the Darbys and the Reynolds.

The place that would have been most affected by the absence of the Autherley–Nantwich link was Ellesmere Port. Without the Midlands traffic, the improvements of the 1830s and 1840s would not have happened, the port would not have thrived

Chapter 11 : The First Canal Age

A busy scene at Ellesmere Port at the end of the 19th century, showing the new flour mills and docks. The iron ore wharf is on the left. Railway & Canal Historical Society: Wilson Collection

nor the town grown. The population of Ellesmere Port now exceeds 60,000. Obviously there would have been some development in this area in the last 170 years, but there seems little reason to believe that the urban centre would have grown to such an extent.

The Ellesmere & Chester Canal may not have built its Middlewich Branch, and it is probable that no railway would have bought or leased the canal company, in which case it is unlikely to have survived much beyond the start of the 20th century. Pontcysyllte Aqueduct would have fallen into disuse and would eventually have been demolished. Hence the Llangollen Canal could never have become the country's most popular leisure canal.

Notes and references

1. Letter from 'An Inhabitant', *Montgomeryshire Journal*, 17 August 1835; *Chester Chronicle*, 17 April 1835.
2. Table of costs: National Library of Wales, Glansevern/13683. Reproduced in Stephen Hughes, *The Archaeology of the Montgomeryshire Canal*, 1988, p.57.
3. G.A. Cooke, *A Topographical and Statistical Description of the Principality of Wales, Part 1, North Wales*, c.1800, p.153
4. Robert Skey, *Report on the present state of competition*, 1841, p.23 [Author's collection]
5. Tom Foxon, *Anderton for Orders*, 1988, p.120
6. *Wrexham Advertiser*, 27 January and 3 March 1877
7. SU Executive Committee, 28 July 1915: TNA, RAIL623/27
8. *Wrexham Advertiser*, 18 December 1880
9. *Wrexham Advertiser*, 14 December 1861

10. *Chester Courant*, 25 October 1831
11. *Chester Chronicle*, 18 December 1847
12. *Wrexham Advertiser*, 8 August 1857 and 28 August 1858
13. Newspaper report of General Meeting on 7 September 1861: TNA, RAIL1110/413
14. George Jebb, *Proof of Evidence to the Royal Commission*, 1907, p.29: CRT Archives, BW/192/1/2/3
15. Ellesmere Canal Provisional Committee, 15 September 1791 and 21 August 1792: TNA, RAIL827/4
16. Robert Skey, *Report on the present state of competition*, 1841 [Author's collection]
17. Royal Commission on Canals 1906–9, Vol.7, paragraph 420

12
Decline (1914–1944)

The First World War

Government control

MANY canal Acts included a clause requiring canal companies to move troops and their equipment free of charge, though this was more concerned with preserving order within the country than for moving troops to embarkation ports for overseas campaigns. Similarly, the importance of railways for the movement of troops had been recognised since the 1830s. The Regulation of the Forces Act 1871 provided for full state control in wartime; from then on, planning was based on the premise that the government would take control of the network on the outbreak of war, giving overall directions to the companies which would continue to manage the operation of their lines.

Railways and railway-owned canals were put under the control of the Railway Executive Committee of the Board of Trade on 4 August 1914, the day war was declared. The Shropshire Union was in an anomalous position – as it was leased to the London & North Western Railway, not owned by it, it stayed outside the controls.

William Whittam, the Shropshire Union's General Manager, attended a meeting on 20 December 1916 chaired by the Director of Munitions Transport. Representatives of canal companies and carriers discussed whether it would be possible to improve the usage of canals for conveying materials of a non-urgent nature, in order to relieve the pressure on railways. A committee was set up, which reported to the Ministry of Munitions on 9 January 1917. Events then moved quickly. The Canal Control Committee was set up, publishing a *Handbook* which explained its aim:

> It is desirable that senders of heavy goods, manufacturers, and traders throughout the Country should render every possible assistance to the Government in dealing with the difficulties which have arisen in the transport of goods. The necessity is becoming more urgent as the War proceeds, and it will, therefore, be a patriotic step on behalf of all who can do so, if they will use the inland waterways of the Country, when they are suitable for the transport of their commodities between one point and another.

The Government took charge of the independent canals with effect from 1 March 1917, placing them under the control of the Canal Control Committee. Later that year responsibility for the Shropshire Union was transferred to the Railway Executive Committee, with the financial arrangements backdated to 1 January 1917.

Requisitions

IN the opening weeks of the war, six cartage horses and sets of harness, together with three vehicles, were taken by the Army Authorities from the Company's stables at Birmingham, and two more horses at Etruria. Compensation of £347 was paid, which was not considered adequate. There is no further mention in the minutes of similar requisitions, so presumably instructions had been given that companies transporting essential goods were not to be affected.

More serious was the requisitioning of the *Ralph Brocklebank* and *W.E. Dorrington*, together with ten of the Company's men. These steam tug-tenders had been built in 1903 and 1906 respectively for the Shropshire Union's cross-Mersey traffic. They were taken on 31 October 1914 and returned on 26 November, having been used on patrol duties in the Bristol Channel. During their absence the SU's third steam tug-tender, *Lord Stalbridge*, was worked with a double crew, assistance with docking was provided by the Manchester Ship Canal Company, and passenger carrying temporarily ceased. The sum of £1,632 was claimed in compensation, and £1,400 was paid. (The *Ralph Brocklebank* was renamed *Daniel Adamson* in 1936, and has survived into preservation.)

The following summer the Admiralty enquired about using one or more of the SU's steamers on patrol work in the Mediterranean. Their unsuitability for working such waters was pointed out, as was the dislocation which would be caused to the Company's business, which was itself largely concerned with the conveyance of foodstuffs and war materials.

THE SHROPSHIRE UNION CANAL

European War

List of Staff who served with the colours.
1914 – 1919

No	Name	Capacity	Regiment
	Baker. W	Sub-Inspector	Kings Shropshire Light Infantry
1	Hawkins A	Clerk	Royal Air Force
4	Mainwaring J	Joiner	Royal Air Force
5	Griffiths G	"	Kings Shropshire Light Infantry
6	Miner H	"	
7	Price J	App Joiner	Royal Air Force
14	Thomas J W	Boatbuilder	Royal Engineers
15	Edwards G H	"	"
18	Coleman H	Sawyer	Kings Shropshire Light Infantry
21	Whiston A	Fitter	Worcestershire Regiment
22	Parling L	"	Royal Navy
23	Union J	App Fitter	Loyal South Lancs
24	Cartwright S	"	Lancashire Fusiliers
30	Powell W	Striker	Kings Shropshire Light Infantry
33	Hall C	Painter	Royal Engineers
34	Price A	"	Kings Shropshire Light Infantry
35	Thomas A	"	Shropshire Yeomanry
36	Griffiths C	"	Kings Shropshire Light Infantry
43	Roberts J	Bricklayer	"
44	Davies J A	Bricklayers Asst	Royal Field Artillery
45	Parker H	Labourer	Kings Shropshire Light Infantry
48	Powell C	"	"
49	Carsley W	"	Royal Horse Artillery
51	Powell J	Stoker	Kings Shropshire Light Infantry
54	Sides A	Labourer	Royal Horse Artillery
57	Davies C	"	Kings Shropshire Light Infantry
69	Davies H	Banktender	"
75	Roden J	Labourer	"
87	Dean J Junr	Banktender	Shropshire Yeomanry
94	Collins G	"	Kings Shropshire Light Infantry
95	Saywell J	"	"
105	Pitt W	Sluice Attendant	Royal Navy
Extra	Walsh J H	Labourer	Royal Welsh Fusiliers
–	Johnson A E	Labourer	Welsh Cycling Corps
Killed	Shidlow W	Carpenter	Kings Shropshire Light Infantry
–	Woodvette L	Striker	

Until the early 2010s a Roll of Honour hung in Ellesmere Depot listing the Shropshire Union employees from there who served in the forces in the First World War. Because this was badly affected by damp and fading, a reproduction has been made matching closely the original style and lettering.
Canal & River Trust

Nevertheless, the *W.E. Dorrington* was requisitioned for a short period from 30 May 1917 for urgent service at Le Havre, the Government agreeing to accept all expenses and risks.

Recruitment and its effects

RECRUITMENT into the armed forces was initially voluntary, though there was considerable social pressure on young men. To try to reduce that pressure, in the autumn of 1915 the SU issued a war badge to all those men of military age in the Engineering Department who could not be spared from their duties.

Because voluntary recruitment had proved inadequate, Lord Derby, the Director-General of Recruiting, introduced a scheme whereby men aged 18 to 40 were told that they could continue to enlist voluntarily, or attest with an obligation to come if called up. In the event, voluntary recruitment ceased in December 1915 and progressive calling-up of the attested men started the following month. The Military Service Act 1916 removed any voluntary aspect – all eligible men could be called up. There was an exception if it was 'expedient in the national interests that he should be engaged in other work'. Boatmen aged 25 and over, together with certain other canal workers, were deemed to satisfy this criterion.

The number of Shropshire Union men on war service progressively increased:

– December 1914   96
– December 1915   213
– December 1916   223
– December 1917   301
– December 1918   326   Engineering Dept 102, Carrying Dept 224

Thus about a fifth of the men in the Engineering Department and a quarter of the men in the Carrying Department had joined the forces by the end of the war.

Maintenance of the canal suffered, not helped by exception gales in the winter of 1915/16, very icy conditions in the winters of 1916/17 and 1917/18, and periods of heavy rainfall resulting in several breaches of the canal. All non-urgent maintenance was deferred, the Engineer, George Jebb, repeatedly warning about the catching-up which would be needed when hostilities ceased and men returned from the armed forces.

There was some assistance from the Transport Workers Battalion of the York & Lancaster Regiment. A detachment of 50 men helped in the Tilstone Lock and Stanthorne Lock areas during the planned summer stoppage in 1917, several of them staying on for other work through the autumn. In total, 4,559 days were worked for the SU by men from the Battalion.

Men also left to go into better-paid munitions work. This was noted as a particular problem at Chester boatyard, where their specialist skills were necessary for boat maintenance. Representations were made to the Ministry of Munitions, and the men were allowed to remain with the Company.

From July 1916, women started working in the warehouses at Ellesmere Port; initially 30 were taken on, plus a 'forewoman'. Although they were reported as 'working satisfactorily' there does not seem to have been any further positive decision to employ women; however, there are a few passing mentions in the minutes of women being appointed to such jobs as ticket clerks, usually widows or daughters taking over from male former employees.

By the end of 1916 the shortage of steerers was becoming serious, with boats standing idle. The following June, with even more boats not being used, it was decided that no more boats should built for the time being.

It seems that some men were returned from active service to man the boats, though no record has been found of this scheme in the SU minutes or in Government archives. Jack Roberts, an SU boatman from 1908 until 1921, joined up in January 1915. In his memoirs he stated:

> After about two and a half years, during my third leave in England, I was on Chester Station, waiting for my train to Ellesmere Port. I was approached by my old canal inspector, Mr Talbot, and we both got on the train to Hooton. We had a chat, and he asked me if I would like to go back on the canal. I thought he was joking but he said he was serious, so I said I would.

A few weeks later, after a short period abroad, he was posted to Huntingdon where he was told he could return home and resume boating.[1]

Because there was less traffic, the number of boats in the fleet reduced from 660 in June 1914 to 608 in December 1919. Over the same period the number of horses was reduced from 492 to 414.

Surprisingly, the SU's minutes make no mention of the fatalities which must have been suffered by the employees who served with the armed forces, nor is there any discussion of the implications of the men returning to canal employment after the war.

The SU men who died were included in the LNWR's Roll of Honour: 12 were specifically listed as being SU employees, and a further 20 were almost certainly so, because of their job and/or location. There were several others who may well have been SU employees, for example, those described as 'Labourer, Ellesmere Port' or 'Carter, Wolverhampton'. Thus, in total, it is probable that about 40 SU men lost their lives in the First World War.[2]

The fear of air raids

AN immediate fear when war was declared was air raids, so night watchmen were employed at the places thought most vulnerable: Pontcysyllte, Chirk and Nantwich Aqueducts and Belvide Reservoir. These were intended to be temporary appointments, but those at Pontcysyllte, Nantwich and Belvide lasted until the end of the war. When the military authorities established an observation post near Stretton Aqueduct, it was hoped that they would take over watching Belvide Reservoir, but that was never agreed.

Chapter 12 : Decline (1914–1944)

The names and addresses of the Canal Company's District Inspectors and of the men in charge of canal works were given to the various Chief Constables, asking that where possible early notice of the approach of enemy aircraft should be sent to them. The Chief Constables promised to do all in their power. Special instructions were issued about what to do if an air raid happened. Also, measures were taken to restrict or obscure lights, in accordance with the Defence of the Realm Regulations.

In 1916 insurance was taken out against damage from air raids: the reinstatement value of the Company's property was assessed as £1,516,805, and a premium of £2,313 paid. The insurance was not renewed in later years.

The Mersey ports were strategically vulnerable, and in 1917, under the Regulations, it was deemed necessary for the telephone at Ellesmere Port docks to be manned continuously. Daytime manning was no problem, and it was thought that a telephone extension could be put into the hydraulic engine house, as that was manned all night. This did not prove practicable, and an extra person was employed overnight in the general office.

In fact the Mersey ports were never bombed, nor was anywhere in the area served by the Shropshire Union's canals. However, the SU's canal boats also served the Black Country and the Potteries. During a Zeppelin raid on the night of 31 January 1916, Tipton, Bradley, Wednesbury and Walsall were bombed, killing more than 30 people – this had an emotional effect far in excess of the casualties and damage caused, as it showed that the whole country was at risk. On the night of 27 November 1916, Kidsgrove, Tunstall, Fenton and Trentham suffered an air raid; a warning had been passed to the SU, and men were called out in the Norbury, Chester and Ellesmere districts.

The breach on the Weston Branch

On 5 May 1917 the Weston Branch breached at Dandyford, a little over 1½ miles east of Hordley Bridge, isolating the wharfs at Weston and Shade Oak. The embankment, about ten feet high, had shifted on the soft underlying peat. When Jebb examined the area he found that the embankments on the branch were unstable in several places. He recommended that the only way to prevent future trouble would be to line the bed and sides with clay puddle for more than one and a quarter miles of the canal, at an estimated cost of about £14,000. The company analysed the receipts for the first half of 1914 and calculated that of the £614 taken on the Weston Branch, only £50 related to the portion east of Hordley wharf. Because the income from the branch was minimal, the Committee decided that the expense was not justified. In any case, in the short term, neither men nor materials could be procured for the job.

An application was made to the Board of Trade for permanent closure on the grounds that the canal was 'unnecessary for the purposes of public navigation'. Ellesmere Rural District Council was the major objector because it would incur extra costs in transporting road-stone and because it was needed for conveying cattle feed. The ministry's inspector thought the estimated cost of restoration was not excessive but wondered whether something lesser might answer the purpose.

Nevertheless, he seemed persuaded by Jebb's contention that, unless the repairs were carried out in a substantial manner, further and probably more serious breaches might be expected when the canal was refilled with water. The Minister's decision not to prevent closure was given in 1920.

Labour relations

The support of the labour force was vital to the war effort. One effect was that the power of the unions inevitably increased, especially in large organisations such as the major railways, and this power continued once peace returned. Many men were members of the Shropshire Union Employees Union; others, including boatmen as well as engineering and depot staff, were members of the National Union of Railwaymen. It is evident from the minutes of the Executive Committee that employee relationships began to take up a lot of time at every meeting. A new post of Chief Staff Clerk was created in January 1918, Arthur Thompson being appointed specifically to deal with applications from groups of employees, interviews with the men's representatives, and arbitration and other proceedings.

Wartime brought inflation, prices more than doubling between 1914 and 1919, which inevitably resulted in demands for pay increases. These were given by supplements known as 'war bonuses'. Their amount was a matter for the Executive Committee to decide, but the SU tended to follow whatever had been decided by the London & North Western Railway, though the railwaymen's circumstances might be quite different. Each group of workers was dealt with separately; the negotiations might have been less protracted if the management had taken the initiative and had dealt with all groups together, rather than reacting to demands.

One day's pay, granted to all employees in celebration of Armistice Day, must have seemed little compensation for the struggles of the previous four years.

After the war

Once the war had ended, the national mood of jubilation did not last long. 'Spanish flu' killed an estimated quarter of a million people in Britain, young adults being especially susceptible. Male unemployment quickly rose to over two million men; in addition many women who may have wished to have worked were displaced by men returning from the armed forces. Price inflation continued. With the end of war orders, a serious depression hit the economy by 1921. The whole decade was one of stagnation and deflation, which exacerbated labour disputes.

Peacetime did not bring a return to what had been considered pre-war normality for the transport industry. The Shropshire Union emerged from the war seriously weakened. Arrears of maintenance had built up. Trading patterns had altered; and as the Shropshire Union was very dependent on export and import traffic between the Midlands and the Mersey ports, it suffered more than most.

Throughout the war, toll increases were under government control. As these did not keep pace with cost increases, the government guaranteed the pre-war level of profit through the payment of a subsidy. Government control, effectively nationalisation, met with little or no resistance. Canal finances were so bad that Government aid was positively welcomed.

On 31 August 1920 most canals reverted to private control, although the Minister of Transport agreed to continue nominal government control of certain waterways for a time – in the case of the SU, this was until 14 August 1921. The SU minutes are strangely quiet about this. It can be inferred from later correspondence that the SU was permitted to increase tolls by 150% in late 1920.

Competition and charging

WAR accelerates improvements in technology. The change which was to have the greatest effect on the canals (and on the railways) in the medium term was the improvement in the performance and reliability of motor vehicles. By the end of the war, manufacturers were geared for large-scale production, and by then of course there were many men trained to maintain and drive vehicles. Motor lorries could provide door-to-door transport, and one lorry and driver could move much more in a week than could a boat with its crew of two. Relatively little capital was required to enter the business, and there was virtually no regulation.

Canals were best suited for bulk boat-sized loads between canalside premises. If either the source or destination – the mine, quarry, factory, mill or dock – were away from the canal, transhipment and local haulage became necessary, adding to costs. These considerations applied as much to railways as to canals, but by 1921 railways had access to far many more locations.

Canals (and railways) were also hampered by the legislation concerning their charges: maximum rates were specified by law, but reductions were permitted providing the reduced rates were available to all customers. This had been appropriate when the railway companies had a monopoly or oligopoly for much freight traffic, but by the mid-1920s road transport provided genuine competition in many circumstances.

Furthermore, the maximum rates were based on the value of the items being carried – more valuable freights had a higher charge per mile – whereas road transport priced according to its costs, which were of course unrelated to the value of the goods.

In summary, the war did not cause the economic decline of the canals – it accelerated trends which were already present.

Labour relations

LARGELY as a result of the stresses caused by wartime inflation, relations between management and men had soured. Labour relations had changed from paternalistic to confrontational.

The phrase 'war bonuses' implied that once things returned to normal, the extra would cease being paid – but of course, prices never did revert to prewar levels, so after the war the bonuses were consolidated into pay rates.

Pay was one issue; conditions of service another. Inevitably there was pressure for the conditions of service negotiated for railway employees of the LNWR to apply to the canal staff too. The 48-hour week and various other conditions came to be applied to staff in the Engineering Department; management resisted doing this for the Carrying Department because of the very different circumstances under which boatmen worked, but eventually agreed to pay overtime at a time and a quarter for hours worked in excess of 48 a week.

In September 1919, railwaymen went on strike for just over a week, and the NUR members employed on the canal did so too. The management made arrangements for the horses to be fed and looked after, though in some instances this was done by the strikers themselves.

Closure of the Shropshire Union's carrying company

SINCE the late 1840s, the majority of the carrying on the canal had been by the Shropshire Union's own carrying subsidiary, the Shropshire Union Railways & Canal Carrying Company (SURCC). With 427 narrow boats, 112 Mersey flats and various other vessels, in 1898 this was the largest fleet in the country. The narrow boats were mainly trading between Ellesmere Port and the West Midlands conurbation with a substantial number operating on the Birmingham Canal network, this being owned by the LNWR.

A steady flow of new narrow boats boats entered the fleet in the early years of the 20th century, mainly being built at the company boatyard at Tower Wharf, Chester, with some being built at its boatyards at Ellesmere Port. During the war six boats were built at Trevor because of a strike at Chester. The last boat built was *Witness*, which joined the fleet in March 1917. Like all the SURCC's cargo-carrying canal fleet, it was horse-drawn.

For most traffics, horse-drawn boats stood little chance in competition with more modern forms of transport. Steam-powered tugs hauled some of the boats on the lock-free section between Ellesmere Port and Chester and also between Tyrley (just to the south of Market Drayton) and Autherley Junction, this section having only one lock in its 25 miles. Even when motor boats, operated by national or regional firms, started to appear on the Shropshire Union Main Line and Middlewich Branch, as far as can be ascertained they never travelled on the other branches.

In the early years of the 20th century the carrying business had made small surpluses, but the First World War changed this. The view was taken that it would not be possible to return the carrying fleet to profitability after the government's financial support ceased on 14 August 1921, so on 1 June 1921 the SU announced that it would cease to accept traffic after 31 August that year. The rail interchange facilities at Calveley were also to be closed.

The SU was estimated to be losing about £80,000 a year, and by ceasing to be a carrier the losses could be reduced to

Chapter 12 : Decline (1914–1944)

£44,000. A major operational problem was that a large proportion of the traffic was to or from Liverpool; as narrow boats were unsuitable for crossing the Mersey, everything had to be transhipped at Ellesmere Port, adding significantly to the cost.

At that time the SURCC was conveying about 80% of the traffic on its canals, mainly grain, iron and steel – much of the other 20% being carried in traders' own boats.

The government had been consulted in the April but refused to sanction the cessation of carrying whilst it still had responsibilities. It was concerned that about a thousand men would be made unemployed; in fact the number of boatmen whose services were terminated was just over seven hundred. A second concern was that there were several firms and one corn mill (Maesbury) more than three miles from a railway station. An internal ministerial memo makes it clear that cessation of carrying was inevitable, but it wanted the decision delayed until government control ended, so that it would not be blamed.[3]

The *Montgomery County Times* presented the news sentimentally:

> There is a picturesque charm about the meandering waterway, and a sense of restfulness about the leisurely pace of the barges with their easy-going occupants, which are in pleasant contrast to the clatter and rush of the dust-raising tractors that have quite destroyed the amenity of our highways.[4]

The local authorities in the Border Counties area were concerned by the decision, mainly because they feared it was a prelude to full closure of the Welsh canals. It was asserted that poor maintenance had reduced the carrying capacity of boats to between 10 and 15 tons, though it was rather an exaggeration that they could previously carry 25 tons, as 20 tons would have been more accurate.

The most vocal opposition came from the millers at Ellesmere Port who claimed to be entitled to have the existing arrangements continue, arguing that the existence of cheap transport had induced them to build their mills at Ellesmere Port in the first instance; they also complained about the short length of the notice period. However, the SU had no legal obligation to continue carrying – and certainly not at a financial loss – and it took only five days to demonstrate that there would be no difficulty in obtaining outside contractors to provide the carrying service.

Not everybody was unhappy about the prospect: when asked by the Ministry for comments, Samuel Williamson, the General Manager of the Cambrian Railways Company, replied that any restriction of traffic on the canal suited them as the canal had been an active competitor. He added that in his negotiations with the Great Western Railway he had pointed out that this 'will, in all probability, add substantially to the value of the undertaking' – the reality was surely that the resultant transfer of trade at Newtown, Welshpool, Oswestry and Ellesmere would have been negligible. (At this time the grouping of railway companies into the 'Big Four' was being planned, so naturally the valuation of railway companies was a significant issue.)[5]

Alternative arrangements

DESPITE the short time which existed between the formal notice being issued on 1 June 1921 and the actual cessation of carrying on 1 September, the substitute arrangements seem to have come in into place smoothly. The flour millers and galvanised iron manufacturers of Ellesmere Port made their arrangements with barge owners. The Chester & Liverpool Lighterage & Warehousing Company, based in Chester and Whitchurch, started a general carrying company between Ellesmere Port and Wolverhampton and also to the towns on the Welsh Branch. (Despite its name, it did not carry across the Mersey; the cross-Mersey traffics were operated by an associated company, Harris Barges, and other undertakings.) Messrs A. & A. Peate began conveying grain between Ellesmere Port and their mill at Maesbury. National and regional carrying firms increased their operations on the Main Line.

Wharfs and warehouses at various locations were leased to carriers. The Chester & Liverpool Lighterage & Warehousing Company took possession of the Cow Lane Depot (except for the bonded stores), an office and stables at Dee Basin, Chester, and premises at Nantwich, Whitchurch and Newport. No other firm leased more than two wharfs. The boatyard and dry dock at Tower Wharf, Chester, were leased to J. & H. Taylor & Sons.

The boating service which had been provided by the SURCC within the South Staffordshire area, which included journeys to Kidderminster and Stourport, was taken over by the LNWR with effect from 2 January 1922, several boats being transferred from the SURCC fleet. Other boats joined the maintenance fleet.

The fleet, which at the end of carrying had totalled 469 of which 331 were narrow boats, was put up for sale. Significant purchasers of narrow boats were the Chester & Liverpool Lighterage & Warehousing Company (33), Midlands & Coast Carriers (28), Fellows, Morton & Clayton (25), the Anderton Company (13), and A.&A. Peate of Maesbury Mill (10).

Purchasers of broad-beamed boats included the Bishop's Wharf Carrying Company (at least 14), Richard Abel & Sons (at least 7) and William Bate & Co. (3). But over half the river and canal barges, some over 100 years old, remained unsold by 1927. By 1935 most of the remaining craft had been moved to the Dee Basin at Chester. (When the basin was in-filled in 1952, contractors removed the parts above water level, and the hulls were buried under rubble.)

The tug-tenders, *W.E. Dorrington*, *Ralph Brocklebank* and *Lord Stalbridge*, were sold to the Manchester Ship Canal for £9,125.

The men

EVEN before the transfer of the South Staffordshire area boats, about 90 of the approximately 700 men made redundant had been found jobs with the LNWR. A pension and gratuity scheme was devised for the rest. The amount paid depended on whether the man was a member of the Provident &

215

Pension Society. For those who were not, the scheme for *ex gratia* payments was:

- Aged 65 and over – 5*s* a week
- Aged 60 to 64 – between 3*s*.6*d* and 5*s* a week, depending on length of service
- Under 60 with 10 years service – lump sum of between £2 and £25, depending on age and service

Those in the Society received the full pension of 7*s* or 10*s* a week if they were aged 60 or over, or half pension of 3*s*.6*d* or 5*s* if they were between 55 and 59. In addition the SU paid them a lump sum gratuity of between £10 and £50, depending on age and service. Those aged under 55 with more than ten years service were paid a lump sum gratuity of between £3 and £14. Men who had less than ten years service received no gratuity.

Regrettably, there is no record of how many men came into each category, nor how many found alternative employment.

Ellesmere Port Docks

IN the autumn of 1921, talks were held with the Manchester Ship Canal Company with a view to it taking over the docks at Ellesmere Port, as it was thought that the MSC would be better placed to develop them. By 1922 terms for a fifty-year lease had been agreed and the formal transfer happened on 1 April. The change was made with no difficulties; there was no interruption of business, which was conducted on the same lines as before. The MSC continued to employ most of the 45 waged dock-workers.

As part of the agreement, the carrying firm Fellows, Morton & Clayton transferred its traffic between the West Midlands and Liverpool to the SU route instead of using the Bridgewater Canal (owned by the MSC) and the Trent & Mersey Canal. This traffic, estimated at 50,000 tons a year, would bring in about £11,000 in tolls. Fellows, Morton & Clayton also acquired the freehold of the SU's premises at Crescent Wharf in the centre of Birmingham on the Newhall Branch Canal.

The lease to the MSC proved beneficial to all, with significant developments being made in the dock facilities over the next couple of decades.

The London Midland & Scottish Railway

WITH wartime control of railways ceasing in 1921, there was fairly general agreement that the benefits of unified operation should continue. The result was the passing of the Railways Act 1921 which grouped virtually all the country's railways into four regional companies, one of which was the London Midland & Scottish Railway (LMSR),

This was created on 1 January 1923 by the merger of the LNWR and seven other major railway companies – some were willing, some were forced – and several minor ones. As well as 6,900 miles of railways, 10,200 locomotives, 19,600 carriages and 207,000 wagons, the LMSR inherited a large shipping fleet and several hotels. At the outset it claimed to be the largest transport organisation in the world and the largest private enterprise business in Europe. However, it suffered from management problems, particularly in its early years, and from financial difficulties, especially in the 1930s. No dividend was paid on ordinary shares from 1932 to 1935 nor in 1938, for example.

Amongst the assets inherited by the LMSR were 644 miles of canals, including the Trent & Mersey and Birmingham Canals as well as the Shropshire Union system. Unsurprisingly, its canal activities were of little or no interest to senior management. There was not even a 'Canal Committee' or its equivalent.

The former Shropshire Union under the LMSR

IN anticipation of Grouping, on 29 December 1922 the Railway Amalgamation Tribunal had formally approved the Shropshire Union Railways & Canal Company being absorbed by the LNWR, the effective date being back-dated to 1 January 1922. The accounts of the SU had actually been merged with those of the LNWR from the beginning of the year. Less than £25,000 of SU stock was exchanged for LNWR stock at this preliminary absorption – most of the rest of the stock created in 1846 had been exchanged for LNWR stock many decades earlier. This shows clearly how the Shropshire Union as a separate company was little more than a fiction by 1922.

No major engineering works were carried out during the LMSR's twenty-five years of ownership of the Shropshire Union system. The most significant development was the agreement with Wolverhampton Corporation to take water from Barnhurst Sewage Works, since when there has rarely been a water shortage problem even in the driest summers.

Repairs were carried out to the dam and the outlet valve chamber of Arenig Fawr Reservoir in 1926/27, but in 1931 it was noted that it had not been necessary to use the water in this lake for either the canal or the flannel factory at Bala during the year. As the reservoir was no longer needed, it was passed to Bala Urban District Council in about 1946 and is now owned by Welsh Water.[6]

In order to avoid expenditure on maintenance, in 1932 the level of the water in Arenig Fach Reservoir was reduced to that of the output valve. At some date, probably later in the 1930s, this reservoir was passed to the local land-owner.[7]

By the end of the LMSR era the number of lock-keepers and lengthsmen had been greatly reduced and all wharves were privately operated. Many of the isolated properties no longer had an acceptable standard of water supply or sewage disposal, there was no prospect of getting an electricity supply to them, and some even had no access by road or track. Hence many of the canal houses had been sold or demolished.

When Jack Roberts, the former fly-boat captain, returned to employment on the canal in the late 1930s after fifteen years absence, he found quite a change:

> All the pride in appearance had diminished and the traffic was different as it was now a toll canal. All the old fly-boats had gone, and also the men from the various warehouses

Chapter 12 : Decline (1914–1944)

A notice photographed at Carreghofa in 2004, which by 2018 had been removed – this was a rare physical reminder of the LMS period of ownership.
Author

and depots. These buildings were almost all locked up and rusting. Some of the old stables had been demolished.[8]

Nevertheless, and contrary to the general impression given today, railway ownership actually enabled many canals to survive. Some privately-owned canals just died – when income no longer covered the costs, maintenance ceased, weeds grew unchecked, silt was deposited, and nature (or neighbouring landowners) took over. In contrast, the law required railway-owned canals to be maintained in good working condition.

Not that closure was impossible. The law offered three options:

- the canal's owner could make an application to the Minister of Transport if the canal was 'unnecessary for the purposes of public navigation'; or
- any local authority or three adjacent landowners could apply if the canal had become derelict, that is, had not been used for navigation for at least three years; or
- the railway company could obtain a private Act of Parliament giving the consent to closure.

Traffic and revenues

FORTUNATELY, statistics for the tonnage conveyed on the Shropshire Union during most of the LMSR period are available. These do not distinguish between the various sections of the canal, but it is reasonable to assume that the great majority of the traffic was on the Main Line and the Middlewich Branch.

The tonnage carried increased substantially during the 1920s, from 325,000 tons in 1922 to a peak of 484,000 tons in 1928, only 20% short of the 1905 figure of 605,000 tons, then decreased slightly to 397,000 tons in 1931. Direct imports at Ellesmere Port virtually ceased in August 1932, whereas previously they had accounted for some 60,000 tons of traffic a year. Other traffic through Ellesmere Port declined slowly but steadily through the rest of the 1930s, whereas traffic passing through Middlewich fluctuated between 85,000 to 115,000 tons a year. By 1938 the total tonnage had fallen to 215,000.

The financial position in 1938 (the last peacetime year) was:

	£	£
Expenditure		
Maintenance	28,837	
Superintendence & wages	4,038	
Other expenditure	8,499	
Transfer to Renewal Account	1,920	43,294
Income		
Tolls	21,487	
Rents and other receipts	13,042	34,529
Loss on canal		8,765
Share of profit, Ellesmere Port (from MSC)		6,829
Overall loss		1,936

As can be seen, the payment by the Manchester Ship Canal with respect to the Shropshire Union's share of the profit at Ellesmere Port made all the difference.[9]

The other receipts included sale of water. In 1922 Brunner Mond at Middlewich was paying £500 for taking and returning to the canal 200,000 gallons a day. It wished to take and retain 400,000 gallons, which the SU thought practicable except in times of drought. An agreement was made for 300,000 gallons a day, the revenue forecast to be between £1,800 and £2,400 a year. Pipes with 6in. valves were installed at the locks. The supply had probably ceased by 1940.

The Main Line and Middlewich Branch

THE Shropshire Union Main Line was not as deep as many other trunk canals. For example, a pair of boats could carry only 45 tons, compared with at least 54 tons between Birmingham and London.

One boatman later wrote:

> Its mud was of a particularly tenacious quality and empty boats were in danger of becoming embedded in it every time they met a loaded vessel, so restricted was the channel. On the exposed embankments the wind waited to seize the high fore-ends of empty boats and blow them ashore ... Quite often a boat would get off the mud only to be blown ashore again immediately. No wonder boatmen had a picturesque vocabulary.[10]

When working as a pair, one option was to use a long line – five 90ft lines joined together – to come up the narrow Hack Green, Audlem, Adderley and Tyrley locks so that the motor, albeit above the lock, could still tow the butty. This technique needed good teamwork with the butty steerer signalling when the butty had reached the lock, the final pulling in being done by hand. The butty's tiller was held in position with strings. In this way a pair could be worked with a crew of only two. This system of long lines did not work going downhill, but boats going north were often empty.

Following the demise of the SU's carrying subsidiary, much of the traffics on the Main Line and Middlewich Branch were taken over by Fellows, Morton & Clayton, the largest firm of canal carriers in the country. This brought a regular service of powered boats onto the Shropshire Union for the first time. The firm had first operated steamers in 1860 (though it is unlikely that these were ever used on the SU waters) and boats with Bolinder semi-diesel engines in 1912. However, it mechanised its services from London to Birmingham, Leicester and Nottingham before its services north of Birmingham. Significant cargoes from Ellesmere Port included sugar to the Midlands, and bagged flour to Wolverhampton and Bloxwich. Fellows, Morton & Clayton's boats between Manchester and the Midlands started going via the SU Main Line instead of via the Trent & Mersey Canal through Harecastle Tunnel; metals were a particularly important traffic on this route.

Noah Hingley & Sons of Netherton Ironworks had traditionally employed the SURCC and were concerned about being totally dependent on the railways. They therefore established Midlands & Coast Canal Carriers principally to continue to convey their products and others to Ellesmere Port, though they also carried some traffic down to London. In 1922 the firm took a sub-lease of Broad Street Depot in Wolverhampton. In 1938 the fleet was sold to Fellows, Morton & Clayton.

The Anderton Company, which was based at Stoke-on-Trent, took over the china clay traffic from Ellesmere Port to the Potteries.

The oil refinery at Stanlow, opened in 1924, gave rise to a trade in fuel oil and gas oil, mainly to the Shellmex depot at Langley Green at the top of the Titford Branch locks, in the boats of Thomas Clayton (Oldbury), specialist carriers of liquid products. Until 1937 these boats were horse-drawn and usually worked in pairs. A tug took the boats the short distance up the MSC from Ellesmere Port to the refinery; this continued even after the introduction of motor boats, it being 1953 before boats were allowed to do this stage under their own power. Whilst Langley Green was the main destination, gas oil was taken regularly to Birmingham and to Nottingham, and fuel oil was delivered to Saltley, Walsall, Wolverhampton, and occasionally to Leamington Spa. The company also conveyed naphtha from Oldbury to Manchester.

Other companies which operated on the Main Line included Richard Abel & Sons and Bishops Wharf Carrying Co. of Liverpool, E. Thomas of Walsall, George & Matthews of Wolverhampton, and one local firm, J. Parr of the Junction Inn, Norbury.

Cowburn & Cowpar transported chemicals from Trafford

Motor boat at Tyrley top lock, showing the use of the long line to draw in the butty boat.
Neil Jenkins

Chapter 12 : Decline (1914–1944)

Cadbury's factory at Knighton, with the churn tower at the back of the wharf.
Knighton Foods

Park, Manchester, and Weston Point to the Courtaulds works at Wolverhampton, starting in 1926 and ceasing in 1951. The principal cargo was carbon disuphide, but various acids, solvents, acetone, caustic soda and oils were also conveyed.

In 1911 Cadbury's had built a factory at Knighton to make chocolate crumb. Boats brought mass chocolate (ground cocoa beans made into blocks) from Bournville and sugar from Liverpool and Colwick (on the river Trent, just east of Nottingham) to Knighton, where the ingredients were mixed and the milk added. The resulting product was boated back to Bournville. Farmers along the canal would arrange for their milk to be collected from the various wharves or from newly-constructed stagings adjacent to their land – an example can be seen just to the south of the embankment at Market Drayton. Cadbury's built a milk concentrating station at High Onn in 1924. This milk traffic continued until the 1930s, when the trade was lost to road transport, but the chocolate crumb traffic continued.

Most traffic was transit traffic, passing to or from the former Shropshire Union system at Autherley Junction or Middlewich. More local traffic included grain carried to mills at Chester, Waverton, Calveley and Gnosall. Coal went to these mills and other canalside industries in Chester and to coal merchants at Market Drayton and various village wharfs.

The Shrewsbury Branch

Trench Incline operated for the last time on 31 August 1921; it had worked for 124 years, a testament to the soundness of its design. For some years the only traffic had been grain from Ellesmere Port going up to Donnington Wood mill. The closure date coincided with the SURCC ceasing to be a carrier. The legal formalities approving closure of the incline and the canal above it were not finalised until 1931.

It is not clear when the last loads passed on the branch below the incline. Traffic would have needed one of the especially narrow Trench boats, but only one was sold from the former SURCC's fleet – that sale was in 1925, but the records do not show the purchaser – most of the others becoming maintenance boats. One former major customer, the Trench Iron Works, closed in 1931, and traffic to Joseph Sankey & Co. (previously known as the 'Castle Works') is likely to have ended before 1927 when the firm sought to fill in the basin there and remove the bridge.

The Humber Arm had been principally used in connection with the Lilleshall Company's private railway line to its collieries and iron works. The Duke of Sutherland's property on the Humber Arm was auctioned on 28 June 1922. The wharf was sold to the owner of the adjacent farm, and the freehold of the railway to the Lilleshall Company. Having no further use for them, the SU sold the one-ton crane, donkey pump, weighbridge and railway material to the Lilleshall Company. The track remained for a period – on 24 August that year two wagons loaded with sand ran away down the gradient, smashing the crossing gates and the warehouse doors. In 1924 the track was lifted for the first mile south from the Humber Arm and the land sold, thus ending the possibility of further transhipment.

Shrewsbury Basin was closed and a Warrant of Abandonment obtained in 1922 in order to save the cost, estimated as £1,000, of a new swing bridge across the entrance.

The traffic in by-products from Shrewsbury Gas Works carried by Thomas Clayton (Oldbury) and by Chance & Hunt ceased in 1927 and 1931 respectively. Using the provisions of the Road & Rail Traffic Act 1933, Shropshire County Council applied for a Warrant of Abandonment for the canal from Shrewsbury to Withington, where there was no longer any traffic, so that they could lower bridges. Shrewsbury Borough Council agreed a joint application for the section within the Borough boundary. The objections to the Warrant mainly concerned agricultural water supplies or the prospects of dereliction. The LMSR proposed an undertaking to carry out minimal maintenance to ensure water supplies, drainage and public health; an assurance was also given about the future maintenance of Berwick Tunnel. The objectors seemed to have been satisfied by 1937, but legal problems delayed the matter and it got tangled up with the objections to abandonment of the Montgomery Canal, as discussed later. Shropshire County Council withdrew its application but Shrewsbury Borough Council continued. An objection was raised by someone who owned land east of Comet Bridge (the more northerly of the two bridges at Ditherington) over the loss of water supplies. The Council compromised by restricting the length closed to that between the terminal basin and a point 266ft east of Comet Bridge. The Warrant was granted in 1939.

The canal was intended to have been filled in but the war intervened and there were concerns about the cost. By 1945, residents and some councillors, backed by the Local Medical Officer of Health, were concerned that the lowered water level was a health hazard and a breeding ground for mosquitoes. A successful appeal was made to the Minister of Health and draining the canal started that autumn.

Revenue from tolls in the nine months to 30 September 1935 totalled only £66. The last proved commercial traffic to Withington was in 1935; the last traffic to Long Lane was a coal boat about every six weeks until 1939. The final traffic on any part of the branch was in 1944: tar from Newport Gas Works to the Black Country, carried by Thomas Clayton (Oldbury).

The occasional pleasure boat used the canal before the Second World War. One such hirer of *Joyce*, a small cabin cruiser, who got as far as Berwick Tunnel in July 1939 reported that in the flight of seventeen locks down from Norbury Junction 'the surface of the water was lost between masses of weed and green slime, the ironwork of the gates was rusty, and the paint thereof had long since peeled off'. The first two miles beyond Newport were particularly thickly covered with weeds and water lilies; after that the going got easier until the section between the Eyton locks. From Withington conditions got steadily worse until at Berwick Wharf the boat was brought to a final halt by solid masses of green slime. The steerer walked on and found that

> the shallow cutting preparatory to entering Berwick Tunnel ... seemed like the Valley of Desolation. There was a sickly, nauseating smell arising from the stagnant waters and, all over, there was silence.[11]

Hurleston Junction to Llangollen and its branches

WHEREAS the Main Line was kept in reasonable condition, by 1929 the Welsh Branch was reported as being shallow in places, limiting boat loads to 15 tons.

After the closure of the SURCC, traffic on the Llangollen line

Peaceful scene at Uffington, c.1930.
Shrewsbury & Newport Canals Trust

Chapter 12 : Decline (1914–1944)

Boys fishing at Whitchurch Basin in the early 1930s, with ex-SURCC *Cuckmere*, then owned by the Whitchurch Warehousing Company. *Waterway Images Library*

The weekly boat carrying coal to Quina Brook at the end of the Prees Branch had probably ceased by the start of the First World War, and Edstaston wharf may not have seen any trade after the demise of the SURCC. The last recorded loads on the Prees Branch were coal from Tunstall (in the Potteries) to Whixall – probably Waterloo, a mile further on – in 1933, roadstone from Chirk to Whixall in 1934 and coal and cinders, again probably from Tunstall, to Waterloo in November 1934. After that the first mile of the branch continued to be used by maintenance boats taking puddling clay from Whixall.

The grocery and cheese traffics at Whitchurch ceased when the SURCC stopped operating but other traffics such as coal, stone and gas tar continued for a while. Grain from Ellesmere Port was carried by the Chester & Liverpool Lighterage & Warehousing Company until it went into receivership in 1933; at least two of its craft were taken over by a new company, the Whitchurch Warehousing Company. The last definite record of commercial carrying to Whitchurch was a load of flour in 1936.

Frankton Junction to Newtown

IN the second half of the 1920s, maintenance standards on the branch from Frankton Junction to Newtown, what we now call the 'Montgomery Canal', were reduced, which must have made navigation more difficult. In 1925 the annual maintenance cost was £4,213; by 1933 it was £2,719. Part of the saving came through closing the Welshpool engineering yard in 1926, but most came through reducing the number of full-time staff to seventeen plus four part-time staff employed for 10 to 12 weeks a year.

Closure of the Guilsfield Arm had been considered in 1924 but no action was taken at that time.

Following the cessation of trading by the SURCC, ten of its boats were bought by A.&A. Peate of Maesbury to enable them to continue to bring grain from Ellesmere Port to their mill, together with corn and maize from local wharves. They also brought coal from Black Park Colliery at Chirk. Return loads, when they could be found, were generally roadstone, sand or timber. During the 1920s and early 1930s Peate's built up a fleet of about a dozen Foden steam wagons, both for local deliveries and for bringing grain from Birkenhead and Liverpool. The first wagon had metal front wheels and solid rubber-tyred rear wheels, the maximum speed being 5mph, and was presumably used only for local deliveries. The last had pneumatic tyres all round and a good turn of speed, and during a (long) day could do a round trip to Liverpool, picking up a 10-ton load. This proved more economical than canal transport, which they ceased in February 1934.

Before the War, the toll charged from Ellesmere Port to Maesbury was 2s.2½d a ton. Following the wartime inflation in wages and other costs, this was increased to 5s.6¼d in late 1920, then reduced progressively to 4s.5d in 1921 and 3s.10d in 1922. The following year a special reduction to 2s.6d was made for Peate's traffic to Maesbury, and this was further reduced to 2s.0d in 1928. It cannot therefore be said that Peate's traffic was squeezed off by excessive charges.

was mainly in the hands of the Chester & Liverpool Lighterage & Warehousing Company, which leased the warehouse at Whitchurch, and various bye-traders. Apart from grain to Peate's mills at Maesbury which passed off the Llangollen line at Frankton Junction, none of the traffic flows were substantial, and as time went on they petered out. Thomas Clayton (Oldbury) took creosote from Oldbury to Cefn Mawr. Transport of some loads of cement traffic appears to have lasted until the closure of the works at Ellesmere Port in 1932. Various wharfs along the branch received coal from Black Park Colliery, Chirk, until 1933 and roadstone from Froncysyllte until 1934. Roadstone brought down from the Ceiriog Granite Company's quarry to the wharf at Chirk was conveyed to Platt Lane in 1935. The last records of flour and offals carrying are in 1936 from Ellesmere Port to Bettisfield and to Wrenbury. After that, little was carried on the Llangollen line – one ton of timber from Hampton Bank to St Martin's Moor in 1938 and finally some peat from Whixall Moss to Autherley Junction (the ultimate destination was not recorded) between 1937 and February 1939.

As mentioned earlier, on 5 May 1917 the Weston Branch breached at Dandyford, making Hordley wharf the terminus of the branch. It is not known when this wharf was last used.

By the start of the 1930s, Peate's were overwhelmingly the most important trader on the branch, accounting for over 80% of the tonnage. Next in importance were Jones Evans & Co., flannel manufacturers of Newtown. In 1934 they brought 26 boat-loads (463 tons) of coal from Black Park Colliery, the portion of the tolls attributable to the Montgomery Canal being £37. The firm closed in June 1935.

By 1934 other individual traffics were insignificant. That year the portion of their tolls attributable to the Montgomery Canal totalled £39:

- T. Edwards of Maesbury brought six loads (99 tons) of coal from Black Park and four loads (72 tons) via Autherley Junction (probably from the Cannock area);
- J.B. Jones of Queen's Head took nine loads (144 tons) of sand to Welshpool, eight loads (126 tons) to the Powis Estate yard and four loads (50 tons) to Black Park – he also arranged for one part load of timber (just 5cwt) from below Frankton Locks to St Martins;
- R.T. Jones, also of Queen's Head, took four loads of sand (53 tons) to Llanymynech, three loads (44 tons) to Pant and one load (16 tons) to Welshpool, bringing one part load of hay (10cwt) back from Pant to Maesbury; and
- the Montgomery Farmers Association took four loads (72 tons) from Autherley to Aberbechan.

The people and firms named above are the ones with whom the contracts were made – they were not themselves boat owners. No doubt most of the work was done by George Beck, who in 1936 was noted as being the only trader remaining on the canal.

The Agent for the Powis Estate stated in late 1936: 'Only this year we have conveyed by canal several cubic feet of timber at a cost far beneath that charged by either the railway or road transport.' In fact the load was 73 tons of timber from Abbey Bridge (between Pool Quay and Buttington) to the Powis Estate yard, a journey of only 3¾ miles through Welshpool, so conveyance by railway would not have been an option.[12]

When the Manchester Grammar School's Rover Scouts boated to Newtown in September 1933 they found:

> the backwater used for turning at the end of the canal did not appear to have been used for years whilst the cut was full of weeds and green algae and was rather unpleasant.[13]

Once Peate's of Maesbury ceased carrying in February 1934, the case for closure seemed strong. The annual income from commercial tolls was only £76 with a further £282 coming from the sale of water (half of that being to the Great Western Railway at Welshpool), £62 from pleasure boat licences, £26 from fishing and £7 from rents and wharfage.

However, the area engineer thought that the annual cost of maintenance which was about £2,700 could be reduced by only a little over £400 if weed-cutting and dredging ceased and grass-mowing reduced. He warned that lengthsmen would still be needed because much of the canal was on a hillside where in times of heavy rainfall a large volume of water flowed into the canal, requiring prompt action to control the levels in order to prevent the canal overflowing, possibly breaching an embankment. Furthermore, if the canal was neglected but had to be reopened following a legal challenge, it was thought that the expenditure then required would be out of all proportion to the savings which had been made. It was therefore decided to take no action about closure.

The breach at the Perry Aqueduct

THE branch from Frankton Junction to Newtown breached near the Perry Aqueduct on 5 February 1936. Repairs would have cost about £600, which the LMSR was unwilling to pay, thus effectively closing the canal.

Three boats were trapped below the breach: a private pleasure boat owned by Herbert Openshaw (a wealthy man living at Llanfechain, some five miles west of Llanymynech), Beck's *Perseverance*, and the canal company's *Berriew*. A temporary repair enabled enough water to be in the canal to float out Openshaw's boat. Beck was paid £80 compensation.

There was a little traffic after the breach: 64 tons of sand from Queen's Head to the Powis Estate yard in April 1936, for example, and what was probably the last load, one ton of timber from Freestone Lock to Brithdir in December 1938.

In his seminal book *Narrow Boat*, published in 1944, Tom Rolt discussed the breach:

> It was not a serious matter, for canal lengthsmen have since told me that it would have taken only a few days' work to restore the canal to navigable condition, but this was not to be. For the Railway Company it was a welcome pretext to abandon a liability.[14]

The following year Rolt wrote that he had inspected the breach and it was of negligible proportions. He added that the former Welsh Section Inspector had told him that the Ellesmere workshop assembled the men and materials to repair it but then received instructions not to carry out the work.[15] He also related a story told to him by the lock-keeper at Frankton. Soon after the bank collapse happened, the lock-keeper said that the breach was stopped unofficially by a boater who wished to pass through. The LMSR Engineer sternly objected and ordered him to dismantle his work. Rolt commented, 'If it is true, it is the most classic example of railway sabotage that has come our way yet.'[16]

The District Engineer considered that the annual cost of maintaining the canal to 'ordinary navigation standard' would be about £3,000. It was estimated that 27,500 tons of traffic a year – about 27 fully-laden boats per week – would be needed to cover this maintenance cost. The calculation did not take account of the fact that much of the cost would continue even if navigation ceased; on the other hand, the income assumed was for the whole journey (two-thirds of journeys assumed to be from Ellesmere Port) and not just the part attributable to the mileage on the Montgomery Canal.

Mr Thompson, the Shropshire Union Canal Agent based at

Chapter 12 : Decline (1914–1944)

Chester, gave his opinion about why trade on this canal was so difficult to get:

> The principal cause operating against the canal carrier in this district is that it is purely agricultural and there is no back loading. Moreover with the development of road vehicles traders and farmers placed practically all the heavy traffic on the roads and left the light – such as bran – on the canal – a boat capable of carrying 20 tons ... was full with about 15 tons of low rated traffic on which the boatman had to be paid a higher tonnage rate to compensate for less weight.[17]

The LMSR's Board agreed to apply to the Minister to abandon the canal; this was confirmed at a Special General Meeting of shareholders, as required by Section 45(2)(b) of the Railway & Canal Traffic Act 1888. The formal application was made on 24 March 1937.

Mr C. Pemberton from the LMSR's legal section accompanied by Mr Thompson then met the Clerks of the various local authorities affected to explain the reasons and to assure them that as long as the company owned the canal, they would not seek to diminish their existing responsibilities in relation to matters other than navigation. In other words, water levels would be controlled, land drainage duties honoured, and bridges and boundary fences maintained. Closure could help the local authorities, in that road improvements would be made easier and cheaper. No Clerk could give a commitment without consulting his council, of course, but Mr Pemberton gained the impression that there was not likely to be any substantial opposition from any council. The Chairman of Newtown Urban District Council blamed the closure on railway companies' general policies concerning their canals, but Mr George, their Clerk, said that notwithstanding the Chairman's views, he would report that they had no good grounds for spending any money in connection with objections and public inquiries.

A draft agreement with the local authorities was formulated. This stated that as long as the company owned the canal it would continue to undertake its responsibilities. Water would continue to be supplied 'for the use of those persons who are being supplied [from the canal] for farm or domestic purposes which supply shall not be diminished below its normal level by any act on the part of the company'.

Seven of the local authorities signed the draft agreement. Shropshire County Council, in particular, were keen to support closure so that various road bridges could be improved.

Press reaction to the notice of abandonment was unfavourable. The *Shrewsbury Chronicle* exhorted the National Farmers' Union to take action:

> It would be disastrous for many farms, where the canal has for generations provided a water supply, to be cut off. In this abandonment too, there is the danger of leaving a muddy quagmire in which, for years, animals can founder or bedaub themselves, to say nothing of the attraction for the most venomous species of mosquitoes, dragon-flies and other winged and creeping pests. Awake, O Farmers' Union, delay may be disastrous.[18]

A protest meeting was held at Pool Quay on 6 August 1937. The lack of use of the canal was attributed to the railway company doing everything possible to divert its traffic to the railways. The formal resolution stated:

> The canal has been in existence for nearly a century and a half, with the result that gradually the whole district has come to look upon it as a permanent feature of the landscape, and not only is it the main source of water supply for the whole district, but land has been bought and sold and divided up, using the canal as a boundary.[19]

The main concern was the loss of the water. If farmers had been using the canal for over a hundred years, it was thought that surely they had acquired prescriptive rights, whether or not they had a formal agreement. One farmer said that if the water level dropped by only six inches, part of his farm would be practically useless. It was also thought that the promise to maintain the water level was ineffective because there was no guarantee that if part of the canal was sold, the duty would pass to the purchaser.

The LMSR argued that some people paid to extract water, and these contracts could be terminated on giving the required notice. Others had rights from the original canal Acts because streams had been intercepted. However, the amount taken out of the canal was vastly greater than the amount which went in from the streams – indeed those streams often became dry in summer. Most farmers took water without a statutory right and without payment, so they were not entitled to a continued supply or to compensation. Only three landowners had rights to water enshrined in the original Acts: the Powis, Glansevern and Glanhafren Estates.

Most of the formal written objections to the Minister came from farmers and concerned water supplies. Major Marriott, the Agent for the Powis Estate, was the only objector who had actually used the canal for transport. He felt that the canal was 'a useful means of transport and that, if allowed to compete with the railway could undercut them in dealing with quite a considerable amount of transport'. However, the Powis Estate's toll payments had averaged less than £5 over the previous four years. In addition, the owner of one wharf made a formal complaint – Henry Platt Hall of Newbridge Wharf, at the south end of the Vyrnwy Aqueduct – though the records showed that no traffic had passed at that wharf for at least the previous sixteen years.

Despite various local authorities accepting the draft agreement concerning future maintenance, the Ministry of Transport sided with the objectors. It was felt the agreement did not go far enough, and it should be in perpetuity. Attention was drawn to the Act passed the previous year to enable the London & North Eastern Railway to end the right of navigation on part of the Nottingham Canal, where Parliament had deemed that the

223

Cressy, which had been built by the SU at Trevor in 1915, had been owned by Peate's before being bought by Kyrle Williams. In 1929 it was converted for pleasure use at John Beech's boatyard below the third lock of the Frankton flight. A small steam engine was installed and a new cabin created forward of the engine, leaving the existing fore-cabin intact. Williams invited his wife's god-son, Tom Rolt, on the first trial a short way up the Llangollen Canal, then, the following March, to be in the crew for the initial longer voyage to Middlewich – and out of the Shropshire Union system. *Waterway Images*

company must continue with full responsibility for maintaining the canal.

A new agreement was drafted, with two major changes. The words 'for such period as [the canal] remains in their ownership' which had proved so controversial were removed. On the other hand, the wording concerning who was entitled to water was considerably tightened to 'those persons who are entitled to have watering places for cattle under section 49 of the Canal Act 1794'. This time every local authority except for Welshpool Borough refused to sign – even Shropshire County Council. The pressure from the farming lobby seemed to have succeeded.

The LMSR resubmitted its application to the Minister on 14 June 1938, specifically saying that it did not intend to seek a Special Act.

The decision letter sent on 17 August 1938 stated that the Minister refused the application on the grounds that the question of compensation had not been dealt with. This was not an issue that had been raised earlier, so then followed an exchange of letters in which the LMSR tried to get the Ministry to state who it felt was entitled to compensation, but the Ministry refused to be drawn, implying that it would be a matter for the courts to decide. A further complication was that the objectors felt that the LMSR had no powers to make the necessary undertaking. Again, the unhelpful reply was 'It is not for the Minister to adjudicate on that question'. Instead, the Minister recommended that the LMSR apply for an Act of Parliament.

The LMSR's Solicitor's Office was quite relaxed about the Minister's attitude, writing to the Chief Commercial Manager saying: 'The Company's interests are prejudiced in no way by the delay, in fact the position is getting more favourable from the

Chapter 12: Decline (1914–1944)

point of view of proving the Company's case.' This does seem to have missed the point that by then the issue was not public navigation but maintenance of the watercourse in perpetuity.

Pleasure boating

Commercial services

As was discussed in Chapter 10, 'Captain' Samuel Jones started a pleasure trip boat service at Llangollen in 1884. After his death in 1908 Isaac Roberts took over the boats; later they were operated by his sons, Richard and Albert Roberts. This horse-drawn service, under successive managements, has continued to the present day, interrupted only by the two World Wars.

At the other end of the Shropshire Union system, before the First World War, Arthur Beech of Compton advertised steamer trips from Newbridge (on the Staffordshire & Worcestershire Canal) to Brewood as an occasional alternative to Coven or Calf Heath. This service was revived after the war and lasted until about 1925.

Private boats

MOTOR boats made private canal boating easier. Tolls were calculated for the whole trip; the mileage scale was complex, but with a minimum charge if a lock was passed. In 1939, for example, this minimum charge for 'steam, motor or electrically powered boats' on the former Shropshire Union system was 8s for the outward journey and 4s for the return journey.

Because of the novelty, memoirs of a few trips were published in books and magazines. For example, in July 1913 Austin Neal piloted his converted ship's lifeboat *Hectic* from the Derby Canal to Llangollen, entering the Shropshire Union system at Autherley Junction at 6pm and continuing until running out of petrol at 11pm. The next day they proceeded to above Baddiley Locks, and on the third continued to Llangollen – a total of 85 miles in 26½ hours cruising time. After taking the boat right up to Horseshoe Falls, they returned to Hurleston Junction then went down to Christleton. The return journey was via the Shropshire Union Main Line. Neil found the 'fir-clad ravines ... indescribably beautiful' and admired 'Telford's wonderful aqueduct'. The lift bridges on the Ellesmere Canal gave William, the junior member of the crew, some problems:

> He could only just reach the uplifted bridge with the boat-hook; and being unable to give a sufficiently long and strong pull to return the bridge to the horizontal, it occasionally took command of the proceedings, and, when about a third of the way down, majestically lifted itself up again, carrying the struggling William into the air with it.

Regrettably Neal's account does not mention the commercial traffic.[20]

Between the wars several private boats visited these canals, perhaps many more than one now imagines, as only those few whose diaries have survived and been published are known about. That pleasure-boating was not rare is hinted at in a statement of

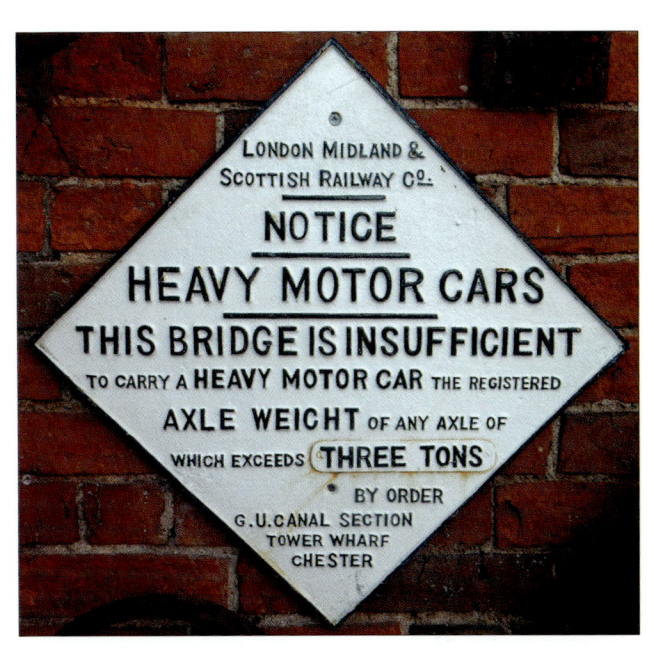

London Midland & Scottish Railway bridge sign.
Neil Cook

tolls taken in 1934 for travelling on the canal in the section between Frankton Junction and Newtown:

12 owners residing in District	£15. 5s. 0d
[this may include rowing boats for hire at Welshpool]	
8 owners not residing in District but paying for the privilege of travelling over this section	£16.13s. 6d
Casual trips	£29. 3s. 0d

Hire boats

AN advertisement in *The English Lakes*, a guidebook published by the London Midland & Scottish Railway in 1926, promised 'A Novel Holiday':

> You probably have no idea what enjoyment can be derived from a Motor or Pleasure Boat cruise on such a quiet, romantic waterway as the Shropshire Union Canal. New vistas of beauty confront the traveller at every bend of its course, which runs through quaint, delightful old Chester, alongside the lovely meres of Shropshire, across the glorious valleys of the Ceinog and Dee and 'neath Breidden Hills, famed as the site of the battle between Caractacus and Ostorius.[21]

Readers were invited to contact the Manager of the Shropshire Union Canal Section at Chester. Unfortunately, nothing else is known about these holidays. Did you hire an ex-commercial narrowboat? Did you sleep under canvas in the hold or stay in hotels at the towns you visited? Was the horse and crew provided for you? Indeed, did anyone ever respond to the advertisement?

225

Two narrow boats, *Cuckmere* and *Tangmere* (ex-SURCC *Scipio* and *Good Hope*), were acquired from the Chester & Liverpool Lighterage & Warehousing Company by the Whitchurch Warehousing Company. Both seem to have been used mainly for hiring for group or family holidays, with a horse and with or without a boatman, although they probably also carried cargoes when the opportunities arose. For example, in 1933 *Tangmere* was hired by Manchester Grammar School's Rover Scouts for a fortnight at the end of the summer holidays; they travelled beyond Llangollen at least as far as the Chain Bridge and also reached Newtown. Despite heavy showers, strong winds and cold nights, they must have enjoyed themselves, as they returned the following year.

The first hire boat, in the modern sense, on a British canal is thought to have been in the early 1930s: *The Rambler*, based at Stoak on the Wirral Line. A more substantial concern was the Inland Cruising Association, based at Christleton, south-east of Chester. By 1939 the firm had 13 craft. Their publicity material invited hirers to cruise up the Welsh Branch to Llangollen. This was the preferred route as it was quiet, whereas the Main Line was considered 'dirty and busy' – the reference to 'dirty' presumably being because the water of the Welsh Branch was clear as the sparse commercial traffic used horse-drawn boats whereas the propellers of the motor boats on the Main Line caused turbidity. One hirer though that this comment was unfair, but reported:

> If there is any complaint about the main canal, it is that one has to be especially careful in choosing one's night mooring, to avoid being hit or pulled away from the bank by passing motor barges. Whilst the vast majority of watermen fully uphold their reputation for courtesy by easing down, it is regretted that a few, always either girls or young lads, do ignore one's presence and cause one an anxious moment as they sweep by.[22]

During part at least of the inter-war period, rowing boats or canoes could be hired at Whitchurch and Welshpool, as well as at Llangollen. Some canalside landowners also had boats, the agreements stating that the boats could not pass locks.

Thus by the Second World War pleasure boating on canals was not unknown, but it was still a very unusual holiday.

The Second World War

ON the day war was declared the government took control of railways and railway-owned canals, including the Shropshire Union network. Six Regional Canal Committees were established to accept collective responsibility for water-borne traffic in their regions and, if the need arose, to exercise executive powers. The canal companies and the carriers were represented on these committees, together with the appropriate ministries and labour union.

As in the First World War, because of men entering the armed forces there was a shortage of boatmen, though boatmen aged 25 or more were exempt from call-up. The Ministry of War Transport had a much-publicised scheme for employing volunteer women, but they never seem to have worked on the narrow canals north of Birmingham.

The tonnage carried on the Shropshire Union during the first four years of the war stayed reasonably steady, averaging just under two-thirds of the figure for 1938. Revenues reduced despite the government approving an increase in rates, whereas costs increased significantly.

In 1941 Frank Pick, the recently-retired Chief Executive Officer of the London Transport Passenger Board, was asked by the Ministry of War Transport to recommend ways of improving the effectiveness of the contribution of canals to the war effort. Reporting back after only nine weeks, he recommended strengthening the Regional Canal Committees' supervision of the canals in their areas, making canals protected industries for employment purposes and bringing their financial guarantees in line with those of the railways.[23] This last point did not apply to the Shropshire Union, as railway-owned canals were already covered under the railway guarantee. He also identified the problem that the canals seemed unable to secure 'their fair share' of the traffic from the Midlands to the ports, including the Shropshire Union route to Ellesmere Port.

Pick compared the four Mersey transhipment facilities, praising Weston Point but being highly critical of Runcorn and Preston Brook. Of Ellesmere Port his report stated:

> It is tidy and well maintained but again goes back over a long period of time. Its facilities were however skilfully designed for the purposes of trans-shipment. Its cranes are hydraulic. Some of them have been removed so that they tend to be insufficient at this present time.

He was generally critical of canals being 'improvident and careless' in letting land off piecemeal and so losing control of their property, instancing the Shropshire Union at Chester as an example.

The report was never published but was sent to the Canal Association and the carriers' association. A civil servant commented with evident frustration:

> There has been a curious lack of comment. Succeeding generations in the canal industry are apparently less and less inclined towards activity; their general attitude seems to be a desire to be left in peace.[24]

Certain new traffics developed during the war, partly because the east coast ports had become more vulnerable. These included: fuel oil from Stanlow to Nottingham; grain, flour and Canadian cheese to warehouses for buffer stocks in both the West and East Midlands; and aluminium from the Mersey to Amblecote, near Stourbridge. A feature of wartime control was that traffic to and from South Staffordshire was worked through Ellesmere Port, Weston Point and Runcorn indiscriminately.

Many large military supply depots were located in Shropshire and its environs because it was thought to be beyond places likely to be subjected to heavy bombing. None were canalside, and canals took little or no part in transporting war materials to or from them.

Chapter 12: Decline (1914–1944)

The area also had many airfields, becoming the main training centre for airman, both RAF and American. It therefore suffered a disproportionate number of aircraft crashes, including one into the canal at Wheaton Aston, where on 4 July 1944 a Thunderbolt undershot the nearby aerodrome after its engine had cut out at 3,000 feet. The pilot was unhurt.

Western Command Stop Line No.8 was constructed in 1940 between Shrewsbury and Newport and on to Nantwich, and pillboxes were erected to guard some of the canal bridges, including Type 24 (hexagonal) pillboxes by High Bridge, Norbury, and Newcastle Road Bridge, Market Drayton.

The SU network was never seriously damaged by enemy action. In 1942 an aircraft dropped a bomb which destroyed the cottage at Wharton's Lock (on the former Chester Canal). Luckily the lock-keeper's wife was visiting a neighbour at the time; her husband was in the RAF. The second incident was when a bomb was dropped on the towpath near Pendeford, breaching the low embankment. Two oil boats were passing at the time and got stuck as the water level fell. The damage was soon repaired.

Ellesmere Port and Stanlow, unlike Liverpool, were never bombed, despite being obvious targets.

An improved canal to the Midlands?

PROPOSALS for a canal from the Mersey to Birmingham capable of taking boats carrying 100 tons were first mooted in 1890, became a recommendation of the Royal Commission on Canals in 1909, and were presented again in 1925. These all would have affected the Shropshire Union commercially but not physically.

Then in 1943 a scheme was put forward by the Ministry of War Transport for the river Weaver to be made navigable from Winsford to the Shropshire Union Canal a little north of Audlem; the canal southwards would be widened and deepened to a new basin at Pendeford, on the edge of Wolverhampton.

The survey by Christopher Marsh, the Weaver Navigation's Engineer and Manager, envisaged eight new locks would be needed on the Weaver, two lifts at Audlem, further lifts at Adderley and Tyrley, and rebuilding the lock at Wheaton Aston. All the bridges would be removed or replaced with a standard design giving two clear 21ft channels either side of a central pier with an air draught of at least 12ft. Designed for boats 93ft long and 14ft 8in. beam with a draught of up to 5ft 4in. and carrying 100 tons, the cost including the terminal basin but excluding wharfs and warehouses was estimated to be about £2¾ million. The first part of this scheme, from Winsford to Northwich, was authorised by the Weaver Navigation Act 1945.

Needless to say, nothing came of these ideas. There is no doubt that all would have been expensive failures as a 100-ton standard was hopelessly out-of-date, water supply would have been problematical, and the cost of transhipment at Wolverhampton would discourage use. By way of comparison, in France, Freycinet's Act back in 1879 set the standard minimum dimensions of locks on principal waterways as 126ft by 17ft, the canal to have a depth of 6½ft – these dimensions suiting the 300 tonne péniche. This was successful in competing with railways but by the 1920s road hauliers were beginning to take away much of their non-mineral traffic.

The 1944 Acts

As early as 1928 the LMSR management identified the problem of its loss-making canals but no action was taken, presumably because of the opposition that would inevitably be stirred up. In practice, it preferred abandonment proceedings to be initiated by highways authorities but the experience of trying to close the Montgomery Canal showed how uncertain that method could be.

One paragraph of the Pick Report of 1941 dealt with the closure of 'useless or neglected canals':

> Then there are canals to be closed because their traffic value is wholly disproportionate to the cost of their upkeep. Such for example [include] ... the western branches of the Shropshire Union Canal ... By pruning away the dead wood, there should be a healthier tree and more likelihood of growth in usefulness.[25]

Unfortunately no summary of tonnages carried, costs and revenues survives for the Shropshire Union branches separately from the Main Line.

Ashton Davies, Vice President of the LMSR, wrote a memorandum to its Executive Committee stating that as regards abandonment, he agreed with Mr Pick's recommendations. In addition to the branches of the Shropshire Union, which totalled 121¼ miles in length, he added the 1¼ miles of the Shropshire Canal from Madeley to Coalport which had never been formally closed despite being unused for several decades, plus the Huddersfield Narrow Canal, the Ulverston Canal and parts of the Cromford, Ashby and Caldon Canals (a total of a further 44¼ miles).

The London Midland & Scottish Railway (Canals) Act 1944

As stated earlier, in 1938 the Ministry of Transport had recommended that the LMSR apply for an Act of Parliament if it wished to permanently close the Montgomery Canal. Action was held in abeyance until 1943 when a Bill covering all the canals specified by Mr Davies was prepared.

The Ministry of War Transport was not opposed to the Bill. The Inland Waterways Division recommended encouraging its passage, as did the Highways Division. The note of a meeting with the latter stated that one of the principal desires of the Department was the get rid of 'humpy bridges', noting that there were a number on the 'Newton/Frampton' (no doubt meaning Newtown/Frankton) section which they were particularly anxious to deal with. The Ministry of Agriculture was concerned about farms no longer being able to water cattle, but the Inland Waterways Division replied to the effect that they do so without payment, and it would be for the courts to decide if there are such rights and the compensation to be paid.

THE SHROPSHIRE UNION CANAL

This topic was raised in the Parliamentary hearing. Ashton Davies attempted to explain the company's attitude towards agricultural water supplies, saying that if the farmer had been taking water and it was known that it had been a common practice to have the supply, then the intention was that he should continue having it. However, the farmer would have to prove that he had a prescriptive right. The cross-examining barrister pointed out that this could only be done by an expensive action in the High Court, which most farmers could not afford. Davies replied that the company would endeavour to be reasonable, but it did not want any fresh obligations put upon it.

In this, the company succeeded. Section 3(b) of the Act stated: 'the Company shall continue to be subject to ... all obligations (if any) to supply or permit the abstraction or use of water'. This would include any duties imposed by the original Acts authorising the construction of the canal and any subsequent contracts. Whether prescriptive rights had been created by long usage was left to the Courts to decide. Section 10(14) required the water level to be kept at the level of the overflow weirs unless the Minister of Agriculture & Fisheries approved it being lowered, the Minister having to consider the requirements of land owners and occupiers for water for domestic or agricultural purposes. Section 8 stated that if any part of the canal was sold, the purchaser would continue to have the same duties as the company.

Members of Parliament contributed little to the debate. Mr Crawford Greene, the MP for Worcester, was concerned about the effect that abstraction from the Upper Severn would have on the supply of clean water for drinking at Worcester. He seemed unaware that the abstraction which worried him had been going on for well over a hundred years, and that most of the water was returned to the Severn anyway.

The London Midland & Scottish Railway (Canals) Act 1944 was duly passed. Under section 3(1)(a) not only were all rights of navigation extinguished but it was made explicit that 'the closed canals shall not be used for navigation' (unless required by the Minister of War Transport). However, Section 9 permitted pleasure boats to use any open stretch of the closed canals in Cheshire, Denbighshire and Flintshire – which prompts the question – why not in Shropshire, Montgomeryshire or Staffordshire? The reference to Denbighshire is understandable, as there was a long-established pleasure boat operation in the Llangollen area, but the only section of the canal in Flintshire was a couple of miles in the Bettisfield area.

The 1944 Act required the water extracted from the Dee to be measured and recorded, so that compliance could be proved. A gauging house was therefore built at the intake at Horseshoe Falls. *Author*

Chapter 12 : Decline (1914–1944)

The London Midland & Scottish Railway Act 1944

THE Welsh Branch had long being used to supply water to the engine sheds of the LMSR at Chester and to canalside farmers; water was also being sold to several industries such as Monsanto (at Cefn Mawr) and United Dairies (Ellesmere). The River Dee Company had queried the legality of water sales as early as 1884 but a formal legal challenge had always been averted – one which the Shropshire Union or its successor would almost certainly have lost.

Because the various industries would be unable to replace these water supplies in the short term, the LMSR considered it necessary to add protective clauses to another Act in 1944 which it was promoting. These permitted a daily average of 11½ million gallons to be taken from the Dee, reducing to almost 6¼ million gallons after 1954, by which time all sales to industry were to have ceased. This lower volume was still needed for canal purposes, in particular for the deep locks of the Middlewich branch.

This second Act was passed on the same day as the Act to close the branch canals.

London Midland & Scottish Railway boundary stone.
Cathy O'Brien

Notes and references

The principal source for the events up to 1922 is the minutes of the Executive Committee of the SU (TNA, RAIL623/27–28).
The 25 years of LMSR ownership have proved the most difficult to research because of the sparsity of surviving official records. As noted earlier, there was no 'Canal Committee' or equivalent. The correspondence concerning the closure of the Montgomery Canal is contained in file C299/49/7/1/5 at the West Yorkshire Archives, Wakefield. Joseph Boughey, 'Declining traffics on branches of the Shropshire Union Canal', *Waterways Journal 4*, 2002, provides much detailed information.

1. Jack Roberts, *Shropshire Union Fly-Boats*, 2015, pp.144–5
2. Statistics derived from an analysis of the LNWR Roll of Honour, as listed on the website of the LNWRS Society: www.lnwrs.org.uk/SHG/RollHon/index
3. Briefing memorandum for the Minister of Transport, 27 April 1921: TNA, MT49/107; SURCC formal notice, 1 June 1921: TNA, RAIL1053/1959
4. *Montgomery County Times*, 11 June 1921
5. Letter from Cambrian Railways to Ministry of Transport, 2 July 1921: TNA, RAIL1053/1959
6. LMS Engineering Department letters, 18 December 1931 and 7 June 1932 (now held by CRT, Leeds); email from Welsh Water, 10 July 2017 (with thanks to David Brown of CRT)
7. LMS Engineering Department letter, 7 June 1932 (now held by CRT, Leeds) (with thanks to David Brown of CRT)
8. Roberts, *op.cit.*, p.151
9. LMS evidence to Pick, 1942: TNA, RAIL1007/515
10. Tom Foxon, *Anderton for Orders*, 1988, pp.37–8
11. T. Wheeldon, 'A journey into the heart of Shropshire', *Motor Boat & Yachting*, 29 September 1939, reproduced in *Cuttings*, December 2012, pp.43–5
12. Letter from Powis Estates, 10 December 1936; traffic statement, 4 January 1937
13. Logbook of the Rover Scouts of the 1st Manchester Grammar School Scout Troop, 3 September 1933, quoted in Alan Jones, 'Rover Scouts' cruises on *Tangmere*, 1933 and 1934', *Waterways Journal 14*, 2012, p.47
14. Tom Rolt, *Narrow Boat*, 1946, pp.14–5
15. David Bolton, 'Escape from the Llangollen', *Waterways World*, August 2007, pp.85–6
16. David Bolton, 'The ascent of the Llangollen', *Waterways World*, July 2007, p.65
17. Memorandum from the Shropshire Union Canal Agent (Chester), 13 September 1937
18. *Shrewsbury Chronicle*, 16 July 1937
19. *Oswestry & Border Counties Advertizer*, 11 August 1937
20. Austin E Neal, *Canals, Cruises and Contentment*, 1915, pp.121–41
21. A copy of the advertisement is found as item D7821 in the archives of the Canal & River Trust at Ellesmere Port. 'Ceinog' is presumably a misprint for 'Ceiriog'. The site of the decisive battle between British and Roman forces is unknown; traditionally Cefn Carnedd between Caersws and Llanidloes has been considered the most convincing site, though an alternative is Dolforwyn Castle, three miles east of Newtown (and on the Montgomeryshire Canal). However, the latter is some fifteen miles from the Briedden Hills.
22. T. Wheeldon, 'A journey into the heart of Shropshire', *Motor Boat & Yachting*, 29 September 1939, reproduced in *Cuttings*, December 2012, p.42
23. Report on Canals and Inland Waterways ('Pick Report'), 1941: TNA, MT52/109/2
24. Memorandum (signature unreadable), 21 November 1941: TNA, MT52/109
25. Frank Pick, *Report on Canals and Inland Waterways*, Ministry of War Transport, 1941 (unpublished): TNA, MT52/109

13
Revival

Heralding the revival: *Narrow Boat*

As well as the passing of the Act which formally closed over half the Shropshire Union system, 1944 saw the publication of *Narrow Boat*, a book which caught the public imagination and heralded the revival of Britain's canals. Written by Chester-born Tom Rolt, *Narrow Boat* is a nostalgic elegy based on his journey round Midlands canals in 1939–40. Both the book and Rolt's boat *Cressy* had links with the Shropshire Union system.

Cressy, the former SUCCC boat which had been bought and converted by Kyrle Willans, was acquired by Rolt in 1939. By then its steam engine had been replaced by a petrol engine. He arranged for the cabin accommodation to be rebuilt, then set off, newly-married to Angela, with the boat as their home. They travelled north on the Trent & Mersey Canal and reached Middlewich on the day war was declared. For the next two months they were moored at Church Minshull whilst Rolt worked at Rolls Royce's aero-engine factory at Crewe. Then, having accepted the offer of a job in Hampshire, they set off south via Nantwich, Market Drayton and Autherley Junction. It was on the Shropshire Union during the first stage of this journey that Rolt started writing *Narrow Boat*.

Having read *Narrow Boat*, Robert Aickman, a literary agent, visited Tom Rolt in 1946 on *Cressy*, which was then moored at Tardebigge on the Worcester & Birmingham Canal, to suggest the formation of a voluntary organisation to campaign for the greater use of the canals. An open meeting was called at Aickman's Bloomsbury apartment, and the Inland Waterways Association (IWA) was born.

The national scene

Nationalisation

Most canals were nationalised on 1 January 1948, together with the railways. The financial brief was to break even, taking one year with another. The umbrella organisation, the British Transport Commission (BTC), regarded most of the canal network as an obsolete economic embarrassment, the principal exceptions being the commercial rivers – the Trent, Severn and Weaver – and the Aire & Calder Navigation. Below it, the Docks & Inland Waterways Executive (DIWE) had little more sympathy, its main concerns being the 32 ex-railway docks which it managed, though a few senior officers and many of the staff 'on the towpath' could see a future for some canals. In 1949 a DIWE paper stated that 'the future of the artificial waterways is obviously considered doubtful'.[1]

The focus was on integrated transport, the BTC controlling not only the railways and canals but also road haulage, acquiring some 4,000 private companies by 1950. (Road haulage was largely denationalised in 1953.) Within such a large organisation and in a time of so much change, canals inevitably had only a low priority.

Canals struggled to retain their existing traffics. Other sources of power were replacing coal, canals' staple load. New factories were not being located canalside. Road transport was getting more efficient with vehicles increasing in capacity and the road system being improved. Canals had their traditional problems of ice in winter and water shortages in summer, to which must be added the difficulty in obtaining good crews at a time of full employment and improving working conditions. The decline in commercial canal traffic was inevitable. Some carrying firms ceased trading when they became loss-making, and the nationalised fleet took over their boats and contracts on the grounds that the toll income would exceed the losses from carrying.

The BTC's policy for the little-used canals was that they should be transferred to other organisations such as river boards and local authorities, who could then develop them for other purposes. A list totalling some 600 miles was prepared but few organisations were interested in taking on the responsibilities.

British Transport Waterways

After the DIWE was abolished in 1953, the canals were administered by a board of management, British Transport Waterways (BTW), still under the BTC.

In April 1955 the Report of the Board of Survey (the 'Rusholme Report') which had been commissioned by the BTC stated that 'possible uses are for pleasure boating and fishing, and several waterways constitute valuable amenities'. However, these seem to have been regarded as problems not opportunities: 'The existence of these ancillary uses has in the past proved an obstacle to physical abandonment.'[2]

Towards the end of 1955 the BTC showed signs of softening its attitude. When the BTC's Bill was published on 28 November the canals nationally proposed for abandonment totalled 90 miles, not the 771 implied by the Rusholme Report. Sir Brian Robertson, who had become BTC Chairman in September 1953, stated that he regretted that the Board of Survey had not had a more independent basis. Sir Reginald Kerr, newly-appointed Chairman & General Manager of BTW, whilst favouring the retention only of selected waterways, encouraged the pleasure use of canals; he also had some experience of canal restoration and appreciated the role of volunteers.

Whereas the DIWE's magazine *Lock and Quay* never mentioned pleasure cruising, an editorial in *Waterways*, its successor published by BTW, in the summer of 1957 announced:

> Now cruising is not and never will be our main business. But our efforts in this direction are a symbol of the spirit that today animates British Waterways, the spirit that recognises not only the need to develop our waterways commercially, but also the many opportunities they can afford to the community for the healthy enjoyment of leisure hours and holidays.

That year BTW started publication of a series of booklets under the general title of cruising guides. The General Manager's introduction said this was 'a series which is being prepared as a guide to holiday-makers and others cruising on the waterways of British Transport, in the hope that the information given will help towards the enjoyment of their cruise'. This was a further public recognition that the future of much of the canal network lay in pleasure boating, not in commercial carrying.

The following summer an editorial in *Waterways* said: 'British Waterways are doing more and more to encourage pleasure cruising of all kinds on the canals', and went on to welcome 'the private owner, the firm with craft to hire and the enthusiasts who hire them'. Meanwhile BTW was taking tentative steps to start its own hire fleet.

By 1958 the toll system had been replaced by a general system of boat licensing, which encouraged pleasure cruising.

The report of the Bowes Committee in 1958 recommended dividing all navigations into three categories: category A comprising the major river navigations plus a few short extensions of them into the canal network, category B being the canals still regularly being used by commercial traffic, and category C the little-used canals. These latter were to be referred to an independent committee, the Inland Waterways Redevelopment Advisory Committee (IWRAC), which would consider the future of the canal, either closure or retention for pleasure boating. A few canals were closed in the period up to 1962. Judging from the IWRAC's reports on the canals in the Shropshire Union area, the main consideration was financial. Little regard was paid to amenity, and none to the wider economy, the built heritage or wildlife. Nor do these reports mention the Inland Waterways Association or any representations from the general public.

During the 1950s and early 1960s the efforts of the IWA and the rest of the voluntary sector were mainly targeted towards keeping the existing system open, the biggest (though unsuccessful) campaign concerning the Kennet & Avon Canal. There were the beginnings of restoration, most notably Linton Lock on the Yorkshire Ouse (1949), the Lower Avon in Warwickshire (1950–62) and the southern part of the Stratford-upon-Avon Canal (1960–64). None of these projects involved such major engineering works as reinstating or realigning road bridges.

British Waterways Board

THE BTC was abolished in 1963, canals becoming a separate nationalised industry controlled by the British Waterways Board (BWB) – but this meant that they could no longer benefit from cross-subsidisation. Canal closures ceased, except for a few sections of the canals in Birmingham and the Black Country.

The BWB's 1964 Report acknowledged for the first time that the future of most of the waterways lay in their leisure use. The same year the nationalised carrying fleet was finally disbanded. Some independent carriers struggled on for a few more years.

The Transport Act 1968 divided the waterways into three categories: commercial, cruising 'to be principally available for cruising, fishing and other recreational purposes', and the remainder. The BWB was placed under a duty to deal with remainder waterways 'in the most economical manner possible ... whether by retaining and managing the waterway, by developing or eliminating it, or by disposing of it'. Of the former Shropshire Union system, the Main Line was declared a cruising waterway, together with the branches to the river Dee, to Middlewich and to Llangollen.

With the long term future of the main canal network secured, during the next ten years the number of hire boats more than trebled and of private boats more than doubled. Recognising a growing problem of linear moorings, the BWB started encouraging the construction of off-line moorings and marinas.

Relations with the IWA and the various canal societies generally became more cooperative, and often there was local authority support. The waterways societies were particularly good in exploiting various government initiatives such as the Job Creation Scheme in the second half of the 1970s, Derelict Land Grants in the 1980s and 1990s, and the Heritage Lottery Fund since 1994. The restoration volunteers nationally became formalised as the Waterway Recovery Group (WRG) in 1970. Major projects included the Ashton and Peak Forest Canals (1965–74), the Basingstoke Canal (1976–91), and the Kennet & Avon Canal and the river Kennet (1967–90). The economic as well as the amenity benefits from restoration became apparent, leading to the major restoration schemes largely financed by the Millennium Fund: the Huddersfield Narrow Canal (including the 3¼ mile long Standedge Tunnel), the Rochdale Canal, and the Forth & Clyde and Union Canals – the last including the construction of the iconic Falkirk Wheel.

However, restoration inevitably disturbs the natural habitats which had developed in the derelict canal, and these often contained rare plants or wildlife. The Nature Conservancy Council (later English Nature) declared some lengths of canals as Sites of Special Scientific Interest (SSSI), and sought to restrict boat movements. This seriously affected the newly reopened Basingstoke Canal, for example. Environmental legislation was strengthened during the 1990s and has become a major consideration in any restoration proposals – Natural England (the successor to English Nature) and its Welsh equivalent now effectively have the power to veto schemes.

Canal & River Trust

ON 2 July 2012 the responsibilities of the former British Waterways were transferred to a specially created charitable company limited by guarantee, the Canal & River Trust (CRT). The heritage assets are owned by the Waterways Infrastructure Trust, of which the CRT is managing trustee, but if the government ever considers the CRT to be in serious breach of its duties or is becoming insolvent, it can transfer the management role to another charity.

Organisation in the Shropshire Union area

ALTHOUGH the canals were nationalised on 1 January 1948, the Shropshire Union system was not transferred from the Railway Executive to the DIWE until 25 July 1948.

Over the years since nationalisation, the organisational arrangements have been changed several times, sometimes into smaller units to give improved 'customer focus', sometimes to larger units to get the benefits of scale. For much of the 1990s the administrative area virtually coincided with the former Shropshire Union area but in 2003 the Chester office was closed and Northwich became the administrative and engineering centre. A further reorganisation in 2015 saw engineering responsibility removed from the area office and relocated to Birmingham.

The workshop at Market Drayton made concrete products such as piles, fence-posts and the exceptionally ugly containers for stop-planks. *Canal & River Trust*

A more drastic reorganisation is planned for the summer of 2018; details are not known at the time of writing, but it is probable that the Shropshire Union network will be divided between the proposed West Midlands and North West Regions, with special arrangements being made for the sections in Wales.

Ellesmere Depot had been making wooden lock gates for the whole of the former Shropshire Union system and sometimes for locations further away. This came to an end in early 1961, when lock-making for the north-western canals was centralised on the more modern facilities at Northwich. Since then it, like Norbury, has merely been the base and stores for the local bank staff.

For a period in the first half of the 1950s Market Drayton had a small plant making concrete products for use on the canals.

The Shropshire Union Main Line and Middlewich Branch

THE unusual transhipment warehouse at Barbridge, with its roof spanning the canal, was demolished in the late 1950s but other important buildings have survived, such as Taylor's Yard at Chester, the stables at Bunbury and the buildings at the maintenance depot at Norbury Junction. The early 20th-century

A fine job has been made of turning the stables at Church Minshull into domestic accommodation. *Author*

Chapter 13 : Revival

warehouses at Audlem and Market Drayton have found new uses and the warehouse at Chester has been sympathetically converted into the 'Telford's Warehouse' bar and restaurant.

Plants such as ferns and orchids thrive in the damp sunless conditions of Woodseaves Cutting, south of Market Drayton; it has been declared an SSSI, though mainly for its geological interest. Its steep sides have suffered a number of slippages over the years.

The embankments at Shelmore and Shebdon have also continued to give trouble, with £1.7m being spent on the former in the winter of 2002/3 and £0.6m on the latter in the late summer of 2009. Closure of the canal for several months during the boating season demonstrated its economic importance – in particular, the shops at Audlem lost a lot of trade in 2009, as did the various canalside pubs. In Market Drayton the canal was said to be as quiet as it usually was in a January.

Two major breaches have happened on the Middlewich Branch: on 10 October 1958 near Church Minshull and on 15 March 2018 close to the aqueduct over the river Wheelock.

The breach near Church Minshull in 1958. The water from a four-mile length scoured a hole in the canal to about 40ft below towpath level.
Railway & Canal Historical Society: Shearing Collection

THE SHROPSHIRE UNION CANAL

Collingwood passing through Lock 14 of the Audlem flight on 30 August 1959. In the 1950s and 1960s washing detergents caused foam at weirs and locks on waterways where the water supply came from sewage works, a problem later overcome by reformulation of the detergents. *Railway & Canal Historical Society, Shearing Collection*

The end of commercial carrying

THE Manchester Ship Canal (MSC) was not nationalised because it was regarded as a port rather than a canal. The docks at Ellesmere Port formed part of the publicly-owned estate of the DIWE, but the fifty-year lease to the MSC continued. Transhipment there reduced in 1948 when the Manchester Ship Canal's Bridgewater Department suspended its loss-making lighterage and transhipment operations. Cross-Mersey services operated by Richard Abel & Sons continued until at least 1956, final loads transhipped including sugar to Wolverhampton and rubber to Birmingham.

Following nationalisation, British Waterways' own fleet was the principal carrier on the Shropshire Union Main Line. Typical traffics from Ellesmere Port to Wolverhampton and Birmingham were flour and sugar. Longer-lasting were various traffics which originated at Weston Point Docks, Runcorn or Manchester, using the Middlewich Branch then the Main Line south from Barbridge Junction. These included aluminium and copper going to various destinations in the Black Country and bentonite powder (a type of absorbent clay with numerous industrial uses) from Manchester to Wolverhampton. 'Tank house slime' (a waste product of the copper industry) was conveyed northwards, from Walsall to Manchester. Although Cadbury's milk traffic had long ceased, chocolate crumb continued to be carried between Knighton and Bournville until 1961. With diminishing traffic, British Waterways ceased carrying in narrow boats in October 1964.

In 1952 the public were invited to have a week's holiday taking narrow boat *Kimberley* from Autherley Junction to Weston Point, loading a cargo of metal, delivering it to Birmingham, then returning the boat to its base. Over 180 miles, 126 locks and the Anderton Lift twice, plus the time loading and unloading – getting on for 100 hours work – in a week! For this the crew would be paid £6. Sam Lomas, the toll-taker at Autherley described this as: 'Your Holidays with Pay. See the Canals of England Free. The Green Fields and Wild Rabbits. It's an Education. It's a Thrill.' Unsurprisingly the experiment was a failure. A member of the first crew broke his ankle; crews could not achieve the round trip in the time; the boat was badly treated; and other boatmen resented the amateurs being given priority in loading.[3] However, this does highlight what was expected as a matter of routine from professional boaters.

Of the other transport firms using the Main Line, the most successful was Thomas Clayton (Oldbury), specialist carrier of liquid products, who until 1955 had a contract for conveying fuel oil from Stanlow to the Shellmex depot at Langley Green at the top of the Titford Branch locks.

After the war, almost all the traffic comprised a single motor boat or a motor boat pulling an unpowered butty. The last pair of horse-drawn boats passed in 1953, with 73-year-old Steve Dulson in charge. He didn't retire; after a short period on other canals, he returned in charge of a motor boat. However, he found problems he hadn't encountered before, running out of

Chapter 13 : Revival

The arched warehouses at Ellesmere Port after the fire. These were generally considered the finest canal warehouses in the country, so their loss was a real tragedy. It is not known how the fire started. *Canal & River Trust*

fuel on one occasion, and he said that an engine was more difficult to start in the morning than a horse.[4]

The 1958 Bowes Report suggested enlargement of the Weaver–Wolverhampton route as a commercial route, envisaging something on the lines of what had been proposed in 1944, but this was far too late to be seriously considered – the contracts for the parallel M6 were let in 1960–61 and completed two years later.

Commercial traffic declined throughout the period. The amount carried on the Shropshire Union system in 1938 had been 215,000 tons, virtually all of that being on the Main Line and Middlewich Branch. Wartime traffics up to 1944 averaged about 130,000 tons. After this traffic diminished steadily, to 73,000 tons in 1947, 55,000 tons in 1949 and 32,000 tons in 1953. By 1960 it was a mere 5,800 tons.

When British Waterways ceased carrying, Willow Wren took over its traffic and leased several of its boats. In 1967, when Seddons of Middlewich ceased to have coal brought from Stoke-on-Trent, Willow Wren withdrew from carrying in the north-west, but their local manager, Alan Galley, then set up the Anderton Carrying Company (reviving a historic name) and continued for several more years. A significant traffic in these final years was aluminium from Weston Point to Wolverhampton.

Another firm which attempted to keep commercial carrying alive was the Birmingham & Midland Canal Carrying Company, which was set up in 1965 by some enthusiastic members of the IWA in the Midlands. Their short-lived traffics on the Shropshire Union included aluminium ingots from Walsall to Liverpool, Duckham's motor lubricating oil from Ellesmere Port to Aldridge (the first attempt sunk the boat *Yeoford*, as the centre of gravity of the tank was too high) and bicycles from Birmingham to Ellesmere Port. However, by the end of the 1980s, commercial traffic had ceased.

The transformation of Ellesmere Port

By 1968 the run-down condition of Ellesmere Port and the Wirral Line were giving great cause for concern. The grain trade from Liverpool to the mills in the basin had ceased. Because the bottom gates of the entrance lock were left open, wash from the vessels on the MSC brought silt into the lock, making it difficult to use. Proposals for a motorway and link road were to affect the canal; despite protests, a bridge was built which restricts the width of boats to 9ft, instead of the 14ft which the rest of the canal up to Nantwich can accommodate.

On 31 March 1970 the arched warehouses at Ellesmere Port burnt down. The other large warehouses in the Lower Basin, the great grain elevator and eventually the flour mills were all demolished in the early 1970s; only the lighthouse and the clay shed, now the leisure centre for the Holiday Inn, remain at this level. Fortunately the Island Warehouse and most of the ancillary buildings above the locks survived.

The fifty year lease to the MSC was not renewed in 1972, so the site reverted to British Waterways.

When teacher Diana Skilbeck visited Ellesmere Port in 1973 she was horrified with what she saw: 'The water was filled with oil drums and planks, while in the lower basin a group of men hacked up concrete barges.' She responded constructively, bringing a party of staff and girls from her school in order to help clear the basin and generally tidy up.[5]

The most important development in the last fifty years on the Shropshire Union Main Line has been the creation of the boat museum at Ellesmere Port. The North Western Museum of Inland Navigation was formed in 1971 by a group of enthusiasts who were concerned that old working craft from the canals and rivers would completely disappear as the nature of the waterway system changed from freight transport to leisure use. Their first public exhibition was opened for the summer of 1976. With the support of the then Ellesmere Port & Neston Borough Council this grew into a fully professional operation and was renamed The Boat Museum, the volunteer organisation becoming the Boat Museum Society. The Queen and Prince Philip visited the museum in November 1979, recognising what had been achieved in a relatively short time. Since 1999, rebranded as the National Waterways Museum, it has been managed by The Waterways Trust and its successor, the Canal & River Trust. With Heritage Lottery funding, new displays have been made and the Heritage Boatyard created. The CRT's archives have been brought together here too.

The Shropshire Union Canal

The pleasure boating era

THE Main Line between Chester and Autherley Junction and the Middlewich Branch were never seriously under threat of closure, largely because the decrease in commercial traffic was compensated for by an increase in pleasure boating. The Inland Cruising Association, based at Christleton, resumed hiring after the war, but with only four boats instead of the thirteen they had in 1939. In 1949 Messrs Adams and Littler, started hiring boats from Old Wharf, Market Drayton. The company was later sold to John Haines and renamed 'Holidays Afloat' in 1951.

In 1956 the North Western Division decided to convert a working boat into a pleasure cruiser. This was probably the initiative of Christopher Marsh, the enterprising Divisional Manager. The boat chosen was *Arabia*, which had been constructed in 1907 as a butty by Fellows, Morton & Clayton in their Saltley boatyard and converted into a motor boat by Yarwood's of Northwich in 1937. It was shortened to 46ft by James Mayor & Co. of Tarleton and fitted with a 20hp Parsons air-cooled diesel engine. Renamed *Water Arabis*, it had six berths with Dunlopillo mattresses, with hot & cold water to the basins, and electric light throughout. Based at Chester, hiring started in July 1956. The experiment proved successful, and in the next two years *Water Bulrush* and *Water Crocus*, both four-berth boats, were added to the fleet there. In 1962 the local base was moved from Chester to Middlewich, then from the 1969 season Nantwich Basin replaced Middlewich. Improvements were made there in 1985 but BW ceased to operate a hire fleet in 1992.

Several more independent hire firms were established on the Main Line in the 1960s and 1970s; by 2018 hire boats were operating from Beeston, Bunbury, Audlem, Norbury, Brewood and Autherley Junction.

The Nantwich & Border Counties Yachting Club was founded in 1953. Its members' boats first moored in Nantwich Basin, then after 1961 linear moorings were created along the bank to the north; the new basin was opened in 1973. At the southern end of the Main Line, the Wolverhampton Boat Club started in 1961 as the Autherley Boat Club and moved to its current site in Pendeford in 1966.

The first marina in the former Shropshire Union area was Venetian Marina, below Cholmondley Lock on the Middlewich Branch. Opening in 1971, it soon grew to have 150 berths, then the largest in the country; now it would be considered to be relatively small. Its design differs from more modern marinas in that its water cannot be isolated from that of the canal. Surprisingly no marinas were constructed on the Main Line until Overwater Marina opened below Audlem Locks in 2010, followed by Tattenhall Marina on the former Chester Canal and Aqueduct Marina on the Middlewich Branch.

The layby at Market Drayton which holds just over 50 boats was made in the 1960s for Ladyline.

This canal has unusually large lengths of linear moorings, particularly between Cheswardine and High Offley and also in the Tattenhall area, the latter having in excess of 120 boats in one continuous line. Linear moorings are unpopular with other boaters because they can be unsightly and have to be passed very slowly.

The 'Holidays Afloat' hire base at Market Drayton in the early 1950s.
On the wharf is one of the early hire boats, converted from a wartime bridge pontoon with a body made of plywood, and equipped with both gas and electricity. *Neil Jenkins*

CHAPTER 13 : REVIVAL

Happy holidaymakers preparing for their week's cruising on a BW hire boat based at Nantwich.
Canal & River Trust

Ladyline was once one of the biggest chandlery, boat sales and hire businesses in the country, its headquarters being at Market Drayton. The site is now a housing estate (where the author lives), but the moorings have survived.
Shropshire Council

237

The Shropshire Union Canal

The Llangollen Canal

As stated in the last chapter, the London Midland & Scottish Railway (Canals) Act 1944 closed what is now known as the Llangollen Canal to navigation except for certain sections, most importantly, between Chirk and Horseshoe Falls.

The Ministry of War Transport insisted that it should have the right to require canals which were currently navigable to remain navigable until six months after the end of the war, and a suitable clause was included in the Act. In fact, the legal definition of the end of the war was not when fighting ceased in Europe (May 1945) or even in the Far East (August 1945) but when the 'War Emergency' was deemed to be at an end, which was not until 8 October 1950; however, the Ministry did not exercise its right in the specific case of the Llangollen Canal.

The 1945 breach

At about 3.30am on 7 September 1945 the canal breached between Sun Trevor and Wenffrwd Bridges, washing away a 100ft section of the embankment of the Ruabon–Llangollen railway line which ran 37ft lower down the hillside. The Great Western Railway's morning mail and newspaper train plunged into the gap, killing driver Jones. Remarkably fireman Joy was thrown clear; despite suffering a broken wrist and severe shock, he walked the 1½ miles to Llangollen to report the accident.

The hillside there is formed of semi-porous glacial moraine, a mixture of boulders, nodules, clay and sand. The puddle clay under the canal bed and under the towpath did not seem to have failed. The two railway companies' mining engineers concluded that the natural drainage from the uplying lands had been passing through the glacial moraine, forming subterranean channels and voids, and the crust overlying one of these had collapsed. Lt.-Col. Wilson, the accident inspector, concurred, adding that the cumulative effect of vibration from heavy motor traffic on the main road slightly further up the slope may have contributed.

He felt that there was still a risk to the railway for about 200 yards either side of this breach, and queried whether there was any necessity to retain the canal, now that there was no obligation to keep it open for navigation. He recognised that it was necessary to maintain the flow of water for industrial purposes and for feeding the Main Line. The available fall (about ¼ inch in 400 yards) was so small that a very large bore pipe would be required to carry the flow of 11½ million gallons of water a day, and the risk of subsidence leading to pipe fracture would remain. This could be largely overcome if multiple pipes were used, but this would require a pump. The LMSR adopted the simplest remedy in the short term, which was to reinstate the canal.[6]

Pleasure boating and the IWA

At this time the Grundy family's cabin cruiser *Heron* was one of the few private boats using the canal. When purchased it was lying below Frankton Locks, which it ascended in August 1945. Every year from 1946 onwards it was taken up to Llangollen.

On 1 March 1948 Robert Aickman and Tom Rolt, by then Chairman and Secretary respectively of the newly-formed IWA,

The wreckage of the train derailed by the collapse of the embankment which was washed away following the breach in the canal.
Llangollen Museum, Muriel Thomas Collection

met Sir Cyril Hurcomb, Chairman of the BTC, to discuss the future of the canals. During this meeting attention was drawn to the Llangollen Canal, their concern being that this canal was under a special threat because the legal powers for abandonment had already been granted. The IWA representatives said that the Act should be rescinded because the bridges could be lowered at any time. A few days later Robert Davidson, a member of the DIWE, wrote saying that the IWA's views 'in many ways harmonise with our own'. Then on 27 May a 'very satisfactory' meeting was held with Sir Reginald Hill, the DIWE Chairman, which ended with a promise of an investigation into the 'scandalous matter' (in Aickman's words) of the Llangollen Canal.[7]

In an interview with the *Liverpool Daily Post*, Robert Davidson was quoted as saying:

> The Executive ... is sympathetic towards the use of canals for pleasure and may set aside for this purpose stretches not now used commercially, such as the Lancaster Canal and the Welsh reaches of the Shropshire Union, and is prepared to look kindly upon firms starting boat hire.[8]

When invited to state which canals it considered should receive first consideration for the encouragement of pleasure traffic, the IWA responded that they should be the Kennet & Avon and the Llangollen Canals. Prospects for the retention of the canal therefore looked promising.

Christopher Marsh

CHRISTOPHER MARSH was Divisional Waterways Officer for the North Western Division of the Docks & Inland Waterways Executive, later designated Divisional Manager.

Tom Rolt referred to him as 'the only member of the senior staff of the new Executive who had canal water in his veins'. After gaining wide engineering experience in the docks of South Wales, waterways in Belgium, flood prevention works in Ceylon and five years as Resident Engineer at Sunderland Docks, Marsh had been appointed Engineer & Manager of the Weaver Navigation in 1934. He gave technical assistance to the Ministry of War Transport in their consideration of the Bills leading to the 1944 Acts. It was largely through his efforts that the Llangollen Canal was saved from closure. Regarded by some as autocratic, he was very much the 'boss' in the North West and sometimes openly disagreed with the powers-that-be in London, which may be why he was passed over for jobs at the highest level in the DIWE and British Waterways despite his ability. However, he was well-known to his staff and respected by them.

With great difficulty mainly because of weed growth and low water levels Tom Rolt got *Cressy* as far as Ellesmere in 1947. Rolt reported that he succeeded in getting up to the Horseshoe Falls aboard *Heron* in about May 1948. From Trevor to a mile short of Llangollen the boat had to be bow-hauled much of the way; at that point stop planks had been inserted which gave a reasonable depth of water for the horse-drawn pleasure boats operating from Llangollen wharf.

In the summer of 1949 the Grundys took *Heron* to Horseshoe Falls again and Cecile Dorward, another IWA member, reached Trevor on her narrow boat *Phosphorus*, as did Rolt on *Cressy*. They reported that the canal was in a much better condition – higher water levels and less weed.

Bridges

UNDER the 1944 Act, from 1 April 1945 the responsibility for maintaining bridges carrying highways passed to the appropriate local authorities or, for trunk roads, to the Ministry of Transport. The canal company had to pay lump sums equivalent to the estimated capitalised cost of future maintenance. The amounts were subject to negotiation, the final settlements not being until the 1950s. On the other hand, the Act required the highways authorities to reimburse the DIWE for any extra cost of maintaining the canal caused by bridge lowering in those cases where the canal had to continue to be maintained as a water supply channel. This was of course especially relevant for the Llangollen Canal.

By 1949 the fear about highways authorities lowering bridges had become a real threat. Shropshire was proposing to lower St Martin's Moor Bridge carrying the B5069 Gobowen–Overton road; Denbighshire wanted to lower Wenffrwd Bridge carrying the A539 Ruabon–Llangollen road. The IWA wrote to both County Councils pointing out that the natural levels of road and canal were such as to allow full navigable headroom and good road alignment. Members were urged to make representations about the 'folly and destructiveness' of the proposals.

Tom Rolt enlisted the assistance of the Council for the Preservation of Rural Wales and the Council for the Preservation of Rural England; discussions were held with the Town Planning Institute and the Chief Planning Officer of Shropshire. The Llangollen Urban District Council (UDC) backed the campaign, as did various local newspapers. Contact was also made with the National Farmers Union as the Shropshire Farmers' Union was lobbying for the lowering of all the bridges on the canal.

In October 1950 the County Surveyor of Shropshire reported on 19 road bridges over canals. He considered that a 4ft headroom would enable maintenance boats to continue to pass through, but Christopher Marsh, Divisional Waterways Officer for the North Western Division of the DIWE, insisted that they needed 7ft 6in. for their maintenance craft. He asserted that it would be more expensive to maintain the canal without using boats and would not respond to the suggestion that these be adapted.[9]

The two bridges which were the responsibility of the Ministry

St Martin's Moor Bridge, as rebuilt with full headroom in 1955/56. It has since been replaced.
Trevor Ellis

of Transport, at Grindley Brook (A41: Whitchurch–Chester) and Moreton Bridge (A5: Oswestry–Llangollen), presented no problems as the required headway of 7ft 6in. could easily be provided. Similarly, two of the county bridges gave no problems. For ten, the extra expense of providing a 7ft 6in. headway would add £20,000 to the total cost. To retain the required headway at the other five bridges would make road improvements impossible. The report referred to 'dangerous hump-backed bridges' and stated: 'There is no doubt that from the highway interest point of view, the lower headroom for these bridges is vital.'

The report commented: 'The position is again complicated by the attitude and campaign of members of the Inland Waterways Association, whose interest is to preserve canals for pleasure craft. They claim that this particular length of canal is one of the most beautiful in England, and on no account should it be obstructed below 7ft 6in. (or very slightly lower) and thereby prevent its use for this purpose.' He also noted that 'certain trade interests also seem to be arising ... with boats for hire' and that 'local press comments are supporting the non-lowering of these bridges'. It was agreed that a joint conference should be called, though subsequent minutes do not mention whether it was held.

Because the St Martin's Moor Bridge was particularly dangerous and the works there urgent, the County Surveyor put forward a scheme which would give the desired height, though it would increase the cost by £2,500 to £8,500. This was approved, subject to the Ministry of Transport agreeing to pay its 60% grant. The Ministry did not give its approval for several years, and it was not until the 1955/56 financial year that the work was done, by which time it cost £11,000.[10]

In May 1952 Robert Aickman claimed 'a major success for our Association': Denbighshire County Council had decided not to lower the A539 bridge but instead to improve the road approaches. The report in the *IWA Bulletin* also noted that the Shropshire bridges had been reprieved for a less noble (but equally effective) reason, budget cuts caused by the national financial crisis.

Pleasure boating and the IWA (continued)

MEANWHILE the canal was being dredged, the water depth was better than it had been, and a weed-cutter had started to be used. Nevertheless, the canal was still difficult to navigate, particularly for full size narrow boats. Many lock walls bulged; if the boat had 'spread' through old age it could be necessary to use a winch or ask passers-by to help to pull the boat into or out of the lock. Mr Hughes, the Section Inspector, though helpful to boaters was especially interested in fishing so did not want to discourage weed growth. As engines of narrow boats were then generally cooled using water from the canal, filters frequently blocked.

To publicise the potential of the canal, the North-Western Branch of the IWA held a rally at Llangollen from 18 to 21 June 1952. This was the second boat rally which the IWA had organised, but the first with the specific aim of campaigning. Festivities started with a dinner at the Boat House Restaurant by the Mere at Ellesmere on the preceding Monday, Christopher Marsh being a guest of honour. The twenty-one boats moved on to Llangollen, arriving there on the Wednesday. The boats, decorated with bunting, were ranged out on the off side of the canal, the official rally site being the field by the winding hole, opposite the café. A public exhibition was held in Mr Moore's Old Welsh Flower Shop, adjacent to the Bridge End Hotel. On the Thursday the Chairman of Llangollen Urban District

Chapter 13 : Revival

The rally plaque, whose current owner when a boy earned five shillings from ferrying people to and from the site in the family dinghy. *John Alderson*

From front to back, Lt.-Com. Sharpe's *Ulass*, Dr Wallis's *Obsession* and Ray Slack's *Glenrosa* at the Llangollen Rally. *Martin Grundy*

Council gave an official welcome at the Royal Hotel before the start of a film show. The following afternoon Mr Roberts organised an outing to Horseshoe Falls in his horse-drawn trip boats, giving all the takings to the IWA Branch funds. The well-attended rally dinner was held that evening at the Bridge End Hotel, several more films being shown afterwards.

The DIWE helped make the rally a success by clearing and dredging the canal and by repairing various lock gates. Boaters attending the rally were given a 50% discount on their tolls.

The report in the Branch newsletter, *The Nor' Wester* concluded: 'Altogether the rally well fulfilled the objects for which it was arranged, in that it provided a very happy week of social pleasures for those taking part, it showed the general public that the canal was open for use and capable of providing first-class holidays, and it reminded the canal authorities of the serious regard which the Branch has for this waterway.'

However, it did not actually generate much publicity: the *Shrewsbury Chronicle*, for example, did not mention it.

Despite the efforts, in the years 1951 to 1953 the income of the Llangollen Canal was less than 15% of the expenditure, and the annual loss averaged £21,700.

Early in 1953 the DIWE announced that they had started negotiations nationally for the transfer of non-commercial waterways to water authorities or to the local authorities through which they ran, who could then develop them for other purposes. The list included the Llangollen Canal. The Ellesmere Rural District Council (RDC) resolved that it was 'in favour of the retention of the canal only in so far as it was of use to farmers, and that they had no interest in its maintenance as a thing of beauty or as a means of attracting visitors to the area'.

Anthony Hill, an IWA member, leased the DIWE's boatyard at Trevor in 1953. Later that year it was said there were five boat-hiring companies within easy reach of the canal, with more than 30 boats between them, and that more than 400 boat trips had been made during the year.

On 23 November 1953, the North-Western Branch convened a meeting involving some forty national and local organisations and commercial undertakings with an interest in the Llangollen Canal. Support for the retention of the canal was expressed by various local authority representatives, industrialists, farmers, anglers, the Ramblers Association (if only for the use of the towpath, part of which it considered should be included in a long-distance path from Prestatyn to Chepstow), the Council for the Protection of Rural Wales and the Country Landowners Association, amongst others. Stan Offley, Chairman of the North-Western Branch of the IWA, commented that the officers of the DIWE had been most helpful. Alderman E.A. Cross of Wrexham said that he was also a member of the Dee & Clwyd River Board; he thought that a lot depended on the scheme to enlarge the capacity of Bala Lake, as that was going to have a great effect on the amount of water that would be available to put into the canal. It was unanimously resolved to support the canal's maintenance in good navigable order and as a means of water supply.

It was also agreed to create the Welsh Border Canal Preservation Committee with 20 members, including a number of IWA representatives. The Chairman was Mr R.J. Edwards, a member of Wrexham RDC, and the Secretary Trevor Williams, Clerk to Wrexham RDC. Unfortunately, little was actually achieved by the Committee. In August 1955 a report in *The Nor'Wester* said disenchantedly:

> It is a mistake to pack committees with important people who are there because they add tone and dignity to the proceedings. The only real test is genuine enthusiasm, and this is much more important than education or an important position in society, though neither of these attributes disqualify. ... We have some people who are really keen, some who would do good work if they were kept at it, some who approve in a general way but are never likely to take an active part, and some who are hardly interested and in one or two cases appear to be the nominees of hostile interests.[11]

Because the new Chairman of Llangollen UDC had been expressing his concern, the IWA Branch Committee decided to get in touch with him; this resulted in 'a more united and energetic body' being created, though that too seems to have achieved little.

In late 1953 and early 1954 there were many pro-canal reports in the national, regional and local press which must also have influenced public opinion. Stan Offley wrote to all the MPs in the north-west of England about potential closures. Seventy-seven replies were received: almost half expressed unequivocal support; two were opposed; and the rest (Offley stated) were 'politicians' letters in which they refrained from committing themselves although they indicated that the matter 'was constantly in their minds'.[12]

Water supply

IN 1950 the Mid & South East Cheshire Water Board considered taking over the Llangollen Canal in order to acquire 18 million gallons of water a day but, having ascertained that this would require heavy expenditure, had decided not to proceed with the scheme. The IWA had heard rumours that the intention was to replace the locks with weirs.

Using the canal to supply water to the Nantwich area was not a totally new proposal: the Nantwich Local Board of Health had requested it in 1852 but the Shropshire Union Canal Company had responded by saying that it did not have the necessary legal powers to do so.

In 1953 the DIWE repeated its request to the Water Board to take over responsibility for the Llangollen Canal but the Water Board refused, instead proposing contributing a sum towards its maintenance. As before, the IWA was particularly concerned about the possibility of this meaning that locks would be replaced by weirs.

The 1960 breach near Millars bridge. The canal here, as in all other sections on a steep hillside, is now in a concrete trough.
Railway & Canal Historical Society, Weaver Collection

Chapter 13 : Revival

The Water Board erected this unattractive building just below Pontcysyllte Aqueduct. Water is pumped from the river Dee up to the canal whenever the aqueduct has to be drained. Author

A three-week test to see the implications of a flow of 8 million gallons a day was undertaken: depth markers were placed along the canal and a 24-hour watch kept to see whether there was any sudden drop in the level, which would indicate that the canal could not cope with the extra water. The test was successful: the water level was maintained.

The British Transport Commission Act 1954 included the power to supply water from the Llangollen Canal to industrial customers in perpetuity and for the Mid & South East Cheshire Water Board to convey water from Froncysyllte to the canal reservoir at Hurleston.

When the Bill was discussed in the House of Commons, Mr Garner Evans, the MP for Denbigh, called the Llangollen Canal 'the most beautiful canal in the country', but he was unable to get a clause added giving the explicit right of navigation.

When in 1955 the domestic water supply proposals were formally discussed at a public inquiry, the representative of the BTW (the DIWE by then having been abolished) stated that there was no intention of interfering in any way with boating or fishing. The Water Board would pay BTW an annual sum commencing at £6,000 and rising after six or seven years to £19,000, which was then said to be slightly more than the maintenance cost of the whole canal, though the figures quoted below dispute this. The agreement was to last until March 1989, and then to continue unless terminated by either party giving four years' notice.

The principal negotiator on behalf of BTW was again Christopher Marsh. The IWA was delighted with the outcome, describing it as 'a demonstration of what can be done ... by multi-functional utilisation'. The formal agreement was signed in 1957; the supply started in May 1958; and the enlarged Hurleston Reservoir was officially opened on 18 September 1959.

From the IWA's point of view, the main worry was when the Dee & Clwyd River Board proposed bye-laws which would have made it illegal to discharge overboard even washing-up water. Following strong objections from the North-Western Branch the draft was amended to exclude boats on waterways controlled by the British Transport Commission.

Progress

ONCE the decision was made to use the canal for water supply, more time and money was put into maintaining it. In particular, it was dredged where years of neglect had allowed it to silt up.

Meanwhile, the numbers of visiting boats was increasing. In 1956 it was reported that 94 boats had reached Llangollen by the end of July, as evidenced by their masters signing the visitors book at the Llangollen Pottery. Some 200 boats visited Llangollen in 1957.

That year British Transport Waterways published 'Inland Cruising Booklet No.1', titled *Cruising the Llangollen Canal*, prepared by Stanley Hall under the direction of Christopher Marsh. This booklet seems to have been the first public use of the name 'Llangollen Canal' by which the canal is now invariably known. Presumably this was considered better for marketing purposes than the alternatives.

On 5 September 1960 the canal breached near Millars Bridge on the Trevor–Llangollen section and was repaired promptly. To the outside world it seemed evident that the Llangollen Canal was now safe from any threat of closure to navigation.

Behind the scenes

HOWEVER, the canal's legal status was still that it was closed to navigation. The case was therefore considered by the Inland Waterways Redevelopment Advisory Committee.

In July 1960 BTW provided the background information, including a summary of the finances for the previous five years:

	1954	1956	1958
	£	£	£
Maintenance of canal, buildings, plant etc	27,619	32,411	29,770
Water supply	326	738	508
Rents	470	181	209
Rates	409	568	783
Depreciation	852	330	1,795
Other	61	36	685
Total direct costs (excluding central charges)	29,737	34,264	33,749
Sale of water	1,759	1,155	18,888
Rents, commercial licences, fishing rights etc	1,458	1,588	2,139
Pleasure boat tolls	175	320	417
Other income	63	73	455
Total income	3,455	3,136	21,899
Net cost	26,282	31,128	11,850

To maintain the passage of water to the Water Board and other industrial supplies (principally Monsanto) and to provide adequate bank protection arising from increased use of the canal by pleasure craft, it was anticipated that some £80,000 would have to be spent in excess of normal maintenance expenditure over the coming three years. The report concluded by saying that income from pleasure boating, fishing and particularly the Water Board and Monsanto 'will go some way in offsetting this expenditure and make the branch self-supporting with the result that the [British Transport] Commission are prepared to retain the waterway for the present'.[13]

The IWRAC went further: it recommended that the canal be retained *permanently* to allow passage of boats of 2ft 6in. draught not only for its importance as a water channel but also for its established amenity value.

The first (January 1961) draft report by a junior civil servant of the Ministry of Transport said it was 'possible though doubtful' that income would rise sufficiently to cover the normal outgoings, but that it was 'most improbable' that the revenue could ever cover the interest charges on the £80,000 extra expenditure, let alone interest on any further capital expenditure that might be thought necessary. These liabilities would have to be borne by the taxpayer. Nevertheless, this might be justifiable: special aid should be considered for the preservation in the national interest of selected canals with high 'amenity' value. (Interestingly, this point had *not* been made by the IWRAC.) The writer added that the Llangollen Canal passes through very attractive country and has on it several structures of historic interest, Pontcysyllte Aqueduct being considered by the BTC to be one of the fourteen most important historic canal structures in the country. The first draft of the Ministry of Transport's report therefore made no firm recommendation, concluding (in civil-service-speak) that 'it would therefore be inadvisable to prejudice its future' but also 'inadvisable to commit ... the Exchequer to an indefinite liability'.[14]

The BWB then provided up-dated revenue information showing a provisional net deficit of £8,750 in 1960 and an estimated deficit of £7,600 in 1961. It was still seeking authority to spend the £80,000 on bank protection and other works. The Ministry discussed this with the Board's engineers and discovered that much of the cost was attributable to the wash of the boats using the canal. Nevertheless, the second (February 1961) draft had similar conclusions to the first: retention for the present.

After some polishing, a third draft of the report was written in July 1961, but before David Serpell, the Deputy Secretary at the Ministry of Transport, would submit it to John Hay, Parliamentary Secretary, for a decision he asked some awkward questions.[15] In particular he stated:

> The role of pleasure craft needs to be considered, since it is for them that bridges would have to be maintained ... they are said to contribute to maintenance by distributing weed, and to add to its cost through the damage caused by their wash; the gross receipts from pleasure craft are scarcely significant (some £400 towards a maintenance bill of £29,500).

After reminding his colleagues of the statement made by the Chancellor of the Exchequer just that week that investment expenditure was to be avoided where this can be done without damaging the provision of essential services, he suggested the Water Board's needs could be met by pipes. He considered that the final decision largely depended on the 'suitability' of the agreement with the Water Board.[16]

BTW subsequently considered that the immediate capital expenditure needed was £105,000, with the certainty that there would have to be further such expenditure. In response to Serpell's request it estimated that lowering the water level and putting weirs at the locks would reduce the capital expenditure required to £49,000 and give net annual savings of £8,000, with the additional benefit that the risk of breaches in the Horseshoe Falls to Chirk Bank section would be minimised.

CHAPTER 13 : REVIVAL

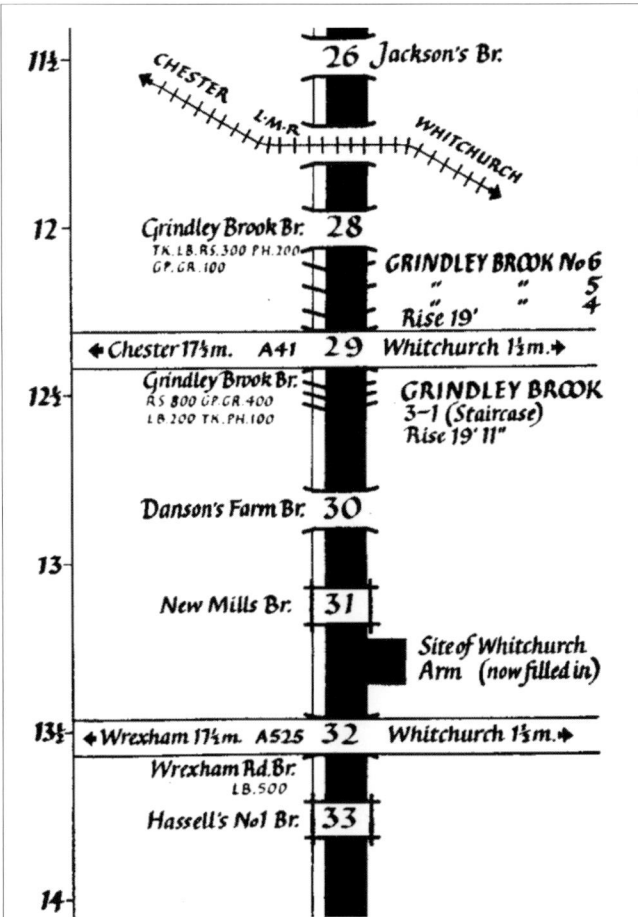

> A mile or so farther on, under the railway bridge carrying the Whitchurch–Chester line over the canal, there is a sharp left turn, inviting careful navigation, which leads into the first of the six *Grindley Brook* locks. While the three locks in the lower group are of the usual type, with independent chambers and short separating pounds, the upper three locks are grouped into what is known as a 'staircase' or step-lock, in which one chamber leads directly into the next and four gates suffice to control the three locks. A note of the special procedure required to negotiate the 'staircase' appears on page 30. For about a mile before Grindley Brook the canal forms the boundary between Cheshire and Shropshire, and at the railway bridge the canal passes into the latter.
>
> Between Grindley Brook and *Platt Lane* the canal has more bends as the ground becomes more broken, but the countryside is still of an agricultural character. About one mile after leaving the locks at Grindley Brook, at a sharp right-hand bend, the site of the former Whitchurch Arm can be located.
>
> *Whitchurch* is a little over a mile distant along the road from Grindley Brook Locks. Here the usual full range of town amenities is available.

An extract from *Cruising the Llangollen Canal*. Since 1957 this section has gained two road bridges, lost the railway, and seen the first section of the Whitchurch Arm reopen.

However, the Ministry of Transport delayed for two years making any firm recommendations – which meant, in effect, that the junior civil servant's recommendation of 'carry on as now' happened – and the whole issue was then deferred again pending establishment of the new British Waterways Board created by the Transport Act 1963.

The Llangollen Canal came to be regarded as one of the 'amenity' canals where the IWRAC had recommended considerable financial outlay for maintaining canals for pleasure boating and amenity generally. The Board stated that it was undertaking a review of the whole of its waterways system as required by the Act, and would be paying particular attention to this case. The relevant IWRAC papers were passed to the Board, of which Admiral Parham, the IWRAC's chairman, was a member.

Who saved the Llangollen Canal?

So who should get the credit for saving the Llangollen Canal? The local authorities, with the notable exception of Llangollen UDC, did little actively to save it. Their decisions not to lower bridges were made to minimise the cost to them, not because they thought they were making the right decisions for the local economy or the environment. The money from the Mid & South East Cheshire Water Board was crucial, but there seems no evidence that its motives were anything other than obtaining a suitable water supply at a reasonable cost; the wider benefits probably had no influence on its decision. The IWA played an important role, first by making people aware of the issues, then by mobilising public opinion and influencing decision-makers. In the 1940s Tom Rolt himself was particularly active; in the 1950s the initiative lay mainly with the North-Western Branch, especially its indefatigable Chairman, Stan Offley, and Secretary, Ray Slack.

However, two groups whose impact should not be understated are the hire firms and the private boat owners. The evidence of the increasing usage of the canal, albeit for leisure rather than commercial carrying, was probably a major factor in demonstrating the economic value of its retention for navigation. In particular, hiring introduced many people to the waterways, enthusing some of them to become members of the IWA, lobbyists and boat-owners. It is generally true that government

245

Wrenbury, 1957: The hotel boat *Saturn* has just passed through the lift bridge and is moored outside the mill, now the 'Dusty Miller' restaurant. *Saturn* started life as a SURCC fly-boat. It has now been restored (or reconstructed, some would say) and is actively involved in educating youngsters about the canals and canal life. *Owen Prosser / Ian Wright*

bodies are more influenced by people's actions, in this case their willingness to invest, than by their petitions and letters.

From 1948 and through the 1950s, the legislation under which the waterways and railways operated was that they were purely transport organisations. The minutes of the DIWE make no mention of non-commercial use of the canals, except for a couple of passing references to fees. It is therefore not surprising that the senior staff were either indifferent to the closure of the Llangollen Canal or keen on seeing responsibility passed to another body.

The one exception was Christopher Marsh, Divisional Waterways Officer for the North Western Division, whom Tom Rolt referred to as 'the only member of the senior staff of the new Executive who had canal water in his veins'.[17] Marsh himself claimed the principal credit for having saved the Llangollen Canal. For example, at the IWA Branch dinner in 1957 he said that he had invoked the clause which effectively prevented the local authorities from lowering bridges, and that he had been negotiating with the Water Board for seven years.[18] It does seem a fair assessment that his vision and persistence were the principal reasons why the Llangollen Canal remained open to navigation, though what his personal motives were can only be guessed.

Cruiseway

THE Llangollen Canal was designated a cruising waterway by Schedule 12 of the Transport Act 1968, though in law much of the canal was still closed to navigation by the 1944 Act. This anomaly wasn't sorted out until 1988, when a short Act was passed permitting navigation on the whole of the canal.

In the last four decades, the most serious engineering problems have been breaches in the canal. In 1978 efforts to stop a leak into a house by the towpath moorings in Llangollen closed the canal from July to September. Worse, in March 1982 a massive section of embankment failed a mile west of Trevor, causing the canal to be closed for fourteen months whilst the channel was rebuilt as a concrete trough. At the end of 1984 further subsidence caused a short closure, then in January 1985 the biggest collapse on this section occurred, taking away much of the concrete section built only two years earlier. This time a full structural survey was made of the Trevor–Llangollen and Chirk Bank sections, resulting in a £5 million contract to put much of the channel in a concrete trough with effective under-drains.

In recent years there have been two breaches in the embankment near Bettisfield, close to the England/Wales border. The first was caused by badgers – they find the softer soil of canal

Chapter 13 : Revival

Professor Castensson photographs Pontcysyllte Aqueduct whilst the rest of the group waits for his questions. This day of the visit was done using the author's boat Dorabella, *seen on the right.* Author

embankments particularly suitable for burrows, and they are of course a protected species – and the second was probably attributable to contractors doing piling work nearby. Whenever a breach occurs, an immediate priority is to arrange a bypass pipe for the water being conveyed to Hurleston Reservoir.

Pontcysyllte Aqueduct, the principal engineering structure on the Llangollen Canal, was designated a Scheduled Ancient Monument of National Importance in 1958, one of the first industrial monuments to be so recognised and thus given statutory protection.

In 1975 it was discovered that movement in the south abutment had caused the two inside girders of the southernmost arch to fail and for the outside pair to be buckled – the trough itself was carrying virtually the full structural burden. The original cast-iron girders were replaced by steel spans, the consulting engineers considering that if emergency action had not been taken, 'the piers might have collapsed one after another like dominoes'. Further remedial and conservation works were carried out in 2003/4 to protect it from corrosion, replace selected bolts using wrought iron, refurbish the towpath and handrail, repair masonry and reduce leakage.

A continuing problem is the wear on the bridges, particularly below water level. The flowing water carries silt in suspension. The channel is constricted at bridges, exacerbated by the frequent passage of powered craft, and the strong flow of water scours out the mortared joints and fines. This is made worse by the occasional boating impact which dislodges brickwork.

World Heritage Canal

SINCE the United Nations Educational, Scientific and Cultural Organization (UNESCO) started its list of properties forming part of the cultural and natural heritage 'of outstanding universal value' in 1972, over 1,000 World Heritage sites have been designated worldwide. Britain is well represented on the list; the Ironbridge Gorge site includes the Shropshire Canal from Coalport to Blists Hill. Designation involves strict rules about the long-term preservation of the site; it is possible to be taken off the list if the site is under threat.

Wrexham County Borough Council conceived the idea of seeking designation mainly to assist in promoting economic development and tourism in a run-down area. Its original idea was to apply for designation of Pontcysyllte Aqueduct and its immediate hinterland. Following advice, this was expanded to the whole of the canal corridor from Chirk Bank (Gledrid Bridge) to Horseshoe Falls, eleven miles of waterway, with a buffer zone comprising the important views. It included all the principal engineering features of the canal: the two major aqueducts of Pontcysyllte and Chirk plus two others, Chirk and

Whitehouses Tunnels, 31 bridges, Horseshoe Falls and two floodweirs, 15 embankments, 16 cuttings, 18 culverts, and the associated canal buildings at Chirk Bank, Froncysyllte, Trevor, Llangollen and Llantisilio. The expanded area crossed the England/Wales border into Shropshire and extended into Denbighshire, so the neighbouring councils were brought in as partners. The other major partner was British Waterways. Such organisations as Cadw, the Royal Commission on the Ancient & Historic Monuments of Wales and English Heritage were also represented.

Against strong competition, this was chosen as Britain's nomination for 2009. Every structure and historic property in the bid area was surveyed and its condition established. The history was researched in detail and an assessment made of how Pontcysyllte and Chirk Aqueducts influenced future aqueduct and viaduct designs. Writings and paintings contemporary with its construction and early days were collected, as the canal in its landscape was a great attraction even then. Planning and conservation policies were documented, a task made harder by part of the site being in England, where the rules differed from those applying in Wales. Management plans were devised for the canal and its surroundings. Visitor surveys were undertaken; weaknesses in provision were noted and plans for improvement devised.

The Nomination Document and Management Plan was ready by the end of 2007, signed by the relevant ministers, and sent to UNESCO headquarters in Paris where a 'desk assessment' was done of the submission. In September 2008 UNESCO's independent assessor, Professor Reinhold Castensson of Linköping University, Sweden, appropriately an expert on the Göta Canal and Thomas Telford, visited the site for three days. On the first day he had an overview (literally – from a helicopter); on the second day he went by boat from Chirk Bank to Trevor; and on the third day he concentrated on the Llangollen end. Throughout this time he asked pertinent questions of the members of the group.

In March 2009 it was announced that the bid would be formally considered at UNESCO's meeting in Seville in June. A small team went there to make a brief presentation and answer questions. The hall held over a thousand delegates, and there were more than twenty countries represented on the decision-making panel. The order in which the thirty bids would be heard was known, but not the exact timetable. The bid heard immediately before this involved seven hours of tough cross-

During the late 1950s and early 1960s, extensive repairs were carried out to the trough sides and the parapet railing was replaced with a replica of Hazledine's original.
Railway & Canal Historical Society, Weaver Collection

Chapter 13 : Revival

An impression of what the incline would have looked like. The assumption that boaters could operate the incline without supervision seems optimistic.
Whitchurch Waterway Trust

examination. The team found this nerve-wracking and were most apprehensive. At 7.30pm on the Saturday evening the stage was theirs – and 24 minutes (and just three easily-answered questions) later, unanimous approval was given. A couple of countries' representatives said it was the best bid they had ever seen. In total, only thirteen of the bids from across the world were approved.

Thus the top section of the Llangollen Canal has now been formally recognised by UNESCO as an international masterpiece of the 'heroic age' of civil engineering. The citation states:

> The Pontcysyllte Aqueduct and Canal are early and outstanding examples of the innovations brought about by the Industrial Revolution in Britain, where they made decisive development in transport capacities possible. They bear witness to very substantial international interchanges and influences in the fields of inland waterways, civil engineering, land-use planning, and the application of iron in structural design.

Designation doesn't automatically bring new funds, but it makes fund-raising easier. British Waterways gave a public commitment that they would maintain the structures to the best historical and environmental standards. Marketing, nationally and internationally, is more effective, especially with regards to non-boating visitors. Above all, it gives everybody involved a special pride in the canal – demonstrating that the top end of the Llangollen Canal is not just a beautiful canal, its importance is internationally recognised.

Branches off the Llangollen Canal

The Whitchurch Arm

THIS mile long branch was formally closed by the 1944 Act. The following year it experienced an unusual use: for the watering of elephants by a circus visiting the canalside Jubilee Park.

The section south of Sherrymill Bridge was sold in 1948; the rest of the branch had been sold by 1968. The local council filled in much of the canal using domestic refuse. The westernmost end of the canal was filled in by BTW employees in about 1955. The part immediately to the south of Sherrymill Bridge became part of the park. Much of the section from Sherrymill Bridge to Chemistry Bridge eventually had houses built on it.

Proposals for the restoration of canals are usually initiated by waterways enthusiasts. The Whitchurch proposals were unusual in that the project was initiated by Whitchurch Town Council, with the support of North Shropshire District Council and Shropshire County Council. This came about because in 1982 the Town Council commissioned a study from Liverpool Polytechnic on methods of regenerating the town. The report identified reopening of the canal as giving significant economic benefits. Because houses had been built on part of the old line, the suggestion was made that instead use be made of the Stags Brook. Boats would negotiate the 11ft difference in water levels by means of an inclined plane, a unique feature on a British canal, and therefore potentially a significant tourist attraction. Below the plane there would be a lake, with moorings towards the eastern end.

The Whitchurch Waterway Trust, a charitable company limited by guarantee, was created in 1985 to progress the project. The local authorities were supportive. As part of the agreement accompanying the granting of planning permission for housing, land was donated by Ashdale Homes (1984) and Wilcon (1995) to the North Shropshire District Council. The bridge at Greenfield Rise built in anticipation of the lake was completed in 1988 – it is actually slightly too low – and that at Meadowcroft in 1995.

Shropshire County Council managed the restoration of the section from the canal junction to Chemistry Bridge, largely financed by a Derelict Land Grant. Opened in 1993 in the presence of Red Rum, the Grand National veteran, this section is owned and operated by the Whitchurch Waterway Trust.

It is well used by visiting boaters as well as having a few revenue-generating permanent moorings. The rest of the project was Shropshire's bid for Millennium Commission funding in 1996. It was one of the 16 finalists in the national round but was not chosen.

The all-ability footway and cycleway from Greenfield Rise to Sherrymill Hill was completed in 2000, the repair work to Chemistry Bridge in 2001 and the construction of the car park at Chemistry later the same year.

A planning application was made in October 2002 for the weir, the lake, an inclined plane, visitor mooring basin, operations centre, sanitary station and a visitor car park. Outline planning permission was granted on 17 June 2004, subject to twenty conditions, several of which required extra researches to be undertaken. However, this planning permission expired three years later because the details of the development had not been submitted to the Planning Authority in accordance with various conditions.

At an Extraordinary General Meeting of the Trust held in March 2006, it was agreed that the first priority should be the lake and park, with the canal being joined to it later.

Land ownership was not a problem. Following local government reorganisation in 2009, ownership of all the land needed for the project passed to the new unitary Shropshire Council.

Over the years, numerous reports have been commissioned from consultants. These included:

– the plans and estimates of cost which were prepared by Platt White, engineering consultants, for the planning application;

– Stags Brook Hydraulic Study, Enviros, February 2004 – highly technical, but reaching the conclusion that the proposed development would slightly reduce the risk of flooding;

– Key Issues Report, RSKENSR Group, November 2005 – a clear preliminary assessment of the implications of the site's geology, hydrology, ecology, landscape and archaeology, with recommendations about mitigation and further research; and

– Consolidation Report, Peter Brown, July 2009 – costing the Water Park proposal, stating what further reports would be necessary, and discussing the capital and revenue funding options.

As a result of the last-named report, the project was reassessed, and the Trust decided to concentrate first on extending the canal under Chemistry Bridge to a new roadside basin, but doing so in such a way that it did not prejudice the creation of a Water Park and link for boats at a later date.

The design work was done to the satisfaction of CRT and planning consent obtained, but more problematical has been the raising of about £650,000 to make the scheme a reality. A bid for funding was turned down from the Heritage Lottery Fund. At the end of 2016 funding of £61,000 was awarded from European Agricultural Fund for Rural Development, which will allow works including levelling of the ground, improvement of existing paths to a wheelchair-friendly standard, creation of a new accessible path and a new picnic area.

The Prees Branch

IN October 1960 the IWRAC concurred with British Waterways' recommendation that part of the Prees Branch be transferred

Whixall Marina is on the Prees Branch, in a former pit where clay was dug for puddling the canal. The nature reserve starts on the right hand side of this photograph.
Canal & River Trust: British Waterways Marinas Ltd.

Chapter 13 : Revival

On the Prees Branch in 1959 or 1960 – possibly the last pleasure boat ever to use the waterway. *Railway & Canal Historical Society: Weaver Collection*

to the Wem Rural District Council for use as a refuse tip. The infilling was to be orderly and continuous, and when complete was to be earthed over, so that ultimately it could be sold to adjacent landowners for use for agricultural purposes. It is not clear exactly what length this referred to.

In its first report in 1971, the Inland Waterways Amenity Advisory Council (IWAAC), an independent advisory body set up under the Transport Act 1968, declared the Prees Branch to have 'no amenity value in its present condition' but thought it had a 'high potential' as a mooring site. It supported BWB's proposals to retain the first mile for navigation purposes, develop the next mile as a nature reserve, and abandon and dispose of the remaining 2½ miles. This is indeed what happened. The former pit for clay puddle at Whixall became a marina, the approach canal with its two attractive bascule bridges being restored. The nature reserve, which is managed by the Shropshire Wildlife Trust, was designated as a Site of Special Scientific Interest because it contained some very rare pondweeds; also found present were uncommon plants such as monkey flower, frogbit, skullcap and water violet.

An assessment of the effect of restoration on the ecology of the Prees Branch in 1979 concluded that the restored section had lost most of its rich flora. The nature reserve wasn't without problems: shading from the alder trees, accumulation of organic sediment, and choking of some parts of the canal by excessive growth of yellow water-lily and other parts by excessive growth of reedswamp species. However, with suitable management, it was thought that the reserve could support a rich flora and fauna.

The Montgomery Canal

Reopening what we now call the Montgomery Canal has long been an aspiration of canal enthusiasts. For example, Emlyn Garner-Evans, MP for Denbigh, speaking at the IWA North-Western Branch dinner in 1956 said that a new waterways policy should make provision for the rehabilitation of waterways made away by selfish interests in the past, such as 'the beautiful waterway from Frankton to Welshpool and Newtown'. The Welshpool Angling Association hand-dredged certain sections of the canal to improve the habitat for fishing. Mr R.D.R. Corser of the IWA Midlands Branch wrote to Montgomeryshire County Council in 1963 suggesting that the disused canal could be used for commercial and pleasure craft, which would enhance Welshpool as a pleasure resort and have a similar effect at Llanymynech. Others weren't so keen: a *Montgomeryshire Express* article of 1962 declared that living near the canal was 'a nightmare' because of the stagnant water, the stench, rats and vermin.[19]

The Inland Waterways Redevelopment Advisory Committee

The report by the BWB to the IWRAC in July 1960 detailed the condition of the canal at that time:

– The first 2 miles from Newtown to Freestone Lock, which is the lock adjacent to the end of the feeder from Penarth Weir, had been de-watered. During the period 1952–5 discussions had been held with Newtown Urban District Council about the transfer of Newtown basin and a short section of the canal. The position was complicated by the fact that houses adjoining the basin which were formerly owned by the canal company had been sold with various rights of drainage into the basin. Because of this, the condition of the basin had deteriorated and the Council had on several occasions served notices to abate the nuisance. Approval to de-water the basin was given by the Ministry of Transport in May 1955, subject to BW making arrangements to deal with the foul sewage entering the basin. Once the works were done, the site was sold to Central Dairies.

- The next section of 21¼ miles between Freestone Lock and Carreghofa – in other words, between the feeder from the Severn and the feeder from the Tanat, was in water but obstructed by several culverts where bridges had been lowered.
- About 1¼ miles of the 5¼ mile section between Carreghofa and Maesbury Marsh had been de-watered and piped to avoid heavy seepage.
- Part of the final 6 miles to Frankton Junction had been de-watered following the 1936 breach.
- The Guilsfield Arm, 2¼ miles long, had previously been considered for de-watering but the farmers' demands for alternative water supplies, as expressed through the Agricultural Executive Committee, were so excessive that no action was taken. The Montgomery Field Society and the Nature Conservancy had asked for the length to be scheduled as a Site of Special Scientific Interest (SSSI) because of certain aquatic plants found there; however they felt they were unable to take over the maintenance.

Ten of the 59 road bridges, all by then owned by the highways authorities, had been lowered and the watercourse culverted. Furthermore, navigation on the otherwise open lengths was not possible because of the condition of the locks and because the channel was silted up and heavily overgrown with weeds.

The principal use of the canal was agricultural water supplies. In 1958, the last year for which figures could be produced, there was a small amount of income from the sale of water (£421), fishing rights (£308) and rents etc (£562). Expenditure (excluding an apportionment of the District Engineer's office) totalled £7,213. Thus the net annual avoidable cost of the Montgomery Branch was £5,922.

BW recommended discussions with adjacent landowners with a view to eliminating the canal and disposing of the land, most of which would be taken into agricultural use. The cost of providing alternative water supplies, diverting drainage, opening of culverts, providing fencing and infilling locks was estimated at £150,000, to which they would expect some contribution from those benefiting. Alternatively, the canal could be adapted as a water channel at a cost of £13,000, in which case the annual deficit would continue virtually unchanged.

After consulting relevant government departments and outside bodies, the IWRAC considered that a comprehensive scheme of elimination would involve needless expense. Instead, lengths where there was no immediate need to eliminate the canal should be kept in water with maintenance minimised consistent with the avoidance of danger or nuisance. Opportunities should be taken to negotiate with landowners and farmers where alternative water supplies could be made available. In Welshpool it was thought that the local authority might want to use the length for roads or other purposes.

Unsurprisingly, the civil servants of the Ministry of Transport were content to endorse the Committee's recommendations – in effect, carry on as before, with minimum expenditure. However, because both the Montgomery Branch and the Llangollen Branch had up until then been considered together, the Minister had never been asked formally to make a decision about the future of the former, despite all parties being in agreement.

Welshpool Bypass?

THE Welsh section of the Montgomery Canal slept quietly on until 1967 when it was rumoured that the Welsh Office had proposals for a bypass for the A483 at Welshpool, and that it was intended to follow the line of the canal. It seems implausible that this was the first local knowledge of this, as BWB's report to the IWRAC of July 1960 refers to it. Welshpool certainly needed a bypass but the local activists who formed the Welshpool Bypass Action Committee felt that a dual carriageway on the line of the canal was too close to the town centre, and a route by the railway would be much preferable. The Shropshire Union Canal Society (SUCS) realised that if the canal route was adopted, all hopes of reopening the canal through to Newtown would be lost. They carried out surveys and consultations, and John Boulton prepared a restoration report.

The Action Committee, chaired by Claude Millington, wrote to SUCS in June 1969, saying that the project had reached the planning stage though the route was still officially secret, and asking if SUCS would assist in any way to defeat the proposal. A meeting of the two organisations was held to discuss how best to make some form of positive display in Welshpool, and it was decided to clear as much of the canal as could be done in a weekend. They then contacted Graham Palmer, editor of *Navvies Notebook* who had organised the successful 'Operation Ashton' the previous autumn. (This growing band of restoration volunteers did not adopt the name 'Waterway Recovery Group' until 1970.)

The proposed route was officially displayed at a packed meeting of the Welshpool Borough Council meeting on 9 September. The Town Clerk read objections and correspondence from various bodies, including the Action Committee, and the Mayor held aloft a copy of SUCS's restoration report. The Council resolved to approve the need for a bypass but to request the Welsh Office to put forward alternative routes. The following day a delegation from the Council went to Market Drayton at the invitation of SUCS and saw for themselves the benefits from having a thriving canal.

The Action Committee, SUCS and Graham Palmer worked together to organise the restoration of about three-quarters of

CHAPTER 13 : REVIVAL

Welshpool 1969: No hard hats, no hi-viz jackets – just everybody enjoying themselves.
Waterway Images

a mile of the canal through the town during the weekend of 18/19 October. A local firm, Buttington Contractors, agreed to provide the plant; other local volunteers organised accommodation and catering.

Some 180 volunteers (another report says nearly 300) came from all parts of the country for the week-end; using JCBs, a Hy-Mac, pumps and several lorries they cleared the canal and towpath. The top gates of the lock, which had previously been taken to Stoke Bruerne, were refitted and some white paint applied. Towards the end of the Sunday the Mayor of Welshpool, Cllr Elwyn Davies, was taken in a boat along the length of the worksite.

The weekend – later sometimes called the 'Big Dig' – was a great success. Much press publicity was obtained, and it had a major effect on local public opinion. The goodwill was further increased the following year when SUCS put a trip-boat, *Powis Princess*, on the canal and held a dinghy rally.

The IWAAC gave its support, saying that the Montgomery Branch was 'high in importance regionally if restored and could become of national importance if the traffic on the Llangollen Canal increases'.

The Public Inquiry into the by-pass scheme was held in July 1971. The Welsh Office's evidence included the following:

> This canal has been out of use for a considerable number of years, except for irrigation purposes and fishing. It has been culverted in a number of places north and south of Welshpool, and has been completely cut just north of the County boundary at Llanymynech. Any proposal to reinstate this section as part of the national system of canals would therefore be prohibitively expensive. Even a limited extension of the use of the canal in the County would be expensive and difficult to achieve.
>
> Plans to restore the canal cannot be based on work by volunteers and prisoners, and public enthusiasm is inclined to grow less in time. The State would not get the canal work done for nothing and in fact public funds would be required.
>
> Only about a mile would be lost, and the waterways to the north and south of the town would still be available for amenity purposes.

The Borough Council had passed a resolution endorsing the bypass scheme, but that was only because they had been told by

The Inland Waterways Amenity Advisory Council at Welshpool in 1971, having disembarked from *Powis Princess* at the aqueduct over the Lledan Brook. The Aqueduct Warehouse is visible on the left; opposite it was the wharf where stone was brought from Stondart Quarry. *Powis Princess* was a former working boat with the top created from two London Transport RT buses, driven by a Hotchkiss Cone engine. *Waterway Images*

CHAPTER 13 : REVIVAL

The Prince of Wales steers the newly-delivered *Heulwen/Sunshine* through Moors Farm Lift Bridge on 23 May 1976 when he formally reopened the section north of Welshpool.
Waterway Images

255

the Welsh Office that if they did not support it there would be no bypass. In the actual hearing, the Council raised many objections and supported the points made by the Action Committee. David Hutchings, who had organised the restoration of the Stratford-upon-Avon Canal and the Upper Avon Navigation, was the principal witness for the canal lobby, demolishing the Welsh Office's suggestion that the canal could never be restored and advocating the setting up of a charitable trust.[20]

The following year the Inspector gave his decision: the canal should not be used as the route for the by-pass. He added:

> In view of public demand and need of outdoor recreation, the voluntary organisations should be encouraged in their work of providing both funds and labour for nation-wide canal projects, and the severing of the Welsh Frankton–Newtown canal section at Welshpool could be avoided and the canal retained as an important local amenity and part of a restored national canal system.[21]

This gave the enthusiasts just the fillip they needed and, most importantly, made the local authorities and government departments realise that restoration was both possible and desirable. Indeed, in the long run the bypass proposal proved beneficial – it prompted the action to raise awareness of the canal locally and nationally, and kick-started the action to restore it.

In 1972 the plans for Abermule bypass showed that the canal would be culverted with a depth of 2½ft and headroom of 5½ft. Following representations from the IWA, SUCS and British Waterways, the Welsh Office agreed that these dimensions would be amended to a depth of 4½ft and headroom of 6½ft, making the bridge suitable for navigation.

Restoration plans

RESTORATION work commenced with Welshpool Town Lock, where the gates from Dolfor Lock (the second lock north of Newtown) were re-used. This was formally reopened by the Prince of Wales who had personally become involved in the revival of the Montgomery Canal, visiting it several times between then and 1993. The Prince of Wales' Committee, precursor of the Prince's Trust, raised the money for the restoration of the canal from below Burgedin Locks to Gallowstree Bridge (at the north end of Welshpool) including the four Pool Quay locks – this became known as the 'Prince of Wales Length'. Funding largely came from the Variety Club of Great Britain, which saw the restored canal as an opportunity for waterway cruises for disadvantaged children with physical disabilities.

Joan Heap, wife of the then Chairman of the IWA, together with 'the ladies of the IWA' raised the £5,482 for a boat designed for easy access by people in wheelchairs, the first of its kind, to be constructed by Birkenhead shipyard apprentices.

The Prince of Wales' Committee was involved in several other activities which are now commonplace on canal restorations but were then innovative. An Interpretive Officer was appointed to develop people's interest and involvement through organising a diary of events including local history tours, guided walks, rallies and fishing competitions. Publicity and background material was produced with the help of three previously unemployed young people, taking advantage of the Job Creation Scheme. A display and information centre was planned for an empty warehouse at Welshpool; this has subsequently developed into the Powysland Museum.

Full restoration of the canal became less likely when the section from Newtown to Freestone Lock was sold to the Mid-Wales Development Corporation in 1973. The Corporation was keen to acquire it as the route for its trunk sewer to the treatment works near Penarth Weir. Much of the land is now owned by Severn Trent plc and part by Natural Resources Wales; the route is a well-surfaced and well-used footpath and cycleway.

The attitude of the BWB towards the restoration of the canal had been neutral at the time of the 'Big Dig' but, in contrast to its then attitude to most other restoration schemes, it began to give practical support though still often staying frustratingly secretive. A case in point was the proposed new bridge at Arddleen, where the main A483 crossed the canal. The canal societies were concerned that if the bridge was lowered it would prevent the long-term aim of connecting the 'Prince of Wales Section' to the national network. The BWB claimed that it was working with the Welsh Office to ensure the headroom was adequate but was not forthcoming about the state of negotiations. In 1973 the Welsh Office had agreed to a suggestion by the BWB to incorporate in the bridge design a boxed culvert capable of incorporating a dropped lock. As a consequence of difficulties having arisen with this suggestion, a meeting was held on 20 October 1976 – in answer to a question in the House of Lords, this was described by Baron Elwyn-Jones, the Lord Chancellor, as 'a conference of all concerned', though neither the IWA nor SUCS had been invited. Although no conclusion had been reached, he stated that the bridge would be navigable. (The Earl of Cranbrook commented that this most attractive canal is an excellent nature reserve, and warned that this may be ruined if too many motor boats use the canal. The Lord Chancellor responded enigmatically: 'My Lords, that is yet another illustration of the many-sidedness of Truth.')

In 1975 the BWB gave approval to the IWA preparing a scheme to restore the four miles from Frankton Junction to Queen's Head, subject to an engineering survey being done by an independent consultant so that the extent of the work to be undertaken could be officially agreed. This was the first occasion that such permission had been given to a group to undertake unsupervised restoration work. Following a meeting of the Montgomery Waterway Restoration (Steering) Group, which included representatives of BWB, the Inland Waterways Amenity Advisory Committee (IWAAC) and the Prince of Wales' Committee, held at Buckingham Palace chaired by the Prince of Wales, Messrs Allott & Lomax of Sale were appointed as consultants. Their proposed restoration methods look inappropriate by later standards, with very long sheet piling through the peat to the underlying soil. The consultants' main concern

Chapter 13 : Revival

proved to be water supplies; for example, they recommended that any water coming down Frankton Locks must be pumped back. In the event this did not prove necessary. The finance for restoring Frankton Locks was raised by donations and sales, as no public sector money was forthcoming. The work was completed in 1987 but was not usable until the next stage of the canal was reinstated. Restoration purely by volunteers was a slow process but it proved to the decision-makers that reopening the Montgomery Canal was both possible and genuinely desired.

A further physical obstacle was created in August 1980: the lowering of Williams Bridge, where the B4398 crossed the canal to the north of the Vyrnwy Aqueduct. Powys County Council faced a genuine problem: the canal was here on an embankment, the road had a double bend which made the humped-back bridge even more awkward, it had a weight limit of 8¾ tons, and traffic was controlled by lights. The parapet had been damaged in the past and was then a temporary affair. The best long term solution would probably have been an electrically operated lift bridge, but the much cheaper expediency of culvert pipes was adopted instead. These were on site even before approval had been obtained. The waterways societies organised a campaign, including a full-page advertisement in the *Shropshire Star* and interviews on Radio Shropshire. *The Times* carried a picture on its front page on 28 July 1980. Over 200 letters were written to MPs, MEPs and local councillors but without success.

A significant development in 1980 was the Examination in Public into the first Powys County Structure Plan. Michael Limbrey represented the IWA and Michael Handford, SUCS. They succeeded in getting the County's policy amended to the effect that nothing would be done to obstruct restoration (possibly excluding highway works).

In 1981, following a meeting called by Sir Frank Price, Chairman of the BWB, the Montgomery Waterway Restoration Trust was formed with the support of the Prince of Wales' Committee to co-ordinate the whole of the restoration. The Trust had representatives from the BWB, the local authorities, statutory bodies, and voluntary bodies concerned with the project, including the naturalists. By this time the canal societies had come to recognise that recreation and amenity were not the most effective arguments to use when advocating canal restoration: rather, they had to concentrate on the jobs and business opportunities that restoration would create.

The British Waterways Board had a financial crisis in 1982 which led to it issuing a statement saying that future restoration of the canal was uncertain and that no new works were to be commenced after Frankton (where the WRG were working) and Carreghofa (SUCS). The Trust asked for a meeting with Sir Frank Price, at which it was agreed that an economic study would be undertaken of the viability of restoration. W.S. Atkins were engaged to undertake this cost-benefit analysis, the first time such an analysis for a canal restoration scheme had been commissioned from a consultant. The report, published in 1983, stated that full restoration from Frankton Junction to Newtown Pump House including the Guilsfield Arm would cost £9.4 million but the return to the local community from increased tourist expenditure would be over £1 million a year, as well as giving a much improved recreational and leisure facility for all.[22]

Nature conservation

Part of the Welsh section had been designated a Site of Special Scientific Interest (SSSI) back in 1959, and sections in England were so designated in 1963.

In May 1984 an ecological report commissioned by the Nature Conservancy Council showed the complexity of the issues concerning aquatic vegetation. The species were particularly diverse because the canal occupied a transition zone between the acid uplands to the west and the fertile planes to the east. Some species were spreading westwards, others eastwards; some plants, and also some molluscs, had spread beyond their normal range of distribution. The dredging which had been done was found to promote species diversity, though there was much variation in the effect on individual species. Boating levels were too low to have had a detectable effect on the aquatic vegetation, but it was thought that any increase would probably have a damaging effect. The report concluded: 'The canal flora appears in fact to have benefited from the restoration and the current management regime could be regarded as ideal for nature conservation.'

It was clear from the report that, paradoxical as it may sound, nature must be actively managed. For example, removal or thinning of trees benefits the submerged flora and increases its diversity, but it also benefits the emergent reeds and increases the problems of reedswamp encroachment. The plants of most interest to naturalists tend to be the 'first colonisers', but the management issue is then how to prevent the 'successor colonisers' from taking over. Thus disturbance can sometimes be good: for example, cattle trampling the edges of the canal inhibits the growth of reedswamp and encourages small marsh plants to grow free from competition.[23]

A Job Creation Scheme was formulated to record the current populations of flora and fauna on the canal, prior to further restoration activity. The project also included the making of off-line reserves, the first of these being at Rednal, in the former interchange basin.

Restoration agreed – and frustrated

The British Waterways Board published its consultation paper in 1986. This included details of the engineering works necessary, the most significant ones being, in summary:

– a fifth lock at Frankton so that the water level would be some 1ft 8in. lower than originally – this was thought desirable because the embankment across the valley of the river Perry had suffered considerable subsidence as a result of improved land drainage – with a consequential lowering of the top cill of Aston Top Lock;

- lining and rewatering the dry canal between Gronwen and Llanymynech;
- realigning the B4398 to pass over a new bridge, replacing Williams Bridge;
- building a new lock to the north-west of Maerdy Bridge and lowering the water level by 5ft 7in. between Maerdy Bridge and Burgedin – Maerdy Bridge would need to be rebuilt but the new Arddleen Bridge would be suitable for the canal channel, which would be in a cutting throughout this length. Burgedin Top Lock would also need to be rebuilt;
- diverting the canal at Gallowstree Bridge to pass under a new bridge higher up the road;
- diverting the canal at Whitehouse Bridge and raising the level of the road;
- diverting the canal at Refail to pass under a new bridge at a higher point;
- realigning the A483 at Garthmyl to the east for three-quarters of a mile, with a quarter of a mile of new canal constructed between the old and new roads, with one new bridge;
- further realignments of the A483 and new bridges to replace Halfway House and Red House Bridges;
- reinstating the 1½ miles of the canal between Freestone Lock and the former Newtown Pumphouse and providing a winding basin at the latter point; and
- a new pumping station to provide water from the river Severn to the top pound.

The consultation paper referred to the nature conservation requirements to retain the rich abundance of plant life – it was thought that these would be met by using redundant lengths of canal and lay-byes. The Board were in discussions with the Nature Conservancy Council about ways to maintain the existing SSSIs using sensible waterways management. The paper also set out the draft contents and timetable for a Bill to be presented to Parliament.

With government permission, the private Act of Parliament received Royal Assent in January 1987, this being the only occasion when canal restoration has been explicitly sanctioned by an Act. (This Act also formally recognised the name 'Montgomery Canal' for the canal between Frankton Junction and Newtown.) Funding the £8 million needed in Wales was agreed in principle by the Powys County Council, Montgomeryshire District Council, the Wales Tourist Board and the Mid-Wales Development Board. Their commitment unlocked European Union funds. Full restoration was estimated to take three to five years.

Success seemed assured – the Council of SUCS even asked, 'Upon what should the Society turn its spotlight once the Monty finally retires from the Campaign stage?'

Late in 1988 Peter Walker, the Secretary of State for Wales, vetoed the scheme. This decision, in turn, denied access to a 40% European Regional Development Fund grant. The public bodies withdrew their funding, whist continuing to express support. A petition with over 12,000 signatories was presented to the Welsh Office asking for the Secretary of State to reconsider his decision, but without success.

Actually, there had been an earlier hint that permission might not be forthcoming. For the local authorities to make their grants, they needed the sanction of the Welsh Office – and it asked for a further cost-benefit analysis, which was commissioned from Coopers & Lybrand. It came to somewhat different but in some ways more favourable conclusions than the previous Atkins report, forecasting a total of 280 new jobs and an additional regional income of £1.9 million a year. Nevertheless, the Welsh Office still were not totally satisfied and had asked for further discussions.

Piecemeal restoration resumes

AFTER the disappointment of Peter Walker's decision, the one piece of good news was that Humphrey Symonds, a former Secretary

Creating the nature reserve alongside Aston Top Lock. It seems paradoxical that the biggest single job done by the Waterway Recovery Group (to 2018) should be to make a watercourse that will never have boats. *Bob Dewey*

CHAPTER 13 : REVIVAL

of the Shrewsbury & Border Counties Branch of the IWA, left over £200,000 with the condition that it was used for the restoration of the Montgomery Canal. Much of this money was used to finance the nature reserve by Aston Locks, described below; the rest proved invaluable in unlocking other funds – most grant-givers require a portion of the funds to be raised from elsewhere by the applicant.

Piecemeal restoration works continued. The progress of restoration, including the opening dates of the various sections, is given in detail in Appendix B.

Most notably the two lowered bridges on main roads either side of Welshpool, Gallowstree Bridge and Whitehouse Bridge, were reconstructed, opening in 1992 and 1995 respectively. When SUCS rebuilt the Burgedin Locks, the water level of the Arddleen pound was kept at its full original height, not the substantially reduced level proposed in BWB's 1986 consultation paper. By 1998 the eleven miles from near Arddleen to Refail had been reopened and moorings and a slipway (for launching boats up to about 25ft long) constructed at Welshpool. This was rightly regarded as a tremendous achievement.

The northern section of the canal, from the foot of Frankton Locks to just short of the river Perry, was undertaken under the umbrella of Shropshire County Council using grants from various sources, including the Derelict Land Grant scheme. This was a significant change in attitude by Shropshire County Council; as recently as 1979 the County's draft Structure Plan gave no protection to the line of the canal – it was the Secretary of State for the Environment who added a statement that no permanent planning permission would be given which would prejudice the restoration of the canal.

As expected, the major problem encountered was that the land across Perry Moor had dried out, so the whole bed of the canal had sunk, necessitating the insertion of a new lock with a drop of 2½ft – this was called the Graham Palmer Lock, after the founder of the WRG. Modern lining methods had to be used for the canal across the valley, a combination of butyl, concrete and gabions, but the section south of Keeper's Bridge did not require lining. The first 100 yards of the Weston Arm was also restored. The contract was awarded to Wrekin Construction in late 1993. The section from Frankton Junction to Queen's Head was reopened in 1996.

Meanwhile, the most ambitious project had started: the construction of a nature reserve around the top of the three Aston Locks. British Waterways bought the land for £20,000. Five ponds were excavated, lined with butyl rubber membrane, with weirs in the linking channels. The whole area was equivalent to about a mile of canal. WRG carried out the works, a great

Stephen Lees, who drafted the Conservation Management Strategy, gathering a sample of floating water plantain on the Vyrnwy Aqueduct. He was specifically licensed to have permission to do this. *Author*

contribution being made by Kent & East Sussex Canal Restoration Group. It was estimated that contractors would have cost £250,000 whereas volunteers achieved it for £100,000 for equipment hire and materials.

This has proved more successful than the earlier nature reserves associated with the Shropshire Union canals, mainly because its slowly flowing water mimics the conditions in the canal. However, it has also shown that it is essential to have an active maintenance programme in order to avoid the mix of the ecology slowly changing.

At the same time as the nature reserve was being created, Aston Locks were restored, though the reopening of the canal through them as far as Gronwen had to wait until 2003, by which time the nature reserve was deemed to be mature.

SUCS restored three locks south of Garthmyl: Brynderwen, Byles and Newhouse Locks. Because of lowered bridges, including three crossings by the A483, this section cannot yet be used by powered boats. However, it is important that it is kept reasonably unobstructed, as it provides the feeder channel for water from the Penarth Weir to the navigable section.

In December 1997 a bid was made to the Heritage Lottery Fund (HLF) for a project then estimated to cost £34 million to link the restored sections of the canal, the Fund administrators having requested that there should be one complete bid, rather than it being staged. Matched funding had been identified for 25% of the overall cost. The bid was supported by a detailed submission covering every aspect of the restoration: engineering, natural and built environment, landscape evaluation, interpretation, public support, marketing, and so on. Unfortunately the HLF was itself in financial difficulties – in particular, the then new government required funds to be diverted to schools and hospitals. Also, there were numerous bids for canal restoration, and the Millennium Fund had approved three major projects: the Huddersfield Narrow Canal including Standedge Tunnel, the Rochdale Canal, and the Scottish Lowland Canals. After protracted discussions, the bid was turned down in September 1998.

The Montgomery Canal Partnership

THE Montgomery Canal Partnership was set up in 1999, with membership from all interested organisations, including British Waterways, the local authorities, the various wildlife trusts and heritage organisations, and representatives of volunteers. It commissioned several reports, the most important being the Conservation Management Strategy, largely financed by the HLF. Stephen Lees, whose background was in environmental management but who was also a boater, was appointed to draft the Strategy and to co-ordinate the restoration proposals.

By this time the law governing nature conservation had changed. The whole of the Welsh section had been designated a Special Area of Conservation under the European Habitats Directive (1994) due especially to the presence of the internationally important floating water plantain *(Luronium natans)*. The Countryside & Rights of Way Act 2000 imposed further duties on owners of SSSI sites to positively manage them in order to maintain the nature conservation value. In effect, in the eyes of the law, though not generally in the opinion of the public, nature conservation now overrode all other considerations.

The nature organisations and the waterways organisations had worked together reasonably well over the years, evidenced most notably by the agreements of 1984 and 1986, which had led directly to the creation of the Aston Nature Reserve. However, although the nature organisations were members of the Trust and the Partnership, the relationship had tended to be fragile. In 1998 the Shropshire Wildlife Trust broke ranks and published a leaflet, *Montgomery Canal: The Way Ahead*, which included criticisms of the nature conservation works which would have been better discussed with the other partners first. Then in 2003 English Nature and the Countryside Council for Wales signed up to the principles which were to be the basis of a Conservation Management Strategy, but when the first draft was produced, they declared that these principles were wrong, delaying the final report by more than a year.

After long discussions, all parties felt able to sign up to the Conservation Management Strategy in 2005. This recognised that if nothing were done, nature conservation interest declines, with the rare aquatic habitat disappearing into a reed grass swamp. Periodic dredging and weed-cutting was necessary, and the trees should not be allowed to grow to excessively shade the canal. It also pointed out that the built heritage decays, and if the Vyrnwy and Aberbechan Aqueducts failed, the sources of water to maintain the ecology would also be lost.

The Strategy stated that off-line reserves equal in water area to the canal channel would be created and actively managed. (English Nature originally demanded reserves equal to the pre-1936 water area.) Until these were mature, no additional boating would be allowed in the sensitive areas. Boat movements would be subject to an annual limit. In the English section the maximum would initially be 2,500 movements a year ('there and back' being counted as two movements), rising by stages to a maximum of 5,000 if the effect of boating had not proved to be detrimental. In Wales the target maximum would be 2,500; initially it would be nil in the sections currently not navigable by powered boats and 500 in the section between Arddleen and Refail.[24] In sensitive sections of the canal there would be a 2mph speed limit. The possibility of boats being towed through the most sensitive section of all, in the area of the Vyrnwy Aqueduct, was suggested. The limits were all subject to review (up or down) depending on how the various plants thrived.

The Strategy was launched at the Welsh Assembly and, the day after, at the Houses of Parliament.

British Waterways commissioned an economic appraisal from Rural Solutions, a planning consultancy based at Skipton, Yorkshire. Its report, over 250 pages long, concluded that the canal's reopening would 'provide a valuable vehicle for regeneration of the local economy within its hinterland and potentially impact upon the region as a whole'. However, it was felt that the stakeholders were too inward looking and needed to generate more support from other parties who could assist in delivering the projects. Active co-operative promotion would be necessary during and after restoration.

Post-restoration the Montgomery Canal was forecast to attract 1.65 million visits per year, around half being new visits to the waterway. A total of £21 million would be spent by canal visitors each year within the local authority districts of Powys, Oswestry and North Shropshire, of which £3.0 million would be net additional spend within the economies of these local authorities. 105 new tourism and leisure related jobs would be created within the local economies of Powys and Shropshire by the increased canal-based activity.

In addition, there was potential to deliver over 5,000m^2 of new commercial floorspace through the direct development of canal-side sites by the Restoration Partnership, accommodating a predicted 233 jobs (but this included 35 already counted as relating to tourism and leisure), some 80% of which would be new jobs to the area. The principal development opportunities were thought to be at Welshpool (72 jobs), Queen's Head (67) and the Powis Castle Sawmill site (56). The development of all the sites identified would cost about £11m.[25]

Progress since 2005

BRITISH Waterways had a statutory limitation preventing them from adopting additional costs outside those necessary to fulfil the limited remit for 'remainder waterways' such as the Montgomery Canal. Securing a long-term agreement for funding of maintenance works was to be essential before major capital works could be undertaken – and the local authorities were the only bodies likely to be able to commit to year-by-year funding. The Canal & River Trust, British Waterways' successor, does not have the statutory constraint though of course its budgets are still limited. On the other hand, the local authorities have suffered major cuts in their funding, especially since 2010, and their ability to spend on projects which are not a statutory requirement has been greatly reduced.

The first 'Dinghy Dawdle' was held on the Montgomery Canal in 1987. In the early years the participants claimed to be 'exercising the right of navigation' over blocked bridges: a cooperative police constable would stop the traffic, and the motorists would be handed a leaflet (without official police approval) complaining about 'highwaymen' blocking the canal. Dinghy Dawdles became an annual event, the last being in 2011. In 2012 the event was transformed into the Montgomery Canal Triathlon – a 13½ mile cycle ride followed by 11 miles canoeing and a 10½ mile walk – 180 people taking part. Similar events were held in subsequent years which have been so popular that the number of participants has had to be limited.

The IWA had held its National Trailboat Rally at Welshpool in 1996; it was repeated in 2008 as part of the 'Monty08' festival, with other events based on Maesbury and Llanymynech. A rally has been held at Maesbury in the autumn in several later years. In 2015 the Welsh Waterway Festival was held at Welshpool.

In the mid-2010s much of the towpath was upgraded for walkers and cyclists, at a cost of over £1 million. The section from Redwith Bridge to Pryce's Bridge was re-watered in 2014, though there were some problems with leaks.

In the autumn of 2016 the HLF approved a grant of £2.53 million towards a £4.2 million package of works, of which £326,000 represented the value of work by volunteers. The package is enabling the navigable section to be extended by 1¼ miles from Gronwen to Crickheath, new nature reserves (including a third reserve by Aston Locks) to be created, and improvements to almost four miles of towpath between Welshpool and Llanymynech. This leaves a dry section of just two miles between Crickheath and Llanymynech.

The Shrewsbury and Newport Canals

FOLLOWING the 1944 Act, the section between Shrewsbury and Uffington was drained and some of it filled in. Minimal maintenance using a cut-down boat continued on the rest of the canal until the mid 1960s in order to maintain the land drainage capability though a report by British Waterways in January 1960 stated that many farmers wanted the canal returned to being agricultural land. One culvert, it was said, impeded the flow of a drainage course from the adjoining low-lying land extending to some 4,000 acres. Three lift bridges had been replaced by low level concrete bridges. It was estimated that it would cost £39,000 to do the necessary works on the section between Wappenshall and Uffington: demolishing occupation bridges and aqueducts, opening up culverts, diverting drainage and filling in the locks. The net annual avoidable costs in 1958 were £1,892.

A BW report in February 1960 on the section between Norbury Junction and Wappenshall stated that 16 of the 23 top gates of the locks had been replaced by concrete weirs.

Particularly west of Newport many of the farmers wanted to incorporate the canal into their land. Works necessary to effect closure of the canal were estimated to cost £63,000. The net annual avoidable costs in 1958 were £628, this relatively small figure being attributable to income from various rents totalling £1,021. The Humber Arm had recently been disposed of.

Both reports mentioned that the costs of closure were likely to be lower than the figures stated because it was thought that many of the farmers could be persuaded to undertake some of the works at their own expense.

These reports do not seem to have been considered by the IWRAC, presumably because closure had already been approved and the only remaining issues were thought to be approving the disposal of the land and of any expenditure necessary to enable this to be done.

In the summer of 1964 British Waterways put forward formal proposals to dewater the canal and sell the land to the adjacent landowners. The Newport Urban District Council objected to this, and the press report of their decision prompted Major C.O. Hilditch to contact other potential protesters. Assisted by Captain Lionel Munk, Chairman of the Inland Waterways Association, the resultant informal group wrote to British Waterways and the various local authorities. A public meeting on 25 June 1965 in the ballroom of the Royal Victoria Hotel, Newport, was attended by some 250 people, and from this the Shrewsbury & Newport Canal Association (SNCA) was born. Its formal aims were:

– to restore to navigability the length of canal from Norbury Junction to Shrewsbury – 'or as near as we can possibly get'; and

– to link the canal with the river Severn above Shrewsbury Weir (which of course the Shrewsbury Canal had never done).

The existence of a group advocating restoration prompted an opposition group of farmers who also met a representative of the BWB. It was rumoured that promises were made about the sale of parts of the canal to certain farmers.

Dr Cyril Boucher, the IWA's Honorary Consulting Engineer, was commissioned to report on the practicability and cost of restoration. The nineteen locks between Norbury Junction and Newport were generally in excellent condition, he stated, though it would be necessary to remove the concrete weirs and provide new cills, gates and paddle gear. Between Newport and Wappenshall Junction the three locks would need similar treatment and one bridge would need to be rebuilt. The two Eyton locks should be restored with guillotine gates; one bridge would need raising. The Long Lane to Uffington section would require the most civil engineering. The Wellington–Whitchurch (A442) road crossing had been culverted, necessitating a new large reinforced concrete bridge at Long Lane. West of there, thirteen minor bridges had been lowered; these would need raising and the necessary approaches constructing. Some repairs were needed to Berwick Tunnel, and just beyond the tunnel was a leak. Because restoring the former line from Uffington into

Shrewsbury would be difficult and expensive, Dr Boucher recommended linking the canal to the river Severn by constructing four locks with a fall totalling 32ft. It would be necessary to raise the river level 4ft by constructing a weir at Uffington and also to provide a lock at the existing weir just below Shrewsbury. He estimated that the works would cost about £140,000. The SNCA's Committee considered that the cost excluding the link to the Severn could be reduced to £82,000 since much of the labour would be voluntary.

After lengthy correspondence, representatives of the SNCA met Arnold Allen, BWB's General Manager, on 31 March 1965 and talked for about two and a half hours. The major point of difference about the works to be done concerned bank protection. Whereas Dr Boucher considered the majority of the banks to be in quite good condition, the BWB thought that piling was needed for the 40% of the canal which was on an embankment plus parts of the rest, the total cost for this being some £150,000. The second issue was that the BWB considered that the cost of gates was about double that estimated by Dr Boucher. Although at the beginning of the meeting it was said that BWB had not yet made a decision, as the meeting went on the SNCA representatives sensed that it had already been decided to eliminate the canal.

Following the meeting the BWB sent a letter which stated that as this was a canal which had been physically run down over a long period, they could not bring themselves to believe that restoration was feasible. It concluded: 'The obstacles to restoration are overwhelming ... there is no alternative but for us to proceed with disposal.'

Within a few weeks, dewatering started below Eyton Bottom Lock. Two sections east of Rodington were sold off, field drains laid along the canal bed, hedges grubbed out and the land levelled. The SNCA requested Barbara Castle, the Minister of Transport, to stop further elimination until a full appeal to her had been prepared, but the formal response stated that this was 'not a case in which the Minister could see her way to intervene'. A meeting was offered but before arrangements for it were made it was decided to try to rouse public opinion though a publicity campaign, a petition, and involvement of MPs and local authorities. Articles appeared in two national and all the regional and local papers, and the issue was also the subject of five minutes of television time. The petition contained just over 8,000 signatures, but as the Director of the Anglers' Co-operative Association said it was signed 'on behalf of their 11,846 members', the SNCA claimed a 'moral' 20,000. Armed with the petition and expressions of support, a meeting was held with an official of the Ministry of Transport. The latter stressed that they were unable to issue a directive to the BWB in this matter; all they could do was to pass on the comments and act as an intermediary. It all had no effect: the BWB did not change its mind. By the autumn the negotiations for the transfer of land to adjacent owners was complete.

During the next three decades the canal from Norbury Junction to Uffington became lost in the farming landscape. In some places it is not even possible to tell where the canal had been. Some ironwork and other items were removed, with permission, much of it being used to help restore the Stratford-upon-Avon Canal. Rodington Aqueduct was demolished. The biggest heritage loss was the destruction of the ornamented iron aqueduct over the Duke's Drive near Kynnersley.

It is a matter of lasting regret that the local authorities did not even designate the towpath as a public footpath although for a long time it was shown on the Shropshire County Structure Plan as being appropriate for conversion to a cycle path.

Even worse, various new main roads were created which crossed the line of the canal at or near water level, with no provision being made for its eventual restoration:

– Newport bypass (A41);
– the A5 extension of the M54, which was built alongside the Wolverhampton to Shrewsbury railway, cutting the line of the canal twice, thus isolating Berwick Wharf and Berwick Tunnel;
– Shrewsbury's eastern bypass (A49); and
– Telford Way, Shrewsbury's inner ring road (A5112).

A reminder of the history of the Shropshire Union was lost when the railway yard at what had been Shrewsbury Wharf was closed on 5 April 1971. The access from the station was bricked up in August 1985 but can still be seen. The site subsequently became a car park.

Slow progress

ALTHOUGH the battle for the Shrewsbury & Newport Canals seemed to have been lost, the SNCA did not totally give up. Instead it reconstituted itself as the Shropshire Union Canal Society, with a brief covering the whole of the former Shropshire Union system. As noted above, three years later it was to get heavily involved in the restoration of the Montgomery Canal.

Newport Urban District Council acquired the 1½ mile section of the canal within the town boundary in 1967. With the £3,500 payment from British Waterways intended for the long-term maintenance of bridges, the Council cleaned out the length and using water pumped from the Strine Brook restored it for fishing. Meretown Lock was buried, whilst the Fishers, Town and Tickethouse Locks were partly filled, a cascade replacing the bottom gates.

In 1970 Shropshire County Council removed the granite setts from Newport High Street, dumping some of them on the side of the canal west of Town Lock. Unfortunately the weight caused the newly-excavated canal bed to rise and a 100yd section had to be filled in, with a new narrow water channel directed across it. The following year the headroom under the Town Bridge was reduced when the Strine Valley Sewer was laid. The 1½ miles of canal through Newport was designated a Site of Special Scientific Interest in 1986 because of its aquatic plants.

The Wrekin District Council protected the part under their

CHAPTER 13 : REVIVAL

Duke's Drive, Kynnersley, about 1954. *Railway & Canal Historical Society*

planning control from the erection of permanent structures across the alignment.

The volunteers had not totally forgotten the canal. In the late 1970s some clearance work was carried out in the Berwick area by the short-lived Shrewsbury & Newport Canal Group. This was wound up in 1983, its fund balance of £105 being donated to the Waterway Recovery Group of the IWA. SUCS set up a Shrewsbury & Newport Sub-Committee in 1988. Amongst other activities, a questionnaire concerning their attitude to restoration was sent to farmers; of the eighteen replies received, only one was positive.

Telford Development Corporation encouraged the creation of public open space in the Hadley Park area, and the Wrekin College Canal Restoration Group received a Shell Award for their work on the two surviving locks with their guillotine gates; this work was later continued by the British Trust for Conservation Volunteers. Also on the Trench Branch, a lock within the GKN Sankey works was regated.

The importance of Longdon Aqueduct was formally recognised when it was added to the List of Buildings of Special Architectural or Historic Interest in 1983 (Grade I, the highest designation) and was restored using a 100% grant from the Department of the Environment.

In 1992 SUCS commissioned a survey by the Civil Engineering and Building Department of Coventry University. East of Newport the line of the canal was generally clear, and those structures which had been inspected were in reasonable or good condition. Between Newport and the crossing of the Duke's Drive much of the line was virtually untraceable. Restoration of the next section, past Wappenshall Junction to Eyton, was thought to be reasonably easy. From Pave Lane westwards there were several major problems: the road crossings at Pave Lane, the A5 (M54 extension) twice and Shrewsbury bypass, and the aqueducts at Longdon and Rodington. The report concluded that reconstruction on the original line was possible as far as Longdon and that although many engineering works would be required, there was no particular difficulty apart from the cost. It continued, 'Whilst not beyond the bounds of possibility, the west end of the canal to Shrewsbury should be seen as a second stage.'

The attitude of the local authorities concerning restoration was generally becoming positive. In 1992 Shropshire County Council repaired Wappenshall Bridge, a listed structure, after serious subsidence had occurred. The following year Shrewsbury Borough Council designated the canal from Ditherington to the bypass as an all-ability nature trail, several stretches being dug out as nature pools. In 1994 Wrekin District Council relined and renovated the section of the canal through Newport. In 2000 the skew bridge at Forton was cleared and repaired by Staffordshire County Council.

The Shrewsbury & Newport Canals Trust

THE Shrewsbury & Newport Canals Trust (SNCT) was formed following a public meeting in Newport in June 2000. Its aims included:

- seeking to preserve the canal's remaining features;
- promoting restoration amongst the local authorities and other organisations, and developing partnerships;
- seeking to ensure that local authorities' Structure and Local Plans were favourable to the restoration of the canals; and
- carrying out projects to raise public awareness in the history of the canals and of the benefits of restoration.

The Trust has proved generally successful in encouraging the local authorities to support restoration. Members have carried out much valuable work including clearance of parts of the canal, its structures and its towpath, digging out Meretown Lock, giving guiding walks, and organising a boat rally most years at Norbury Junction.

In 2004, W.S. Atkins, a leading firm of engineering consultants, published a detailed study of the state of the canal and the options for restoration. It found that from Norbury Junction to Edgmond much of the canal had been infilled but the locks and bridges appeared to be restorable. From Edgmond to the terminus at Shrewsbury all the road bridges had been demolished and the roads flattened and straightened.

The engineering solutions identified to the various obstacles were:

- The crossing of Newport bypass (A41) would be achieved by realigning the canal and relocating Meretown Lock to the west of a new road bridge. (Because of its large scale and high cost, this proposal for crossing the A41 has been superceded by a plan for a pair of locks on the original line of the canal similar to those proposed for Long Lane.)
- Two options were put forward for Long Lane (A442), either a 'dropped lock' – a descending lock before the main road, with a second ascending lock after the minor road bridge – or diverting the canal nearly half a mile to the south and raising the level of the main road.
- The 2½ mile long loop via Berwick Wharf and Berwick Tunnel south of the A5 where it runs parallel with the railway would be avoided by a cut-and-cover tunnel to the north of the railway.
- The canal would be lowered by some ten feet by a lock at Uffington, which would enable it to pass below Shrewsbury bypass (A49).
- The canal would continue at its lower level until shortly before Telford Way (A5112), where there would be a junction. The northern arm would pass under the road then rise by a lock to the canal's original route past Ditherington Mill to the terminus at the former Butter Market. The southern arm would lock down to river level just above Shrewsbury Weir.
- Minor roads would have lift bridges.

The condition and historical importance of Longdon Aqueduct would not allow it to be reused; instead the canal would be diverted to the south and across a new aqueduct. However, at a village meeting the majority opinion of the residents was that they would prefer the old line of the canal to be used.

The cost of the whole project was estimated as £86 million, of which £19 million would be for the 10½ miles from Norbury Junction to Wappenshall and £67 million for the 14½ miles continuation to Shrewsbury. The annual economic benefits were assessed as £4 million.[26]

The Trust adopted the aim of restoration from Norbury Junction to Wappenshall Junction, whilst ensuring that nothing was done to prejudice the eventual extension to Shrewsbury. In the short run, it was decided to concentrate on three areas: north-east Shrewsbury including the Flax Mill; Wappenshall Wharf; and Newport Wharf. At Shrewsbury the original route of the canal was preferred, contrary to Atkins' recommendation, with a link to the river from the terminus. It had been hoped that the local authorities would enter into a formal partnership with the Trust and help finance a Project Manager, but the local authorities preferred a looser arrangement.

A 'Living Lottery' bid was made in 2006 for the Norbury–Wappenshall section but it did not make the 'long list'. One feature included in the bid came in for much criticism locally: an inclined plane coming down from Shelmore Embankment, instead of reinstating the first twelve locks in the flight down from Norbury Junction.

This counterbalanced inclined plane was conceived principally in response to two issues: British Waterways had said that there was insufficient water in summer to supply the Shrewsbury & Newport Canal; and it was thought that major funders liked there to be something special, ideally 'iconic', about projects they supported. It added some £10 million to the cost but would be a visitor attraction of regional significance – this was not an unreasonable assumption, the Falkirk Wheel having proved to be a great public success. However, despite the proposal including a new road to keep traffic out of the village, the residents of Norbury were almost all opposed to the concept, as were some SNCT members who felt the traditional locks should be reinstated.

The dispute prompted the formation of the Norbury to Newport Canal Restoration Community Interest Company early in 2011, an organisation centred on Norbury, and having the aim of restoring the canal using the original route. Near the end of the year the two organisations signed a Memorandum of Understanding under which they both agreed to pursue the common goal of restoring the canal on its original line as far as possible, with the CIC concentrating on the section from Norbury to the A41 Newport bypass. The SNCT formally dropped the idea of the inclined plane and committed itself to the restoration of this section of canal along the original line of the canal. By then, British Waterways had changed its opinion concerning water, saying that some was available for the branch. The CIC was dissolved in 2018.

Chapter 13 : Revival

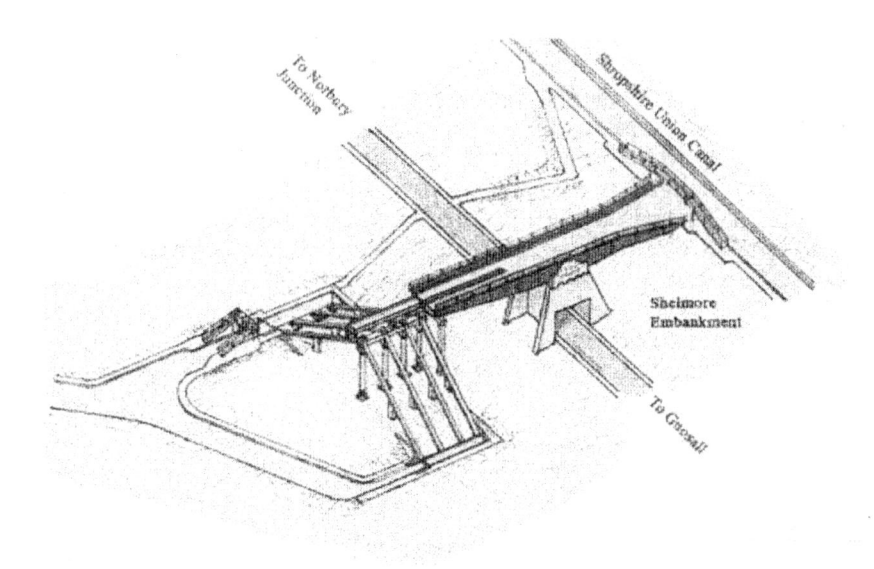

The counterbalanced double-inclined plane was designed by the Trust's Honorary Engineer, Dennis Rogers. The boats would float in caissons; as one caisson rose up on one side, the other caisson would fall on the other side – a solution requiring little energy to be used as the weight on both sides would always be equal. Shrewsbury & Newport Canals Trust

An opportunity for action came when Wappenshall Wharf with its two warehouses came on the market. After lengthy negotiations the site was bought by Telford & Wrekin Council (the unitary authority which was the successor to Wrekin District Council) in 2009 for £395,000 and leased to the Trust, which wished to restore the buildings and convert them for use as a base for the volunteers with exhibition, education and other public facilities.

The Trust commissioned a study from Astley Associates into the reinstatement and rewatering of 2¾ miles of canal from Wappenshall Wharf to Lubstree Wharf. The total cost was estimated as £8¼ million, of which some £1¼ million would be for work to the warehouses. This was thought to give very significant economic, tourism, recreational, educational and heritage benefits.

The further phases were envisaged to be as follows (2010 costs):

– Restoration of 4½ miles between Newport Town Basin and the junction with the Humber Arm, which would connect Newport to the Wappenshall section. Costing some £9½ million, there would be low economic benefits directly from this section, the main benefits coming once the connection was made with the main canal network.

– Restoration of 1¼ miles from Forton Bridge to Newport Town Basin, including passing under Newport bypass. The cost was estimated at £3½ million but there was thought to be significant economic, regeneration and heritage benefits to the town of Newport.

– Restoration of the 2¾ mile section from the Shropshire Union Canal at Norbury Junction or Shelmore to Forton Bridge. The cost could be from £13 million to £23 million, depending on whether all the original locks are restored or an inclined plane constructed to bypass locks 1 to 12. Although the most expensive section, its construction would enable very significant additional economic benefits to be achieved on the other sections from boat traffic being able to travel to and from the national network.[27]

In 2009 Telford & Wrekin Council allocated £1½ million to be spent in Newport in ways which accorded with local people's wishes. The fund was administered by the Newport Regeneration Partnership, which included representatives of the leading organisations in the town, together with the Town and Borough Councils. Improvements to the canal proved popular in a local survey, and the initial plan was to realign the sewer, re-excavate, line and re-water the canal, and re-gate Town Lock. In the end, all that was achieved was to create the attractive Canal Corner adjacent to the Town Lock.

In 2014 the Heritage Lottery Fund approved a grant of £1 million towards an estimated £1.5 million cost of restoring the Wappenshall warehouses, the creation of a visitor centre and rewatering the basin. However, the grant offer was withdrawn in 2017, despite over £300,000 being raised through donations and pledges.

The warehouses at Wappenshall in 2002, awaiting restoration. *Author*

Notes and references

The basic information concerning the saving of the Llangollen Canal derives from *Waterways*, the magazine of the Inland Waterways Association. For the restoration of the Montgomery Canal and the Shrewsbury & Newport Canals the main sources used were *Nor'Wester* and *Shroppie Fly Papers*, the magazines of the IWA's North-Western Branch and its successor, the Shrewsbury & North Wales Branch, and *Cuttings*, the magazine of the Shropshire Union Canal Society.

1. BTC Supporting Papers, 9/9/1949: TNA, AN85/2 (quoted in *Hadfield's British Canals*, 1994, p.263)
2. *Canals and Inland Waterways: Report of the Board of Survey* ('The Rusholme Report'), 1955, paragraph 220: TNA, MT115/101. One should not be too quick to condemn the report: the authors' brief was to make an ailing transport business financially successful.
3. *IWA Bulletin*, May & August 1952
4. *Nor'Wester*, February & June 1954 and October 1955
5. *Nor'Wester*, March 1975.
6. Inspector's Report: TNA, RAIL1053/131/7
7. *IWA Bulletin 14*, [?June] 1948, pp.1, 12. There is no reference in the minutes of the DIWE to this meeting – indeed there are only two references to the IWA in the whole of the six years' life of the DIWE.
8. *Liverpool Daily Post*, 7 June 1948
9. Shropshire County Council, Roads & Bridges Committee, 10 October 1950, minute 8: Shropshire Archives (SA), SC3/1A/1/14. The St Martin's Moor Bridge scheme was not new – the LMSR and Shropshire County Council had signed an agreement on 13 June 1940 to transfer the bridge. (DIWE, 3 July 1951, minute 1805(a): TNA, AN77/3)
10. Shropshire County Council, Roads & Bridges Committee, 10 October 1950, minute 8; 31 March 1953, minute 6 and capital programme: SA, SC3/1A/1/14

11. *Nor'Wester*, August 1955, p.2: CRT, D7370/05
12. ibid, p.1; October 1955, 5: CRT, D7370/05
13. BW report, 29 July 1960: TNA, MT124/163
14. MoT report, 25 January 1961: TNA, MT124/163
15. David Serpell was to gain notoriety in 1983 as the author of a report on Britain's railways which postulated reducing the network from 10,300 to 1,630 miles. This was only one of the five options he put forward, but it is the one which people remember.
16. MoT report, 27 July 1961, and comments, 28 July 1961: TNA, MT124/163
17. Tom Rolt, *Landscape with Canals*, 1977 (reprinted 1984), p.147
18. *Nor'Wester*, June 1957, 3–4: CRT, D7370/07; also information from Martin Grundy, 31 July 2005
19. *Montgomeryshire Express*, 24 November 1962, quoted in *IWA Bulletin*, November 1963, pp.16–7
20. *Cuttings*, 12, Autumn 1971, pp.16–23; *Nor'Wester*, September 1971 and August 1972
21. *Nor'Wester*, August 1972
22. W.S. Atkins, *The Costs and Benefits of Restoration*, 1983; *Cuttings*, p.74, Aug/Sep 1983, pp.9–11
23. Catriona G.A. Paskell, *An investigation of the ecological effects of renewed navigation and maintenance on disused parts of the Shropshire Union Canal system*, May 1984: TNA, FT568
24. Montgomery Canal Partnership, *Montgomery Canal: Regeneration through Sustainable Restoration (A Conservation Management Strategy)*, September 2005
25. Rural Solutions, *The Montgomery Canal Restoration Project*, April 2004
26. W.S. Atkins, *Feasibility Study*, 2004; *S&News*, p.19, Summer 2005, pp.8–9
27. Astley Associates, *Norbury Junction to Forton Bridge – initial appraisal of the economic, heritage, social, leisure and economic benefits*, 2010

14
The Second Canal Age

In the decades following the First World War, commercial traffic on the canals faded away. But since the Second World War the canals have become a popular leisure asset. Many are now busier than they have ever been – we are truly living in the Second Canal Age. What can the history of the Shropshire Union area tell us about these changes?

Was the decline of freight inevitable?

By 1914 the canals had lived with railway competition for fifty years; each mode accommodated the traffic best suited to it. Canal tolls and freight prices had been squeezed because of the competition, and the long-term trends in the location of industry may have caused concern, but (contrary to what is often said) the evidence is that in the case of the Shropshire Union, railways were not the ultimate cause of the canal's demise.

During the two decades following the end of the First World War, the motor lorry became an effective competitor, especially as it could provide a door-to-door service, avoiding any need for expensive transhipment. We have seen that cost increases led to the closure of the Shropshire Union Canal Company's carrying subsidiary in 1921, and seen the example of how A.&A. Peate of Maesbury disposed of their boats when they found it more economical to move grain by road. Traffic on the branches to the west of the former Shropshire Union Main Line faded away during the 1920s and virtually ceased in the 1930s, a trend shared by rural canals elsewhere.

It is interesting to compare this experience with that of rural railway stations. The Great Western Railway kept detailed statistics of the quantities of goods and minerals handled at each of their stations. As a typical example, those for the large village of Audlem during this period are shown in Table A.[1]

It is therefore evident that rural railways' main period of decline was the same as the final period of decline of the rural canals. It was motor lorries, not railways, which eventually killed the rural canals as a mode of transport. (Passenger numbers at rural railway stations also suffered, reducing greatly during the period from 1923 to 1928 when bus services were being introduced.)

The traffic of trunk canals such as the Shropshire Union Main Line held on rather longer, the period of final decline being the 1950s. But again the main cause was motor lorries which became more powerful and hence faster; there was also a relatively small increase in their permitted weight. Roads too improved, though the main period of improvement came later, in the 1960s and 1970s.

Following Grouping in 1923, the Shropshire Union was directly managed by the London Midland & Scottish Railway, its policy concerning canals seeming to be merely to minimise the loss. Did the LMS miss an opportunity to modernise the Main Line?

During the period from 1932 to 1934 the Grand Union Canal's locks south of Birmingham were doubled in width to a little over 14ft and bridges were rebuilt to take wider boats. In practice narrow boats continued to be used in pairs, usually with a total crew of three. In the case of the Shropshire Union, making the 28 locks of the former Birmingham & Liverpool Junction Canal broad without altering the rest of the channel would have speeded pairs of narrow boats but not have fundamentally changed anything.

To make the route suitable for broad boats would have needed the rebuilding of over 90 bridges; an even greater cost would have been the earthworks necessary to widen the cuttings and embankments, to deepen the channel and to make it possible for broad boats to pass each other. The main benefit would have been that boats could work through from Liverpool without transhipment of cargoes at Ellesmere Port. However, unless the

Table A : Audlem Station	1913	1923	1928	1933	1938
Goods received (tons)					
General merchandise	1,768	1,991	978	627	915
Coal and minerals	6,022	3,334	6,016	2,701	972
Goods dispatched (tons)					
General merchandise	439	241	117	67	41
Minerals	57	20	152	5	68
Receipts	£2,282	£3,439	£3,304	£1,794	£1,261

21 locks of the Birmingham Canal rising to Wolverhampton were also rebuilt, transhipment to narrow boats or lorries would have been needed at Autherley.

This was also a fundamental problem with both the Royal Commission's proposals in 1911 and those of the Ministry of War Transport of 1943. Both would have required transhipment for the final stage of the journey. Neither of these proposals would have permitted use by sea-going vessels. Even the Manchester Ship Canal, which is able to accommodate inter-continental cargo liners, found that the increasing size of ships and the growth of containerisation during the 1970s and 1980s led to a decrease in traffic from a peak of 20 million tons in 1958 to about 8 million tons in 2011, with little traffic now passing beyond Runcorn.

The obvious conclusion is that any major investment in the Shropshire Union Main Line and Middlewich Branch would not have been productive. Any extra income would have been insufficient to cover the cost of financing the works.

No doubt minor improvements could have been made, particularly with regard to mechanisation of loading and unloading at the ports and the inland wharves, but that would never have reversed the long-term trends.

Should the Perry Aqueduct breach have been repaired, and was the 1944 Act justified?

As mentioned earlier, Tom Rolt used the phrase 'railway sabotage' in connection with the LMSR's non-repair of the Perry Aqueduct breach in 1936. He and many other writers on canal history have been very critical of this and of the promotion of the 1944 Act which closed most of the branch canals to navigation. But are their comments fair?

When the breach on the Montgomeryshire Canal occurred in 1936, the LMSR had the legal duty to repair it if anybody had objected on the grounds of maintaining the right of navigation. However, nobody did object – at least not until a year and a half later. The only trader who could probably have validly objected had been bought off.

By the time the canal breached, trading had virtually ceased. As recently as 1932, 8,992 tons of traffic had brought in tolls of £805, but in 1935 the commercial traffic was down to 974 tons and the tolls to £58.

Railway companies were transport businesses, not environmental or social charities. Their financial turnover was large, but that does not mean they were profitable. The LMSR made losses for much of the 1930s and for several years paid its ordinary shareholders no dividends; indeed in some years it did not even pay all its preference shareholders.

In a business context, it seems unreasonable to expect railway companies to invest in their canals when they could see no likely prospect of any return on their investment, let alone an adequate return. We regret it when businesses close loss-making factories, but we don't object to the principle. Nobody now criticises canal companies for having closed their tramroads when they ceased to feed enough traffic to their canals to justify their upkeep. In my opinion it is unreasonable to criticise railway companies for not predicting that 50 years later, canals would become a major leisure asset – albeit one which requires a large public subsidy.

Ironically, some of the provisions in the 1944 Acts had the unintended consequence of enabling the Llangollen Canal to be saved.

How was the attitude to canals changed?

In the early years following Nationalisation canals were regarded as businesses, albeit generally failing businesses. Management's aim was to minimise the losses. It was not until the 1960s that non-commercial reasons for retaining the canal system came to be generally accepted – and this relied on the agreement of politicians and the public of the need for a large annual contribution from the taxpayers.

Tom Rolt's *Narrow Boat* was published in 1944 and was a Readers Union choice in 1946. It was not the first book to bring canals to the attention of the general public, but it certainly caught a nostalgic post-war mood. As stated in the last chapter, Rolt started writing it (in a former SURCC boat) whilst on the Shropshire Union system, though this does not feature much in it. *Idle Women* by Susan Woolfitt (1947) and *Maidens' Trip* by Emma Smith (1948) were reminiscences of the wartime boatwomen's experiences on the Grand Union and south Midlands canals. *Painted Boats*, a dramatised documentary film of 1945 based on the Grand Union, also created awareness of canals amongst a wider audience. Rolt's *Inland Waterways of England* and Charles Hadfield's *British Canals*, both published in 1950, showed the history of the canals. Both Rolt and Hadfield were founder members of the Inland Waterways Association, and Robert Aickman, its Chairman, proved to be an indefatigable publicist.

But petitions, rallies and local press articles are not sufficient to influence events: decision-makers need to be convinced. People's actions are far more convincing than their words. Actions in this context includes boating holidays, which had started in a small way before the Second World War, expanded in the 1950s and became a significant economic activity in the 1960s. Men such as Geoffrey Wain and the other founders of the Inland Cruising Association showed they were willing to invest in this new holiday venture. Others followed, their enterprises providing all-year maintenance and administrative jobs, and seasonal part-time employment. The growth in boat ownership and the services needed to support this was also significant. Most of the extra jobs created have been in rural areas.

Many villages have benefited from the canal. Audlem, for example, has become a favourite overnight stop for boaters; without the extra trade the village would be unlikely to have its excellent range of shops or three pubs. A popular pastime for boaters and local residents is visiting a canalside pub, of which there are more than 25 (in 2018) in the Shropshire Union area. It is unlikely that every one of the pubs at Shebdon, Norbury Junction, Cheswardine Wharf, Welsh Frankton or Hindford, for example, would survive if the canal were not active.

Chapter 14: The Second Canal Age

Thus I would contend that it was the proved economic benefits of canals which was the crucial factor in changing the views of the decision-makers from the late 1950s onwards. By the end of the century the perception of the environmental and social benefits had also become important.

An early but untypical example of reinvigoration of a legally lost canal was the Llangollen Canal, discussed in detail in the last chapter. In this case the actions of one waterways manager, Christopher Marsh, were crucial.

More typical is the story of the slow restoration of the Montgomery Canal which started in 1969 and by 2018 had reintroduced boating into just over half of the route. Here the process was started by volunteers working on site and evidence of popularity provided by the success of the Shropshire Union Canal Society's trip boat and the establishment of the Heulwen Trust providing services to disabled young people. The argument was progressed effectively by the pioneering commissioning of cost-benefit analyses demonstrating the wider economic benefits to the community.

What are the lessons from the restoration schemes?

Two sorts of people have been involved in the restoration movement: those whose skill is to lobby and persuade, and those who carry out work, increasingly to a high standard. The former are usually motivated by a strong interest in 'heritage' and the countryside, and are often boaters; the latter enjoy the physical activity, achievement and comradeship of the work, and are not necessarily so interested in the long-term benefits of what they have created. Both are needed for success.

Local support

The first stage for promoting any restoration scheme is to create public awareness. Publicity can come through talks to local societies, exhibitions and social media. Volunteers carrying out basic work such as scrub clearance can make good copy for local newspapers, which are always seeking pictorial news. The next stage is usually the formation of a supporters' organisation.

The deeper the local support, the more likely the campaign is to be effective and the more easily potential local opposition – often based on the fear of change – can be overcome. Schools and colleges can be invaluable supporters, as can be local businesses.

With the support of the local councillors, preservation of the line of the canal can be incorporated in the formal planning process. This is an essential preliminary stage in order to prevent new development from impeding restoration.

The local authority may be persuaded to give more active support, as when Telford & Wrekin Council bought Wappenshall Wharf and leased it to the Shrewsbury & Newport Canals Trust. Although local authorities finances are now more constrained, their support is still important. Shropshire and Powys Councils are members of the Montgomery Canal Restoration Trust, which has no doubt helped with funding applications.

The line of the canal

The experience in the Shropshire Union area shows that more than enthusiasm and local support is required. Firstly, it is a great help if the land has not been sold, which is one reason why the Montgomery Canal restoration has been more successful than the Shrewsbury & Newport. Land assembly in the absence of compulsory purchase powers is difficult and slow. Furthermore, if the land has been sold, many of the owners may be actively opposed to restoration as they may see change as being directly detrimental to their interests, making it impossible to show general support amongst the local community.

In hindsight, it is a pity that the local authorities did not make the former towpath of the Newport Branch and the Shrewsbury Canal into a public footpath or bridleway. That would at least have kept the line of the canal as a leisure route.

The environmental impact

Secondly, the environmental stewards – the county wildlife societies and their active supporters – must be convinced that the restoration package will not damage the wildlife. Best is if they can be recruited into the restoration movement, as has been achieved for the Montgomery Canal, where they are members of the Montgomery Waterway Restoration Trust.

In 2009 John Eaton of Liverpool University produced a report for the Trust which increased the understanding of the effect of boat movements on channel-growing plants. The report showed that a key factor is the ratio of the boat displacement to the channel size. Preferably the boat's draught should not be more than 70% of the depth of the channel. Damage is also proportional to the cube of the power put in, hence the need for a speed limit. Actually the return flow (the rush of water past the boat) is more important than the propeller jet when the boat is moving at a constant speed; the propeller jet is more important when starting. A second major issue is the composition of the bed of the canal, the ideal option being a mixture of small stones (for cohesion of the roots) plus silt infill (for penetrability). The report also emphasised the importance of light for plants. Shade reduces light by some 80–90%, so it is essential to control tree growth. Light is also lost through turbidity caused by propeller action.

Hence restoration schemes must now incorporate nature reserves and other mitigation measures. Experience of, for example, the reserves in the Prees and Guilsfield Branches, has shown that these need to be actively managed if they are to retain the special characteristics of most significance to the naturalists.

However, with the exception perhaps of the reserves by the Aston locks, these nature reserves are neither particularly attractive nor interesting for the general public, to whom 'nature' tends to mean birds such as ducks, swans, herons and kingfishers and the more obvious wild flowers. Better interpretation is needed, as is done for Fens Moss, adjacent to the Llangollen Canal.

The environment of course is a wider concept than just wildlife and plants. Benefits from canal restoration which can be stressed include landscape – water unless polluted is invariably attractive – and the built heritage, as canals usually have century-old engineering structures and buildings constructed with vernacular materials.

Finance

THIRDLY, and crucially, money is needed. The scale of some of the engineering works, such as those involving major road crossings, is far beyond what volunteers can achieve, necessitating the employment of contractors.

The canal restoration movement has been particularly successful in making use of government initiatives such as derelict land grants and job creation schemes in the 1970s and 1980s, and regional development funds and local authority finance in the later years of the 20th century.

Lottery funding made possible the major canal restorations leading up to the millennium – the Huddersfield Narrow and Rochdale Canals and the Falkirk Wheel – and, on a smaller scale, it has continued to be the principal source of finance. However, other than for small grants, the Heritage Lottery Fund requires the applicant organisation to make a contribution towards the project. This 'partnership funding' can be made up of cash, volunteer time, non-cash contributions, or a combination of all of these, but some must be from the organisation's own resources. This requirement for 'matched funding' can be a major problem – it is the reason why the Wappenshall project did not go ahead in 2017, despite gaining lottery funding approval.

For smaller schemes grants can often be obtained from the various environmental trusts administering the Landfill Communities Fund. Successful bids have also been made to national charities such as the Esmée Fairbairn Foundation and to more locally-focussed charities.

Since the economic crisis of 2008 and the change of government in 2010, local authorities' finances have been so severely squeezed that there is little money available for services which are not statutory obligations. As a result, local authority financial contributions to canal projects have virtually ceased.

Cost-benefit analysis

POTENTIAL funders need to be convinced of the wider benefits from restoration, which has had the merit of forcing enthusiasts to realise that restoration is not an end in itself – it has to produce demonstrable economic and social benefits.

Canals clearly generate tourism income, but they also enhance commercial development which provide further local employment. This may prove to be a key factor in the eventual redevelopment of the derelict industrial area alongside the route of the former Plas Kynaston Canal. It is noticeable that the factors taken into account in cost-benefit analyses have changed over time: in 1983 the Atkins report on the Montgomery Canal assumed that 55% of the additional benefit would come as a result of private and hire boats, whereas the 2004 Rural Solutions report attributed just over 2% to this source. A further financial effect is that a canalside location increases the value of houses; surprisingly little advantage has been made of this in the 'Shropshire Union' area.

Social benefits can include improvements to health, education and training, and involvement of disadvantaged groups or minorities. The case made for canal restoration now inevitably involves informal recreation such as towpath walking. The benefits can be enhanced by upgrading the towpaths for cycling, as has happened on the Welsh section of the Montgomery Canal. More organised leisure activities include canoeing, one of the particular successes on the Montgomery Canal being Shropshire PaddleSport at Queen's Head, which also provides facilities for disabled persons. Education is an important element in the planned restoration of warehouses at Wappenshall.

The present (2018) and the future

ALTHOUGH this book has concentrated on the history of the Shropshire Union system, I cannot resist making some personal observations as a boater and a local resident. I hope I have not been too pessimistic about some of the restoration proposals – all forecasts are fallible!

The Shropshire Union Main Line

BOTH the Main Line south of Barbridge and the Middlewich Branch are popular cruising routes, being part of the 'Four Counties Ring' (completed by the Trent & Mersey Canal through Harecastle Tunnel and the Staffordshire & Worcestershire Canal). The northern section of the Main Line is less popular, with relatively few boaters travelling north of Christleton, despite the attraction of the National Waterways Museum at its terminus.

Chester, though very much a tourist town, has not benefited greatly from the growth in leisure-boat holidays in the last fifty years; indeed it has unjustifiably acquired a reputation for being unwelcoming to boaters. Nor is the canal within the city picturesque enough to attract many of the vast numbers of people visiting the shops and cathedral within the old walls. Apart from the restaurant boat on the canal, most visitors' water-related experiences concern the Dee and its trip boats. The Chester Canal Heritage Trust is working to address these issues.

Access to the river from the Dee Branch has not been possible since 2005 because of silting in the basin and problems with the tail of the river lock. Currently this is the only canal in the country categorised as a cruising waterway which is not usable. The benefits of reopening the lock would be considerably enhanced if another project being promoted by the Chester Canal Heritage Trust came about: building a lock adjacent to the Dee weir on the Handbridge (south) side of the river. This would enable inland craft to access more than a dozen miles of the river.

The National Waterways Museum has an unrivalled collection of inland and estuarial craft and superb historic buildings, but visitor numbers are down to about 30,000 a year from a peak of about 150,000. Ellesmere Port is not an obvious tourist destination, whereas nearby Liverpool has several free museums and art galleries. It is a pity that the government has never accepted that this should be regarded as a museum of national

Chapter 14 : The Second Canal Age

The Inland Waterways Association held its 2008 National Campaign Rally on the Montgomery Canal to encourage local people to support restoration by showing them what a lively and colourful place the canal could be. On display at Welshpool are (from left to right) *Dorabella* (the author's boat), *Snowgoose* (powered by electricity) and *Vulcan* (steam). *Author*

importance, unlike the National Railway Museum at York, the RAF Museum at Cosford and more than a half a dozen museums in London – because so much is free, the public now tends to be reluctant to pay for entry to museums.

With many of the wooden craft requiring extensive preservation works, some for the second time, it needs a change in policy so that more of the boats are kept out of the water and under cover, not necessarily within the historic site. This implies a major one-off cost and would not itself attract more visitors. Perhaps one answer lies in getting a boat restoration firm working within the site, with conditions being that the public must be able to see easily what is being done and that there has to be significant activity at weekends. People enjoy watching others working.

Another project being discussed which would increase the use of the northern section of the Main Line would be an agreement with Peel Holdings, owners of the Manchester Ship Canal, for the creation of a 'ring' making use of the Ship Canal, the river Weaver, Anderton Lift, and the Trent & Mersey and Shropshire Union Canals. The principal engineering requirement would be the reopening of Frodsham Lock. I hope that Peel Holdings' justifiable concerns about safety can be overcome, as this would be a superb leisure boating route.

The Llangollen Canal

THE main line of the Llangollen Canal is now amongst the busiest in the country, with New Marton Locks, the most westerly on the canal, having some 11,000 boat movements a year. (A boat going up the lock and later returning down it counts as two boat movements.) During high summer there can sometimes be long delays at New Marton Locks, at the four locks at the entrance to the canal at Hurleston, and at Grindley Brook, where there are three conventional locks plus a 'staircase' of three more, a location supervised by the lock-keeper who normally works the flight on the basis of 'three boats up, then three down'. The Fraenkel Report of 1974–7 actually recommended duplicating these locks.

The canal between Trevor and Llangollen contains two long sections where two boats going in opposite directions cannot pass each other and each end is not visible from the other. Boaters are advised to send one member of their crew ahead to check that the way is clear – this is made easier by using mobile phones – but obviously single-handed boaters cannot do that. Queues can build up at these narrows and also at Pontcysyllte Aqueduct where a succession of boats crossing slowly from one end can mean a long wait for anyone coming the other way.

This canal has the highest proportion of hire boats compared with private boats. Because 'change-over day' is still generally at a weekend there tends to be a movement of boats towards Llangollen in the first half of the week, returning in the second half of the week. This put great pressure on the limited moorings at Llangollen at mid-week, especially on Tuesday evenings, which led British Waterways to create a large new mooring basin in 2003 and to introduce overnight mooring charges – the only place this is done on the whole of the CRT's system.

There are currently marinas at Swanley, Whixall, Ellesmere and Chirk and hire bases at these locations and at Whitchurch, Welsh Frankton and Trevor. Further marinas have been approved at Ellesmere and Wrenbury. Whether the canal can cope with much extra demand without seriously injuring the pleasure of boating holidays is questionable.

Although a popular choice for inexperienced boaters, it is not generally realised that this is actually one of the most difficult canals to navigate because, unlike most other canals, it has perceptibly flowing water. This makes steering 'downstream' more difficult and causes awkward flows below locks which tend to push the boat sideways. Progress 'upstream' is impeded through the tunnels. A minor benefit from the flowing water is that this canal is less likely to freeze during the winter, making it ideal for Christmas cruising.

The planned extension of the canal branch at Whitchurch to a new basin for visitor moorings would certainly bring economic benefits to the town, which currently tends to be by-passed by boaters, but it is difficult to be optimistic about the necessary funds being found.

The quarter-mile-long Ellesmere Arm is a popular place for mooring overnight and this helps the town's economy. The adjacent land on the western side already has planning permission for housing. The scheme which so far has only received outline permission showed building coming right up to the towpath. My fear is that residents who purchase there may well object to boats mooring outside their front doors on environmental and 'nuisance' grounds, eventually leading to mooring being banned.

On the eastern side of this arm is the former Shropshire Union warehouse which has been derelict for a couple of decades and is now in a sorry state. Planning permission was given several years ago for conversion into a restaurant. This is the most significant canalside building at risk in the former Shropshire Union system.

Ellesmere Depot is certainly the finest historic canal maintenance depot in the country, and perhaps the most complete early 19th-century workshop of any sort. This is planned to be developed as a tourism asset but it is to be hoped that it does not lose its 'working' atmosphere.

The first boat-hire firm on the Llangollen Canal started at Trevor in 1953; its successor's fleet, which includes several day boats, now tends to dominate the entrance to the basin. A restaurant boat works from the other end of the basin, providing trips over Pontcysyllte Aqueduct. The aqueduct is now an international tourist attraction, with over 300,000 visitors a year, though not yet providing a commensurate local 'spend'.

Slow progress is being made with improving the visitor experience in the area of the World Heritage Site. The towpaths have been resurfaced, though there are now some problems with speeding bikers between Trevor and Llangollen. Art works have been installed. The small visitor centre by Pontcysyllte Aqueduct has been extended; a more ambitious scheme for a visitor centre looks increasing unlikely in view of the pressures on local government finance. The first section of the former Plas Kynaston Canal could possibly be reopened and the hire boats relocated there, which would considerably open up Trevor Basin for public use. The further reinstatement of the Plas Kynaston Canal would be an ideal focus for the redevelopment of the vacant (but heavily polluted) Monsanto site. However, it is important that the doubts of local residents are allayed: some have seen the increase in visitor numbers as merely increasing the pressures on local facilities such as parking, without any real benefits coming to the local community.

At Llangollen it would be desirable to make visitors more aware of the canal, which suffers from not being visible to people in the town (unlike the heritage steam railway) and from being up a steep hill on the far side of the river.

The Montgomery Canal

REGRETTABLY, the restoration of the Montgomery Canal has had little economic impact so far. Only one directly canal-related business has been established, 'Canal Central' at Maesbury Marsh, though the inns at Queen's Head and Maesbury Marsh have no doubt seen more trade. The major success has been Shropshire PaddleSport, the canoe and kayak club at Queen's Head, which is thriving.

The English section, the seven miles from Frankton Junction to Gronwen, currently has about 1,100 boat movements a year, well short of the current authorised maximum of 2,500 movements, and a number which has been decreasing steadily since the Conservation Management Strategy was approved in 2005. The numbers are rationed by the very limited hours that boats may pass through Frankton Locks. The next mile is being restored, and there is every hope that the further three miles to Llanymynech will be restored within the next five years, thanks partly to a £70,000 legacy from Tony Harrison, formerly the IWA's Honorary Engineer. When the 2016 programme of works is completed, it is hoped that the maximum number of boat movements can be increased to 5,000, which could enable a small marina to be built at Queen's Head.

The five miles between Llanymynech and Ardleen include two lowered bridges on the main A483 and Williams Bridge (on the B4398 near the Vyrnwy Aqueduct) which was lowered as recently as 1980. The Aqueduct is in poor condition, needing repairs estimated to cost at least £1½ million. However, the biggest problem to restoration is that this section has the greatest nature interest, including the most prolific growth of *Luronium natans* in Western Europe.

Chapter 14 : The Second Canal Age

The current state of the eleven miles which have been restored to navigation in Wales is disappointing. The first hire boat, *Clifton*, had been craned in during 1992; the Welshpool-based fleet later grew to three boats, but they were removed in about 2003. *Maldwyn*, a restaurant boat also based at Welshpool, operated from the mid 1990s to 2005. The horse-drawn holiday boat *Sian* lasted only a few seasons to 2009. Few private boats are based on the canal. The one success story is the Heulwen Trust, with its second boat being launched in 1993.

In 2013 there were only about 100 boat movements through Pool Quay Locks and well under half this number through Belan Locks, though the number of movements has subsequently slightly increased thanks to the *Heulwen* boats. Boat movements help keep down weeds and also help to keep the channel clear. Despite the Canal & River Trust's efforts, the canal is deteriorating. Even the museum in the warehouse has changed its emphasis from the canal to Welshpool generally.

Prospects seem bleak for the section south of Refail. There are three lowered bridges on the A483. The approach to Newtown would be particularly difficult to reinstate. And, with boat movements limited to 1,000 a year in Wales – in practice the number of movements would be considerably lower, the further south one gets – it would be difficult to make a good economic case for restoration.

How can more boats be attracted to the isolated section? CRT offers a mere 25% discount for boats which remain exclusively on it – this should be a much larger discount to reflect the severely limited cruising range, indeed the CRT would lose little financially by offering (say) a five-year licence-free period, and the extra boat movements would help keep the unwanted vegetation down and the channel clear.

The second need is day boats for hire, and preferably a couple of 'short break' hire boats too. Realistically, there isn't currently enough potential for this to be a business in itself, but it could be a side-line for another business, a pub or a garage, for example. CRT must not kill enterprise by demanding excessive hire and mooring charges – it needs to look at the Welshpool section of the Montgomery as something special, and not as an errant part of the main network. And how about all these hire boats being electric, which is so much better for appreciating the wildlife? They could then be marketed through nature magazines in addition to the usual places. Electric day boats are used on the Broads, carrying enough charge for eight hours cruising. This would need electric points being put in at Welshpool and in at least two (preferably four) other places, but this is the sort of initiative which would be likely to attract funding.

Thirdly, but crucially, the canal needs enthusiastic management, seeking opportunities (and not merely for funding), encouraging businesses and organising activities for locals and visitors, punctuated with regular special events such as steamboat or electric-boat rallies. Volunteers can do a lot – indeed, they already do a lot – but they are rarely a real substitute for somebody full-time committed to making a success of this marvellous community asset.

The Shrewsbury & Newport Canal

The Shrewsbury & Newport Canal has the biggest membership of the restoration schemes in the former Shropshire Union area, but also has the largest task. Unlike the Montgomery Canal, where the land is still owned by the CRT, most of the line of the Shrewsbury & Newport Canal would have to be repurchased.

Despite the failure to get matched funding for the full proposals for the Wappenshall Wharf area, no doubt a more limited scheme for the buildings will be developed and be implemented. This will absorb much of the energies of the Trust for a few years, but it should also provide encouragement for further piecemeal restoration.

Reopening the four miles from Norbury Junction to Newport, the key to long-term restoration, seems less assured as it will be difficult to demonstrate the social and economic benefits needed in order to get lottery and other grant funding. It would also almost certainly be necessary to obtain an Order under the Transport & Works Act 1992. The Canal & River Trust is concerned about the adequacy of water supply were the locks down from Norbury to be restored, though its attitude seems more positive than it was a few years ago. The actual engineering to reopen this section is relatively easy apart from the crossing of the A41.

Reconstruction of the next six miles from Newport to Wappenshall Junction would be relatively straight-forward, as indeed would the following two miles to Long Lane. After that, however, the practical and engineering issues of the final twelve miles are so large as to make success doubtful: crossing the A422 at Long Lane and the A49 Shrewsbury Bypass; crossing the Tern Valley in a way which leaves Longdon Aqueduct untouched; a whole new line in a cutting parallel with the A5 and the railway, thus avoiding the loop through Berwick Tunnel (unless some cheaper alternative can be found); and a whole set of issues about what to do where the canal enters Shrewsbury.

It is to be hoped that success at Wappenshall Wharf will encourage success elsewhere on the canal.

The Canal & River Trust

CRT's charitable objects are wide and cover all inland waterways in England and Wales, and also embrace canal restoration. However, in practice it concentrates on the canals and rivers of the former British Waterways.

Whereas British Transport Waterways had regarded its prime purpose as commercial carrying, the British Waterways Board initially concentrated on the leisure users of the water, especially boaters and anglers. In the 21st century BW began to pay much more regard to the users of its towpaths. For its first six years the Canal & River Trust developed those policies. Of particular local importance, it greatly increased local involvement and volunteer support. Several sections of the Shropshire Union canals have been adopted by community groups – the Tyrley Locks area by the local prison – assisting in lock-painting, hedge-laying and other improvements. Volunteers assist CRT

The former 'Ladyline' site at Market Drayton is the best example on the former Shropshire Union system of housing taking full advantage of a waterside site. *Author*

employees at Grindley Brook, Hurleston and Audlem Locks and staff 'welcome points' at Trevor and Norbury. In 2018 CRT started actively promoting itself as a 'wellbeing provider', that is, helping to make people healthier and happier. Walkers and cyclists have long been numerically the biggest users of the canals – now CRT seems to regard them as its main customers.

Some final thoughts

A recurring theme has been how what has happened often differed greatly from that which was planned or was expected.

The first investors in the Chester Canal had to wait over forty years before a dividend was paid. The Ellesmere Canal was intended to run north–south, but when it eventually fully opened its main line ran east–west. The Birmingham & Liverpool Junction Canal was promoted in response to the threat of a railway being built, and due to delays in construction opened only two years before Britain's first trunk railway, which was in direct competition; it also cost 50% more than intended.

The London & Birmingham Railway negotiated to lease the Shropshire Union system principally as a way of creating a line to the north and to Ireland independent of the Grand Junction Railway, but then the two railway companies merged. In the medium and long term the canal was a financial burden on them, rather than being an asset. Nevertheless, this railway-controlled company eventually came to have the biggest fleet of canal boats in Britain.

The 1944 Act formally closed all the branches to boating, yet, more than fifty years later, what is now called the Llangollen Canal had been transformed into the most popular leisure canal in the country.

And, when one thinks about the Montgomery Canal, the optimist would think how marvellous it is that half of this long-derelict canal has reopened, whereas the pessimist would say how slow the progress has been since the 'Big Dig' of 1969.

The canals have never been as popular as now, judging from the number of televisions programmes, all enthusiastic and positive, which have been broadcast in recent years. The future of canals seems assured, and in the Canal & River Trust, the Inland Waterways Association and the various local canal societies they have worthy champions. No doubt the future will also hold surprises – let us hope they are mainly pleasant ones.

Notes and references

1. Great Western Railway, Traffics dealt with at stations and goods depots: TNA: RAIL266/43 & RAIL266/53

Timothy West, the author and a duck wait for Prunella Scales during the filming of an episode of 'Great Canal Journeys'. *Quita Brown*

Appendices

Appendix A

Shropshire Union Canal : mileage and locks

		m f	m f	locks
Chester	Nantwich – Chester		19 0	14
Ellesmere	Chester – Ellesmere Port	8 5		3
	Dee Branch	0 1		3
	Hurleston J – Frankton J	29 0		1
	Whitchurch Branch	1 0		0
	Prees Branch	3 6		0
	Ellesmere Branch	0 2		0
	Frankton J – Carreghofa	11 4		7
	Frankton J – Llantisilio	17 0		2
	Weston Branch	6 0	77 2	0
Ellesmere & Chester	Middlewich Branch		10 0	3
Mongomeryshire (Eastern)	Carreghofa – Garthmyl	16 2		13
	Guilsfield Branch	2 2	18 4	0
Montgomeryshire (Western)	Garthmyl – Newtown		7 3	6
Birmingham & Liverpool J	Nantwich – Autherley J	38 7		29
	Norbury J – Wappenshall J	10 4		23
	Humber Branch	0 6	50 1	0
Shrewsbury	Wappenshall J – Shrewsbury	14 4		2
	Wappenshall J – Wrockwardine Wood	3 6	18 2	9
			200 4	133

Notes
1. Distances stated in miles and furlongs.
2. Source: *Bradshaw's Canals and Navigable Rivers*, 1904.
3. Excludes the Shropshire Canal, which was leased to the Shropshire Union from 1849 to 1858.
4. In addition to 11 locks, the Shrewsbury Canal had an inclined plane raising boats 75ft.
5. When the Montgomery Canal was restored, an additional lock was added to what was originally the section of the Ellesmere Canal between Frankton Junction and Carreghofa.

Appendix B

Montgomery Canal : progress of restoration (to 2018)

Frankton Locks	opened 1987; into use 1995
Graham Palmer Lock – Queen's Head	opened 1996
Queen's Head – Gronwen	locks restored and reserve created 1998; opened 2003
Gronwen – Crickheath	part re-watered; being restored
Crickheath – Llanymynech	dry; one lowered bridge
Llanymynech	short section restored and used by trip boat
Llanymynech – Carreghofa	in water but not usable; one lowered bridge
Carreghofa – Arddleen	in water but not usable; locks restored 1986; three lowered bridges
Arddleen – Burgedin	locks opened 1998
Burgedin – Gallowstree Bridge ('The Prince of Wales Length')	opened 1976
Gallowstree Bridge	opened 1992
Gallowstree Bridge – Whitehouse Bridge	Town Lock opened 1974
Whitehouse Bridge	opened 1995
Whitehouse Bridge – Refail	opened 1996
Refail – below Freestone Lock	in water but not usable; both locks restored; five lowered bridges
Freestone Lock – Newtown	dry; line of canal not owned by CRT

Note
The sections shown as 'not usable' may be used by portable boats such as canoes.

Appendix C

Shropshire Union Canal : chronology

1768	Nov.25	Meeting called to promote an Act for a canal to Chester
1772	April 1	Chester Canal Act: Chester to Middlewich and Nantwich
1776	*July 4*	*American Declaration of Independence*
1779	April 2	Chester Canal: decision not to build to Middlewich
1779	Nov.	Chester Canal: opened to Nantwich
1787		Wombridge Canal constructed
1787	Nov.	Chester Canal: collapse of Beeston Brook Lock
1791	June 28	Meeting at Overton to promote a canal between Shrewsbury, Chester and the Mersey
1793	*Feb.1*	*War with France declared*
1793	April 30	Ellesmere Canal Act
1793	June 3	Shrewsbury Canal Act
1794	March 28	Montgomeryshire Canal Act
1795	Feb.10–12	Floods – Longdon-on-Tern Aqueduct damaged
1795	Oct.	Chester Canal: financial reconstruction
1797	March (?)	Shrewsbury Canal: opened
1797	summer	Montgomeryshire Canal: opened to Garthmyl
1797	summer/ autumn	Ellesmere Canal: Wirral Branch linked to Chester Canal
1805	*Oct. 21*	*Battle of Trafalgar*
1805	Nov.26	Ellesmere Canal: Pontcysyllte Aqueduct and Grindley Brook to Hurleston Junction link opened
1808		Ellesmere Canal: 'Water Line' from river Dee to Pontcysyllte opened
1813	July 1	Ellesmere and Chester Canals: merger
1815	*June 18*	*Battle of Waterloo*
1815	June 22	Montgomeryshire Canal Act – extension to Newtown
1819	March	Montgomeryshire Canal: Garthmyl to Newtown opened, though water supply restricted use until 1821
1826	May 26	Birmingham & Liverpool Junction Canal Act – main line
1827	March 21	Birmingham & Liverpool Junction Canal Act – Newport Branch
1827	June 21	Ellesmere & Chester Canal Act – Middlewich Branch
1832	*June 7*	*Great Reform Act*
1833	Sept.1	Ellesmere & Chester Canal: Middlewich Branch opened
1835	March 2	Birmingham & Liverpool Junction Canal: full opening
1837	*June 20*	*Accession of Queen Victoria*
1843	Sept.	Formal opening of the new works at Ellesmere Docks
1845	May 8	Act authorising merger of E&C and B&LJ Canals
1846	Aug.3	Acts changing name to SURCC and authorising conversion of much of the canal system to railways; Shrewsbury Canal sold to SURCC
1846	Dec.4	SURCC Extraordinary General Meeting approved terms of lease to LNWR
1847	Jan.1	Montgomeryshire Canal (Eastern Branch) sold to SURCC
1849	June 1	Opening of Shropshire Union Railway
1849	July 1	Lease of SURCC to LNWR came into effect
1849	Nov.1	Shropshire Canal leased by SURCC
1850	Feb.5	Montgomeryshire Canal (Western Branch) bought by SURCC
1851	*May–Oct.*	*The Great Exhibition (Crystal Palace)*
1858	Feb.	Shropshire Canal sold to LNWR
1863	Jan.1	LNWR took over operation of the Shropshire Union Railway
1863	April 24	Richard Moon appointed to Executive Committee
1867	spring	Reopening of the Pontcysyllte Railway after conversion
1879	March	LNWR took over secretarial and financial functions
1891	May 7	Death of Third Earl of Powis (the last connection with the 'old' SU)
1896	Feb.12	Sale of Pontcysyllte Railway to the Great Western Railway
1914	*Aug.4*	*Start of First World War*
1917	May 5	Breach at Dandyford truncated the Weston Branch
1918	*Nov.11*	*End of First World War*
1921	Aug.31	Last day of carrying by SURCC; last use of Trench Incline
1922	Jan.1	LNWR absorbed SURCC
1922	April 1	Lease of Ellesmere Port Docks to Manchester Ship Canal
1922	Dec.29	Railway Amalgamation Tribunal approved transfer to LNWR
1923	Jan.1	Creation of LMSR
1933		Last commercial traffic from Shrewsbury
1936	Feb.5	Breach at the Perry Aqueduct closed the branch to Newtown
1939		Last commercial traffic on 'Welsh Branch'
1939	*Sept.3*	*Start of Second World War*
1944	Dec.	LMSR and LMSR (Canals) Acts formally closed much of SU canals
1948	Jan.1	Nationalisation; creation of the British Transport Commission
1952	June 18–21	IWA rally at Llangollen
1963	April 1	Creation of the British Waterways Board
1965		Norbury Junction to Uffington de-watered
1966	Nov.9	Formation of the Shropshire Union Canal Society
1988	July 29	Act permitting use for navigation of canals closed by 1944 Act
2009	June 29	Pontcysyllte Aqueduct & Canal designated a World Heritage Site
2012	July 2	Creation of the Canal & River Trust

The Shropshire Union Canal

Appendix D

Dividends

Year	Shrewsbury	Montgomeryshire (Eastern Branch)	Ellesmere & Chester	Year	Shrewsbury	Montgomeryshire (Eastern Branch)	Ellesmere & Chester
1798	£2.10s	—		1823	£10	£2.10s	£3
1799	£2.10s	—		1824	£10	£2.10s	£3.10s
1800	£2.10s	—		1825	£10	£2.10s	£3.15s
1801	£3. 3s	—		1826	£10	£2.10s	£3.15s
1802	£3.10s	—		1827	£11	£4	£3.15s
1803	£8	—		1828	£11	£4	£3.15s
1804	£4	—		1829	£11	£4	£3.15s
1805	£4	£2.10s		1830	£11	£4	£3.15s
1806	—	£2.10s		1831	£11	£4	£3.15s
1807	£4	—		1832	£11	£4	£3.15s
1808	£4	£5		1833	£10	£4	£3.15s
1809	£4	£4		1834	£9	£4.10s	—
1810	£4	£4		1835	£9.10s	£4.10s	—
1811	£4	£4		1836	£16	£4.10s	£3
1812	£4	£5		1837	£15	£4.10s	£4
1813	£4	£5.10s	—	1838	£14	£4.10s	£4
1814	£4	£5.10s	£2	1839	£16	£5	£4
1815	£4	£4.10s	£4	1840	£15	£5	£4
1816	£4.10s	£3	£3	1841	£13	£5	£4
1817	£8	£3	£2	1842	£12	£5	£4
1818	£8	£4	£2	1843	£10	£5	£4
1819	£1.10s	—	£4	1844	£10	£5	£4
1820	£4.10s	—	£3	1845	£10	£5	£4
1821	£9	£2.10s	£3	1846	£10	£5	£4
1822	£5	£2.10s	£3				

Notes

1. The total investment per share was: Shrewsbury £125; Montgomery (Eastern Branch) £100; Ellesmere & Chester £133 (former Ellesmere Canal investors). Thus, for example, a Shrewsbury Canal dividend of £2.10s represented a 2% return on the original investment.
2. The Chester Canal, Ellesmere Canal and Montgomeryshire Canal (Western Branch) never paid a dividend. The first two merged in 1813, and dividends started to be paid in the following year.
3. From 1842 the Shrewsbury Canal and the Ellesmere & Chester Canal paid their dividends 'clear of income tax'. In that year income tax had been reintroduced at the rate of 7d in the pound on all annual incomes greater than £150. In other words, the true dividend was slightly higher than the figures shown.
4. After the lease to the LNWR, the dividend was half that paid to holders of LNWR Ordinary Shares.

Appendix E
Senior Officers

Birmingham & Liverpool Junction Canal

Collector of the Rates, Tolls and Dues Equivalent to General Agent
1835–1845   Robert Skey
Engineer
1835–1845   Alexander Easton

Chester Canal

Clerk
1772–1773   Philip Norbury
1773–1782   John Moon
1782–1799   Charles Hill   then for several years, nobody appointed
1806–1807   Thomas Broster
1808–1809   Charles Tomlinson
1810–1813   William Cross
Engineer
1772–1774   Samuel Weston
1774–1777   Thomas Morris
1778   Josiah Clowes   After 1778 a committee member undertook the role: Joseph Turner (to 1795) and John Fletcher (thereafter)

Ellesmere Canal

General Agent
1793–1805   Thomas Telford   Continued as Consulting Engineer until 1834
1805–1813   Thomas Stanton   From 1811 included engineering role
Engineer
1795–1803   John Duncombe
1803–1811   Thomas Denson

Ellesmere & Chester Canal

General Agent
1813–1845   Thomas Stanton   Included engineering role
1845–1846   Robert Skey   After merger with B&LJC
Engineer
1845–1846   Alexander Easton   After merger with B&LJC

Montgomeryshire Canal, Eastern Branch

Clerk & Engineer   The title varied over the years
1798–1802   Richard Cross
1802–1819   Joseph Hill
1819–1833   George Buck
1833–1839   James Sword
1839–1847   Edward Johnes

Montgomeryshire Canal, Western Branch

Clerk & Engineer
1819–1832   John Williams
1832–1833   George Buck
1833–1850   T.G. Newnham

Shrewsbury Canal

Agent & General Superintendent
1797–1837   Henry Williams
Engineer & General Superintendent
1837–1846   John Beech
Tonnage Clerk
1837–1846   John Hewitt

Shropshire Canal

Agent
1794–1839   Henry Williams
1839–1850   John Hewitt

Shropshire Union Railways & Canal

General Manager
1846–1863   Robert Skey
1863–1872   Alfred Wragge   included role of Secretary
1912–1921   William Whittam
1921–1922   J. Mathison
Traffic Manager (sometimes referred to as General Traffic Manager)
1872–1879   William Jones   1876–79 also LNWR District Manager
1879–1911   Thomas Hales
Secretary
1846–1850   William Cowan
1853–1863   Alfred Wragge
1872–1879   James Hope   From 1879 Hope continued with reduced duties, retiring in 1911 after more than 60 years' service
1879–1922   The Secretary of the LNWR was also Secretary of the Shropshire Union but was not involved in day-to-day management
Engineer
1846–1851   Alexander Easton   Continued as Consulting Engineer until 1854
1851–1863   John Beech & Edward Johnes
1863–1869   John Beech
1869–1919   George Jebb   Continued as Consulting Engineer after 1919
1919–1922   Harry Jones

Appendix F

The Egerton and Leveson-Gower Families

The two families, which had a complex relationship, played a key role in the development and financing of the canals of Shropshire and Cheshire.

Samuel Egerton (1711–1780) was the great-grandson of John Egerton, the 2nd Earl of Bridgewater. He was an MP for Cheshire from 1754 until his death, his only one reported speech being on the Chester Canal Bill, 22 April 1771. He became master of Tatton Park in 1738 and twenty years later inherited a vast legacy from his uncle, Samuel Hill.

When the Trent & Mersey Canal obtained its Act in 1766, he held fifteen £200 shares, the single biggest shareholding, and in 1772 he lent the money which enabled that canal to be finished; his total commitment was £46,500. He owned five shares in the Chester Canal and in 1775 agreed to underwrite its borrowings to the extent of £20,000, without which the canal could never have been completed to Nantwich.

Francis Egerton, 3rd Duke of Bridgewater and 6th Earl of Bridgewater (1736–1803), was son of Scroope Egerton, the 1st Duke of Bridgewater and 4th Earl of Bridgewater. He was thus a second cousin of Samuel Egerton, who with Francis's mother, was his official guardian during his minority.

Sometimes known as the 'Canal Duke', he personally financed the Bridgewater Canal and was an investor in the Trent & Mersey Canal. These investments, together with incomes from the various estates he inherited, made him extremely wealthy. He died unmarried. He had no son, so the title of Duke died with him.

His will was complex and had implications for the development of what became the Shropshire Union network. As well as assigning his landed estates it created the Bridgewater Trust, comprising the profits on the Bridgewater Canal and the Lancashire coal mines, which were said to total £75,000 a year. However, the management remained with Trustees, not the beneficiary, which caused conflicts of interest. The Trust did not terminate until 1903.

John Egerton, 7th Earl of Bridgewater (1753–1823), the son and grandson of bishops, was a professional soldier who served with distinction throughout the French wars, rising to the ranks of Major-General in 1795 and full General in 1812. He was also MP for Morpeth (1777–1780) and Brackley (1780–1803).

On the death in 1803 of the 'Canal Duke', the Earldom and much of his estate, including the lands at Ellesmere but not the Bridgewater Canal, were inherited by John Egerton. It always rankled with the 7th Earl that he was not a Duke. He devised a will which required that his property go to Lord Brownlow, whose family house was at Belton near Grantham, on condition that Brownlow became at least a Marquess. After a long and expensive law suit the courts decided that the will should stand without the condition.

The Earl's principal residence was Ashridge in Buckinghamshire, which he restored at a cost of some £300,000. However, although non-resident, he obviously took a great interest in Ellesmere. He rapidly built up a holding of 50 shares in the Ellesmere Canal and chaired meetings from 1805. When in 1806 the company needed £15,000 to pay creditors and complete the works, the Earl of Bridgewater gave a temporary loan.

Granville Leveson-Gower, 1st Marquess of Stafford (1721–1803), owned large estates in Staffordshire, Shropshire and Yorkshire. He succeeded his father as Earl Gower in 1754 and was created Marquess of Stafford in 1786 in recognition of his political activities. His second wife, Lady Louisa Egerton, whom he married in 1748, was the sister of the 'Canal Duke'.

His partnership with Thomas and John Gilbert (who were also closely associated with the 'Canal Duke') constructed the Donnington Wood Canal, sometimes referred to as the Marquess of Stafford's Canal. He was a significant investor in the Shropshire and Shrewsbury Canals, but took no part in their management.

George Granville Leveson-Gower, 1st Duke of Sutherland (1758–1833), became the 2nd Marquess of Stafford in 1803 on the death of his father. He was a politician and, from 1800 to 1802, Ambassador to France. His marriage to Elizabeth, Countess of Sutherland in her own right, added a huge area of northern Scotland to his existing estates.

His mother was a sister of the 'Canal Duke'. Because of this connection and their personal friendship, from 1803 he was the beneficiary of the first life interest in the Bridgewater Trust. In the year of his death he was created 1st Duke of Sutherland; at this time he was thought to be the richest man in the country.

Despite his canal interests, he was the largest investor in the Liverpool & Manchester Railway. Nevertheless, it was his backing of the proposals for the Middlewich Branch of the Ellesmere & Chester Canal and for the Birmingham & Liverpool Junction Canal which was probably decisive in enabling those schemes to go ahead.

George Granville Leveson-Gower, 2nd Duke of Sutherland (1786–1861), as Lord Gower, owned Lilleshall Hall and estates in Shropshire even before the death of his father. He inherited his father's extensive personal land-holdings together with the (virtually worthless) shares in the Birmingham & Liverpool Junction Canal. However, he did not inherit the second life interest in the Bridgewater Trust as that had been willed by the 'Canal Duke' to George's younger brother, Francis (who changed his surname to Egerton). Thus his income was considerably lower than his father's but his propensity to spend was not less.

Through his Agent, James Loch, he encouraged the creation of the Shropshire Union.

Appendix G

The Plas Kynaston Canal

The Plas Kynaston Canal was the only significant private canal built off what became the Shropshire Union network.

Between Trevor Basin and Cefn Mawr – appropriately meaning 'big ridge' – is a valley through which runs the Tref-y-nant Brook, which was then the boundary between the large parishes of Llangollen and Ruabon. The land between Trevor Basin and the stream was owned by Rice Thomas of Coed Helen (near Caernarvon). This had come to him as a result of his marriage to Margaret, the daughter of John Lloyd of Trevor Hall. He died in 1814, she in 1826, the Trevor Hall estate being left to six co-heirs.

On the east side of the Tref-y-nant Brook was the Plas Kynaston estate, in 1805 owned by William Owen. He had inherited it from his father of the same name, who had been one of the original promoters of the Ellesmere Canal. However, his father had been a reckless spender and gambler, leaving huge debts which his son endeavoured to pay off. The estate was advertised for sale in 1813 but two days before the auction was due to take place it was withdrawn and at least a large part of it was sold by private treaty to Sir Watkin Williams Wynn, the owner of the nearby Wynnstay estate.

The Plas Kynaston estate was a rich source of minerals, particularly coal and ironstone, and a location for several small mines and the Plas Kynaston Foundry, owned by William Hazledine, which provided ironwork for Pontcysyllte Aqueduct, the Conway and Menai suspension bridges, Waterloo Bridge at Betws-y-coed and lock gates on the Caledonian Canal, amongst other places.

The Pickering family

The Pickering family were entrepreneurs based in Cefn Mawr. There were three men with the name Exuperius Pickering – father, son and grandson – and one cannot always tell who was responsible for any particular project.

Exuperius Pickering senior (c.1760–1838) usually described himself as a 'coal master', leasing various mines over the years; for example, in 1802, together with two other men, he leased 'all mines of coal and ironstone under commons called Cefn Mawr, Cefn Bychan and Rhosymedre in Ruabon' for 21 years. It was he who with Edward Rowland patented the flotation canal lift which was trialed in 1796 in the Ruabon area.

Exuperius Pickering junior (c.1785–1835) became a partner in the lease of Oernant slate quarry in the Horseshoe Pass about 4½ miles north-west of Llangollen in 1807. He acted as agent for Sir Watkin Williams Wynn with regard to his coal and other interests in the Ruabon area, at least from 1819 until 1829. He seems to have had a wider range of industrial interests than his father. For example, in 1823 he was given permission to erect a blast furnace on land at Trevor on the south side of the feeder canal between the first bridge and where the footbridge is now, on what may have been the site of the construction yard for the aqueduct; he probably did not actually smelt iron there but certainly built a rolling mill and forge. As is noted later, he also became involved in lime burning.

The Pickerings developed a thriving business supplying coal to as far away as Newtown and Nantwich. One or both was also responsible for the building of the Chain Bridge over the river Dee near the Horseshoe Falls in 1817, which enabled coal to be taken up the valley to Corwen.

Some time in the 1810s, perhaps after the sale to Sir Watkin Williams Wynn, the Pickerings came to be tenants of much of the Plas Kynaston estate, including occupying Plas Kynaston Hall. However, they had left the Hall by 1830, later documents usually having the address of Newbridge Cottage, Ruabon.

After the death of the two elder Pickerings and with the general economic depression, the businesses seem to have run into trouble. Owed some £20,000, the North & South Wales Bank took possession of Cefn Colliery in 1843. The ironworks had been sold by 1838, the lime works probably shortly afterwards.

The facts about the construction of the Plas Kynaston Canal are particularly difficult to establish for certain – it has not been possible to prove exactly who did what and when. The records show what was intended, not necessarily what actually happened, so the following account of the construction of the canal includes several inferences and a little guesswork.

In 1820 the Ellesmere & Chester Canal Company gave Exuperius Pickering junior permission to make a canal from Trevor Basin to the site of his projected new colliery. So far it has not been possible to prove beyond doubt which colliery this was, but the most likely is Cefn Colliery, one of the largest collieries in the area in the middle of the 19th century and which certainly was operated in the 1830s and early 1840s by the Pickering dynasty. It is probable that a map in Canal & River Trust's archives shows Pickering's intentions, and that a double line at right angles to the end of the curve of the canal referred to a proposed tramroad inclined plane.

The principal objection to this suggestion is that Cefn Colliery lay not far from the hairpin bend on the Ruabon Brook Railway; it also lay at virtually the same height as the bend, whereas the canal was some fifty feet lower. Thus the colliery already had reasonable transport facilities. Of course, Pickering may have preferred to tranship the coal at the wharf at Cefn Mawr rather than at Trevor Basin, where several other coal-owners' coal would be needing to be transhipped.

Pickering could use his canal free of tolls, but if others used it instead of the Ruabon Brook Railway, compensation equivalent to the lost revenue would have to be paid to the canal company. This would have been relevant for the Plas Kynaston Foundry which lay close to the intended route of the canal and also near the railway which passed behind the foundry, a little higher up the hill. Thus if the foundry used the canal in preference to the tramroad it would pay more but avoid the necessity for transhipment at Trevor Basin. The canal company reserved the right to buy the canal at cost or at valuation.

The minutes and the surviving archival records do not mention any agreements with the owners of the land on which the canal was to be built: Margaret Thomas of Trevor Hall for the first 400 yards from Trevor Basin, and Sir Watkin Williams Wynn of Wynnstay for the rest.

The 1820 agreement refers to the possibility of a lime works, so

Pickering obviously had it in mind at that time. In fact, the only part of his proposed canal which he seems to have built was about 300 yards to a bank of limekilns on the west (Trevor) side of the Tref-y-nant Brook. This may have been done in 1825 when he leased some limestone quarries at Llanymynech. A directory of 1835 records him as a lime-burner as well as a coal proprietor.

Thomas Edward Ward

THE other leading entrepreneur of the Cefn Mawr area in the first half of the 19th century was T.E. Ward (c.1780–1854), but rather less is known about him. In 1805 he leased the Black Park Colliery, Chirk, from the Chirk Castle estates, and is said to have spent £30,000 on developing the mines; by the middle of the century it had annual sales of 50,000 tons and employed 200 men. In the 1820s he began developing the Plas Kynaston Colliery which lay on the east side of the Cefn Mawr ridge. A later colliery with the same name (active 1865–97) was to the east of Cefn Station on the GWR's Chester–Shrewsbury line; Ward's colliery was probably immediately west of the future position of the railway line.

Like the Pickerings, he used the Ellesmere & Chester Canal to distribute his coal, probably mainly sourced from Black Park Colliery, and like them diversified into ironworks. In the long run his businesses proved more successful. However, he sounds a harsh employer. When interviewed in 1841 by H. Herbert Jones on behalf of the Children's Employment Commission he stated that he was averse to extending education amongst the lower orders as he had never known any good to come from teaching them writing and arithmetic.

In 1825 the canal company agreed that Thomas Ward could extend Pickering's canal 'of a length of 1,700 to 1,800 yards' to his Plas Kynaston Colliery. A map in the Denbighshire Record Office, presumably of Ward's proposal, shows Pickering's canal from the northern end of Trevor Basin going only as far as his limeworks. It also shows a proposed canal, not joining Pickering's canal, but instead starting further south in the basin, duplicating Pickering's canal going north-east before curving round to the south following the contour on the hillside; it then curves round the end of the ridge before continuing north-east, terminating near the Plas Kynaston Colliery. If the proposed canal had joined Pickering's canal in the obvious place, it would have been just short of 1,800 yards long, corresponding with the length mentioned in the minutes. One can only speculate about the reason for the duplication, but the most likely explanation is that Pickering refused to cooperate with his rival.

On 6 August 1829 the General Committee of the Ellesmere & Chester Canal Company decided 'that Mr Lee and Mr Stanton on the part of this Company be authorized to endeavour to effect an arrangement with the representatives of the late Mrs Thomas to enable the Company to complete the Canal between Plas Kynaston Works and the Ellesmere & Chester Canal so as to render application to Parliament in the ensuing session for that purpose unnecessary'. The minute should not be taken as implying that the foundry was now the intended destination of the canal, merely that the route of the first section as far as the foundry was in doubt.

As mentioned earlier, the Trevor Hall estate owned the freehold of the land west of the Tref-y-nant Brook. No doubt they had objected to two canals over their land, when the obvious natural solution was that which Ward had originally proposed: an extension of Pickering's canal. The existence of a statutory deposit map implies that the negotiations were not initially successful, but clearly the matter was settled before it came before Parliament. It is possible that the canal company entered into a lease of the land between Pickering's canal and the Tref-y-nant Brook as a later map has an annotation stating that in 1832 the company agreed not to erect any lime kiln or wharf by this section of canal without consent. However, in 1838 the tithe assessment shows Ward as being the occupier.

Thus it seems that Ward built some 800 yards of the 1,000-yard length of the Plas Kynaston Canal, though he did not continue it for the full distance originally envisaged. The canal was taken from a junction about 200 yards along Pickering's canal, north-east across the Tref-y-nant Brook into the Plas Kynaston estate lands, then south-east, with a wharf at the bend. It terminated just before a spur off the Cefn Mawr ridge, near where the Queen's Hotel was built a few years later.

The new canal was lock-free, at the 310ft summit level of the Ellesmere & Chester Canal. As construction was relatively simple, it was probably completed in 1830 or shortly afterwards. The maps consulted do not show a winding hole at the end, so the boats were probably pulled backwards to where the canal widened at the bend.

From the 1873 Ordnance Survey map one can infer that a tramroad 1,000 yards long was constructed from the end of the canal, through a short tunnel, and round the end of the ridge to the colliery. This would have been a simpler and cheaper option than taking the canal the full length of the way.

However, there is no hint of the tramroad on the on the statutory deposit maps for railway proposals in 1845 and 1846. Assuming these maps are accurate, and they certainly seem to be in other respects, there are two obvious possibilities. Ward could have built the tramroad but it had been abandoned by 1845; if it had not become used as a footpath, it may not have been considered worth noting by the various surveyors. Then for some reason it was reinstated in later years. Alternatively, it was not made until after 1845.

In 1845 the Shrewsbury–Chester railway was being planned, its route virtually passing through the site of Ward's Plas Kynaston Colliery. Ward died in 1854 but the colliery continued for several years. A new Plas Kynaston colliery was sunk to the east of the GWR line, and was active from 1865 until 1897. For the colliery owners to build an old-fashioned horse-drawn tramroad to a canal after the railway had opened seems illogical, yet in 1873 this tramroad certainly existed and was owned by the colliery company.

Robert Graesser and Monsanto

ROBERT Graesser (1844–1911) established the Plaskynaston Chemical Works in 1867 to extract paraffin oil and wax from shale, a waste product of the local collieries. This provides a possible explanation for the reopening of Ward's tramroad. The old Plas Kynaston Colliery had been one of the largest collieries in the area, so would have been an appropriate source of the raw material. Indeed, the 1873 map shows that the railway did not terminate at the end of the canal but crossed it and went past the pottery to the chemical works. After a few years cheap oil started coming from America, making its production from shale uneconomic. A reference to Graesser's original product survives in the name 'Oilworks Road'.

When the production of oil became uneconomic, Graesser developed processes to distil phenols and cresols from coal-tar acids. The plant was successively expanded, products including dyes and an ingredient for making explosives. Until the 1890s, over half of Britain's phenol production was at Cefn Mawr; after that date the United States and Germany came to dominate the world market, though Graesser's phenol continued to command a premium because of its quality. The early years of the 20th century saw increasing outlets for phenol, notably when Bakelite, the world's first synthetic plastic, was developed in 1907–9.

After the First World War, Monsanto, the American chemical firm, bought a half share in the works. The product range expanded to include saccharin (which ceased after only three months), vanillin and aspirin, and phenol-based synthetic resins were developed. The joint company came to an end in 1928, Monsanto continuing on this site. Expansion continued, and the site was increased by the purchase of the former Plas Kynaston Foundry. At its peak over 2,000 people were employed. Rubber-processing additives were developed in the 1950s; towards the end of the 20th century these became the main products produced. In 1994 the rubber chemicals businesses of Monsanto and Akzo Nobel were combined with the formation of a new company, Flexsys; this later became a subsidiary of Solutia Inc., a divestiture from Monsanto. The factory was progressively closed, the last employment on the site being in 2015.

Operation

RECORDS have not survived concerning the actual usage of the canal. Nevertheless it seems reasonable to suppose that as well as Pickering's and Ward's own operations it was used by the various businesses which were located canalside but never rail-connected. The Plas Kynaston Foundry remained in Hazledine's ownership, possibly until his death in 1840; it continued in operation until the 1930s. Other canalside industries created in the mid-19th century included the Plas Kynaston Pottery, the Sylvester Screw Bolt works and a tube works.

It is now not clear who was actually responsible for the Plas Kynaston Canal: the Wynnstay estate or the managers of the canalside industries. The available evidence seems to show that everybody assumed it was someone else. Boats were not charged for using the canal, and little or no maintenance was done.

The Plas Kynaston Canal was involved in two deaths at the end of the 19th century. When the 19-year-old Edward Hughes attempted to jump across it, as he often did, he stepped backwards to get a run for his jump but fell 40 feet into a disused lime kiln. And when Algernon Fletcher, an expert swimmer, was giving lessons in the Plas Kynaston Canal to some of his fellow workers he caught typhoid from the water polluted with effluent from Cefn Mawr, dying a fortnight later.

The canal was certainly used to bring the raw materials from various gasworks and to take the manufactured chemical products to their markets. In 1885, Graesser said that dredging was needed to enable boats to reach his wharf, and offered to pay part of the cost. A couple of years later the SU agreed to do whatever was necessary to ensure the stability of the banks, at an estimated cost of £32. The canal is shown on a map produced by the Shropshire Union Canal in 1895.

In 1903 repairs estimated to cost £426 were needed. Sir Herbert Williams Wynn, the 7th baronet, then owner of the Wynnstay estate, had declared he was not willing to contribute. The Shropshire Union's Executive Committee wished to see the Plas Kynaston Canal kept open, as it was still being used by the SU's boats, so the Traffic Manager was instructed to consult the Agent of the Wynnstay estate and Messrs Graessers. The minutes do not record the outcome, and it seems likely that little or nothing was done.

Closure

IT is not known when a boat last travelled loaded on the Plas Kynaston Canal. It is not mentioned in *Bradshaw's Canals and Navigable Rivers of England and Wales*, published in 1904. However, Jack Roberts records in his memoirs collecting a load of drums containing caustic from Graesser's works in 1910.

The 1912 Ordnance Survey map shows the part beyond the bend as filled with water plants, so presumably no longer navigable. Part of this section was cleared about 1916 so that boats could reach the sodium nitrate store. A postcard said to be dated 1918 depicts the wharf at the bend, known as Ward's Wharf, as full of reeds, implying that it had not been used for several years. The 1938 OS map has the canal still in water for its full length – none appears to have actually been in-filled by then.

The canal continued to be used by Monsanto as a water supply channel until after the Second World War. The breach on the 'Water Line' in 1945 showed the vulnerability of this source of water; Monsanto therefore started using water pumped up from the river Dee. Most of the Plas Kynaston Canal was then filled in. As the canal had been constructed without needing an Act of Parliament, it was not subject to a formal closure procedure.

With the closure of the industry, the site became the largest single area of derelict land in north-east Wales. A favoured proposal is for the Plas Kynaston Canal to be re-excavated as a central feature of the redevelopment, which is likely to be for a mix of industry and housing. The Plas Kynaston Canal Group is pressing (2018) for this to be done, which would also have the benefit of bringing tourists closer to the village of Cefn Mawr, assisting with its economic regeneration.

Bibliography

Books

Harry Arnold, *The Llangollen Canal*, 2008

Harry Arnold, *The Montgomery Canal and its Restoration*, 2003

Peter Aspinall and Daphne Hudson, *Ellesmere Port: the making of an industrial borough*, 1982

Joseph Boughey and Charles Hadfield, *British Canals: the standard history*, 2008

Anthony Burton, *Thomas Telford*, 1999

Gordon Emery (Editor), *The Old Chester Canal*, c.2005

Charles Hadfield, *Canals of the West Midlands*, second edition, 1969

Charles Hadfield, *Thomas Telford's Temptation*, 1993

Charles Hadfield and A.W. Skempton, *William Jessop, Engineer*, 1979

Stephen Hughes, *The Archaeology of the Montgomeryshire Canal*, fourth edition, 1988

John Milner and Beryl Williams, *Rails to Glyn Ceiriog: the history of the Glyn Valley Tramway, Part 1, 1857–1903*, 2011

Jonathan Morris, *The Shropshire Union Canal: a towpath guide to the Birmingham & Liverpool Junction Canal from Autherley to Nantwich*, 1991

Andrew Pattison, *William Hazledine, Shropshire ironmaster and millwright*, 2017

Alastair Penfold (Editor), *Thomas Telford: Engineer*, 1980

Ron Quenby, *Thomas Telford's Aqueducts on the Shropshire Union Canal*, 1992

Jack Roberts, *Shropshire Union Fly-Boats*, 2015

Peter Wakelin, *Pontcysyllte Aqueduct & Canal World Heritage Site*, 2015

Edward Wilson, *The Ellesmere and Llangollen Canal*, 1975

Wrexham CBC and RCAHMW, *Pontcysyllte Aqueduct & Canal: Nomination as a World Heritage Site*, 2008

Articles

Harry Arnold, 'Memories of Ellesmere Yard', *NarrowBoat*, Winter 2011/12

Joseph Boughey, 'Declining traffics on branches of the Shropshire Union Canal', *Waterways Journal* 4, 2002

Joseph Boughey, 'Early pleasure boating on the Shropshire Union Canal', *Waterways Journal* 7, 2005

Joseph Boughey, 'Postscript on Shropshire Union pleasure boating', *Waterways Journal* 17, 2015

Peter Brown, 'How the Llangollen Canal was saved', *Waterways Journal* 9, 2007

Peter Brown, 'Longer but better? The proposed deviation of the Montgomeryshire Canal, 1821', *RCHS Journal*, March 2010

Peter Brown, 'John Fletcher of Chester', *Waterways Journal* 17, 2015

Peter Brown, 'Thomas Telford and the Ellesmere Canal, 1793–1813', *RCHS Journal*, July 2007

Peter Brown, 'Wappenshall Wharf', *RCHS Journal*, July & November 2005

Neil Clarke, 'William Reynolds and the East Shropshire tub boat system', *RCHS Journal*, November 2009

Richard Dean, 'The metamorphosis of the Ellesmere Canal', *RCHS Journal*, November 1985

Alan Faulkner, 'Famous fleets: Shropshire Union Railways & Canal Co.', *NarrowBoat*, Summer 2010

Alan Faulkner, 'Chester & Liverpool Lighterage & Warehousing Company', *Waterways Journal* 14, 2012

David Gwyn, '"Best adapted to the general carriage": railways of the Llangollen Canal, their history and archaeology', *Industrial Patrimony* 18, 2007

John Herson, 'A canal in its context: transport in the Chester area in the early nineteenth century', *Waterways Journal* 12, 2010

Terry Kavanagh, 'The early Birmingham & Liverpool Junction Canal tugs', *Waterways Journal* 2, 2000

Terry Kavanagh, 'The Life and Times of a Shroppie Fly Boatman', *Waterways Journal* 5, 2003

Terry Kavanagh, 'Aspects of Family Boating on the Shropshire Union Canal', *Waterways Journal* 11, 2009

Tony Lewery, 'For Alice and Bill: revisiting some aspects of horse boating', *Waterways Journal* 2, 2000

Andrew Pattison, 'Thomas Telford's Shrewsbury Team: Telford, Hazledine and Simpson', *RCHS Journal*, November 2007

Timothy Peters and Stephen Brown, 'Repairs to the Llangollen arm of the Shropshire Union Canal', *Proceedings of the Institution of Civil Engineers*, paper 1500007, 2015

Edwin Shearing, 'Chester Canal projects', *RCHS Journal*, November 1984 and January 1985

Edwin Shearing, 'Planning and construction in the Norbury district', *RCHS Journal*, July and November 1990

Edwin Shearing, 'The Shropshire Union Canal and the Peatswood Estate at Tyrley, *RCHS Journal*, November 1987

Barrie Trinder & David Gwyn, '"Images bold and thoughts sublime": the cultural landscape of the Llangollen Canal', *Industrial Patrimony* 18, 2007

Cath Turpin, 'Grain traffic on the northern Shropshire Union', *NarrowBoat*, Winter 2017

Index

Biographical box-outs shown in **bold**

Accidents and incidents, 35, 55, 72, 88, 97, 160, 167, 178, 179, 183, 203, 204, 213, 227, 238, 282
Adderley, 113, 123
Anson, 2nd Viscount, 113, 115
Arddleen, 258, 259
Arenig Lakes (reservoirs), 101, 102, 216
Aston (near Oswestry), 257–259, 261, 269
Audlem, 120, 123, 233, 234, 267, 268, 274
Autherley, 118–120, 123, 154, 163, 173, 174, 176, 185
Autherley Junction toll, 112, 120, 163

Baker, William, 136, 143, 152, 154
Bala Lake, 75, 78, 102, 152, 170, 241
Barbridge, 32, 33, 100, 184, 185, 203, 232
Bather, John, 95, 105, 106
Beech, John, 52, 143, 148, 149, 152, 154
Beeston, 28, 32–35, 97, 151
Belan, 90, 91
Belvide Reservoir, 118, 119, 154, 155, 212
Berriew, 85, 150, 151
Berwick, 156
Berwick Tunnel, 50, 54, 220, 261, 273
Bettisfield, 246, 247
Birmingham Canal, 19, 98, 111, 123, 131, 132, 146, 163
Birmingham & Liverpool Junction Canal, 52, 98, 110–125, 128–137, 206, 207, 275, 278
Birmingham – see 'South Staffordshire' traffic
'Black Country, The' – see 'South Staffordshire' traffic
Boat clubs, 236
Boats
    Committee/inspection boats, 51, 146, 177
    Flats and floats, 105, 106, 177
    Flyboats, 92, 106, 121, 172–176, 181
    Ice-breakers, 51, 178
    Market boats, 28
    Motor boats, 176, 214, 217, 218
    Narrowboats (other), 172–174, 176, 177, 214, 215
    Passenger boats, 76, 166, 167
    Steam-powered, 106, 123, 124, 129, 171, 175, 176, 210, 212, 215
    Tub-boats, 39, 41, 177, 179

Boats mentioned by name
    British Waterways, *Collingwood* 234, *Kimberley* 234, *Water Arabis* 236, *Water Bulrush* 236, *Water Crocus* 236
    Chester Canal, *Bootle* 31, 32, *Egerton* 31, *Peplow* 31, 32, *Speed* 31
    Shropshire Union Canal, *Bancroft* 183, *Berriew* 222, *Cressy* 224, *Duchess* 183, *Earl of Powis* 178, *Eyton* 183, *George Stanton* 178, *Good Hope* 226, *Havoc* 176, *Hind* 184, *Hussar* 185, *Lancaster* 176, *Leader* 176, *Lord Stalbridge* 210, 215, *Luna* 176, *Magnet* 175, *Merlin* 183, *Nettle* 176, *Oak* 184, *Pioneer* 176, *Ralph Brocklebank* 210, 215, *Redwing* 175, *Saturn* 246, *Scipio* 226, *Seal* 179, *Test* 175, *W.E. Dorrington* 210, 215, *Witness* 214, *Wolf* 176
    Other carriers, *Perseverance* 222, *Yeoford* 235
    Community/charity boats, *Heulwen* 255, 256, *Powis Princess* 254
    Hire boats (not BW), *Clifton* 273, *Cuckmere* 221, 226, *Tangmere* 226, *The Rambler* 226
    Hotel/restaurant boats, *Maldwyn* 273, *Saturn* 246, *Sian* 273
    Private boats, *Cressy* 224, 230, 239, *Dorabella* 247, 271, *Dragonfly* 168, *Glen Rosa* 241, *Hectic* 225, *Heron* 238, 239, *Obsession* 241, *Phosphorus* 239, *Ranger* 168, *Snowgoose* 271, *Ulass* 241, *Vulcan* 271, *Wanderer* 168
Boat lift, 68
Boatyards, 178, 180, 195, 197, 200, 214
Breaches, 97, 143, 152, 213, 222, 233, 238, 242, 246, 247
Brewood, 159, 202, 225
Bridgewater
    3rd Duke ('The Canal Duke') (**279**), 18, 22, 24, 94, 279
    7th Earl (**279**), 76, 77, 79, 94, 279
Bridgewater Canal, 18, 21, 98
Bridgewater Trustees, 106, 112, 279
Brierly Hill Branch, 43, 46
Brindley, James, 17, 18, 21, 25
British Transport Commission, 230, 261, 238
'British Waterways', 7, 230, 231, 234–237, 243, 244, 251, 252, 256–262, 273
Brocklebank, Ralph, 141
Buck, George (**86**), 84–89, 97
Bunbury, 174, 232
Bunbury Heath Reservoir, 28

Calveley, 135, 157, 160, 168
Cambrian Railways (and constituents), 147, 148, 164, 208, 215
Canal & River Trust, 232, 235, 260, 261, 273, 274
Carreghofa, 74, 84–86, 88, 153, 252, 257

Carriers
    SURCC, 107, 172–185, 214–216
    Other, 104–107, 121, 164, 171, 172, 215, 216, 218, 219, 222, 234, 235
Cartage, 174
Cefn Mawr, 57, 65, 69, 97, 160, 197, 221, 229, 280–282
Chain Bridge, 97, 167
Chamberlaine, John, 22, 24, 27, 31
Chester, 12, 14, 15, 17, 18, 21, 22, 26–29, 32, 35–37, 65, 66, 76, 77, 104–107, 142, 146, 155, 157, 169, 173–175, 178, 180, 184, 185, 194, 203, 215, 229, 232, 233, 236, 270
Chester Canal, 20–37, 59, 61, 65, 74, 94, 97, 206, 207, 275, 278
Chester & Birkenhead Railway, 127, 131, 133, 134
Chester & Holyhead Railway, 127, 134, 135
Chirk, 72, 91, 97, 147, 157, 159, 160, 162, 167, 191, 202, 221
Chirk Aqueduct, 72, 73, 143, 147, 151, 212, 247, 248
Chirk Tunnel, 72, 97
Church Minshull, 174, 229, 232, 233
Clive, Lord – see Powis
Closure of canals, 149, 213, 217, 219, 220–225, 230, 231, 246, 261, 268, 282
Clowes, Josiah (**50**), 25, 26, 28, 50
Coalbrookdale Company, 42, 45, 46, 50, 54, 164
Coalport, 43, 44, 46
Commercial Canal, 34
Competition
    Coastal shipping, 104, 105, 205
    Other canals, 106, 108, 122, 205
    Railway, 111–113, 122, 123, 126–131, 144, 145, 147, 149, 163–165, 205, 206, 208
    River, 12, 92, 205
    Road, 16, 17, 54, 78, 92, 104, 106, 122, 167, 204, 205, 214, 221, 230, 267
    Tramroad, 42, 45
Constables, 96
Cotes, John, 40, 114
Crime, 203, 204
Cubitt, William, (**95**), 89, 93, 95, 102, 103, 106, 116–118, 120–122, 133–135

Dadford family (**83**), 50, 81, 83, 88
Dee Branch, 270
Dee Conservancy Board, 169, 170
Dee Navigation, 14, 12, 26, 27, 32, 34, 66, 169
Denson, Thomas, 62, 63, 77, 97
Dividends, 46, 47, 55, 93, 108, 207, 277
Docks & Inland Waterways Executive, 230–232, 239, 241, 242, 246
Donkeys, 171, 172
Donnington Wood Canal, 39–41, 44, 50, 113, 114
Drought, 155
Duncombe, John (**59**), 57, 59, 60, 62, 63, 65, 66, 74, 77

Easton, Alexander, 99, 100, 113, 116, 121, 123, 124, 142, 143
Edstaston, 97, 156, 173, 196
Egerton, Samuel (**279**), 24, 30, 31
Egerton, William, 31–34, 74
Ellesmere, 60, 61, 77, 94–96, 135, 143, 155, 159, 198–200, 211, 229, 232, 272
Ellesmere Canal, 33–37, 56–79, 81–84, 93–97, 206, 207, 278
Ellesmere & Chester Canal, 55, 86, 93, 94–109, 128–137, 275, 277, 278
Ellesmere Port, 9, 65, 76, 77, 97, 102–106, 143, 145, 146, 150, 151, 155, 163, 170, 173, 181, 182, 184, 185, 195, 208, 209, 212, 213, 215–218, 226, 227, 235, 270
Ellesmere Tunnel, 135
Employees
    Conditions of employment, 179–182, 214
    Disputes, 182, 183, 213, 214
    Education, 184
    Housing, 181, 182, 203, 216
    Religious provision, 184, 185
    Retirement and pensions, 185, 215, 216
    Welfare, 183–185
Exchequer Bill Loan Commissioners, 89, 90, 124, 125, 134
Eyton, Thomas (**49**), 49–51, 55, 61, 95

Fenns Moss, 135
Ffrwd Branch, 64, 66
Finance, 22, 29–37, 43, 44, 47, 49, 55, 60, 79, 81, 84, 89, 90, 92, 93, 108, 109, 124, 125, 134, 137–139, 173, 186, 187, 206, 207, 213, 214, 216, 217, 222, 244, 268, 270
Fletcher, John (**35**), 34–37, 65, 66, 73–75, 77, 104, 105, 111
Ford, Thomas, 43, 50, 73, 74
Forton, 115
Frankton Junction, 73, 74, 224, 257, 259, 272
Froncysyllte, 71, 72, 152, 202, 221

Garthmyl, 84, 85, 88, 90, 91, 202, 258
Gas works, 51, 159, 160, 168, 195, 198, 199, 202
Giffard, Thomas, 120, 154
Gilbert brothers, 18, 22, 40, 41, 43, 44, 49
Glyn, George Carr, 128, 131, 133
Glyn Valley Tramway, 190–192
Gnosall, 202
Golbourne, John, 25–27
Government, national, 165, 166, 210, 212–215, 223, 224, 226–229, 238, 244, 245, 253, 256, 258, 262
Gower
    1st Earl – see Stafford, 1st Marquess
    2nd Earl – see Sutherland, 1st Duke
Gowy Aqueduct, 25
Graesser, Thomas, 168, 197, 281, 282
Grand Junction Railway, 55, 122, 126–133, 135, 136, 208
Great Western Railway, 55, 127, 136, 147, 148, 157, 163, 164, 238
Grindley Brook, 75, 169, 271, 274

Grub Street Cutting, 116, 117
Guilsfield Branch, 86–88, 221, 252

Hack Green, 123, 173
Hales, Thomas, 142, 165, 173
Hampton Bank, 75
Hay Incline, 43–46, 149
Hazledine, William, (**71**), 52, 68, 72, 83, 84, 91, 97, 99, 102, 120, 121, 124, 197, 280
Heritage Lottery Fund, 235, 250, 259–261, 270
Heulwen Trust, 255, 256, 273
High Offley, 114, 115
High Onn, 115, 219
Hill, Sir John (**58**), 58, 61, 76, 94
Hill, Joseph, 84, 86, 88
Holyoake, Francis, 102
Holyoake, George, 113, 137
Hordley, 73, 149, 221
Horses, 172–175, 210, 212, 214, 234, 235
Horseshoe Falls, 75, 97, 152, 153, 170, 228
Houghton, James, 43, 50, 73, 74
Hugh's Bridge Incline, 41, 44
Humber Branch, 114, 156, 196, 219, 261, 265
Hunt, Rowland (**58**), 57, 58, 63, 78, 79, 111
Hurleston, 36, 177, 181, 274
Hurleston Reservoir, 100, 243

Ice, 51, 54, 155, 205
Inclines (proposed), 249, 250, 264, 265
Inland Waterways Amenity Advisory Council, 251, 253, 254, 256
Inland Waterways Association, 230, 231, 238–243, 245, 246, 251, 256, 257, 259, 261
Inland Waterways Redevelopment Advisory Committee, 231, 244, 245, 250–252

Jebb, George (**142**), 149, 150, 153, 176, 206, 212
Jessop, Josias, 86, 88, 89
Jessop, William (**60**), 27, 28, 34, 36, 43, 50, 59, 60, 62–67, 69, 71, 73, 74, 81, 84
Johnes, Edward, 86, 93, 143

Ketley Canal, 42, 43
Ketley Incline, 42–44
Kirk, Richard, 57, 64, 66
Knighton, 202, 219
Knighton Reservoir, 116, 118, 143, 154
Knockin, 78, 79
Kynaston(-Powell), (Sir) John (**58**), 57, 58, 76, 94
Kynnersley, 263

Lea Hall Embankment, 143, 151, 152
Leisure use of canals
   Fishing, 171
   Private and hire boats, 168, 181, 225, 226, 230, 231, 236–241, 243–247, 268, 269, 272
   Trip boats, 15, 167, 225, 253, 254
   Other, 171, 203, 261, 268, 270, 272–274
Lilleshall, 39–41
Lilleshall Company, 41, 45, 54, 113, 114, 148, 149, 219
Lime kilns, 40, 76, 77, 90, 91, 160, 198, 199, 201, 202, 280, 281
Liverpool, 103, 136, 146, 158, 185
Llangollen, 75, 152, 156, 166–169, 200, 202, 225, 226, 240, 238, 241, 271, 272
Llanymynech, 57, 72–74, 76, 82, 90, 92, 135, 157, 202
Lloyd, John Robert (**58**), 57, 58, 73, 74, 97
Local authorities, 16, 21, 27, 73, 213, 215, 219, 220, 223, 224, 239, 242, 245, 249, 252, 253, 257–263, 265, 262, 269
Loch, George, 133, 137
Loch, James (**112**), 98, 99, 112–116, 122, 123, 129, 130, 208
London & Birmingham Railway, 55, 122, 126–128, 131–133, 135, 136, 138
London & North Western Railway, 47, 128, 137–149, 157, 163, 164, 173, 208
London Midland & Scottish Railway, 216, 217, 222–225, 227–229, 268
Long Lane, 261, 264, 273
Longdon Aqueduct, 50–52, 151, 263, 264, 273

Maesbury, 73, 74, 77, 160, 197, 202, 221, 252, 272
Manchester & Birmingham Railway, 127, 128, 134–136
Manchester Ship Canal, 150, 216, 217, 234, 271
Manchester traffic, 98, 112, 120, 157, 160, 161, 193, 202, 218
Marinas, 236, 251, 272
Market Drayton, 113, 115, 120, 123, 152, 155, 156, 174, 200, 201, 232, 236, 237, 274
Marsh, Christopher (**239**), 227, 236, 239, 240, 243, 244, 246, 269
Mersey, cross-Mersey traffic, 9, 105, 106, 151, 165, 172, 173, 178, 179
Mid & SE Cheshire Water Board, 242, 243
Middlewich, 21–24, 27, 30, 98, 99, 168, 236
Middlewich Branch, 23, 98–100, 209
Middlewich Junction toll, 99, 162, 163
Monsanto, 197, 229, 272, 282
'Montgomery Canal', 221–225, 227–229, 251–261, 272, 273, 275
Montgomery Canal Partnership, 260
Montgomery Waterway Restoration Trust, 257
Montgomeryshire Canal, 72, 73, 80–93, 133, 138, 139, 206, 207, 275, 277, 278
Moon, John, 25–31
Moon, (Sir) Richard (**141**), 141, 144–146, 192
Morris, Thomas (probably father & son), 25–27, 30, 35, 36

Names of canals, 57, 136, 244, 258
Nantwich, 22, 27, 28, 32, 35, 108, 113, 115, 135, 173, 185, 198, 212, 236, 237
National Waterways Museum (and predecessors), 235, 270, 271
Nationalisation, 230
Nature Conservancy Council & successors, 232, 252, 257, 260
Nature conservation and reserves, 232, 251, 252, 257–261, 269, 272
Newport, 120, 156, 185, 220, 262, 264
Newport Branch, 114–117, 120, 124
Newport Canal Restoration CIC, 264
Newtown, 81, 88–92, 89, 135, 147, 148, 152, 153, 157, 166, 167, 199, 200, 222, 251, 256, 258, 265, 273
Norbury, 113, 120, 123, 155, 173, 181, 185, 203, 232, 264, 265, 274
North Staffordshire Railway, 148, 162

Oswestry, 73, 199
Owen, William (**58**), 57, 58, 74, 97
Owen, William Mostyn, (**58**), 57, 58, 74

Pant, 202
Passenger services, 76, 106, 107, 166, 167, 205, 225
Pave Lane, 40, 41, 113
Peate, A&A, 215, 221, 222
Penarth Weir, 152, 153, 168
Pentrefelin, 97, 157, 158
Perry Aqueduct, 222, 268
Pick, Frank, 226, 227
Pickering, Exuperius (father & son), 68, 95, 97, 197, 280–282
Pinkerton, James, 27, 28
Plas Kynaston Canal, 97, 270, 272, 280–282
Pontcysyllte Aqueduct, 60, 69–72, 151, 209, 212, 243, 246–249, 272
Pontcysyllte Railway, 187–189
Pool Quay, 92
Porth-y-Waen, 73, 81–84, 90, 202
'Potteries, The', 9, 21, 22, 24, 28, 34, 98, 146, 160, 161, 165, 174, 182, 185, 218
Potts family of solicitors, 22, 49, 57, 61, 76, 94, 95, 136, 143
Powis
  2nd Earl of the 2nd Creation, 57, 73, 81, 89, 90
  2nd Earl of the 3rd Creation (**94**), 94, 99, 111, 128, 131, 133, 136, 140
  3rd Earl of the 3rd Creation (**140**), 140, 141, 148
Prees Branch, 74, 75, 221, 250, 251
Prince of Wales Committee, 256
Proposed canals (not built), 18, 19, 31, 65, 75, 81, 86, 87, 89, 102, 112, 114, 123, 150, 162, 163, 227
Provis, William (**96**), 96, 99, 102, 103, 108, 115, 118, 131
Pugh, William (**90**), 89, 90

Queen's Head, 183, 199, 222, 259, 260, 270, 272
Quina Brook, 75, 160, 221

Railway & Canal Traffic Act 1888, 165, 166
Railway/canal interchanges, 156, 157
Randlay Reservoir, 148
Rednal, 156, 157, 166, 167, 202
Rents and wayleaves, 170, 171
Reservoirs, 28, 51, 75, 78, 100–102, 118, 119, 148, 154, 155, 212, 216
Restoration (general comments), 269, 270
Reynolds, William (**42**), 39, 41, 42, 43, 45, 50, 51, 54, 61, 72
Rhoswiel, 169
Roberts, Jack, 176, 212, 216, 217
Rodington Aqueduct, 50
Rolt, Tom, 222, 230, 238, 239, 245, 268
Rowland, Edward, 57, 68, 197
Royal Commission on Canals 1906–9, 151, 161, 165, 208
Ruabon, 12, 60, 65–67, 193, 196–198
Ruabon Brook Railway, 67, 68, 187–190, 197

St Martin's, 239, 240
Salmon Fisheries Acts, 152, 153
Salt, 28, 151, 152, 160
Severn Navigation, 13–15, 44, 46, 49, 57, 92
Shebdon Embankment, 117, 233
Shelmore Embankment, 113, 115–117, 233
Shrewsbury, 12, 14, 49, 53, 54, 55, 74, 77, 92, 97, 107, 143, 144, 159, 173, 185, 194, 195, 219, 262, 264, 273
Shrewsbury & Birmingham Railway, 47, 55, 127, 132, 133, 147, 148
Shrewsbury & Chester Railway, 126, 147, 156
'Shrewsbury & Newport Canal', 219, 220, 261–265, 273
Shrewsbury & Newport Canal Association, 261, 262
Shrewsbury & Newport Canals Trust, 264, 265
Shrewsbury Canal, 48–55, 74, 133, 137–139, 148, 206, 207, 275, 277, 278
Shropshire Canal, 42–47, 139, 148, 149, 206, 207, 227, 278
Shropshire Union Canal Society, 252, 253, 256–259, 263
Shropshire Union Railway, 133, 134, 136, 144, 145
Simpson, John (**68**), 67, 69, 72, 75, 77, 83, 84, 91
Skey, Robert, 120, 123, 130, 131, 136, 141, 142, 145, 148, 149, 166, 175, 205, 208
Soudley, 143, 152
'South Staffordshire' traffic, 9, 102, 111, 112, 120, 146, 158–161, 172–174, 182, 185, 193, 202, 214, 215, 218, 226, 234, 235
Stafford
  1st Marquess (**279**), 17, 18, 22, 39–41, 43, 44, 49, 279
  2nd Marquess – see Sutherland, 1st Duke
Staffordshire & Worcestershire Canal, 18, 112, 118–120, 122, 163
Stanlow, 234
Stanton, George, 95, 96, 140, 141

Stanton, John, 78, 102
Stanton, Thomas, 63, 77, 78, 95, 96, 102, 103, 105, 107, 108, 111, 130, 131, 136
Stephenson, Robert, 133–137, 144, 148
Stretton Aqueduct, 124
Subsidence, 45, 148–149, 151–152
Sundays, canal closure, 96, 181
Sutherland
    1st Duke (**279**), 98, 99, 112, 129, 208, 279
    2nd Duke (**279**), 114, 137, 208, 279

Tanat Weir, 85, 152, 153
Tattenhall, 74
Telegraph, 170, 171
Telford (east Shropshire coalfield), 11, 12, 39, 42, 43, 148, 149, 195, 196, 263
Telford, Thomas, (**62**), 50, 51, 61–64, 66, 69, 71, 72, 76–78, 84, 94, 95, 97, 99,102, 103, 111, 113–120, 124, 128, 129
Tolls (pleasure boats), 168, 225, 231
Tolls (tonnage), 35, 44–46, 54, 55, 92, 104, 105, 108, 120, 122, 161, 162, 214
Tomkinson, James, 31–34
Tootal, Henry, 137, 141
Towing, by locomotive, 176, 177
Traffics
    Agricultural produce, 106, 160, 161, 202, 226
    Bricks & tiles, 160, 171
    Chemicals, 161, 218, 219, 234, 282
    Coal, 28, 33, 41, 49, 51, 54, 57, 90–92, 104, 106, 121, 159, 161, 171, 172, 195–199, 202, 205, 221
    Grain, 104, 121, 160, 161, 171, 205, 215, 218, 219, 221, 226, 234
    Iron products, 104, 106, 121, 122, 158, 159, 196–198, 215, 218
    Ironstone, 104, 106, 121, 147, 159, 196, 197, 199
    Limestone, 40, 49, 54, 57, 90, 91, 104, 106, 108, 121, 159, 172, 182, 196, 197, 199, 201, 202
    Merchandise, 92, 104, 106, 121, 204, 205, 206
    Oil and petrol, 121, 160, 195, 218, 226, 234, 235
    Pottery and china clay, 28, 160, 218
    Slates & stone, 57, 92, 104, 106, 121, 157, 160, 221
    Timber, 92, 106, 121, 160, 161, 205, 221
    Other traffics, 33, 55, 121, 160, 161, 171, 219, 226, 234, 23
Tramroads – see also Glyn Valley T and Ruabon Brook R, 45, 46, 66, 92, 97, 114, 150, 151, 157, 158
Trench Branch, 53, 54, 156, 196, 219, 263
Trench Incline, 44, 50, 54, 148, 156, 166, 219
Trench Pool (reservoir), 51
Trent & Mersey Canal, 18, 21–24, 31, 34, 35, 98, 99, 102, 108, 162, 163
Trevor, 65–68, 97, 160, 168, 174, 186–190, 196, 241, 242, 246, 272, 274, 280, 281
Trevor Rocks, 96, 108, 157, 159, 184, 202
Turner, Joseph (**28**), 26, 28, 32–35, 59, 61

Turner, William, 59, 62, 69, 75, 76
Turnpike roads, 16, 17, 54, 78, 79, 93
Tyrley, 113, 115, 118, 119, 122, 123, 173, 176, 218, 273

Uffington, 51, 52, 220, 261, 264

Vyrnwy Aqueduct, 84, 85, 151, 257, 272

Wappenshall, 52, 54, 114, 121, 122, 156, 164, 201–203, 263, 265, 273
Ward, Thomas, 91, 97, 102, 281
Wartime, 210–213, 226, 227, 238
Water, sale, 33, 168–170, 196, 217, 223, 224, 228, 229, 242–244, 246
Waterway Recovery Group, 231, 252
Waterways Infrastructure Trust, 232
Weaver Navigation, 16, 102, 152
Wellington, 49, 143, 164, 201
Welshpool, 81, 86, 92, 135, 155–157, 159, 166, 169, 173, 199, 221, 226, 252–256, 258–260, 271, 273
Westhead, Joshua, 136, 137
Westminster, Marquesses of, 102, 103, 150
Weston, Samuel, 21, 25, 31, 34, 65
Weston Branch, 149, 213, 221, 259
Weston Lullingfields, 74, 77, 97
Wharves and warehouses (rural), 28, 33, 77, 155–158, 173, 202
Wheaton Aston, 113, 119, 120
Wheelock, 28, 35
Whitchurch, 61, 74–77, 135, 156, 159, 173, 198, 221, 226, 249, 250, 272
Whitchurch Waterway Trust, 249, 250
Whitehouses Tunnel, 72, 97, 157, 167
Whitworth, Sir Richard, 18, 19
Whixall, 155, 250
Whixall Moss, 75, 143, 152, 221
Wilkinson, John, 12, 43, 44, 49, 57, 59, 60, 65, 72, 78, 79
Williams, Henry (**44**), 44, 46, 50–53, 66
Wilson family of contractors (**114**), 118, 124, 138
Windmill Farm Incline, 44–46
Wolverhampton, 141, 155, 184, 185, 216
Wombridge Canal, 41, 42, 50
Woodseaves Cutting, 115–117, 152, 170, 233
Worcester, 134, 137
World Heritage Site, 247–249, 272
Wrenbury, 74, 160, 246
Wrockwardine Wood, 39–41, 49
Wrockwardine Wood Incline, 44, 45, 148, 149
Wynn, Sir Watkin Williams, 5th Baronet, 66, 75, 85, 280
Wyrley & Essington Canal, 119

Yeoman, Thomas, 22, 23, 25, 27
Young, George, 41, 43, 50

SHROPSHIRE UNION RAILWAYS & CANAL COMPANY NOTICE
THIS PATH ON SUFFERANCE ONLY

CYCLING ON THE COMPANYS TOWING PATH IS STRICTLY PROHIBITED
3.1901   BY ORDER

In 1901 towpaths were not open to the public and cycling was banned. Now towpaths are open to all and cyclists are welcomed. [page 274]

Welshpool Lock in 1959, showing George Buck's unique design of paddle gear. The cast-iron lock gates and balance beams were re-erected outside the canal museum at Stoke Bruerne; they are now at the National Waterfront Museum in Swansea. [page 86] *Railway & Canal Historical Society*

Virtually unrecognisable now is this 1957 view of Wardle Lock, Middlewich, overshadowed by the Murgatroyd Mid-Cheshire Salt Works. *Malvern* is tied up on the left. Although now thought of as part of the Middlewich branch, Wardle Lock was built by the Trent & Mersey Canal so that it could control the junction and extract 'ransom' tolls. [page 98] *Railway & Canal Historical Society: Shearing Collection*